The Purposeful Writer

A RHETORIC WITH READINGS

Second Edition

Donna Gorrell

St. Cloud State University

ALLYN AND BACON

Boston   London   Toronto   Sydney   Tokyo   Singapore

Editor in Chief, Humanities: Joseph Opiela
Senior Editorial Assistant: Brenda Conaway
Production Administrator: Rowena Dores
Editorial-Production Service: York Production Services
Text Designer: Pat Torelli
Cover Administrator: Linda Dickinson
Composition and Manufacturing Buyer: Louise Richardson

Library of Congress Cataloging-in-Publication Data

Gorrell, Donna.
    The purposeful writer : a rhetoric with readings /
Donna Gorrell — 2nd ed.
        p.   cm.
    Includes index.
    ISBN 0–205–14618–X
    1. English language—Rhetoric. 2. English language—
Grammar—1950–   3. College readers. I. Title.
PE1408.G629 1993
808'.042—dc20   92–32297
                                                          CIP

 This textbook is printed on recycled, acid-free paper.

Credits

Page 7. Neil Postman, from *Amusing Ourselves to Death.* Copyright © 1985 by Neil Postman. Reprinted by permission of Viking Penguin, a division of Penguin Books USA Inc.

Pages 17–18. Loren Eiseley, "How I Learned to Read" from *All the Strange Hours.* Reprinted with permission of Charles Scribner's Sons, an imprint of Macmillan Publishing Company from *All the Strange Hours* by Loren Eiseley. Copyright © 1975 Loren Eiseley.

Credits continued on page 579, which constitutes an extension of the copyright page.

Printed in the United States of America
10 9 8 7 6 5 4 3 2 1   97 96 95 94 93 92

Contents

3   *The Writing Process: Prewriting*   *40*

4   *The Writing Process: Drafting*   *62*

Part II   The Practice of Purposeful Writing   121

8   *Writing to Entertain and Move*   *207*

13   *Writing to Instruct*

Contents by Method of Development

Preface

Like the first edition of *The Purposeful Writer*, the revised and expanded second edition derives from the fundamental idea that writers—authors of books and stories and essays—are the best teachers of writing. They are effective because they are always available, always instructive, always right on track, always supportive. They are always ready with examples of excellent writing, often demonstrative of problems writers have in expressing ideas. They show how words go together to make up sentences, how sentences join to make paragraphs, how paragraphs contribute to the development of a central idea. They show how writers like themselves achieve coherence and a tone appropriate to the situation. They show the many ways of developing ideas and the multitude of purposes for writing.

Experienced writers know that they can learn from other writers, and they know how to *read as writers* in order to learn from others—how to read for style and structure as well as for meaning. This kind of reading, for them, is often so automatic as to be unconscious. But many writers have not acquired this skill of reading as writers, and some are even ineffectual in reading as readers. They read, but not actively and critically. Many college students have not yet come to understand that reading for what a writer *does* as well as for what a writer *says* can increase both comprehension of content and skill in writing.

This book is based on the premise that the goal of writing classes—mature, capable writing—can be aided by active reading. In learning writing from other writers, students can discover how to develop ideas and achieve coherence and tone; they can acquire a sense that tells them when a phrase is right, when it is time to begin a new paragraph, and how the occasion dictates all the other decisions that must be made in writing. Realizing that most writing textbooks do not truly bring together reading and writing, in this book I have attempted a genuine integration of readings that illustrate and model the purposes of writing and writings that enable student writers to practice the things writers do to attain those purposes. Because of this integration, *The Purposeful Writer* serves as both rhetoric and reader. With the addition of a handbook of usage, it is now also a source of information at the sentence level.

Purpose is a key term in this book, determining its arrangement, selection of readings, discussions, and assignments. Writers write for particular purposes: to inform, to entertain, to reflect, to record, and so on. How they develop their ideas—by classification, comparison, causal analysis, and so on—depends on what they need in order to achieve their purposes. So purpose has been my organizing principle, with methods of development, invention, and revision being treated within the context of writing. (Teachers looking for particular methods of development will find them listed in a supplementary table of contents.) My selection of purposes relies in part on James Moffett's categories of recording, reporting, informing, and generalizing (or explaining), plus extensions to other kinds of writing that student writers do: summarizing, responding, showing what they know, and conducting research. Preferring to treat writing holistically, I've also included purposes for writing beyond those usually required in school, purposes such as reflecting, personal corresponding, entertaining, and praising.

Part I, The Principles of Purposeful Writing, establishes the position that writing and reading are related inseparably. Addressing students as writers and readers, Chapter 1 discusses a variety of writing processes and the number of ways that readers read, according to their purposes and experience. The chapter makes specific suggestions for developing active reading and encourages students to read as writers. Chapter 2 presents an overview of rhetorical principles. Because rhetoric is part of everyday life, a knowledge of its principles can make better informed readers and writers. Moreover, by applying the principles to specific rhetorical situations, student writers can see that in many cases their varying roles are real and that their persuasive appeals are a consideration for the needs and interests of the audience.

Chapters 3, 4, and 5 then examine prewriting, drafting, and revising. The process of writing, as we know, varies from individual to individual and from situation to situation. It may be recursive, all-at-once (concursive), sequential, or linear, depending on the writer's purpose for writing and familiarity with the subject. Invention may occur at any point, as may drafting and revision. But while the mind can prewrite, draft, and revise almost simultaneously, the parts must be separated for instruction and may indeed be called *stages*, considering that stages are not necessarily linear, may allow for backtracking, and may even be conflated. Chapter 3 covers invention, Chapter 4 development and arrangement, and Chapter 5 revision. Each chapter in Part I is illustrated with examples from student and professional writing and has exercises to augment the discussion.

Part II, The Practice of Purposeful Writing, begins with composing that is close to the self (reflection), follows with writing meant to persuade or move an audience, and then covers the multiple purposes that emphasize the subject. Subject-emphasis writing, observing Moffett's scheme, begins with that which is closest to the self (recording) and proceeds through reporting, informing, and explaining. The remaining three subject-emphasis chapters present other common purposes for writing: instructing, praising or censuring, and summarizing and responding. The final chapter is completely new and responds to the need for instruction and practice in conducting and reporting research. In a style that is both respectful of the product and sensitive to the producer, this chapter takes students through the entire process, from using library resources to completing the paper in MLA or APA form. The chapter concludes with a complete student paper with MLA citations and sample pages of the same paper revised for APA form.

Except for Chapters 15 and 16, the chapters in Part II all follow a similar pattern: a discussion of the writing purpose, or aim, and then several pieces of writing that illustrate specific purposes, accompanied by discussion questions, analyses, exercises, and writing assignments. In each chapter, the readings suit the type of discourse covered, illustrating some of the specific purposes encompassed by the general aim. And since most writing has more than one purpose—not just to inform, for example, but to entertain as well, not just to reflect but also to persuade and inform—readers undoubtedly will discover purposes other than the ones targeted.

My students tell me they like topics that are relevant to their lives, humorous, and timely. Acknowledging the aging of the average college student and the diversity of backgrounds in the writing classroom, I've tried to select themes of interest and relevance to students of whatever age and whatever culture: nature and the environment, drugs, the Vietnam war, people, and the family, to name a few. I have also included numerous student essays to show that students are capable of interesting, sometimes enormously powerful and moving writing. Because these writings are not overly polished, they still read as if they were written by students.

Writing assignments are closely integrated with readings short enough to function as examples and models of how other writers have achieved their purposes. Accompanying discussion questions, analyses, and exercises further explore the purpose or topic. The writing assignments are process-oriented, often referring students to methods of prewriting, relating features of the reading, and suggesting possible trouble spots in revision. They are written in such a way, too, that teachers can easily revise and augment them as desired.

The coordinated exercises invite students to explore ideas rather than arrive at pat answers. Almost all the exercises require some writing. Most of them appeared in the first edition in a slightly different form; I've relabeled them to indicate the nature of the activity. Those under the heading "The Exploring Writer" are appropriate for journal writing or other individualized work; those labeled "The Community of Writers" are especially appropriate for group or pair activity.

Teachers can use chapters from both parts in any order, adapting them to their own teaching styles and local constraints. A workable plan is to begin with principles in Chapter 1, move to one of the Part II chapters for practice, and then continue to integrate Part I chapters with assignments in Part II. The flexibility of the book allows teachers to skip entire chapters, move back and forth within Part II, assign several readings and one writing within a chapter, and have students select a writing from a chapter in which some of the readings have been considered in class. The index, the glossary, and cross-referencing permit access to discussions of particular aspects of writing such as coherence, tone, and methods of development, which are treated in contextual discussions throughout the text.

A new feature of this edition that greatly expands its flexibility is the appendix, which begins with "Handbook: A Guide to Clear Sentences." Writers using *The Purposeful Writer* now have a reference on matters of usage, punctuation, and mechanics. Its arrangement is based on the assumption that students turn to a handbook mainly for solutions to problems. They will therefore find sections on sentence boundaries, sentence inconsistencies, problems with modification, verbs, pronouns, and style, plus treatments of punctuation, mechanics, and spelling. Section symbols facilitate the referral and location of relevant discussions. Appendix B, "The Making of English Sentences," discusses the coordinating and subordinating aspects of English sentences.

Acknowledgments

Readers familiar with scholarship in rhetoric will recognize themes and echoes from various camps and theorists. I am reluctant to name them, however, because of the alterations the ideas may have undergone before appearing here. James Moffett, for example, would hardly lay claim to the transmutation of his theories as they appear in this book. Even Frank Smith, to whom I am indebted for his compelling ideas on reading as a writer, would no doubt be reluctant to receive attribution for my treatment of such reading. I'm not claiming that my discussions are Aristotelian, Kinneavyan, Brittonist, Vygotskyan, Burkean, or whatever, but the influences are there, in altered form.

There are some people, however, who must be acknowledged because of their direct influence on the outcome of this book. I owe a tremendous debt to the colleagues who took the time and trouble to review early drafts and offer encouragement and specific suggestions for revisions. Reviewers are as follows: Joseph Barwick, Central Piedmont Community College; Kathleen Bell, Old Dominion University; Patrick Bizzaro, East

Carolina University; Patricia Connors, Memphis State University; Charles Dodson, UNC-Wilmington; Theresa Enos, University of Arizona; Patricia Graves, Georgia State University; Stephen Hahn, William Paterson College; Douglas Hesse, Illinois State University; C. Jeriel Howard, Northeastern Illinois University; Robert Inkster, St. Cloud State University; Peggy Jolly, University of Alabama; William Lalicker, Murray State University; Mary McGann, University of Indianapolis; George Miller, University of Delaware; James Porter, Purdue University at Fort Wayne; Robert Schwegler, University of Rhode Island; Christopher Thaiss, George Mason University; Nancy Walker, Southwest Missouri State University; Irwin Weiser, Purdue University; and Richard Zbaracki, Iowa State University.

At Allyn and Bacon, many people were actively involved in getting this book into print. I especially want to thank Joe Opiela, Executive Editor, Brenda Conaway, Editorial Assistant, and Rowena Dores, Production Editor.

Closer to home, let me acknowledge my students—for encouraging me at each stage of production and especially for creating some lively, thoughtful writing and then allowing me to include it here. Thanks also to my teaching assistants for their insightful comments and suggestions on the first edition, to fellow faculty member Lynn Bryce for sharing the extraordinary research paper written by her student Brian Woods, to Brian for graciously allowing me to display it, and to Judith Kilborn and the student contributors to *Kalaidoscope:* BernaDette Wilson, Wang Xiao, and Yong Il Song. Finally, I thank Ken, who, while I labored at crafting a book in my workroom, worked in his woodshop crafting objects at least as functional—the degree of function depending on one's purpose, of course.

Donna Gorrell
St. Cloud, Minnesota

PART I

The Principles of Purposeful Writing

CHAPTER 1

The Writer/Reader

Everyone who becomes a competent writer uses authors in exactly the same way. . . . They must read like a writer in order to learn how to write like a writer. There is no other way in which the intricate complexity of a writer's knowledge can be acquired.

—*Frank Smith*

You are a writer. Any time you put pen to paper or compose at the word processor, you are a writer. You may think you're just a student in a college writing class, doing assignments to get a grade and fulfill a requirement. You may think school writing is not real writing, not what professional writers do. There may even have been times when you would have *liked* to think of yourself as a "real" writer, maybe not in the company of Ernest Hemingway or Alice Walker, but a writer all the same. Or perhaps you *do* like to think that doing school writing makes you a writer but are hesitant to call yourself one. Whether or not you want to be a writer or have ever thought of yourself as one, you *are* one. In writing your assignments, you do some of the things professional writers do, and you think in some of the ways all writers think.

Being a writer means that you, like other writers, work with ideas. Your ideas may originate outside yourself—say in a lecture, something you've read or observed, or a discussion with friends. Then your mind does something with those ideas: bounces them around, turns them upside down, looks at them in different ways, relates them to and compares them with other ideas, sorts them out, takes them apart and looks at the components, questions what they mean. You may talk about these ideas with other people. And you put them down on paper. Eventually they get to a reader.

Paths Writing Takes

Writers have various ways of getting their thoughts on paper, ready for readers. These differences depend somewhat on the writer's preferences, but often they are decided more by the subject and purpose of the writing. When you are working with new ideas or new ways of looking at ideas, or in other ways striking out into uncharted territory, you can't map the plan in advance. First you explore; then you draw the map. But when the writing is familiar or routine, perhaps with its own structure, such as the narration of an incident, you already have an idea of what you're going to say. Picture these different approaches to writing as walks through the woods, sometimes slow and meandering, sometimes direct.

The Discovery Route

You take the slow discovery route when you don't know precisely what you want to say. With just a general idea in mind, you start writing about your thoughts, developing them as you go, not worrying about where you're heading because you can always go back and mark the path later, or take another path, or take a shortcut. At this stage you're not interested in following a map, such as an outline of some sort. You're interested only in exploring, to see where your ideas will take you, where you will end up, or whether you have to go back and start over. You're *discovering* now.

Only later, when you start thinking about an audience—someone who needs to follow you—do you begin to mark your path clearly. Then you write a thesis sentence as an overall guide to where your paper is going, you make your paragraphs coherent and complete, you add details as necessary, you delete irrelevant side trips, you add transitional sentences to connect paragraphs, and you write a concluding paragraph that clearly marks the end of this particular journey.

The Direct Route

At other times, you mark your path before you begin. You've been over this territory before and know the quickest way of getting to your destination. You know how to avoid pitfalls, obstructions, and wrong turns. You stay on familiar paths. When faced with this kind of writing, you engage in considerable thinking; you make an outline of some sort; you plan your examples, details, and arguments; you think about who your audience is and what you need to say to satisfy that audience. When you begin to compose, you follow your plan, making adjustments if necessary but for the most part using it as your guide. When you finish, your work is in decent order; it may need some revisions at the sentence level and some additions of overlooked details, but you don't have to move parts around or delete large chunks of unrelated material.

The Combination

Probably most of your writing combines the discovery and direct routes. You've been in these woods before, written this kind of paper before, but not by this path. Before you write, you think about what you are going to say and why you want to say it. You explore your ideas, either in your head or on paper, informally or through specific strategies. You may do some reading to find out what others have said. But at some time you feel the need to mark a plan for your ideas. As you write you do more discovering, because new ideas and new ways of looking at ideas come during composition. And you may revise your plan. Some of your writing goes quickly and easily, because you know what you want to say, and some of it is a struggle, because you're still working with your ideas.

Exercise: The Community of Writers

Here are three writing assignments on the general topic breakfast. *Write a short paragraph on each one. Then with a group of classmates exchange papers and discuss the methods for writing each paragraph as (a) discovery route, (b) direct route, or (c) combination.*

1. Describe what you ate for breakfast this morning.
2. Compare the breakfast you ate this morning with the kind of breakfast you usually had as a child.
3. Discuss the relative merits of eating breakfast or of skipping the meal.

Whatever your process for producing a piece of writing, being a writer means that at least at some stage—at the beginning, at the end, or all the way through—you think about your readers and order your thoughts so that your readers know where you are going, won't take any wrong turns, and won't get lost or frustrated along the way. As a writer, then, you *revise*, not just correcting and polishing but standing back and seeing the piece of writing again, through a reader's eyes, and making whatever changes are necessary—adding details, transitions, explanations; deleting unnecessary repetitions and empty words; working with awkward sentences;

rearranging paragraphs that are not in logical order; substituting words, sentences, and new ideas.

All this work and more is what it means to be a writer. And you are a writer.

Ways to Read

You're also a reader. This is not news to you; in your lifetime you've read assignments too numerous to count, and here you are, on the fifth page of this book, having just read about being a writer and what that means. You probably also know that there is more than one way of reading—of looking at those black-and-white marks on a page and making sense of them. You don't read a college textbook in the same way you read a romantic novel. If you did, you would probably fail the exam. Nor do you read a letter from the telephone company telling you that your account is a month overdue in the same way you read a letter from a good friend.

The way you read, like the way you write, is determined by your purpose. If you read for artistic appreciation when you need to remember and understand facts, you may overlook some of those facts. If you read for appreciation or facts when you need to proofread, you may overlook errors. When you read a news article in the newspaper, you seek information, and you expect it to be accurate and objective. But when you turn to the editorial page, you seek opinions on the news; the facts may be accurate here too, but the writer may have been strongly biased in selecting them, and you know you can disagree. Much of your reading, like writing, is probably done with a combination of purposes; when you read a poem, for instance, you no doubt have some desire to appreciate its artistry but surely also to understand what it has to say. Readers always have a purpose for reading, and they read according to their purpose and the requirements of the situation.

Reading for Meaning

If your purpose for reading is to prepare for an exam, then you read closely for a particular kind of meaning. You want to understand and remember everything that might be important and might be on the exam. You pay close attention to facts, charts, boldfaced type, and other clues to what is significant. You try to relate facts to ideas, so that they're more meaningful to you and therefore more likely to stick in your memory. If, in contrast, your purpose for reading is to enjoy a story just to relax and forget about your own world, you read fast, and in your eagerness to find out what the characters do next you may pass quickly over whatever seems insignificant. When you finish, you can vividly recount the plot and describe the characters, because you've just shared their experience of life, but when it comes to specific facts you may have little to say, because you passed over them too quickly.

Meaning Making Is Individual

Reading for meaning is a complex activity, more than just decoding marks on the page. Each time you read, whatever you read, you bring to that reading your own knowledge and experience, and your own purpose. To make meaning of the marks you see, you relate them to what you already know. If, for example, you were to read "The day was frustrating from start to finish," you would remember the frustrating days you've known. You might think of missed buses, rain pouring down when you forgot your umbrella, long lines at the bookstore, or other unfortunate times when everything went wrong. But what *you* see in the words is not quite the same as what someone else—a classmate also reading the book, perhaps—sees. You and other readers all envision different frustrating days. And none of them may be what the writer had in mind.

The writer is responsible for giving you more information than is presented in that sentence, and for doing so as clearly and explicitly as possible. In fact, as a reader you would *expect* the writer to tell you more. If the writer is careful in describing the frustrating day, you and other readers may be able to imagine a frustrating day that is similar to the one the writer intended. Your responsibility as a reader is to read the words in their context and not to make something else of them.

Active Reading

When reading for information or someone else's opinions, you need to read actively and critically, searching for the information you want, getting involved in what the writer is saying, but not allowing yourself to be swayed by faulty appeals to your emotions. To understand what writers are saying, active readers ask themselves questions like these:

Questions for Active Reading

1. What is the writer's purpose in writing?
2. What is the writer's main point?
3. Does the writer imply more than he or she is saying?
4. Is the information accurate?
5. Are the explanations clear?
6. Is the writer biased?

> ### *Questions (continued)*
> 7. Does the writer suppress or overlook some important information?
> 8. Does the writer attempt to pass off opinions as facts?
> 9. What is the writer's attitude toward the subject?
> 10. Is the writer an expert on the subject—or just pretending to be one?

(These types of questions are discussed and illustrated in Part II. See in particular Chapter 7, Writing To Persuade.)

If you are naturally skeptical, you probably already—perhaps unconsciously—question whatever you read. If you tend not to question what people say, you will find that you learn more about what you read if you actively seek answers to questions like these. You might also ask questions about the writer's relationship with the audience, like those listed on page 26–27.

Exercise: The Community of Writers

Read the following paragraph carefully and critically, asking the questions for active reading *and discussing your answers with a group of classmates.*

There is an evangelical preacher on television who goes by the name of Reverend Terry. She appears to be in her early fifties, and features a coiffure of which it has been said that it cannot be mussed, only broken. Reverend Terry is energetic and folksy, and uses a style of preaching modeled on early Milton Berle. When her audiences are shown in reaction shots, they are almost always laughing. As a consequence, it would be difficult to distinguish them from audiences, say, at the Sands Hotel in Las Vegas, except for the fact that they have a slightly cleaner, more wholesome look. Reverend Terry tries to persuade them, as well as those "at home," to change their ways by finding Jesus Christ. To help her do this, she offers a "prosperity Campaign Kit," which appears to have a dual purpose: As it brings one nearer to Jesus, it also provides advice on how to increase one's bank account. This makes her followers extremely happy and confirms their predisposition to believe that prosperity is the true aim of religion. Perhaps God disagrees. As of this writing, Reverend Terry has been obliged to declare bankruptcy and temporarily halt her ministrations.

—Neil Postman, *Amusing Ourselves to Death*

Reading as a Writer

Sometimes when you read, your primary purpose is not to make meaning of the words and marks on the page. Instead of directing your attention to what the marks represent, you scrutinize the marks themselves. The most obvious example of this purpose is proofreading your own writing for error. With this kind of reading, you pay attention to every word, dot, and squiggle you've written, so that you can find any mistakes you might have made in typing or copying. If you don't notice the errors and correct them, you may be giving your readers false signals. On a broader scale, you read your own writing for the purpose of revising: to determine whether your sentences are phrased clearly, to assess the accuracy and adequacy of your details, to see whether you've supported your thesis and whether you've gone off your topic, and so on. Reading to revise is essential for writers. (This kind of reading is discussed in greater detail in Chapter 5.)

Another purpose for reading other than to gain information is just to see how other writers express their thoughts. *You read as a writer.* This is a second kind of critical reading, in which you read not only for meaning but for style and structure as well. You notice how other writers organize their ideas, how they arrange words in their sentences, what words they use, how they fill up their paragraphs and then shift to new paragraphs, how they connect their paragraphs and sentences, how they begin, and how they end. This kind of reading is helpful even to experienced writers, because they, like all writers, struggle with their writing and want to know how others have solved similar problems. You too can read as a writer, learning writing from other writers.

Reading as a writer is often an unconscious act, done as an aside while reading for meaning. But it is an acquired way of reading; people can learn how to do it. The following list gives examples of questions readers might ask when they read as writers. Try applying these questions to essays, chapters, newspaper and magazine articles, and anything else you read.

Questions for Reading as a Writer

1. How does the writer begin?
2. How does the writer end?
3. Where does the writer state the main idea of the whole piece (thesis)?
4. How long are the writer's paragraphs?
5. Where does the writer express the main idea (topic sentence) of each paragraph?

Questions (continued)

6. How does the writer support ideas (examples, explanations, statements of authorities [testimony], statistics, comparisons, analogies, and so on)?
7. How does the writer use long sentences?
8. How does the writer use short sentences?
9. How does the writer connect ideas?
10. What kind of repetition does the writer use?
11. Does the writer repeat any grammatical structures (parallelism)?
12. Does the writer use any figurative language (metaphors, similes, and so on)?
13. Does the writer use any unusual words?
14. How does the writer use commas and other punctuation marks?

Exercise: The Community of Writers

Here is a paragraph by Henry David Thoreau. Reading it as a reader, you would ask questions like the active reading questions on page 6—in other words, you would want to know What does he say? When you read it as a writer, *however, you ask How does he say it? How does he connect related ideas? How does he emphasize important ideas? How does he begin and end? And so on. Read the paragraph first as a* reader *to determine what Thoreau says. Then read it as a* writer *to determine how he has written his ideas. After your second reading, discuss with your groupmates the questions that follow.*

I went to the woods because I wished to live deliberately, to front only the essential facts of life, and see if I could not learn what it had to teach, and not, when I came to die, discover that I had not lived. I did not wish to live what was not life, living is so dear; nor did I wish to practise resignation, unless it was quite necessary. I wanted to live deep and suck out all the marrow of life, to live so sturdily and Spartan-like as to put to rout all that was not life, to cut a broad swath and shave close, to drive life into a corner, and reduce it to its lowest terms, and, if it proved to be mean, why then to get the whole and genuine meanness of it, and publish its meanness to the world; or if it were sublime, to know it by experience, and be able to give a true account of it in my next excursion. For most men, it appears to me, are in a strange uncertainty about it, whether it is of the devil or of God, and have *somewhat hastily* concluded that it is the chief end of man here to "glorify God and enjoy him forever."

—Walden

1. Writers emphasize their main ideas through repetition. How many times does Thoreau repeat *life* and related words? How many additional times does he refer to life by means of the pronoun *it?*
2. Writers connect related ideas by means of parallel structures. What ideas are connected by the parallel infinitives in sentence 1—*to live, to front, see, discover?*
3. Writers sometimes use figurative language in the form of similes, metaphors, or analogies to make their writing vivid. "Suck out all the marrow of life" is one example of figurative language. Find other figures in this paragraph.
4. Writers often begin directly, plunging into the heart of the matter. What does Thoreau's direct beginning tell you about the main idea of this paragraph?

In the chapters in Part II you are asked to read both ways: as a reader and as a writer.

Learning Writing

This book is based on the assumption that reading aids writing. People who have studied writing know that effective writing can be achieved in three ways:

1. Through writing,
2. Through instruction and feedback, and
3. Through reading.

Improvement in writing requires all three techniques; one or two of the three is not enough. To write well, you need (1) plenty of writing; (2) someone to tell you how other writers write, what you're doing well, and how you can make your writing better; and (3) the special kind of reading just discussed—reading as a writer.

Writing

Much can be said for native ability. The best tennis players probably start out with an inherited predisposition for muscular coordination, strength, and build, together with mental alertness and speed. But the presence of these characteristics is not enough. If John McEnroe and Martina Navratilova had depended only on their inherited abilities, they would never have been good enough to play professional tennis. Only when inherited predispositions are developed through use can physical potential become physical prowess. Furthermore, and this is good news for the rest of us, even people whose genes don't make them the strongest or fastest or best coordinated can develop the characteristics they did inherit. They may not become the next Wimbledon champions, but with practice they can become skilled enough to enjoy an occasional game of tennis.

As with physical prowess, some people seem to be born with an inclination toward writing ability. They have an active imagination, an excellent memory for detail, and a sense of order and arrangement. They may start writing stories while they're still in elementary school, and in secondary school they may enter essay contests—and win. They get A's on their papers. They may become professional writers. But they, like athletes, must exercise their abilities if they want to use them well. The mental activities involved in writing, like physical skills, can be improved with use or can deteriorate with disuse. Even the less skilled writer can become skilled enough to enjoy writing. But there are no shortcuts. To write well, you must write and write and write.

It's not easy. It's not easy to be a very good tennis player, and it's not easy to be a very good writer. Both require work. And the difficulty of that work is not equally distributed. You may find some writing tasks relatively easy and others quite hard, while what's easy for you may be difficult for someone else. Very few people find all writing tasks easy. Some find all writing tasks hard. Analytical writing is almost always difficult, because it requires close reading, an open yet skeptical mind, comprehension, a critical response, and the skill for conveying this response to an audience. Narration of a personal experience, in contrast, is frequently easier, because it requires mainly remembering the experience and making sense of it for a reader.

Writing is difficult because it is a complex activity, involving many mental processes that are all tied up with knowledge and experience, attitudes toward subjects and audiences, and even physical ability to get words on the page. And to complicate matters, ideas and attitudes change even as we write. No one really knows everything that happens when someone writes. But we do know that through practice we can exercise the skills required for writing.

Instruction and Feedback

Tennis players need trainers and coaches—people to tell them how to handle the racquet and move their feet, what happens when a play doesn't work, what is getting better, what is good about their style, what still needs improvement. This instruction and feedback is meant to develop natural ability and to assist practice and training.

Writers too need instruction and feedback. Just writing, practicing the skills, isn't enough. You need someone to help you see when an idea doesn't come across clearly, which details could be added and which ones omitted, how your sentences might be improved, what is strong and good about your writing style, and so on. In this way you learn to look critically at your own writing. For student writers, this kind of feedback usually comes from the teacher or from classmates.

Everybody seems to fear criticism. We all want to think that what we've done is perfect and couldn't possibly be improved on, so, when other people tell us that they don't see how our third paragraph relates to our thesis, or that our conclusion is weak, or that other aspects of our writing are faulty, we're defensive. But criticism is part of writing. Remember that criticism can be favorable too. Doesn't it make you feel good when someone tells you what he or she really likes about something you've written? And even if the criticism is negative, isn't it better to get that feedback while you can still make changes, rather than after your work is completed? Writing always has readers, and reading is a matter of comprehending not only *what* writers say but *how* they say it. When the *how* is done well, readers are less conscious of it and concentrate more on the *what*. When writing is done poorly, the inaccuracies stand in the way of meaning, and readers notice the *how* instead of the *what*.

Don't underestimate the value of your classmates' opinions, and don't be afraid to ask for their feedback. Also, consider asking for criticism from other willing readers—roommates, parents, friends. Finally, learn to be your own best critic. Don't read your writing as if it's already perfect and the best you can do. Instead, look at it as something like a lump of wet clay on a potter's wheel. With a light touch here and there, or sometimes with a heavy hand, you can form a vase, then alter its style, redesign its shape, clarify your intentions—change the vase from just a pot to one that is both functional and lovely.

Reading

One way of learning to look at your writing as others might see it is to look critically at what others have written. As we have discussed, there are two kinds of **critical reading:** asking what the writer has said and asking how the writer has said it. Both can happen at the same time, while you are reading for meaning. You may have noticed when reading poetry that your attention focuses on both meaning and style, and that meaning, in fact, depends on style. This dual reading occurs at other times too, most often unconsciously. You may not even be aware that the style of a piece of writing has affected you as you read it. For example, read these sentences:

I began to read everything I could lay my hands on.

I began to read everything I could get.

In reading the first sentence, you probably paid no notice to the phrase "lay my hands on," yet your reading of the phrase affected your understanding of the sentence. When you read the second sentence, however, your attention was no doubt drawn to the word *get* simply because it is what makes the second sentence different from the first. Then you probably began thinking about any difference in meaning the change may have brought about. You shifted from unconscious to conscious perception of style; you were looking at *how* and *how well*.

When you read critically, you make the unconscious act of analysis a conscious one. You observe that something was said particularly well, or badly, and you pause to notice the phrasing. You come across a word you have never seen in print, and you observe how it's spelled and how it fits the context. Your attention is drawn to a single-sentence paragraph, and you stop for a second to wonder why it's so short. Maybe you've never read in this way before, but that's not to say you can't do it. It's not something you want to do every time you read, because it does slow your reading. But you will find that, as you practice being a conscious critical reader, your unconscious analytical powers will increase. At the same time, your appreciation of good writing will increase. When you analyze the work of other writers, trying to understand not only *what* they have said but *how* they have said it and *how well* they have said it, you have become a critical reader.

You can learn to apply this kind of critical reading to your own writing, to step back and look at *how* you've written as well as *what* you've written—to be your own, your first, critical reader.

Reading, Writing, and Thinking

What do you know about how you write? If you've ever written about your process of writing, the chances are good that you went into great detail on early stages (brainstorming, outlining, or whatever you do when you begin), and you devoted some time to what you do with a completed draft (how you revise). But what about the part in the middle? Can you describe what happens while you compose your draft? Many people, when asked, can't. They may know what they do before they start composing, and they can often describe how they revise, but they usually leave a big gap in between.

Reading this book will help you understand that part of the procedure. When you write, something tells you which words to use, how to combine your words in phrases, when to end a sentence, and so on. Something told Loren Eiseley to say, in the example sentence on page 12, "lay my hands on" instead of "get" or something else. And something tells you when you need an example to illustrate your point or when you're getting off your topic. Something tells you when your conclusion is not right. Where does this "something" come from? On what basis do you make all these decisions? What happens while you compose?

The easy way for you to describe your composing is to observe and record your actions, or to have someone else watch you as your pen moves across paper or your fingers tap keys on the word processor, producing words and sentences and other little marks on the paper or screen. This kind of observation usually reveals periods of fast composing, letters and words easily turning into sentences, sentences into paragraphs. It also reveals pauses, both long and short ones, in which you might stare out the window, pick at your fingernails, get up and walk around, sometimes even pack it up for the day. It reveals deletions, additions, substitutions. These are all observable aspects of composing.

But what is it that tells your fingers to make the letters? How do those fingers even know what a letter is? How do they know which letters go together to make particular words? (And even if you're a poor speller, remember that your fingers get *most* of your words right.) How do those words combine to make sentences? Why those words and not others? Why those sentences and not others?

It is your mind, of course, that propels your fingers, but how does your mind make those decisions? Somehow the mind works on ideas and ways of stating those ideas. It looks for relationships between what has been said and what is yet to be said. The mind asks: Can I say this? Is it true? It it right? Is it accurate? Is it clear? Then: How can I say this to make it clear? The mind looks for words and arrangements of words and for examples and analogies to illustrate the idea. And when the going gets really difficult, the mind backs off, takes a break, observes the caterpillar inching across the windowsill or takes you to the kitchen to inspect the contents of the refrigerator. The mind is not really off the task; it's just resting.

But still unanswered are the questions about how the mind knows what letters and words to choose and how to arrange them. How does a writer decide to say, as in the paragraph preceding the last one,

> But what is it that tells your fingers . . . ?

Why not

> But what is telling your fingers . . . ?

The second sentence is the way it read before revision. You may not even like the revised version; you may prefer the original. Or you may prefer still another version:

> But what tells your fingers . . . ?

All three ways are grammatically correct and say essentially the same thing, so why bother changing the sentence? How can we explain the final choice?

The mind makes its decisions on the basis of past experience. It weighs the truth and accuracy of a statement on the basis of what it has known to be true and accurate. It bases grammatical and stylistic decisions on what it has seen and done before: on *reading* and *writing*. Experience in reading and writing is what informs the decisions writers make. The more experienced the writer, the better informed the decisions.

This is where reading as a writer enters in. When you observe how other writers write, whether consciously or unconsciously, you amass knowledge that you can draw on when you yourself write. You don't copy what other writers have done, but, because you have read those ideas and stylistic choices, you are able to use them to inform your own decisions. When you know many ways to start a sentence, you can select the one that seems to give the emphasis, tone, and stylistic rhythm that you want. Take another look at the three example sentences, and see that even though the grammar is correct in all three and the meaning almost exactly the same, the emphasis, tone, and rhythm are different. Choices on such matters, where there are no rules, can be made only with knowledge gained from reading and from practice in writing.

Being a Reading Writer

This chapter carries the idea that reading is purposeful. You may read for various reasons, such as for information, for pleasure, for revising and correcting, and, as suggested here, for learning from other writers. The chapters in Part II of this book are designed to help you to be a *reading* writer, analyzing how other writers have met specific purposes in writing, and then to be a *writing* writer, writing to meet similar purposes. You will read the ideas of other writers as a means of generating new ideas. You will study how those writers express their ideas in writing, and perhaps you'll learn from their experience.

The remaining chapters in Part I will give you some background on what writing is and what writers do. Chapter 2 introduces purposes for writing and illustrates how purpose influences the emphasis of the writing. Chapters 3 through 5 investigate the process writers engage in as they write: prewriting in Chapter 3, drafting in Chapter 4, and revising in Chapter 5.

Exercise: The Community of Writers

1. With your groupmates, discuss the following questions plus the questions for active reading on page 6.
    a. What does Eiseley say about reading?
    b. What does he say about writing?
    c. What do you learn about his parents?
    d. What do you learn about Eiseley?
    e. What do you think is his opinion on the see-John-run sort of books?
    f. Eiseley recounts two vows he made as a child. What were they?

2. With your groupmates, discuss what Eiseley *does* with the content of his story. Here are some questions to help you focus your analysis:
    a. How does Eiseley use direct quotations? What is their effect?
    b. Eiseley's first sentence is packed with information. List at least five things he tells you in it.
    c. How does Eiseley handle chronology? What does paragraph 3 tell you about when he learned to read? Where does he tell the year of his parents' decision not to send him to kindergarten?
    d. List the words that seem unusual to you. Are they clear in context?
    e. Consider sentence length. Paragraph 1 consists of two long sentences separated by a short one. In paragraph 2, notice the different sentence patterns. Count the sentences and the words in this paragraph. Divide the second number by the first to get an average sentence length. What is the effect of the short sentences in this paragraph?

Exercise: The Exploring Writer

After reading "How I Learned to Read," write a brief account of the circumstances of your learning to read. Consider when it happened, where it occurred, who taught you, the first stories you remember reading, how you felt about reading, problems you had, or something else you recall about the experience. Choose the most interesting aspect and focus on that. Prepare to discuss your experience in class.

How I Learned to Read

Loren Eiseley

It so happened that when I was five years old my parents, in a rare   1
moment of doting agreement, looked upon their solitary child and
decided not to pack him off to kindergarten in that year. One can call
them feckless, kind, or wise, according to one's notions of the result.
Surprisingly, I can remember the gist of their conversation because I
caught in its implications the feel of that looming weather which, in after
years, we know as life.

"Let him be free another year," they said. I remember my astonish-   2
ment at their agreement. "There'll be all his life to learn about the rest.
Let him be free to play just one more time." They both smiled in sudden
affection. The words come back from very far away. I rather think they
are my mother's, though there is a soft inflection in them. For once, just
once, there was total unanimity between my parents. A rare thing. And I
pretended not to have heard that phrase "about the rest." Nevertheless
when I went out to play in the sunshine I felt chilled.

I did not have to go to kindergarten to learn to read. I had already   3
mastered the alphabet at some earlier point. I had little primers of my
own, the see-John-run sort of thing or its equivalent in that year of 1912.
Yes, in that fashion I could read. Sometime in the months that followed,
my elder brother paid a brief visit home. He brought with him a full adult
version of *Robinson Crusoe*. He proceeded to read it to me in spare
moments. I lived for that story. I hung upon my brother's words. Then
abruptly, as was always happening in the world above me in the lamplight,
my brother had departed. We had reached only as far as the discovery of
the footprint on the shore.

He left me the book, to be exact, but no reader. I never asked mother   4
to read because her voice distressed me. Her inability to hear had made
it harsh and jangling. My father read with great grace and beauty but he
worked the long and dreadful hours of those years. There was only one
thing evident to me. I had to get on with it, do it myself, otherwise I would
never learn what happened to Crusoe.

I took Defoe's book and some little inadequate dictionary I found   5
about the house, and proceeded to worry and chew my way like a puppy
through the remaining pages. No doubt I lost the sense of a word here
and there, but I mastered it. I had read it on my own. Papa bought me
Twenty Thousand Leagues Under the Sea as a reward. I read that, too. I began
to read everything I could lay my hands on.

Well, that was a kind of vow made to myself, was it not? Not just to   6
handle ABC's, not to do the minimum for a school teacher, but to read
books, read them for the joy of reading. When critics come to me again

I shall say, "Put Daniel Defoe on the list, and myself, as well," because I kept the vow to read *Robinson Crusoe* and then to try to read all the books in the local library, or at least to examine them. I even learned to scan the papers for what a boy might hopefully understand.

That was 1912 and in the arctic winter of that year three prisoners   7 blasted their way through the gates of the state penitentiary in our town. They left the warden and his deputy dead behind them. A blizzard howled across the landscape. This was long before the time of the fast getaway by car. The convicts were out somewhere shivering in the driving snow with the inevitable ruthless hunters drawing a narrowing circle for the kill.

That night papa tossed the paper on the table with a sigh. "They   8 won't make it," he said and I could see by his eyes he was out there in the snow.

"But papa," I said, "the papers say they are bad men. They killed the   9 warden."

"Yes, son," he said heavily. Then he paused, censoring his words   10 carefully. "There are also bad prisons and bad wardens. You read your books now. Sit here by the lamp. Stay warm. Someday you will know more about people out in the cold. Try to think kindly, until then. These papers," he tapped the one he had brought in, "will not tell you everything. Someday when you are grown up you may remember this."

"Yes, papa," I said, and that was the second vow, though again I did   11 not know it. The memory of that night stayed on, as did the darkness and the howling wind. Long after those fleeing men were dead I would re-enter that year to seek them out. I would dream once more about them. I would be—Never mind, I would be myself a fugitive. When once, just once, through sympathy, one enters the cold, one is always there. One eternally keeps an appointment with one's self, but I was much too young to know.

—*All the Strange Hours*

CHAPTER 2

The Writer's Purposes

Purpose in discourse is all important. The aim of a discourse determines everything else in the process of discourse.
—James L. Kinneavy

Chapter 1 establishes that readers have various purposes for reading, including gaining information, seeking pleasure, revising and correcting, and learning from other writers. In this chapter we investigate purposes for *writing.* Because you are both a reader and a writer, you should be aware of both kinds of purposes.

Writing always has a **purpose.** Think about it: Do you ever write when you don't have a reason for doing so? Even if you're just writing a shopping list or a diary entry, you have a purpose—to remember what to buy or to record thoughts or events. You may not always know what your purpose is; you may think you're writing to inform when your essay ends up being a piece of persuasion. In fact, most times when you write you probably have more than one purpose. The readings in Part II illustrate how writers often have multiple purposes. Jonathan Kozol in Chapter 11, for example, gives a lengthy list of facts about illiteracy ostensibly to inform the reader about its extent, but, in wanting to inform the reader, Kozol very likely wants also to persuade the reader to take action.

Your purpose in writing is related to three other components of the writing situation: the **writer,** the **audience,** and the **subject**—or the *I,* the *you,* and the *it.* Your purpose determines which of the three is being emphasized. When you write a shopping list to remember to buy certain things, the emphasis is on the subject, *it.* But when you write an entry in your diary to express your thoughts, with no intention of letting anyone else read what you've written, the emphasis is on the writer, *I.* By contrast, when you write a humorous essay intending to entertain, the emphasis is on your audience, the *you*.

What we're considering is **rhetoric,** a term that has many definitions. Some definitions of this word are negative, as a result of people using rhetoric for deception. But others are more neutral. One of the clearer definitions comes from a modern rhetorician, Donald C. Bryant: Rhetoric is "adjusting ideas to people and people to ideas." This definition assumes our three components: a subject, "ideas"; an audience, "people"; and a writer or speaker, the person doing the adjusting. Every piece of writing evolves from a **rhetorical situation.**

The Flexible Triangle

Think of the rhetorical situation as a triangle made of a rubber band, with each angle representing a component. The rubber band itself is the writer's purpose, and the area it encloses is the piece of writing: an essay, a story, a journal entry, a grocery list, a book report, and so on. If all angles and sides of the rhetorical triangle are equal, no one component is emphasized. Visualize it as in Figure 2-1. But the equilateral triangle is probably more common in geometry than in rhetoric. In rhetoric, the triangle is usually pulled in one direction or another, because the purpose generally emphasizes one component. Visualize it as one of those in Figure 2-2.

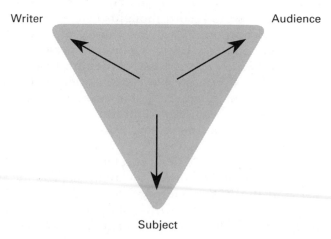

Figure 2-1. Rhetorical Triangle with Equal Emphasis on Components.

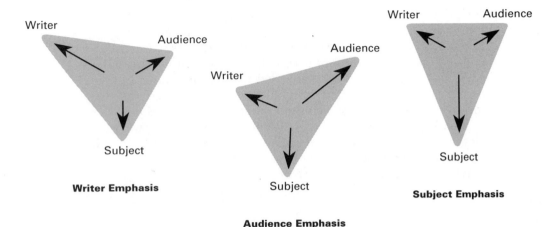

Figure 2-2. Rhetorical Triangles with Emphasis on Various Components.

Exercise: The Community of Writers

Each of the following passages illustrates writer-emphasis, audience-emphasis, or subject-emphasis writing. Read each passage to decide which component of the rhetorical situation is dominant and how the other two components enter in. Discuss your decisions with your groupmates, supporting your decisions with evidence from the passages.

1. "What's wrong with your language behavior? Have you said the wrong thing one too many times? When your back's against the wall, will you know what to say? In this book, best-selling author Dr. Elgin will show you how to develop verbal and nonverbal communication skills to control your language behavior and trigger positive responses from listeners."
    —From back cover of Suzette Haden Elgin, *The Last Word on the Gentle Art of Verbal Self-Defense*

2. "Without warning, in the middle of my thirties, I had a breakdown of nerve. It never occurred to me that while winging along in my happiest and most productive stage, all of a sudden simply staying afloat would require a massive exertion of will. Or of some power greater than will.

    "I was talking to a young boy in Northern Ireland where I was on assignment for a magazine when a bullet blew his face off. That was how fast it all changed."
    —Gail Sheehy, introduction to *Passages*

3. "On May 23, 1987, the *New York Times* ran a long obituary of Archie Carr, a zoologist who spent his entire fifty-five-year career studying the giant sea turtle. I had never heard of Professor Carr, but I enjoyed reading the story of his life. Operating mainly from a field camp in Costa Rica, he reestablished turtle populations in many countries where they had been almost exterminated for their food, developed tagging techniques that partly solved the mystery of their breeding cycle and their 1,200-mile migrations, and wrote eleven books that created a popular understanding of the work he and his colleagues were doing to save the species."
—William Zinsser, *Writing to Learn*

Writer-Emphasis Writing

The writer is always present in a piece of writing. As its originator, he or she must be there. Sometimes the writer's presence is barely discernible, as in most scientific and technical writing. In writer-emphasis writing, however, the *I* is dominant. Some instances of this writing may be autobiographical like Gail Sheehy's paragraphs, being *about* the writer and intended for an external audience. Others may be *for* the writer, with no other audience intended.

Writing in which the writer is the initial intended audience is often caged *reflective* writing, because it looks into the writer's thoughts. In Chapter 6 Mark Baker examines evil as it is encouraged in warfare, and two student writers reflect on growing up with alcoholic parents. These writers first used a personal style to explore their topics, then revised their drafts for another audience.

Another example of writer-emphasis writing is journal writing, in which the writer records experiences and impressions for personal purposes: to set down ideas for future reference, to think through confusing issues, to work out emotional reactions, and so on. Like the explorative type of reflective writing, journal writing sometimes yields topics that can be rewritten for an external audience. You can read more about reflective writing and journal writing in Chapter 6.

Autobiography and Credibility

As a reader, you will sometimes encounter entire pieces of autobiographical writing, writing *about* the writer that was intended for an audience other than the writer. More often, you will find such writing in introductions, where writers establish *credibility*, or their authority to write on a given subject. For instance, in her paragraphs on page 21, Gail

Sheehy introduces herself and an experience that propelled her into the writing of her book. A few pages later she announces, "It was this experience that made me eager to find out everything I could about this thing called *midlife crisis.*" As in much writing, she found it necessary first to clarify her relationship to her subject.

Writers establish their credibility primarily by being informed about their subjects. If you don't know about cataloging library books, you don't write about it. But if you are an accomplished swimmer, you can give authoritative instructions on how to do the backstroke. Given that you know your subject, you can increase your believability by projecting a role appropriate for the rhetorical situation.

Writer's Roles

People have many legitimate roles. You are probably not quite the same person in the classroom as you are when you're out with your friends or at home with your family. Depending on the situation, you present various facets of your character. You do this by the language you use, your tone of voice, the way you laugh and what you laugh at, the way you listen, even the clothes you wear. And though these facets of your character are all different, they are all valid; they're all you.

The same is true in writing. The facet of your character that presents a formal report is not quite the same as the part of you that writes an entry in your journal. In fact, the facet of your character that writes a paper for an English class is different from the one that writes a lab report. And as the role changes, the expression of it—the voice—changes too. Like your spoken voice, your written voice changes with your role. You would no more write an English paper the way you write a letter to a friend than you would talk in a classroom the way you would talk at a party. This is not to say that the role or the language in the classroom is better than at the party, just different.

Why is the role different? Because the other components of the rhetorical situation are different. The writer's role changes according to the audience and the subject. You are casual with friends, more formal with teachers. You can be frivolous at a party but must be serious in writing a paper.

Roles in Academic Writing

The features of the writer's role in academic writing are similar to those in writing for an employer or in any formal writing. When you write a paper, at school or on the job, you assume a **voice** that shows you are serious about your subject and respectful of your audience. You avoid slang and colloquial expressions, use vocabulary befitting the situation, and carefully edit errors. To appear informed about your subject, you try to be thorough and specific. To give the impression of an orderly mind, you organize your writing logically.

Your role as a writer is evident, then, in your vocabulary, grammar, style, tone, organization, treatment of details, and subject. This formality is not a fake role—no more than the *you* in dress clothes is any less real than the *you* in faded blue jeans and ragged sweatshirt. The more formal *you* is simply appropriate for the more formal situation.

These adjustments are often unconscious. Before beginning a piece of writing, you probably don't sit down and decide what role you need to assume. But when you write you do need to consider consciously the total rhetorical situation. Many inexperienced writers begin by considering only their subject, overlooking their own roles as writers, their audiences, and their purposes for writing. But what you say and how you say it are determined at least as much by the audience you're saying it to and your relationships with that audience and with your subject as they are by the subject itself.

Exercise: The Community of Writers

Discuss with your groupmates the variety of roles you each experience and the ways in which each role differs from the others. Discuss the legitimacy of each role.

Exercise: The Exploring Writer

Use the following information to write two paragraphs, the first in your English classroom role, the second in another role of your choice, one that seems to you decidedly different from the first. By vocabulary, grammar, style, tone, organization, and selection and treatment of details, express your role in the appropriate voice. Use as much information as you need and whatever order suits your purpose.

1. The copyright law of 1790, 1831, and 1909 was amended in 1976.
2. The amended law came into effect on January 1, 1978.
3. Copyright law gives ownership to authors of books, periodicals, computer programs, and other literary works; musical compositions, dramas, pantomimes, motion pictures, videotapes, and sound recordings.
4. With a few exceptions, the owner of a copyright has exclusive rights to reproduce the copyrighted work.
5. To declare a copyright, the author affixes a notice on the work by means of the letter *c* in a circle, the word *copyright,* or the abbrevi-

ation *copr.,* plus the date and the name of the owner of the copyright. Example: Copyright 1990 John Doe.

6. Owners may register their copyrights with the U.S. Copyright
   Office, The Library of Congress, Washington, DC 20559.

Audience-Emphasis Writing

Audience-emphasis writing tends to be more consciously persuasive
in purpose than some other kinds of writing. The writer appeals to
characteristics of the reader's personality and background to move that
reader to believe as the writer does. The first passage in the exercise on
page 21 appears on the back cover of the book it advertises, appealing to
the bookstore-browsing reader to purchase the volume. Reading this sales
pitch, you might suddenly remember all those embarrassing moments
when you said the wrong thing.

Some audience-emphasis writing is written strictly for entertainment.
Like persuasive writing, writing for entertainment makes certain assumptions about its readers: that they share experiences and knowledge upon
which humor or pleasure can be based.

If your purpose is to persuade or to entertain, your audience will be
the most important consideration, and knowing something about your
readers will be essential; at the very least, you should be able to make
reasonable guesses about their character and preferences. (You will find
writing for persuasion and entertainment treated in more detail in Chapters 7 and 8.)

Exercise: The Community of Writers

*Read the following paragraphs and discuss with your groupmates the shared
knowledge they depend on.*

Take the experience of the couple from Lorain [Ohio] who bought   1
a house trailer and went on a vacation trip to Florida. All went well until
the return trip home. The husband grew weary after many hours at the
wheel and finally abdicated the driver's seat in favor of his wife, while he
went back to the trailer and fell asleep.

It was a nervous sleep, to be sure. He had never before trusted his   2
wife at the wheel, and he was naturally uneasy over the risks involved.
When the vehicle suddenly came to an abrupt, screeching stop, he
immediately assumed the worst and leaped out of the back of the house
trailer to see what had gone wrong.

All that had happened, actually, was that a traffic signal suddenly had 3
turned red and the wife had found it necessary to slam on the brake. By
the time the husband, dressed only in his underwear, made his exit to the
street and in his slow, sleep-fogged way sized up the situation, the light
had turned green and the wife blithely drove away, leaving him in the
middle of the intersection in his underdrawers. That's where a police
cruiser came upon him a few minutes later.

"I can explain it all, officer!" said the husband to the policeman as 4
his shivering shanks were hustled into the cop car. No doubt he did, in
time, but the explanation could not possibly have been an easy one.

—George E. Condon, *Cleveland Plain Dealer*

Audience Considerations

Whatever the rhetorical situation, writers need to consider their audience. What you write will most likely be read by people who have
backgrounds, experiences, and perceptions of your subject that are quite
different from yours. As noted in Chapter 1, a writer must give readers
enough information to allow them to read as the writer intended. To
know what information is necessary, you need to know something about
your readers.

Here are some questions you might ask as you write—while you're
exploring the subject, while you're composing, and as you revise.

Questions About Audience for Writing

1. Who is my audience?
2. What does my audience know about my subject?
3. What does my audience know about me?
4. What is my relationship to my audience?
5. How interested is my audience in my subject?
6. How can I stimulate audience interest?
7. What is my audience's attitude toward my subject?
8. What is my audience's attitude toward me?
9. Do I want to change what my audience knows or how it feels
   about me and my subject?
10. What experiences and knowledge do I share with my audience?
11. How can I use those experiences and that knowledge to
    present my subject?

Questions (continued)

12. How does my audience perceive the rhetorical situation in which I am writing: reflective, persuasive, informative, or something else?
13. What does my audience expect of my grammar, style, and vocabulary?

Answers to questions about your audience—these or others you may ask—can help you make decisions about your approach to your subject, what details to include and omit, how to organize your material, what words to use, what level of formality is appropriate, and so on. You won't always have answers to all your questions, but ask them anyway (even if your audience is "just" your teacher) and *guess* the answer. You'll probably be close to right, and that's better than not considering the audience at all.

Questions about audience are useful for reading as well for analyzing your own writing or that of other people. Use them along with the questions for active reading on page 6.

Answers to these questions can give you insights into the relationship writers establish with their audiences.

Questions About Audience for Reading

1. Who is the intended audience? Am I among that group?
2. What does the writer assume the audience knows about the subject?
3. What does the writer seem to know about the audience?
4. What is the writer's relationship to the audience?
5. How interested am I, as audience, in the subject?
6. What does the writer do to stimulate my interest?
7. What is my attitude toward the subject?
8. What is my attitude toward the writer?
9. Does the writer want to change what I know or how I feel about the writer and the subject?
10. What experiences and knowledge does the writer assume we share?
11. How does the writer use those experiences and that knowledge to present the subject?

> **Questions (continued)**
> 12. How do I perceive the rhetorical situation of this piece of writing: reflective, persuasive, informative, or something else?
> 13. What assumptions does the writer make about my expectations of grammar, style, and vocabulary?

Exercise: The Community of Writers

Read the following column, being particularly sensitive to the writer-audience relationship. Then discuss the questions about audience for reading, supporting your answers with details from the column.

Medicine That Purrs

Ellen Goodman

Not long ago, I read a small story about a cardiac study in Baltimore and filed it away in my mind under the heading "Pets Heal Broken Hearts."   1

The story was about a biologist, Erika Friedman, who had studied ninety-two heart patients for a year after they left the hospital. She wanted to see whether there were any special social reasons why some of them did better than others.   2

It turned out that there was something called a Pet Factor. Only three of the fifty-seven patients with pets died during that year, compared to eleven of the thirty-nine without pets.   3

I am, by habit, wildly skeptical about the sort of studies that end up in pop form. Their authors are usually found a few months later jogging through *People* magazine in expensive terrycloth shorts, followed by their children and their paperback rights. So I have no idea whether the American Heart Association should start filling out prescription pads for budgies and beagles.   4

Nevertheless, the study piqued the curiosity I've had about people and pets since I bought my first turtle at my first circus. It has often occurred to me that pet owning is not a two-way relationship, but is, rather, two one-way relationships.   5

I currently live under the same roof with two large, black dogs that eat mail in lieu of the mailman. In my life as a dog owner, I have grown to realize that people and pets do not really have very much in common except each other. I have to give credit for this thought to William James, who once said: "Take our dogs and ourselves, connected as we are by a   6 tie more intimate than most and yet . . . how insensible each of us is to all that makes life significant for the other—we to the rapture of bones under hedges, or smell of trees and lamp posts, they to the delights of literature and art."

The truth is that we have hung out together for lo these million years   7 out of convenient mutual needs. The need of a pet for a person is as clear-cut as a bowl of food. The only true love song uttered by a dog in the entire history of Anthropomorphism is the one Snoopy howls called "Suppertime." The chorus goes like this: "Suppertime, suppertime, suppertime. . . ."

The average dog or cat will do almost anything to reinforce human   8 supper-giving behavior. Ogden Nash once glowingly wrote:

I marvel that such
Small Ribs as These
Harbor such a
Desire to Please.

But to the less romantic among us, this behavior is a matter of thousands of years of natural selection. The dogs that did not "desire to please" ended up in dog pounds that stretched from the Fertile Crescent to the Golden Gate.

But the need of a person for a pet is something entirely different.   9 Except for Doberman pinschers, the average urban-suburban pet owner is looking for a living thing that (1) needs him and (2) can't talk back.

In short, we seek an uncritical constant companion that can never   10 spill the beans. Millions of dog owners commit themselves to a lifetime of walking in the rain simply because the animal on the other end of the leash will never sue . . . for malparenting. Thousands prowl the streets of Manhattan with scoopers and paper bags in order to have something wagging its tail when they get home. Millions more become devoted to kitty litter so that they can lecture something which will only come back with a purr, and never say, "You're neurotic."

I'm not talking about the crazies, the 141-cat-ladies, and people who   11 build monuments to their Welsh terriers and leave trust funds to their Siamese. They always knew that one dog was worth ten doctors.

We are in this case talking about your better-basic-hamster owner, the   12 full professor who talks baby-talk to his schnauzer and the bureaucrat who worries if he has to leave his bunny at a strange kennel.

This study suggests, just suggests mind you, what we may need for our   13 health. "Taking care" may be as important as taking digitalis. A loyal and friendly companion may be a perfect pacemaker. We all seem to need to be needed, and we thrive on a dose of uncritical companionship. If we can't get it on two legs, we'll take it on four. We'll even take it on the wing.

Subject-Emphasis Writing

Most writing emphasizes the subject. In academic writing, as in business, technical, and other nonfiction writing, the primary purpose is to convey information—to compile it and transmit it, to show you have learned it, to learn it through writing it, sometimes even to show that you know the conventions of conveying it. If you think of most of the school writing you've done, you'll probably realize that the emphasis was not on you, the writer, or on your intended audience. Rather, the emphasis was on the subject—again with the qualification that the writer and audience components of the rhetorical situation were present. Refer to the paragraph by William Zinsser in the exercise on page 22. There you see an emphasis on the subject, Professor Carr, for the purpose of informing the reader about Zinsser's newly discovered knowledge about him. Note that even though the passage has a subject emphasis, Zinsser includes a bit of himself: "I had never heard of Professor Carr, but I enjoyed reading the story of his life."

In much school writing, not only is the subject emphasized but it is determined by someone else. You write a sentence, a paragraph, or an essay in response to a teacher's question. By so doing you show what you know about the subject, and you often learn something new about it. Or you read about an assigned subject and then summarize and/or respond to what you've read, showing that you have done the reading and understand it. In such assignments, you don't need any means of discovering a subject. In other cases, though, you have to find your subject, especially in writing classes when your teacher assigns a particular kind of writing (for example, a narrative essay) or a particular purpose (such as telling someone how to make something). Whether the subject is assigned or not, you need ways of exploring it, generating ideas related to it, and deciding what you will say about it. (Writers have many ways of exploring ideas, some of which will be discussed in Chapter 3 under "Discovering Ideas" and "Invention." In addition, each chapter in Part II suggests things you can do to discover what you have to say.)

People have many **purposes** for conveying information. Some of these are *to record, to report, to inform, to explain, to instruct, to praise or censure, to summarize and respond,* and *to ask and answer questions.* This chapter takes a brief look at these purposes; each one is explained and illustrated in more detail in Part II.

Subject-emphasis purposes for writing overlap a great deal. In this book the essays illustrating **recording** as a purpose can generally be viewed as telling *what is happening;* for example, saying, "By exercising, you are reducing the cholesterol in your blood." In contrast, the essays illustrating **reporting** look back on *what happened;* you might say, "You reduced the cholesterol in your blood by exercising." The essays illustrating **informing** tell *what happens* under given circumstances; they generalize about events. For example, you might say, "Exercise reduces cholesterol in the blood." Two other subject-emphasis purposes, **explaining** and **instructing,** tell *why something happens or happened* and *how something is done or how to do it:* why exercising reduces cholesterol in the blood and how to exercise to reduce cholesterol in the blood.*

To Record

Writers **record** something as it happens for the purpose of preserving the information: "The temperature is 96°F." "The committee agrees to hear the petition." Your class lecture notes and lab notes are records, as are notes you make on your reading. You may record individual and group activities, for later summarizing and reporting. Records are often informal, telegraphic, and fragmented. When they are prepared for another audience, however, as for a teacher or a supervisor, they are rewritten in a more complete form.

The following paragraph records the end of a tennis match. Notice in its terminology the assumptions it makes about the audience's knowledge. Notice too the present tense of verbs and the relative absence of the writer's opinions.

> Taylor lobs. Laver runs back, gets under the bouncing ball, kneels, and drives it into the net. He is now down 1-5. He is serving. He wins three points, but then he volleys into the net, again he volleys into the net, and again he volleys into the net—deuce. He serves. He moves forward. He volleys into the net. Advantage Taylor—match point. The sound of the crowd is cruel. "Quiet, please!" the umpire says. Laver serves, into the net. He appears to be trembling. He serves again. The ball does not touch the ground until it is out of the court beyond the base line.
>
> —John McPhee, *Pieces of the Frame*

No writing can be totally objective. It can represent information only as the writer perceives it. In this paragraph, the sentences "The sound of the crowd is cruel" and "He appears to be trembling" record the writer's impressions of what he observes. (Chapter 9 has further examples of writing to record.)

To Report

Reporting is related to recording in that something that is reported may first be recorded. In other words, a thing is *recorded* as it happens; it

---

*I am loosely borrowing from and amplifying James Moffett's *Teaching the Universe of Discourse* (Boston: Houghton Mifflin, 1968).

is *reported* after it happens. Reporting is also related to *informing* in that most reports convey information.

School writing, as well as much business and scientific writing, requires a great deal of reporting. You might do book reports, lab reports, news reports, reports of library research, and reports of individual or group activities. In much of this kind of writing, the personality and opinions of the writer are not important or relevant. Moreover, the audience is assumed to be interested, so there is often no need to appeal to its preferences. It is important, however, to know who the audience is and what its level of expertise on the subject is, because this knowledge will determine your vocabulary and selection of details. The subject is presented as clearly and directly as possible, using as much detail as is necessary for the audience. The style is usually formal, but not extremely so. The verbs are mainly in the past tense.

In Chapter 10, Rachel L. Carson reports objectively on conditions in the Sargasso Sea, but when student writer Janice Anderson reports an experience at the state fair, she includes her reactions. The following paragraph concentrates on the subject, telling you little about the writer's opinions.

> Ominous black clouds boiled up into the afternoon sky over eastern Iowa one day in September 1972, and shortly before 2 p.m. a tornado touched down northeast of Cedar Rapids. It was a giant twister. It plowed through the countryside for 66 miles, staying on the ground six times longer than the average tornado and leaving a mile-wide swath of destruction.
>
> —*Wall Street Journal*

(Chapter 10 has more examples of writing that reports.)

To Inform

In writing that focuses on the subject, **informing** may be the most common purpose. Much of what is written in magazines and books is for the purpose of passing on information to an audience, sometimes with an ancillary aim of entertaining or persuading. Your textbooks are written to inform and to instruct. Many of the essays you write in an English class are for informing, with the additional purpose of improving your writing. In practice, informing can incorporate almost every other subject-emphasis purpose, and even purposes with an emphasis on the writer or the audience. Writing that informs may also report, explain, instruct, praise, and so on.

The writer of a magazine article not only wants to inform and entertain you, she also may want to persuade you, as well as to make money and become known as a writer. You write an essay in class not just to inform your reader and summarize an assigned reading but to get a grade as well. So, when you think of informing as your purpose for writing, you might well probe a little deeper and see what submerged purposes you have. If, for example, persuasion is one of your aims, you will need to give a different kind of attention to your audience than if you want only to inform. In careful reading, too, you ought to be aware of the writer's possible multiple intentions.

Audience is always a consideration in informative writing. To inform successfully, you must make some guesses about what the audience knows. Otherwise you risk boring your readers with something they already know or frustrating them by saying too little. With informative writing, you should always have answers to questions like those on page 26. In the following example, the audience is assumed to be student writers who might want to learn from professional writers.

> Professional writers begin by trying to interest readers. They never start by saying, "How can I avoid making mistakes?" They ask themselves this question instead: "How can I make people pay attention to what I am saying and take my writing seriously?" Good writers want to be correct. They know that if they use incorrect spelling, sloppy punctuation, erratic grammar, and rough syntax they will destroy the effect of their writing—just as a pianist who hits a few wrong notes will destroy the effect of a Beethoven concerto. But professional writers never assume that correctness is enough in itself. They want to engage readers and keep them engaged.
>
> —Richard Marius, *The Writer's Companion*

This paragraph borders on instruction, as well it might since it comes from a textbook. You may find that much writing to inform has instruction as a secondary purpose. But compare this paragraph with the example in the section "To Instruct" to see how instruction as a primary purpose influences writing. (You will find more examples of informative writing in Chapter 11.)

To Explain

Although explaining is similar to both informing and instructing, **explaining** tells *why* something is the way it is or works the way it does. Sometimes it analyzes *how* something works. Explaining may intend to justify actions, for example why you missed class. It aims for understanding through analysis of parts or causes. In Chapter 12, Judith Viorst explains, through classification analysis, how she perceives friendships; Jonathan Schell explains, by causal analysis, what the consequences of the detonation of a one-megaton bomb would be; and student writer Terry Splett explains, through comparison, how her family celebrated both

Chanukah and Christmas. (Other essays in Chapter 12 further illustrate explaining as a purpose for writing.) Here's a brief example that explains how lie detectors work:

> As I understand it, a human being cannot tell a lie, even a small one, without setting off a kind of smoke alarm somewhere deep in a dark lobule of the brain, resulting in the sudden discharge of nerve impulses, or the sudden outpouring of neurohormones of some sort, or both. The outcome, recorded by the lie-detector gadgetry, is a highly reproducible cascade of changes in the electrical conductivity of the skin, the heart rate, and the manner of breathing, similar to the responses to various kinds of stress.
>
> —Lewis Thomas, "The Lie Detector"

To Instruct

You may think that much of what you read in school has been written for the purpose of instruction, and in a way that's true. However, the distinction here is between instructing *that* and instructing *how*. Instructing *that*—relating facts, information, conjectures, and so on, or analyzing causes, actions, or relationships—falls more within our categories of informing or explaining as a purpose. **Instructing** as a purpose of writing in this book means instructing *how*. This kind of writing usually addresses the reader directly, while concentrating on the subject. In Chapter 13, Campbell Morris tells how to make a smooth-flying paper airplane, and Tom Bodett, with tongue in cheek, discusses a new sport, "ditch diving." Here is a brief example of instruction:

> Don't ever hesitate to imitate another writer—every artist learning his craft needs some models. Eventually you'll find your own voice and shed the skin of the writer you imitated. But pick only the best models. If you want to write about medicine, read Lewis Thomas; if you want to write literary criticism, read Edmund Wilson and Alfred Kazin.
>
> —William Zinsser, *On Writing Well*

In this paragraph, the imperative mood ("don't ever hesitate") and the pronoun *you* speak directly to the reader, telling *how* to write. (You will find other examples of instruction in Chapter 13.)

To Praise or Censure

Praising and **censuring** are more common in writing outside school. But even in school you know their effects: You read biographies, sometimes book length or essay length but more often short pieces describing an author, a scientist, a diplomat, and so on. Often these pieces are more than information; they extol the individual. And you may be familiar with the necessity of having letters of recommendation, highlighting your good points and, you hope, omitting your weaknesses. On the other side, there is censure—less common than praise and certainly less welcome. In Chapter 14, a student criticizes a former teacher, and Tom Wolfe takes a cynical look at people who want to be like everyone else.

You probably remember Marc Antony's speech in Shakespeare's *Julius Caesar* that begins

> Friends, Romans, countrymen, lend me your ears;
> I come to bury Caesar, not to praise him.
> The evil that men do lives after them,
> The good is often interred with their bones;
> So let it be with Caesar.

Then Antony does just the opposite of what he proposes: He praises Caesar, as well as censuring Brutus, inciting the crowd against Brutus and the other traitors. This speech shows how both praise and censure can be effective. You'll find other examples of praise and censure in Chapter 14.

To Summarize

Although **summarizing** usually accompanies other kinds of writing, it also stands alone as a primary aim in both student writing and writing on the job. Summarizing is an essential skill. It is a component of reporting: You summarize lecture or lab notes, reading assignments, articles you've read in your library research, and individual or group activities. Summarizing is also integral to reviewing or responding to reading. Your teachers sometimes assign summaries of required reading because they know that the act of summarizing will aid both your remembering and your understanding. Abstracts, which are a type of summary, and executive summaries are almost always parts of business and other professional reports, serving to focus the reader's attention and save valuable time.

To summarize well, go to the heart of the matter first, then add other essential information—not quoted sentences and phrases—from the original. In the following opening paragraph of summary, you can see that the writer makes an overall statement of what the summarized book is about.

> The newly single man has the reputation of being lucky: freed from the old ball and chain at last, he can pursue his every whim. But divorced and widowed men suffer and often suffer alone, as Jane Burgess explains in *The Single-Again Man.* . . . Burgess describes how these men cope with their feelings and their children and how they readjust.
>
> —Pamela Black, *Psychology Today*

(Chapter 15 gives you an opportunity to work on your summarizing skills.)

To Respond

Response, a common purpose, is a companion to summary. Think of the millions of letters and memos written every day in response to other letters and memos. Think of all the requests for information which bring about responses that furnish the information (in which case a secondary purpose is to inform). People also respond to arguments, with the added purpose of persuasion. Book and article reviews are a type of response that includes summary. Response can be either information or opinions, sometimes a statement of the writer's opinion based on evidence or authority.

Here is a very brief book review that includes both summary and response:

> Mr. Dovlatov's "Russian Family Album" consists of ironically deadpan sketches of his relatives. That is, he claims the characters are his relatives, but he uses them to present a satirical picture of Soviet society in its more pretentious and irrational aspects. This small book is tart, funny, and maliciously deflative.
>
> —Phoebe-Lou Adams, review of *Ours* by Sergei Dovlatov, from *The Atlantic*

(Chapter 15 also covers response.)

To Ask Questions

Students are often thought of as the ones who *answer* questions, but serious students learn to *ask* them too. You have probably known times when you realized that to ask the right question you had to be informed. In class, for example, your questions and the way you frame them reveal that you've read the assignment. When you ask an informed question, you not only show what you know but also get more information. You see a remarkable increase in your learning simply by doing your assignments and then asking questions about what you don't understand. In writing too, asking informed questions is appropriate. Questions are common in the business world, where letters and memos are written to elicit information and clarify points.

In writing, asking questions is a way of beginning essays and ending them, a way of responding to required reading, a way of beginning research and looking at its implications. Sometimes writers use questions as the organizing principle of an entire piece of writing. Here is the way Sydney J. Harris opens one of his essays:

> If there should be, on Christmas night, a second coming, would there not be soon a second crucifixion?

And this time, not by the Romans or the Jews, but by those who proudly call themselves Christians?

I wonder. I wonder how we today would regard and treat this man with His strange and frightening and "impractical" doctrines of human behavior and relationships. Would we believe and follow, any more than the masses of people in His day believed and followed?

Would not the militarists among us assail Him as a cowardly pacifist because He urges us not to resist evil?

—"If Christ Returned on Christmas"

Harris continues asking questions that begin "Would not," and he ends the essay with the quizzical statement "I wonder." Though such extensive use of questions is rare, it does happen. These questions are not so much to solicit answers as to stimulate thought. For this reason, they are effective at the beginning and end of an essay.

To Answer Questions

Paired with asking questions is answering them. This purpose for writing appears to be informing; however, there is a fundamental difference between the two. When you inform, you assume that the audience doesn't know what you know. But when you answer questions *to show what you know,* as in exams, your audience knows more than you do and will evaluate your learning on the basis of what you write. That's not a very desirable writing situation, and it's not as much fun as most other kinds of writing, but it's a fact of school life (and often of business and professional life) and a valid aim for writing. When you are in this situation, you must

1. Focus on the larger picture to show that you understand the information,
2. Add supporting details to show that you can handle the facts,
3. Use vocabulary appropriate to the subject or field,
4. Organize carefully, again to show that you understand your material, but also to make the reading easier, and
5. Edit for gross errors that will impede reading.

Essay examinations are a specialized type of writing in which answering questions is the major purpose.

You might say that showing that you know a subject well is an aspect of all writing, because you never want to appear uninformed when you write. But in those cases your main purpose is something else, and you probably know more about your subject than your reader does. (Essay-examination writing is discussed in more detail in Chapter 15.)

A Rhetorical Blend

Writer emphasis, audience emphasis, subject emphasis—these are some of the important purposes for writing. This chapter has established that all writing has a rhetorical situation: a writer, an audience, and a subject, all of which are affected by the purpose for writing. We have concentrated on each component separately and described the related purposes. Yet it is important to remember that, even when writing emphasizes one of the components, the other components are present. You always have your role as a writer; you have an audience, usually other readers but sometimes yourself; and you have something to write about, your subject. It may be the presence of all three components that accounts for writers often having more than one purpose when they write. As you will see in Part II, multiple purposes are common, even while one purpose is dominant. In the next chapter we will begin looking at what writers do to produce a piece of writing.

Exercise: The Community of Writers

Read the following short essays and discuss these questions with your groupmates.

1. What is the purpose of the essay? Can you find secondary purposes?
2. Is the emphasis of the essayist on the writer, the audience, or the subject?
3. What role does the writer seem to assume?
4. What is the writer's attitude toward the subject?
5. Whom does the writer seem to assume as audience?
6. What do you see as the main idea of the essay? Write that idea in a single sentence.

Writers at Work

Kenneth Roberts' working methods and ours differ so widely it is hard to realize we are in the same line of business. We've just been looking through his book "I Wanted to Write" and marvelling at his stamina and his discipline. The thought of writing apparently stimulates Roberts and causes him to sit upright at a desk, put in requests to libraries, write friends, examine sources, and generally raise hell throughout the daylight hours and far into the night. He works at home (where his privacy is guarded), writes in longhand, counts the words, keeps a record of moneys received, and gets a great deal done. Now turn for a moment to your correspondent. The thought of writing hangs over our mind like an ugly cloud, making us apprehensive and depressed, as before a summer storm, so that we begin the day by subsiding after breakfast, or by going away, often to seedy and inconclusive destinations: the nearest zoo, or a branch post office to buy a few stamped envelopes. Our professional life has been a long, shameless exercise in avoidance. Our home is designed for the maximum of interruption, our office is the place where we never are. From his remarks, we gather that Roberts is contemptuous of this temperament and setup, regards it as largely a pose and certainly as a deficiency in blood. It has occurred to us that perhaps we are not a writer at all but merely a bright clerk who persists in crowding his destiny. Yet the record is there. Not even lying down and closing the blinds stops us from writing; not even our family, and our preoccupation with same, stops us. We have never counted the words, but we estimated them once and the estimate was staggering. The only conclusion we can draw is that there is no such thing as "the writing man," and that after you have waded through a book like "I Wanted to Write" you still don't know the half of it, and would be a fool to try and find out.

—E. B. White, *The Second Tree from the Corner*

Sick of Slipping and Sliding on Icy Streets?

Imagine walking across all of the thin, slick patches of ice on sidewalks and streets without the worry of slipping and falling. A revolutionary product is now available which will save you the pain and embarrassment of slipping on ice and packed snow. Shoe chains. 1

Sure, you may feel a little strange at first to be the only person walking down the street with chains on the bottom of your shoes or boots, but once others realize how carefree you are when you walk across the icy sidewalks, they'll want shoe chains too. 2

Shoe chains are designed to give traction the same way tire chains work for cars. Just slip them around your shoes and you're ready to tackle the ice and snow without worry Shoe chains don't weigh down your feet and will last many snowy, slippery winters. They come in three sizes made to fit all shoes. 3

If you are ready to give up all the needless worry of an embarrassing fall on the ice, just fill out the enclosed order form, which includes a size chart to help you determine your shoe chains size. For only $10.00 you can abandon the hassle of slippery sidewalks and streets. Order shoe chains for friends and family as Christmas gifts and save $2.00 on every additional pair. 4

If you are in need of traction and stability for winter walking, shoe chains are for you! 5

—Michele (student writer)

CHAPTER 3

The Writing Process: Prewriting

The teacher may demonstrate the technique of systematic questioning, but the students must apply the technique for themselves if they are really to learn its usefulness.
—Richard L. Larson

There is no single writing process. The way you write a report is probably very different from the way you write a persuasive piece. Writing a letter to a friend is different from writing a letter to your employer. Your process of writing is determined by who you are as a writer, who your audience is, what you're writing about, and what your purpose is for writing.

Whatever your procedure for producing a piece of writing, you decide what to write, **prewriting;** get it down in words, **drafting;** and make some changes, **revising.** When you write a lengthy report, you may spend much of your time searching for, reading, and sifting information. By the time you are ready to begin your first draft, you may already have a thick stack of note cards, a thesis sentence, an outline, and an odd assortment of jottings. After you've composed your first draft, you revise carefully and repeatedly to produce a paper that represents your best work. When you write a friendly letter, by contrast, you may start writing as soon as the paper is in front of you, you discover your ideas as you write, one idea leads to another, and you cross out and substitute words as you go, so that whatever revisions you make are done while you are composing.

Most writing, however, is somewhere between these extremes. You start with some kind of prewriting or planning, then do your drafting, then work on revising. Even with the friendly letter, you are likely to begin thinking about what you want to say before you get the paper out and then to read over and correct what you've written before you fold it up and drop it in the mail. Thinking in advance is part of the writing process just as surely as forming the words on the page or crossing out and revising are.

The scale of this process is not necessarily the entire essay or letter. More likely, the scope is smaller, such as a paragraph or even a sentence. The "stages" of writing may occur within a single sentence, as when you pause to decide what you want to say in your next sentence, draft the sentence, then reread and revise it, or when you plan and revise even while composing the sentence. Prewriting, then, to look at it literally, is what you do before you draft, and revising is what you do after there's something to revise, either in your thoughts or on paper. In practice, prewriting, drafting, and revising occur so concurrently that you barely distinguish them as stages. Let's just say that **prewriting** is all the decisions you make before you write.

Discovering Ideas

Ideas for writing may originate in the middle of a conversation when a word or an idea opens up a flood of new thoughts, or in a sensory impression when a particular scent or sight evokes half-forgotten images. Ideas may begin in class discussions or something you hear on radio or television. Some of your best ideas occur quite unconsciously while you're reading: What another writer says spurs you to begin looking at a thing in a fresh way. If you pursue those thoughts, you may discover something you want to save or write: new insights into a familiar subject, an opinion you want to share, knowledge that someone else could use.

Sometimes, though, ideas do not originate unless you make a conscious effort to stir them up. You may have to prod your mind until you discover something that you realize you can write about. Discovering is not as simple as pulling ideas out of a file drawer. It's more like starting a fire. Although some fires erupt spontaneously (like some ideas), most of the time a good fire requires careful preparation of combustible materials (reading, study, and experience) and a spark to ignite them. Even after the fire is started, it may need some fanning and poking for the flame to keep going. While the fire is burning, it is *active*. Like ideas, it *does* things. It generates heat and light. In so doing, a fire, like ideas, can be immensely destructive. But fires and ideas are also capable of generating untold benefits.

Prewriting may be a spoken or written effort to explore ideas (such as freewriting, listing, or questioning), or it may be the mulling over of thoughts as you go about other business. Some of the best prewriting is done while the writer is doing something else: driving the car, riding the bus, taking a walk, running, or washing the dishes. The methods described in the next section can assist you in discovering an idea and in exploring your thoughts once you have a topic in mind. You can use these methods in three ways:

1. In writing, by discovering ideas on paper;
2. In speech, by talking out a subject with someone else;
3. In your mind, by talking out a subject with yourself.

Invention

Prewriting uses methods of **invention:** ways of discovering and exploring ideas and how to express them. As you read about these methods, bear in mind that you discover and explore at all points in your writing, while you're drafting and revising as well as while you're planning. While you draft, you use some type of invention when you pause to consider what to write next; while you revise, the methods of invention are particularly useful in discovering how to rethink. Writing is inventing. In this chapter, ten of the common methods of invention are described, and some of them recur in Chapter 5 on revising. In Part II you can apply invention to specific writing assignments. You will probably find the methods of invention most productive when you combine two or more for a single writing project.

Reading

In your search for ideas, you may overlook an obvious source: **reading.** Consider the wealth of ideas residing between the covers of books and magazines and on the pages of newspapers, on microfilm and microfiche, and in computer data banks. Much of what is written is based on what someone else has already written. When you read, you think not only of what the writer has said but also of something the writer has not said, a new angle, a new application. In other words, you are an *active reader.* When you ask questions like the active reading questions in Chapter 1 (page 6), you may discover new things to say. Here are some additional questions you might ask:

Questions for Discovering Ideas in Reading

1. Do I agree with what the writer is saying?
2. How might this idea be expressed better?
3. How does this information relate to what I know?

Questions (continued)

4. How can I apply this information to what I know?
5. What could I add to what this writer has said?
6. How do I feel when reading this piece of writing?
7. What does this writing contribute to my experience?
8. How significant is this writing to my experience?
9. What new idea does this writing give me?

These questions are similar to those in Chapter 1, but they probe deeper into what the writing might mean to you.

Ideas may come serendipitously, as unexpected gifts, while you're reading for another purpose, or you may deliberately pursue a topic to learn more about it. When you're looking for information on a topic, you can use your library's card catalog or online catalog and indexes. If you're just casting around for something that interests you, you can browse in your library or your own bookshelves or magazine rack, skimming until you find something that appeals to you. Then read; if you read actively, the ideas you gain are likely to engender new thoughts. To explore these thoughts further, you can take up another method of invention. Next you might return to reading, to fill in the gaps you discover in your knowledge.

When you get around to writing, you may need to credit the other writer for his or her ideas. (See Chapters 15 and 16.) In so doing you will also give your reader information on how your ideas developed, and your statements will be based not only on your own credibility but on the authority of the other writer as well. Here's an example of how reading leads to new thoughts. First is the reading, a portion of an article in *The Atlantic* about dolphins ensnared in tuna nets, then the new writing. Note how the second writer credits the ideas of the first.

The beaks of Sam LaBudde's first dolphins strained against the net 1
that had formed a canopy over them. Their flukes churned the ocean white. They thronged at the surface, desperate to force slack in the net sufficient to free their blowholes for a breath. Their shrieks and squeals began high in the hearing range of humans and climbed inaudible scales above. LaBudde wanted to scream himself.

The net was brailed, or hauled in. Its red mesh was scarcely visible, 2
and the dolphins snagged in it seemed to levitate from the sea. High above the deck the great spool of the power block, turning by fits and starts, raised and gathered the seine, conveying the dolphins—some

drowned, some still struggling feebly—up toward the block's tight aperture. The net passed through the block, crushing the dolphins, and then slowly descended to the deck. LaBudde stepped forward with his shipmates and began disentangling dead and dying dolphins from the mesh. The dying trembled in their death throes. The dead stared with eyes wide open. LaBudde noticed that the hue of the iris was different in each animal—dolphins are individuals even in death. He noticed his own red arms. A dolphin, the first he had ever touched in his life, had left him bloody to the elbows.

Months later, on land, Sam LaBudde's sleep would be troubled by a recurrent dream in which injured dolphins spoke in cryptic tongues. He might have spared himself the dream, perhaps, had he given vent to his feelings at sea. He could not. LaBudde was not what he seemed—just another crewman on a Panamanian purse seiner in the eastern tropical Pacific. LaBudde was a spy.

—Kenneth Brower, "The Destruction of Dolphins"

The second writer, stirred by the emotional impact of Brower's description of the wanton killing of dolphins ensnared in tuna nets, decides to write on human disregard for all nonhuman life.

Writing based on reading

Perhaps the wrong species has been given dominion over the creatures of the earth. We seem to think that "subduing" them means killing off whatever we want or whatever gets in our way. Kenneth Brower in "The Destruction of Dolphins" shows in graphic terms how indifferent we are to the lives of other creatures. Instead of fishing in ways that catch only the tuna they want to catch, fishermen use purse seines that entrap not only the tuna but the dolphins that travel with the tuna. As a result, when the nets are drawn in, sometimes hundreds of dolphins, intelligent creatures that Brower describes as "individuals even in death," are crushed, dismembered, and killed (37).

The parenthetical number following the quotation refers to the page number in Brower's article. If she had not included his name in her paragraph, the second writer would also have named the author within the parentheses, like this: (Brower 37). At the end of her paper, this writer cited the article as follows:

Work Cited

Brower, Kenneth. "The Destruction of Dolphins." *The Atlantic* July 1989: 35–58.

Questions About Audience

Sometimes asking **questions about audience**—to establish who your audience is and what it knows about your subject—provides ideas for writing and helps you know what sort of details you need to use. If, for example, you want to persuade people who do not use seat belts that they should buckle up, you might decide to collect statistics about accident victims who were not wearing seat belts or to paint a picture of the traumatic effects on the families of accident victims whose lives might have been saved had they been buckled. Refer again to the questions about audience for writing in Chapter 2 (page 26). Answers to questions such as Who is my audience? How interested is my audience in my subject? and What experiences and knowledge do I share with my audience? can be a big help in determining what to say and what you need to find out.

Listing or Brainstorming

One of the simplest ways to prewrite is to **list,** or **brainstorm.** One dictionary defines brainstorming as "a disturbance in the brain." As a method of invention, brainstorming is an intense prodding for the purpose of uncovering memories, thoughts, and images and making new relationships among them, leading to new ideas. The brain becomes "disturbed," stirred up, and remembers forgotten ideas and details. When you brainstorm or list, you begin with a given topic and write down everything that occurs to you on that topic, whether it seems related or not. You try to work fast.

When you've finished, you go back over the list and strike out unlikely ideas, group according to similarities those that are left, and brainstorm again to fill in gaps. As an alternative, choose one item, and from it start a new list. This method works well in collaboration with one or more other people. You can work together on building a list, or, after you have brainstormed alone for a while, you can ask someone else for input.

Here's a sample brainstormed list on the topic "human disregard for all nonhuman life":

    killing of dolphins
    killing of baby seals
    Greenpeace
    Marine Mammal Fund
    tuna fishing
    veal production
    chicken houses
    vivisection

The writer got this far in her list and decided that she would rather explore "human disregard for dolphin life." So she proceeded from her first item:

killing of dolphins
tuna fishing
Greenpeace
Marine Mammal Fund
laws—U.S.
international law
numbers of dolphins killed
intelligence of dolphins
inhumanity of killing intelligent creatures
fishermen's point of view
need for tuna

This writer could have gone on, but she realized from the items she already had that she would need more information. She read the rest of the *Atlantic* article and went to her library to search for information on dolphins, the tuna-fishing industry, and relevant laws.

Mapping or Clustering

A variation of listing is **mapping,** or **clustering,** a discovery technique borrowed from instruction in reading. Again, you start by jotting down everything that occurs to you on a topic. The difference is that you write the ideas in clusters and then map out related thoughts, as in Figure 3-1. The topic is in the center, double-circled; it is the starting place. From there, related thoughts are jotted down and circled, then connected to associated ideas by lines.

Mapping allows you to see how parts of your topic relate to the whole. The writer of this map could see a pattern developing, in that every cluster seems to lead to the costs of drought, so he underlined each type of cost. His next step would be to explore that thought further and develop it as a controlling idea, stating it as a thesis (see pages 58–60). The clustering might evolve into an outline like the ones on pages 56–57.

Try mapping on any topic you want to explore. If no clear idea emerges from your first exploration, you might, as with listing, choose one thought and begin mapping again.

Figure 3-1. Mapping, or Clustering.

Exercise: The Community of Writers

Use mapping, or clustering, as a discovery technique for reading comprehension. After reading the following essay, write the main idea in the center of a sheet of paper and double-circle it. Then jot down supporting and related ideas, circle them, and connect associated ideas to one another by lines. In class, compare your map with those of your groupmates. The maps will be different, because you each will have read the essay out of your own experience. But your sense of the main idea will probably be similar.

The hot-spot hypothesis was put forward in the early nineteen-sixties   1
by J. Tuzo Wilson, of the University of Toronto, as a consequence of a stopover in Hawaii and one look at the islands. The situation seemed obvious. James Hutton, on whose eighteenth-century "Theory of the Earth"

the science of geology has been built, understood in a general way that great heat from deep sources stirs the actions of the earth ("There has been exerted an extreme degree of heat below the strata formed at the bottom of the sea"), but no one to this day knows exactly how it works. Heat rising from hot spots apparently lubricates the asthenosphere—the layer on which the plates slide. According to theory, the plates would stop moving if the hot spots were not there. Why the hot spots are there in the first place is a question that seeks its own Hutton. For the moment, all Jason Morgan can offer is another shrug and smile. "I don't know," he says. "It must have something to do with the way heat gets out of the lower mantle."

From very deep in the mantle (and perhaps all the way from the core) the heat is thought to rise in a concentrated column, and for this reason is alternatively called a plume. Its surface features are not proof in themselves that they are the product of some plant-stem phenomenon that is (or was) standing in the mantle far below. The chemistry of hot-spot lavas suggests that the rock is coming from below the asthenosphere, but there is no direct evidence of fixed hot spots in the mantle. They exist on inference alone. There is no way to sample the mantle. It can only be sensed—with vibrational waves, with viscosity computations, with thermodynamic calculations of what minerals do at different temperatures and pressures. Sound waves move slowly in soft rock, and some modes of the sound can be stopped completely when the rock is molten. The speed and patterns of seismic waves tell the story of the rock. Seismology is not quite sophisticated enough to look through the earth and count hot spots, but it approaches that capability, and when it gets there hot spots should appear on the screen like downspouts in a summer storm. If they don't, that may be the end of the second-greatest story in the youthful explorations of geological geophysics.

—John McPhee, *Rising from the Plains*

Journalist's Questions

Another variation of list making is using questions to assist your brainstorming. Sometimes known as the five W's and an H, these interrogatory words will start your **journalist's questions:** *who, what, where, when, why* and *how.* Use each word as often and as many times as you can. You'll be amazed at how many answers you'll get. On the topic of drought, for example, you might start by asking questions like these:

Who is affected by drought?
How are people affected by drought?
Where is drought most serious?
What is drought?

Why is there drought?
How does drought begin?
When do people first notice a drought?
What can be done about drought?
How is my neighborhood affected by drought?
How is my state affected by drought?
Why is insufficient rainfall a problem?

The first round of questions could go on for another page or two, or you could take one question, such as "How is my neighborhood affected by drought?" and ask further questions along that line. For example:

How is my neighborhood affected by drought?
Who seems to be the most affected?
Why are those people affected the most?
What are they doing about insufficient rainfall?

You go on until a controlling idea begins to emerge and you're ready to write a tentative thesis sentence. The next step would be to organize your ideas under that thesis sentence or to begin focused freewriting using the ideas you have generated so far. The outline on pages 56–57 shows how one writer developed an essay on drought.

Exercise: The Exploring Writer

The journalist's questions can be used to discover ideas in reading. Using these questions will make you an active reader, and, if you apply them to much of your reading, they may help you discover ideas for your writing as well. As you read the following paragraph, ask questions that begin with who, what, where, when, why, *and* how: *like Who is the writer? Who is he writing about? What is he saying? When do the events take place?*

For those who fought, the war had other features unknown to those who looked on or got the war mediated through journalism. One such feature was the rate at which it destroyed human beings—friendly as well as enemy. Training for infantry fighting, few American soldiers were tough-minded enough to accept the full, awful implications of the term "replacement" in the designation of their Replacement Training Centers. (The proposed euphemism "reinforcement" never caught on.) What was going to happen to the soldiers they were being trained to replace? Why should so many "replacements"—hundreds of thousands of them, actually—be required? The answers came soon enough in the European theater, in Italy, France, and finally Germany. In six weeks of fighting in

Normandy, the 90th Infantry Division had to replace 150 percent of its officers and more than 100 percent of its men. If a division was engaged for more than three months, the probability was that every one of its second lieutenants, all 132 of them, would be killed or wounded. For those being prepared as replacements at officer candidate schools, it was not mentally healthy to dwell on the oddity of the schools' turning out hundreds of new junior officers weekly after the army had reached its full wartime strength. Only experience would make the need clear. The commanding officer of the 6th King's Own Scottish Borderers, which finally arrived in Hamburg in 1945 after fighting all the way from Normandy, found an average of five original men remaining (out of around 200) in each rifle company. "I was appalled," he said. "I had no idea it was going to be like that."

—Paul Fussell, "The Real War, 1939–1945," *The Atlantic*

Classical Probes

The ancient rhetoricians knew that people have a great deal more knowledge than they usually use. To draw out what they knew about a specific topic, the rhetoricians devised six specific categories called the **classical probes:** *identification, comparison and contrast, classification, causes and effects, process analysis,* and *exemplification.* These categories, they thought, coincide with ways the mind collects and stores information. People want to know how? and why? and what? So under each category the rhetoricians asked related questions. Here are some of the questions you can ask when exploring a topic:

Identification
What is it?
What does it look like?
What does it feel like?

Comparison and contrast
How is it like other things?
How is it different from other things?

Classification
What are its parts?
How does it relate to other things?
How are its parts interrelated?

Causes and effects
What are its causes?
What are its effects?

Process analysis
How does it operate?
How is it produced?

Exemplification
What are some examples of it?

As with other methods of exploring ideas, this one can feed itself. You can take the answer to any question and ask additional questions about that idea.

Exercise: The Community of Writers

Working with a partner, use the classical probes to explore the topic greenhouse effect *(or another topic of your choosing). Here are some questions to begin a probe on* greenhouse effect. *Answer these and compose further questions that fit the topic. You may find that your questions begin to center on one or two probes.*

What is the greenhouse effect? *(identification)*
Is the greenhouse effect like anything else I know? *(comparison)*
How is the greenhouse effect different from normal climatic features? *(contrast)*
What causes the greenhouse effect? *(cause)*
What effects does it bring about? *(effect)*
Can the causes of the greenhouse effect be described in groups? *(classification)*
How does the greenhouse effect operate? *(process analysis)*
What are some examples of the greenhouse effect? *(exemplification)*

Cubing

Related to the classical probes is **cubing,** a strategy that allows you to visualize prewriting. Imagine your topic or problem enclosed in a cube—a six-sided square box—in which each side represents a way of looking into your topic or problem (see Figure 3-2). Here are some sample cubing questions to ask about your topic:

Classify It	*Describe It*	*Analyze It*
To what group does it belong?	What does it look like?	What are its parts?
How is it like others in the group?	What is its shape?	What is it made of?

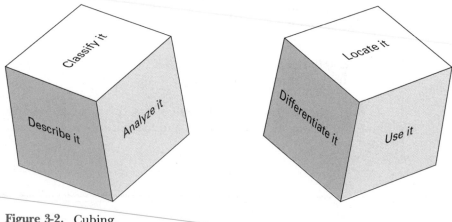

Figure 3-2. Cubing.

Differentiate It	*Locate It*	*Use It*
What makes it different from other things?	Where can I find it?	What is it good for? What does it do?

Your process of discovery can continue to add related questions. In other words, as you discover ideas, keep turning the cube so that other sides reveal your topic. As with the classical probes, one or two aspects of the cube may be the most helpful for a particular topic. The advantage of cubing is that you can objectify your topic, putting it in front of you and examining it from all sides. If you're a visually oriented person, this may be an especially useful strategy for you. Once you have uncovered ideas, you can proceed to another prewriting strategy—devising a tentative thesis, outlining if you have a structured topic and thesis, freewriting (see page 54), or reading if you're still exploring.

You can also use the cubing strategy to discover a topic. In this case, you examine the assignment. Here are examples of the kinds of questions you might ask:

Classify It	*Describe It*	*Analyze It*
How is it like other assignments?	How does it look rephrased in my own words?	What are its parts?

Differentiate It	*Locate It*	*Use It*
How is it different from other assignments?	Where can I find more information on this assignment?	What can I learn from this assignment?

Finally, cubing is a strategy for active reading. To comprehend a reading assignment thoroughly, think of it as a cube and examine it from all sides by asking questions similar to those in the six categories.

Exercise: The Community of Writers

With your groupmates, use cubing for an active reading of the following paragraph about life in 1900. Imagine the paragraph enclosed in a cube, and, as you view the paragraph through each of the cube's six sides, beginning anywhere—

Classify it—How does this information relate to what I already know about the subject?
Describe it—What is the subject?
Analyze it—What is the main point, and how does the author support it?
Differentiate it—How is it different from other information on the subject?
Locate it—Where would I expect to find information like this?
Use it—How can I apply this information?

These implacable costumes, male and female, reflected the prevailing credo as to the relations between the sexes. The ideal woman was the sheltered lady, swathed not only in silk and muslin but in innocence and propriety, and the ideal man, whether a pillar of rectitude or a gay dog, virtuously protected the person and reputation of such tender creatures as were entrusted to his care. If unmarried, a girl must be accompanied by a chaperone whenever she ventured out to an evening's entertainment in the city. If she were a daughter of the rich, a maid might take the place of the chaperone; it was never quite clear, under these circumstances, who was supposed to protect the maid's virtue. Eleanor Roosevelt has recorded in her autobiography her relief when, at the age of twenty or so, she found that her friend Bob Ferguson was considered close enough to the family to be permitted to escort her home from evening parties at the studio of Bay Emmet the painter. "Otherwise I always had to have a maid wait for me—that was one of the rules my grandmother had laid down." And James W. Gerard has added his testimony as to the iron code which still governed New York Society in that period. "Even when I was thirty years old," wrote Gerard in his old age, "if I had asked a girl to dine with me alone, I would have been kicked down her front steps. If I had offered her a cocktail, I would have been tossed out of Society for my boorish effrontery." Needless to add that a woman must never be seen in a bar—or even a smoking car.
—Frederick Lewis Allen, *The Big Change: America Transforms Itself, 1900–1950*

Freewriting

One way of exploring ideas that involves neither making lists nor answering questions is focused **freewriting.** You just write on a particular topic, without stopping, without planning, without making corrections or worrying about what word to use or how to spell it. Like most methods of invention, freewriting is based on the classical notion that people accumulate a wealth of knowledge and may need a strategy for tapping that knowledge. It also derives from the modern theory that people learn— generate ideas—by writing. That is, when you freewrite you not only draw information from your memory bank but you also *do* something with that information: analyze it, compare it, combine it with other information, actually *engender new thoughts* as you write.

Sometimes freewriting is used without a focusing topic. In such a case, you begin writing whatever is on your mind. If nothing comes, or until something comes, just write "I can't think of anything to write" or "I wonder what will come of this" or anything else that keeps your pen moving across the paper or your fingers tapping on the keyboard. Sooner or later, something emerges—perhaps not a usable idea, but then again it may be one that leads to something better.

Exercise: The Exploring Writer

Freewrite on the general topic freedom *or on one of the ideas suggested by the readings on pages 47, 49, or 53. Write fast for ten minutes without stopping or correcting errors, putting down whatever occurs to you. If the ideas you generate look usable, apply another invention strategy to explore them further and possibly develop a paper from them.*

Imitation

Imitation is an old practice enabling less experienced writers to learn from the more experienced. One form focuses on acquiring stylistic variations. You may be asked to write in the style of Ernest Hemingway, for example, so you would write a series of short sentences and a few that seem to go on and on with clauses joined by conjunctions. Or you may be asked to imitate sentences that have features you often write incorrectly. Many writers, for example, have trouble with compound sentences in which two clauses must be separated by a semicolon, so they imitate such sentences, patterning correct writing instead of remedying mistakes. At other times, writers imitate entire essays to acquire a sense of essay components: thesis sentences, for example, or paragraph development and methods of achieving coherence. There are many ways of using imitation for improving style and structure.

Another, often overlooked, feature of imitation is that, by imitating the writing of others, the writer discovers new ideas. As you write that paragraph imitating Hemingway's style, your own ideas come to you. If you study a model essay and then write an essay patterned on it, you find that while you concentrate on the form of the original you discover ideas of your own. You find something that fits. Once you have begun to generate ideas, you can depart from the pattern and write an essay that is not only your own ideas but your own pattern.

Exercise: The Exploring Writer

Write an imitation of the following paragraph, substituting another action, something you know, like building a house, decorating a room, or moving to college. Choose your own topic. "Millions of years ago" can be "several days ago" or "a score of years ago." Sample first sentence: "Several months ago my twelve-year-old brother built a tree house in the crotch of an old maple tree."

Millions of years ago, a volcano built a mountain on the floor of the Atlantic. In eruption after eruption, it pushed up a great pile of volcanic rock, until it had accumulated a mass a hundred miles across at its base, reaching upward toward the surface of the sea. Finally its cone emerged as an island with an area of about 200 square miles. Thousands of years passed, and thousands of thousands. Eventually the waves of the Atlantic cut down the cone and reduced it to a shoal—all of it, that is, but a small fragment which remained above the water. This fragment we know as Bermuda.

—Rachel L. Carson, *The Sea Around Us*

If you like the idea that develops, explore it further with other invention strategies— freewriting, perhaps, or the journalist's questions.

Outlining

As a method of exploring ideas, **outlining** is last in this discussion because it works best after you have used other methods. In fact, after employing one or two other methods of invention you may not even need an outline. Your list, cluster, or whatever may be all you require as a guide for writing. Or you may be one of those people who prefer to use outlining as a next step. Outlining systemizes the thoughts you have generated with other methods. It has the advantage of forcing you to clarify distinctions by means of parallel and subordinate categories.

Some people almost always use some kind of outline when they write; others rarely use one. Most people probably use one only part of the time, as, for example, with a complex subject, a large amount of material, or a very formal paper. Here is a conventional pattern for formal outlines:

I. Main topic
   A. First subtopic of I
   B. Second subtopic of I
      1. First subtopic of B
      2. Second subtopic of B
         a. First subtopic of 2
         b. Second subtopic of 2
            (1) First subtopic of b
            (2) Second subtopic of b
               (a) First subtopic of (2)
               (b) Second subtopic of (2)

Each level has at least two items, since subcategories *divide* the preceding item; however, a level may have as many more items as necessary. Most outlines go no further than the fourth level, designated by lowercase letters *(a, b)*.

Here is a formal topic outline based on the ideas generated in the drought cluster on page 47:

I. Introduction
   A. "Greenhouse effect"
      1. Increased carbon dioxide in the atmosphere
      2. Higher average temperatures
      3. Lack of rainfall
   B. Definition of drought
   C. *Thesis: Drought is everybody's business because it escalates the cost of living.*
II. Costs from the farm
   A. Dry fields
      1. Need for irrigation
      2. Expense of water and equipment
   B. Lower yields
      1. Higher costs for farmers
      2. Higher food prices

III. Costs from technology

    A. Lower water tables—quote statistics

    B. Need to drill more wells

    C. Higher water bills

IV. Medical costs

    A. Respiratory problems

        1. Dust in the air

        2. Pollen in the air

    B. Need for medical care and medicine

 V. Conclusion

    A. Other effects

        1. Dry lawns

        2. Dirty houses and cars

    B. Need for concern and understanding

This outline has three levels, the first represented by roman numerals, the second by capital letters, and the third by arabic numerals. The items at each level are parallel. In drafting, the section under each roman numeral would probably represent a paragraph, filled in with supporting details.

In a sentence outline, each item in the topic outline would be rephrased as a complete sentence. Here is section I:

  I. Changes in the earth's climate are making the periodic occurrence of droughts a very real possibility.

    A. Some people call these changes the "greenhouse effect" and attribute them to misuse of our environment.

        1. We pour excessive carbon dioxide into the atmosphere.

        2. The result is a warming of the earth.

        3. Warmer temperatures contribute to lack of rainfall.

    B. Drought can be defined as a severe lack of rainfall that results in low crop yields, burned up lawns, dead trees and shrubs, lowered water tables and lakes, reduced flow in rivers and streams, and dust everywhere.

    C. *Thesis: Drought is everybody's business because it escalates the cost of living.*

Often a working outline, no more than a list of items in the order in which you will use them, is enough. But because a formal outline is a guide not only to the order of development but to the relationships among items as well, you should know how to make one so that you can use it with facility when you need it. Note how Chapter 5 suggests outlining as a revision strategy.

Developing a Thesis Sentence

The preceding formal outline includes a thesis sentence: "Drought is everybody's business because it escalates the cost of living." A **thesis sentence** states the main idea of an essay. It is not just a statement of subject: not just "This essay is about drought" or "The purpose of this essay is to discuss the drought situation." These are both statements of subject only—despite the wording of the second one implying purpose.

In stating the main idea of an essay, a thesis sentence (1) declares the subject and (2) asserts what is being said about the subject. It sometimes also (3) states the method of development. Purpose is implied. The thesis sentence in the preceding outline declares the subject ("drought") and makes an assertion about it ("is everybody's business"). The thesis sentence also states the method of development.

Subject: drought
Assertion: is everybody's business
Development: because it escalates the cost of living

The main idea of this proposed essay is that drought is everybody's business. The essay would be developed causally, showing why drought is everybody's business (because it escalates the cost of living). Through their phrasing, thesis sentences imply an informative or persuasive purpose—or both. The "because" clause of the sentence of drought implies an informative purpose ("drought escalates the cost of living"), but the main clause is clearly persuasive ("drought is everybody's business"). If you glance again at the outline, you see that to support the persuasive purpose the writer had to develop the informative one.

Thesis sentences often develop during prewriting. In exploring a subject, you may discover that you have something to say, that you are forming an attitude toward your subject, and that you are taking a position on it. Knowing what you want to say beforehand and stating your assertion in your thesis makes your drafting easier than beginning with only a vague idea. In fact, a well-phrased thesis sentence is sometimes the only guide necessary for writing a short essay, a business memo or letter, or some other uncomplicated composition with a single subject. However, there are no doubt times when you do not have a thesis until after you have done some drafting, when you discover your thesis as you write. The result is that, after drafting, you must carry out extensive revision to make your draft support your thesis. You delete irrelevant material, add details, work on coherence, adjust your phrasing, and so on. (Chapter 5 deals with revision.)

Sample Thesis Sentences

Thesis sentences are as varied as are subjects for writing. Read the following thesis sentences and note how they state both subject and assertion, or point, with the purpose implied.

> To understand how your paper airplane flies is a step in making your plane fly well.—Campbell Morris

Subject: how a paper airplane flies
Assertion: understanding helps you to fly your plane well
Purpose: to inform readers about flight theory

> We haven't yet developed a clear idea of the ethics of picture-taking.
> —Ellen Goodman

Subject: ethics of picture taking
Assertion: we haven't yet developed a clear idea
Purpose: to persuade readers to develop an ethical position

> We must learn the rules, courtesies, and etiquette of attending a concert or recital.—Lynette Frohrip (student writer)

Subject: the rules, courtesies, and etiquette of attending a concert or recital
Assertion: we must learn them
Purpose: to persuade readers to adopt courteous behavior

> Despite this tragic object lesson, we seem bent on repeating precisely the same mistake in the handling of drugs.—Milton Friedman

Subject: the handling of drugs
Assertion: we seem bent on repeating a mistake
Purpose: to persuade to a different action

> At Mr. Duggleby's I nearly landed in the biggest trouble of all.
> —James Herriot

Subject: a barely averted trouble
Assertion: it was the biggest trouble
Purpose: to inform (and entertain)

Writing Workable Thesis Sentences

Writers sometimes compose thesis sentences that hinder writing instead of aiding it. Theses that are broad, general, or mixed present problems. In constructing your thesis, concentrate on making it *limited, specific,* and *unified,* as these examples illustrate.

> *Limited.* "There are still barriers to political action. Let me discuss five of them."—Senator Albert Gore. Of all the barriers to political action on the environment, Gore will discuss five.
>
> *Specific.* "Thousands of balloons released at sporting events may be a deceptive threat to wildlife."—*Audubon.* As opposed to a general thesis, such as "Balloons are a problem," this thesis states what the problem is in particular terms.
>
> *Unified.* "As Mickey's personality softened, his appearance changed." —Stephen Jay Gould. Main ideas are stated in *main clauses.* Gould will write about Mickey Mouse's appearance, not his personality. Had he written his thesis as two main clauses ("Mickey's personality softened, and his appearance changed"), his main idea would not have been clear.

Placement of Thesis Sentences

In academic writing and in most business writing, the thesis, or point, is stated explicitly. These statements usually occur in the introduction— often at the end of the introduction, after background or related information has been given. An alternative location is at the end of the piece of writing, an arrangement that occurs frequently in narrative writing in which the writer recounts a story before declaring its significance. Sometimes the writer who holds the statement of thesis until the end will begin by asking a question, which is answered when the thesis is stated.

At times, the thesis is left unstated. Such usage occurs especially in some professional writing, where the writer is able to maintain tight control over the essay development without an explicit statement. In such writing, readers are generally able to identify the controlling idea because the entire essay supports it.

(Additional discussions of thesis sentences and their development accompany the readings in Part II.)

Increasing Your Options

This chapter has presented ways of discovering and exploring ideas. You may have been familiar with some of them before reading, but now you can expand your prewriting options by trying others. In Chapters 4 and 5, you will see how the same invention techniques that assist your prewriting are useful also in drafting and revising.

Exercise: The Community of Writers

1. With your groupmates, discuss the subjects and assertions in the following thesis sentences.

    a. "The Big Bang is the earliest event about which we have any record."
    —Carl Sagan

    b. "The wind is the most fundamental fact of life in Patagonia."
    —George Gaylord Simpson

    c. "Consider these varieties of friendship."
    —Judith Viorst

    d. "Probably the most vexing new question for writers is what to do about the 'he-she' pronoun."
    —William Zinsser

    e. "If you become one of the nearly two million taxpayers audited by the Internal Revenue Service, here are a few things to keep in mind."

    f. "We now know that 'Sesame Street' undermines what the traditional idea of schooling represents."
    —Neil Postman

    g. "One such superstition is the belief that black magic is all powerful."
    —Virginia Buckmire (student writer)

2. With a partner in class, select a topic for joint exploration and use three methods of invention to explore that topic. Work together on two methods, like brainstorming and clustering, and individually on one, for example freewriting. Then compare notes and together write a thesis sentence and/or an outline.

CHAPTER 4

The Writing Process: Drafting

Thought is not merely expressed in words; it comes into existence through them.

—*Lev Vygotsky*

Drafting is what many people think of as writing: putting the pen to the page, the fingers to the keyboard. Drafting is working your way through a writing project, getting your ideas down and creating new ones as you go, arriving at the last period, when you can breathe a sigh of relief and take a well-earned rest before you start purposeful revising.

Drafting, or composing, is more than choosing words. It's more than developing and arranging your ideas. In fact, you can be composing even when your pen and fingers are still. When you stare out the window, thinking about how to phrase your next sentence, you are composing. When you stretch out on your bed to think through your next paragraph, you are composing—just as truly as when you're tapping keys on the word processor or pushing your pen across the page. Drafting is so closely tied to prewriting and to revising that it's difficult to separate it, for purposes of discussion, from the entire process of writing. This chapter will treat drafting as the portion of writing that concerns putting ideas on the page: matters of paragraphing, developing and arranging ideas, and beginning and ending essays. At the same time, it will be based on the assumption stated in Chapter 3: that prewriting, drafting, and revising may be as close together as the composition of a single sentence.

How People Write

When you develop a guide in prewriting—a list, a cluster, an outline, a thesis sentence, or maybe just some first thoughts—you probably try to follow it as you write, changing that plan as your ideas develop. Think of your plans as controls against getting bogged down in irrelevancies or losing your sense of direction, not as rigid road maps that prevent you from staying a little longer on one idea or skipping another that you realize doesn't require your attention.

While composing your first drafts you probably work alone. You may have consulted other people as you were exploring ideas, and you may ask someone to give you feedback when you're ready to revise, but while drafting you're on your own. You're the one to make decisions about how to arrange your ideas, how to illustrate and explain your points, what words to use, how to frame your sentences, and so on. Drafting is a private act and a very personal one, even while you consider your future audience.

The way people write is determined by the specific rhetorical situation: the purpose, the role of the writer, the audience, and the subject. Yet people write in their own ways. Some people are *fast* writers, and some proceed at an agonizingly *slow* pace. Some might be termed *inch-at-a-time* writers, pausing after every sentence or phrase to get it right; others are *chunk-at-a-time* writers, writing whole paragraphs or essays before looking back. Some require a working outline *before* they begin, and others write an outline as part of their revising.

You probably know people who are *planners* when they write, who spend hours and days deciding what they will say, how they will explain their main ideas, who their likely audience will be, and what characteristics of that audience are significant for the writing. They outline their ideas or use some other means of arranging them, and, when their first draft is completed, it may require very little revision. You probably have other acquaintances who are *revisers*. They do very little planning, choosing instead to draft their ideas quickly and then spend hours and days rearranging, adding, deleting, and substituting. They need to identify a controlling idea in their drafts and then revise to support it. Finally, you may know people who are *drafters*. They sit down to write with little apparent prewriting, and, except for reading over their drafts to correct spelling and punctuation, they do no revising either. Most writers, including most professional writers, can't write without prewriting and revision. To develop their ideas with the depth and insight necessary to make their writing worth reading, they need to plan and revise as well as to draft.

Exercise: The Community of Writers

Here are three writers' accounts of how they write. Two are by student writers and one by a professional writer. As you read these accounts, try to characterize each writer's process. Are the writers planners, revisers, or drafters? Are they inch-at-a-time writers or chunk-at-a-time? Fast or slow? Outliners before or after drafting? You may find more than one characteristic for each person. With your groupmates, characterize the process of each writer, then compare the processes with one another and with your own writing processes.

For me, the process of writing is the same, regardless of the piece. I tend to meditate or think about my topic for a long, long time before I sit down to write even the first draft. Sometimes it seems like I write the entire piece in my mind, so when I finally sit down to write, the first draft comes fairly easily and is normally pretty good. I do have a tendency to dwell on a particular sentence for long periods of time, until I get it right. Getting it right basically amounts to expressing the idea in the exact way in which I want it to be received, taking into account word choice, sentence structure, and tone. I love to experiment with a variety of sentence structures. This doesn't come easily because I am extremely critical of my own work.

I spend a lot of time reading my piece out loud when I am writing and also when I am revising. I look for consistency in tone, variety in sentence arrangement, rhythm, parallelism, wordiness, spelling, verb tense, and repetitive word choice. Then I work on my transitions and organization, making sure that the piece is clear, well-directed toward my purpose, and flows smoothly. Finally, I try to come up with a title. This is usually the most difficult part for me.

I've found that there is always room for revision, and what I like one day may not be what suits me the next. Generally, I am very satisfied with a piece before I read it to anyone or turn it in to an instructor. I am very pleased with my final drafts of "A Pain in the Name" [see Chapter 8] and "We Celebrated Chanukah and Christmas" [see Chapter 12]. 1 am also very satisfied with the titles. "A Pain in the Name" took a bit more work than "We Celebrated," probably because it dealt with humor, which I found challenging—I hate bad humor!

"We Celebrated" is of particular importance to me. I read the piece to my mom and dad, and both were very emotionally moved by it. When I read the piece, I am even moved by it. It seems that I said exactly what I needed to say, sincerely and effectively. My writing seems to reflect a very strong voice, which is evident in "We Celebrated."

—Terry Splett (student writer, "We Celebrated Chanukah and Christmas" in Chapter 12 and "A Pain in the Name" in Chapter 8)

When I initially get an idea for a paper, I am usually in some incon- 1
venient place like in the bathtub soaking, in my car driving, or in a classroom where I am supposed to be actively participating or taking notes. I
have learned that no matter how inconvenient it is, I must obtain a piece
of paper and a writing implement (pen, pencil, or crayon) and write the
idea down. If I don't, I will either forget the concept or spend the entire
time thinking about the idea without paying attention to what I am doing.

The second step, although a relatively subconscious act at first, is to 2
think. Writers have called this prethinking; for me it is more like
daydreaming. I generally come up with a blockbuster title that I seldom
use, because by the time I am finished with my prethinking, the title does
not apply anymore.

When I first began to take writing seriously, I would use the clustering 3
method, which consists of a small circle which contains the central idea, with
spider-like lines emerging from the outer rim. Attached to these lines are
additional lines relating to the central theme. Spawning from these circles
are supporting ideas and tidbits of information. The next step was to decide
which direction I was going and eliminate ideas which were not supportive of the direction I had taken. Finally I would write the paper in longhand,
type it, and submit it for acclaim or condemnation. Sometimes the work
was good and the revisions were few; often it was my tenses which needed
help. Rewrite, rewrite, and, one day, I had a paper worth reading.

After a time, I found that I was eliminating the clustering on paper 4
and replacing it with mind clustering. It became more efficient for me to
do additional prethinking and then type my thoughts. I use a computer,
so it is easy to reword as I reread and to change paragraphs and sentences
before I turn in the finished product.

I found that as I developed my typing skills, I eventually could keep 5
up with my racing mind. For me it is imperative that I get my ideas down
before I forget them, and if I think too much about the structuring I lose
the flavor of what I am writing.

The first paragraph is the most important to me, because it is there 6
that I capture my readers and seduce them into reading further. I spend
more critical time on the first paragraph than I do on the rest of the
paper, generally speaking. Conclusions or ending paragraphs are second
to me in importance, because I want the readers to be satisfied that I have
ended and not left them hanging.

—Susan Wollack (student writer, "The Poetry of Sister Margarete"
in Chapter 14)

Interviewers: Is the act of writing easy for you? 1

[James] Thurber: For me it's mostly a question of rewriting. It's part 2
of a constant attempt on my part to make the finished version smooth, to

make it seem effortless. A story I've been working on—"The Train on Track Six," it's called—was rewritten fifteen complete times. There must have been close to 240,000 words in all the manuscripts put together, and I must have spent two thousand hours working at it. Yet the finished version can't be more than twenty thousand words.

Interviewers: Then it's rare that your work comes out right the first time?   3

Thurber: Well, my wife took a look at the first version of something I   4 was doing not long ago and said, "Goddamn it, Thurber, that's high-school stuff." I have to tell her to wait until the seventh draft, it'll work out all right. I don't know why that should be so, that the first or second draft of everything I write reads as if it was turned out by a charwoman. I've only written one piece quickly. I wrote a thing called "File and Forget" in one afternoon—but only because it was a series of letters just as one would ordinarily dictate. And I'd have to admit that the last letter of the series, after doing all the others that one afternoon, took me a week. It was the end of the piece and I had to fuss over it.

Interviewers: Does the fact that you're dealing with humor slow down   5 the production?

Thurber: It's possible. With humor you have to look out for traps.   6 You're likely to be very gleeful with what you've first put down, and you think it's fine, very funny. One reason you go over and over it is to make the piece sound less as if you were having a lot of fun with it yourself. You try to play it down. In fact, if there's such a thing as a New Yorker style, that would be it—playing it down. . . .

Interviewers: Does it bother you to talk about the stories on which   7 you're working? It bothers many writers, though it would seem that particularly the humorous story is polished through retelling.

Thurber: Oh, yes. I often tell them at parties and places. And I write   8 them there too.

Interviewers: You write them?   9

Thurber: I never quite know when I'm not writing. Sometimes my   10 wife comes up to me at a party and says, "Dammit, Thurber, stop writing." She usually catches me in the middle of a paragraph. Or my daughter will look up from the dinner table and ask, "Is he sick?" "No," my wife says, "he's writing something." I have to do it that way on account of my eyes. I still write occasionally—in the proper sense of the word—using black crayon on yellow paper and getting perhaps twenty words to the page. My usual method, though, is to spend the mornings turning over the text in my mind. Then in the afternoon, between two and five, I call in a secretary and dictate to her. I can do about two thousand words. It took me about ten years to learn.

—James Thurber, *Writers at Work, First Series*

Exercise: The Exploring Writer

Write an essay that explains your usual method of writing an essay. Consider questions like these:

Which portion of the process gets your primary attention: prewriting, drafting, or revising?

How do you handle each part?

Where do your ideas come from?

How do you develop your ideas?

What do you do about titles?

Do you use an outline?

Paragraphs

Essays usually develop as a series of interconnected paragraphs, all supporting a single main idea expressed (or sometimes unexpressed) in a thesis sentence. The way the paragraphs develop is sometimes established by the thesis sentence, as Chapter 3 explains. In the following thesis sentence, for example, the method of development is included with the statement of subject and the assertion about the subject:

> The art of ditch diving is in the elegance with which you perform three distinct actions.—Tom Bodett, "Ditch Diving"

Here the subject is ditch diving and the assertion is that to make ditch diving an art you need to perform three actions elegantly. In reading this essay, you expect to read not only about something called ditch diving but also about three actions that are important to it, possibly explained in three paragraphs.

A paragraph is a unit of writing, an unspecified number of sentences that focus on a central idea. The central idea is often expressed in a topic sentence—often appearing at the beginning of the paragraph, sometimes at the end, and sometimes in the middle. The ideas in paragraphs are developed in many ways, as the remaining sections of this chapter explain.

When you develop your essay from an outline, especially a sentence outline, your topic sentence and its support represent a major section of the outline. When you develop your essay from freewriting, you may end up with one long unit that you need to examine to determine where your paragraph shifts occur. You may also need to add topic sentences to assist your reader in seeing how your paragraphs are connected to your thesis sentence.

Exercise: The Community of Writers

Here is an essay in which the paragraph breaks have been removed. First read it through yourself and mark (¶) the places where you think natural paragraph divisions should occur. Some paragraphs may have topic sentences and some may not, but all paragraphs should concern a central idea. When you have made your decisions, compare your paragraphing with that of your groupmates and try to explain disagreements.

Youngster's Goosefish Catch Remains as a Vivid Memory

[1]I snagged the prehistoric-looking goosefish when I was ten years old. [2]I caught it on my new fishing pole. [3]I miss the times when I could claim any fish that was caught on my fishing pole simply because it got hooked on my pole. [4]Did it matter that my dad hauled in the fish most of the way? [5]No. [6]The catch was still mine, because it liked my worm better—and I didn't even put it on the hook. [7]The Massachusetts inlet called Cape Cod Bay was where I hooked swimmers such as flounder, striped bass, bluefish, tautog, skates, and eels. [8]I spent every early June of my childhood in Truro with my family. [9]And every June I claimed nearly every fish. [10]And there was Dad. [11]He'd prepare the lines, bait the hooks, reel in the fish, remove the hooks, clean the fish . . . and allow me to take the credit, as I so often did. [12]Most years we stayed with the Bardwells, a transplanted family from my hometown of Emden, Illinois. [13]"Doc" Bardwell had delivered me and been my doctor for my first few years. [14]Doc is a cigar-puffing, pipe-smoking man of many expletives. [15]He'd complain plenty as we tried to get out the door to go fishing, wondering if we had all the equipment, or enough to eat. [16]But despite all the hassle, he was always more than willing to take Dad and me on little fishing excursions on his boat. [17]On one of the these trips, I caught the most exotic fish I had ever snagged before the goosefish. [18]I hooked a dogfish—I had a knack for catching the fish with other animal names attached to them. [19]Of course, a dogfish looks nothing like a dog. [20]It's actually a small shark, and this one was small—a couple feet long at the most. [21]But the goosefish. . . . [22]I had heard of it, probably from Dad and Doc. [23]Dad had read that a fisherman found seven whole ducks in one gutted goosefish. [24]"Sure," I thought. [25]That morning we were jigging for mackerel to use as trolling bait for bluefish. [26]But I preferred to fish for the familiar flounder, which usually camp out on the ocean floor. [27]So Dad had rigged my line and I'd set it deep. [28]Doc caught a squid, which he decided to keep for bait. [29]As he was poking at it, trying to get it to squirt its cloaking substance, I saw my pole dip. [30]I thought the largest flounder on record must've been at the end of my line. [31]I attempted to reel it in, but I barely even budged the line. [32]Good ol' Dad stepped in once again. [33]The goosefish broke the water. [34]All I saw was a mouth—at least a foot wide.

[35]And teeth. [36]Teeth upon teeth. [37]"What is that? [38]What d'ya got there?" Doc bellowed. [39]"Geez, is that a goosefish? [40]Hold on," he said as he killed the engine and grabbed the gaff hook. [41]As Doc swung the hook toward the angered monster, the fish snapped and broke the line. [42]The goosefish slowly settled to its dark underwater home. [43]That fish was by far the ugliest, scariest-looking creature I'd seen in my life. [44]And I'd only seen the mouth. [45]I owe my clear image of it now to a book of fish I looked at. [46]The goosefish is brown, two to three feet long, and can weigh up to 50 pounds. [47]I wish I could've just weighed it. [48]I'm sure we would have had no intention of keeping the thing. [49]But if I had known then what I know now. . . . [50]The goosefish is also called a monkfish, in restaurants anyway. [51]Supposedly it's quite tasty, very similar to lobster. [52]If people only knew how that creature really looks. [53]Of course, lobsters aren't the most friendly looking seafood either. [54]But then, you wouldn't find seven whole ducks inside a lobster.

—Louisa Gorrell, *Milwaukee Sentinel*

How Writers Develop and Arrange Ideas

Some writers arrange their thoughts by making an outline or list and using it as a guide (see Chapter 3, "Outlining"). They feel that they work better if outlining is part of their prewriting. Some kinds of writing work especially well with this method—for example, research papers, reports, and other papers with circumscribed formats. Other writers prefer to let the form develop from their ideas. They discover what they mean to say through freewriting and rough drafting, then arrange and rearrange their ideas through extensive revision. This strategy can work well when writers are still exploring a topic and when they know the forms that a particular kind of writing conventionally takes. For some writers, letting the form develop without conscious effort results in a piece of writing that is disorganized, with parts off the topic and no controlling idea. Whenever you begin your writing without a plan, think of it as freewriting and the resulting piece of writing as a rough draft, one that will require extensive revision.

Knowledge of conventional forms is useful at all stages of writing: prewriting, drafting, and revising. Consciously or unconsciously, writers need to know answers to such questions as these:

What makes a group of sentences a paragraph?
Where are thesis sentences commonly located?
How are paragraphs developed?
How are essays concluded?

One way of acquiring knowledge of this sort is to have someone *tell* you what essays and other pieces of writing are supposed to look like: "Thesis sentences frequently occur at the end of the introduction" or "Don't introduce any new information in your conclusion."

But learning by being told is much less efficient than learning by observing, imitating, and practicing. Think of how you learned to speak. It was not so much by having someone *tell* you how as by listening to other people speak. When you first learned to repeat a sound you had heard your mother say, something like "Da Da," and found that your father was exceedingly pleased when you uttered it, you continued making the sound. You had learned a word. Later on, as your family read you stories, you learned certain things about stories, such as the way they begin: phrases like "Once upon a time" or "There was once" or "Long ago in a faraway land." And when you wrote your first stories, you used these phrases. Throughout your education, you have used imitation, perhaps more than you realize.

Similarly, you can learn how other writers arrange their ideas, as explained in Chapter 1. Writers learn from other writers. By practicing methods of arrangement similar to those of other writers, you learn some of the limitless variations of language. This kind of learning works with both a structured and an unstructured approach that draws your attention to the way other writers use ideas and words. The next section presents a quick overview of the most common methods of developing and arranging ideas for writing. The longer discussions in Part II give you a context for reading and writing that draws on these methods.

Methods of Developing and Arranging Paragraphs and Essays

In most writing, ideas are developed and arranged in a variety of patterns. Used singly or more often in combination, these patterns develop individual paragraphs or entire essays. You can use them as an aid to both reading and writing. In writing, you can use them in prewriting, drafting, and revising.

In your *reading*, you can increase your comprehension and retention, and perhaps even improve your reading speed, with an understanding of the writer's method of organization and idea development. If you know, for example, that a paragraph, an essay, or a textbook chapter is arranged by cause and effect, you will read actively for effects and causes. By relating the information in a causal way, you will make more sense of it and thus remember it better.

In your *writing*, these methods of development and arrangement can assist you not only in organizing your ideas but in developing, or discovering, them as well. You will notice similarities to the invention strategies suggested in Chapter 3. You can examine a topic *spatially*, for example, discovering details and relationships, and you can *compare* a new topic with something you are familiar with, examining similarities and differences and drawing conclusions. If you observe in your prewriting that you are asking mainly *when* questions, you may need chronology for arranging your ideas; if you ask mainly *why* questions, you may need cause and effect. Taking advantage of the way methods of development and arrangement relate to methods of invention can make your writing easier.

Sometimes the arrangement of ideas evolves as one writes. Topics and thesis sentences often determine the arrangement. In Chapter 11, for example, John McPhee sets out to explain the burning of a fireplace fire, and his ideas develop *chronologically*. If, after drafting the essay, he wanted to check the completeness and clarity of his details, he could read the draft chronologically to see if he had omitted anything or had events out of order.

The common methods for developing and arranging ideas are explained in the following sections.

Chronology or Sequence (Narration)

Narrations of events and explanations of processes are arranged chronologically. **Chronology** is simple time order. Writers use it for telling stories, both fiction and nonfiction. Novels are usually developed chronologically, as are biographies, anecdotes, reports, and instructions. The following example comes from a book-length narrative of a rafting adventure across the Pacific:

> Four men lay snoring in the bamboo cabin while Torstein sat clicking with the Morse key and I was on steering watch. Just before midnight I caught sight of a quite unusual sea which came breaking astern of us right across the whole of my disturbed field of vision. Behind it I could see here and there the foaming crests of two more huge seas like the first, following hard on its heels. If we ourselves had not just passed the place, I should have been convinced that what I saw was high surf flung up over a dangerous shoal. I gave a warning shout, as the first sea came like a long wall sweeping after us in the moonlight, and wrenched the raft into position to take what was coming.
>
> —Thor Heyerdahl, *Kon-Tiki*

In reading the paragraph, you may have noticed that each occurrence relates to the previous one. To connect the parts of his narrative, Heyerdahl provides clues to the chronology: *Just before midnight, as the first sea came.* Writers might use other connecting clues to connect time-related events: *first, second, next, later, at the same time, while, after, before, when,* and so on.

Although some narratives, such as *Kon-Tiki,* are book-length, many are often only a portion of a piece of writing, sometimes an anecdote, a brief story, or an introduction and sometimes an illustrative example. Jonathan Kozol, for instance, introduces his essay on illiteracy with a narrative account of a day in the life of an illiterate man (see Chapter 11). In "Thinking Like a Mountain" (Chapter 6), Aldo Leopold supports his point about the extinction of wolves by narrating a hunting incident from his own life.

A number of the readings in this book are developed chronologically. "The Principle" by Maya Angelou (Chapter 10) is an autobiographical account of an experience with racism. Chronology is effective not only in narrating or reporting something that happened but also in telling readers how something happens, as John McPhee does in describing how a fire burns (Chapter 11), or telling how something should be done, as in "Smooth Flyer" (Chapter 13) on how to make a paper airplane. Use chronology whenever you want to connect events sequentially by time. (See also "Narrating a Personal Experience," pages 276–86, and "Reporting an Observed Incident," pages 286–92.)

Space (Description)

Descriptions are often arranged **spatially,** usually from a single perspective. Imagine yourself walking into a room and telling someone what you see. You could start anywhere, perhaps with what strikes your eye first. If you are describing something purposefully, however, the sequence will likely not be so random. In "Nursing Homes and Growing Old" (Chapter 8), for example, student writer Jeff Hedin describes entering the building through the "steel-framed" nursing home door and proceeding down the "bone-white" hall, conveying with his concrete words the impression of a sterile, institutional atmosphere. In the sample paragraph for chronology, Thor Heyerdahl uses description to report the awesomeness of the wall of water that swept over his raft.

Objects may be described vertically, horizontally, circularly—whatever is appropriate for the situation. In the following paragraph, note how the writer describes Sable Island, an ark of sand in the North Atlantic "where no land should be" and consequently a graveyard for sailors and ships.

If reminders of death are everywhere on Sable, one realizes that he is also in the midst of great fecundity. Anytime I cast my eye around, seals were feeding in the water or sunning on the beach, horses were grazing in the marram [grass] or galloping beside the surf, seabirds were filling the air with shrill sound. Sable is sanctuary as well as graveyard. Oppressive in light of human history, it is nevertheless a majestic natural place.

—Harry Thurston, "The Devil's Work Is an Ark of Sand"

To make his point that Sable Island is teeming with life despite its reputation for death, Thurston describes the island as he sees it. Wherever he looks, he sees life.

Rachel L. Carson, on the other hand, describes the Sargasso Sea (Chapter 10) sequentially: the water, the weeds in the water, the animal life in the weeds. She thus achieves a purpose not only of describing the total environment but also of showing the interrelatedness of the parts. When student writer Susan Wollack spatially describes a teacher (Chapter 14), she makes her point of disapproval by remarking on the teacher's "cool green eyes" and "too straight teeth." (See also the section "Describing a Natural Phenomenon" in Chapter 10.)

Exercise: The Exploring Writer

In Thurston's paragraph, arranged spatially, identify the topic sentence and the details that develop it. What is the function of the final sentence?

Classification

Some topics are arranged according to how they are **classified.** An essay on computer printers, for example, might be arranged by the method of printing: dot matrix, daisy wheel, laser, and others. The following paragraph introduces a chapter on the uses of computers in education:

The uses of computers can be categorized in many arbitrary ways. I shall focus on five of their most visible contemporary functions, as (1) gameplaying devices, (2) information sources, (3) teaching machines, (4) creative tools, and (5) communication links. Most of my opening comments will focus on negative aspects of computers, but I shall end on a more optimistic note.

—Frank Smith, *Joining the Literacy Club*

Classification is our way of making sense of the world. Life is much more comprehensible if we can group things. When we classify music, we do not look at every piece and performance separately from all others;

we look at groups—country western, reggae, hard rock, and so on. Classification helps us remember and keep track of things by imposing order on them. That's why it is a common means for arranging topics. In Chapter 7, Senator Albert Gore uses classification in "What Is Wrong with Us?" to explain what he sees as five barriers to effective political action on the global environment. Lewis Thomas, in Chapter 8, uses classification to give a humorous explanation (and illustration) of punctuation marks.

When we classify things, we do so according to certain principles, which are decided by our subject and what we mean to say. Smith classifies computer uses according to "their most visible contemporary functions." Gore classifies environmental lethargy as five "barriers to political action." Thomas's principles of classification are punctuation marks. In "Friends, Good Friends—and Such Good Friends" (Chapter 12), Judith Viorst classifies friends according to variety and intensity. Whatever your subject, your principles of classification are the shared characteristics that determine how you group or divide its features or elements.

Your essay will probably develop along classification lines if your prewriting centers on questions such as What are its parts? and How can it be categorized? and How does it relate to other things? As in the Smith example above, you'd develop each part in a sequential order determined by your subject and purpose, remembering that the most emphatic positions are first and last. (See also the section Explaining by Classification in Chapter 12.)

Comparison

Arrangement by **comparison** is called for when an essayist considers two or more subjects. Like classification, comparison is a way of thinking that helps us make sense of the world. It assists us in understanding and judging the things we come in contact with. We compare colleges, teachers, VCRs, athletic shoes, and so on. Sometimes, as a result of our comparison, we make decisions—to attend a particular college or to buy a particular type of shoes. At other times, we use comparison to achieve other purposes—to persuade someone to vote a certain way or to show an audience how different (or similar) two U.S. presidents were.

The following paragraphs explain, tongue in cheek, how to "get rich" by refraining from buying high-ticket items. After saving $150,000 a year by not renting an expensive apartment, the author saves more money by not buying a Mercedes-Benz.

A short time later, while my wife and I were still just *nouveaux riches,* I saw one of those Mercedes-Benz station wagons. It was parked in front of the liquor store. The car was so new that it still had the dealer's price sticker in the window. Do you know what the manufacturer's suggested retail price was? It was almost $50,000.

I was shocked. My wife and I have a station wagon, but it's just one of the normal brands. It has a front seat, a back seat, and a "way back," just like the Mercedes, and it cost only about a quarter as much. I did some on-the-spot arithmetic and decided not to trade up—a deal that left roughly $35,000 on the table for my wife and me.

—David Owen, "How to Get Rich Quick"

The comparison arrangement here is simple: In the first paragraph Owen describes the Mercedes, and in the second he compares the couple's station wagon with it.

Comparison as a method of arranging ideas has several subcategories. When you *compare* two things, you concentrate on likenesses and differences. If you give your attention mostly to differences, however, you are engaging in *contrast.* For example, if you were comparing Thomas Jefferson and Abraham Lincoln, you might start from the common ground that they were both lawyers and U.S. Presidents. From there you would show how they differed—perhaps in economic background, achievements as presidents, methods of arguing their legal cases, and so on. Your methods would be *contrast,* because your purpose would be to show differences. But if you wanted to show that Jefferson and Lincoln were similar, you would begin with their differences—such as backgrounds and presidencies—and then concentrate on the facts that they were both successful lawyers, both devoted to careful study, and so on—*comparison.*

Writers wanting to show similarities or differences encounter the special difficulties of handling two (or more) subjects. A comparison or contrast requires that both subjects be examined on the same points. To compare the taste of an orange with the shape of a lemon, for example, does not make sense. To compare Jefferson's presidency with Lincoln's law practice is, again, useless information.

Comparisons can be organized point by point or subject by subject. Point-by-point arrangement would compare Jefferson and Lincoln first, perhaps, on economic background, then study habits, then law practice, and finally presidency. Subject-by-subject arrangement would deal first with Jefferson on economic background, study habits, and whatever else was covered, then with Lincoln on the same points. For extensive comparisons, point-by-point arrangement is probably easier for readers to follow. For a simple comparison like that of oranges and lemons, subject-by-subject arrangement might be manageable.

Because of the multiple subjects in comparison, **coherence** may present special problems for writers. To ensure that your readers understand which subject is under discussion, use transitional markers that show the shifts, such as *however, on the other hand, although, in contrast, similarly,* *likewise,* and *but.* In addition, repeating key words, such as the names of the two subjects, will help your reader keep up with you. (For more on coherence, see pages 296–97 and 319–320.)

Writers sometimes use comparison to develop a portion of an essay. In "Senses" (Chapter 11), for example, George R. Harrison devotes two paragraphs to the limitations of the human eye in an essay dedicated to praising the eye. For further discussions and illustrations of comparison/contrast, see Reflecting on Human Folly, pages 145–51 (Chapter 6), and "We Celebrated Chanukah and Christmas," pages 366–69 (Chapter 12), in which student writer Terry Splett shows how a Judeo-Christian family celebrated two holidays.

Exercise: The Community of Writers

In magazines, newspapers, or books find an example of comparison *and one of* classification *as methods of development and bring them to class. With a partner, discover what features your comparisons have in common and what features your classification samples share. Then discuss what makes the comparisons different from the classification samples.*

Analogy

As a method of developing and arranging ideas, **analogy** has some similarities to comparison, but its function is different. Unlike comparison, which focuses on two or more subjects somewhat equally, analogy concentrates on one subject, explaining it with references to the second. It is often used to explain something abstract or unfamiliar by relating it to something concrete or familiar. Love, for example, is like a roller-coaster ride, with frequent ups and downs, the downs being more exciting than the ups but also more stressful. In this example, notice that the language is that of a roller-coaster ride but describes love. In "Senses" in Chapter 11, George R. Harrison describes the eye by means of the terminology for cameras. Analogy takes the form "Subject A is like Subject B," in which the writer is focusing on Subject A, an unknown or difficult concept, and relating it to Subject B, a familiar concept or object.

In the following paragraph, Mark Twain only apparently describes knowledge of a New York City street. He is really using this description to present a pilot's knowledge of the Mississippi River, since his readers are more likely to know about walking urban streets, be they in New York or any large city, than to know about navigating the Mississippi.

One cannot easily realize what a tremendous thing it is to know every trivial detail of twelve hundred miles of river and know it with absolute exactness. If you will take the longest street in New York and travel up and down it, conning its features patiently until you know every house and window and lamppost and big and little sign by heart, and know them so accurately that you can instantly name the one you are abreast of when you are set down at random in that street in the middle of an inky black night, you will then have a tolerable notion of the amount and exactness of a pilot's knowledge who carries the Mississippi River in his head. And then, if you will go on until you know every street-crossing, the character, size, and position of the crossing-stones, and the varying depth of mud in each of these numberless places, you will have some idea of what the pilot must know in order to keep a Mississippi steamer out of trouble. Next, if you will take half of the signs in that long street, and *change their places* once a month, and still manage to know their new positions accurately on dark nights, and keep up with these repeated changes without making any mistakes, you will understand what is required of a pilot's peerless memory by the fickle Mississippi.

—*Life on the Mississippi*

Analogy is more often used as one method of developing an essay than as a single method of development. In "What Is Wrong with Us?" (Chapter 7), Senator Gore uses the following analogy:

There is an old science experiment in which a frog is put into a pan of water, and the water is slowly heated to the boiling point. The frog sits there and boils because its nervous system will not react to the gradual increase. But if you boil the water first and then put the frog in it, it immediately jumps out.

The subject of Gore's essay is not frogs; rather, he uses this story as an analogy to explain the real point of his essay: why people are so slow to react to dangers to the environment. "We are at the environmental boiling point right now," he says. In another example, Lewis Thomas explains intuition by analogy to the ability to see things out of "The Corner of the Eye" (Chapter 12). Analogy is useful in explaining. Use it with caution, however, bearing in mind that analogous things are never alike in all ways. City streets and the Mississippi River, for example, have obvious differences.

For a further discussion of analogy, see the section "Explaining by Analogy and Exemplification" in Chapter 12.

Exercise: The Exploring Writer

Take Twain's analogy a little further, trying to uncover other ways in which a river is like a city street. Find additional examples of analogies in your reading.

Cause and Effect

A very common method of arrangement is **cause and effect**—common because it answers questions that begin Why? and What will happen if? We want to know why tuition is so high, why so few people got out to vote, why crime is so extensive, why families split up. And we want to know what the effects of an action will be: What would happen if marijuana were legalized? Will I pass the exam if I stay up all night studying? Will I be able to meet my expenses if I take on a part-time job? What effect does styrofoam have on the environment? Like other methods of development, cause and effect is effective because it relates to the way people think. If you find in exploring your topic that you are asking questions beginning *why* and *what if,* your essay will probably develop along the lines of cause and effect.

One of the hazards of cause-and-effect development is attributing something to cause when in fact the relationship is simply one thing following another in time. This fallacy is commonly called "post hoc," from the Latin phrase *post hoc, ergo propter hoc,* meaning "after this, therefore because of this." It's actually an oversimplification, as when someone says "Education has improved in this state since the new governor took office." The new governor *may* have had something to do with the improvement of education, but his taking office didn't alone have that effect. A writer wanting to make this point would have to show what steps the governor took to make that change.

Writers using this method of development sometimes begin with a single cause, like lack of rainfall, and then discuss several effects, like decreased crop yields, lower water tables, and increased respiratory illnesses. Or they may begin with an effect and discuss causes—for example, several causes of increased respiratory illnesses.

Here is a paragraph that begins with a single cause, sodium cyanide—called "magic" by its Filipino fish collectors—and ends with its effects:

> A squirt into the coral, and all the fish hiding there come out spinning and jerking. Any angelfish, triggerfish, squirrelfish, or blue tangs the diver catches in his hand. Most of the rest are unmarketable and left spiraling and fluttering amid poisoned corals. For every fish

captured alive by cyanide, nine die, by the estimate of Steve Robinson of the International Marinelife Alliance. "Magic" is black magic. Cyanide fishing is an effective method in the short term, disastrous in the long. The chemical is bad for the health of the divers, who suffer skin lesions and hair loss and sometimes fatally poison themselves; bad for the longevity of the cyanide-shocked fish; and fatal for the coral upon which the aquarium-fish business—and millions of Filipinos—depend.

—Kenneth Brower, "State of the Reef"

A more complicated cause-and-effect arrangement is a causal chain, in which the writer starts with either a cause or an effect and then works backward or forward with related causes and effects. Figure 4-1 starts with a cause, lack of rainfall, and traces related causes and effects. In this chain, each effect becomes the next cause. The first cause, lack of rainfall, results in the ultimate effect, higher water costs.

As a reader and as a writer, you can make use of transitional words and phrases as clues to cause-and-effect relationships—words such as *therefore, so, consequently, because, for this reason,* and *as a result.* Among key words related specifically to the topic, *cause* and *effect* are also effective in achieving coherence, as in phrases such as *the foremost cause* and *the final effect.*

Some of the readings in this book use cause and effect as the primary method of development, others for developing part of an essay. In Chapter 11, *Audubon* magazine charges that celebratory releases of balloons cause harm to wildlife. Joan Didion in Chapter 9 describes the effects of the Santa Ana wind. But in "Winter of Man" (Chapter 8), Loren Eiseley uses cause and effect along with other methods of development to describe the fearful effects of our own technology. In "I Have a Dream" (also in Chapter 8), Martin Luther King, Jr. uses cause and effect and other methods to develop his famous speech. Other readings using cause-and-

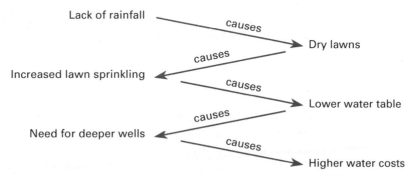

Figure 4-1. Causal chain.

effect development are listed in the front of this book in the section entitled "Contents by Method of Development." Further discussions of cause and effect can be found on pages 328 and 346–51.

Exercise: The Exploring Writer

List the effects of cyanide poisoning detailed in the paragraph by Kenneth Brower. Find other examples of cause-and-effect development in your reading.

Exemplification

Exemplification is one of the most common methods of development. We make a statement and then explain it with an example. In the following paragraph, a specific illustration explains the topic (first) sentence:

> Here and there we find dramatic illustration of the fact that the tides affect the whole ocean, from its surface to its floor. The meeting of opposing tidal currents in the Strait of Messina creates whirlpools (one of them is Charybdis of classical fame) which so deeply stir the waters of the strait that fish bearing all the marks of abyssal existence, their eyes atrophied or abnormally large, their bodies studded with phosphorescent organs, frequently are cast up on the lighthouse beach, and the whole area yields a rich collection of deep-sea fauna for the Institute of Marine Biology at Messina.
>
> —Rachel L. Carson, *The Sea Around Us*

This paragraph shows how methods of development are often combined: Most of the paragraph *exemplifies* the topic sentence—through *description*. In addition, the topic sentence implies cause and effect, so the descriptive sentences show the effects brought about by the ocean tides. You will find development through exemplification throughout this book.

You are probably familiar with the words that writers use to lead into exemplification: *for example, for instance, such as, a leading example, can be illustrated by,* and so on. In "The Corner of the Eye" (Chapter 12), Lewis Thomas introduces an example with the words: "Take, for example, the metaphors we use in everyday speech to tell ourselves who we are, where we live, and where we come from." What follows are words we use to describe ourselves and our worlds. Examples are not always introduced by transitional expressions. In "Aggression Defined" (Chapter 12), Elliott Aronson introduces a series of several examples with this sentence: "It is difficult to present a clear definition of *aggression* because the term is used in so many different ways in common speech." And student writer Terry Splett in "A Pain in the Name" (Chapter 8) sprinkles her essay liberally with names that strike her as odd: "I'm forever grateful to Mom for the fact that none of us was named Nanette Nat, Nick Nat, Pat Nat or Zack Nat!"

Definition

Definitions of terms are frequently necessary in writing. Sometimes you encounter an entire essay devoted to definition, but more frequently you find paragraphs clarifying terms. Any time you use terms that your readers may not understand—whether the terms are totally unfamiliar or are unfamiliar only in the way you are using them—you need to define them. In the following paragraph, the author takes a familiar term and tells his readers how he is using it:

> "Now . . . this" is commonly used on radio and television newscasts to indicate that what one has just heard or seen has no relevance to what one is about to hear or see, or possibly to anything one is ever likely to hear or see. The phrase is a means of acknowledging the fact that the world as mapped by the speeded-up electronic media has no order or meaning and is not to be taken seriously. There is no murder so brutal, no earthquake so devastating, no political blunder so costly—for that matter, no ball score so tantalizing or weather report so threatening—that it cannot be erased from our minds by a newscaster saying, "Now . . . this." The newscaster means that you have thought long enough on the previous matter (approximately forty-five seconds), that you must not be morbidly preoccupied with it (let us say, for ninety seconds), and that you must now give your attention to another fragment of news or a commercial.
>
> —Neil Postman, *Amusing Ourselves to Death*

Definitions often use methods of development other than telling what a term means. In "Taste," in Chapter 11, William Zinsser defines an intangible subject, taste in writing, mainly through exemplification—giving examples of taste in clothing and in the arts, plus examples of what he calls timeless taste. In "A Third of the Nation Cannot Read These Words," also in Chapter 11, Jonathan Kozol uses a narration (chronology) and specific details (exemplification) to define illiteracy.

Definitions in essays ordinarily do not use dictionary definitions, because most readers have dictionaries and do not need to be given a formal definition of a given word. The primary reason for a definition is to explain to readers how the writer is using a particular term, making the dictionary definition superfluous.

For more on definition, see pages 168–69, 329–33, and 351–56.

Other Methods of Arrangement

The preceding methods of development relate closely to your methods of discovering and exploring ideas. Ideas that you explore causally usually end up in *cause-and-effect* development; those explored by means of examples end up as *exemplification*. The methods that follow are possible ways of *arranging* items within your methods of development. For example, with *emphasis* you might save your strongest example for last, and with *problem and solution* you might pose a cause-and-effect problem and then suggest some possible solutions. In "Deadly Danger in a Spray Can" (Chapter 11), Michael D. Lemonick deals with cause and effect in just this way.

Question and Answer

Writers sometimes like to lead into their subjects by asking questions. They then develop the paragraph or essay with answers. Here is such a paragraph:

> Have you ever stopped to wonder what it would be like to see two completely different visions simultaneously, one with each eye? That, of course, is what fish do. Our eyes focused on the same object report a single merged image to the brain; the fish's brain receives two images at once, for its eyes face in opposite directions and cannot focus simultaneously on the same object.
>
> —Eugenie Clark, *Lady with a Spear*

The writer, a noted ichthyologist, then devotes several more paragraphs to answering her question, asking another challenging question along the way: "Can a fish remember with its left eye something it has learned with its right?"

Beginning a paragraph or an essay with a question assists the reader in sharing the writer's interest in the subject. It focuses the subject for both writer and reader. In Chapter 7, Albert Gore asks "What Is Wrong with Us?" and other questions regarding treatment of the global environment, and, because the answers to these questions are not readily discovered, readers read on.

Exercise: The Exploring Writer

Rewrite the Rachel L. Carson paragraph on page 80 to begin with a question. What changes do you notice accompanying the changes in phrasing? Consider features such as emphasis, audience attention, and style.

Problem and Solution

The **problem and solution** method of arrangement is similar to the question and answer method, except that it sets up a problem instead of asking a question. Here is an example:

> It's Friday afternoon, and you have almost survived another week of classes. You are just looking forward dreamily to the week end when the English instructor says: "For Monday you will turn in a five-hundred word composition on college football."
>
> Well, that puts a good big hole in the week end. You don't have any strong views on college football one way or the other. You get rather excited during the season and go to all the home games and find it rather more fun than not. On the other hand, the class has been reading Robert Hutchins in the anthology and perhaps Shaw's "Eighty-Yard Run," and from the class discussion you have got the idea that the instructor thinks college football is for the birds. You are no fool. You can figure out what side to take.
>
> —Paul Roberts, "How to Say Nothing in Five Hundred Words"

The problem is established: trying to please the teacher with an essay. In the remainder of the essay, the author attempts a solution.

Like question-and-answer arrangement, problem and solution challenges the reader to contemplate a situation with the writer. The introduction to Terry Splett's essay on Chanukah and Christmas in Chapter 12 sets up the problem of how a Judeo-Christian family celebrates the December holidays, beginning with the children trying to understand the family's Sunday morning habit of the children going off to Sunday school while their father stays home and makes breakfast for them. Splett's readers are thus involved in a situation they may not have considered previously.

Emphasis

The **emphatic** method of arrangement is based on the idea that the most notable positions in a piece of writing are the beginning and the end. Writers therefore may start with the most important point and work to the least important, or start with the least significant and move toward the strongest point. Sometimes they place the weakest point in the middle. In this example, the writer saves his emphasis for the end:

> When I was seven I was playing dodgeball on a warm March day at the school playground next to my house. A huge, cloudy icicle hung from the school roof, three stories up. It was a seven-foot dagger that heroically withstood a daily cannonade of snowballs as my playmates and I tried to pick off icicle after icicle.
>
> I stood beneath Fang, poised in case the ball was thrown my way. Suddenly, the guy who was "it" whirled and flung the ball at my head. I ducked, scooted to my right, then instinctively flinched as I heard a monstrous, growling explosion. Ice was skidding everywhere. Fang had fallen—right where I had been standing.
>
> —Gary Legwold, "The Crystalline Challenge"

John McPhee uses emphasis in his description of fire in "Firewood," Chapter 11. While using chronology to explain the process of burning, he saves for his last sentence his identification of the burning compounds.

Exercise: The Community of Writers

With your groupmates, reread Gary Legwold's paragraphs and identify words and phrases that set you up for the ending. Then collaboratively rewrite the paragraphs so that they state at the beginning the fact that the icicle fell. Notice the change in emphasis and use of details.

General to Specific and Specific to General

Two related ways of arranging ideas are from general to specific and from specific to general. A writer using the common **general to specific** method would start with a thesis or topic sentence and develop it with specific statements and illustrations. A writer using the **specific to general** method would accumulate illustrations and specific statements, finally arriving at a statement of thesis or topic. Narratives are sometimes developed this way, as are reflections.

The following paragraph is developed from general to specific, beginning with a topic sentence followed by specific statements that develop the topic:

Wherever climate has permitted it, men have evaporated salt from sea water for many centuries. Under the burning sun of the tropics the ancient Greeks, Romans, and Egyptians harvested the salt men and animals everywhere must have in order to live. Even today in parts of the world that are hot and dry and where drying winds blow, solar evaporation of salt is practiced—on the shores of the Persian Gulf, in China, India, and Japan, in the Philippines, and on the coast of California and the alkali flats of Utah.

—Rachel L. Carson, *The Sea Around Us*

This next example is arranged from specific to general. The paragraphs have the specific statements first, with the final sentence stating the topic.

Given a paycheck and the stub that lists the usual deductions, 26 percent of adult Americans cannot determine if their paycheck is correct. Thirty-six percent, given a W-4 form, cannot enter the right number of exemptions in the proper places on the form. Forty-four percent, when given a series of "help wanted" ads, cannot match their qualifications to the job requirements. Twenty-two percent cannot address a letter well enough to guarantee that it will reach its destination. Twenty-four percent cannot add their own correct return address to the same envelope. Twenty percent cannot understand an "equal opportunity" announcement. Over 60 percent, given a series of "for sale" advertisements for products new and used, cannot calculate the difference between prices for a new and used appliance. Over 20 percent cannot write a check that will be processed by their bank—or will be processed in the right amount. Over 40 percent are unable to determine the correct amount of change they should receive, given a cash register receipt and the denomination of the bill used for payment.

From these and other forms of evidence, the APL* concludes that 30 million men and women are now "functionally incompetent." Another 54 million "just get by." This total of 84 million far exceeds all other estimates that we have seen.

—Jonathan Kozol, *Illiterate America*

These two methods of arrangement, like emphasis, are usually used with another type of development. Carson's paragraph, for example, uses *exemplification,* naming specific examples of salt harvests. The Kozol paragraphs likewise use *exemplification,* piling up statistical evidence of illiteracy.

A number of readings in this book are arranged from general to specific (thesis first) and from specific to general (thesis last). Aldo

---

*Adult Performance Level: A study carried out in 1973 at the University of Texas to identify how many adults were unable to cope with the responsibilities of everyday life.—D.G.

Leopold's "Thinking Like a Mountain" in Chapter 6 is a reflective piece that presents details about wolves before stating the thesis in the last paragraph. Thesis-first essays, being more common, will occur more frequently.

Summary of Methods

These, then, are some of the common methods of developing ideas in writing: chronology, space, classification, comparison, analogy, cause and effect, exemplification, and definition. These methods combine with types of arrangement: question and answer, problem and solution, emphasis, general to specific, and specific to general. The combinations are methods of developing and organizing paragraphs and entire essays.

You may be thinking that usually when you read you are unconscious of the writer's method of development, just as you are unconscious of grammar and punctuation. When the form and conventions are what you expect, you don't notice them. If you sometimes read *as a writer,* however, you *will* notice how other writers develop and arrange their ideas and possibly give yourself more options when you write.

Introductions, Conclusions, and Titles

Introductions, conclusions, and titles are often the most troublesome parts of writing. Whether you are writing essays for school, letters for business or personal communication, or reports, if you're like many writers you may tell yourself that you'll be fine if you can just get started. Then when you get to the end, you're stumped all over again: How can you finish it up?

Introductions

Here are several introductory paragraphs from essays in Part II. Read them and see what you anticipate happening in the essays.

A deep chesty bawl echoes from rimrock to rimrock, rolls down the mountain, and fades into the far blackness of the night. It is an outburst of wild defiant sorrow, and of contempt for all the adversities of the world.

—Aldo Leopold, "Thinking Like a Mountain"

I had a little puppy for a while in Vietnam. For a period of three days, I would take this little puppy and squeeze it until it would yelp. Or twist its little paw.

—Mark Baker, "The Taste of Evil"

When I announced I was running for President, I said the greenhouse effect, the depletion of the ozone layer, and the global ecological crisis will, by the end of this election year, be recognized as the most serious issue facing this country and the world. Three days later, a George Will column ridiculed the naiveté of a politician who could imagine that issues of this kind would be politically salable.

I guess he was partly right and partly wrong. I was right in that the issue has, during this year, attained enormous importance and new recognition. But he was right, since it didn't do me any good politically. There are still barriers to political action. Let me discuss five of them.

—Albert Gore, "What Is Wrong with Us?"

Appearing at times as if an artist has splashed paint on tree trunks and across the faces of rocks, lichens present a display as vibrant as wildflowers. Yet most people know very little about these exotic plants. Striking in variety as well as in color, lichens are useful to humans and serve as excellent reminders of both nature's fragility and its resilience.

—Kathleen Almy, "Lichens: Nature's Paintbox"

If a neatly adjusted time machine could take you back to the Main Street of an American town in 1900, to look about you with your present-day eyes, your first exclamation would probably be, "But look at all those horses!"

—Frederick Lewis Allen, "The Way It Was"

Life is filled with things that are assumed to be true because they are "obvious" or "self-evident." It's always a shock to learn that one of those things is not true at all. It gives you a chance to imagine what it was like to hear from the town crier that the world was round rather than, as was obvious and self-evident, flat.

Among the set of self-evident myths is the idea that if you want to lie you're better off doing it on the phone, where people can't see you and you are therefore more likely to get away with it. That happens to be false; it is in fact easier for people to spot a lie when they hear it on the phone than when they hear it from a person present at the time.

—Suzette Haden Elgin, "Telephone Listening"

One fairly clear observation from these introductory paragraphs is that there are many right ways to begin an essay. Consistent with the purposes of the essays they introduce, they employ some of these means of heightening interest:

Attention-getting statements
Curiosity-arousing details
Background statements
Humor
Challenging statements
Questions
Quotations
Statistics
Narratives

Frederick Lewis Allen's essay describes town life in 1900, so his introduction sets the scene. Mark Baker's introduction tells you that the essay will describe something unpleasant. Two of the introductions use the first-person pronoun *I,* placing the writer within the context of the essay; two address the reader, *you,* thus establishing a familiar tone for the remainder of the essay.

The **tone** of an essay can be as varied as a person's emotions or intentions: humorous, serious, objective, cynical, sad, contentious, angry—to name a few examples. Tone in writing is comparable to the sound of your voice. The way you sound in writing reflects your attitude toward your subject and your audience. Leopold's and Baker's introductions establish a reflective tone, while Almy's and Elgin's are more objective and explanatory. The tone established in an introduction should be consistent throughout the essay.

The common location for **thesis sentences** is the introduction; the thesis sentence is often the final sentence of the introduction. But theses are sometimes stated in conclusions, as with essays arranged from specific to general, and are sometimes even left unstated, being implied instead. In three of these introductions, the thesis of the essay does not appear because it is expressed in the conclusion. In the Gore, Almy, and Elgin examples, however, the thesis appears at the end of the introduction. Each introduction is appropriate for its essay, establishing its subject, a relationship between writer and reader, and the tone. Each attempts to interest the reader in the subject and implies the purpose of the essay.

Your introductions may be easier to write if you think of them as temporary placeholders. They don't have to be perfect before you get on with the essay. After you find out what your essay actually says, you can always revise your beginning to tell your reader what to expect. At that time you can see that your introduction is appropriate for your essay. Sometimes writers even postpone writing an introduction until after they have composed the essay. The introductions sampled here are likely not as they first appeared when the writers began writing. As part of revised essays, these introductions probably went through several changes before arriving at their published form. Don't be distressed, then, if your introductions don't initially sound the way you want them to.

To summarize, your *revised* introductions, those that are ready for the reader, should have five features. They should:

1. Be consistent with the purpose of the essay,
2. Be interesting,
3. Usually present the subject and your position on it (thesis),
4. Establish the essay's tone, and
5. Establish a relationship between you and your audience.

Exercise: The Community of Writers

With a partner or a group, examine tone in the sample introductions. What features contribute to the tone? What does the tone tell you about each writer's attitude toward subject and audience?

Conclusions

A **conclusion** does more than mark the end of a piece of writing; it *finishes* it. It winds it up, makes a final statement, completes what the introduction started, and gives the reader a last word. It doesn't leave the reader asking "So what?" and wondering about the point of the essay. It might accomplish this state of completion in a number of ways.

The easiest way to write a **conclusion** is to reread your entire essay, then concentrate on the introduction, in particular the thesis sentence, and write something that finishes what you started. Restate your thesis, answer a question you asked, refer to an anecdote you began with, or summarize your solution to the problem you introduced. Put yourself in the reader's place: Are there any loose ends you haven't tied up?

Make your conclusion consistent with each of the features for introductions established above. If the purpose of your essay is reflection or information, don't suddenly shift to trying to persuade your reader to particular actions. If you began with a serious tone, don't end by trying to be funny. And don't begin addressing the reader directly if you didn't do so in your introduction.

Conclusions are usually only a few sentences long. They normally do not present new information, examples, or opinions. These features are customarily used as support for points made within the essay, and their appearance seems out of place at the end, where all the points of the essay are being pulled together. Some writers like to end with an apt quotation. Before you do so, ask yourself whether you want somebody else to take over the final, emphatic position and have the last word in your essay.

If you don't write your essay at the last minute, you can let it rest for a while, then reread it later, when a conclusion may easily occur to you.

Titles

Unless you have a great idea for a **title** before you begin an essay, save its composition for last, because you will have a much better idea of how to describe your essay *after* you've written it. Titles should be descriptive: "The Eyes of Fishes," "Basic Flight Theory." They should also be short; in fact, they're usually fragments: *Illiterate America,* "The Decline of Heroes," "Command Performance." And they should be interesting, for it is usually the title that convinces a reader to pay attention to what you've written: "Bringing Back the Beast of Lore," "Pondering the Personal Pronoun Problem."

Do not underline the title of your essay or enclose it in quotation marks. Just center it near the top of your first page.

Completing the First Draft

Drafting is more than arranging ideas. When you write you examine your knowledge in new ways, and you *make new ideas.* Through the complex activity of engaging in composition, you not only communicate with a reader; you also sometimes surprise yourself with new insights by the time you get to your final period and your first draft is finished. You have probably already done some revising, but you still have much ahead of you. Chapter 5 discusses some techniques.

Exercise: The Community of Writers

Read the following paragraphs and identify examples of these methods of development and arrangement:

Chronology
Space
Classification
Comparison
Analogy
Cause and effect
Exemplification

Definition
Question and answer
Problem and solution
Emphasis
General to specific and specific to general

You are likely to find more than one method for most paragraphs. In what other ways might each paragraph be developed and arranged?

1. "Now that *Ms.* has made it, we're going to have to settle the problem of the masculine pronoun's taking charge when the gender is undetermined, as in 'Each member should supply *his* own utensils.' Today, a great many people are laboriously conscientious in saying things like 'his or her own utensils' or 'his/her own utensils.' In the past few years, I've received dozens of suggestions for new pronouns to cover both genders. The most recent was from Thomas S. Jackson, a Washington, D.C., lawyer, who says that the use of 'him or her,' 'he or she,' and so on, 'is both awkward and wasteful.' He suggests some new pronouns."

    —Thomas H. Middleton, "Pondering the Personal Pronoun Problem"

2. "Until recently, seeking has been done primarily by boys and merging by girls. Girls could seek scholarship so long as it didn't interfere with popularity. It was fine to take a summer job, but not to embark on a serious career. They could train their talents in dance lessons, drama clubs, piano recitals, church choirs, any of which would suit them well for a lifetime of pleasing. Unless—and this apprehension lurked always in the back of the mind—they turned out to be gifted. For then they would be forced to make a painful choice: either marriage or mastery of their art. Most of them gave up the lessons."

    —Gail Sheehy, *Passages*

3. "If direct taxes upon the wages of labour have not always occasioned a proportionable rise in those wages, it is because they have generally occasioned a considerable fall in the demand for labour. The declension of industry, the decrease of employment for the poor, the diminution of the annual produce of the land and labour of the country, have generally been the effects of such taxes. In consequence of them, however, the price of labour must always be higher than it otherwise would have been in the actual state of the demand: and this enhancement of price, together with the profit of those who advance it, must always be finally paid by the landlords and consumers."

    —Adam Smith, *The Wisdom of Adam Smith*

4. "I used to worry that computers would become so powerful and sophisticated as to take the place of human minds. The notion of Artificial Intelligence used to scare me half to death. Already, a large enough machine can do all sorts of intelligent things beyond our capacities: calculate in a split second the answers to mathematical problems requiring years for a human brain, draw accurate pictures from memory, even manufacture successions of sounds with a disarming resemblance to real music. Computers can translate textbooks, write dissertations of their own for doctorates, even speak in machine-tooled, inhuman phonemes any words read off from a printed page. They can communicate with one another, holding consultations and committee meetings of their own in networks around the earth."

—Lewis Thomas, "The Corner of the Eye"

5. "The Pilgrims were not nineteenth century pietists, or quietists. They were not pale plaster saints, hollow and bloodless. They were men—and women, too—of courage and conviction, strong and positive in their attitudes, prepared to sacrifice much for their principles, even their very lives. Far from being Victorians, they were children of another and a greater age, the Elizabethan, and in their lives reflected many of the qualities of that amazing age— its restlessness and impatience with old ways, its passionate enthusiasms, its eager curiosity and daring speculation in all fields, its boldness in action, its abounding and apparently inexhaustible energies."

—George F. Willison, *Saints and Strangers*

CHAPTER 5

The Writing Process: Revising

> *Revision is, indeed, re-seeing and it goes on continually in the composing process.*
>
> —*Ann Berthoff*

Writers **revise.** They want to make their meaning clearer, more explicit, self-explanatory. They want to see if they have said everything they intended to say, if they have said anything they want to retract or rephrase before someone else reads it, and if they have made all the necessary connections. They want to make their style clear, direct, precise, concise, and appropriate to the situation—taking into account their readers, the subject and purpose of the writing, and their roles as writers. Writers want to avoid offending or confusing their audiences. They want to speak with authority. They want to say everything necessary for clarity but no more than necessary. They want to use the right words, spell them correctly, arrange them in their sentences to prevent awkwardness, avoid inappropriate usage, have smooth and logical transitions between sentences and paragraphs, relate all their paragraphs to their thesis sentences, give appropriate signals with punctuation, and so on.

This is what revising is. It's not just correcting spelling and punctuation, though correcting is part of revising. It's not just replacing words with synonyms, though it is that too. Nor is it just searching for sentence fragments or faulty verbs or dangling modifiers, though revision does include those chores. It's not even just checking organization or coherence or thought development. Revising is more like *reconsidering, rethinking,* and *reseeing.* James Thurber, a noted humorist whose thoughts on writing are quoted in Chapter 4, admits that his writing often does not take shape until the seventh draft.

In writing your school papers, you probably don't have time to complete seven drafts. But you do have time to revise. If you use your available time well and understand revising thoroughly, you can produce papers unlike Thurber's first drafts that his wife calls "high-school stuff." Remember that revising occurs at all stages of writing. You may revise while prewriting—altering your plans even before you begin drafting, adjusting your outline or thesis, deleting thoughts you decide are no longer important, considering and reconsidering how you will begin, and so on. And, like most people, you probably also revise while drafting—adding or deleting sentences, rearranging words, correcting typing errors, and making all the other changes writers make when, pausing to consider what to say next, they go back and reread what they have just written.

But even with the adjustments you make as you compose, the writing is likely not perfect when you have finally put down your last period. You may know now what you want to say, but your draft is not ready for a reader. This first draft is often called a "rough draft," and sometimes not even a "first" but a "zero" draft, after which counting begins; sometimes writers call it a "discovery" draft, a "writer-based" draft appropriate only for the writer's eyes, or a "speculative" draft. Call it what you will, it can be improved.

Revising, like drafting, is something only the writer can do. Other people can give you suggestions, but only you, the writer, can make the changes. Only you know what details you can add, how you planned to connect two ideas, which ideas are irrelevant, and whether rephrasing a sentence alters the meaning you intended. Revising, like drafting, is making and discovering meaning, clarifying thoughts by putting them into words and adjusting those words. When you write something, you discover what you mean to say and your purpose for saying it. Because others may read for different meanings and purposes, they may not see what you intended. At the same time, however, audience response is crucial information for a writer, since the main point of writing is to get an idea across. So ask for and accept the feedback of other readers; then weigh their criticisms with your own intentions and clarify your writing as necessary.

This chapter will show you some ways of reconsidering, rethinking, and reseeing your writing. We will look mainly at *reading as a reader, using invention questions, mapping or outlining, applying a checklist,* and *getting feedback from others.* The chapter treats revision as that part of the writing process usually needed after drafting; however, bear in mind that revision occurs anywhere in the procedure. The end of the chapter will treat two related parts of writing: *editing* and *proofreading.*

Reading as a Reader

Chapter 1 recommends that you read as a *writer* to develop a sensitivity to how other writers express their ideas. This chapter now advises you, when reading what you have written, to read as a *reader*—to put yourself in your reader's place. Whatever method you use for revising your writing, you have to go back and reread. You are, after all, your first reader. If you don't like or understand what you read, you can probably assume other readers won't either. Novelist William Styron, discussing his writing process, says, "Every day I pick up the story or whatever it is I've been working on and read it through. If I enjoy it as a reader then I know I'm getting along all right." *Enjoyment* is his criterion for criticism. "The writer," he says, "must criticize his own work as a reader" (*Writers at Work*, 1st series, 278).

Can you put some distance between yourself and your drafts and read them as a reader, not as their writer and creator? Your readers are limited to the words you put on a page; they can't read your mind, and they can't ask you questions. So if, when you set out to revise, you read your drafts critically as a *reader*, you may discover that you have omitted some details or that you did not make all your connections clear. As a *writer*, you know what those details are, and to you everything seems to flow logically. Reading as a reader, you see what is missing and unclear.

When you reread your first draft, you will probably find parts that you enjoy and others that are too rough for even you to appreciate. These parts you pause to tinker with, trying to clarify your sentences and paragraphs so that they say what you meant to say. *Meaning* is undoubtedly the major object of criticism. If your writing doesn't say—directly and unambiguously—what you intended, then it must be revised. With your first draft, ask questions like these:

Does my main idea come through clearly?
Do my details lend sufficient support to that central idea?
Is it clear how all parts of my essay are connected to one another?

Revising Is Changing Meaning

Anything you do to change the meaning of your writing is revising. You can alter meaning in four ways:

Adding   Substituting
Deleting   Rearranging

These four actions operate on a number of levels. You can **add** a paragraph or a whole section, significantly building on your meaning, or you can add a brief example, even an adjective, a comma, a transition, or an underline. You can **delete** a paragraph, a sentence, a comma, or a conjunction, eliminating wordiness and repetition and combining sentences to achieve conciseness and variety. You can **substitute** a verb, a phrase, an example, a paragraph, a sentence. And you can **rearrange** a paragraph, some examples, the spelling of a word, words in a sentence.

Let's examine more closely how changes such as these qualify as changes in meaning. Correcting spelling is usually thought of as editing, something anyone, even a computer, can do because meaning is not involved. Adjusting punctuation, too, is often thought of as editing. Changing meaning, then, is thought of as occurring on a global scale, affecting the entire essay: revising a thesis sentence, adding or omitting a paragraph, altering one's writing voice. These are significant revisions, to be sure. However, sometimes just adding a comma or changing spelling alters meaning. Consider what happens when you add commas to this sentence:

My brother who is still in elementary school won a new Mazda in a raffle.

My brother, who is still in elementary school, won a new Mazda in a raffle.

In the second version, the meaning is different. The first version implies more than one brother, with the *who* clause identifying which one; the second implies a single brother, and the *who* clause supplies additional information about him. Since only the writer is likely to know how many brothers are involved, only the writer can revise such a sentence; only the writer knows what changes can be made without saying something other than what was meant. Unless the writer makes those changes, the reader may be misled.

When you revise, you do change the meaning—sometimes slightly, sometimes a great deal. If you revise "dirty cars" to "dust-covered cars," you've changed the meaning a little, yet significantly. If you correct your spelling from "hop" to "hope," you've changed the meaning more significantly. And if you change the order of your paragraphs so that they read from least emphatic to most emphatic instead of the other way around, you have made a greatly significant change.

Read your essay as many times as necessary to get it in shape for a reader. At some point you may need to make a fresh, preferably typed, copy because the original is getting too messy. Then continue revising. On one of your readings, read your essay aloud so you can listen for awkward phrases and sentences.

Revising with a Word Processor

If you do your composing on a word processor, revising is easier in many ways than it would be with typed or handwritten copies. You can add or delete on the screen and still have a clean, readable text. You can rearrange easily, moving large chunks from one part of your text to another. In an overtype mode, you can substitute words and sentences without first deleting the originals. But the process of drafting and revising on the word processor has features that you should guard against. Because of the ease of revision, you might muddy your writing by making unnecessary additions and substitutions. Through deletion you could lose some sentences you wish you had kept; perhaps you can retrieve them, perhaps not. In moving your paragraphs around, you may undo your original connections.

Here are some tips for revising on the word processor:

1. Unless your word-processing program saves automatically, save your composition frequently—and always before printing a paper copy. The best of us make mistakes or encounter power failures. While drafting or revising, save text every few minutes.
2. Always print a paper copy to refer to while you are revising; then work with both the paper copy and the screen.
3. Look for repetitions and inconsistencies that occurred as a result of your having before you only one screen at a time while you composed.
4. Look for digressions and irrelevancies that might have occurred because composing is so easy on the word processor.

You are more likely to achieve the distance you need for reading as a *reader* when you revise from your paper draft than when you read from the screen, where you have been the writer. Also, with a paper draft you can more readily conceptualize your paper as a whole and avoid inconsistencies in structure and development; you can see how well you have connected sections and can detect unnecessary repetitions.

Exercise: The Community of Writers

Here are the first four drafts of a paragraph that introduces an essay about the advantages of low-intensity workouts. Read each draft and decide, with your groupmates, how the writer uses (1) addition, (2) deletion, (3) substitution, and (4) rearrangement. Then ask, How does the writer discover meaning through revising?

First Draft

Most people think exercise is too much work. They're too busy or it makes them too tired. They're satisfied being couch potatoes. They tried working out and pushed themselves to the limit. Finally they become frustrated and used one of the many excuses to drop out: too busy, too tired, sick or injured and unable to continue.

Second Draft

Many people don't get enough exercise because they think it's too much work. They're satisfied being couch potatoes. When they tried working out, they pushed themselves to their limits, telling themselves, "No pain, no gain." Finally they became frustrated and used one of the many excuses for dropping out: too busy, too tired, sick or injured and unable to continue. Instead, a low-intensity workout may be the answer.

Third Draft

Many people don't get enough exercise because they think that exercising is too much work. They tried working out once or twice, even signed up for sixteen weeks of Nautilus, telling themselves, "No pain, no gain," but they finally became frustrated. They didn't see any improvement in their health or appearance, and they were tired of being tired and sweaty. So they used one of the many excuses for dropping out: too busy, too tired, or sick or injured. What they didn't know was that a low-intensity workout provides the same benefits of improved health and appearance but at a more enjoyable pace.

Fourth Draft

Are you one of the many people who don't get enough exercise because you think that exercising is too much work? Perhaps you've tried working out once or twice or even signed up for sixteen weeks of Nautilus, exercising at a high intensity and telling yourself all the time, "No pain, no gain." But then you became frustrated. You didn't see any improvement in your health or appearance, and you were tired of being tired and sweaty. You finally dropped out, using one of the many excuses: too busy, too tired, sick, or injured. Well, here's the good news: you can improve your cardiovascular fitness, lose weight, and increase muscle mass with a low-intensity workout.

Using Invention Questions

If you're sometimes at a loss as to how to proceed with revision, try applying the methods of invention discussed in Chapter 3. Since these methods are ways of discovering ideas, they can be particularly useful for revealing incomplete development of thoughts and for discovering information that should be added to clarify your meaning. Here we'll consider the journalist's questions, the classical probes, and questions about audience, but you might find some of the other invention methods useful as well, particularly cubing and brainstorming.

Journalist's Questions

Try asking the **journalist's questions,** the five **W's** and an **H:** *Who? What? Where? When? Why?* and *How?* Asking these questions about the ideas you've put down can tell you whether you've explained yourself adequately. If you were the writer of the paragraph in the preceding Community of Writers exercise, you could ask questions such as these about your essay:

Who will read this?
Who exercises?
How do people exercise?
Why do people not exercise?
What are the benefits of exercise?
What is harmful about exercise?
What kind of exercise is best?
Where can people get exercise?
When is a good time to exercise?
Why should people exercise?

Questions like these could reveal a wealth of details for enriching the paragraph and the essay that it introduces. Using these interrogatory words can help you to see what you are saying and what you are not saying.

Classical Probes

Another way of asking questions about your draft is to use the **classical probes:** asking questions about *identification, comparison and contrast, classification, causes and effects, process analysis,* and *exemplification.* For example:

What is exercise? (*identification*)
What kinds of exercise do I discuss? (*classification*)
How do I say exercise improves health and fitness? (*process analysis*)
What do I say are the effects of intense workouts? low-intensity workouts? (*causes and effects*)
How do I compare intense workouts with low-intensity workouts? (*comparison*)
What examples of intense workouts do I use? What examples of low-intensity workouts do I use? (*exemplification*)

This type of questioning might continue until you are sure your draft includes answers to all the questions you consider important for developing your point. As with using the classical probes during prewriting, you might find you are concentrating on one or two probes, for example asking a number of comparison questions if your essay compares two subjects, as the one on exercises seems to do.

Questions About Audience

Even though in prewriting you establish who your intended audience is and how much you know about it, you might find it useful to ask some **questions about audience** after you have a draft in front of you. Here are the audience questions from Chapter 2, rephrased for revision. For a given essay, ask as many as apply.

Questions About Audience for Revision

1. Who is my intended audience?
2. What does my audience know about my subject?
3. Do I establish my credibility in relation to my subject?
4. Do I establish my relationship with my audience?
5. What do I say to interest my audience in my subject?
6. Do I say anything that promotes positive attitudes toward my subject?
7. Do I say anything that promotes positive attitudes toward me?
8. Do I want to change audience attitudes toward my subject or me?
9. Do I establish ties with my audience by means of shared experiences and knowledge?
10. Do I use shared experiences and knowledge in presenting my subject?
11. How will my audience perceive the rhetorical situation in which I am writing: reflective, persuasive, informative, or something else?
12. How will my audience react to my grammar, style, and vocabulary?

Exercise: The Exploring Writer

Select two methods of invention to use for revising a draft of your writing. Apply these methods to your draft to see if there is anything you should add, delete, substitute, or rearrange.

Exercise: The Community of Writers

Here is the rough draft of a student's letter to the president of his university. When his teacher read this draft, she told him that his argument was weak and needed more thought and development. With your groupmates, apply the journalist's questions, the classical probes, and the questions about audience from a reader's perspective to discover how the writer might strengthen his case. If you were the university president receiving this letter, how would you react and what else would you want to know?

Dear Mr. Campbell:

1   The parking problem at this university is becoming a big problem because there is nowhere to park. I was advised by other older students to take early classes to prevent the problem of parking. But even students with 9:00 A.M. classes have to walk five or six blocks and sometimes even farther to get to class. This is a real problem when the temperature is below 0. It is frustrating to go to school and not find a close parking spot. The only way is to go to school a couple of hours before class.

2   Another problem with the parking tickets. A lot of students are receiving parking tickets because they have to park in illegal places so they don't have to walk far to classes. The parking tickets are a disadvantage to the students who live off campus. These students should be able to go to school knowing that they can find a parking spot a couple of blocks from school.

3   I hope you will take this problem into consideration and try to have something done.

4   I would like to see something done so students wouldn't face this problem in the future. Maybe the school could pay for a parking lot or ramp close to school. There is not enough parking for the students who attend this university so something has to be done.

Sincerely,
John Martinez

Outlining or Mapping

Although invention questions are useful for revealing omissions, outlining your draft helps you check for irrelevant information and faulty organization, as well as omissions. Outlining or mapping a completed draft is a good idea especially for writers who compose without an outline, who begin instead by freewriting or following a loose mental plan. You may produce an outline only when a teacher requires you to submit one; legitimize it now as a part of your writing process.

Outlining

To **outline** your rough draft, state the main idea of each paragraph in a sentence, using a roman numeral for each paragraph. These should be your topic sentences, whether you expressed them explicitly in your essay or not. Use sublevels to show the development of each paragraph. When you are finished, you should be able to see the connections between all your topic sentences. You should also be able to see whether each paragraph is adequately developed and whether it has irrelevant information. (Refer to "Outlining" in Chapter 3 for a fuller discussion.)

Mapping

Mapping, as described in Chapter 3, is a method of listing and visually organizing ideas. A visual map of your paper may help you revise it. To **map** your rough draft, place the main idea of your essay, or the thesis, in the center of a sheet of paper and enclose it in a double circle. Then around that circle write the main ideas of your paragraphs, circle them, and add your supporting information. Draw lines to connect related information. If you end up with an idea you haven't been able to connect to anything else, it may be irrelevant to this essay. If it is truly unnecessary to your essay, discard it. It may, however, be critical information that needs more development. If so, go back to some kind of invention questions to discover how to develop that idea.

Exercise: The Community of Writers

Here's the student essay on exercise, followed by a partial outline of its organization and development. Each roman numeral in the outline represents a paragraph in the essay. With your groupmates, complete the outline, using the essay and the filled-in outline items as guides. Note that the outline has some flaws; these are clues to flaws in the essay's organization. As you complete the outline and study it, you will discover undeveloped ideas and ineffective organization. Discuss needed revisions in development or organization of the essay.

As an alternate exercise, read the student essay on exercise and check its organization and development with mapping.

No Pain, No Gain?

(student writer)

Are you one of the many people who don't get enough exercise   1
because you think that exercising is too much work? Perhaps you've tried working out once or twice or even signed up for sixteen weeks of Nauti-

lus, exercising at a high intensity and telling yourself all the time, "No pain, no gain." But then you became frustrated. You didn't see any improvement in your health or appearance, and you were tired of being tired and sweaty. You finally dropped out, using one of the many excuses: too busy, too tired, sick, or injured. Well, here's good news: you can improve your cardiovascular fitness, lose weight, and increase muscle mass with a low-intensity workout.

A common misconception is that the greater the exercise intensity, the more fat burned. In reality, fat can only be utilized when oxygen is present. For fat to be converted into energy it must be converted into energy by being broken down to fatty acids. This is done when the fat molecule combines with oxygen. It is only possible in an aerobic workout. Intense workouts are anaerobic, therfore, they can only use carbohydrates and protein for sources of energy. If you think about it the process is logical. When the body is working at a high intensity, it naturally uses its most efficient fuel, carbohydrates. When working at lower intensities, the body can afford to fall back on its less efficiently burned caloric sources, such as fat.

A similar misconception is that exercising at higher intensities burns significally more fat. In fact it does not. Kath and McCardle cite the following in their book *Nutrition, Weight Control and Exercise.* "A 150 pound person expends about 110 kilocalories while jogging one mile in twelve minutes. If the same person runs the mile in five and a half minutes, only about 130 kilocalories are expended."

You may be surprised to learn that only twenty additional calories were expended by exercising twice as hard. Are you willing to exercise that hard and triple your chance of injuring yourself or dropping out? An ideal exercise program is one that is low enough to use fat as an energy source, but high enough to elicit a cardiovascular training effect.

One example would be walking instead of running. If you run you should run at a pace where you can still talk comfortably. In chosing an exercise you should pick one that you enjoy, and remember that variety is the spice of life. If you enjoy your workouts you will look forward to each session. It has always been easier for people to find time in their busy schedules to do activities they enjoy. Aerobic exercise should be done three times a week for at least thirty minutes. This advice has become the first commandment of physical fitness—the requirement needed by the body to keep the heart and lungs healthy.

The important factor to remember when developing a fitness routine is that duration of exercise, not the intensity, is the critical factor for burning more calories. And longer duration is acheived by lowering the intensity. As you maintain an exercise program year after year, a healthy lifestyle will come more and more naturally and you will keep looking and feeling healthier.

Outline

I. Introduction of the subject

   A. Audience and exercise

   B.

   C.

   D. Thesis: You can improve your cardiovascular fitness, lose weight, and increase muscle mass with a low-intensity workout.

II. Common misconception that intense workouts burn more fat

   A. Reality: fat utilized in presence of oxygen

      1. Broken down into fatty acids

      2.

      3. Anaerobic workouts

   B. Logical process

III. Similar misconception that intense workouts burn more fat

   A. Kath and McCardle quotation

IV. Difference in caloric expenditure

   A.

   B. Ideal exercise program

      1.

      2.

V. Example of ideal exercise program

   A. Advice on exercise

      1.

      2.

      3.

      4.

VI. Conclusion: duration not intensity as critical factor

   A.

   B.

Applying a Checklist

Every revision is specific to a piece of writing, so no revision checklist applies to all situations. There are general guides, however. As just discussed, the invention questions can be adapted to revisions of many pieces of writing; outlining and mapping can also often apply. In addition, you might try a checklist such as this one:

Revision Checklist

1. Is my *purpose* apparent throughout the essay?
2. Does my *thesis sentence* state both the point of my essay and my subject?
3. Are all *paragraphs* clearly related to my thesis?
4. Is each *paragraph* developed fully enough that my readers aren't left with unanswered questions?
5. Do I have any *paragraphs* that should be combined? Any that should be separated?
6. Are my *paragraphs* clearly connected to one another?
7. Does my *introduction* appeal to the interests of my audience, and does it prepare my audience for what I am about to say?
8. Does my *conclusion* end with the point I stated in my thesis?
9. Do I have a clear, authoritative *voice* that is appropriate for my subject, my audience, and my purpose?
10. Is there anything I should delete to avoid inappropriate *repetition or inconsistencies*?
11. Is there anything I should add to *clarify my position*?
12. Do the *grammar and usage* in my sentences clearly express my meaning?
13. Have I used *words* that convey my meaning accurately and unambiguously, without bias, pretensions, and unintended connotations?
14. Have I shown how the parts of my essay *relate* to my thesis and *connect* to one another?
15. Does my *title* both describe my subject and interest my audience?

A checklist like this points out that revision goes on at several levels: essay, paragraph, sentence, and word. At all levels you look for clarity and completeness, for connections between parts, for unity and consistency. Revision usually does not concentrate on one level at a time—say, working at the essay level before looking at sentences and words—and the preceding checklist reflects this roving of the revising eye. Some writers even prefer to do some editing—correcting spelling or usage errors—before beginning their larger revising projects, just so these errors won't distract them. In practice, you will probably revise and edit (see "Editing") at the same time.

Essay-Level Revisions

To apply the revision checklist at the essay level, use questions 1, 2, 7, 8, 9, 10, 13, and 14. At this level, look for a coherent whole: Do all parts relate to a thesis that states your central idea clearly and precisely? Is your purpose or are your purposes for writing apparent and consistent throughout the essay? If your purpose is to report a factual occurrence, for example, is it appropriate for you to speculate? Is your tone, or voice, consistent, and does it coincide with your purpose? Lapsing into humor or cynicism is not appropriate for a serious report. Does your conclusion reiterate the central idea you began with—by summary, restatement, or some other means? (Chapter 4 has more on conclusions.) Is your title consistent with the whole essay, reflecting your central idea in an interesting way—as does the title for the essay on exercise, "No Pain, No Gain?"

Paragraph-Level Revisions

To analyze your paragraphs, use questions 3, 4, 5, 6, and 13. Paragraphs sometimes are not developed adequately and sometimes do not focus on a single idea. Sometimes they are excessively long and need to be divided; at other times the essay would be easier to follow if two paragraphs were combined. If your paragraphs need further development, refer back to Chapter 3 for methods of discovering and exploring ideas.

Coherence

In a well-written essay, all the paragraphs relate to the main idea (expressed in the thesis sentence) and connect to one another. If all these connections are made, the essay has **coherence.** Writers relate their ideas in a number of ways. The primary means for making an essay coherent is to express the main idea in a *thesis sentence* (pp. 58–60). A clearly stated thesis, first, gives the reader an idea to build on. In addition, it is stated in *key words,* and each time these words are repeated, the reader is able to connect to the thesis. For example, in the following thesis sentence, the key words are *wind* and *Patagonia.*

The wind is the most fundamental fact of life in Patagonia.

With each occurrence of these key words, a connection is made to the thesis.

The effect of another coherence device is similar to that of the thesis sentence. A *topic sentence* expresses the main idea of a paragraph much like a thesis sentence does for an essay. Unlike a thesis sentence, a topic sentence does not always make an assertion, but, in one way or another, it names the subject of the paragraph, thus providing a key idea to hold the paragraph together. Usually the first sentence of a paragraph lets readers know what the paragraph will be about. Many writers use the topic sentence not only for giving coherence to its own paragraph but also for connecting the paragraph to the preceding one. As an example of this twofold coherence gained from topic sentences, here is the first sentence from one of Michael D. Lemonick's paragraphs in "Deadly Danger in a Spray Can" (pp. 334–36):

> While recycling will help, the only sure way to save the ozone is a complete ban on CFC manufacture.

The first phrase, "While recycling will help," refers back to the preceding paragraph, while the remainder of the sentence declares the subject of the present paragraph. Here's another example. It's from "Aggression Defined" by Elliott Aronson (pp. 352–55).

> But this distinction is not altogether satisfactory because, by concentrating on an outcome alone, it ignores the intention of the person perpetrating the act, and this is the crucial aspect of aggression.

In this example, the first three words, "But this distinction," relate to the previous paragraph, and the rest of the sentence makes a new statement, which will be explained in the remainder of the paragraph.

These are the major methods for achieving coherence between paragraphs. (You'll find other discussions on pages 296–97, 319–20, and 386.) Within paragraphs, writers often use transitional words and phrases to show how their sentences relate to one another. By using the right transitional word, you can indicate contrasting ideas, similarities, examples, chronology, and so on. By themselves, transitional words only signal relationships; to be truly coherent, the sentences themselves must be related. Here are some of the more common words and phrases that achieve this type of coherence. They are arranged by function.

Transitional Words and Phrases

SIGNAL	*WORDS*
Addition	and, again, also, in addition, moreover, furthermore, besides, next, then, finally
Comparison	in comparison, likewise, similarly, in the same way
Concession	of course, although, granted, to be sure, after all, at the same time, even though

Transitional Words and Phrases (continued)

Contrast	but, however, although, nevertheless, on the contrary, yet, on the other hand, conversely, otherwise
Examples	for example, for instance, in fact, specifically, as an illustration, in particular
Location	here, there, next, beside, in front of, behind, above, below, nearby
Result	so, therefore, thus, consequently, then, as a result
Summary	in conclusion, to summarize, to sum up, in other words, in brief, finally
Time	first (etc.), next, then, later, meanwhile, subsequently, currently, afterwards, finally, before, soon

Sentence-Level Revisions

At this level, see that your sentences follow one another smoothly, that you are not omitting details and connections. Grammar and usage should not stand in the way of the ideas you want to express; your usage should be like what you find in published writing of the same type. To develop a style that employs conventional sentence patterns and usage, study the sentences of other writers. Read some of the essays in Part II to gain a sense of usage, voice, and level of formality for expository writing. Try to make your sentences sound like written, not spoken, sentences you have encountered. Questions 8, 9, and 11 can assist you on this level.

Word-Level Revisions

Question 12 directs your attention to the words you use. If any word stands out as a little odd, give it a close look. Does it express your meaning accurately? *Flout* and *flaunt,* for example, have very different meanings. In the context of your essay, could a word have a double meaning? For instance, in the phrase "exercise more naturally," does *more* relate to *exercise* or *naturally?* Could a word you use give the impression that you are biased, such as the pronouns *he, his,* and *him* to refer to persons of both sexes? Is a word pretentious, such as *endeavor* instead of *try,* or *deem* instead of *think?* Does a word convey meanings that you didn't intend because of the connotative baggage it carries—*gloomy* rather than *dim,* for example? Mark Twain said that the "difference between the right word and the almost-right word is the difference between lightning and a lightning-bug." You are the best judge of what is the right word for your essay, so you must revise for the exactly right word.

Getting Feedback from Others

As noted earlier, your first drafts are probably not the sort of thing you want someone else to read. They express the thoughts you had while you were still discovering what you wanted to say. First drafts may have irrelevant material, gaps where explanations are necessary, unclear pronoun references, shifts in focus. You revise your writing so readers will understand what you mean and think well of you. There may be times, however, when, to see clearly what changes you should make, you need to let someone else read your draft, with all its inaccuracies and imprecisions.

When you ask other people for **feedback,** tell them how you want them to read your writing, what you want them to look for. If you're concerned about focus, tell your readers to consider whether your essay concentrates on a central idea or seems to slip off at times. If you think your examples might not be concrete enough, tell your readers you want them to give close attention to how you illustrate your points. If you want an overall assessment, you might ask your readers to use the revision checklist questions in the previous section.

Sometimes you voluntarily request feedback, and sometimes it is an assigned part of a course. For whatever reason you get reader response, and whether it's from teacher or peers, you'll probably need to moderate your natural sensitivity to criticism. If you're like most writers, you feel as if your writing is an extension of yourself, as if criticism of your writing is criticism of you. However, suggestions for improvement of early drafts can be thought of as collaborative aids, as helpful pointers that can make your final draft better. This is why you *want* feedback from others.

A readily available and often overlooked kind of feedback is what you can get from other writers. Published writers are always available, through their writing, for guidance and instruction. If you have questions about how to revise your introduction, observe how other writers begin their essays. Do you want to know how to lead into an example? See how other writers do it. Writers can show you how to connect paragraphs, how to subordinate less important information in your sentences, how to use transitional words and phrases, how to conclude your essays, and so on. They don't *tell* you; they *show* you in their own sentences and paragraphs and essays. All you need to do is apply the principles to your own writing.

Exercise: The Community of Writers

1. *Exchange recent drafts of an essay with a classmate and give each other feedback on ways to revise them. Discuss what is troubling you about your paper, where you think the problems are, what kind of response you want. Use the revision checklist questions on page 105 if you want an overall response.*
2. *Working with a partner in class, apply the revision checklist (page 105) or the questions about audience for revising (page 100) to the student essay "No Pain, No Gain?" on pages 102–03. What advice on revision would you give its writer?*

Editing

Related to revising is **editing.** Unlike revising, editing can often be done by other people as well as by the writer, although the writer ought to be the *first* editor (and the *last*). Sometimes teachers are editors, sometimes classmates, sometimes friends, sometimes people called *editors* who prepare writing for publication. Editing is preparing a revised draft for presentation to other people. It usually does not change meaning, at least not significantly. When writers edit, they correct spelling and punctuation and make other changes so that their writing conforms to conventional standards. Editing is therefore one of the last steps in writing. Still, many writers do some editing as they draft and revise. If when rereading their drafts they see a misspelled word or a misplaced comma, they correct it so that it doesn't distract them while they concentrate on the broader issues.

The way to edit is to look for the kinds of errors that usually crop up in your writing. If you commonly write sentence fragments, look for fragments. If pronoun reference is a problem, make sure that every time you use a pronoun (for example, *it, this, they, he, she*) the noun it refers to is absolutely evident. If you have a problem with the forms of your verbs, read your essay through once looking only at verbs. You probably can't get your editing done in one pass through. Most writers need to go over their writing repeatedly to make all the corrections they have to make. At some point in your editing, type a clean copy; then continue to read carefully for errors and faulty phrasing.

Checklists are sometimes helpful as reminders of what to look for when you edit. Each writer and each writing situation requires a particular kind of editing, but you can use the following checklist as a guide, adapting it for each piece of writing you edit.

Editing Checklist

1. Does my *punctuation* follow conventional usage?
2. Should I check the *spelling* of any of my words?
3. Does every *verb* agree with its subject, especially in sentences where subjects and verbs are widely separated?
4. Are the *tenses* of my verbs consistent with the way I want to use them?
5. Does every *pronoun* (particularly *it, this, they, he, she*) clearly refer to a noun or another pronoun?
6. Does every *modifier* have an obvious connection to the word I want it to modify?
7. When I have used *coordinating conjunctions (and, but, or, nor, for, so, yet)*, are the sentence parts they connect equivalent in grammar and in meaning?
8. Do I use *capitals, abbreviations, numbers,* and *underlines* according to conventional usage?
9. Do I have unnecessarily *wordy constructions,* such as those that begin *there are* or those that have a verb plus a noun, or a verb plus an adjective, when a verb will do ("they *took notice of*" instead of "they *noticed*" and "they *are desirous of*" instead of "they *want*").
10. Do I have any *clichés,* overworked figures of speech such as "rat race" and "to top it off"?

Editing with a Word Processor

If you have drafted with a word processor, begin your editing on the screen. Word processors make editing so easy that it's no problem to pass through an essay or other piece of writing several times to correct errors. If you have a spelling checker, use it, remembering that you need to watch for words it doesn't flag—homonyms like *to/too/two,* for example. If you tend to overuse or misuse words such as *there* or *this,* use your "search" function to locate them; then decide whether each usage is appropriate.

Before considering your editing ended, print a paper copy and continue reading for errors and inappropriate usage. Mark your corrections with a red pen so you won't miss any when you transfer them to your word-processing disk.

Exercise: The Exploring Writer

Edit the following paragraph, applying the editing checklist as appropriate and writing a clean copy.

The wolf is an often misunderstood creature. It's reputation paints a picture of a cold blooded killer but in fact the wolf is a very important part of natures ecolgical balance. For instance as depicted in the movie *Never Cry Wolf* the wolf was thought to be a major contributer to the decline of the great caribu heards. Research proved however, that the wolf packs only hunted to survive, and to provide for the young pups. The decline of the caribu came from overkill from man, and disease within the heard. The wolfs while hunting, would single out the young, old, and weak caribu; therefore letting the strong, healthy caribu move on to mate again. By hunting only out of necessiry and survival, the wolves actually contributed to the propagation of the caribu heard.

Proofreading

Also related to revising is **proofreading,** which, like editing, can be done by either the writer or someone else. Ultimately, however, the responsibility is the writer's. The errors that go under your name are *yours,* no matter who the typist or proofreader is. Proofreading is done on the final copy, to make sure it conforms to conventional standards—that there are no errors in typing, spelling, or punctuation, no unintentionally omitted or repeated words, no strikeovers or smudges—in other words, that the copy is clean and ready for presentation to a reader.

Proofreading is difficult to do, because reading is usually for meaning, and this kind of reading is precisely what writers must *not* do when proofreading. When you proofread, you must read for *error,* and nothing else. When reading for meaning, a person's eyes take in two or three words at a time, focusing on one of them and giving the outlying words only scant attention. You can appreciate the implications for proofreading, especially for the words at the beginnings and ends of lines. Here are some tips for meticulous proofreading:

Proofreading Tips

1. Look at every word and punctuation mark.
2. Resist the temptation to overlook the first and last words on a line.
3. Read aloud; doing so slows your reading.
4. Point at each word as you read.
5. Read backward from the end of the essay.

Do whatever you need to in order to avoid reading fast and for meaning. Catch all your final errors, because whatever errors remain are *yours*. Teachers often think it is a shame when a student spends hours writing a paper and then submits it with errors that could have been eliminated by careful proofreading.

Proofreading on a Word Processor

If you have composed with a word processor, always proofread your final paper copy. To prevent a possible need for reprinting, however, give your document a careful last reading on your screen. If you generally read too fast, keep the line you are proofreading at the *bottom* of your screen, and scroll to the next line only after you've read the last word on the line you're reading. If you still skip words, move the cursor to each word as you read. Reading with the cursor is tedious, though, and you will have to train your eyes to slow down.

A Final Word

Revising is a lot of work, often requiring a great deal of time. But the payoff is a piece of writing you can be proud of as a representation of you. It expresses your thoughts to another person, in words and a style that you have made as good as you can. To know when to quit revising, you might follow the practice of novelist John Dos Passos: "I usually write to a point where the work is getting worse instead of better. That's the point to stop."

Exercise: The Community of Writers

1. *Apply the editing checklist on page 111 to John Martinez's letter on page 101.*
2. *With a partner, observe how your eyes move when you read. First, read paragraph 1 in this exercise. Have your partner count the number of times your eyes stop as you read each line. Compare the number of stops with the number*

of words per line. Then observe as your partner reads. Next, read paragraph 2 and have your partner count the stops your eyes make; compare the number of stops with the number of words per line. Then reverse with your partner. Your findings will fall in these categories:

a. Eye stops are equal to the number of words.
b. Eye stops are fewer than the number of words.
c. Eye stops are more than the number of words.

Don't be surprised if your eyes also make backward movements. Discuss the implications of your findings with your partner and your class.

The cold late October air was biting my arms, legs, and face. My uniform, consisting of a pair of cotton shorts and a t-shirt, wasn't enough to keep anyone warm in October, especially on such a chilly day. The athletic socks covering my arms to my elbows made me pretend that my fingers weren't as numb as my frozen toes. I didn't even notice the numbness of my nose because my concern was for my lungs, which ached from the cold, brisk air. Yet the heavy breath billowing from my lungs was warm enough to create steam when it escaped through my mouth.

—Deneen Young, student

We're not good enouhg to be on a leauge team, Buzz always ends up getting too drunk and starts goofing off. He likes to see how far he can throw his ball using an overhand delivery the league guys do'nt like that. Besides, you have to have your own bowling shoes to be on a team. I'll be damned if I'll pay 25 bucks for a pair of shoes I can only wear on Wendsday nites. We do'nt even rent bowling shoes, we tell Jerry that we all have enormous feet—size 17. He does'nt have any rentals that big so he let's us bowl in our socks.

3. *Here is the final draft of "No Pain, No Gain?" Compare it with the rough draft on pages 102–03 and answer the following questions.*

  a. *Did the writer reconcile her problems with organization?*
  b. *Did her revisions clear up problems with development?*
  c. *Does her essay as revised develop her thesis as revised?*
  d. *What problems still remain?*

  Now apply the revision checklist (page 105) to the revised essay and be prepared to discuss in class whatever revisions you think should be made.

No Pain, No Gain?

(student writer)

Are you one of the many people who don't get enough exercise   1
because you think that exercising is too much work? Perhaps you've tried working out once or twice or even signed up for sixteen weeks of Nauti-

lus, exercising at a high intensity and telling yourself all the time, "No pain, no gain." But then you became frustrated. You didn't see any improvement in your health or appearance, and you were tired of being tired and sweaty. You finally dropped out, using one of the many excuses: too busy, too tired, sick, or injured. Well, here's good news: you can improve your cardiovascular fitness and lose weight with a low-intensity workout.

A common misconception is that the greater the exercise intensity, 2 the more fat burned. In reality, fat can be utilized more efficiently in low-intensity workouts. For fat to be converted into energy it must be broken down to fatty acids. This can be achieved only in the presence of oxygen, because the fat molecule must combine with oxygen. This conversion is possible only in an aerobic, low-intensity workout, which promotes the body's ability to utilize oxygen. Because anaerobic workouts are less likely to circulate oxygen throughout the body, they can only use carbohydrates and protein for sources of energy. When the body is working at a high intensity, it naturally uses its most efficient fuel, carbohydrates. When working at lower intensities, the body can afford to fall back on its less efficiently burned caloric sources such as fat.

A similar misconception is that exercising at higher intensities 3 burns significantly more fat. In fact it does not. According to Katch and McArdle in their book *Nutrition, Weight Control, and Exercise,* a 150-pound person expends about 110 kilocalories while jogging one mile in twelve minutes, but if the same person runs the mile in five and a half minutes, only about 130 kilocalories are expended. You may be surprised to learn that only twenty additional calories were expended by exercising twice as hard. Are you willing to exercise that hard and increase your chance of injuring yourself or dropping out?

An ideal exercise program is one that is low enough to use fat as an 4 energy source but high enough to elicit a cardiovascular training effect in which heart, lungs, and circulatory system utilize increased oxygen. Good examples are swimming, rowing, walking, cycling, and running. Because walking allows exercise over a longer period, it has an advantage over running. If you run, you should run at a pace that allows you to still talk comfortably. In choosing an exercise, pick one that you enjoy. If you enjoy your workouts you will look forward to each session. It has always been easier for people to find time in their busy schedules to do activities they enjoy.

Aerobic exercise should be done three times a week for at least 5 thirty minutes—the requirement for keeping the heart and lungs healthy. If you want to burn more calories, the important factor to remember when developing your fitness routine is duration of exercise, not the intensity. And longer duration is achieved by lowering the intensity. As you maintain an exercise program year after year, a healthy lifestyle will come more and more naturally and you will keep looking and feeling healthier.

Work Cited

Katch, Frank I., and William D. McArdle. *Nutrition, Weight Control, and Exercise.* Boston: Houghton, 1977.

4. *Here's Chapter 2 of British author Joyce Cary's* The Horse's Mouth *(New York: Harper, 1944), a novel about a talented but slightly disreputable painter. Just released from prison for "uttering menaces," Gulley Jimson returns to the old boathouse where he had left a massive unfinished painting. Read the chapter first for the enjoyment of getting to know this old rascal; then read it for what it says about revision. Be prepared to discuss your responses in class. What does the chapter tell you about—*

   a. *Reseeing a creative work after a period of rest?*
   b. *Response from other people?*
   c. *What an artist (or writer) can do with responses from others?*
   d. *"Big holes" and "little holes" in creative work?*
   e. *The artist's (or writer's) attitude toward revision?*

from *The Horse's Mouth*

Joyce Cary

I could see my studio from where I stood, an old boathouse down by the water wall. A bit rotten in places, but I had been glad to get it. My trouble is I get big ideas. My last one was the Fall, twelve by fifteen, and you can't get room for an idea like that in a brick studio under two hundred pounds a year. So I was glad to get the boathouse. It had a loft. I took the planks off the beams at one end and got a very nice wall, seventeen foot high. When I had my canvas up, it was two foot off the floor, which just suited me. I like to keep my pictures above dog level.

Well, I thought, the walls and roof are there still. They haven't got blown away yet. No one has leant up against 'em. I was pleased. But I didn't go along in a hurry. One thing at a time. Last time I was locked up, in thirty-seven, I left a regular establishment behind. Nice little wife, two kids, flat and a studio with a tin roof. Watertight all round. North light. Half-finished picture, eight by twelve. The Living God. Cartoons, drawings, studies, two painter's ladders, two chairs, kettle, frypan, and an oil stove. All you could want.

When I came back, there was nothing. Wife and kids had gone back to her mama. Flat let to people who didn't even know my name. And the studio was a coal store. As for the Living God, my drawings, cartoons, ladders, they'd just melted. I hadn't expected to see the frypan and kettle again. You can't leave things like that about for a month in any friendly neighbourhood and expect to find them in the same place. But the

Living God with his stretchers and stiffeners weighed a couple of hundredweight. When I came back from gaol even the smell had gone. Coker said that someone said the landlord took it for the rent. The landlord swore he had never seen it. I daresay he had hidden it somewhere in an attic telling himself that it might be worth thousands as soon as I was dead, and the more I was worried, the sooner that would be.

The top of my boathouse suddenly nodded its head at me, as if 4 saying, "That's it, old man." Then I saw that a couple of kids were taking a plank off the roof. More patrons, I thought. When they saw me coming, they slid off the roof and ran. But not far. Crouching round like a couple of wolves waiting for the old horse to drop. I didn't need to unlock the door. Somebody had done it for me by knocking off the hasp of the padlock. And when I opened it, two more kids got out of the window on their heads. "Don't hurry," I said, "there's plenty of time before dinner."

There was nothing inside except a lot of pools on the floor from last 5 night's rain. And the picture. I got another surprise. A big one. It was still there. Why, I thought, it's not bad in places. It might be a good thing. The serpent wants to be a bit thicker, and I could bring his tail round to make a nice curl over the tree. Adam is a bit too blue, and Eve could be redder—to bring up the blues. Yes, yes, I thought, getting a bit excited, as I always do when I come back to work after a holiday, I've got something there. Adam's right leg is a gift, whatever you may say. Nobody has done that before with a leg. What a shape. I must have been tight or walking in my sleep when I knocked that off. And yet it's leggy all right. If that limb could speak, it would say, "I walk for you, I run for you, I kneel for you. But I have my self-respect."

Just then a stone came and knocked out the last window-pane that 6 wasn't broken already. And I heard a voice, "Ya, mister, how did you like chokey?" Those kids had had a fright and they were getting their own back.

Next minute I heard a different kind of yell, and when I went to the 7 window I saw them making for the street with young Nosy on their tails.

He came in two minutes later, blowing, with the sweat on his nose 8 and his cap falling off the back of the head. "It's a shushame, Mr. Jimson. I hope they haven't done any damage."

"Not to speak of. There's quite a lot left. And it's an expensive canvas. 9 Make a good floorcloth for any scullery." "Why, it's all f-full of holes, and they've cut a piece out."

For somebody had been shooting at the birds with an air-gun and 10 there was a piece about a foot square cut out of Adam's middle with a blunt knife. "What a shushame," said Nosy, and his nose turned pink. "You ought to tell the po-police." "Well," I said, "Adam hadn't got a bathing-dress." "It's disgusting." "So he was, and somebody has made him respectable. Some mother, I expect. Anxious about her children. There's a lot of very good mothers in this district. You'd be surprised." "But the p-picture's ruined." "Oh no, I can easily put in a patch. It's the little holes are the nuisance. Are you going to school yet?" for I wanted to get rid of him. I wanted to get on with my work. "Nun-no," he said, "it's dinner-time." "Don't you do any work in your dinner-time?" "S-s-sometimes." "If you want to get that scholarship and go to Oxford and get into the Civil Service and be a great man and have two thousand pounds a year and a nice clean wife with hot and cold and a kid with real eyes that open and close and a garage for two cars and a savings' book, you'll have to work in your dinner-time. All the good boys round here work in their dinner-time."

"They've been writing names all over Eve, Mr. Ji-jimson. It's b-beastly,   11
b-beastly." "Yes, they seem to have appreciated my picture a whole lot." "I wonder you can go on pa-painting, Mr. Jijimson, for such people." "I like painting. That's been my trouble all my life." "I wuwish I could paint." "Now, young chap, you go home quick; before you catch anything." And I chased him out.

Exercise: The Exploring Writer

The following draft of an assigned paper was written by a student who asked both a classmate and his teacher to read it and respond to it before he revised it. He wanted to know if they felt his organization was right, if they detected any irrelevancies, if they saw any problems in his tone, and if there was any informa-tion he should add. Finally, he wanted an overall revision check. Put yourself in the place of his classmate, and write a response to assist him in his revision. Answer his questions, and tell him what your major problems are as a reader of this paper.

The Dive

Jason Fisher (student writer)

Staring above me, watching the bubbles, I find myself in another   1
world. A trance, damned to be reality, a joy beyond belief. Floating like a leaf, anxious to be part of the deep blue, I dive deeper and deeper into the ocean.

Being so excited to dive, I became part of the ocean. Swimming as if   2
I was one of the underworld creatures, a small tear formed inside my mask. Little did I know an incident frightning beyond reason was about to take place. This incident brought me so close to death, I swore never to this type of dive again. If I had the power to change anything in my life, I would remove this incident.

On this particular dive, we were doing wreck dives off the northern   3
coast of the Grand Cayman. In a wreck dive, you find a sunken ship and search the rooms for artifacts. In this case, I was in training to become a

diving instructor. I had to go alone into the wreck. To fully grasp the horror of diving into a wreck alone, you must first realize that as soon as you hit the water you are disorientated. If I was to swim ten feet away from the boat, unless I knew the surroundings very well, I would need to do a complete turn or use a compass to find my way back to the boat. Therefore, in a sunken ship, amongst unknown surroundings, it is easy to become lost. There are precautions to take, tieing a rope to a belt around your waist which is connected to the boat is an easy way to find your way out of the wreck.

As I sat on the boat, getting my gear ready for an important and dangerous dive, I gazed through the blue water that surrounded us. Forgetting all possible danger, I was mesmerized by the silent world below. After a careful check of my gear, I rolled backwards off the boat. Only to make a nightmare reality. Desending into the light blue at a resonable speed, I found the wreck. The wreck was located at sixty-four feet below surface. I swam towrds it, pulling the rope behind me. Following through the welcoming door, I turned my flashlight on. Looking around, I proceeded into the heart of the ship. Only to find darker and darker rooms. 4

In confused realization, I discovered a horrible aspect about myself. At least it was horrible to find out about it now. I discovered that I am claustrophobic. As the room got darker and darker, and smaller and smaller, I felt as though I would be flattened inside the room. In all the anxiety and panic, I kicked the rope from my belt. The room began to crush me, so I quickly swam in and out of rooms, only to find smaller rooms. I felt as though I had to squeeze my way through minute chambers. Finally, grabbing hold of myself, I remembered the rope. Not knowing that I had kicked it off about six rooms back. I was scared and lost in sixty-four feet of water. In all dives your tank holds 3000psi, whick basically means you have 20–40 minutes of diving, depending on the dive and depth. At 1000psi, the amount of air you have is questionable. At 500psi, you could only have 20psi, because SCUBA gauges cannot read below that level. Although, most tanks come equipt with 3000psi. 5

In fifteen short minutes I had drained my tank from 3000psi to 1200psi, and was breathing as if I had just ran a marathon. In my nine years of diving which accumulated 125 dives, not including my dives to become an instructor, I never dreamed that the ocean could hurt me. I looked at my gauge which now read 900psi, and I began to panic. Swimming furiously through the wreck, I gave up. I sat to quietly die. During my last outrage I found out later, I kicked the rope. Which made the rope move in a straight line. At this point I was laying on the floor watching my gauge drop from 900psi to 500psi. I saw a light flash through the room. A diver was looking for me! He helped me up and we slowly proceeded out of the wreck. To my surprise, before we reached the door to leave, my tank ran dry, as my gauge read 430psi. We buddy breathed 6 out of the wreck and to the surface. When you buddy breathe you share the rig, which releases air from the tank. Later I found out that they were worried about me, because my rope had not moved for a considerable amount of time. Then, when it did, it moved abruptly in one direction. I thank God they came to find me. If not, when approximately two more minutes passed, my breathing aparatus would have stopped disprsing air.

Still today I love the ocean. Nothing will ever be able to change that. The ocean, in all its power, beauty, and might, is the most unpredictable creation in this world. I had the idea in my head that nothing would ever hurt me when I was below. Now I know that is not true. Although this is an incident I would like to forget and remove from my life, I respect the ocean a quite deal more because of it. The scariest part of my incident, was at the edge of death, as I layed watching my last pockets of air rise to the surface, I felt a comfort in death.

PART II

The Practice of Purposeful Writing

CHAPTER 6

Writing to Reflect

> *Until writing, most kinds of thoughts we are used to thinking today simply could not be thought.*
>
> —*Walter Ong*

Reflection is something people usually do for themselves rather than for an audience. Usually it doesn't even get onto paper, occurring instead in the mind. **Reflection** is careful, deliberate thought prompted by a specific circumstance, a purposeful consideration of a particular subject. A reflection tends to be philosophical, seeking meaning to one's environment. Here is an illustration, a poem by William Wordsworth prompted by the sight of a rainbow:

> My heart leaps up when I behold
>   A rainbow in the sky:
> So was it when my life began;
> So is it now I am a man;
> So be it when I shall grow old,
>   Or let me die!
> The Child is father of the Man;
> And I could wish my days to be
> Bound each to each by natural piety.

In this verse, the poet's view of a rainbow recalls similar instances in the past, leading to contemplation on the continuity within a life span.

Reflections also explore and express emotions—sometimes only in the mind but at other times in writing. Love letters are a common type of reflective writing. Whatever their end, whether sent to the object of love or left to languish in a drawer, the writer probably feels better for having written them. People experiencing bereavement sometimes seek an outlet for their emotions by writing about the experience, working through the anger, grief, discouragement, and the entire complex of emotions that accompany it. People overcome by emotions that are difficult to handle may keep a notebook in which they record feelings and their immediate causes, with the hope of achieving control over them.

Because it is naturally close to the self, reflective writing often is more autobiographical than other types. Reflections evolve from experiences, and a writer can hardly tell the story of his or her life without reflection. Thoreau's reflection in "A Fire in the Woods" constitutes a piece of his life, Leopold's reflection on "Thinking Like a Mountain" includes an autobiographical narrative, and student writers Lorrie Anderson and Lorna Marro reflect on events in their own lives. You are likely to find too that when you reflect you write autobiographically.

Even though reflection occurs most commonly as a mental act, it is sometimes done best in writing. Some thoughts are just too complex to hold in one's mind. Writing assists reflective thought for the same reason that some arithmetic problems must be done on paper—the limits of the short-term memory. For example, it is likely that you can multiply 7 times 6 in your head by relying on your memory; you can probably even multiply 7 times 68 without pencil and paper, if you force yourself a little. But multiplying 87 times 96 probably exceeds the limits of your ability to carry out all the steps and to hold the numbers in your mind while you work with them.* Similarly, if you want to analyze a complicated chain of events, you might need to take some notes instead of trying to remember and connect each incident. Also, you are more likely to remember and comprehend much of your schoolwork if you use writing in addition to your reading.

The Journal

Some people keep a regular record of their reflections and activities in a special notebook for the purpose, commonly called a **journal.** Because journals record reflections as they occur, many writers find them a tremendous source of ideas for writing. You may already be one of those people. If not, now is a good time to start. Get yourself a notebook: some writers prefer a spiral composition book, some a loose-leaf binder, some a lined tablet, and others a pocket folder with loose lined paper. Set aside a special portion of your day for journal writing; if you don't reserve a certain time, you will forget to write. Then *use* your journal. Here are some ways some people use journals.

---

*This idea is explained by Richard Young and Patricia Sullivan in "Why Write? A Reconsideration," *Essays on Classical Rhetoric and Modern Discourse,* ed. Robert J. Connors, Lisa S. Ede, and Andrea A. Lunsford. Southern Ill. U. Press, 1984.

> ### *Ways to Use a Journal*
>
> 1. Record thoughts, observations, activities, and impressions you want to remember.
> 2. Analyze your feelings about certain events.
> 3. Explore problems that need solutions.
> 4. Ask questions that need answers.
> 5. Summarize class lecture notes.
> 6. Summarize reading assignments.
> 7. Analyze or compare reading assignments.
> 8. React to books you've read, plays you've seen, music you've heard.
> 9. Respond to newspaper commentaries and editorials.
> 10. Begin drafts of writing assignments.
> 11. Analyze the dynamics of a conversation.

(Academic journals are also discussed under "Notes" in Chapter 9.)

In a journal, you write for yourself. Journal entries sometimes lead to public writing with an intended audience and purpose; at other times they remain informal and private. Here are some examples of student journal entries. Do you see any possibilities of their leading to writing that is more formal and public? Do you see any evidence that the writers of these samples thought they would be read by someone else?

Hajimemashite . . . How do you do. Watashi wa hima o arimasen . . . I have no free time. The Japanese language has got to be the hardest foreign language to take. My roommate has Russian. The amount of homework he is putting into the class and receiving a passing grade is slightly between one or two minutes a week. The only time he practices is when he says "Nyet" and that's only when I'm into his food.

Smell the air. It's fresh and cool with a touch of autumn. The only thing on my mind today is hunting. Hunting is more than killing. Picture yourself in camouflaged garments, a twelve-gauge at your side. Black lab, ammo, duck call, bologna sandwiches and sunflower seeds. It's a cloud-covered day and the grass is tan. Trees of October have started to appear. The dry grass rustles like a snare drum crescendoing over the rolling hills. I lie in the grass, tired but spirited. The grass has a distinct smell like a barn full of sweet hay mixed with a little breeze of fresh air and evaporating dew. I let my head rest on the cushion of grass and watch the clouds turn different shades of grey as they move on towards tomorrow.

9-18. Since my grandmother died eight days ago, life just isn't the same. My parents said, "She got to see so many things: the four oldest grandchildren graduate and her granddaughter's wedding. But what are we going to do with Grandpa?"

9-19. I am wondering how lonely my grandpa is to be married sixty years and then lose what he was living for. The last time I talked to him he said, "I'll be with her soon." This just makes me crumble inside.

9-22. All of a sudden I feel someone tapping me on my shoulder. It is my sister, crying. "I tried calling but the phone was busy. Grandpa died last night." I've never felt so helpless in my life.

9-25. The day of the funeral. I was just here two weeks ago, doing the same thing, feeling the same way. It's like I could feel part of my grandpa leave me. The worst part was when they played taps, and the flag was presented to my dad. It was only the second time I've seen my dad cry.

If you keep a journal regularly, making entries three or four times a week, you will inevitably incur benefits. Writing may become easier for you. You will have a source of ideas for formal writing needs. And you are likely to have a greater understanding of the coursework and other subjects you summarize and analyze. You will probably, though, have ambivalent feelings toward your journal: disliking to sit down to write in it even while appreciating the advantages that derive from doing so.

Journals Made Public

Henry David Thoreau kept a journal for years. His sixteen published volumes are examples of journal writing that began as personal records, sources of ideas for lectures and essays, but gradually became more refined in style, as if he thought they might someday have other readers. Regarding journal writing, he wrote: "Of all strange and unaccountable things this journalizing is the strangest. It will allow nothing to be predicated of it; its good is not good, nor its bad bad" (*Journal,* I, January 29, 1841). He seems to be asking, "What can one say about a journal?" and answering "One can simply say, it exists." One of Thoreau's journal entries, "A Fire in the Woods," is included in this chapter.

Like Thoreau, Annie Dillard took a secluded house and kept a journal for recording her reflections on nature, life, and whatever else occurred to her. In *Pilgrim at Tinker Creek* we find private reflections prepared for a public audience. Here are a few excerpts to further illustrate what journal writing can be: recollections of childhood, wonderings on paper, records of dreams. What ideas do they give you for your journal?

Like the bear who went over the mountain, I went out to see what I could see. And, I might as well warn you, like the bear, all that I could see was the other side of the mountain: more of same. On a good day I might catch a glimpse of another wooded ridge rolling under the sun like water, another bivouac. I propose to keep here what Thoreau called "a meteorological journal of the mind," telling some tales and describing some of the sights of this rather tamed valley, and exploring, in fear and trembling, some of the unmapped dim reaches and unholy fastnesses to which those tales and sights so dizzyingly lead.

When I was six or seven years old, growing up in Pittsburgh, I used to take a precious penny of my own and hide it for someone else to find. It was a curious compulsion; sadly, I've never been seized by it since. For some reason I always "hid" the penny along the same stretch of sidewalk up the street. I would cradle it at the roots of a sycamore, say, or in a hole left by a chipped-off piece of sidewalk. Then I would take a piece of chalk, and, starting at either end of the block, draw huge arrows leading up to the penny from both directions. After I learned to write I labeled the arrows: SURPRISE AHEAD or MONEY THIS WAY. I was greatly excited, during all this arrow-drawing, at the thought of the first lucky passer-by who would receive in this way, regardless of merit, a free gift from the universe. But I never lurked about. I would go straight home and not give the matter another thought, until, some months later, I would be gripped again by the impulse to hide another penny.

I wonder how long it would take you to notice the regular recurrence of the seasons if you were the first man on earth. What would it be like to live in open-ended time broken only by days and nights? You could say, "it's cold again; it was cold before," but you couldn't make the key connection and say, "it was cold this time last year," because the notion of "year" is precisely the one you lack. Assuming that you hadn't yet noticed any orderly progression of heavenly bodies, how long would you have to live on earth before you could feel with any assurance that any one particular long period of cold would, in fact, end? "While the earth remaineth, seedtime and harvest, and cold and heat, and summer and winter, and day and night shall not cease": God makes this guarantee very early in Genesis to a people whose fears on this point had perhaps not been completely allayed.

I had a curious dream last night that stirred me. I visited the house of my childhood, and the basement there was covered with a fine sifting of snow. I lifted a snow-covered rug and found underneath it a bound sheaf of ink drawings I had made when I was six. Next to the basement, but unattached to it, extended a prayer tunnel.

The prayer tunnel was a tunnel fully enclosed by solid snow. It was cylindrical, and its diameter was the height of a man. Only an Eskimo, and then only very rarely, could survive in the prayer tunnel. There was, however, no exit or entrance; but I nevertheless understood that if I—if almost anyone—volunteered to enter it, death would follow after a long and bitter struggle. Inside the tunnel it was killingly cold, and a hollow wind like broadswords never ceased to blow. But there was little breathe-able air, and that soon gone. It was utterly without light, and from all eternity it snowed the same fine, unmelting, wind-hurled snow.

Exercise: The Exploring Writer

Write a journal entry on (1) a recollected childhood incident, (2) something you wonder about, or (3) a remembered dream. Think of it as writing for yourself that you might eventually revise for an audience.

Shared Reflections

Dillard's reflections, Wordsworth's poem, and the other readings in this chapter are evidence that people sometimes want to share their thoughts with others. Reflections that we write for ourselves are often very personal. The thoughts may be incomplete, undeveloped, disorganized, and characterized by digressions and irrelevancies. In form, they may be fragmentary, loosely punctuated, unparagraphed, with vague and incomplete references. They may have doodles and drawings made during writing pauses.

Writing for others, however, is usually organized in some logical way, its ideas developed enough for readers to understand them as the writer intends and connected so that readers can see how they are related. Shared reflections are revised with the reader outside the self in mind. Here's an example of a reflective paragraph before it was revised for a reader:

> Bart and I went to the lake today. We backed the car out of the garage carefully and then drove over to Robert's and picked up him and Charles. When we got to the lake, we discovered that Mr. Ciatti's boat had come unmoored, so we spent the rest of the day tying up the boat and repairing the damage.

While this paragraph may be perfectly clear to the writer, as a reader you probably have a few questions. For instance, who is Bart? And who are Robert and Charles and Mr. Ciatti? What lake? Why did they go to the lake? Is there something significant in backing the car out of the garage *carefully*? How badly was the boat damaged? How does the writer feel about the incident? Here's a revision that answers some of these questions. The new parts are italicized.

> *My Brother* Bart and I went to Lake *Kenilworth* today, *as we usually do on the Fourth of July, to do a little fishing off the boat of our dad's boss, Mr. Ciatti. Since Mr. Ciatti was out of town on a business trip, he asked us to use his boat so that someone would be keeping track of it. Excited about the prospect of spending the day on Mr. Ciatti's cabin cruiser, we hopped into our dad's new Oldsmobile* and drove off to pick up *our friends* Robert and Charles. *We were beginning to count our fish already and were making bets about who would catch the biggest. Little did we know that we would not be doing any fishing that day.* When we got to the lake, we discovered that Mr. Ciatti's boat had come unmoored. *Though the damage was slight,* we had to spend the rest of the day getting it tied up again and repairing the damage.

In the revised paragraph, the writer provides more details as well as the significance of certain details.

Exercise: The Exploring Writer

Rewrite your journal entry from the preceding exercise, adjusting it for an audience other than yourself by adding or deleting details that may increase understanding of the incident, reflection, or dream.

The essays in this chapter represent reflective writing written or revised for readers. They illustrate reflections on nature, on evil, and on student pressures, for purposes of exploring, discovering, and comprehending.

REFLECTING IN A JOURNAL ENTRY

Journals are a familiar form of reflective writing. Reflections in journals are usually written for the self for the purpose of exploring ideas or recording events and the writer's reactions to them. Academic journals have the specific purpose of recording, summarizing, and analyzing school-related lectures and reading. At times, writers will revise their journals or portions of them to make them public. Before reading the journal entry below, read the discussion of journals on pages 123–27 in this chapter.

Reading

"A Fire in the Woods" is a disturbing entry in Henry David Thoreau's journal that records a thoughtless act which leads to a potentially dangerous fire, loss of property, and cooperative fire-fighting efforts. In writing about the fire, Thoreau seems to be trying to work out his own feelings concerning it. He begins recording the incident, just narrating the events as they occurred, but then finds himself reacting to the incident, trying to discover meaning in it and his feelings toward it.

As you read this entry, think about whether Thoreau intended for an audience to read it. On what features do you base your decision? How does Thoreau feel about the fire?

A Fire in the Woods

Henry David Thoreau

I once set fire to the woods. Having set out, one April day, to go to the sources of Concord River in a boat with a single companion, meaning to camp on the bank at night or seek a lodging in some neighboring country inn or farmhouse, we took fishing tackle with us that we might fitly procure our food from the stream, Indian-like. At the shoemaker's near the river, we obtained a match, which we had forgotten. Though it was thus early in the spring, the river was low, for there had not been much rain, and we succeeded in catching a mess of fish sufficient for our dinner before we had left the town, and by the shores of Fair Haven Pond we proceeded to cook them. The earth was uncommonly dry, and our fire, kindled far from the woods in a sunny recess in the hillside on the east of the pond, suddenly caught the dry grass of the previous year which grew about the stump on which it was kindled. We sprang to extinguish it at first with our hands and feet, and then we fought it with a board obtained from the boat, but in a few minutes it was beyond our reach; being on the side of a hill, it spread rapidly upward, through the long, dry, wiry grass interspersed with bushes. 1

"Well, where will this end?" asked my companion. I saw that it might be bounded by Well Meadow Brook on one side, but would, perchance, go to the village side of the brook. "It will go to town," I answered. While my companion took the boat back down the river, I set out through the woods to inform the owners and to raise the town. The fire had already spread a dozen rods on every side and went leaping and crackling wildly and irreclaimably toward the wood. That way went the flames with wild delight, and we felt that we had no control over the demonic creature to 2 which we had given birth. We had kindled many fires in the woods before, burning a clear space in the grass, without ever kindling such a fire as this.

As I ran toward the town through the woods, I could see the smoke over the woods behind me marking the spot and the progress of the flames. The first farmer whom I met driving a team, after leaving the woods, inquired the cause of the smoke. I told him. "Well," said he, "it is none of my stuff," and drove along. The next I met was the owner in his field, with whom I returned at once to the woods, running all the way. I had already run two miles. When at length we got into the neighborhood of the flames, we met a carpenter who had been hewing timber, an infirm man who had been driven off by the fire, fleeing with his axe. The farmer returned to hasten more assistance. I, who was spent with running, remained. What could I do alone against a front of flame half a mile wide?

I walked slowly through the wood to Fair Haven Cliff, climbed to the highest rock, and sat down upon it to observe the progress of the flames, which were rapidly approaching me, now about a mile distant from the spot where the fire was kindled. Presently I heard the sound of the distant bell giving the alarm, and I knew that the town was on its way to the scene. Hitherto I had felt like a guilty person—nothing but shame and regret. But now I settled the matter with myself shortly. I said to myself, "Who are these men who are said to be the owners of these woods, and how am I related to them? I have set fire to the forest, but I have done no wrong therein, and now it is as if the lightning had done it. These flames are but consuming their natural food." (It has never troubled me from that day to this more than if the lightning had done it. The trivial fishing was all that disturbed me and disturbs me still.) So shortly I settled it with myself and stood to watch the approaching flames. It was a glorious spectacle, and I was the only one there to enjoy it. The fire now reached the base of the cliff and then rushed up its sides. The squirrels ran before it in blind haste, and three pigeons dashed into the midst of the smoke. The flames flashed up the pines to their tops, as if they were powder.

When I found I was about to be surrounded by the fire, I retreated and joined the forces now arriving from the town. It took us several hours to surround the flames with our hoes and shovels and by back fires subdue them. In the midst of all I saw the farmer whom I first met, who had turned indifferently away saying it was none of his stuff, striving earnestly to save his corded wood, his stuff, which the fire had already seized and which it after all consumed.

It burned over a hundred acres or more and destroyed much young wood. When I returned home late in the day, with others of my townsmen, I could not help noticing that the crowd who were so ready to condemn the individual who had kindled the fire did not sympathize with the owners of the wood, but were in fact highly elated and as it were thankful for the opportunity which had afforded them so much sport; and it was only half a dozen owners, so called, though not all of them, who looked sour or grieved, and I felt that I had a deeper interest in the woods, knew them better, and should feel their loss more, than any or all of them. The farmer whom I had first conducted to the woods was obliged to ask me the shortest way back, through his own lot. Why, then, should the half-dozen owners [and] the individuals who set the fire alone feel sorrow for the loss of the wood, while the rest of the town have their spirits raised? Some of the owners, however, bore their loss like men, but other some declared behind my back that I was a "damned rascal;" and a flibbertigibbet or two, who crowed like the old cock, shouted some reminiscences of "burnt woods" from safe recesses for some years after. I have had nothing to say to any of them. The locomotive engine has since burned over nearly all the same ground and more, and in some measure blotted out the memory of the previous fire. For a long time after I had learned this lesson I marvelled that while matches and tinder were contemporaries the world was not consumed; why the houses that have hearths were not burned before another day; if the flames were not as hungry now as when I waked them. I at once ceased to regard the owners and my own fault—if fault there was any in the matter—and attended to the phenomenon before me, determined to make the most of it. To be sure, I felt a little ashamed when I reflected on what a trivial occasion this had happened, that at the time I was no better employed than my townsmen.

That night I watched the fire, where some stumps still flamed at 7 midnight in the midst of the blackened waste, wandering through the woods by myself: and far in the night I threaded my way to the spot where the fire had taken, and discovered the now broiled fish—which had been dressed—scattered over the burnt grass.

Questions: The Community of Writers

1. Recount the progress of the fire and the fire-fighting efforts. What does this account tell you about chronological development?
2. Trace Thoreau's changing reactions to the fire. How does he feel at the beginning of the fire? At its end? How does he feel about the fire at the time of writing the journal entry? What do you think is his primary attitude toward the fire?
3. What were the effects of the fire? Which did the fire affect most, land or people?
4. Do you see any evidence of Thoreau's intending to have an audience read this journal entry? Explain your answer.

Analysis

Thoreau's journal entry begins with his story about how the fire started: "I once set fire to the woods." He describes the circumstances and the setting, what he and his companion did to try to extinguish the fire, the progress of the fire, and the actions aimed at putting it out. In describing the incident, he also explores his attitudes to it, being a concerned citizen, assessing fault, being curious, and so on.

Development

Thoreau's **narrative** of the fire's development is **chronological,** one event following another: First he and his companion catch some fish for their dinner, but their cooking fire ignites the dry grass surrounding the stump on which they've kindled it, and suddenly the fire is out of control. Thoreau's entry also uses **cause and effect analysis.** From the first cause, the spread of the cooking fire, he recounts a number of effects.

Exercise: The Exploring Writer

In your journal, write an entry about fire.

Writing

Use your journal entry about fire or the one you wrote for the exercise on page 127 and expand it into an essay. Do some brainstorming or use the classical probes (see Chapter 3) to discover additional details and ideas to make this reflective piece interesting for an audience. To assist you in making this mainly private writing public, ask the Questions about Audience for Writing on page 26. Also, ask yourself how you feel about your subject, since your reactions will tell the audience why you are writing.

Because this essay is largely reflective writing, you can expect to be using the personal pronoun *I.* However, if you discover as you revise that the pronoun is recurring too frequently—for example, every sentence or so—try revising your sentences to eliminate some of the incidences. Note how the following sentences are revised:

> *I* was crying as *I* got into the backseat with my brother. *I* reached for the box of tissues that my mother had had the foresight to bring. *I* was thinking about the silence in the car as we set out for the funeral service.

For some reason *I* could not explain, *I* was remembering my grand-mother's Swedish meatballs and the way *I* used to watch *The Sound of Music* with her.

Revised: I was crying as my brother and *I* got into the backseat. Fortunately, my mother had had the foresight to bring a box of tissues, and in silence *I* reached for them as we set out for the funeral service. For some unexplained reason, *I* was remembering my grandmother's Swe-dish meatballs and the way we used to watch *The Sound of Music* together.

The revised passage has four *I's* as opposed to seven in the original version. The passage is still personal, relating one writer's thoughts on the death of her grandmother, but the repetition no longer calls attention to itself.

REFLECTING ON NATURE

Quality of life is inextricably tied to environment. Yet the evidence is clear that the greatest enemy to the global environment is the species with the most intelligence and sensitivity for maintaining it—humankind. Wit-ness denuded mountains, rain forests stripped bare, parklands burned off by careless campfires, topsoil washed into the sea, species decimated and endangered. Environmentalists are often charged with standing in the way of progress, and frequently they are as strident in expressing their convictions as are those who would replace clean water and air with pollution or kill dolphins along with tuna or cut down trees to build more houses.

At the same time, there is the quiet voice of reflection. People sit on the dock and watch the incoming waves as the sun sets; they walk through the park and listen to the ripple of leaves or the unremitting call of the wren; they run along the footpath and feel on their faces the refreshing morning air; they are surprised by a rainbow and pause to admire it. There is much to appreciate about nature. Often our reflections do not get onto paper; the moment passes and the thoughts are gone. Occasion-ally we remember how good the air felt or how we glowed on sighting the rainbow; we may tell someone about the experience, or we may keep it to ourselves. Times like these give us reasons for carrying a pocket-size journal, for recording our thoughts while they are fresh.

Reading

Aldo Leopold recorded his reflections on nature in a widely read book, *A Sand County Almanac.* In the excerpt here, he reflects on the fate of wolves—and deer and mountains—in a world controlled by humans.

As you read, note his attitude toward his subject and how he acquired that attitude. Observe also how a reflective, or personal, piece of writing can be intended for an audience other than the self, and how as public writing it can be powerfully persuasive; it acquires a more decisive purpose upon publication.

Thinking Like a Mountain

Aldo Leopold

A deep chesty bawl echoes from rimrock to rimrock, rolls down the mountain, and fades into the far blackness of the night. It is an outburst of wild defiant sorrow, and of contempt for all the adversities of the world.   1

Every living thing (and perhaps many a dead one as well) pays heed to that call. To the deer it is a reminder of the way of all flesh, to the pine a forecast of midnight scuffles and of blood upon the snow, to the coyote a promise of gleanings to come, to the cowman a threat of red ink at the bank, to the hunter a challenge of fang against bullet. Yet behind these obvious and immediate hopes and fears there lies a deeper meaning, known only to the mountain itself. Only the mountain has lived long enough to listen objectively to the howl of a wolf.   2

Those unable to decipher the hidden meaning know nevertheless that it is there, for it is felt in all wolf country, and distinguishes that country from all other land. It tingles in the spine of all who hear wolves by night, or who scan their tracks by day. Even without sight or sound of wolf, it is implicit in a hundred small events: the midnight whinny of a pack horse, the rattle of rolling rocks, the bound of a fleeing deer, the way shadows lie under the spruces. Only the ineducable tyro can fail to sense the presence or absence of wolves, or the fact that mountains have a secret opinion about them.   3

My own conviction on this score dates from the day I saw a wolf die. We were eating lunch on a high rimrock, at the foot of which a turbulent river elbowed its way. We saw what we thought was a doe fording the torrent, her breast awash in white water. When she climbed the bank toward us and shook out her tail, we realized our error: it was a wolf. A half-dozen others, evidently grown pups, sprang from the willows and all joined in a welcoming mêlée of wagging tails and playful maulings. What was literally a pile of wolves writhed and tumbled in the center of an open flat at the foot of our rimrock.   4

In those days we had never heard of passing up a chance to kill a wolf. In a second we were pumping lead into the pack, but with more excitement than accuracy: how to aim a steep downhill shot is always confusing. When our rifles were empty, the old wolf was down, and a pup was dragging a leg into impassable slide-rocks.   5

We reached the old wolf in time to watch a fierce green fire dying in   6
her eyes. I realized then, and have known ever since, that there was
something new to me in those eyes—something known only to her and
to the mountain. I was young then, and full of trigger-itch; I thought that
because fewer wolves meant more deer, that no wolves would mean
hunters' paradise. But after seeing the green fire die, I sensed that
neither the wolf nor the mountain agreed with such a view.

Since then I have lived to see state after state extirpate its wolves. I   7
have watched the face of many a newly wolfless mountain, and seen the
southfacing slopes wrinkle with a maze of new deer trails. I have seen every
edible bush and seedling browsed, first to anaemic desuetude, and then
to death. I have seen every edible tree defoliated to the height of a saddle-
horn. Such a mountain looks as if someone had given God a new pruning
shears, and forbidden Him all other exercise. In the end the starved
bones of the hoped-for deer herd, dead of its own too-much, bleach with
the bones of the dead sage, or molder under the high-lined junipers.

I now suspect that just as a deer herd lives in mortal fear of its wolves,   8
so does a mountain live in mortal fear of its deer. And perhaps with better
cause, for while a buck pulled down by wolves can be replaced in two or
three years, a range pulled down by too many deer may fail of replacement in as many decades.

So also with cows. The cowman who cleans his range of wolves does   9
not realize that he is taking over the wolf's job of trimming the herd to
fit the range. He has not learned to think like a mountain. Hence we have
dustbowls, and rivers washing the future into the sea.

We all strive for safety, prosperity, comfort, long life, and dullness.   10
The deer strives with his supple legs, the cowman with trap and poison,
the statesman with pen, the most of us with machines, votes, and dollars,
but it all comes to the same thing: peace in our time. A measure of success
in this is all well enough, and perhaps is a requisite to objective thinking,
but too much safety seems to yield only danger in the long run. Perhaps
this is behind Thoreau's dictum: In wildness is the salvation of the world.
Perhaps this is the hidden meaning in the howl of the wolf, long known
among mountains, but seldom perceived among men.

Questions: The Community of Writers

1. What does Leopold mean by "thinking like a mountain"?

2. What does the mountain understand that the deer, the coyote, the cowman,
   and the young hunter Leopold do not?

3. How does Leopold use narration to support his point?

4. What does the "fierce green fire" that died in the eyes of the wolf tell the
   young hunter Leopold about nature?

5. How did you feel when you read the essay? What aspects of the story affected
   you as you read?

6. Is Leopold advocating a prohibition on killing wolves? What does he mean in paragraph 8 when he says, "so does a mountain live in mortal fear of its deer"?

7. What do you understand in Leopold's indirect quotation from Thoreau in paragraph 10: "In wildness is the salvation of the world"?

8. In your own words, state Leopold's persuasive purpose for publishing this reflective essay.

Analysis

Leopold's reflections begin with hearing the call of a wolf. He reflects on the "hidden meaning" of the call and then remembers how he came to understand that meaning himself, ending with "thinking like a mountain." In reflecting on the change in his attitude toward killing wolves, Leopold urges the reader to change with him: to witness the death of the old wolf and to understand the implications of senseless extermination of a species. When he says in paragraph 7 "Since then I have lived to see state after state extirpate its wolves," he clearly regards this destruction as a mistake.

This position is echoed by another writer, Ted Williams, who, in an article called "Bringing Back the Beast of Lore," chronicles how thoroughly humans have eliminated wolves:

> For centuries we trapped them, poisoned them, shot them, and burned their pups alive in their dens. In 1905 we even tried biological warfare, infecting them with mange. Ten years later Congress passed a law requiring their elimination from federal lands. We had cleansed Yellowstone Park by 1926. It hasn't been easy, but finally we have won against the wolf.

Williams reports barely a thousand of the animals still living in the late 1980s in the contiguous forty-eight states. Though openly informative in purpose, his article, like Leopold's essay, is strongly persuasive about the wanton destruction of natural species.

Rather than use historic facts as Williams does, Leopold attempts to persuade by recounting a personal story about the death of a mother wolf and her family. Reflecting on his change of attitude and quoting another naturalist, Henry David Thoreau, Leopold invites the reader to participate in tolerance for nature.

Thesis

As a piece of reflective writing, this essay does not have an explicitly stated **thesis.** Yet it does have a controlling idea—an unstated thesis that makes the piece a coherent whole, holding its parts together and determining what the author includes and what he omits. In fact, it may have two theses, one *informative* and one *persuasive*. The informative thesis might be phrased something like this: "The mountain understands the balance of nature." Leopold develops his informative thesis by narrating his hunting story and explaining how nature maintains its own balance.

If we understand Leopold's purpose to include persuasion, we will express the thesis differently, perhaps "People should allow nature to maintain its own balance." Leopold's final sentences would seem to support such a thesis.

Exercise: The Exploring Writer

Leopold uses mostly familiar words and moderate-length sentences (twenty to twenty-five words). Such a style enables reading at a comfortable pace with a high degree of comprehension. But a few words in this essay may have been unfamiliar to you or used in an unfamiliar way, impeding your comprehension. From the context, you probably guessed at their meaning. List those words now and look them up in a dictionary, searching for a meaning suitable to Leopold's essay. Then write sentences that use these words in what you perceive to be the same way Leopold uses them.

Writing

Reflect on an aspect of nature. Like Leopold, concentrate on an incident you've observed or experienced that contributed to an insight. Look around you. Even in urban settings you will find a natural world: pigeons and squirrels if not wolves and deer; sunsets and clouds and trees and rain showers. Thoreau once wrote about ants, John Steinbeck about a turtle.

Begin with a first draft that is truly a personal reflection, intended only for your own reading. If you are keeping a journal, you may want to use one of your journal entries or to begin this assignment as a new journal entry. Explore the natural incident in detail, including your feelings and thoughts when it occurred. At this point, don't give a great deal of attention to vocabulary, sentence style, or even thesis. Because your essay is personal, it may start out loosely structured, digressive, and disconnected.

As a controlling idea begins to emerge, you can develop it by adding details and eliminating irrelevant information. Your finished essay will still be reflective in tone—highly personal, and not instructive or argumentative. But it will be a coherent whole, organized and developed around a specific thesis or controlling idea. It will explain and illustrate your reflections in enough detail that they will have meaning for an audience other than yourself.

REFLECTING ON HUMAN WEAKNESS

All of us have a darker side—an aspect of our personalities that we're not proud of, one that we've learned we must keep in check. We may remember beating up on a younger brother or sister and recall with discomfort how we enjoyed it, knowing that that urge is still with us. Behind the wheel of a vehicle, the personalities of many people change from placid sociability to aggressive competitiveness. People lie sometimes when they don't want to acknowledge the truth; they cheat, slander, torment, and insult.

People ordinarily try to refrain from such behavior and even from admitting that they indulge in it. When our reflective writing brings to the fore the unpleasant aspects of our personalities and the acts they have caused, we usually don't want to reveal such admissions. Sometimes, however, we realize that others can learn from our experience, and we make our darker thoughts public.

Reading

The essay that follows is a reflection of how warfare encourages and thrives on humanity's darker side and how the prompting of this evil affects the soldiers, who are encouraged to be ruthless. The author, Mark Baker, is a Vietnam veteran recounting the stories of other Vietnam veterans. As you read this essay, which is an introduction to one of the chapters in his book *Nam: The Vietnam War in the Words of the Men and Women Who Fought There,* try to discover Baker's attitude toward warfare's encouragement of expressions of evil. Does he have a purpose for writing other than reflection? (For other views on the Vietnam War, see "Walking Point" on pages 152–54 and "Mom and Dad" on pages 243–46.)

The Taste of Evil

Mark Baker

"I had a little puppy for a while in Vietnam. For a period of three   1
days, I would take this little puppy and squeeze it until it would yelp. Or twist its little paw.

"I knew what I was doing. I knew that I was transferring something to   2
this little puppy. Somebody or something had to suffer for all the pain inside of me, and it was going to be the puppy.

"I was so horrified by my behavior that I gave the puppy to someone else. I had to get it out of my sight. I don't think I would have killed it, but I didn't quite know where this spark of sadism was going to lead me. It went against the grain of who I thought I was. I had a sense of being split in two."

It rises like a wave of nausea in your throat, out of nowhere, uncontrolled, the dry, bitter taste of evil. You're walking the dog and in canine goofiness he insists on sniffing one empty square of sidewalk, holding his ground until you jerk the leash so hard the choke chain almost cuts his windpipe in two. A child says "No" at just the wrong time and you swallow hard when you find yourself towering over your own flesh and blood with murder in your eye. You actually slam on the brakes, jump out of the car, and run back to rip the throat out of the tailgater behind you before he can roll up his windows. An uneasy joke escapes from the knot of petty viciousness inside you and you seem to stand outside yourself as you watch it metamorphosize to malicious teasing. Suddenly you're tormenting some other human being—usually someone you love—until he's ready to take a wild swing at you.

The feeling passes quickly leaving you shaking with every thump of your heart, wondering where in this sane and ordered world a psycho like that comes from. But that psycho was you, the other you, the darker side, the one who knows all the nasty things you've done or thought in the privacy of your mind, the flipside of your conscience that hoards the merest slights and demands revenge no matter how petty, how misdirected.

No eighteen-year-old kid went to Vietnam thinking, "Oh boy, now I'm going to be evil." But most of them met their darker sides face to face in that war. A few of them had an adolescent meanness which blossomed ugly, nurtured by the circumstances they found in Vietnam. Many of them indulged the ruthlessness they discovered as part of the instinct to survive.

For all the glory words like duty, honor, and valor, war runs best on evil, a breeder reactor that vomits out a hell full of pain for the little spark of sadism people feed into it. Evil was encouraged with rewards of medals, time off from the horror, a hot meal. How else can you convince boys to kill one another day after day? And when the darker side grabs the upper hand, takes control, how else can it be excused?

Vietnam veterans do not have the luxury of dismissing evil as a momentary aberration in an otherwise civilized world. They have seen the ugliness humans are capable of inflicting—that they themselves are capable of inflicting.

The brutal stories are delivered with a nervous chuckle, dirty jokes from another world that don't quite survive translation. "I guess you had to be there." But there is no enjoyment in the telling. The hesitant laughter is self-defense, a shaky feint to keep the evil at arm's length. If the mortal slapstick can be kept in a cartoon life, maybe the shadow of inhumanity can be denied a little longer, the personal pain can be buried a little deeper.

Questions: The Community of Writers

1. What is your first reaction upon reading the essay? What does Baker do to promote your reaction? What is his attitude toward his subject?
2. How does audience reaction relate to Baker's purpose in writing?
3. What persuasive purpose might Baker have had for writing?
4. Who might Baker be quoting in the first three paragraphs?
5. What does Baker say about evil in the final four paragraphs?
6. What does he say about people's ability to control their baser instincts in situations where those instincts are encouraged?
7. What sentence might be regarded as Baker's thesis?

Analysis

"The Taste of Evil" is not meant to be pleasant reading. It reflects on an undesirable aspect of human nature. One of Baker's purposes may be to inform readers about a burden that Vietnam veterans brought home with them and about the horrors of war. But his foremost purpose seems to be to reflect on the nature of evil and how it figures into warfare. While reflections are first of all personal, the philosophical insights that derive from them can achieve other purposes when they are shared with an audience.

Development

In developing his essay, Baker begins by quoting a veteran's experience with a puppy and the veteran's horror at his behavior. Baker then attempts in paragraphs 4 and 5 to define the "dry, bitter taste of evil" with examples, getting the reader directly involved through use of the second-person *you:* "You're walking the dog," "you seem to stand outside yourself," "that psycho was you." The effect of these paragraphs might have been different if Baker had used third person: "Someone is walking the dog," "people seem to stand outside themselves," "that psycho was someone's best friend."

Baker devotes the remainder of the essay to the Vietnam experience. "War," he says, "runs best on evil," and Vietnam veterans know firsthand what evil and ugliness people, themselves included, can inflict. After his introductory **narrative** (paragraphs 1–3) and his **definition** of evil with examples (paragraphs 4–5), Baker applies his definition to specific circumstances (paragraphs 6–9). The first sentence of paragraph 8 seems to sum up the various parts of the essay—the definition of evil, the relating of war and evil, the specific references to Vietnam. Given his persuasive purpose, this sentence might also be viewed as Baker's *thesis.*

Style

Consider Baker's use of *passive voice.* In paragraph 7 he says, "Evil was encouraged with rewards of medals, time off from the horror, a hot meal." The passive verb *"was encouraged"* does not say who did the encouraging. Would you prefer that the writer name the encourager? Again, in paragraph 9, Baker writes, "The brutal stories are delivered with a nervous chuckle." Would the sentence have been better if he'd said, "The veterans deliver the brutal stories with a nervous chuckle"? Writers ordinarily use active voice—as in this proposed revision naming the persons doing the delivering—unless they have a reason for using passive voice. In active voice, the subject of the sentence performs the action of the verb ("veterans deliver"). In passive voice, the performer of the action follows the verb, usually in a *by* phrase, or is not included, as in the two examples from paragraphs 7 and 9.

Ordinarily, writers want to tell who is performing the action of their verbs. Sometimes, however, as in these four circumstances, they do not:

When the performer is not known ("The window was broken").

When the performer is not important ("The program was printed").

When the writer wants to conceal the identity of the performer ("The money was embezzled").

When the writer has stylistic reasons, such as to keep subjects consistent in a series of sentences or to shift the emphasis in a sentence.

The two sentences quoted from Baker's essay illustrate stylistic reasons for using passive voice. In both, Baker has placed in subject position the topical subjects. The first sentence is about evil, the second about brutal stories. By using passive voice, Baker emphasizes evil and brutality, the focus of his essay. The best rule to follow about passive voice is to use it if you have a good reason; otherwise avoid it.

Exercises: The Exploring Writer

1. Baker's final paragraph has another sentence with passive voice. Find the sentence and rewrite it to make the passive verbs active. Add subjects as necessary, but do not otherwise change the meaning. Then compare your revised version with the original. How has the effect changed?

2. *Examine a piece of your own writing for occurrences of passive voice. Consider your reasons for writing in the passive, and revise if you think that doing so would improve the sentences.*

Writing

Reflect on a common human weakness, one that, like the baser instincts Baker describes, requires training and constant attention to keep it in check. Some examples might be:

- Rudeness
- Prejudice
- Lying
- Procrastination
- Greed

Reflection can take many paths when it explores a subject. The classical probes (see Chapter 3) are especially useful tools for prompting reflective thoughts: *identify* the subject, *compare* it with similar things, *classify* it, *analyze* its *causes and effects*, tell how it works (*process*), and give some *examples* of it.

As you revise your reflections for an audience, you may choose to organize your essay as Baker does, begin with a narrative illustration, then define your subject with examples, and finally relate your subject to a specific circumstance. Remember that reflections revised for an audience include details and explanations that may be unnecessary when the writer is the only reader.

REMEMBERING A PAINFUL EXPERIENCE

We've all had painful experiences. They may have been caused by other people, been brought on by our own actions, or just happened. We may have unwittingly caused a fire, as Thoreau remembers in his journal entry, or caused someone mental or physical anguish. Recalling such occurrences often brings remorse and a wish that we could undo our actions. Some of our recollections concern the hurtful actions of other people, and in recalling the pain we also try to make sense of these incidents. Such recollections may come to the surface almost against our wills when we write reflectively in our personal journals.

Reading

"Whimpering Puppies," written by a college student, recalls a painful childhood experience. Like Baker's "The Taste of Evil," this essay explores the effect of unchecked evil, but from the perspective of a recipient of abusive behavior. This essay, though, is somewhat narrower in scope than Baker's, focusing on a personal experience and the writer's understanding of it. On the basis of the title, what do you think the writer's purpose is?

Whimpering Puppies

Lorrie Anderson (student writer)

For years I never fully realized anything had been wrong with my childhood. I only knew one thing: I thought I was going crazy. I felt different from everyone else. I couldn't seem to have close relationships with people. I didn't have many close friends. None of my social relationships lasted longer than a few days or a couple of weeks at the most. I felt insecure and unsure of myself in social situations and at school. I really didn't know what self-esteem was at that time, but I knew I lacked confidence in my abilities. I honestly didn't think I was good at anything. My parents seemed to confirm this thought by their constant badgering and insults. My father was an alcoholic, and his illness affected us all.

One of my most vivid memories was of one of my father's alcoholic rampages when I was in about fifth grade. My parents had been fighting, which usually happened whenever my father had been drinking. As their voices grew louder, their tone became more abusive. I was huddled in a bedroom with two of my sisters, neither of whom acknowledged that there was anything wrong. I prayed that the fight would not involve any of my brothers or sisters.

Suddenly I heard louder noises and screaming. It sounded as if someone was being killed. My mother had been on the receiving end of my father's temper many times. Now I was afraid she was being hurt . . . no, I was actually afraid my father was going to kill her. I raced out of the bedroom to stop the fight.

When I came into the kitchen, I saw what had caused all the noise. My father had thrown a cupboard full of pots and pans all over the kitchen. He was screaming at my mother, who just stood there taking his abuse and not trying to stop him. I jumped between them trying to shut out the verbal beating my father was giving me.

"Stop it, just stop it!" I yelled, I think at both of them. My father grabbed my arm in a drunken rage. My mother tried to protect me and grabbed onto my other arm. They pulled at me from opposite directions, and my father screamed: "Okay, who do you love?"

This sort of abuse occurs in alcoholic families. My father would get   6
drunk and would start fighting with my mother. He would tire of her as a target, and then the kids would be involved. That's why my brothers and sisters and I would disappear as quickly as we could whenever fighting started. We were like puppies, cowering under the bed or in a closet or whimpering in a corner until our angry master passed out or tired of his rampage.

Questions: The Community of Writers

1. Do you agree with the writer's analogy of whimpering puppies? Does it seem an appropriate way to describe the reactions of the children to their father's behavior?

2. How does the analogy connect to the lack of self-esteem the writer describes in her introductory paragraph?

3. How did you react to the narrative when reading it?

4. Read paragraph 6 without the first sentence. Does this sentence seem out of place in this personal essay? Discuss your reasons.

5. What does this incident tell you about children dealing with parental alcoholism?

6. What kind of reader does the essay seem to be written for—one who has not grown up in an alcoholic family, one who has had no contact with alcoholic families, or one who has experienced alcoholism?

7. What do you think is Anderson's purpose for making this experience public?

Analysis

This is a reflective essay—a writer's recollections about a painful childhood experience, one incident to illustrate her point about an unhealthful family situation. Notice her personal reactions to the incident:

> I was huddled in a bedroom.
> I prayed that the fight would not involve any of my brothers or sisters.
> I was afraid [my mother] was being hurt.

The details about the incident are specific, and the reactions are clear. But the writer says nothing about the causes of her father's alcoholism or treatments for alcoholism, because that is not her purpose.

Purpose and Thesis

The first sentence in paragraph 6—"This sort of abuse occurs in alcoholic families"—seems to indicate a purpose other than reflection, an audience other than the writer. However, it is the only sentence in her essay that generalizes beyond the writer's specific situation. The generalized statement seems to be more *informative* than persuasive, in that it does not require action from the reader. Consider the likelihood of the statement as the essay's *thesis*. A narrower, more specific sentence occurs at the end of paragraph 1: "My father was an alcoholic, and his illness affected us all." Do you feel that this is a more likely thesis sentence? Does it sum up the subject and point of the essay?

Exercise: The Exploring Writer

Anderson does not answer the question screamed by her father: "Okay, who do you love?" Write a paragraph in which you assume the writer's role and try to answer this question. Make it a paragraph that would be appropriate inserted before the final paragraph in the essay and would resolve the problems posed in the first paragraph.

Writing

Reflect on an experience that was difficult or painful for you—one that, like the one in "Whimpering Puppies"—was caused by another person, or one that was a result of accidental occurrences or your own carelessness. Since this is a personal experience, connect it to something you've learned about yourself

When you revise for your audience, delete information that you don't want others to know and add details that an interested audience would like to read. Your readers will want to know not only what happened but also how you reacted.

REFLECTING ON HUMAN FOLLY

Every now and then, we all begin to contemplate how foolish we all are. Isn't it folly to build magnificent new skyscrapers while the homeless wander on the streets below? Isn't it idiocy to pump water out of the eons-old aquifers beneath the earth's surface in order to maintain lush green lawns for a season? And we continue to pump oil out of the earth at a furious pace to keep up with our insatiable energy demands. We continue to use chlorofluorocarbons even though we know they are destroying the ozone layer that protects us from the sun's harmful ultraviolet rays.

Pick up any newsmagazine or newspaper and you will find writers decrying human folly. Such writings are usually informative or persuasive in purpose, intended to effect change. Sometimes, however, we turn to the foolish ways of humankind in our reflections. We reflect on what the world will be like for our children: Are we damaging the earth so irreparably that living as we know it now will be impossible for them? Will there be space and resources on this earth for the generations to come? Such reflections, like informative writings, may have persuasion as a purpose, especially when the writers make them public.

Reading

In "Late Night Thoughts on Listening to Mahler's Ninth Symphony," Lewis Thomas asks if it is not irresponsible to build bombs and missiles when what we want to achieve is a world for our young people to grow up and grow old in. A noted scientist, a physician, and a widely published writer, Thomas also enjoys fine music. In this essay, he records reflections on how his listening has changed over the years. As a result of nuclear armament, he can no longer assume that the earth will endure, and this thought affects the way he hears music. Perhaps you listen to music as Thomas does—in part tuned in to the music, in part absorbed in your own thoughts, with the result that music and thoughts blend into a new way of hearing the music and a fresh insight that would not have occurred without the music's input. As you read, note how the strains of the symphony prompt Thomas's contemplation.

Note also the persistent use of *I*. As a record of the writer's own thoughts, the first-person pronoun is appropriate. At the same time, this essay has been published, so we can assume that Thomas intended it for an audience beyond himself.

Late Night Thoughts on Listening to Mahler's Ninth Symphony

Lewis Thomas

I cannot listen to Mahler's Ninth Symphony with anything like the   1
old melancholy mixed with the high pleasure I used to take from this music. There was a time, not long ago, when what I heard, especially in the final movement, was an open acknowledgment of death and at the same time a quiet celebration of the tranquillity connected to the process. I took this music as a metaphor for reassurance, confirming my own strong hunch that the dying of every living creature, the most natural of all experiences, has to be a peaceful experience. I rely on nature. The

long passages on all the strings at the end, as close as music can come to expressing silence itself, I used to hear as Mahler's idea of leave-taking at its best. But always, I have heard this music as a solitary, private listener, thinking about death.

Now I hear it differently. I cannot listen to the last movement of the Mahler Ninth without the door-smashing intrusion of a huge new thought: death everywhere, the dying of everything, the end of humanity. The easy sadness expressed with such gentleness and delicacy by that repeated phrase on faded strings, over and over again, no longer comes to me as old, familiar news of the cycle of living and dying. All through the last notes my mind swarms with images of a world in which the thermonuclear bombs have begun to explode, in New York and San Francisco, in Moscow and Leningrad, in Paris, in Paris, in Paris. In Oxford and Cambridge, in Edinburgh. I cannot push away the thought of a cloud of radioactivity drifting along the Engadin, from the Moloja Pass to Ftan, killing off part of the earth I love more than any other part.

I am old enough by this time to be used to the notion of dying, saddened by the glimpse when it has occurred but only transiently knocked down, able to regain my feet quickly at the thought of continuity, any day. I have acquired and held in affection until very recently another sideline of an idea which serves me well at dark times: the life of the earth is the same as the life of an organism: the great round being possesses a mind: the mind contains an infinite number of thoughts and memories: when I reach my time I may find myself still hanging around in some sort of midair, one of those small thoughts, drawn back into the memory of the earth: in that peculiar sense I will be alive.

Now all that has changed. I cannot think that way anymore. Not while those things are still in place, aimed everywhere, ready for launching.

This is a bad enough thing for the people in my generation. We can put up with it, I suppose, since we must. We are moving along anyway, like it or not. I can even set aside my private fancy about hanging around, in midair.

What I cannot imagine, what I cannot put up with, the thought that keeps grinding its way into my mind, making the Mahler into a hideous noise close to killing me, is what it would be like to be young. How do the young stand it? How can they keep their sanity? If I were very young, sixteen or seventeen years old, I think I would begin, perhaps very slowly and imperceptibly, to go crazy.

There is a short passage near the very end of the Mahler in which the almost vanishing violins, all engaged in a sustained backward glance, are edged aside for a few bars by the cellos. Those lower notes pick up fragments from the first movement, as though prepared to begin everything all over again, and then the cellos subside and disappear, like an exhalation. I used to hear this as a wonderful few seconds of encouragement: we'll be back, we're still here, keep going, keep going.

Now, with a pamphlet in front of me on a corner of my desk,   8
published by the Congressional Office of Technology Assessment, entitled *MX Basing*, an analysis of all the alternative strategies for placement
and protection of hundreds of these missiles, each capable of creating
artificial suns to vaporize a hundred Hiroshimas, collectively capable of
destroying the life of any continent, I cannot hear the same Mahler. Now,
those cellos sound in my mind like the opening of all the hatches and the
instant before ignition.

If I were sixteen or seventeen years old, I would not feel the cracking   9
of my own brain, but I would know for sure that the whole world was
coming unhinged. I can remember with some clarity what it was like to
be sixteen. I had discovered the Brahms symphonies. I knew that there
was something going on in the late Beethoven quartets that I would have
to figure out, and I knew that there was plenty of time ahead for all the
figuring I would ever have to do. I had never heard of Mahler. I was in
no hurry. I was a college sophomore and had decided that Wallace
Stevens and I possessed a comprehensive understanding of everything
needed for a life. The years stretched away forever ahead, forever. My
great-great grandfather had come from Wales, leaving his signature in
the family Bible on the same page that carried, a century later, my
father's signature. It never crossed my mind to wonder about the twenty-
first century; it was just there, given, somewhere in the sure distance.

The man on television, Sunday midday, middle-aged and solid, nice-   10
looking chap, all the facts at his fingertips, more dependable looking
than most high-school principals, is talking about civilian defense, his
responsibility in Washington. It can make an enormous difference, he is
saying. Instead of the outright death of eighty million American citizens
in twenty minutes, he says, we can, by careful planning and practice, get
that number down to only forty million, maybe even twenty. The thing to
do, he says, is to evacuate the cities quickly and have everyone get under
shelter in the countryside. That way we can recover, and meanwhile we
will have retaliated, incinerating all of Soviet society, he says. What about
radioactive fallout? he is asked. Well, he says. Anyway, he says, if the
Russians know they can only destroy forty million of us instead of eighty
million, this will deter them. Of course, he adds, they have the capacity
to kill all two hundred and twenty million of us if they were to try real
hard, but they know we can do the same to them. If the figure is only forty
million this will deter them, not worth the trouble, not worth the risk.
Eighty million would be another matter, we should guard ourselves
against losing that many all at once, he says.

If I were sixteen or seventeen years old and had to listen to that, or   11
read things like that, I would want to give up listening and reading. I
would begin thinking up new kinds of sounds, different from any music
heard before, and I would be twisting and turning to rid myself of human
language.

Questions: The Community of Writers

1. What two specific occurrences alter the nature of Thomas's thoughts?

2. Locate instances in the essay that express Thomas's changes in attitude toward death and toward Mahler's symphony.

3. Who do you think Thomas's intended audience is? Does his final paragraph assume a youthful audience, sixteen- or seventeen-year-olds? Explain your answer with evidence from the essay.

4. Can you think of any reason for Thomas to select "sixteen or seventeen" for his "If I were" statements?

5. Are Thomas's personal reflections generalizable? In other words, do his thoughts on listening to Mahler relate to you and other readers?

Analysis

One of the primary themes of Thomas's essay seems to be thoughts of death—how he once thought of death and how he thinks of it now. For years, Thomas listened to Mahler's symphony contemplating only his own death. But, after reading the graphic descriptions in the congressional pamphlet *MX Basing*, he could think only about global death and destruction. With this alteration in focus came a change in attitude toward death and toward the symphony.

Thesis

Thomas's *thesis* is in his very first sentence: "I cannot listen to Mahler's Ninth Symphony with anything like the old melancholy mixed with the high pleasure I used to take from this music." This thesis states his subject, his assertion about his subject, and his method of development:

Subject: Listening to Mahler's Ninth Symphony
Assertion: I cannot listen as I did in the past.
Method of development: Contrast of present with past

Development

As implied in his thesis, Thomas's reflections develop along the lines of **comparison/contrast.** He contrasts the present with the past, the "now" with the "not long ago." Beginning with the past, he relates how he once listened to Mahler's symphony; then in paragraph 2 he presents a contrast with "now," relating his thoughts while listening. Paragraph 3 shifts again to past contemplations, then back to "now" in paragraphs 4 through 6. In paragraph 7 Thomas again relates the "used to" of his listening, contrasting in paragraph 8 with a specific occurrence that prompted his new thoughts. Paragraph 9 shifts back to the past, and the remainder of the essay addresses the full import of Thomas's present reflections. The pattern looks like this:

Not Long Ago	*Now*
Paragraph 1	Paragraph 2
Paragraph 3	Paragraphs 4–6
Paragraph 7	Paragraph 8
Paragraph 9	Paragraphs 10–11

The essay is a combination of philosophical *reflection, reminiscence,* and a *record* of the present. In part Thomas states his beliefs and ideas, and in part he records events and actions. Paragraphs 1 through 7 and 11 are mainly statements of beliefs and ideas, whereas paragraphs 8 through 10 primarily relate events and actions.

Purpose and Audience

Look again at the concluding paragraph. Its opening clause, "If I were sixteen or seventeen years old," repeats the opening of paragraph 9, in which Thomas remembers what it was like to be sixteen, and his first reference in paragraph 6: "If I were very young, sixteen or seventeen years old, I think I would begin, perhaps very slowly and imperceptibly, to go crazy." The "If I were" statement seems to be a thread that ties the essay together. Imagine Thomas writing this reflective essay: listening to Mahler's symphony, his thoughts roaming, recalling past reflections, being sixteen or seventeen, the civil defense official on television, the pamphlet on his desk, the symphony and thoughts of death, what life was like when he was sixteen or seventeen, how the world has changed, worldwide death and destruction, what life will be like for people who are sixteen or seventeen now. Reflections are often tied by recurring thoughts: the symphony, death, a particular time in life.

Thomas's first audience for this reflective essay was undoubtedly himself and his purpose only to reflect—to record his thoughts while listening to Mahler's Ninth Symphony. In making his reflections public, however, his audience broadened—probably including sixteen- and seventeen-year olds but not limited to them. And his purpose? Reflections intended for an audience usually have purposes beyond the exploration of ideas. If we study Thomas's final paragraph, we might decide that his purpose, other than to record reflections, is to *persuade* readers to work toward nuclear disarmament, to *explain* how awareness of the nuclear age alters even the small things in life, or perhaps only to inspire further *reflections* in his readers.

Exercises: The Exploring Writer

1. *In your journal or elsewhere, write an exploration of why Thomas would select sixteen or seventeen years of age as the basis for his reflections. Are these just ages picked out of the air? Since you are closer to sixteen or seventeen years old than Thomas is, do you think his reactions to nuclear armament are appropriate and helpful?*
2. *For Thomas, reflecting while listening to music yielded important insights. Try it yourself. Turn on some music that you enjoy listening to, and while you listen do a freewriting (see Chapter 3) on whatever thoughts occur to you. If you're keeping a journal, do the writing in your journal and keep it as a source of ideas. Or use this exercise as prewriting for the following writing assignment.*

Writing

Reflect on a change in attitude, a difference in how you look at something now from how you viewed it in the past. Here are some ideas:

- Studying
- Reading
- A kind of music
- Parental rules
- A place

First do a freewriting, possibly accompanied by music, concentrating on "now" and "not long ago," exploring your change in attitude, and establishing what caused the change. Through your reflections you may discover some things about how you have changed and why, and about how these insights might relate to what's important to other people.

Your comparisons are likely to end up, like Thomas's, as a balanced essay of contrasting paragraphs. (See the section on comparison in Chapter 4.) As you revise, insert the cause of the change where appropriate, and bring in enough reminiscence, records of present actions, and philosophical insights to interest and inform an audience about the change. While reflective essays sometimes rely on an implicit thesis or controlling idea (Leopold's, page 134) and others state the thesis at the end (Baker's, page 138), for this essay consider *beginning* with a thesis sentence that sets up your comparison. Because this essay will report *your* experiences and reflections, incidents from your own life are appropriate.

ADDITIONAL READINGS FOR DISCUSSION

Reading

The following essay expresses a nontraditional student's reflections on the Vietnam War as seen by a high school student whose boyfriend is "over there." On looking back twenty years later, she finds meaning in the experience. Other readings on the Vietnam War are "The Taste of Evil" in this chapter and "Mom and Dad" in Chapter 9.

Walking Point

Teri Anderson Brown

I "came of age" comfortably uncomfortable in a cozy little valley in Utah during the heat of the Vietnam War. Words such as *Tet Offensive, platoon, Khmer Rouge,* the *DMZ* became part of my high school lingo via Walter Cronkite and the evening news. I also learned words like *grunt, jungle rot, shotgunning, walking point, dinks,* and *Charlie* through fifty-eight letters written by a boy barely nineteen and wandering the jungles of Southeast Asia with his surest friend, an M-16, slung over his shoulder.   1

I still have those letters. Twenty years later I look at the word *free*   2 written in the stamp corner signifying no dues required on mail coming from a war zone. Somehow when I was sixteen the irony of that word on his letters escaped my notice. Somehow the poignant innocence and confusion of a small-town farm boy blew over my head like a breathless wind. Somehow it took me two decades to read between the lines of those letters written from transport planes, firebases, and jungles during monsoon rains that made the inky words weep and fade on the paper as though they had been written millennia before by someone who was crying. Thank God I kept them. They are my link to the past, my window to the future.

Not long ago a friend was telling me about a portable replica of the   3 Vietnam Memorial. It is on a cross-country exhibit for those who would never make it to Washington, D.C., to see the original. She called it the "portable wall." Through years of searching for an understanding of how the events of Vietnam changed me personally, I have learned that each one of us has a portable wall: a private, invisible memorial mirroring people and events. It is a memorial of memories that helps us create a personal interpretation of our universe, of our life, of what difference we can make to any of it. I have been erecting my own portable wall for years.

My wall has only one name on it, but words and pictures from those 4
crazy days come together in a muted collage of memory that will be
engraved there forever. I can see my own reflection, a junior hippie in
conservative caricature, aching to be part of what was "happening." I was
the only girl in my class with a boyfriend "over there." It gave me license
to snub prom queens, football jocks, and the juvenile tedium of the high
school scene. My Vietnam letters, combined with the nightly news,
helped me ace all the current event quizzes. My peers treated me with a
unique respect because of my direct line of communication to "Nam." I
could make them see what was "coming down" in the deltas and high-
lands of Asia better than Cronkite ever could. I burned incense every
night and while the Doors rocked on my turntable I read my letters and
watched the smoke, like a lonesome spirit, thread through the beads and
shadows of my room.

Now when I face my invisible wall I remember myself, as if in soft 5
pencil sketches, sluffing algebra, sneaking home to check the mailbox,
hiding in the maple tree with a copy of Rupert Brooke's "1914" sonnets,
ironing my hair for a Cream concert, water skiing at the lake in a red
bikini, cramming nine girls into my fluorescent green VW, defying my
parents, writing letters.

But there are ghosts and images that haunt my memorial—like the 6
stark photo of an arm, just an arm, ripped and rotting at the stump,
hanging naked and exposed on a barbed wire fence. On the backside is
the simple explanation "Charlie's arm." Another image, less vivid, of
some ambassador from somewhere saying something about a little cor-
ruption oiling the machinery crowds for its own space in my memory.
Always in his proper place looms the carefully posed LBJ praying earnestly for our dear boys in the service of their country. His form nearly
overpowers that of a boy, thousands of miles from home, shirtless, smiling, love beads and a peace sign hanging on his hairless chest, a can of
beer in his hand, a headband stitched with "VIET WAR NAM" fitted like
a fallen halo around his forehead. Words of a once-popular song echo
softly through my soul, "old enough to kill, but not to vote."

My "Nam" letters were an education in and of themselves. I learned 7
from them what nothing else could have taught me. In one letter I heard
the phrase "walking point" for the first time. "I walked point today. That's
when a squad of six to eight of us scope out an area looking for dinks.
The point man leads the way. It's damn scary knowing you're the first one
to stumble into shit. I was scared as hell. They always seem to know where
we are. I guess that only makes sense; it's their playground."

In the very heart of my wall memorial I carry the figure of a boy 8
whose face I can no longer see. His letters are the poetry of my wall. Their
eloquence lies in the understatement of emotion, the unconscious effort
of a bewildered youth to be casual while standing at the gates of hell.

I did not marry the author of those letters. Not long before the end   9
of his tour of duty the letters stopped coming. He came home from
Vietnam in a body bag. I married another vet, whom I have borne a
daughter and three sons. As I watch my children grow, I wonder about
suffering, sacrifice, the future, and if the letters of their generation will
have *free* written in the stamp corner. I wonder about their portable walls
and the day they will find themselves walking point.

After two decades I find myself painfully giving birth to a poem that   10
was conceived long ago.

> Nineteen years of leaf-thin dreams
> tagged, sealed
> lifeless in a black-bag womb,
> offspring of whatever silence reigns
> where guns no longer issue
> their point-blank madness.
>
> No blithe crowds,
> no roses on cheeks of painted girls
> dimpled with come-on smiles,
> no swaying banners, no bands,
> only small-town friends
> hushed with innocence.
>
> Parents bowed in curious disbelief,
> cut in desperate calm,
> faces smooth as stones
> buried in backwash of a wild river,
> the sure bead drawn
> on comfort of their common days.

Over time the lines of my "Nam" letters have quietly receded from   11
my memory. Occasionally I have read them when I am feeling my mortality. Every now and then I take them out of my dresser drawer, and a
remembered picture or phrase will joust with my emotions, will stand me
face to face with my portable wall.

There is one line of one letter that has become a part of the symme-   12
try of my world, juxtaposed with the past, present, and future. It was
written in a state of exhaustion after hours of toting a rifle and radio in
air too thick to breathe through someone else's jungle. It was written by
a boy grown older than his years who was facing death while questioning
life and pondering the risks every person must take, whether in the wreck
of war or the serenity of peace.

"Maybe life is walking point."   13

Questions: The Community of Writers

1. How does the information about the Vietnam War compare with the "official" version from television news?

2. What is "walking point"? What does the phrase tell you about the reality of the Vietnam War? Discuss its meaning as a description of life: "Maybe life is walking point."

3. What does Teri Anderson Brown's poem tell you about her reflections?

4. How does her present understanding of the war differ from the way she saw it at the age of sixteen?

5. What does she mean when she says that her letters are her "window to the future"?

Reading

Campus life is often stressful, full of pressures such as parental expectations, the difficulty of keeping grades up, balancing work and studies, learning to be responsible for one's own life, and so on. In this essay, a student writer reflects on those familiar pressures.

Holding On

Kim (student writer)

The trip went too fast. I was home before I knew it. Even though I'd been away three weeks, nothing had changed. Well O.K.! Maybe the house was cleaner. I am sure my parents never stopped noticing that. It was cleaner because I was gone. 1

No one was around. I knew where Mom was. She was at school. Besides working fifty-plus hours a week with an hour drive both ways, she still insisted that she go to school. So she took classes at a college almost three hours away every other weekend. She always wanted more. 2

After I searched the house for my father, I ventured outside to find out what kind of job he would be doing. Did I mention it was Saturday? My dad was pulling weeds out of the lawn with his bare hands. He could have gone to the drugstore and got some weed killer, and the job could have been done in less than half the time. But no! I mentioned the word *job* on purpose. Although it was Saturday, you still could not be just relaxing—you must be working. 3

Then I knew it was my turn. I didn't dare go in the house and plop down in an easychair. What kind of work would I do? It would have to be somewhat involved—it couldn't just be homework. Well, I figured out 4 what I would do. I decided to begin reading one of my textbooks, but I also threw in doing some laundry.

Every minute of studying sent my mind wandering off even more. 5 Nothing had changed. Even my cat was as mean as ever. They don't understand! I am not like they are! Just what is important to me? This is a question my parents are always asking. What is important to me? Maybe it is not so much what is important as what can I handle? The scary part is that I seem capable of handling less and less each day. Work with its unbreakable schedules, school with its constant work, home with my insensitive parents, and friends who don't understand that you need them too sometimes—all are pressures, each seeming to multiply the others.

I knew I had to concentrate on my reading. Just as I got settled in, 6 the dryer buzzer went off. The clothes were not dry. "Damn!" Nothing was going right. The day ended with little conversation between my dad and me. We each kept to our own area of the house, each doing our own work.

Sunday morning church seemed so early at 8:00 A.M., but you can't 7 sleep in until ten o'clock church because you would waste half the day. There were things to be done. I wondered what they would do all day. I hadn't seen Mom in weeks. I knew I would see her at breakfast.

Breakfast was uneventful. Just the same old questions. "How are your 8 classes?" "How are your roommates?" "How are your instructors?" I handled them in the usual manner—"Fine!"

The ride home from Perkins Restaurant was no more eventful than 9 I expected. It was the same old story: "You need to organize your finances." "A student loan isn't the answer." "Move back into the dorms; it's cheaper."

I felt as if I were losing my grip. I wanted to scream, but all I could 10 manage to do was cry. Don't they understand that is not the problem? The problem is their expectations. Sixteen credits, 3.5 G.P.A. or better, and still work. Don't they understand! I can't do it! I am tired all the time. I know people can do it. I guess that is why I still try. The more I try, however, the farther behind I become. It is hard to get up when you are down.

We finally got home, and the first thing I did was call my ride back to 11 school. "I am ready to go back." My parents didn't understand why I had to go back so soon; after all, it was only eleven o'clock in the morning. I made up some excuse. Don't they understand? It is them!

I sank into the car seat and settled in for the three-hour ride back to 12 school. This time the ride couldn't go fast enough. It felt good to pull onto the highway. I knew my problems didn't go away, but it did feel good to be closed up in a car, far away from everyone else.

As I burst into the doorway of my apartment, my roommates welcomed me home. I knew I would be O.K. 13

Questions: The Community of Writers

1. What pressures of student life does Kim identify in this essay?
2. Characterize how Kim sees her relationship with her parents.
3. Why does she feel better when she returns to school?
4. Do you think Kim would want her parents to read this essay? What reasons might she have for wanting them to read it? for not wanting them to read it?
5. Collaboratively write a note to Kim advising her on how she might revise this essay before slipping it under her parents' door.

Reading

In this essay, a nontraditional student writer reflects on the effects of growing up in an alcoholic home. As you read the essay and speculate on the problems it presents, you might compare it with "Whimpering Puppies" earlier in this chapter.

Epitaph for a Childhood

Lorna Marro

It was during my turbulent childhood that the Vietnam War raged in a land I had never known existed. It meant nothing more to me than a few glimpses on the "Evening News" and hushed conversations between adults. I could not fathom the fear, anger, and horror that shrouded all those involved in the fighting; I could not feel it; it was not real to me. I was struggling to survive in another war. A war that had live combat, P.O.W.'s, and excessive cruelty; a war that crushed all hope of peace like a bug under a heel of a boot; a war where the dark, incessant nights held no faith that a renaissance of a new day would dawn; a war where I lay eternally on the verge of sleep welcoming the exhaustion that would block out the pain of reality; a war where the closing of the garage door was enough to jolt me back into the truth to tell me that now it would begin again; a war that was called alcoholism. 1

Some soldiers hid in foxholes and trenches; I hid under my bed. Those same men prayed to God to spare their lives; I could only pray to end mine. They spoke in whispers—the enemy was near; I could not speak at all—the enemy was here. The Nation mourned for the sons who had given their lives to fight the "Communist Enemy"; no one grieved for the death of a little girl's childhood given in sacrifice to a bottle of "Russian Vodka." 2

I was a prisoner in my own house, and I spent hours staring out the window of the cell that was assigned me for sleeping. From the loneliness of that room I watched the unaware world go by, leaving me behind. I felt 3 the weight of the universe crushing, crushing, crushing my young shoulders until all my feelings and emotions lay dead around my feet. The only thing that kept me behind those invisible bars, and from shouting my rage to the four corners of the earth, was the binding, unspoken code of an alcoholic home: at all costs I must protect the secret sickness that thrives within the family; I must tell no outsider what is going on; I must pretend, lie, or make excuses if someone questions me; I must not ask friends over to play because they might see something that is forbidden; I must not go out and play with them because there is no one to protect my mother.

This was the burden of a child. The hours my mother spent crying;   4
the angry shouts and curses that echoed through the night; the Antarctic cold that permeated every fiber of everything living and non-living in our house; the all-consuming fear that enveloped me like layers of clothing on a winter day—these were the only things that I could rely on. Too afraid to speak the truth, I silently begged visitors with my eyes to look past the facade; to look past the frozen smiles; to look into—the child that hovered in the background. The people saw, but didn't see; the people heard, but didn't hear; and through it all I drifted alone. I had no survival training; I had no weapons; I could not fight the unseen enemy inside my father. Alcoholism: the killer of whole families that pledges to maim and wound without leaving the home. It knows no gender, age, race, or creed; it shows no prejudice.

As an adult not able to cry since childhood, I received the news of my   5
father's death with numbness mixed with anger. Looking down upon his face for the last time, I saw him as he really was—an angry, old man consumed by a disease and tortured with the memories that tormented all of his family. I felt my throat constrict as the first of a universe of bottled-up tears slowly slid down my cheeks. I understood in those few moments what my hate had hidden for a lifetime—I still loved my father. The healing had begun.

Questions: The Community of Writers

1. Lorna Marro's reflective essay began as a journal entry, one she felt she had to write for her own self-discovery. But she also felt it was something that had to be said to an audience, so she spent hours revising and refining the essay, through it all discovering more about herself and her subject. As readers you bring your own experiences to reading, and they affect your reading. The writer of "Whimpering Puppies" would read this essay one way, the writer of "Holding On" another way. Discuss your reactions to the essay.

2. Marro uses repetition and parallel structure extensively. What uses did you find particularly effective? Are there any places where she overuses these stylistic devices?

3. How does Marro's use of analogy contribute to the effectiveness of the essay?

4. How does she achieve emphasis?

Reading

Here are three reflective poems, the first a narrative, the second a description, and the third a narrative record. What additional purposes might each poet have for writing?

Painting Minnesota

Steve Crow

I begin painting with words
as we fly northwest toward
the lingering sunset afire
above the hazy horizon.
The subtle ripples of northern
Minnesota spread in every
direction, yellowish-brown,
each of the many visible
contours suddenly brushed
with soft puddles of darkness
as shadows appear upon every
eastward undulation in the
leeward-light of the sun.
The sky, pale blue, curves
toward the infinity of another
night. Streams and rivers
snake southbound. Hundreds
of lakes in sizes and shapes
span far beyond us while one
straight line of lakes glows
in a narrow pathway of light
all the way to the sun, cold
winter waters touched by a
hovering star. Then, as the
perfect circle of sun slips
nearer the earth, the sun
seems to flatten and become
egg-like, the blinding color
of sunlight burning yellow
beyond yellow as the light
beyond life reaches us as
we watch the last breath
of yellow sink into the haze
like a thin sliver of ember
disappearing in the dark
of a cold fire.

Incident

Countee Cullen

Once riding in old Baltimore,
Heart-filled, head-filled with glee,
I saw a Baltimorean
Keep looking straight at me.

Now I was eight and very small,
And he was no whit bigger,
And so I smiled, but he poked out
His tongue, and called me, "Nigger."

I saw the whole of Baltimore
From May until December;
Of all the things that happened there
That's all that I remember.

On the Lake in St. John's

Wang Xiao (Student Writer)

Early spring
Ice is melting
Tiptoeing
Tiptoeing
I start

Intuitively I step
On the white parts
Covered with snow
That should be safer
Than pure ice

I can hardly breathe
On the brink of death
Uncertain if I can make it
Through the lake
To the other end

What will my parents think in China
Will my mother blame me
I am too bold
But it is too late
The lake's heart embraces me already

Hopping desperately
Upon a solid rock
I stomp my feet
Taking a long long breath
I am safe, mother at home

I realize
The life-death line
Is thin
Paper thin
After all

Questions: The Community of Writers

1. Do poets write simply for themselves or do they want to achieve some purpose with an audience?

2. What effect do you think each poet hopes to have on his or her audience?

3. Discuss the autobiographical elements of each poem.

4. What are the reflective elements in each poem?

5. Compare the ways the three poets use punctuation.

CHAPTER 7

Writing to Persuade

> *Wherever there is persuasion, there is rhetoric. And wherever there is "meaning" there is "persuasion."*
>
> *—Kenneth Burke*

To **persuade** is to use various means for changing someone else's beliefs or opinions or for moving someone to a particular action. You live with persuasion every day. Advertising companies try to persuade you to buy their clients' products. Television networks and stations want you to watch their programs. Colleges and universities want you to enroll in their classes. Fund-raisers of all kinds ask you to contribute to their projects. At the same time, you are daily in the role of persuader: "Let's watch this program." "My absence from class was unavoidable." "Will you give us an extra day to complete this assignment?"

Most language uses are at least partly persuasive in intent. Even though you may have another primary purpose when you write, persuasion cannot easily be separated from that purpose. While you inform or praise, for example, you may also be trying to persuade. Moreover, when your primary intention is to persuade, you also have other purposes: informing, praising, reporting, or something else. Many of the readings in this book have purposes that are persuasive in addition to their other purposes. In this chapter the essays are primarily persuasive, but as you read you will notice other purposes as well.

Persuasive Appeals

There are three basic ways to persuade, and they overlap. One of the most famous rhetoricians, Aristotle, said that people persuade by the **appeal of their own good character** *(ethos)*, by an **appeal to the minds and**

emotions of their audience *(pathos),* and by an **appeal based on logical reasoning** *(logos).* Let's examine each of these appeals.

Appeal of Character (Ethos)

Persuasion is sometimes thought to assume an adversarial relationship between writer and reader; that is, persuasion is necessitated by opposing viewpoints. Once the audience is confronted and persuaded, and its views have become similar to those of the writer, the adversarial relationship is ended. But thinking of your readers as adversaries may not be the most effective attitude if you want to persuade. More effective is to *identify* with them. Appeal to things you have in common. Show how you are on their side. Try to see things the readers' way. Demonstrate how your ideas could benefit them.

Candidates for political office never give the impression that their constituents are their adversaries; rather, they try to be seen as being on the voters' side by shaking hands, holding babies, wearing windbreakers and baseball caps, and so on. And they offer benefits—new highways, cleaner environment, more scholarship money, higher employment, no new taxes. Identification wins votes.

It also sells products. An automobile manufacturer says that buying its cars is "A great way to teach your kids the value of the dollar." The beef industry boasts of "Real food for real people." A cleansing tissue "feels just wonderful next to your skin." A typewriter is "the simplest typewriter in memory." All these slogans identify with the audience by promising some kind of benefit: a good buy, a great taste, a good feeling, and something easy to do. At the same time, they're just ambiguous enough that they don't commit the manufacturer. The "simplest typewriter" ad, for example, has a double meaning for the word *memory:* the audience's memory and the typewriter's. How can the manufacturer be held to one or the other?

But this kind of deception is identification gone awry, and such manipulation gives persuasion a bad name. When you know that an advertiser or a political candidate is trying to manipulate you, you become skeptical, distrusting. When as a critical reader you discern that a writer is trying to persuade you, you react accordingly, judging the merits of the case instead of being mindlessly swayed. Persuasion is not intrinsically a bad thing. Manufacturers must sell their wares, political candidates must be elected, actions must be taken. But when the persuaders are not truthful, they lose what they need most: respect and credibility in the long term.

The Greek rhetorician Aristotle had a word for the *appeal of character: ethos.* Think of a person you respect and trust. What do you admire about that person? What has that person done that makes you so trustful? Ordinarily, the people who are the most believable are those who have earned respect for their honesty, integrity, fairness, wisdom, self-control, and concern for others. We respect them because of past behaviors that have shown they keep their word. They have made right decisions, have weighed the facts intelligently, and have acted for the good of others, not purely out of self-interest. This kind of credibility is difficult to achieve. At the same time, it's extremely easy to lose. One lie or exaggerated truth will do it. As Cicero, a noted Roman orator, observed, "We give no credit to a liar even when he speaks the truth." Honesty increases credibility, and credibility improves persuasion.

Respect and trust must be earned in writing as well. Credible writers support their opinions with facts, check the truth of their facts, and use emotional appeals with restraint. They know their subject well, and they understand and identify with their audience. They maintain a tone that is calm and reasoned, not sarcastic or angry. They write carefully, using conventional grammar and punctuation. Credible writers do not falsify or invent facts. Nor do they misrepresent facts and twist them to suit their own purposes. They do not represent the ideas of other people as their own. In other words, they do not attempt to deceive their audience.

Careful readers test writers' credibility by looking for clues in how they handle both their facts and their relationship with their audience. In "What Is Wrong with Us?" an essay in this chapter, Senator Albert Gore establishes his credibility in the first two paragraphs by noting his professed concern for the "global ecological crisis" and his failure to win the 1988 presidential nomination as a result of the apparent unpopularity of that interest. He thus establishes his authority as an environmentalist-politician. In an essay in Chapter 6, "The Taste of Evil," author Mark Baker establishes his authority as a Vietnam veteran to write about Vietnam. Readers generally want to know where the writer derives the authority to discuss a given subject.

While you prepare to write persuasively, answer the following questions regarding your *ethos:*

1. How expert am I on the subject?
2. Do I need to back my credibility with the expertise of others?
3. How should I reveal my expertise?
4. Why should my audience respect and trust me?
5. What do I have in common with my audience?
6. How can I show the audience I am honest?

Appeal to the Minds and Emotions of the Audience (Pathos)

To identify with an audience, you must first understand it. To persuade an audience to your point of view, first try to find out what you have in common, what beliefs, interests, and values you share. If you want to write a letter to the campus newspaper in response to a recent editorial on legalized abortion, for example, you should remember that some people in your audience are strongly opposed and some strongly in favor, that some have had abortions and some have carried unwanted pregnancies to term, and, though you can't identify with everyone in your audience, your effectiveness will be increased with the amount of identification you can achieve. Considering your audience should give you insight into how to begin a persuasive essay, how to develop your points, what assumptions and fears you may have to allay, and so on. Answering the Questions about Audience for Writing on page 26 may help.

An appeal to the audience's minds and emotions (Aristotle called it *pathos*) is a valid part of persuasion. However, both writers and readers approach emotional appeals with care. Children who are good at persuading their parents have acquired just the right balance of tears and attempts to hide them. But when a television evangelist or a speaker of the House of Representatives openly weeps before the cameras while repenting his sins, the audience, like parents deluged by a superabundance of tears, backs off, unconvinced. There's a term for tears like those: *crocodile tears*. Impassioned expressions, like crocodile tears, beg for sympathy and agreement: "My fellow Americans," "the blessing of God," "unjust laws." Other loaded terms evoke fear or anger: "redneck," "Fascist," "broken promise," "grim existence." These are like pouring on the tears, and they generally get agreement only from people who already agree.

Appealing to an audience's minds is also an effective means of persuasion. Senator Gore appeals to his audience by sharing a concern for the environment and a frustration over the difficulties of saving it. Using the first-person plural *we* throughout his essay, he conveys a sense of urgency and appeals to his audience's desire to act now. In another essay in this chapter, "What 'Sesame Street' Teaches," Neil Postman, a parent as well as an educator, appeals to parents' concern for the well-being of their children. He explains how both children and parents "embraced" "Sesame Street" and why children "loved" it. While both writers probably have more differences than commonalties with their audiences, they share with them the common ground of their subjects, and they use emotional appeals that will be acceptable to those audiences.

Answering the following questions may help you prepare to use *pathos* persuasively:

1. (Again) What do I have in common with my audience?
2. Will this audience accept emotional appeals?
3. How much can I rely on emotional appeal?
4. What emotions can I appropriately appeal to (love, anger, fear, patriotism, pity, disillusionment, etc.)?
5. What physical needs can I appropriately appeal to (food, shelter, sex, security, etc.)?

Appeal of Logical Reasoning (Logos)

Mutual interest can be stimulated by the way the writer handles the subject matter. When you begin reading something on a subject you previously had no concern for, what sort of thing keeps your interest? A stimulating narrative? Telling statistics? Forcefully worded opinions backed by facts? You might not have known or cared about a lost clause in the Declaration of Independence before reading "High Cost of Compromise" (in "Additional Readings for Discussion"), in which Sydney J. Harris tells what that clause provided and presents it as a missed opportunity for changing the course of history. Your readers, likewise, may have had no previous interest in a subject you choose to write about—until you stimulate their interest.

An **appeal of logical reasoning** (Aristotle called it *logos*) depends on an **arguable proposition,** or thesis, and evidence to support it. Let's examine the proposition first. A proposition is arguable if it represents a difference of **opinion.** Statements of **fact** are not arguable. The following sentences are verifiable statements of fact and therefore not arguable:

> There are more teenage pregnancies now than ever before. [Could be verified with statistical reference works.]
>
> Communications in business have undergone many changes in the past few years. [Could be verified by observation, encyclopedia entry, and so on.]
>
> "This is not a copy of the original Declaration as written by Thomas Jefferson."—Sydney J. Harris [Could be verified by comparison.]
>
> "He has kept among us in times of peace, Standing Armies without the Consent of our legislatures."—-Declaration of Independence [Could be verified by observation and historical accounts.]

Neither are statements of personal preference, such as these, arguable:

> The smell of cigarette smoke reminds me of burning trash. [My distaste for cigarette smoke may not be yours.]
>
> I don't like walking in the cold from a parking lot five blocks away. [A reader can't dispute your dislikes.]

Opinions that can be supported by facts, however, *are* arguable and therefore qualify as propositions for logical reasoning. Here are six examples:

> If we continue our present actions, we will destroy our environment.
>
> Every public school should educate children about AIDS.
>
> We could solve the drug problem by legalizing marijuana.

"We are at an environmental boiling point right now."—Albert Gore

"Television educates by teaching children to do what television-viewing requires of them."—Neil Postman

To avoid the potential for child abuse, parents should not spank their children.

Statements like these can serve as thesis sentences.

Exercise: The Community of Writers

Read the following statements and decide which are arguable.

1. Political action committees favor incumbent members of the House of Representatives over their challengers.
2. The campaign to clean up America's waterways has many names— Project Mayfly, Adopt-a-Stream, River Watch, and others.
3. The World Bank is one of the most secretive institutions in Washington.
4. Hong Kong symbolizes imperialist power in the Far East.
5. We hold these truths to be self-evident, that all men are created equal.

Supporting the Arguable Proposition

Since facts are not arguable, they are forceful support for the arguable proposition, or supportable opinion. Types of facts you might encounter in your reading and can find useful in making your own arguments are examples, testimony, statistics, and historical evidence.

Types of Facts

Examples

An **example** illustrates or explains a point. You might draw examples from your personal experience, from the experience of people you know, or from your reading and observations. A single example is usually less effective than several examples or an example used with other kinds of facts. A type of example is the analogy, in which the writer uses a familiar example to illustrate something less familiar—for instance Albert Gore's reference to a science experiment with frogs to illustrate the world's response

Types of Facts (continued)

to the environmental crisis, or a description of the atmospheric ozone layer in terms of a blanket.

Testimony

Quotations, or **testimony,** from experts are powerful support for an argument, particularly for a novice writer whose credibility needs bolstering. Quoting an environmental biologist from the University of California at Davis, for example, makes you more than a first-year college student urging environmental safety; you are backing your position with that of an expert. Choose your "experts" well, however; they must be recognized authorities on the subject you are writing about. If you find that they are quoted by other people writing about the same subject, you can probably safely assume their authority.

Statistics

If they are reliable, meaningful to an audience, and applicable to the subject at hand, **statistics** are effective support for an argument. Writers rarely depend on statistics alone, however. Even Jonathan Kozol's essay "A Third of the Nation Cannot Read These Words" (in Chapter 11), which makes abundant use of statistics, uses a narrative example too.

Historical Evidence

Things happen. The nuclear power plant at Chernobyl melted down. Mount St. Helens exploded. Nazi Germany invaded Poland in 1939. Kareem Abdul-Jabbar was born Ferdinand Lewis Alcindor in New York City. Thomas Jefferson drafted the Declaration of Independence at the Second Continental Congress. Such facts are historically verifiable and can be useful in supporting arguments. To be effective, the facts must by true and must relate to the argument.

Other Types of Support

In supporting their arguable propositions, writers of persuasive essays sometimes find it necessary to *define terms* that are unfamiliar to the audience or that they are using in an unfamiliar way. A volatile term like *gun control,* for example, must be defined as the writer is using it, as must the specialized use of a common term such as *feedback.* Definitions are often cleared up in an introduction, especially if their clarity requires several sentences, as in this definition of "China Syndrome":

> The "China Syndrome" refers to the possibility that a reactor might lose its primary coolant and then its emergency core cooling system and backup systems for some reason might also not function, while the temperature of the core continues to increase. In the usual scenario, the core becomes molten and then melts way down through the bottom of the containment vessel, continuing on into the ground where presumably it eventually cools off. Radioactivity would then be released to the atmosphere and perhaps also to the ground water. This event could indeed be disastrous and could lead to many deaths.
>
> —Jack J. Kraushaar and Robert A. Ristinen,
> *Energy and Problems of a Technical Society*

Sometimes definitions are accomplished briefly when the term occurs, inserted in the sentence and set off with parentheses, commas, or dashes; here is an example:

> Radon gas *(a naturally occurring radioactive gas)* may be the cause of 5,000 to 20,000 lung cancer deaths each year.

In addition to supporting their arguments with facts, writers rely on relevant *opinions*. Testimony, for instance, is often the opinion of a recognized authority or someone who has done research on the subject. The following example shows how a writer cites the research of others:

> Two associates at Boston College, Ann Wolbert Burgess, associate professor of nursing, and Lynda Lytle Holmstom, assistant professor of sociology, studied eighty rape victims who came to the emergency ward of Boston City Hospital. They reported their findings in the *American Journal of Nursing*. Burgess and Holmstom found that half the women in their sample had been threatened with a weapon; another twenty-one reported being manhandled, and twelve had succumbed to verbal threats alone. After lengthy interviews with the eighty women, the Boston College professors stated unequivocally, "The primary reaction of almost all women to the rape was fear, that is, fear for their lives."
>
> —Susan Brownmiller, *Against Our Will: Men, Women and Rape*

More frequently, writers support their arguments with their own considered opinions, as in this example:

> In such a world [of tomorrow], the most valued attributes of the industrial era become handicaps. The technology of tomorrow requires not millions of lightly lettered men, ready to work in unison at endlessly

repetitious jobs, it requires not men who take orders in unblinking fashion, aware that the price of bread is mechanical submission to authority, but men who can make critical judgments, who can weave their way through novel environments, who are quick to spot new relationships in the rapidly changing reality.

—Alvin Toffler, *Future Shock*

Any good argument, of course, will be based on facts as well as thoughtful opinions.

As paradoxical as it may seem, an important means of support is the *opposing argument*. In most cases, your audience knows that there are counterarguments to the one you are proposing. To ignore them weakens your credibility; to use them shows that you have considered them and remain convinced your position is the most valid. Don't devote undue space to opposing views, however; in a short paper, a paragraph is probably sufficient. Do give some thought to the best position for this paragraph. Some writers place it at the beginning, stating what "some people" think and then presenting their more reasonable view (see, for example, the beginning of "What Is Wrong with Us?" on pages 174–76). Others deal with it near the end so they can refute it in their conclusion. Still others position it somewhere in the middle, as it suits their argument (see paragraphs 6 and 7 in "Protection from the Prying Camera," pages 186–88). In "Prohibition and Drugs" (pages 196–98), Milton Friedman refutes opposing views at the end and throughout.

Generally weak forms of support are personal *likes and dislikes* and personal *beliefs*. To say that a movie is bad because you don't like science fiction does not convince an audience not to see the movie. To say that abortions should be illegal because you believe a human life begins at conception does not convince the person who believes otherwise. While beliefs often form a portion of an argument, they are usually its weakest portion and must be supported by facts and fact-based opinions.

In supporting their propositions, writers are wise to avoid biased statements and stereotypical characterizations, since references of this type will probably have a negative effect on all but a like-minded audience. Words such as *feebleminded, bigoted, muscle-bound, silly, shifty, lazy, prudish,* and *sexy* insensitively describe people according to our own biases. Such prejudicial terms are not based on knowledge nor do they promote it; therefore they are avoided in careful writing.

Unexpressed Assumptions

Arguable propositions usually have **unexpressed assumptions** that both writer and reader should be aware of. The proposition "If we continue our present actions, we will destroy our environment" assumes that our present actions are destructive to the environment. "Every public school should educate children about AIDS" assumes that if children are educated about AIDS they will be able to avoid contracting the disease. "We could solve the drug problem by legalizing marijuana" assumes that we want to solve the drug problem.

Sometimes the unexpressed assumptions don't require support, as when readers agree with them. This agreement of course depends on who the audience is—one more reason for writers to be sensitive to their audience. A writer might be able to assume audience agreement that the drug problem must be solved. Agreement on AIDS education as a solution to the spread of the disease would be less likely. An argument is weakened when a writer doesn't recognize unexpressed assumptions or presumes that the audience agrees with them.

Exercise: The Community of Writers

Examine the following arguable propositions for their unexpressed assumptions. Then decide whether these assumptions need to be supported or not. Discuss your views, as well as the implications of any differences in views, with your classmates.

1. To avoid the potential for child abuse, parents should not spank their children.
2. "We are at an environmental boiling point right now."—Albert Gore
3. "Television educates by teaching children to do what television-viewing requires of them."—Neil Postman
4. Blaming violent crime on society's shortcomings is easier than attributing it to the lack of the perpetrators' moral character.
5. The NCAA needs rules aimed at reducing criminal misconduct by college athletes.

Fallacies

Errors in logic are called **fallacies;** they are unsound or incomplete reasoning. Whenever they are present, they weaken an argument. Try to avoid them in your writing and watch for them in your reading. Here are the most prominent fallacies:

Broad generalization—a claim that extends beyond what the evidence will support: "Elderly people are poor drivers."
Oversimplification—a statement that tries to make a complex issue seem uncomplicated: "Gasoline prices have gone up because of the oil spill on the West Coast."

Question begging—an argument based on an unproven statement: "Pointless courses like the general education requirements should be eliminated." (The pointlessness of the courses has not been proven.)

Either-or reasoning—an assumption that there are only two positions and only one of them is right: "If we don't increase the number of landbased missiles, we're sure to have war."

Post hoc cause—an assumption that because one event occurs before another, the first causes the second: "If we plan a barbecue, it will rain; it always does when we have one."

Ad hominem—an attack on persons rather than issues: "Because Johnson had a child out of wedlock, she should not be elected to Congress."

Here are some questions you can ask about your *logos* as you prepare to write persuasively:

1. What examples, testimony, statistics, and historical evidence can I use?
2. How can I check the accuracy of my facts?
3. What kind of evidence will be most convincing for this audience?
4. How can I deal fairly with opposing views?
5. What other types of support can I use (supportable opinion, acceptable beliefs, definitions)?
6. What unexpressed assumptions must I bring to the surface and support?
7. What fallacies might be inherent in my argument?

Persuasive writing employs the principles discussed in Part I for all writing—probably because almost all writing is in part persuasive in purpose. Persuasion does make particularly evident the writer's necessity to be sensitive to his or her own credibility and to the beliefs, interests, and values of the audience, as well as to possess adequate knowledge of the subject and competence in writing.

Here is a summary checklist of the special considerations of persuasive writing:

Checklist for Persuasive Writing

1. Be honest and accurate in your representation of facts.
2. Maintain a calm and reasoned tone.
3. Identify your audience, and then identify *with* it on the strength of beliefs, interests, and values you share.

> *Checklist (continued)*
>
> 4. Use restraint with emotional appeals, restricting yourself to those you know your audience will accept.
> 5. Build your persuasion on a thesis sentence that is an arguable proposition—an opinion supportable by facts.
> 6. Present a reasoned argument supported with examples, testimony, statistics, and historical evidence, plus carefully considered opinions.
> 7. Be aware of the unexpressed assumptions of your argument, and support them if necessary.
> 8. Check your argument for fallacies.

As we have seen, you can find persuasion in almost every piece of writing. This chapter has a collection of essays that are primarily persuasive. They are representative of what you might find as you read magazines and books. And they are representative of the kinds of writing you may at times be inclined to do. Look for persuasive purposes in all the reading you do. Examine magazine and newspaper articles, advertisements, even your textbooks for purposes other than reporting, informing, or the like. Be an active, critical reader, seeking evidence of the writer's credibility; sensitivity to the beliefs, interests, and values of the audience; and quality of the logical appeal.

PERSUADING ABOUT A COMMON CAUSE

In the 1960s there was talk about "Spaceship Earth," an analogy that put all of humankind together in one vehicle moving through the universe. On the journey we travelers have only the water and air that accompany us, only the food we can produce with the supplies we take with us, only the inhabitable area on our spaceship's outer surface that is not covered with water. We cannot get off the spaceship, and we cannot take on fresh supplies. The supplies we take with us are renewable only if we manage them carefully—not wasting them, not polluting them, not consuming them too quickly.

In recent years, much has been written about the earth's environment. We read about "the global village." We are warned about oil spills in our oceans, pesticides running into our lakes and streams, smoke and gases polluting the air we breathe, population outpacing our resources, our protective ozone layer being destroyed. We deal with predictions of more skin cancer, more deaths by respiratory diseases, higher ocean levels and consequent flooding of coastal cities, and so on. In short, people are writing about the environment.

The environment may be the most common of causes, because wherever we live we are a part of it. But we do have other common causes: the societal destruction brought on by drugs and other substance abuse, the modern-day plague called AIDS, the escalating cost of education, the charges of decreased learning in education, the reproach of increased homelessness, the perpetual threat of wanton terrorism, the dangers of being on the streets at night, and so on. Common causes are always topics for persuasive writing.

Reading

In the summer of 1988, Senator Albert Gore of Tennessee, chair of the Senate Subcommittee on Science, Space, and Technology, met with scientists, administrators, and political leaders from five continents in a conference to explore environmental issues with the hope of discovering solutions. The essay "What Is Wrong with Us?" is excerpted from his address to that group and was published in a special environmental issue of *Time* magazine. As you read the essay, note how Gore establishes his credibility; how he identifies with, and appeals to, his audience; and how he supports his argument with examples, testimony, statistics, and historical evidence.

What Is Wrong with Us?

Albert Gore

When I announced I was running for President, I said the green- 1
house effect, the depletion of the ozone layer, and the global ecological crisis will, by the end of this election year, be recognized as the most serious issue facing this country and the world. Three days later, a George Will column ridiculed the naiveté of a politician who could imagine that issues of this kind would be politically salable.

I guess he was partly right and partly wrong. I was right in that the 2
issue has, during this year, attained enormous importance and new recognition. But he was right, since it didn't do me any good politically. There are still barriers to political action. Let me discuss five of them.

Number one, there are areas of uncertainty about the greenhouse 3
effect and the dire nature of the ecological crisis we face, which are seized upon as excuses for inaction. This is a psychological problem common to all humanity. If strong responses are needed and yet there is some residual uncertainty about whether you are going to have to make those

responses, the natural psychological tendency is to magnify the uncertainty and say, "Well, maybe we won't really have to face up to it."

But the fact that we face an ecological crisis without any precedent in historic times is no longer a matter of any dispute worthy of recognition. And those who, for the purpose of maintaining balance in debate, take the contrarian view that there is significant uncertainty about whether it's real are hurting our ability to respond. 4

The second barrier to political action is an unwillingness to believe that something so far outside the bounds of historical experience can, in fact, be occurring. To put it another way, this set of problems sounds like the plot of a bad science-fiction movie. People automatically assume it can't be real. 5

The third political barrier is the assumption that it will be easier and more sensible to adapt to whatever climate change occurs than it will be to prevent the crisis. But the change could come so swiftly that adaptation will be all but impossible. 6

The fourth barrier is the lack of widespread awareness among the peoples of the world about the nature of the problem. Most political leaders, let alone their public, are unaware of what is happening and how severe it is. That must be changed. 7

The fifth barrier to political action is the knowledge that many of the ultimate solutions are almost unimaginably difficult. 8

And since they are harder than anything we have done before, and the efforts may all come to naught anyway, why mess with them? Why not conserve our energy and just not even try? That is a formidable barrier, not least because the solutions require international cooperation on a scale that is totally unprecedented in history. 9

Those five barriers must be overcome before the political system reacts. The role of leadership is critical in spreading awareness, in framing solutions, in offering a vision of the future we want to create, as well as a vision of the nightmare we wish to avoid. 10

There is an old science experiment in which a frog is put into a pan of water, and the water is slowly heated to the boiling point. The frog sits there and boils because its nervous system will not react to the gradual increase. But if you boil the water first and then put the frog in it, it immediately jumps out. 11

We are at an environmental boiling point right now. Is the destruction of one football-field's worth of forest every second enough to make the frog react and jump out of the pan? What will it take? If, as in a science-fiction movie, we had a giant invader from space clomping across the rain forests of the world with football field-size feet—going boom, boom, boom every second—would we react? That's essentially what is going on right now. 12

We saw the two whales trapped in the Arctic ice, struggling for air, and the world responded. The United States and the Soviet Union coop- 13 erated. Yet we see 40,000 babies starving every day, and we don't react. What is wrong with us?

There used to be a debate in the '70s about appropriate technology. 14 Now the question is: Did God choose an appropriate technology when he gave human beings dominion over the earth? The jury is still out. And the answer has to come in our lifetime from the political system.

There are precedents. We made human sacrifice, once common- 15 place, obsolete. We made slavery obsolete. These things, just like changes in weather patterns, took a long period of time. But now, just as climate changes are telescoped into a very short period of time, changes in human thinking of a magnitude comparable to the changes that brought about the abolition of slavery must take place in one generation.

We know how to solve the problem. It will be unimaginably difficult. 16 The cooperation required will be unprecedented. But we know what to do. What is required is a change in thinking and a change in the equilibrium of the world's political system.

Right now the political equilibrium is characterized by short-term 17 policies at the expense of long-term policies. It is characterized by actions to confer national advantage at the expense of actions designed to promote global advantage. It is characterized by preparations for war, ignorance, and starvation.

Our challenge as political leaders is to come up with an agenda of 18 solutions, which we are doing. But the larger challenge for all of us is to shift the world's political system into a new state of equilibrium, characterized by more cooperation, global agendas, and a focus on the future. As General Omar Bradley said at the end of World War II, "It is time we steered by the stars and not by the lights of each passing ship."

Questions: The Community of Writers

1. Gore positions himself as an environmentalist-politician addressing the issue of politics and the environment. What evidence do you see of his authority on his subject? How does he establish his credibility?

2. This essay addresses other political leaders. What does Gore propose they do in addition to coming up with a plan for attacking the problem?

3. Given the five "barriers to political action," how possible do you think change is? Which of the barriers do you think is the most formidable?

4. What audience might Gore have besides world political leaders?

5. What does Gore's analogy of the giant and the rain forests tell you about the environmental problem? about Gore? about the knowledge he assumes his audience shares?

6. Examine Gore's essay for other kinds of support. Does he use any statistics? Testimony from experts? Examples other than the analogies? Historical evi-

dence? Opinions? Does he appeal to the beliefs, interests, and values of his audience? What would you say is the most effective support for his argument? Speculate on his choice of kinds of evidence.

Analysis

Gore establishes his credibility in the initial two paragraphs, first by reminding his audience that he had just run for nomination as a candidate for president of the United States and lost and then by declaring himself an environmentalist. In linking the two, observing that his environmental interest did not aid his political aspirations, he introduces the major point of his essay: that politics is not ready to deal with environmental problems.

Audience and Purpose

Even though Gore's essay was addressed to world political leaders for the purpose of influencing them to bring about a change in the world's political system, it has other *audiences*. When it was published in *Time* magazine with Gore's permission, it acquired as its audience all *Time's* subscribers. When it entered this textbook, it gained still another audience—college students who read the text. Do you think the *purpose* of a piece of writing changes as the audience changes? Think first of Gore's purpose for addressing the political leaders, which he makes clear in his final paragraph. Then think of *Time's* purpose for publishing the article in a special environmental issue, which featured on its cover a globe wrapped in knotted ropes as its "Planet of the Year." You might assume that *Time* shares Gore's concern, though the purpose undoubtedly broadened with the wider audience. What reactions might *Time* expect from its readers? Would you say that the essay has the same purpose here in your textbook as it did in *Time* and at the environmental conference?

These are not easy questions, and there are probably no right answers to them, but if you understand what these questions are asking you probably have a good sense of how all aspects of a *rhetorical situation*—writer, audience, subject, and purpose—overlap and interrelate. One change in the triangle of writer, audience, and subject may have a notable effect on the purpose. Though a piece of writing remains the same, its purpose may change as its audience does. You can apply this principle to college writing. If you submit a paper to one teacher according to that teacher's expectations, you may receive an A for it, but when you use the same paper for another class you get a C. Why? Because the rhetorical situation—in this case the teacher's expectations—is different.

Development (analogy, classification, exemplification)

Gore uses *analogies* to illustrate his argument graphically. First with the frog and the boiling water and then with the giant and the rain forests, he tells us something about the environment and our attitude toward it. Analogies are often regarded as a weakness in arguments, because readers can question their validity. Boiling frogs and clomping giants, after all, have very little to do with the environment. At the same time, analogies can be powerfully illustrative. The problem in using them lies in relying too strongly on them, letting them carry the argument.

But Gore uses other methods of developing his argument. After establishing his credibility as a politician who has committed himself to preserving the environment, he divides and **classifies** the problem into what he sees as the major barriers to political action. He thus identifies the issues that must be dealt with. These statements are *informed opinions,* based on *historical evidence* and Gore's political experience dealing with the issues. By examining his essay, you can find other opinions to support his argument. Gore also uses **examples:** He contrasts the international efforts to save two whales with the inaction to save starving babies (using also a *statistic,* the number of starving babies), and he compares the present need for change with precedents, the abolition of human sacrifice and slavery. Finally, he quotes General Omar Bradley, applying Bradley's words to the present context.

Exercise: The Community of Writers

Imagine a piece of your own writing—from an essay to something as simple as a shopping list or a telephone message. Without being changed itself in any way, how would the message change in purpose if it had a different audience? Discuss your perceptions with your classmates.

Exercise: The Exploring Writer

Brainstorm (see Chapter 3) a list of common causes to discover where your interests lie. Let your list lead you to explore a specific issue. Then write a journal entry that speculates on that issue's impact on you and your world.

Writing

What common causes interest you? Do you agree with Senator Gore about the environment? Do you see barriers to political action other than those he names? Are you concerned about a specific aspect of the deteriorating global environment—perhaps something in your own neighborhood? Common causes can have local as well as global implications. Your interest may be as specific as people walking on grass instead of sidewalks or the need for students to collect recyclable containers. You may be concerned about drug use at your school. Or racial or sexual discrimination where you work or go to school. Or ethics in government—local, state, or federal.

Select a subject you are familiar with so you can establish your credibility. Using your journal entry from the preceding exercise as a starting point, think of something you want to say that would persuade others to think or act as you do. You will need to select a realistic audience: fellow students, perhaps, or parents of young children. Related to your selection of audience is your purpose: to convince other students to stay on the sidewalks, to persuade parents to teach recycling habits to their children, and so on. If you like, address your essay to the editor of your school newspaper or some other newspaper, or even write it as a letter to someone who might be able to bring about change—a senator or congressional representative, for example.

Base your persuasion mainly on facts and opinions, using examples, testimony, statistics, and analogies as appropriate. Maintain a reasonable tone, avoiding anger and undue appeals to destructive emotions such as fear and hatred. Use sarcasm only if you are familiar enough with your audience to know it will take your tone as you intend it. To convince your audience, try to see its point of view.

CHALLENGING COMMON ASSUMPTIONS

Say that you are in a parking lot, waiting at a respectable distance as another car backs out of a parking place, and, before you can pull in, someone coming from the other direction slips in ahead of you. You're incensed; you were there first and had a right to the spot. Or say that, after coming in late Saturday night, you want to sleep in on Sunday morning—till 10:30 or so. But at 8:00 A.M. your next-door neighbor is revving up his lawn mower under your window. You're furious; doesn't he know that people don't mow their lawns at eight o'clock on Sunday morning? In each case, the basis of your right is assumption, not law. And that assumption is founded on social conventions.

Our lives are simplified because of the assumptions we make about the world we live in. Because we assume that other automobile drivers will obey the rules of the road—stay on their side of a two-lane highway, stop at red lights, drive with their headlights on at night, and so on—we dare to venture out in our own cars. Because we assume that attending college will provide us with an education to increase our job opportunities and enrich our lives, we commit four or more years to attaining that education. We assume that friends will be loyal, that family will support us through difficult times, that television and newspaper reports of current events are accurate, if not complete.

Our assumptions are not always correct, however. Occasionally people drive on the wrong side of the road, speed through red lights, and drive without their headlights on at night—making life dangerous for us if we happen to be driving by at the time. Friends sometimes betray us, family sometimes is uninterested in our problems, news reports are exaggerated for effect. And the enhancement of our lives from a college education depends more on how much we take than on how much is given.

We can't go about our lives without assumptions based on trust in our fellow human beings. Yet we don't have to be totally trusting. We are alert to other drivers not obeying the rules of the road. We do some research before deciding on a college and question courses and teachers and schools that do not seem to be providing the education we expected. We judge the integrity of our friends and the television news reports.

Persuasive essays sometimes challenge our assumptions. They challenge a university president who assumes he can spend millions to refurbish his official residence, a school system whose students score below the norm on standardized tests, a television evangelist who solicits donations to support missions, a newspaper reporter whose "facts" seem to be invented. Student writers question the value of a textbook, the necessity of grades, the need for gender-free language.

This section has two essays that challenge assumptions, the first concerning what people expect from television, the second concerning what people consider their public rights.

Reading

How much do the media (television, newspapers, magazines, radio) have to do with what you do and think? Does television news decide what you will know about world events? Do the television cameras and newspaper commentaries elect our presidents? Do television commercials and printed advertisements influence you to buy certain products? Do soap operas decide what you're going to do during lunch hour and how you're going to schedule your classes? Media, both print and electronic, are a considerable aspect of our lives—like it or not. And as with most things that are prominent, the media come in for their share of criticism, television perhaps most of all.

Neil Postman is a critic, writer, educator, parent, and communications theorist. One of his books, *Amusing Ourselves to Death: Public Discourse in the Age of Show Business,* exposes everything on television—even news, educational shows, and religious programs—as show business. "The problem," he says, "is not that television presents us with entertaining subject matter but that all subject matter is presented as entertaining, which is another issue altogether." The essay that follows is part of his chapter "Teaching as an Amusing Activity." Read it to discover what assumptions he challenges concerning "Sesame Street," and weigh his position with your own experience. Note his tone and how he supports his argument.

What "Sesame Street" Teaches

Neil Postman

There could not have been a safer bet when it began in 1969 than that "Sesame Street" would be embraced by children, parents, and educators. Children loved it because they were raised on television commercials, which they intuitively knew were the most carefully crafted entertainments on television. To those who had not yet been to school, even to those who had just started, the idea of being *taught* by a series of commercials did not seem peculiar. And that television should entertain them was taken as a matter of course.

Parents embraced "Sesame Street" for several reasons, among them that it assuaged their guilt over the fact that they could not or would not restrict their children's access to television. "Sesame Street" appeared to justify allowing a four- or five-year-old to sit transfixed in front of a television screen for unnatural periods of time. Parents were eager to hope that television could teach their children something other than which breakfast cereal has the most crackle. At the same time, "Sesame Street" relieved them of the responsibility of teaching their preschool children how to read—no small matter in a culture where children are apt to be considered a nuisance. They could also plainly see that in spite of its faults, "Sesame Street" was entirely consonant with the prevailing spirit of America. Its use of cute puppets, celebrities, catchy tunes, and rapid-fire editing was certain to give pleasure to the children and would therefore serve as adequate preparation for their entry into a fun-loving culture.

As for educators, they generally approved of "Sesame Street," too. Contrary to common opinion, they are apt to find new methods congenial, especially if they are told that education can be accomplished more efficiently by means of the new techniques. (That is why such ideas as "teacherproof" textbooks, standardized tests, and, now, micro-computers have been welcomed in the classroom.) "Sesame Street" appeared to be an imaginative aid in solving the growing problem of teaching Americans how to read, while, at the same time, encouraging children to love school.

We now know that "Sesame Street" encourages children to love 4
school only if school is like "Sesame Street." Which is to say, we now know
that "Sesame Street" undermines what the traditional idea of schooling
represents. Whereas a classroom is a place of social interaction, the space
in front of a television set is a private preserve. Whereas in a classroom,
one may ask a teacher questions, one can ask nothing of a television
screen. Whereas school is centered on the development of language,
television demands attention to images. Whereas attending school is a
legal requirement, watching television is an act of choice. Whereas in
school, one fails to attend to the teacher at the risk of punishment, no
penalties exist for failing to attend to the television screen. Whereas to
behave oneself in school means to observe rules of public decorum,
television watching requires no such observances, has no concept of
public decorum. Whereas in a classroom, fun is never more than a means
to an end, on television it is the end in itself.

Yet "Sesame Street" and its progeny, "The Electric Company," are 5
not to be blamed for laughing the traditional classroom out of existence. If the classroom now begins to seem a stale and flat environment
for learning, the inventors of television itself are to blame, not the
Children's Television Workshop. We can hardly expect those who want
to make good television shows to concern themselves with what the
classroom is for. They are concerned with what television is for. This
does not mean that "Sesame Street" is not educational. It is, in fact,
nothing but educational—in the sense that every television show is educational. Just as reading a book—any kind of book—promotes a particular orientation toward learning, watching a television show does the
same. "The Little House on the Prairie," "Cheers," and "The Tonight
Show" are as effective as "Sesame Street" in promoting what might be
called the television style of learning. And this style of learning is, by
its nature, hostile to what has been called book-learning or its hand-
maiden, school-learning. If we are to blame "Sesame Street" for anything, it is for the pretense that it is an ally of the classroom. That,
after all, has been its chief claim on foundation and public money. As
a television show, and a good one, "Sesame Street" does not encourage
children to love school or anything about school. It encourages them
to love television.

Questions: The Community of Writers

1. What assumption about "Sesame Street" does Postman challenge? How does
   he establish his authority to challenge assumptions?

2. What harm does Postman see in the "Sesame Street" style of education?

3. Evaluate Postman's assumptions about classroom learning. Which of these
   would you challenge for accuracy?

4. On the basis of your experience, support or refute Postman's statement that children reared on "Sesame Street" and other educational programs on television expect to be entertained in school.

5. Postman's tone is somewhat sarcastic, especially when he is accounting for the success of "Sesame Street." Which group—children, parents, or educators—receives the worst of Postman's sarcasm?

6. Examine Postman's essay for fallacies in his argument. Which are unacceptable and acceptable in the context?

7. Think of your own experience regarding television. Is Postman correct in his assumptions about the medium? Is he right in challenging those assumptions?

Analysis

"Sesame Street" has "taught" the nation's children for years. You may have watched it as a child and grown familiar with Big Bird and Cookie Monster and other friendly creatures that inhabit the fabled street. Your parents might have thought that watching the show was educational for you, because you were learning your ABC's and your numbers. But Postman charges that "Sesame Street" educates children only toward television-style learning. He does not say that it is a bad program, nor does he say that it is not educational. Postman says that the program teaches children to want their learning to be entertaining. At the end of the chapter from which this essay is excerpted, Postman tells how television's education as entertainment will affect children:

> Mainly, they will have learned that learning is a form of entertainment or, more precisely, that anything worth learning can take the form of an entertainment, and ought to. And they will not rebel if their English teacher asks them to learn the eight parts of speech through the medium of rock music. Or if their social studies teacher sings to them the facts about the War of 1812. Or if their physics comes to them on cookies and T-shirts. Indeed, they will expect it and thus will be well prepared to receive their politics, their religion, their news, and their commerce in the same delightful way.

Thesis and Purpose

Postman states his *thesis* in the fourth paragraph: " 'Sesame Street' undermines what the traditional idea of schooling represents." This is his *arguable proposition.* It has two *unexpressed assumptions:* (1) that "Sesame Street" is something like school, and (2) that traditional schooling is a desirable norm. Unless an audience agrees upon the underlying assumptions of an argument, those assumptions must be supported. Postman supports his first assumption in his first three paragraphs, showing how children, parents, and educators view the television program as similar to school. How does he support the second assumption? And how critical to his argument is his audience's agreement with that assumption?

Think about Postman's purpose for writing this essay. Does it seem that he wants parents to forbid their children to watch "Sesame Street" and other educational-entertainment programs? In this section of his book, at least, he does not seem to be calling for such action. Instead, it seems more likely that he wants to persuade readers to view so-called educational programs as he does—as entertainment. In that case, his thesis may be tied to his final sentence: "It encourages them to love television." In other words, "Sesame Street" and programs like it are acceptable if they're viewed as entertainment, not as education.

Development

As we have seen, Postman's first three paragraphs support the unexpressed assumption of his thesis that "Sesame Street" has been considered educational. After these paragraphs on why the program was widely accepted, paragraph 4 begins the challenge: "We now know. . . ." This paragraph may be Postman's strongest statement on his argument that " 'Sesame Street' undermines what the traditional idea of school represents." In his final paragraph he explains the problem with such programs. Here is a rough outline of the essay's structure:

I. Assumptions about "Sesame Street"
   A. Children love it because it's entertaining.
   B. Parents embrace it because it relieves them of teaching their children.
   C. Educators approve of it because it appears to help them do their jobs.
II. The challenge
   A. Compared with classrooms, "Sesame Street" is more attractive.
   B. The problem with "Sesame Street" is that it undermines traditional schooling.

Postman's argument is based mainly on *informed opinions* and *historical evidence*. The first three paragraphs are mostly opinions. It would be difficult to prove a statement that children accepted "Sesame Street" as a type of commercial, with which they were already familiar, or that parents embraced the show because it was a convenience for them—a baby-sitter, a substitute for their own teaching. This sentence in paragraph 2, "Parents were eager to hope that television could teach their children something other than which breakfast cereal has the most crackle," sounds like a statement of fact, but we have no evidence of its truth, and because of its sarcasm we're not sure if Postman intends it as fact. Postman wants his readers to add support to his argument by recalling their own experiences. In paragraph 4, he develops his contrast of television school with traditional school by a series of "whereas" sentences. These supportive statements are factual and accurate—common knowledge perhaps, but observations that the audience may not have made. The last sentence of the paragraph, however, is opinion again: "Whereas in a classroom, fun is never more than a means to an end, on television it is the end in itself."

You may be able to find some *fallacies* in Postman's argument, *broad generalization,* most notably. In paragraph 3, for example, he says that educators acclaimed "Sesame Street" as an "imaginative aid," which seems to imply that all teachers thought "Sesame Street" was a great idea. In paragraph 1, he states, "Children loved it because they were raised on television commercials," again a broad generalization that assumes all members of the group share the characteristic.

Postman's final paragraph stresses his argument that "Sesame Street" is educational, just as any entertainment is educational, and that it encourages children to love television, not school. In this paragraph in particular, he appeals to the values of his readers to see so-called educational programming for what it is—entertainment.

Tone

The *tone* of Postman's essay might be read as sarcastic. Consider the tone of the following sentence, for example: "Parents were eager to hope that television could teach their children something other than which breakfast cereal has the most crackle." Here, as throughout the essay, Postman satirizes the ready acceptance of "Sesame Street" as entertaining education for children. Do you think the sarcastic tone is appropriate for Postman's purpose? Considering his treatment of the children who grew up with "Sesame Street," the parents who encouraged them to watch it, and the educators who welcomed it as an "imaginative aid," who do you suppose is Postman's intended audience?

Exercise: The Exploring Writer

Write a series of "whereas" sentences like Postman's in paragraph 4. Take a stance either in favor of or against "Sesame Street" or some other television program in which you can make a series of comparisons. In each of your sentences, contrast the program and something not on television, such as books.

Reading

Do you have the right to snap a few photographs of derelicts standing in a doorway, or Mexicans at work, Irish dancers at a local celebration, Native Americans at a reservation store? When is it appropriate to take pictures of other people? Consider another case: Spending the evening with friends, you politely sit through their home slide show with pictures of "natives" watching the affluent Americans point cameras at them. How do you feel? There is no law that prohibits the practice, but when there is no law to govern the exercise of rights, assumptions regarding social conventions must take over.

Social interchange runs on assumptions. Occasionally, however, people challenge those assumptions, as Ellen Goodman does in "Protection from the Prying Camera." As you read, try to determine what Goodman suggests in place of the assumption that we have a right to take pictures of one another. How does she support her argument? Do you note any fallacies? What is her tone?

Protection From the Prying Camera

Ellen Goodman

Maybe it was the year-end picture roundup that finally did it. Maybe it was the double exposure to the same vivid photographs. Or perhaps it was the memory of three amateur photographers carefully standing in the cold last fall, calculating their *f* stops and exposures with light meters, trying to find the best angle, pointing their cameras at a drunk in a doorway. Or maybe it was simply my nine-year-old cousin playing Candid Camera at the family gathering. 1

But whatever the reason, it has finally hit me. We have become a nation of Kodachrome, Nikon, Instamatic addicts. But we haven't yet developed a clear idea of the ethics of picture-taking. We haven't yet determined the parameters of privacy in a world of flash cubes and telescopic lenses. 2

We "take" pictures. As psychologist Stanley Milgram puts it, "A photographer takes a picture, he does not create it or borrow it." But who has given us the right to "take" those pictures and under what circumstances? 3

Since the camera first became portable, we have easily and repeatedly aimed it at public people. It has always been open shooting season on them. With new technology, however, those intrusions have intensified. This year, someone with a camera committed the gross indecency of shooting an unaware Greta Garbo in the nude—and *People* printed it. 4

This year, again, Ron Gallela "took" the image of Jacqueline Onassis and sold it as if it belonged to him. This year, we have pictures of a 5 crumpled Wayne Hays, an indiscreet Nelson Rockefeller, and two presidential candidates in every imaginable pose from the absurd to the embarrassing.

We have accepted the idea that public people are always free targets   6
for the camera—without even a statute of limitations for Jackie or Garbo. We have also accepted the idea that a private person becomes public by being involved in a public event. The earthquake victims of Guatemala, the lynched leftists of Thailand, the terror-stricken of Ireland—their emotions and their bodies become frozen images.

The right of the public to know, to see, and to be affected is consid-   7
ered more important than the right of the individual to mourn, or even die, in privacy.

What happens now, however, when cameras proliferate until they   8
are as common as television sets? What happens when the image being "taken" is that of a butcher, a baker, or a derelict, rather than a public figure? Do we all lose our right to privacy simply by stepping into view?

Should we be allowed to point cameras at each other? To regard each   9
other as objects of art? Does the photographer or the photographed own the image?

Several years ago, *Time* photographer Steve Northup, who had cov-   10
ered Vietnam, and Watergate, took a group of students around Cambridge shooting pictures. He quietly insisted that they ask every pizza-maker, truck driver, and beautician for permission. His attitude toward private citizens was one of careful respect for the power of "exposure." In contrast to this, the average camera bug—like the average tourist—too often goes about snapping "quaint" people, along with "quaint" scenes: See the natives smile, see the natives carrying baskets of fruit, see the native children begging, see the drunk in the doorway. As Milgram wrote, "I find it hard to understand wherein the photographer has derived the right to keep for his own purposes the image of the peasant's face."

Where do we get the right to bring other people home in a canister?   11
Where did we lose the right to control our image?

In a study that Milgram conducted last year, a full 65 percent of the   12
people to whom his students talked in midtown Manhattan refused to have their pictures taken, refused to be photographed. I don't think they were camera shy, in the sense of being vain. Rather, they were reluctant to have their pictures "taken."

The Navahos long believed that the photographer took a piece of   13
them away in his film. Like them, we are coming to understand the power of these frozen images. Photographs can help us to hold on to the truth of our past, to make our history and identity more real. Or they can rip something away from us as precious as the privacy which once clothed Greta Garbo.

Questions: The Community of Writers

1. Which of Goodman's examples did you find most convincing? Which least convincing?

2. What alternative does Goodman suggest to the willy-nilly snapping of pictures?

3. Discuss fallacies in Goodman's argument.

4. How do you feel about being included in Goodman's statement about how "we" feel about picture taking?

5. What facts does Goodman use to support her argument? How does she use examples, testimony, statistics, or historical evidence?

6. Goodman cites the statistic that 65 percent of people surveyed refused to have their pictures taken. She also wonders whether we may all "lose our right to privacy simply by stepping into view." Discuss your attitudes toward taking pictures of people without permission.

Analysis

Even though Goodman's essay was written in 1977, you should have little trouble recalling parallel current instances. Think of public people who have been "exposed" by telephoto lenses, or victims of calamities whose sufferings are laid open to public view. Families of accident victims are interviewed on television. Cameras show drowning victims being pulled from the water. Are these instances all part of the public's right to know? Do you agree with Goodman's challenge to the assumption that we have a right to take whatever pictures we want? Do you think it's acceptable under some circumstances to take pictures of other people? Is there a difference, for instance, between using a telephoto lens to photograph someone in her backyard and snapping someone at a public event?

Thesis

Goodman states her *thesis* in the form of questions:

"Do we all lose our right to privacy simply by stepping into view?"
"Should we be allowed to point cameras at each other?"
"To regard each other as objects of art?"
"Does the photographer or the photographed own the image?"
"Where do we get the right to bring other people home in a canister?"
"Where did we lose the right to control our image?"

Her answers to all her questions are the same: that we do not have the right to "take" pictures of other people without permission. Her arguable proposition is implied in the examples she presents.

Development

Goodman uses the pronoun *we* to present the assumptions she challenges:

> "We have become a nation of Kodachrome, Nikon, Instamatic addicts. But we haven't yet developed a clear idea of the ethics of picture-taking."
> "We have accepted the idea that public people are always free targets for the camera."
> "We have also accepted the idea that a private person becomes public by being involved in a public event."

By *we* Goodman evidently means you and me, as well as all her other readers. Might this phrasing be regarded as the *fallacy* of *broad generalization?*

While her assumptions and some of the support for her argument are her own considered *opinions,* Goodman also rallies some *facts.* She employs testimony several times, quoting psychologist Stanley Milgram and *Time* photographer Steve Northup and reporting a Navaho belief about picture taking. She also includes a *statistic,* that "65 percent of the people to whom [Milgram's] students talked in midtown Manhattan refused to have their pictures taken." And she has *examples* of public people whose private lives have been exposed by the camera.

Tone

Goodman's *tone* seems to be somewhat confrontational. Rather than identifying with her audience, she seems to regard the audience as an adversary. For, even though she says "we," she seems to have separated herself from the rest of the camera bugs ("it has finally hit me"); she might just as well be saying "you." Would the tone be less contentious if she had used third-person: "People haven't yet developed a clear idea of the ethics of picture-taking"? Perhaps her confrontational tone is necessary in an essay that challenges assumptions.

Exercise: The Exploring Writer

Experiment with how tone changes by rewriting the following sentences using third-person nouns and pronouns instead of we *and changing other words that seem too harsh. Then rewrite the sentences again using second-person pronouns:* you. *Which version sounds least confrontational? Which sounds most confrontational?*

1. We have become a nation of Kodachrome, Nikon, Instamatic addicts.
2. But we haven't yet developed a clear idea of the ethics of picture-taking.

3. We haven't yet determined the parameters of privacy in a world of flash cubes and telescopic lenses.
4. We "take" pictures.
5. Since the camera first became portable, we have easily and repeatedly aimed it at public people.
6. We have accepted the idea that public people are always free targets for the camera.
7. Where do we get the right to bring other people home in a canister?

Writing

Write a persuasive essay that, like Postman's "What 'Sesame Street' Teaches" and Goodman's "Protection from the Prying Camera," challenges a common assumption. Like Postman, you might examine an assumption about media—television, radio, newspapers, or magazines—such as one of these:

- Television news—not news but entertainment
- Soap operas—not pulp but therapy
- Docudramas—not truth but lies
- Newsmagazines (or television newsmagazines)—not news but unethical sensationalism

Or consider challenging a custom built into societal interchanges, such as one of these ideas:

- It's all right to dig through other people's trash cans.
- "Finders keepers"—it's all right to keep what you find.
- It's all right to break a date if a better one comes along.
- It's all right to cheat on tests as long as you don't get caught.

Examine your thesis for unexpressed assumptions that may need to be supported. In developing your essay, specify what common assumption you are challenging and then state your challenge, using appropriate evidence. You may want to present a new idea of the ethics concerning your subject or another way of viewing it. If you think you can handle a sarcastic or confrontational tone, try it; or write in a straightforward, serious tone. Give some thought to who your audience will be, and try to identify with that audience.

ADDITIONAL READINGS FOR DISCUSSION

Reading

Perhaps the most famous persuasive document in the United States is the Declaration of Independence, written primarily by Thomas Jefferson and adopted by the Second Continental Congress on July 4, 1776. This document presented reasons why the thirteen American colonies should declare themselves politically independent of Great Britain. As you read, examine its tone and look for types of evidence: examples, testimony, statistics, historical facts, and informed opinions.

The Declaration of Independence

Thomas Jefferson et al.

In Congress, July 4, 1776. The unanimous Declaration of the thirteen united States of America,

When in the Course of human events, it becomes necessary for one   1
people to dissolve the political bands which have connected them with another, and to assume among the powers of the earth, the separate and equal station to which the Laws of Nature and of Nature's God entitle them, a decent respect to the opinions of mankind requires that they should declare the causes which impel them to the separation.—

We hold these truths to be self-evident, that all men are created   2
equal, that they are endowed by their Creator with certain unalienable Rights, that among these are Life, Liberty, and the pursuit of Happiness.—

That to secure these rights, Governments are instituted among Men,   3
deriving their just powers from the consent of the governed,—

That whenever any Form of Government becomes destructive of   4
these ends, it is the Right of the People to alter or to abolish it, and to institute new Government, laying its foundation on such principles and organizing its powers in such form, as to them shall seem most likely to effect their Safety and Happiness. Prudence, indeed, will dictate that Governments long established should not be changed for light and transient causes; and accordingly all experience hath shown, that mankind are more disposed to suffer, while evils are sufferable, than to right themselves by abolishing the forms to which they are accustomed. But when a long train of abuses and usurpations, pursuing invariably the same Object evinces a design to reduce them under absolute Despotism,

it is their right, it is their duty, to throw off such Government, and to provide new Guards for their future security.—

Such has been the patient sufferance of these Colonies; and such is   5 now the necessity which constrains them to alter their former Systems of Government. The history of the present King of Great Britain is a history of repeated injuries and usurpations, all having in direct object the establishment of an absolute Tyranny over these States. To prove this, let Facts be submitted to a candid world.—

He has refused his Assent to Laws, the most wholesome and neces-   6 sary for the public good.—

He has forbidden his Governors to pass Laws of immediate and   7 pressing importance, unless suspended in their operation till his Assent should be obtained; and when so suspended, he has utterly neglected to attend to them.—

He has refused to pass other Laws for the accommodation of large   8 districts of people, unless those people would relinquish the right of Representation in the Legislature, a right inestimable to them and formidable to tyrants only.—

He has called together legislative bodies at places unusual, uncom-   9 fortable, and distant from the depository of their public Records, for the sole purpose of fatiguing them into compliance with his measures.—

He has dissolved Representative Houses repeatedly, for opposing   10 with manly firmness his invasions on the rights of the people.—

He has refused for a long time, after such dissolutions, to cause   11 others to be elected; whereby the Legislative powers, incapable of Annihilation, have returned to the People at large for their exercise; the State remaining in the mean time exposed to all the dangers of invasion from without, and convulsions within.—

He has endeavored to prevent the population of these States; for that   12 purpose obstructing the Laws for Naturalization of Foreigners; refusing to pass others to encourage their migrations hither, and raising the conditions of new Appropriations of Lands.—

He has obstructed the Administration of Justice, by refusing his   13 Assent to Laws for establishing Judiciary powers.—

He has made judges dependent on his Will alone, for the tenure of   14 their offices, and the amount and payment of their salaries.—

He has erected a multitude of New Offices, and sent hither swarms   15 of Officers to harass our people, and eat out their substance.—

He has kept among us in times of peace, Standing Armies without   16 the Consent of our legislatures.—

He has affected to render the Military independent of and superior   17 to the Civil power.—

He has combined with others to subject us to a jurisdiction foreign   18 to our constitution, and unacknowledged by our laws; giving his Assent to their Acts of pretended Legislation:—

For quartering large bodies of armed troops among us:—   19

For protecting them, by a mock Trial, from punishment for any   20
Murders which they should commit on the Inhabitants of these States:—

For cutting off our Trade with all parts of the world:—   21

For imposing Taxes on us without our Consent:—   22

For depriving us in many cases, of the benefits of Trial by jury:—   23

For transporting us beyond Seas to be tried for pretended   24
offences:—

For abolishing the free System of English Laws in a neighboring   25
Province, establishing therein an Arbitrary government, and enlarging
its Boundaries so as to render it at once an example and fit instrument
for introducing the same absolute rule in these Colonies:—

For taking away our Charters, abolishing our most valuable Laws, and   26
altering fundamentally the Forms of our Governments:—

For suspending our own Legislatures, and declaring themselves in   27
vested with power to legislate for us in all cases whatsoever.—

He has abdicated Government here, by declaring us out of his Pro-   28
tection and waging War against us.—

He has plundered our seas, ravaged our Coasts, burnt our towns, and   29
destroyed the lives of our people.—

He is at this time transporting large Armies of foreign Mercenaries   30
to compleat the works of death, desolation, and tyranny, already begun
with circumstances of Cruelty & perfidy scarcely paralleled in the most
barbarous ages, and totally unworthy the Head of a civilized nation.—

He has constrained our fellow Citizens taken Captive on high Seas to   31
bear Arms against their Country, to become the executioners of their
friends and Brethren, or to fall themselves by their Hands.—

He has excited domestic insurrections amongst us, and has endeav-   32
oured to bring on the inhabitants of our frontiers, the merciless Indian
Savages, whose known rule of warfare, is an undistinguished destruction
of all ages, sexes, and conditions.

In every stage of these Oppressions We have Petitioned for Redress   33
in the most humble terms: Our repeated Petitions have been answered
only by repeated injury. A Prince, whose character is thus marked by
every act which may define a Tyrant, is unfit to be the ruler of a free
people.

Nor have We been wanting in attentions to our British brethren. We   34
have warned them from time to time of attempts by their legislature to
extend an unwarrantable jurisdiction over us. We have reminded them
of the circumstances of our emigration and settlement here. We have
appealed to their native justice and magnanimity, and we have conjured
them by the ties of our common kindred to disavow these usurpations,
which, would inevitably interrupt our connections and correspondence.
They too have been deaf to the voice of justice and of consanguinity.
We must, therefore, acquiesce in the necessity, which denounces our

Separation, and hold them, as we hold the rest of mankind, Enemies in War, in Peace Friends.—

We, therefore, the Representatives of the United States of America, in General Congress, Assembled, appealing to the Supreme Judge of the world for the rectitude of our intentions, do, in the Name, and by Authority of the good People of these Colonies, solemnly publish and declare, That these United Colonies are, and of Right ought to be, Free and Independent States; that they are Absolved from all Allegiance to the British Crown, and that all political connection between them and the State of Great Britain, is and ought to be totally dissolved; and that as Free and Independent States, they have full Power to levy War, conclude Peace, contract Alliances, establish Commerce, and do all other Acts and Things which Independent States may of right do.— 35

And for the support of this Declaration, with a firm reliance on the protection of divine Providence, we mutually pledge to each other our Lives, our Fortunes, and our sacred Honor. 36

Questions: The Community of Writers

1. When Jefferson says "we," as in paragraph 2, who does he mean?
2. After careful reading, who do you think was the intended audience for the Declaration?
3. What is the purpose of the Declaration?
4. What is the purpose of including the long list of abuses committed by Great Britain in the person of King George III?
5. Considering the audience and purpose of the Declaration, what is the reason for including paragraphs 3 and 4 on the legality of governments?
6. How is the credibility of the signers established?
7. What is the tone of the document? Name some specific determinants of its tone.
8. What type of evidence is most common in the Declaration? What other types of evidence lend support? Give examples.

Reading

In the essay that follows, newspaper columnist Sydney J. Harris reveals a little-known aspect of the Declaration of Independence—an excluded clause that might have altered the course of history had it not been deleted in a political compromise. In this cause-and-effect essay, he deals with both actual effects and conjectural ones.

High Cost of Compromise

Sydney J. Harris

Schoolchildren who are taken on visits to Washington generally tour   1
the Library of Congress. There, in a glass cage, they can see a copy of the
Declaration of Independence. But this is not a copy of the original
Declaration as written by Thomas Jefferson.

The original sheets, which have been seen only by officials and   2
scholars, are kept in a safe, and they contain a clause which was omitted
from all later copies. No reference is ever made to it in history classes.

In this clause, Jefferson denounces King George and the British   3
government for acquiescing in slavery and the slave trade. The clause was
knocked out by pressure groups from the South, who agreed to accept
other parts of the Declaration only if this part were deleted.

Nobody knows, of course, what history "might have been," but it   4
seems reasonable to assume that the whole social pattern of our country
would have been different if the clause against the slave trade had
remained in the Declaration, putting the new nation on record as favor-
ing its abolition, along with the other civilized nations of the time.

We would have abolished slavery when it was comparatively easy to   5
do so, and the whole tragic and inconclusive episode of the Civil War
would have been averted—an episode for which America is still paying a
heavy price today.

This is the terrible paradox of politics—that, by its very nature, it is   6
incapable of solving basic political problems. For the essence of politics
is compromise, and Jefferson was forced to compromise his ideals and his
good sense in order to obtain the requisite signatures on the Declaration.

But political compromise usually defers, rather than resolves. It   7
closes its eyes to the deeper causes of a problem, in order to treat its
symptoms—and meanwhile, since the causes go unchecked, the disease
breaks out in more virulent form in the future.

The delegates from South Carolina and Georgia, who pressured   8
Jefferson to delete the slavery clause, were also politicians fighting for
what they thought were their regional advantages. But slavery actually
dragged down the South in the long run, and the Civil War engendered
only bitterness and revenge. Slavery deformed the Negro, denigrated the
South, and dragged its evil consequences into the Twentieth Century.

All political issues, if they are fundamental, are at bottom moral   9
issues. They cannot be settled at the political level, and certainly not at
the military level. Yet we cannot work out our moral problems outside the
political process, outside the give-and-take of practical compromise. That
is why genuine progress is so slow. As a man, Jefferson knew slavery was
wrong; as a politician, he had to condone it. And we pay the price.

Questions: The Community of Writers

1. What clause does Harris say was omitted from the Declaration of Independence for political reasons?

2. What does Harris identify as implications of this political compromise?

3. The development of Harris's essay is basically cause and effect. What are the actual effects, and what are the conjectural ones?

4. Explore the following implications and extend them as far as you can:
   a. Civil War averted
   b. Negro slavery ended

5. Read "I Have a Dream" by Martin Luther King, Jr., on page 232, particularly paragraphs 3 and 4, and relate them to Harris's essay.

Reading

Milton Friedman wrote "Prohibition and Drugs" in 1972. With some updating on types of drugs available and their sources, the essay still is timely. Drugs are even more of a problem now than they were then, and legalization is still occasionally presented as a solution. Friedman's major support for his proposal to legalize drugs is an analogy with the prohibition of alcohol. As you read, ask yourself if this analogy is valid.

Prohibition and Drugs

Milton Friedman

"The reign of tears is over. The slums will soon be only a memory. We 1
will turn our prisons into factories and our jails into storehouses and corncribs. Men will walk upright now, women will smile, and the children will laugh. Hell will be forever for rent."

This is how Billy Sunday, the noted evangelist and leading crusader 2
against Demon Rum, greeted the onset of Prohibition in early 1920. We know now how tragically his hopes were doomed. New prisons and jails had to be built to house the criminals spawned by converting the drinking of spirits into a crime against the state. Prohibition undermined respect for the law, corrupted the minions of the law, created a decadent moral climate—but did not stop the consumption of alcohol.

Despite this tragic object lesson, we seem bent on repeating precisely 3
the same mistake in the handling of drugs.

On ethical grounds, do we have the right to use the machinery of 4
government to prevent an individual from becoming an alcoholic or a drug addict? For children, almost everyone would answer at least a qualified yes. But for responsible adults, I, for one, would answer no.

Reason with the potential addict, yes. Tell him the consequences, yes. Pray for and with him, yes. But I believe that we have no right to use force, directly or indirectly, to prevent a fellow man from committing suicide, let alone from drinking alcohol or taking drugs.

I readily grant that the ethical issue is difficult and that men of goodwill may well disagree. Fortunately, we need not resolve the ethical issue to agree on policy. *Prohibition is an attempted cure that makes matters worse—for both the addict and the rest of us.* Hence, even if you regard present policy toward drugs as ethically justified, considerations of expediency make that policy most unwise.

Consider first the addict. Legalizing drugs might increase the number of addicts, but it is not clear that it would. Forbidden fruit is attractive, particularly to the young. More important, many drug addicts are deliberately made by pushers, who give likely prospects their first few doses free. It pays the pusher to do so because, once hooked, the addict is a captive customer. If drugs were legally available, any possible profit from such inhumane activity would disappear, since the addict could buy from the cheapest source.

Whatever happens to the number of addicts, the individual addict would clearly be far better off if drugs were legal. Today, drugs are both incredibly expensive and highly uncertain in quality. Addicts are driven to associate with criminals to get the drugs, become criminals themselves to finance the habit, and risk constant danger of death and disease.

Consider next the rest of us. Here the situation is crystal-clear. The harm to us from the addiction of others arises almost wholly from the fact that drugs are illegal. A recent committee of the American Bar Association estimated that addicts commit one-third to one-half of all street crime in the United States. Legalize drugs, and street crime would drop automatically.

Moreover, addicts and pushers are not the only ones corrupted. Immense sums are at stake. It is inevitable that some relatively low-paid police and other government officials—and some high-paid ones as well—will succumb to the temptation to pick up easy money.

Legalizing drugs would simultaneously reduce the amount of crime and raise the quality of law enforcement. Can you conceive of any other measure that would accomplish so much to promote law and order?

But, you may say, must we accept defeat? Why not simply end the drug traffic? That is where experience under Prohibition is most relevant. We cannot end the drug traffic. We may be able to cut off opium from Turkey—but there are innumerable other places where the opium poppy grows. With French cooperation, we may be able to make Marseilles an unhealthy place to manufacture heroin—but there are innumerable other places where the simple manufacturing operations involved can be carried out. So long as large sums of money are involved—and they are bound to be if drugs are illegal—it is literally hopeless to expect to end the traffic or even reduce seriously its scope.

In drugs, as in other areas, persuasion and example are likely to be far more effective than the use of force to shape others in our image.   12

Questions: The Community of Writers

1. Update paragraph 11 with more recent details.
2. We are still unable to refute Friedman's statement in paragraph 11, "We cannot end the drug traffic." Cite other statements in the essay that are still true.
3. How analogous are drugs and alcohol? Discuss also the validity of the analogy relating the present era to the time of Prohibition.
4. In addition to his major analogy, how does Friedman support his argument?
5. Friedman makes a number of statements that border on fallacies; for example, in paragraph 10, "Legalizing drugs would simultaneously reduce the amount of crime and raise the quality of law enforcement." Find other statements that are not adequately supported.

Readings

Here are two essays about hunting, the first by *Time* magazine contributor John Skow and the second by Universal Press Syndicate writer James Kilpatrick. You will find that these writers, while viewing hunting from opposite sides, have some common ground. Both also take a satirical stance, but notice how satire can have a variety in tone.

Heroes, Bears, and True Baloney

John Skow

Let's say that I am the benevolent and enlightened despot of my exasperating homeland, the U.S.A., and can eliminate any stupidity or foolishness by waving my hand. I have already banished basketball coaches, light beer, and neckties. Now, on the third or fourth day of hand waving, will I decide to ban hunting? My local newspaper, the Concord, N.H., *Monitor,* reports that black bears have migrated southward in our state. I knew this already. I haven't had the luck to see one, but a few weeks ago a neighbor saw three of them, presumably a female and two cubs, at the edge of a pond a few hundred feet from my house in central New Hampshire. We can all rest easy, however, because the state's fish and game commission has opened a five-week bear-hunting season in our county. Since October 1, the hairy-eared fellows who keep two big-game   1 rifles racked in the back windows of their pickups fifty-two weeks each year, in case World War III starts, have been blasting away at the hairy-eared invaders.

The *Monitor* story told of a local farmer who had been pestered by bears getting into his feed corn. Had to shoot two last year, he said. A fish-and-game-commission biologist said, "Rather than have farmers kill the bears, we would rather have sportsmen utilize the resource." You get used to blood-sport bureaucratese; "utilize," or "harvest," is what you do when you get something fuzzy and four-footed in your sights. As in most states, New Hampshire's fish and game policies often seem to be caught in a time warp, perhaps in the decade of the 1820s, when subsistence hunting was an important food source for most families. Bears, these days, behave like large raccoons. They are smart, cute, hungry corn thieves and garbage raiders, happy in the suburbs and virtually harmless. Last year the state paid less than $7,000 to corn farmers because of bear damage. This is a tolerable figure. It would cost more to keep a bear in the zoo. A citizen determined to be grumpy might reflect that while the last recorded human fatality from a bear attack in New Hampshire was in the 1700s, the last recorded human death from a hunter's blunder was last week.

The fact is that in New Hampshire, it is hunters, not bears or deer or moose, that are troublesome pests. For most of the fall, shooting of some kind is legal, and while I am willing to risk a peppering of bird shot, I don't want to be hulled by the antitank ammunition used for bear or moose (fifty-nine moose no longer menace us as the result of a recent three-day shooting season). So most of us stay out of the woods during the year's most beautiful season. Once, during deer season, I rounded a turn on a logging road while running with my dogs. A couple of heroes were sitting in a pickup truck, drinking beer. One had his rifle trained on my midsection. If he had killed me, he would have received a severe talking-to from the authorities. No one I mentioned this to was surprised. They all had similar stories.

So here I sit, leafing through *Meditations on Hunting* by José Ortega y Gasset, who never jumped deer from a pickup truck. His book is a classy volume that hunters like my friend George Butler give, with wry smiles, to nonhunters like me. Butler is a gifted documentary filmmaker (*Pumping Iron* and *Pumping Iron II: The Women*) who was raised in Somalia and Kenya when hunting was a natural way of living in the great, broad grassland. His new documentary, called *In the Blood* and shot in Tanzania, is about hunting. The action builds toward a scene in which his eleven-year-old son Tyssen shoots his first buffalo and is "blooded"—his forehead is smeared with the animal's blood—by a celebrated hunter, Robin Hurt. "Today you were part of nature," Hurt tells the boy. "It is also a sad occasion . . ." This is baloney, of course, but it is true baloney, like the guff about climbing a mountain because it is there. I am not so sure about another remark in the film, that killing is a way of taking responsibility for what you eat. I can't take responsibility for eating meat without hunting, or spending my vacation hacking up beef quarters at an Armour plant.

Still, Hurt is a serious man who believes that Kenya's decision to ban hunting in 1977 has led to the near extinction of elephants there. In the old days his clients and those of other hunters killed about 200 bulls a year, from an elephant population of about 160,000. When the hunters were forced out and game officials no longer patrolled the bush, gangs of ivory poachers moved in from Sudan and Somalia. Hurt is not optimistic about the future of animals or hunters in East Africa. "I don't think we're there for long," he says. But never mind Africa; it's truth time at home: Do I wave my despotic hand and ban hunting in the United States? (Silence. More silence; the despot is thinking hard.) At last, the answer is: no.

It is a glum, unconfident no. The fact is that hunters are pests. Their blather about improving wildlife is mostly self-serving (though the effective Ducks Unlimited effort to preserve wetlands is both self-serving and environment-serving, which is fair enough). But we all need true baloney, even the armed innocents from Massachusetts who drive up here, see three trees standing together in my side yard, and think they have discovered the Big Woods. Their fantasy is bloody and obsolete, but hunting gives them something they can't get watching golf on the tube. Theodore Roosevelt wrote of the hunting life that "when it is gone, there can be no substitute." Probably true, for good or not.

And the bears? Ah, the bears. They have put up with people for a long time. Hunters will kill them, and fish and game will close the season next year. And five or ten years from now, with luck, they will again begin to repopulate central New Hampshire. Maybe then I will see one.

Some Hunting Protesters Are Overzealous Hypocrites

James Kilpatrick

The hunter who appeared on the television screen a few days ago was doing a great job of holding his temper. He was being badgered by a willowy fellow with long hair whose purpose was to spoil the hunter's day. Looking at the screen, I kept hoping the hunter would punch this milksop zealot in the snoot.

It appears that people who profess to be animal lovers are waging a concerted effort this year. In Hawaii they are mad about dolphins as swimming companions. Elsewhere they are out to ruin the lives of trappers who depend upon the fur trade for a living.

The particular game this season appears to involve the provocative harassment of law-abiding sportsmen in the field. Having alerted local TV stations, the animal lovers turn up on public lands where hunting is permitted. There they ring cowbells or take to bullhorns, the better to frighten game. They chase wildly after hunters, asking insipid questions, and the TV cameramen chase wildly after the troublemakers. All this is supposed to preserve wildlife.

One young woman pronounced that "we have as much right as the hunters to do what we please on public lands." Up to a point, this is true. But no one has a constitutional right to interfere physically with the lawful conduct of another. Free speech has its limits, and the animal lovers, so-called, are breaching them.   4

I say "so-called," because one wonders about those who agitate in the name of animal rights. It seems unlikely that all of them are barefoot vegetarians. More probably they eat meat now and then. They may have enjoyed turkey for Thanksgiving. Their diet may include fish, lobster, and crab. If so, then the weight of their hypocrisy must be a terrible weight to bear.   5

Dan Matthews, director of the anti-fur campaign of People for the Ethical Treatment of Animals, finds it morally wrong for people to wear fur. Does the gentleman wear shoes? Does he hold up his pants with a leather belt? Does he find it morally wrong to have bacon with his eggs? If not, why not? The moral distinction between shooting a deer in the wild and slaughtering a pig in a plant is not immediately apparent.   6

In the television incident that involved the Gucci-Pucci pest and the hunter, the ostensible object was to prevent the killing of deer. Let me tell you something about deer. I have lived for twenty-four years in the Blue Ridge Mountains of Virginia. In these parts we are overrun with deer. The animals can destroy a vineyard or devastate a young apple orchard overnight. They are a positive menace on rural roads. Every year hunters take 120,000 deer in Virginia, and the deer population is not affected at all. State wildlife biologists place the deer population at between 750,000 and 1 million.   7

Most of the deer hunters in my county are local hunters. It seems not to have occurred to the Gucci-Puccis that in our low-income area, a deer represents 80 pounds of dressed meat in the freezer. Mountain men are feeding their families. They hunt as a way of life, as their fathers and grandfathers hunted before them.   8

A personal word: I do not hunt. The only gun on our farm is an ancient double-barreled .410 that belonged to my father-in-law. He was a self-taught naturalist who loved and respected all of God's creatures and treated them with respect, and he taught me his values. I fought for adoption of the Endangered Species Act; I have defended snail darters, sea turtles, dune mice, and spotted owls. The abuse of animals in laboratory experiments arouses me to fury.   9

But fanaticism in any form has small appeal, and the thought will not go away that the pro-animal nuts are as offensive as the pro-gun nuts.   10

They are equally nuts. And when it comes to the supposed evils of hunting, let it be said for the record that hunters do more toward the preservation of wildlife than whole battalions of publicity-seeking panty-waists have ever done.

Since enactment of the Pitman-Robertson Act of 1937, wild game   11
hunters have provided more than $2 billion toward the care and propagation of wild animals. Through the duck stamp program, other hunters have preserved wetlands and developed breeding grounds for waterfowl that otherwise would have been lost. These are the true lovers of nature.

The thought will not go away that in harassing the deer hunters, the   12
willowy boys and the earnest girls are not wholly concerned with prolonging the life of a deer. Their companion purpose lies in preventing the pleasure of the hunter. It is a new Puritanism, as selfish and censorious as the old.

Questions: The Community of Writers

1. Collaboratively paraphrase the thesis, or position on hunting, of each writer.
2. What is the occasion that instigated each essay?
3. Compare the two essays for support. How do they use examples, testimony, statistics, and opinion?
4. What points do Skow and Kilpatrick agree on? On what do they disagree? On what do they seem to disagree most strongly?
5. Compare the essays' tone. What is the tone of each? How does each essayist establish his tone?
6. How does each writer establish his credibility on the subject of hunting? How credible is each?
7. In "Thinking Like a Mountain" in Chapter 6, Aldo Leopold makes a point similar to Kilpatrick's, that unhunted deer herds destroy vegetation. Yet, with similarities to Skow's essay, he regrets having killed wolves when he was younger. Where do you stand on hunting? Is it destructive or constructive? Should wild animals be killed for sport? For their meat? How should hunting be regulated?
8. What other questions does the hunting issue raise?

Reading

Cultural diversity initiatives are changing campuses and higher education. Some people favor these changes and others oppose them. Essayist Barbara Ehrenreich takes on both views and, from her own experience, tries to resolve them. As you read, determine what the issues are and what Ehrenreich's position is.

Teach Diversity—with a Smile

Barbara Ehrenreich

Something had to replace the threat of communism, and at last a   1
workable substitute is at hand. "Multiculturalism," as the new menace is
known, has been denounced in the media recently as the new McCar-
thyism, the new fundamentalism, even the new totalitarianism—take
your choice. According to its critics, who include a flock of tenured
conservative scholars, multiculturalism aims to toss out what it sees as the
Eurocentric bias in education and replace Plato with Ntozake Shange
and traditional math with the Yoruba number system. And that's just the
beginning. The Jacobins of the multiculturalist movement, who are described derisively as P.C., or politically correct, are said to have launched
a campus reign of terror against those who slip and innocently say
"freshman" instead of "freshperson," "Indian" instead of "Native American" or may Goddess forgive them, "disabled" instead of "differently
abled."

So you can see what is at stake here: freedom of speech, freedom of   2
thought, Western civilization and a great many professional egos. But
before we get carried away by the mounting backlash against multiculturalism, we ought to reflect for a moment on the system that the P.C.
people aim to replace. I know all about it; in fact it's just about all I *do*
know, since I—along with so many educated white people of my generation—was a victim of monoculturalism.

American history, as it was taught to us, began with Columbus'   3
"discovery" of an apparently unnamed, unpeopled America, and moved
on to the Pilgrims serving pumpkin pie to a handful of grateful red-
skinned folks. College expanded our horizons with courses called Humanities or sometimes Civ, which introduced us to a line of thought that
started with Homer, worked its way through Rabelais and reached a
poignant climax in the pensées of Matthew Arnold. Graduate students
wrote dissertations on what long-dead men had thought of Chaucer's
verse or Shakespeare's dramas; foreign languages meant French or German. If there had been a high technology in ancient China, kingdoms in
black Africa or women anywhere, at any time, doing anything worth
noticing, we did not know it, nor did anyone think to tell us.

Our families and neighborhoods reinforced the dogma of   4
monoculturalism. In our heads, most of us '50s teenagers carried around
a social map that was about as useful as the chart that guided Columbus
to the "Indies." There were "Negroes," "whites" and "Orientals," the latter
meaning Chinese and "Japs." Of religions, only three were known—Prot-
estant, Catholic and Jewish—and not much known about the last two
types. The only remaining human categories were husbands and wives,
and that was all the diversity the monocultural world could handle. Gays,

lesbians, Buddhists, Muslims, Malaysians, Mormons, etc. were simply off the map.

So I applaud—with one hand, anyway—the multiculturalist goal of preparing us all for a wider world. The other hand is tapping its fingers impatiently, because the critics are right about one thing: when advocates of multiculturalism adopt the haughty stance of political correctness, they quickly descend to silliness or worse. It's obnoxious, for example, to rely on university administrations to enforce P.C. standards of verbal inoffensiveness. Racist, sexist and homophobic thoughts cannot, alas, be abolished by fiat but only by the time-honored methods of persuasion, education and exposure to the other guy's—or excuse me, women's point of view.

And it's silly to mistake verbal purification for genuine social reform. Even after all women are "Ms." and all people are "he or she" women will still earn 65¢ for every dollar earned by men. Minorities by any other name, such as "people of color," will still bear a hugely disproportionate burden of poverty and discrimination. Disabilities are not just "different abilities" when there are not enough ramps for wheelchairs, signers for the deaf or special classes for the "specially" endowed. With all due respect for the new politesse, actions still speak louder than fashionable phrases.

But the worst thing about the P.C. people is that they are such poor advocates for the multicultural cause. No one was ever won over to a broader, more inclusive view of life by being bullied or relentlessly "corrected." Tell a 19-year-old white male that he can't say "girl" when he means "teen-age woman," and he will most likely snicker. This may be the reason why, despite the conservative alarms, P.C.-ness remains a relatively tiny trend. Most campuses have more serious and ancient problems: faculties still top-heavy with white males of the monocultural persuasion; fraternities that harass minorities and women; date rape; alcohol abuse; and tuition that excludes all but the upper fringe of the middle class.

So both sides would be well-advised to lighten up. The conservatives ought to realize that criticisms of the great books approach to learning do not amount to totalitarianism. And the advocates of multiculturalism need to regain the sense of humor that enabled their predecessors in the struggle to coin the term P.C. years ago—not in arrogance but in self-mockery.

Beyond that, both sides should realize that the beneficiaries of multi-culturalism are not only the "oppressed peoples" on the standard P.C. list (minorities, gays, etc.). The "unenlightened"—the victims of mono-culturalism—are oppressed too, or at least deprived. Our educations, whether at Yale or at State U, were narrow and parochial and left us ill-equipped to navigate a society that truly is multicultural and is becoming more so every day. The culture that we studied was, in fact, *one* culture and, from a world perspective, all too limited and ingrown. Diversity is challenging, but those of us who have seen the alternative know it is also richer, livelier and ultimately more fun.

Questions: The Community of Writers

1. What is Ehrenreich's thesis?
2. How does Ehrenreich's view of multiculturalism compare with practice on your campus?
3. What assumptions does she make about her audience?
4. How does she establish her credibility to write about cultural diversity?
5. What other appeals does she use to support her position?

Reading

President Abraham Lincoln's Gettysburg Address, delivered at Gettysburg, Pennsylvania, in March 1863, has long been viewed as a model of concise rhetoric. In these 260 words dedicating the cemetery where thousands of Civil War dead had been hastily buried, Lincoln uses powerful language and familiar stylistic devices to express his regret for the lost lives and his resolution to maintain the nation created with the Declaration of Independence in 1776.

Address at the Dedication of the Gettysburg National Cemetery

Abraham Lincoln

Four score and seven years ago our fathers brought forth on this 1 continent, a new nation, conceived in Liberty and dedicated to the proposition that all men are created equal.

Now we are engaged in a great civil war, testing whether that nation, 2 or any nation so conceived and so dedicated, can long endure. We are met on a great battlefield of that war. We have come to dedicate a portion of that field as a final resting-place for those who here gave their lives that the nation might live. It is altogether fitting and proper that we should do this.

But, in a larger sense, we cannot dedicate—we cannot consecrate— 3 we cannot hallow—this ground. The brave men, living and dead, who struggled here have consecrated it, far above our poor power to add or detract. The world will little note, nor long remember what we say here, but it can never forget what they did here. It is for us the living, rather, to be dedicated here to the unfinished work which they who fought here have thus far so nobly advanced. It is rather for us to be here dedicated to the great task remaining before us—that from these honored dead we take increased devotion to that cause for which they gave the last full measure of devotion; that we here highly resolve that these dead shall not have died in vain; that this nation, under God, shall have a new birth of freedom and that government of the people, by the people, for the people, shall not perish from the earth.

Questions: The Community of Writers

1. The parallel structure of Lincoln's final sentence—"of the people, by the people, for the people"—is often quoted as an example of effective repetition. Find other examples of parallel words and repetitive structures. Refer to the Community of Writers exercise on page 9 for a discussion of these stylistic devices.

2. Lincoln's audience was whoever attended the dedication ceremony—probably many dignitaries and families of the dead soldiers—a more or less general audience. Analyze the diction of this address and consider how word usage might have changed since 1863. Are there any words a president would not use today, considering the audience?

3. Analyze the address for sentence length. How many words does Lincoln use in each sentence? What do your findings tell you about sentence length?

4. Presidents Abraham Lincoln and Thomas Jefferson are often compared, having both been lawyers and effective U.S. Presidents coming from widely different backgrounds. Lincoln begins his address by citing the Declaration of Independence, written by Jefferson. Compare Lincoln's address to the Declaration (pages 191–194). You might look at style, purpose, occasion, and intended audience. What similarities do you find in subject matter?

CHAPTER 8

Writing to Entertain and Move

> *If we arouse in someone an attitude of sympathy toward*
> *something, we may be starting him on the road towards*
> *overtly sympathetic action with regard to it.*
> —*Kenneth Burke*

Entertaining and moving are related purposes for writing. **Moving** stirs the emotions of readers, sometimes to encourage some kind of action, sometimes to engender empathy for others. People may be moved to pity, anger, fear—a whole host of emotions. **Entertaining** moves an audience too. It moves to pleasure—with humor, for example, or with a good story and a harmonious combination of word sounds. Both entertaining and moving thus appeal to the emotions of the audience. They usually accompany other purposes for writing, such as persuasion or information.

Shared Experiences

To achieve the aim of entertaining or moving, the writer's primary need is to understand the audience. A writer must know what is important to and what interests the audience. The writer must actually be, or give the impression of being, at one with the audience, sharing similar backgrounds. Entertaining and moving, more even than informing and persuading, depend on common ground.

People who care about animals are more likely to be moved by a statement about the pain and suffering that minks and other animals may undergo so someone can wear their fur. Similarly, since most people care about children, emotional descriptions of starving, abused, or drug-dependent children move most people to pity. But, of course, allusions to a shared worldview make sense only if the audience knows what the writer is referring to. Many people are familiar with the Bible, so quotations from that book and allusions to its stories will often put an audience in a favorable frame of mind. Most people in the United States celebrate Christmas in some way, so allusions to Santa Claus, the Wise Men, or the Nativity draw upon common images and emotions.

For cartoons, jokes, and other humor to be funny, an audience must understand what a writer means by any allusions. Writer and audience must share knowledge about particular people, say the vice president of the United States, or television or film personalities, or television commercials, makes of cars, and so on. A writer can make a humorous parody of the tale of the three little pigs only if the audience knows the original story.

One of the facts of writing humor, then, is that a single piece of humor probably won't appeal to every audience. Humor is often topical, issue-oriented, and thus bound by time. Satires about the current vice president won't be funny a decade from now. Humor based on current events will be outdated next year. Some humor, however, is timeless. Such humor is based on common human experiences: eating, working, paying taxes, raising a family, living with pets, and so on. While not all entertainment is meant to be humorous, all entertainment, like the specialized type humor, provides relief from daily routine and stress.

Style

Both entertaining and moving rely on an exaggerated style. Parody and satire, for example, depend on controlled **exaggeration,** or hyperbole. *Parody* mimics the style and tone of another piece of writing, often to ridicule. In the following excerpt from a piece called "Across the Street and into the Grill," E. B. White parodies Ernest Hemingway's style and manner of telling a story:

> This is my last and best and true and only meal, thought Mr. Perley as he descended at noon and swung east on the beat-up sidewalk of Forty-fifth Street. Just ahead of him was the girl from the reception desk. I am a little fleshed up around the crook of the elbow, thought Perley, but I commute good.
>
> He quickened his step to overtake her and felt the pain again. What a stinking trade it is, he thought. But after what I've done to other assistant treasurers, I can't hate anybody. Sixteen deads, and I don't know how many possibles.

After the manner of Hemingway, White alludes to people and events as if the reader ought to know about them: "the girl from the reception desk" (what girl? what reception desk?); "felt the pain again" (what pain?); "sixteen deads" (dead whats?). And, like Hemingway's, White's sentences rely heavily on coordinating conjunctions: *and* and *but.* If you know Hemingway's writing, you are more likely to appreciate the humor than if you don't.

Satire uses exaggeration too, often with the intent of ridicule or derision. Newspaper columnists sometimes use satire to point out the folly of elected officials and other public figures. In this brief excerpt from a Dorothy Parker story, "From the Diary of a New York Lady," a type of person is satirized. Judge for yourself what the point of the satire is.

> Wednesday. The most terrible thing happened *just this minute.* Broke one of my finger nails *right off short.* Absolutely *the* most horrible thing I ever had happen to me in my life. Called up Miss Rose to come over and shape it for me, but she was out for the day. I do have *the* worst luck in the *entire* world. Now I'll have to go around like this all day and all night, but what *can* you do? *Damn* Miss Rose.

Parker's use of italics further enhances the exaggeration.

Writing for the purpose of moving employs exaggeration too. For example, exaggerated **repetition** draws on the reader's sense of rhythm. Poetry often evokes an emotional response because of its repetitive rhythm, as do some essays and speeches. Notice how Martin Luther King, Jr., a master of rhythmic repetition, employs the technique in this excerpt from his "I Have a Dream" speech:

> So let freedom ring from the prodigious hilltops of New Hampshire. Let freedom ring from the mighty mountains of New York. Let freedom ring from the heightening Alleghenies of Pennsylvania. Let freedom ring from the snowcapped Rockies of Colorado. Let freedom ring from the curvaceous peaks of California.
>
> But not only that. Let freedom ring from Stone Mountain of Georgia. Let freedom ring from Lookout Mountain of Tennessee. Let freedom ring from every hill and molehill of Mississippi. From every mountainside, let freedom ring.

No doubt about it: this is exaggerated repetition. As a piece of writing, "I Have a Dream" relies in part on readers drawing on the *sound* of words. If you have heard recordings of the speech, you probably actually hear King's voice as you read the words. Speeches by their nature rely more heavily on repetition than do essays meant to be read. They appeal to the ear as well as to the eye. The balance between the unexpected, or surprise, and the expected, gained by repetition and other devices, varies between speech and writing. In writing, entertaining and moving are often achieved with a controlled exaggeration, avoiding too frequent repetition and the incidence of a joke or emotional appeal every line. Humorist James Thurber gives this advice about control:

> With humor you have to look out for traps. You're likely to be very gleeful with what you've first put down, and you think it's fine, very funny. One reason you go over and over it is to make the piece sound less as if you were having a lot of fun with it yourself. You try to play it down.

Surprise is difficult to achieve when humor and emotional appeal are unremitting. If you study humorous essays, you will find that they often have breaks in the humor, to prepare readers for the next incidence. Much of moving and entertaining, especially humor, depends on surprising the audience. Surprise is often balanced with fulfilled expectations. In the E. B. White parody, you are first surprised to discover Hemingway's style, but, once you realize what White is doing, you expect additional similarities and enjoy finding them.

The essays in this chapter represent entertaining and moving as purposes for writing. Even though these two purposes are often widely divergent in their ends—laughter as opposed to sympathy, for example—they employ similar means. Both rely on common experiences and worldviews, balancing the expected with the unexpected, using both controlled exaggeration and surprise. As purposes for writing, both entertaining and moving are usually paired with additional purposes—to inform, perhaps, or to persuade. Read these essays to study technique, to gain enjoyment, and to determine their secondary purposes.

ENTERTAINING WITH HUMOR

People who make their living by writing humorous essays and books write about everyday things—subjects they know well. James Thurber wrote "The Night the Bed Fell" (on his father), "University Days," and "The Dog That Bit People" (the family Airedale, named Muggs). Erma Bombeck writes about *Motherhood: The Second Oldest Profession*, including chapters called "So You Want to Be a Mother!" and "Who Are Harder to Raise—Boys or Girls?" Such writers say that it's much easier to be funny about something you're familiar with; it's easier to exaggerate a known humorous situation, they say, than to invent something funny.

The two essays in this section are about things that are ordinary, usually serious, and often unpleasant: names and punctuation. By exaggeration the writers make their subjects funny. The writers also depend on shared backgrounds with their audiences: Everyone has a name and may have had some unpleasant experiences with it, and every reader has had some encounters with punctuation.

Reading

Student writer Terry Splett is pregnant for the first time and has begun to think about names for the expected baby. Not wanting to burden the child with a ridiculous or an intolerable name, she considers her options. As you read, notice how she relies on common backgrounds and how she uses exaggeration, repetition, and surprise to create humor. What point might she be making with this humorous essay?

A Pain in the Name

Terry Splett

I once worked with a man named Daniel Boone. When I came across his name for the first time on a time card, I thought the guys in the warehouse were just pulling my leg, but when I investigated I found out that it wasn't a joke. Daniel Boone did, in fact, work the night shift, and he even had a union card. I wonder what provoked his mother and father to name him Daniel Boone. 1

I went to school with a Ben Hur and a Mary Hartman. I remember when a thoughtless teacher calling roll in an auditorium class yelled "Mary Hartman, Mary Hartman" just like on the TV show, and I'll never forget the look in that poor ninth grader's eyes, or the laughter that echoed through the auditorium that day. I wonder what provoked her parents when they named her. 2

I also know a Roman Rowan, a Becky Beckman, and a Delana Daleiden. I wonder why parents wreck perfectly good last names with rhyming and clashing first names. Don't they know that children get teased and scorned because of their names? 3

As my husband and I, first-time parents-to-be, discuss names for our baby, we are well aware of this fact. We know from experience that it's especially hard for kids whose last names aren't so hot to begin with, and parents have to be especially careful. 4

My family name was Nat, like short for Natalie, N-A-T. As I grew up, there were constant remarks regarding my ancestors, the g-n-a-t gnats, especially at picnics and baseball games. I used to receive mail addressed to Terry Net, Terry Not, Terry Nut, and Terry Nate. Very rarely was my mail addressed to Terry Nat. No one was able to get my name right, which seemed odd because it was so short. At restaurants, when asked for my 5 name, I used to say N-A-T, and the reservationists would stand there as if they expected ten more letters. Even the bank screwed up. When I went to pick up my title card after paying off my first car loan, I found that the car belonged to Terry National. Did they really think that I abbreviated my last name when I signed for the loan?

I guess that even despite all the jokes and confusion, the name Terry Nat wasn't really that bad, and after talking with Mom I knew that it could have been much, much worse. She told me how careful she had been when naming all of us kids, and how she rejected many of the names that she liked the best, for our sake. I'm forever grateful to Mom for the fact that none of us was named Nanette Nat, Nick Nat, Pat Nat, or Zack Nat! For some reason she wasn't provoked like some parents are.   6

When I was growing up, I always thought that when I got married my name problems would be over, and that when I had kids I would be able to name them anything in the world, within reason. What I didn't know then was that I'd marry a man named Splett. It was a real dilemma choosing between Nat and Splett. I had to choose because there was no way that I was going to hyphenate my name and live the rest of my life as Terry Nat-Splett, so I became a Splett.   7

Almost immediately I began to receive mail addressed to Terry Split, Terry Spit, and Terry Spleet. Reservations are still a problem. If the reservationists don't think I'm spitting when I say the name Splett, they mispronounce it. In fact, a girlfriend and I once missed our reservations altogether because I had no idea that when they repeatedly called "Spell-it" over the intercom they were referring to me.   8

Oh, well, if I lived with Nat for twenty-six years I could certainly live with Splett. It's my kids that I'm concerned about though. I guess I'm in the same spot as Mom was because I can't name them Nanette Splett, Pat Splett, or Zack Splett either, no matter how much I like the names. Nothing in the world could provoke me to do that to them. To make matters worse, because my first name is Terry and my husband's is Gary, we both agree that there won't be another "airy" in our family: no Cheri or Larry or Mary or Harry. And because both of us have the same middle name, Lynn is out too.   9

Even though our choices seem limited, I imagine that there are still several names that don't rhyme with "airy" or that don't clash with Splett. We could choose Andrew, Emily, or Christine. They'd work. Yet I can't help praying for a little girl. Little girls grow up and get married, and I have a plan for our daughter. When she's old enough to date, age twenty-one or so, I'd screen the young men like most parents do, not according to age, intentions, or looks, but according to last names, of course. I'll see to it that she marries a man named Anderson or Jones or Johnson, and she'll be grateful to me forever. She won't have to worry about naming her children as I had to do. She'll be able to name them anything in the world, within reason.   10

Questions: The Community of Writers

1. In what ways does Splett use exaggeration in developing her essay?

2. What is the effect of her repetitive use of the word *provoked?*

3. In paragraph 2, Splett assumes that readers have heard of the television soap opera "Mary Hartman, Mary Hartman." What other common knowledge does she assume in developing her essay?

4. Name some details that surprised you and be prepared to explain in class why they did.

5. What did you learn about Splett's personality as you read her essay?

6. What assumptions does she make about women's names after marriage?

7. Splett uses this humorous essay to make a point about names. What is it?

Analysis

Writers establish contracts with their readers as to the nature of a piece of writing. Readers want to know from the beginning how to read the piece. They are often turned away if writers pretend to be sharing information or offering a service when in fact the primary purpose is persuasion to buy a product or support a cause. Readers are often similarly annoyed when a piece of writing turns out to be humorous after a serious beginning or when it purports to be fact but is in reality mainly fiction. In "A Pain in the Name," Splett tells her readers with her title that she is playing with words and that she will be presenting something other than a serious discussion. Her first sentence continues in this vein, as does the second paragraph.

The humor becomes more apparent, however, when she begins discussing her experiences with her own name: the jokes about her "gnat" ancestors, Terry Nut, and Terry National, then the experiences with her married name. Her humor seems to be based mainly on her surprising recollection of details concerning her name, her clever invention of absurd name combinations, and a finely tuned mixture of surprising the audience and meeting its expectations. In paragraph 5, even though she has led you to expect that something unusual would be coming ("Even the bank screwed up"), she probably surprised you when she said that the title card for her car identified her as Terry National.

As for exaggeration, Splett may not be stretching the facts. Even if she is, you are likely to accept them because she has established a contract of humor with you, and readers of humor expect a certain amount of exaggeration. Most of her details are probably factual, though you can suspect that she has invented the names her mother didn't use and the ones she dismissed as possibilities for her own children. She can also be suspected of exaggeration when she envisions her daughter's choice of a married name.

Purpose

The point of Splett's essay is that parents ought to be careful in naming their children. She expresses this point a number of times by repeating the phrase about parents being provoked to certain actions. A secondary purpose then might be *persuasion*. Information is not important in this essay except for its humorous and persuasive effects. It's not important for you to remember Splett's experiences with her names; what is important is that, first, you enjoy the essay, and, second, you think carefully about naming your children when the time comes.

Exercise: The Exploring Writer

Part of the humor of Splett's essay is the invention of names her mother did not use and names she herself would never give her child. Do a similar invention yourself. Write your name at the top of a piece of paper and then brainstorm (see Chapter 3) a list of first names you are glad you do not have. If your list seems productive of a humorous piece of writing, use it as the basis for freewriting.

Reading

This essay is by a professional writer. A noted physician and scientist, Lewis Thomas is best known for his widely read collections of essays. This one deals with an unlikely subject for a humorous essay, punctuation, and you may find that its humor needs to be extracted with an attentive mind. As you read, remember that Thomas is not writing in an English handbook about how to punctuate. What does his purpose seem to be?

Notes on Punctuation

Lewis Thomas

There are no precise rules about punctuation (Fowler lays out some   1
general advice (as best he can under the complex circumstances of English prose (he points out, for example, that we possess only four stops (the comma, the semicolon, the colon, and the period (the question mark and exclamation point are not, strictly speaking, stops; they are indicators of tone (oddly enough, the Greeks employed the semicolon for their question mark (it produces a strange sensation to read a Greek sentence which is a straightforward question: Why weepest thou; (instead

of Why weepest thou? (and, of course, there are parentheses (which are surely a kind of punctuation making this whole matter much more complicated by having to count up the left-handed parentheses in order to be sure of closing with the right number (but if the parentheses were left out, with nothing to work with but the stops, we would have considerably more flexibility in the deploying of layers of meaning than if we tried to separate all the clauses by physical barriers (and in the latter case, while we might have more precision and exactitude for our meaning, we would lose the essential flavor of language, which is its wonderful ambiguity)))))))))))).

The commas are the most useful and usable of all the stops. It is highly important to put them in place as you go along. If you try to come back after doing a paragraph and stick them in the various spots that tempt you you will discover that they tend to swarm like minnows into all sorts of crevices whose existence you hadn't realized and before you know it the whole long sentence becomes immobilized and lashed up squirming in commas. Better to use them sparingly, and with affection, precisely when the need for each one arises, nicely, by itself.

I have grown fond of semicolons in recent years. The semicolon tells you that there is still some question about the preceding full sentence; something needs to be added; it reminds you sometimes of the Greek usage. It is almost always a greater pleasure to come across a semicolon than a period. The period tells you that that is that; if you didn't get all the meaning you wanted or expected, anyway you got all the writer intended to parcel out and now you have to move along. But with a semicolon there you get a pleasant little feeling of expectancy; there is more to come; read on; it will get clearer.

Colons are a lot less attractive for several reasons: firstly, they give you the feeling of being rather ordered around, or at least having your nose pointed in a direction you might not be inclined to take if left to yourself, and, secondly, you suspect you're in for one of those sentences that will be labeling the points to be made: firstly, secondly, and so forth, with the implication that you haven't sense enough to keep track of a sequence of notions without having them numbered. Also, many writers use this system loosely and incompletely, starting out with number one and number two as though counting off on their fingers but then going on and on without the succession of labels you've been led to expect, leaving you floundering about searching for the ninethly or seventeenthly that ought to be there but isn't.

Exclamation points are the most irritating of all. Look! they say, look at what I just said! How amazing is my thought! It is like being forced to watch someone else's small child jumping up and down crazily in the center of the living room shouting to attract attention. If a sentence really has something of importance to say, something quite remarkable, it doesn't need a mark to point it out. And if it is really, after all, a banal sentence needing more zing, the exclamation point simply emphasizes its banality!

Quotation marks should be used honestly and sparingly, when there   6
is a genuine quotation at hand, and it is necessary to be very rigorous about the words enclosed by the marks. If something is to be quoted, the exact words must be used. If part of it must be left out because of space limitations, it is good manners to insert three dots to indicate the omission, but it is unethical to do this if it means connecting two thoughts which the original author did not intend to have tied together. Above all, quotations marks should not be used for ideas that you'd like to disown, things in the air so to speak. Nor should they be put in place around clichés; if you want to use a cliché you must take full responsibility for it yourself and not try to fob it off on anon., or on society. The most objectionable misuse of quotation marks, but one which illustrates the dangers of misuse in ordinary prose, is seen in advertising, especially in advertisements for small restaurants, for example "just around the corner," or "a good place to eat." No single, identifiable, citable person ever really said, for the record, "just around the corner," much less "a good place to eat," least likely of all for restaurants of the type that use this type of prose.

The dash is a handy device, informal and essentially playful, telling   7
you that you're about to take off on a different tack but still in some way connected with the present course—only you have to remember that the dash is there, and either put a second dash at the end of the notion to let the reader know that he's back on course, or else end the sentence, as here, with a period.

The greatest danger in punctuation is for poetry. Here it is necessary   8
to be as economical and parsimonious with commas and periods as with the words themselves, and any marks that seem to carry their own subtle meanings, like dashes and little rows of periods, even semicolons and question marks, should be left out altogether rather than inserted to clog up the thing with ambiguity. A single exclamation point in a poem, no matter what else the poem has to say, is enough to destroy the whole work.

The things I like best in T. S. Eliot's poetry, especially in the *Four*   9
Quartets, are the semicolons. You cannot hear them, but they are there, laying out the connections between the images and the ideas. Sometimes you get a glimpse of a semicolon coming, a few lines farther on, and it is like climbing a steep path through woods and seeing a wooden bench just at a bend in the road ahead, a place where you can expect to sit for a moment, catching your breath.

Commas can't do this sort of thing; they can only tell you how the   10
different parts of a complicated thought are to be fitted together, but you can't sit, not even take a breath, just because of a comma,

Questions: The Community of Writers

1. What assumptions of common knowledge does Thomas make concerning his audience?

2. In what ways does his discussion of punctuation differ from one in an English handbook?

3. What does Thomas tell you about himself in this essay?

4. Thomas begins stating his thesis in his first sentence but is interrupted by the numerous parenthetical details and never returns to it. Complete the sentence: "There are no precise rules about punctuation, but . . . ."

5. Discuss which paragraph you found the most entertaining and why.

6. What purpose other than entertainment might Thomas have had for writing this essay and why?

7. Find examples here of some of the devices of humor: exaggeration, repetition, and surprise.

Analysis

Thomas writes about punctuation as one writer to another. He assumes that other writers, his readers, will enjoy his play with the marks that are the materials all writers work with. In contrast to Terry Splett's essay, which initiates its humor in the title, Thomas's has a title that seems to indicate a serious purpose. But his first paragraph sets the humorous tone, by exaggeration. As you began reading, you may not have known what Thomas was doing in this paragraph; you may have thought that this is a terribly difficult piece of writing to read; however, the backwash of parentheses at the end of the paragraph would have told you that something unexpected was going on.

Thomas's essay seems meant more to be entertaining than to be funny. Yet he uses the same devices of humor Splett does. Exaggeration seems to be his major device: twelve parenthetical phrases in one sentence, for example, and six semicolons in a paragraph. He illustrates exclamation points with an exaggerated use of them and commas with exaggerated omission and then use. Each mark of punctuation is illustrated with extreme examples. Like Splett, Thomas also balances surprise with fulfilled expectations. In the first paragraph, you can expect to see each mark of parenthesis paired with another, so the delay of their appearance until the end of the paragraph comes as a surprise. Having caught on to what he is doing, in each subsequent paragraph you expect to see the marks illustrated; even so, you are probably a little surprised to discover how Thomas has treated each one. His use of repetition is associated mainly with his exaggeration.

Development (classification) and Purpose

Thomas's method of development is **classification.** However, Thomas seems to select the marks of punctuation in no particular order: first parentheses, then commas, semicolons, colons, exclamation points, quotation marks, and the dash. He discusses periods only in regard to other marks, and he doesn't so much as mention apostrophes. Except for beginning with parentheses and his omissions, he does seem to follow H.W Fowler's order in *Modern English Usage,* which he refers to in his first paragraph. Thomas uses Fowler's terminology too, calling the marks "stops." In fact, Thomas may have set out to parody the entry on stops in Fowler's standard reference work. But why begin with parentheses? Probably because doing so sets the tone for the essay better than any other portion of it would.

Thomas's primary purpose in writing undoubtedly was to *entertain.* However, he also seems to have a secondary purpose—to show that even though punctuation marks have "no precise rules," they do perform particular functions and follow certain conventions. Semicolons, for example, give "a pleasant little feeling of expectancy," colons "give you the feeling of being rather ordered around," and exclamation points seem to be "shouting to attract attention." And Thomas does clearly have a preference for the semicolon, returning to it in paragraph 9, praising it as "a place where you can expect to sit for a moment, catching your breath." In Chapter 13, in another essay on punctuation, Roger Garrison declares the semicolon his "personal favorite" too, having "scatter[ed] semicolons with wild abandon" in a first draft and now recommending that his readers "be careful not to overuse" them.

Exercise: The Community of Writers

Select a mark of punctuation from the following list and collaborate with your groupmates in writing a paragraph that, like Thomas's essay, discusses the mark and illustrates it as well. Exaggerate to excess in using the mark.

.	Period
()	Parentheses
;	Semicolon
—	Dash
:	Colon
-	Hyphen
,	Comma
'	Apostrophe

?	Question mark
" "	Quotation marks
!	Exclamation point

Writing

Write an essay that entertains by means of exaggeration, repetition, surprise, and fulfilled expectations. Choose a familiar subject, something that you are well acquainted with and that your readers will be familiar with too. Like Thomas, you might select an aspect of writing, such as spelling or capitalization, or, like Splett, you might select an aspect of your life. Jokes at the writer's own expense are generally more acceptable to readers than those that seem to belittle other people. Splett's essay on names might have inspired some thoughts about names that you would like to write about.

Here are a few other possible topics:

- Books
- Pencils or pens
- Coffee mugs
- Road signs
- Birthdays
- Holidays

Remember Thurber's advice not to be too amused by your own humor (page 210), and remember to control your exaggeration, to spread the humor out rather than have punch lines one on top of another, and to balance surprise with fulfilled expectations.

MOVING AN AUDIENCE TO SERIOUS THOUGHT

A common purpose for writing is to stir the minds of readers to serious thinking about serious issues. Such essays may in part have a persuasive purpose, and they usually derive from the writers' own reflections about the issues; however, mainly they are meant to touch readers, to move them to new thoughts. A writer may write about the sterility of life for residents in a nursing home. Another may consider the relationship between pain and dying, the difficulty of watching a child die, or the pleasure of listening to an elderly man play "O Tannenbaum" on a pan flute. By using techniques of emotional appeal, these writers could stir their readers to think new thoughts.

These techniques are similar to those employed in entertaining: sharing the backgrounds and experiences of the audience, balancing the expected with the unexpected, and repeating emotionally laden terms. To move an audience, a writer must understand what is important to that audience and must touch familiar chords. Most people have known someone in a nursing home, and describing life there makes an appeal to familial ties and memories. Along with the expected, however, the writer keeps audience interest with the unexpected: a father and son playing cribbage in the visitors' lounge of the nursing home, the similarity between a great-grandmother being left in a nursing home and a son or daughter being left at college. A writer appeals also with the repetition of words that carry emotional weight, like *old* or *growing old, loneliness,* and *happiness.*

Essays that are meant to move an audience can appeal to all the emotions people experience—anger, fear, love, pity, hatred, and so on. Emotions are powerful forces, capable of great good and great harm. Writers who appeal to them should therefore do so ethically and responsibly. Appealing to fear or hatred of a group of people can result in dire consequences, though appealing to fear of our own reckless acts can bring about heedful behavior. Writing that sets out to have readers pity themselves has negative effects, whereas writing that appeals to pity for others can bring about social good.

In the two essays that follow, professional writers appeal to the emotions of their readers for the purpose of encouraging serious thought about serious subjects.

Reading

In this excerpt from the essay "The Winter of Man," scientist-essayist Loren Eiseley writes about fear. Observe how he uses repetition and other emotional appeals to identify those things that deserve to be feared and considered.

The Winter of Man

Loren Eiseley

Has the earth's glacial winter, for all our mastery of science, surely   1
subsided? No, the geologist would answer. We merely stand in a transitory
spot of sunshine that takes on the illusion of permanence only because
the human generations are short.

Has the wintry bleakness in the troubled heart of humanity at least   2
equally retreated?—that aspect of man referred to when the Eskimo,
adorned with amulets to ward off evil, reiterated: "Most of all we fear the
secret misdoings of the heedless ones among ourselves."

No, the social scientist would have to answer, the winter of man has   3
not departed. The Eskimo standing in the snow, when questioned about
his beliefs, said: "We do not believe. We only fear. We fear those things
which are about us and of which we have no sure knowledge. . . ."

But surely we can counter that this old man was an ignorant remnant   4
of the Ice Age, fearful of a nature he did not understand. Today we have
science; we do not fear the Eskimo's malevolent ghosts. We do not wear
amulets to ward off evil spirits. We have pierced to the far rim of the
universe. We roam mentally through light-years of time.

Yes, this could be admitted, but we also fear. We fear more deeply   5
than the old man in the snow. It comes to us, if we are honest, that
perhaps nothing has changed the grip of winter in our hearts, that winter
before which we cringed amidst the ice long ages ago.

For what is it that we do? We fear. We do not fear ghosts but we fear   6
the ghost of ourselves. We have come now, in this time, to fear the water
we drink, the air we breathe, the insecticides that are dusted over our
giant fruits. Because of the substances we have poured into our contam-
inated rivers, we fear the food that comes to us from the sea. There are
also those who tell us that by our own heedless acts the sea is dying.

We fear the awesome powers we have lifted out of nature and cannot   7
return to her. We fear the weapons we have made, the hatreds we have
engendered. We fear the crush of fanatic people to whom we readily sell
these weapons. We fear for the value of the money in our pockets that
stands symbolically for food and shelter. We fear the growing power of
the state to take all these things from us. We fear to walk in our streets at
evening. We have come to fear even our scientists and their gifts.

We fear, in short, as that self-sufficient Eskimo of the long night had   8
never feared. Our minds, if not our clothes, are hung with invisible
amulets: nostrums changed each year for our bodies whether it be chlo-
rophyll toothpaste, the signs of astrology, or cold cures that do not cure:
witchcraft nostrums for our society as it fractures into contending multi-
tudes all crying for liberation without responsibility.

We fear, and never in this century will we cease to fear. We fear the   9
end of man as that old shaman in the snow has never had cause to fear
it. There is a winter still about us—the winter of man that has followed
him relentlessly from the caverns and the ice. The old Eskimo spoke well.
It is the winter of the heedless ones. We are in the winter. We have never
left its breath.

Questions: The Community of Writers

1. What does Eiseley mean by "The Winter of Man"?

2. Eiseley uses several terms to refer to magic: *shaman* for the Eskimo, *amulets* and
   nostrums for the paraphernalia of magic, *witchcraft, ghosts,* and *evil spirits.* How
   do these words represent fears of people in our world today? What do we fear?

3. Who are "the heedless ones among ourselves" whom Eiseley says we should fear?

4. In addition to repeated references to magic, how does Eiseley use repetition to appeal to the emotions of the audience?

5. Discuss what purpose you think Eiseley hopes to achieve.

Analysis

Most people don't have much fear of winter. We may not like the cold, and we may acknowledge that snow and ice on the streets and highways are dangerous, but we don't really *fear* winter. Those of us who live in warm climates don't even give it much thought, and those who live in northern regions just put on a warmer coat and heavier boots, try to adjust their driving to the road conditions, and at the end of the day return to a home that is insulated and heated. But Eiseley challenges us to think about a glacial winter that cannot be closed out and protected against, one that any sensible person would fear.

That glacial winter is an **analogy** for something within ourselves that we should fear: the heedlessness with which we commit actions endangering our very lives. And like the Eskimo with amulets to ward off evil, we have our little nostrums that provide us with a feeling of safety from the results of our communal heedless actions. Eiseley thus blends the analogies of winter and magic to show what dangers humanity has placed itself in and what powerless measures we are taking to combat those dangers.

Thesis

In addition to his *repetition* of words related to his two analogies, Eiseley repeats the key word *fear*. Its first incidence is in paragraph 2, where he quotes the Eskimo: "Most of all we fear the secret misdoings of the heedless ones among ourselves." This quotation serves as Eiseley's *thesis* sentence, and the major part of his essay tells what heedless acts we fear. Even though the essay was first published in 1972, the list is timely. We still fear for our water and air and food. We still fear one another. We still fear illness. This, said Eiseley, returning to his analogy, is winter, this fear that we bring upon ourselves.

Exercise: The Community of Writers

With your groupmates, explore the fears of all of us today. What are our common fears? What are their causes? Why are these fears like a relentless glacial winter?

Reading

The following essay begins "This isn't going to be easy. Nor is it going to be funny." It is neither easy nor funny because it is a father's account of his son's funeral. Al Sicherman, a columnist for the Minneapolis *Star Tribune,* usually writes humorous columns, but this time he writes only of sadness. His purpose for writing such a difficult and painful piece is to move his readers to think about the consequences of using drugs. As a parent he writes to other parents, but his message is just as vital to contemporaries of his son.

Sicherman is writing from Minneapolis, Minnesota, about a son who died while at school at the University of Wisconsin at Madison. As you read this essay, notice what techniques Sicherman uses to appeal to the audience.

Be Scared for Your Kids

Al Sicherman

Dear, dear friends: This isn't going to be easy.   1

Nor is it going to be funny.   2

My older son, Joe, of whom I was very, very proud, and whose   3 growing up I've been privileged to chronicle occasionally in the newspaper, died last month in a fall from the window of his seventh-floor dorm room in Madison, Wisconsin. He had taken LSD. He was eighteen years old.

To say he had his whole life ahead of him is unforgivably trite—and   4 unbearably sad.

I saw him a week before he died. It was my birthday, and he spent the   5 weekend with his stepmother and me. He was upbeat, funny, and full of his new activities, including fencing. He did a whole bunch of very impressive lunges and parries for us.

The next time I was with him, he was in a coffin.   6

He must not have known how treacherous LSD can be. I never   7 warned him, because, like most adults, I had no idea it was popular again. I thought it had stopped killing kids twenty years ago. Besides, Joe was bright and responsible; he wouldn't "do" drugs. It didn't occur to me that he might dabble in them.

His mother had warned him about LSD, though; she knew it was back   8 because Joe had told her about a friend who had taken it. Obviously he didn't listen to her advice. At eighteen, kids think they're invulnerable. They're wrong.

Joey was a very sweet, very funny kid. And even before he had anything   9
particularly funny to say, he had great timing. When he was about six, I asked
him what he wanted to be when he grew up. He paused, just long enough, and
said, "A stand-up physicist."

I went to the mortuary in Milwaukee several hours before the funeral   10
to have a chance to be with him. I spent most of the time crying and
saying dumb things like "I would have caught you" and "I would have
traded with you." I wish I could say that I sang him a lullaby, but I didn't
think of it until several days later. I went ahead and did it then, but it was
too late. It would have been too late in any case.

Joe was not a reckless kid: Last summer he turned down my wife's   11
suggestion that the family go on a rafting trip through the Grand Canyon;
although he loved amusement-park rides, he thought that sounded too
risky. So we went sailing and miniature golfing instead. But he took LSD.
Apparently he figured that wasn't as dangerous.

When he was about seven or eight, Joey attended a camp for asthma sufferers.   12
When asked "What do you do at asthma camp?" he responded, cheerfully, "Wheeze!"

The coffin is always closed in traditional Jewish funerals, and as I sat   13
with him that morning before the funeral, I minded that. I felt so far
from him. I finally decided that I had the right to open it briefly, even if
it was against some rule. In fact, I rationalized, Joe probably would like
my breaking the rule. So I raised the lid.

He was in a body bag.   14

I'm not surprised that kids don't listen to their parents about drugs.   15
Adults' standards of risk are different from theirs, and they know it; and
they discount what we tell them. But we must tell them anyway.

Joe's aunt, a teacher, says that when you warn kids about something   16
dangerous—some thing that kills people—they always say "Name one."
OK, I will. Joe Sicherman. You may name him, too. Please.

Joe's first job was in Manchester, New Hampshire, where his mother had   17
moved with him and his younger brother nine years ago. He was a carry-out boy
in a supermarket. One day he came to the rescue of a clerk faced with a customer
who spoke only French and who wanted to use Canadian money. Armed with his
two years of high-school French, Joe stepped forward and explained "Madame,
non!" She seemed not to understand. That, he said, was when he rose to the very
pinnacle of linguistic and supermarket expertise: "Madame," he said, with a
Gallic shrug of his shoulders, "augghhhhh!" The woman nodded and left.

Because the coffin is always closed, nobody expected anyone to look   18
inside. There were blood spatters on the body bag.

It's entirely possible that warning your kids won't scare them away   19
from LSD. But maybe it will. I wish I could tell you how to warn them so
it would work, but I can't.

This is the generation gap reduced to its most basic: It is parents'   20
worst fear that something terrible will happen to their kids; it is kids'
constant struggle to be free of the protection of their parents.

Joe's next job was in Shorewood, Wisconsin, a Milwaukee suburb, where his   21
family moved just before his junior year in high school. It was a summer job as a
soda jerk. He confided to me that he worked alongside a "soda idiot" and that his boss
was "a soda &#%@." Actually I think he enjoyed it. He told me one day that he
was "acquiring meaningful insights into the Sundae Industry." Like: If you say
"yes" to "Do you want a lid on that?" you're going to get less whipped topping.

Traditional Jewish funerals leave no room for the stage of grief that   22
psychologists call "denial." When you leave the cemetery, you can have
no doubt that the person is dead. In fact, you might say that these
funerals are brutal. I could avoid telling you about it, and spare us both
some pain, but I think I owe it to Joe—and to every parent—to let this be
as forceful as possible.

When the graveside prayers were over, workmen lowered Joe's coffin   23
into the ground and then eased a concrete cover down into the hole until
it covered the metal burial vault. The cover had Joe's name on it. They
pulled the green fake-grass cloth off the pile of dirt next to the grave, and
the rabbi and the cantor each threw a shovelful of earth onto the vault
lid.

Then they handed the shovel to Joe's fifteen-year-old brother, David.   24

It occurs to me now that what I might have done is ask Joe what kind   25
of drugs were around. Maybe my genuine alarm at the reemergence of
LSD would have registered with him. I'm certainly going to be less
self-assured about how I deal with this subject with David. He's a wonderful kid, too, and while I don't want to smother him, I don't want to
assume anything, either.

I didn't take Joe for granted; I think I encouraged him and delighted   26
in him and celebrated with him. But I certainly took his *life* for granted.
Parents must not do that. We must be scared for them. They don't know
when to be scared for themselves.

Although his humor had become somewhat acerbic recently, Joe remained a   27
sweet, thoughtful kid. When, as I often did, I wound up apologizing to him because
a weekend or a vacation hadn't worked out the way I'd hoped, he always patted
my hand—literally or figuratively—and let me know he loved me anyway.

He took good care of others, too. He spent most of his grandfather's ninetieth   28
birthday party making sure that his stepmother had somebody to talk to besides my
ex-wife's family.

And on that last birthday visit with me in early October, he talked a little about   29
his concerns and hopes for his brother. One of those concerns was drugs.

Then they handed the shovel to me.   30

Later I overheard my wife say that the expression on my face when I   31
turned away, having shoveled dirt onto my son's coffin, was the most
awful thing she'd ever seen.

Whenever I thought about Joe recently, it was about college and   32
independence and adulthood, and his latest involvements: His attempt
to produce an English paper that was more interesting than what the

instructor had asked for, the raucous rock band he and his friend put together over the summer, his plans to rent a cabin with a bunch of kids at winter break.

Now, suddenly, I'm no longer looking at the moment, but instead at   33
the whole life. And in some automatic averaging-out, in my mind I'm sometimes calling him "Joey," his little-boy name.

He told his mother a year ago that he wanted his senior year in high school to   34
be the best year he'd ever had, and on the drive to Madison to start college this fall,
he told her that, despite lots of typical teenage domestic tension, it had been. He
said he'd accomplished everything he'd set out to do—except to have a mad,
passionate affair with a woman he didn't even know.

She refrained from asking the obvious question.   35

Then they handed the shovel to his mother.   36

Even though it is only three weeks since his death, I find that the   37
reality of Joey is beginning to turn sepia. He will be forever eighteen. And his life will forever stop in 1989. That saddens me so much. It's not just that he won't have a career, maybe get married, have kids, or those things we hope might happen for a promising young person. He won't go out for pizza anymore either, or come into a warm house on a cold night, or imitate Martin Short imitating Katharine Hepburn, or scuff through piles of leaves.

And I won't ever see him again.   38

Joe had been very involved in high-school journalism. He won a statewide   39
award for feature writing in New Hampshire, and he was an editor of the school
paper in Shorewood. He contributed a great deal of that paper's humor edition in
May, including a large advertisement that read, in part:

Attention! All available slightly twisted females: Marry Me! I am a nice guy,   40
a National Merit semifinalist, devastatingly handsome, relatively inexpensive,
housebroken, handy with tools, easily entertained, a gentleman in the truest sense
of the word, and I think I am extremely funny. In fact, I think I am the funniest
guy on earth! . . . Please call immediately. Operators are standing by. (I am in
great demand.) . . . Kids—Please get permission from your parents before calling."

Then they handed the shovel to his stepmother.   41

In his sermon at David's bar mitzvah last year, the rabbi used a phrase   42
I'd never heard before. It caused me to weep at the time; I wasn't sure why. It's come back to me again and again recently. It isn't consoling, nor even helpful. But it is pretty, and in an odd way it puts events into a much larger perspective.

"All things pass into mystery."   43

At one point during that last visit, we went to a craft fair where Joe noticed   44
someone selling hammered dulcimers. He had never played one, but he'd played the
guitar for quite a few years, which must have helped. He picked up the hammers
and began to fool around, and soon he drew a small crowd with something that
sounded like sitar music. He asked about the price; they were expensive. I keep finding
myself thinking that it would be neat to get him one. I should have done it then.

Then they handed the shovel to his only living grandmother; it took   45
her two tries to get enough dirt on the shovel. Neither of his grandfathers
could bring himself to do it. But many of Joe's friends, weeping, took a turn.

I hope someday to be able to write about Joe again; I probably won't   46
be writing a humor column for a while. In the meantime, I want folks to
know how I think he would have turned out. He would have been a
mensch—a decent, sincere man, the kind you're proud to know. He
already was. Damn drugs.

A year or so ago, the four of us played charades, a vacation tradition. Joe drew   47
"The Sun Also Rises," which he did in one clue. He stretched an imaginary horizon
line between his hands then slowly brought his head above it at one end and
traversed an arc, grinning from ear to ear. It took us about five seconds to get it.
Body bag or no, that's how I want to remember him.

The last thing I wrote about him appeared in the newspaper the   48
morning he died. He told me that he and a friend decided one Saturday
afternoon to hitchhike to a rock concert near Milwaukee. He realized, he
said, that now that he was away from home, he didn't have to ask anybody
if he could go or tell anybody that he was going. He just decided to do it,
and he did it. I wrote about what a heady experience that was, to be
independent at last.

There's a fair measure of irony in that column. We're told that the   49
rock concert is where he got the LSD, and where he took his first trip.

That trip, I understand, went OK. This one killed him.   50

Although Joe apparently was with friends most of the evening, the   51
police said he was alone when he went out the window. We'll probably
never know exactly what happened in those last minutes, but judging by
our own reading of him and by what lots of others have told us, we're sure
he wasn't despondent. Many of his friends, including one who spoke at
his funeral, said that he was very happy and enjoying his life in Madison.

The likeliest explanation we've heard is that he had the LSD halluci-   52
nation that makes a person think he can fly. In any case, a little after one
o'clock Sunday morning, October 15, somebody studying across the
courtyard saw a curtain open and then a body fall. Joe didn't cry out.

I have since, many times.   53

Questions: The Community of Writers

1. Characterize the tone of the essay. How does Sicherman establish it?
2. How does he establish his credibility?
3. What facts does Sicherman tell you about his son's use of drugs? What does
   he tell you about the effects of LSD?
4. Does Sicherman blame himself for his son's use of LSD?
5. How does Sicherman use repetition to achieve his intent of moving an
   audience?

6. Discuss which portions of the essay you find particularly effective.

7. This essay appeared three weeks after Joe Sicherman's death. Do you think his father would have changed anything had he written it after more time had elapsed, say several months?

8. Analyze Sicherman's technique in this essay. Consider for example, the use of italicized sections.

Analysis

People expect to attend the funerals of grandparents, parents, and aged aunts and uncles; they do not expect to attend the funerals of their children. Nor did Al Sicherman expect to attend the funeral of his son Joe, and he is obviously grief-stricken. When people try to adjust to the death of someone they care about, they run a gamut of emotions—shock, denial, anger, guilt, and resignation. Rather than avoiding the issue of his son's death and writing a column about some innocuous subject, Sicherman uses this emotional time to move his readers to an awareness of how serious even a limited use of drugs can be. In his essay you may have found evidence of many emotions related to his grief.

Thesis and Development (chronological)

To make his point that drugs are deadly, Sicherman recounts the experience of his son's funeral and his thoughts at the mortuary and the graveside. The development of the essay has a sequential, or **chronological,** framework enclosing his ruminations on the life of his son. With each passing of the shovel, he adds more thoughts. He does not explicitly state his *thesis;* however, throughout the essay he supports the controlling idea that drugs are deadly. Parents should warn their kids, he implies, and kids should stay off drugs.

The *Star Tribune* printed Sicherman's column on the front page of the Sunday edition, and it was read by thousands. One reader's response, "Fatal Trip," is included in Chapter 15. You might want to read it now and compare your response with it.

Exercise: The Exploring Writer

Freewrite (see Chapter 3) for fifteen minutes about a subject that affects you emotionally and that you want other people to think about, perhaps the death or illness of someone you care for. Consider beginning with a controlling analogy as Eiseley does in "The Winter of Man," or a sequential structural framework, as Sicherman does.

Writing

Use your freewriting as the basis for an essay with the purpose of moving an audience to new thoughts. You might want to engender an awareness of threats to our global environment, the dangers of using drugs, the growing problem of AIDS or one of the other "fears" you and your groupmates discussed. Then again, you might concentrate on something positive, like the emotional lift gained from cheering nursing home residents, collecting donations for the Salvation Army, cleaning up a beach or a stretch of highway, and so on. Persuasion and reflection may be secondary aims, but try to focus on moving an audience to feel the way you do.

ADDITIONAL READINGS FOR DISCUSSION

Reading

Student writer Jeff Hedin writes about getting old. His essay is partly reflection but mostly an appeal to the reader to feel as he does about growing old and living in a nursing home. What do you think is Hedin's purpose for writing?

Nursing Homes and Growing Old

Jeff Hedin

Some days time flies. Other days time drags. But still we get older. 1 Eventually, we'll all be old people struggling to carry out our lives. It worries me to be old. I fear how my life will be. Will I be able to care for myself? Will my wife be alive to share my days? Will I end up living in a nursing home? I'm still a 24-year-old college student whose other worries involve graduation, finding a job, and getting married someday.

It may not have crossed your mind about getting old. We're all still 2 young and active. We lead busy lives and have many goals to attain. Who has time to think about growing old? We are living for now. I want to be happy in my old age. The one place I don't want to end up in is a nursing home.

In the past year or so I had my first experience with a nursing home. 3 My grandmother was unable to take care of my great-grandmother and was forced to place her in a nursing home. It was a shock for me to find this out. My great-grandma was a strong, sharp-minded woman. She was always in control of herself and was very active. But physically she was no longer strong. She needed more care than my grandma could give her.

I first visited the home two summers ago. The grounds were tidy and the surroundings were quiet. Entering the shiny steel-framed door, I noticed a group of residents sitting on either side of the doorway. They were quiet and passive. Their frail bodies sat tilted, as if propped up by some invisible support. Their eyes stared in all directions but saw nothing. Some had mouths hung open. Others had trembling lips and teetering heads.   4

I walked down the long hallway. The floor tile was bone white. Fluorescent lights bleached the shadows on the wall. It was so clean and so sterile. A man in a wheelchair slowly pulled himself along the railing mounted to the wall. He had no legs. Another woman in a wheelchair sat in her doorway. Was she waiting for someone? Or had somebody just put her there to get her out of the way?   5

I scanned the small nameplates that marked each room until I found my great-grandma's room. I peered inside her room and she smiled when she saw me. Her hands sat folded on her lap. A small wool blanket covered her knees. She looked good but not as good as she did when she lived at home. It was so strange to see her in this foreign place. She didn't belong here.   6

We talked for a while. I tried to say things that would cheer her up, to make her feel less lonely. I could see she wasn't happy here and that she wanted to go home. But she wouldn't put up a fuss. She didn't want to upset anyone. I was upset, but not from her. My first visit to a nursing home was a depressing and sobering event. I now knew what this place was like, and I felt bad that my great-grandma didn't like being here. I knew I never wanted to live there.   7

Once on a weekend, I visited her with the rest of my family. My dad came in and said "Hello" and gave her a hug. We visited for a few minutes, and then my dad asked me if I wanted to go to the visitors' lounge for a game of cribbage. He wanted to smoke a cigarette but he also didn't like the feeling of this place. Playing a game of cards was the only way he could forget he was visiting here and that his grandmother had to stay.   8

I often picked up my grandma and went with her to visit the home. She tried to go every day. But sometimes the weather was too bad or there was no one to drive her down. Great-grandma would sit in her chair and wait for someone to come. What else could she do? When we did visit it was the same scene over and over. I tried cheering her up and making her laugh. Yet she still seemed lonely and homesick.   9

On last Thanksgiving Day, Grandma and I drove to Melrose for another visit. We were surprised to see Grandma's sister and family already there. We all sat in the lounge, playing cards and drinking coffee. Great-grandma was having a good time. It was the happiest I'd seen her there. As the afternoon wore on we knew we had to get going. What a   10 terrible feeling to have friends and family around and at the end of the day they leave but you have to stay. It reminded me of when my parents moved me to college for the first time. We unloaded my belongings and then went out to dinner. Afterwards, they brought me back to my apartment and left. I didn't want them to leave. I was afraid of being alone. Did Great-grandma feel the same way?

Two days after Thanksgiving I was sleeping on my parents' couch. It was early morning and the telephone rang. Dad answered it and after a few seconds of conversation I could tell that Great-grandma had died. 11

Growing old is a sure thing. One morning I'll wake up gray and wrinkled. But I want to wake up at home, not in some hospital-like environment. A nursing home is not a home. It's an institution. It reminds me of the hospital "dying rooms" of World War I that I learned about in my European history class. These were places where dying soldiers were put so they wouldn't disturb others and so there would be more bed space for others. It's just a final stop before your train comes to an end. 12

What can we do to prevent staying in a nursing home? Do we live with our sons and daughters and grandchildren? They don't want us getting in the way of their young lives. It's too hard for them. Do we try to live on our own? We might be too frail to climb out of bed. Can our spouses take care of us? Sure, if they are even well enough to take care of themselves. 13

It looks to me as if a nursing home is the only alternative. I don't think anyone will discover a drug that stops the aging process by the time I get old. I better reserve a wheelchair. 14

Questions: The Community of Writers

1. What is Hedin's purpose for writing this essay? Who might his intended audience be?

2. Do you agree with Hedin about growing old? How do your feelings differ from his? How might your feelings differ if you were older, say fifty?

3. What does Hedin dislike about nursing homes?

4. Hedin compares the way his great-grandmother must have felt when the family left her with the way he felt when his parents left him at college. In what other ways can you compare nursing home life with college life?

5. Discuss what techniques Hedin uses to appeal to your emotions.

Reading

Black civil rights leader Martin Luther King, Jr., led sit-ins, boycotts, and marches as nonviolent resistance to segregation and unfair practices against African-Americans. On August 28, 1963, he stood on the steps of the Lincoln Memorial and addressed 200,000 people assembled in the nation's capital for the cause of civil rights. "I Have a Dream" is that speech.

I Have a Dream

Martin Luther King, Jr.

Five score years ago, a great American, in whose symbolic shadow we   1
stand, signed the Emancipation Proclamation. This momentous decree came as a great beacon light of hope to millions of Negro slaves who had been seared in the flames of withering injustice. It came as a joyous daybreak to end the long night of captivity.

But one hundred years later, we must face the tragic fact that the   2
Negro is still not free. One hundred years later, the life of the Negro is still sadly crippled by the manacles of segregation and the chains of discrimination. One hundred years later, the Negro lives on a lonely island of poverty in the midst of a vast ocean of material prosperity. One hundred years later, the Negro is still languishing in the corners of American society and finds himself an exile in his own land. So we have come here today to dramatize an appalling condition.

In a sense we have come to our nation's capital to cash a check. When   3
the architects of our republic wrote the magnificent words of the Constitution and the Declaration of Independence, they were signing a promissory note to which every American was to fall heir. This note was a promise that all men—yes, black men as well as white men—would be guaranteed the unalienable rights of life, liberty, and the pursuit of happiness.

It is obvious today that America has defaulted on this promissory   4
note insofar as her citizens of color are concerned. Instead of honoring this sacred obligation, America has given the Negro people a bad check, a check which has come back marked "insufficient funds." But we refuse to believe that there are insufficient funds in the great vaults of opportunity of this nation. So we have come to cash this check—a check that will give us upon demand the riches of freedom and the security of justice. We have also come to this hallowed spot to remind America of the fierce urgency of *now*. This is no time to engage in the luxury of cooling off or to take the tranquilizing drugs of gradualism. *Now* is the time to make real the promises of Democracy. *Now* is the time to rise from the dark and desolate valley of segregation to the sunlit path of racial justice. *Now* is the time to open the doors of opportunity to all of God's children. *Now* is the time to lift our nation from the quicksands of racial injustice to the solid rock of brotherhood.

It would be fatal for the nation to overlook the urgency of the   5
moment and to underestimate the determination of the Negro. This sweltering summer of the Negro's legitimate discontent will not pass until

there is an invigorating autumn of freedom and equality; 1963 is not an end, but a beginning. Those who hope that the Negro needed to blow off steam and will now be content will have a rude awakening if the nation returns to business as usual. There will be neither rest nor tranquility in America until the Negro is granted his citizenship rights. The whirlwinds of revolt will continue to shake the foundations of our nation until the bright day of justice emerges.

But there is something that I must say to my people who stand on the warm threshold which leads into the palace of justice. In the process of gaining our rightful place we must not be guilty of wrongful deeds. Let us not seek to satisfy our thirst for freedom by drinking from the cup of bitterness and hatred. We must forever conduct our struggle on the high plane of dignity and discipline. We must not allow our creative protest to degenerate into physical violence. Again and again we must rise to the majestic heights of meeting physical force with soul force. The marvelous new militancy which has engulfed the Negro community must not lead us to a distrust of all white people, for many of our white brothers, as evidenced by their presence here today, have come to realize that their destiny is tied up with our destiny and their freedom is inextricably bound to our freedom. We cannot walk alone.

And as we walk, we must make the pledge that we shall march ahead. We cannot turn back. There are those who are asking the devotees of civil rights, "When will you be satisfied?" We can never be satisfied as long as the Negro is the victim of the unspeakable horrors of police brutality. We can never be satisfied as long as our bodies, heavy with the fatigue of travel, cannot gain lodging in the motels of the highways and the hotels of the cities. We cannot be satisfied as long as the Negro's basic mobility is from a smaller ghetto to a larger one. We can never be satisfied as long as a Negro in Mississippi cannot vote and a Negro in New York believes he has nothing for which to vote. No, no, we are not satisfied, and we will not be satisfied until justice rolls down like waters and righteousness like a mighty stream.

I am not unmindful that some of you have come here out of great trials and tribulations. Some of you have come fresh from narrow jail cells. Some of you have come from areas where your quest for freedom left you battered by the storms of persecution and staggered by the winds of police brutality. You have been the veterans of creative suffering. Continue to work with the faith that unearned suffering is redemptive.

Go back to Mississippi, go back to Alabama, go back to South Carolina, go back to Georgia, go back to Louisiana, go back to the slums and ghettos of our northern cities, knowing that somehow this situation can and will be changed. Let us not wallow in the valley of despair.

I say to you today, my friends, that in spite of the difficulties and frustrations of the moment I still have a dream. It is a dream deeply rooted in the American dream.

I have a dream that one day this nation will rise up and live out the   11
true meaning of its creed: "We hold these truths to be self-evident, that
all men are created equal."

I have a dream that one day on the red hills of Georgia the sons of   12
former slaves and the sons of former slaveowners will be able to sit down
together at the table of brotherhood.

I have a dream that one day even the state of Mississippi, a desert   13
state sweltering with the heat of injustice and oppression, will be transformed into an oasis of freedom and justice.

I have a dream that my four little children will one day live in a nation   14
where they will not be judged by the color of their skin but by the content
of their character.

I have a dream today.   15

I have a dream that one day the state of Alabama, whose governor's   16
lips are presently dripping with the words of interposition and nullifica-
tion, will be transformed into a situation where little black boys and black
girls will be able to join hands with little white boys and white girls and
walk together as sisters and brothers.

I have a dream today.   17

I have a dream that one day every valley shall be exalted, every hill   18
and mountain shall be made low, the rough places will be made plain,
and the crooked places will be made straight, and the glory of the Lord
shall be revealed, and all flesh shall see it together.*

This is our hope. This is the faith with which I return to the South.   19
With this faith we will be able to hew out of the mountain of despair a
stone of hope. With this faith we will be able to transform the jangling
discords of our nation into a beautiful symphony of brotherhood. With
this faith we will be able to work together, to pray together, to struggle
together, to go to jail together, to stand up for freedom together, knowing
that we will be free one day.

This will be the day when all of God's children will be able to sing   20
with new meaning

My country, 'tis of thee,
Sweet land of liberty,
    Of thee I sing:
Land where my fathers died,
Land of the pilgrims' pride,
From every mountainside,
    Let freedom ring.

So let freedom ring from the prodigious hilltops of New Hampshire.   21
Let freedom ring from the mighty mountains of New York. Let freedom
ring from the heightening Alleghenies of Pennsylvania. Let freedom ring

---

*Isaiah 40:4–5.

from the snowcapped Rockies of Colorado. Let freedom ring from the curvaceous peaks of California.

But not only that. Let freedom ring from Stone Mountain of Georgia. 22
Let freedom ring from Lookout Mountain of Tennessee. Let freedom ring from every hill and molehill of Mississippi. From every mountainside, let freedom ring.

When we let freedom ring, when we let it ring from every village and 23
every hamlet, from every state and every city, we will be able to speed up that day when all of God's children, black men and white men, Jews and Gentiles, Protestants and Catholics, will be able to join hands and sing in the words of the old Negro spiritual, "Free at last! Free at last! Thank God almighty, we are free at last!"

Questions: The Community of Writers

1. What is the effect of King's abundant use of repetition? Consider paragraphs 7, 9, 11–18, and 21–23.
2. What three political documents does King refer to in the first three paragraphs? What other familiar documents does he quote?
3. King uses several analogies in this appeal. In paragraph 3 he describes the civil rights movement as cashing a check. What other analogies does he use, and what does he mean by them?
4. Why does King not support violence for achieving civil rights?

CHAPTER 9

Writing to Record

A writer may attempt to record what is immediately present in his environment, the events, the appearance of things. He is saying what his world is like at that moment.
—*James Britton*

Recording may be one of the oldest purposes for writing. As long ago as 4000 to 3000 B.C., people in the ancient civilizations of Mesopotamia, China, Egypt, and Mexico were using writing to record financial transactions, laws, and important events. Their records were meant to be permanent, and, being inscribed on stone or sun-dried bricks, some have endured to the present day. Today, the most permanent kind of record we keep is probably what we put on gravestones.

Most of our records are meant to be only semipermanent or even short-term. We keep records of conversations, correspondence, interviews, activities, events, impressions, finances, purchases, concerts, dramas, games, and so on. These records may be in the form of minutes, news articles, letters, notes, journal entries, and they may be recorded on paper, film, tape, disk—by means of pen or pencil, typewriter, computer, tape recorder, camera, and so on.

In academic work, you use notetaking as a means of recording lectures, group discussions, readings, laboratory experiments, assignments. When you research a subject, you may interview knowledgeable people and record their responses both on paper and on tape. In both your academic work and your personal life, you may keep records of your activities, feelings, and impressions in a journal or in letters to parents or friends. Undoubtedly your purpose in recording is not to make as permanent a record as the Mesopotamians did with cuneiform on bricks, but you do intend to keep information in a form that you can refer to later or that someone else can read and understand. Records sometimes remain in their rough form, as class notes might, but they also are revised as reports, such as reports of laboratory experiments, of reading and research, interviews, and so on.

Journals

In Chapter 6, journals are presented as a way of recording reflections, personal activities, observed events, and impressions. This chapter reiterates the value of journals as records that may later serve as sources of ideas for writing. If you want to begin keeping a journal, read "The Journal" and "Journals Made Public" in Chapter 6 about how to get started. Then begin recording what is going on around you—what you see, what you think, what you question, what you experience. Once you have set aside a time for writing in your journal, vow to yourself that you will persist. When you occasionally read back over what you've written, you will discover that you have indeed kept a record of your life. You will find details about events you otherwise would remember only vaguely, you may see changes in your attitudes toward particular issues or people, and you might decide that some of this is good writing that could serve as the kernel for more formal writing.

When you write in your journal, you are ordinarily the only audience. Your personal journal is your writing to yourself about the world as you see it. You don't have to worry about how long to make your entries, how to punctuate your sentences and spell your words, or whether you can use language that might offend someone else. It's only when you decide to revise these records as a type of public writing that you need to consider such matters.

Letters

You may sometimes keep personal records in the form of letters to people you care about. Usually the primary purpose of such letters is to maintain that relationship while you are separated by distance and social environment. You record your daily activities, your frustrations, your joys, and so on, hoping that through continuing contact about ordinary things you will keep your relationship close. While you may also be able to achieve this purpose through telephone calls, the advantage of the letter is that it can be read again and again as a reminder of your presence.

Letters are sometimes saved and thus become semipermanent records somewhat like journals. Biographies and histories are often written on the basis of old letters found in attics or shoeboxes. Because of George Washington's letters to Sally Fairfax, we know of his extramarital passion for this wife of his close friend. Lovers and mothers and grandmothers save letters that years later, like photographs, record informally what the world was like at the moment they were written. Letters from people serving in war zones become records of life under combat; two such letters are included in this chapter.

Notes

How many notebooks do you estimate you've gone through since you started school? In your lifetime you have undoubtedly taken innumerable pages of notes, and you can be certain that you have many more to go. Students take notes as records of their learning. Like journal entries, notes are mainly for the writer's eyes, but notes are often more systematic than journal entries in recording subject matter that must be remembered and understood. You take notes on lectures, reading, and group activities because you need those records for reviewing, studying, writing into reports, and so on.

To take efficient notes on a *lecture,* you must first be an active listener, looking for main ideas, key words, definitions, repetitions for emphasis, cues for relative importance of details. You can't allow yourself to be distracted by the speaker's appearance, vocal intonations, or the discomfort of the surroundings. You take your notes in a way that makes them accessible to you. For most people and most lectures, formal outlines are not the most efficient kind of notetaking. However, indention of subordinate material does give a cue to its relative significance. Some people prefer taking notes on paper marked with a wide left margin, as much as two or three inches, so that on the right they can record information from the lecture and on the left their insights, summaries, reviews, and special notes to remember. In the left margin they might also record special notes of related textbook material, which might look like those in Figure 9-1.

Students experienced in notetaking say they have altered and improved their recording habits over time. Here are a few tips they share:

Tips for Taking Notes on Lectures

1. Watch the professor. If he or she conspicuously reads from notes, you know that what is said next is worth taking notes on. It invariably turns up on the exam.
2. Take notes on everything the professor writes on the blackboard.
3. Make a note that applies the concepts of the lecture to something you know. It's easier to remember a personal application.

Lecture notes from political science	11/23

govt. task	One could consider the most important task of any govt to be: Provide for security of people & territorial integrity of the state. Lacking ability to do so would prevent govt from performing other basic functions of a govt.
threats to security	Why external threat remained persistent 1. nature of intl. system--anarchic in nature 2. " " nation/state 3. " " of individuals
reaction to threats to security	First experiment: concert of Europe 1815-1854 --a reaction to Napoleonic threat --maintained peace because supportive connections such as language, religion, marriage, customs --no public opinion
Concert of Europe	<u>2 Principles</u> 1. All had common responsibility to maintain territorial status quo treaties of 1815 2. Changes should be made with all of Concert's formal and common consent --elaborated rules of conduct
end	--system broke down with introduction of nationalism and rise of Bismarck

Figure 9-1. Lecture Notes.

Tips (continued)

4. At the end of the day, review and summarize your lecture notes, phrasing them in your own words. Likewise, review and summarize your highlighted readings. Then at test time you won't have pages of highlights to review, and your own re-phrasings will make it easier to recall information.
5. When you review and rephrase, take time to classify, grouping information into categories that make sense to you.
6. Look for concepts, not individual pieces of information. However, if you don't know what to expect from the teacher, you will probably have to note just about everything.

To take notes on *reading assignments,* plan on going over your assignments more than once. Be an active reader by first skimming the assigned material; get an overall view by reading headings, noting italicized or boldfaced type words, scanning diagrams, and reading the first sentences in paragraphs. If there are questions at the end of the reading, study them; then as you read look for answers. When you take notes, you may want to summarize each chapter or section for later review. (See "Summaries" in Chapter 15.)

The most efficient primary method of taking notes on reading is probably making notes in the text itself—assuming that the book is yours or, in the case of library materials, you have made your own copies. Figure 9-2 shows a sample annotated page from a textbook. You probably already have some system of making notes as you read: highlighting important lines, perhaps, or making checks in the margin. Both systems can be more effective, however, if you refine and elaborate on them. Here are some techniques used by experienced student note takers:

Tips for Taking Notes on Reading

1. Use underlines to further accent highlighted material.
2. Use asterisks to point out information to be memorized.
3. Use circles to call attention to important words.
4. Use question marks to indicate material you want to ask the teacher about.
5. Make page summaries, brief notations on the content of each page.
6. Combine lecture and reading notes on a single summary page.

274   **Energy Conservation**

Table 9-7
Distribution of Energy Use in the Transportation Sector

Mode	Percentage
Automobiles	50
Trucks	24
Air, passenger and freight	7
Military	5
Rail, freight	3
Water	4
Pipeline	4
Miscellaneous passenger, including bus and rail	3

Transportation

The ways energy is used in the transportation sector are shown in Table 9-7. As could have been assumed, trucks and cars dominate the use of energy, and these vehicles largely employ internal combustion engines fueled by gasoline or diesel oil. The dynamics of automobile motion and fuel consumption will be discussed in some detail in Chapter 12 so that only the general aspects of the problem will be brought up here.

Americans have been infatuated with the automobile for 60 or 70 years. We have more cars per capita, and we drive more miles per capita, than the citizens of any other country. In 1972, some 10,400 passenger miles were driven per capita in the United States compared to 5800 in the second leading country, Canada. Western European countries averaged about 4000 passenger miles per capita. In the same year, 349 gallons of gasoline for auto transportation were used per capita in the United States compared to 90 in Europe. The potential for energy conservation in automobile transportation in the United States is clearly tremendous.

The solution to the problem lies in two different areas: the greater use of more efficient modes of transportation and increased efficiency of the automobile. Because of the convenience of the auto, the U.S. public transportation system has deteriorated very badly in the last 50 years or so. The efficiency of various modes of transportation is shown in Table 12-2; it is clear that we have opted for an inefficient mode, because most travel is by little more than one occupant in an auto. Since 1973, there has been effort by federal and local governments to improve public transportation in the cities, but this has not as yet made a major difference in the use of the automobile. Car or van pooling, sharing the ride, and so forth are more widely used for commuting to work where an inadequate bus or train system exists. We are also finally giving thought to urban design so that the distances the average person must travel for employment or for shopping are reduced from those with the present unplanned sprawl.

It appears, however, that the major energy conservation gains that will be made in

Handwritten annotations: 10,400 miles U.S / 5,500 next country / 2 solutions / The U.S is major consumer of energy, for transp., esp. autos. We are making little progress in energy efficiency

Figure 9-2. Annotated Page from a Textbook. (Source: Jack J. Kraushaar and Robert A. Ristinen, *Energy and Problems of a Technical Society*, rev. ed. New York: Wiley, 1988.)

Notetaking is an essential skill for carrying out that familiar academic assignment, the research paper. Careful reading and meticulous recording of material make a huge difference in the quality of the finished paper. Chapter 16 describes this kind of notetaking in greater detail.

Although the most common notetaking in school is in response to lectures and reading, you may sometimes need to fill another recording role—in *group activities*. Being recorder may mean (1) that you will later report to the class as a whole, and (2) that you must keep a record for later reference by the group. Whatever the purpose, your notes must be accurate and thorough. Here are some tips for taking such notes:

Tips for Taking Notes on Group Activities

1. Be an attentive and active listener.
2. Record discussions completely yet briefly.
3. Be objective. Don't be biased in favor of a single view.
4. Ask for clarification when you don't understand.
5. Record differences of opinion.
6. Be especially thorough in noting conclusions.
7. Keep an accurate record of dates and names.

Being recorder for a group is similar to being recording secretary for a committee or an organization; your report is like minutes of a meeting. While the role of recorder is important to successful group work, you may find that the demands of recording limit your ability to participate in discussions, something to consider when you agree to keep the records.

Records are often singular in purpose, merely to keep an account for later reference or review. Notetaking on lectures and reading is like that. But, as we have seen, records also communicate ideas and maintain continuity. Frequently, too, records also are revised for another purpose, such as to report, like most of the documents in Chapter 10. The essays and writing assignments in this chapter represent a few of the many kinds of writing done for the purpose of recording: letters, records of how the weather or some other natural phenomenon affects people, records of group actions, and interviews.

RECORDING IN PERSONAL LETTERS

One of the most common purposes for writing is to contact friends and relatives we know and care about—to tell them what we're doing, what we're thinking, and what matters to us at the moment. The letter serves as a record of our thoughts and experiences. If the recipient of a personal letter has a question about the details of your story or precisely where you will meet her next week, she only needs to get out the letter and refresh her memory. People like to receive letters; your letter is a part of you, sealed up in an envelope and waiting in the mailbox.

Reading

Here are two personal letters by Lynda Van Devanter, an army nurse in Vietnam. The letters, sent to her parents five months apart, told them what her life was like in the war zone and maintained the continuity of her relationship with them. Published in her book *Home before Morning,* the letters serve now as a record of that period in her life. Van Devanter's letters were recorded on paper; between the two letters is a communication from her father recorded on tape. As you read the letters, observe how they record not only events but Van Devanter's changing attitudes also. When you read the transcript of the taped "letter," determine what her father's purposes might have been for saying what he does.

Mom and Dad

Lynda Van Devanter

Dear Mom and Dad,

Things go fairly well here. Monsoon is very heavy right now—have   1
barely seen the sun in a couple of weeks. But this makes the sky that much prettier at night when flares go off. There's a continual mist in the air which makes the flares hazy. At times they look like falling stars; then sometimes they seem to shine like crosses.

At 4:16 A.M. our time the other day, two of our fellow Americans   2
landed on the moon. At that precise moment, Pleiku Air Force Base, in the sheer joy and wonder of it, sent up a whole skyful of flares—white, red, and green. It was as if they were daring the surrounding North Vietnamese Army to try and tackle such a great nation. As we watched it, we couldn't speak at all. The pride in our country filled us to the point that many had tears in their eyes.

It hurts so much sometimes to see the paper full of demonstrators,   3
especially people burning the flag. Fight fire with fire, we ask here. Display the flag, Mom and Dad, please, every day. And tell your friends to do the same. It means so much to us to know we're supported, to know not everyone feels we're making a mistake being here.

Every day we see more and more why we're here. When a whole   4
Montagnard village comes in after being bombed and terrorized by

Charlie, you know. There are helpless people dying every day. The worst of it is the children. Little baby-sans being brutally maimed and killed. They've never hurt anyone. Papa-san comes in with his three babies—one dead and two covered with frag wounds. You try to tell him the boy is dead but he keeps talking to the baby as if that will make him live again. It's enough to break your heart. And through it all, you feel something's missing. There! You put your finger on it. There's not a sound from them. The children don't cry from pain; the parents don't cry from sorrow; they're stoic.

You have to grin sometimes at the primitiveness of these Montagnards. 5 Here in the emergency room, doctors and nurses hustle about fixing up a little girl. There stands her shy little (and I mean little—like four feet tall) Papa-san, face looking down at the floor, in his loin cloth, smoking his long marijuana pipe. He has probably never seen an electric light before, and the ride here in that great noisy bird (helicopter) was too much for him to comprehend. They're such characters. One comes to the hospital and the whole family camps out in the hall or on the ramp and watches over the patient. No, nobody can tell me we don't belong here.

Love,
Lynda

Hi, Lynda, this is your father. Right now, I'm home by myself. After 1 you suggested it, we scooted out to Gem and found ourselves a nice little old cassette recorder and player so we could start sending you tapes. I hope everybody here doesn't suffer from mike fright.

One of the things the moon landing made me realize is how com- 2 monplace everything seems once it's happened. We've all picked up a feeling of ennui. Gee, these guys were up on the moon, they were wandering around on its surface, they shot the thing up there and shot it back down, and an awful lot of people are terribly unimpressed. It sort of reminds me of an old joke: This young boy takes his uncle to a circus where a guy climbs a 150-foot pole and stands on his head. On his right foot he hangs two or three circular horseshoes and twirls them. He does the same thing on his left foot. With his left hand, he juggles three balls, and with the right hand, he plays a clarinet solo. The young boy says to his uncle, "Ain't he the greatest?" The old guy looks at him and says, "A Benny Goodman he ain't."

So many of us look at everything that happens with that attitude. We 3 forget that there are so many wonderful things that people are doing. Regardless of whether these guys had been the first or the twenty-first guys on the moon, we should be proud of them and never take them for granted. It's a great, great achievement for these good old United States.

I guess there were a lot of things that I never did tell you before you 4 left home. One is that I'm proud that you're doing what you're doing.

Even before the Japanese bombed Pearl Harbor, I was trying to get into the service. At the time, I thought I had it made in the Marine Corps. They were taking young college graduates as possible officer candidates, so I went down and saw old Colonel Miller at the Marine Corps Reserve in Washington. When he saw my glasses, he suggested that I take them off when I came back for the eye exam. I had already memorized the chart so I'd have no problem.

When I went for my physical, the doctor started asking me a lot   5
of usual questions. Pretty soon in the game, I suggested taking the eye examination because I was afraid of forgetting the chart. But this guy was a pretty sharp operator. He said, "I know damned well you wear glasses." So I had to show him my glasses. He looked through them and said, "That refraction's too big for the Marines, buddy boy. You go home."

Later, I took the physical for the Army a couple of times but my blood   6
pressure was too high for them. That was about the time that Nancy came along. I went back and appealed my case with the surgeon general. He ordered the Army to give me another physical, but they weren't buying. They wouldn't take me. It wasn't that I was anxious to be there, but I felt like I owed a little something to my country. I guess this is why I'm so pleased that you're in the Army. I'm living vicariously now. You are me and I'm in. As I said before, I'm very proud.

Dear Mom and Dad,

I don't know where to start except to say I'm tired. It seems that's   1
all I ever say anymore. Thank you both for your tapes and all the little goodies in the Christmas packages. Christmas came and went marked only by tragedy. I've been working nights for a couple of weeks and have been spending a great deal of time in post-op. They've been unbelievably busy. I got wrapped up in several patients, one of whom I scrubbed on when we repaired an artery in his leg. It eventually clotted and we did another procedure on him to clear out the artery—all this to save his leg. His name is Clarence Washington.* I came in for duty Christmas Eve and was handed an OR slip for Clarence—above-knee amputation. He had developed gas gangrene. The sad thing was that the artery was pumping away beautifully. Merry Christmas, kid, we have to cut your leg off to save your life. We also had three other GIs die that night. Kids, every one. The war disgusts me. I hate it! I'm beginning to feel like it's all a mistake.

Christmas morning I got off duty and opened all my packages alone.   2
I missed you all so much. I cried myself to sleep. I'm starting to cry again. It's ridiculous. I seem to be crying all the time lately. I hate this place.

---

*Names have been changed to protect individual privacy.

This is now the seventh month of death, destruction, and misery. I'm tired of going to sleep listening to outgoing and incoming rockets, mortars, and artillery. I'm sick of facing, every day, a new bunch of children ripped to pieces. They're just kids—eighteen, nineteen years old! It stinks! Whole lives ahead of them—cut off. I'm sick to death of it. I've got to get out of here.

I'm so glad that Steve finally got out. He was lucky to have made   3
it through a year in this hellhole without getting seriously wounded. I never got to talk to him, but I understand the bitterness in his letters home, now, in a way I couldn't when I first got here. When I finally got someone in his unit on the phone the other day, they said he'd just left for Saigon to catch his Freedom Bird. With any luck, he's somewhere over Japan about now, and free from this green suck. I envy him.

I found out a couple of weeks ago that Barbara has been transferred   4
to a unit near where Steve was. I've written her a few times but gotten no answer, and the phone lines in her area are utterly awful, so I haven't been able to reach her. I hope she's okay.

I just heard another chopper come in. I better go. They need me in   5
the OR.

Peace,
Lynda

Questions: The Community of Writers

1. Compare Van Devanter's attitude toward her work in her first letter, recorded near the beginning of her tour of duty, with her attitude in the second letter, written five months later. What evidence of change do you see?

2. In the first letter, what does Van Devanter tell you about the nature of the work she does as a nurse in Vietnam? What does she tell you in the second letter?

3. The first paragraph of the intervening message introduces Van Devanter's father on the tape recording. What other recording purposes can you discover in the remainder of the message? What purposes other than recording might he have?

4. In her first letter Van Devanter directs her parents to "display the flag," but in a note preceding her second letter she says, "I threw away the rhinestone flag I had previously worn on my uniform." How does this change apply to the change in attitude you discussed in question 1? Relate these attitudes to today's attitudes about flag burning and flag waving.

5. Van Devanter's father responds to her flag-waving letter by saying, "I'm proud that you're doing what you're doing." If you were her father, how would you respond to Lynda's second letter?

6. Discuss what revisions Van Devanter might have made in her letters before including them in her book.

Analysis

As her personal record, Van Devanter's letters tell what her world was like at the moment of writing:

Things *go* fairly well here.
Monsoon *is* very heavy right now.
It *hurts* so much sometimes to see the paper full of demonstrators.
I'm tired.
The war *disgusts* me.
They *need* me in the OR.

Her verbs are present tense, indicating attitudes and actions at the time of the writing. When she uses past tense verbs ("I *missed* you all so much," "Steve finally *got* out"), it is to support present attitudes with past actions.

As letters to her parents, these pieces of writing are personal, but they allow you, an outside viewer, to witness some personal expressions: "I cried myself to sleep," "I missed you all so much." In preparing her book, Van Devanter intentionally included these and other letters to record for a broader audience what service in Vietnam was like. You are therefore able to perceive the daily personal experience of living through a war, to see how initial idealism deteriorates into weariness and anger, and to know the toll that death and dying have on the living as well as the dead.

Do you have occasion to write regularly to your parents or someone else close to you? Perhaps such a record of your college life will be interesting to you a few years from now. Can you imagine your children twenty or thirty years from now reading about what college life was like for you in the 1990s?

Exercise: The Community of Writers

In a group of three to five people, with one of you designated recorder, recall your first impressions of your college campus—its buildings, the older students, the bookstore, whatever you remember. Then compare your current perceptions of the campus. How have your attitudes changed? How do you account for the changes? Do these changes have any parallels to Van Devanter's?

Writing

Write a personal letter to someone you care about. Record what your world is like at this moment—what is happening, what you are thinking, what your attitude toward school is. Write about the things you would talk about if the recipient were with you. The letter may be very personal. Before you send it, revise the letter for a public audience. You may need to add details that you and your personal audience share but your public audience doesn't know. You may need to change slang and other insider language that might be unfamiliar to the broader audience. You may need to identify some of the people whose names turn up in your letter. At the same time, remember that this piece of writing is still a letter addressed to someone you know well. After you've completed your revision, send the personal letter to the intended recipient and use the revision for your class assignment.

RECORDING REACTIONS TO NATURE

People react to their environment. Suicides are more common in winter, riots in summer. Depression responds favorably to light—the more light, the less depression. On cloudy days, people are often as gloomy as the weather; on sunny days, their outlook is brighter. These are just generalizations, of course. Some people like rainy days, and some like winter, but these people too are responding to their environment.

People like to record their reactions to nature. If you talk to a distant relative or friend on the telephone, the conversation is likely to include a discussion of the comparative weather. If you receive a letter from that person, you may get a report of the weather and the writer's reaction to it. People wish it wouldn't rain—or wish it would. They wish the temperature were higher—or lower. They wish the wind would blow—or not blow.

Most of the time our reactions to nature are rather mild, just something to talk or write about when we can't think of anything else to say. Sometimes, however, nature behaves in unexpected ways, and then our reactions are more pointed. Earthquakes, for example, have devastating effects, and the more affected we are by them the stronger our reactions. If you lose your home, you react strongly. If someone you know loses a home, you are still affected. If you see people on television who have lost their homes, you are sympathetic but mostly glad that you haven't experienced the devastation. We have similar reactions to floods, hurricanes, tornadoes, and other extraordinary natural events. Following one of these events, we encounter numerous records of personal and public reactions. We see homeless people interviewed on television, and we read about them in newsmagazines.

Still, not all unexpected natural events are catastrophic. Some just affect the way we feel. An unexpected cool breeze in the middle of the summer refreshes us, and a warm one in the spring lifts our spirits.

Reading

This essay is excerpted from the chapter "Los Angeles Notebook" in Joan Didion's reflective book *Slouching towards Bethlehem.* In these paragraphs, Didion records what the Santa Ana wind is like and how people in Los Angeles react to it. As you read, notice how much of the record is from Didion's own experience and how much from other sources. Find out what is bad about this wind and what its effects are.

The Santa Ana

Joan Didion

There is something uneasy in the Los Angeles air this afternoon, some unnatural stillness, some tension. What it means is that tonight a Santa Ana will begin to blow, a hot wind from the northeast whining down through the Cajon and San Gorgonio Passes, blowing up sandstorms out along Route 66, drying the hills and the nerves to the flash point. For a few days now we will see smoke back in the canyons, and hear sirens in the night. I have neither heard nor read that a Santa Ana is due, but I know it, and almost everyone I have seen today knows it too. We know it because we feel it. The baby frets. The maid sulks. I rekindle a waning argument with the telephone company, then cut my losses and lie down, given over to whatever it is in the air. To live with the Santa Ana is to accept, consciously or unconsciously, a deeply mechanistic view of human behavior.

I recall being told, when I first moved to Los Angeles and was living on an isolated beach, that the Indians would throw themselves into the sea when the bad wind blew. I could see why. The Pacific turned ominously glossy during a Santa Ana period, and one woke in the night troubled not only by the peacocks screaming in the olive trees but by the eerie absence of surf. The heat was surreal. The sky had a yellow cast, the kind of light sometimes called "earthquake weather." My only neighbor would not come out of her house for days, and there were no lights at night, and her husband roamed the place with a machete. One day he would tell me that he had heard a trespasser, the next a rattlesnake.

"On nights like that," Raymond Chandler once wrote about the Santa Ana, "every booze party ends in a fight. Meek little wives feel the edge of the carving knife and study their husbands' necks. Anything can happen." That was the kind of wind it was. I did not know then that there was any basis for the effect it had on all of us, but it turns out to be another of those cases in which science bears out folk wisdom. The Santa Ana, which is named for one of the canyons it rushes through, is a *foehn* wind, like the *foehn* of Austria and Switzerland and the *hamsin* of Israel. There are a number of persistent malevolent winds, perhaps the best known of which are the mistral of France and the Mediterranean sirocco, but a *foehn* wind has distinct characteristics: it occurs on the leeward slope of a mountain range and, although the air begins as a cold mass, it is warmed as it comes down the mountain and appears finally as a hot dry wind. Whenever and wherever a *foehn* blows, doctors hear about headaches and nausea and allergies, about "nervousness," about "depression." In Los Angeles some teachers do not attempt to conduct formal classes during a Santa Ana, because the children become unmanageable. In Switzerland the suicide rate goes up during the *foehn,* and in the courts of some Swiss cantons the wind is considered a mitigating circumstance for crime. Surgeons are said to watch the wind, because blood does not clot normally during a *foehn.* A few years ago an Israeli physicist discovered that not only during such winds, but for the ten or twelve hours which precede them, the air carries an unusually high ratio of positive to negative ions. No one seems to know exactly why that should be; some talk about friction and others suggest solar disturbances. In any case the positive ions are there, and what an excess of positive ions does, in the simplest terms, is make people unhappy. One cannot get much more mechanistic than that.

Easterners commonly complain that there is no "weather" at all in   4
Southern California, that the days and the seasons slip by relentlessly, numbingly bland. That is quite misleading. In fact the climate is characterized by infrequent but violent extremes: two periods of torrential subtropical rains which continue for weeks and wash out the hills and send subdivisions sliding toward the sea; about twenty scattered days a year of the Santa Ana, which, with its incendiary dryness, invariably means fire. At the first prediction of a Santa Ana, the Forest Service flies men and equipment from northern California into the southern forests, and the Los Angeles Fire Department cancels its ordinary non-firefighting routines. The Santa Ana caused Malibu to burn the way it did in 1956, and Bel Air in 1961, and Santa Barbara in 1964. In the winter of 1966–67 eleven men were killed fighting a Santa Ana fire that spread through the San Gabriel Mountains.

Just to watch the front-page news out of Los Angeles during a Santa   5
Ana is to get very close to what it is about the place. The longest single Santa Ana period in recent years was in 1957, and it lasted not the usual three or four days but fourteen days, from November 21 until December 4. On the first day 25,000 acres of the San Gabriel Mountains were burning, with gusts reaching 100 miles an hour. In town, the wind reached Force 12, or hurricane force, on the Beaufort Scale; oil derricks were toppled and people ordered off the downtown streets to avoid injury from flying objects. On November 22 the fire in the San Gabriels was out of control. On November 24 six people were killed in automobile

accidents, and by the end of the week the Los Angeles *Times* was keeping a box score of traffic deaths. On November 26 a prominent Pasadena attorney, depressed about money, shot and killed his wife, their two sons, and himself. On November 27 a South Gate divorcée, twenty-two, was murdered and thrown from a moving car. On November 30 the San Gabriel fire was still out of control, and the wind in town was blowing eighty miles an hour. On the first day of December four people died violently, and on the third the wind began to break.

It is hard for people who have not lived in Los Angeles to realize how   6
radically the Santa Ana figures in the local imagination. The city burning is Los Angeles's deepest image of itself. Nathaniel West perceived that, in *The Day of the Locust,* and at the time of the 1965 Watts riots what struck the imagination most indelibly were the fires. For days one could drive the Harbor Freeway and see the city on fire, just as we had always known it would be in the end. Los Angeles weather is the weather of catastrophe, of apocalypse, and, just as the reliably long and bitter winters of New England determine the way life is lived there, so the violence and the unpredictability of the Santa Ana affect the entire quality of life in Los Angeles, accentuate its impermanence, its unreliability. The wind shows us how close to the edge we are.

Questions: The Community of Writers

1. From Didion's essay, make a list of features describing the Santa Ana wind; then make a list of features describing human reactions to the wind. Relate the two lists and try to draw some inferences, or conclusions, on what features of the wind cause the observed reactions.

2. Didion describes the Santa Ana as a *foehn* wind. What is a *foehn* wind, and what effects is it said to have on people? Which of these effects have scientific support and which are anecdotal? Do you know of other "malevolent" winds?

3. What does Didion tell you about herself in this essay?

4. What does Didion say about how the city of Los Angeles feels about fire?

5. This essay was published in the 1960s. Discuss how it might be updated with more recent accounts of the effects of the Santa Ana or other *foehn* winds?

Analysis

Like Van Devanter's letters recording life in Vietnam, Didion's essay records the present:

There *is* something uneasy in the Los Angeles air this afternoon.
The baby *frets.*
I *recall* being told.
The children *become* unmanageable.

Didion records what Los Angeles is like with the coming of the Santa Ana wind. And, again like Van Devanter, she uses past tense verbs to recall events that support her record of the present:

> The Pacific *turned* ominously glossy.
> The heat *was* surreal.
> The Santa Ana *caused* Malibu to burn the way it did in 1956.

Records of presently occurring events often draw on past events for support and interest.

Development

Didion's essay is developed mainly by **cause and effect.** It introduces a single cause—the Santa Ana wind—and describes various effects on people and the environment. In describing these effects, Didion records her own feelings, the actions of others, and testimony from other people, in both the present and the past. Concerning the effects on herself, she says:

> I rekindle a waning argument with the telephone company, then cut my losses and lie down, given over to whatever it is in the air.

> I could see why [the Indians would throw themselves into the sea]. The Pacific turned ominously glossy during a Santa Ana period, and one woke in the night troubled not only by the peacocks screaming in the olive trees but by the eerie absence of surf. The heat was surreal.

About the effects on others, here are some examples:

> The baby frets. The maid sulks.

> On November 26 a prominent Pasadena attorney, depressed about money, shot and killed his wife, their two sons, and himself. On November 27 a South Gate divorcée, twenty-two, was murdered and thrown from a moving car.

Didion records the testimony of others, referring to the work of an Israeli physicist and other scientists and quoting detective-story writer Raymond Chandler: "On nights like that . . . every booze party ends in a fight. . . . Anything can happen." She also observes the effects on the environment: the "unnatural stillness," the "ominously glossy" sea, the "incendiary dryness" of the forests.

She includes statistics, "front page" history, definition (of the *foehn* wind), and her own inferences. Her final statement may be read as Didion's thesis: "The wind shows us how close to the edge we are." It draws together all her details and makes an inference about them.

Exercise: The Exploring Writer

In your journal or on a separate sheet of paper, write a paragraph that, like Didion's first paragraph, begins "There is something _____ in the air" to describe something that is going on around you—perhaps related to the weather, perhaps anticipating an event (such as exams, a holiday, the end of the term). Describe how you feel and what you observe.

Writing

Keep a daily record for a week, noting the weather and the reactions to it in yourself, the people around you, and your environment. Note what people say about the weather and whatever changes you observe in their behavior that may be weather related. Some people, for example, get sinus headaches when the weather is about to change; some respond favorably to sunshine and gloomily to clouds and rain; some lose their tempers easily in hot and muggy conditions. Record their weather-related stories and your reflections on the kind of weather you are experiencing. Be a close observer, and make your notes as complete as necessary for you to carry out the second part of this project.

After keeping your record for a week, select *one* weather condition you have described and use it to write a *public* record. Describe the weather conditions and record the reactions you have observed. Add weather-related stories you may have heard; any statistics you may have gleaned from radio, television, or newspapers; any inferences you have made from your observations. If you have experienced similar or contrasting weather in other locales, you may be able to make some comparative observations. To give your record immediacy, use present tense verbs, as Didion does, to describe the weather as it is happening, but use past tense as appropriate when relating stories or past weather occurrences.

In revision, see that your essay is now a *public* record rather than the collection of private notes it began with. While your notes may have been cryptic or truncated—for example, "Rain again, gloom again"—in your public record you need to fill out your sentences and explain your statements. Also, you may have to identify your locale, the dates you are covering, and something about yourself, such as your age or length of time at this locale and your usual attitude toward weather. Think of your readers; they probably have weather-related stories they could tell too, so make yours one they can relate to.

RECORDING INTERVIEWS

An important source of information for essays and reports is interviews of experts. When acquiring information, you can learn from many sources: textbooks, encyclopedias, almanacs, newspapers, professional journals, popular magazines, and so on. But in an interview you may be able to get firsthand information that is not available any other way. If you want to write a persuasive essay about the need for adequate parking space on your campus, you can greatly strengthen your case by knowing what the university is planning to do to make adequate parking space available, information that can be gained from your buildings and grounds supervisor. In writing about the need for more street lighting, you can find out from the city engineer what the plans, problems, and possibilities are for improvements. If you want information about the use of DNA "fingerprinting" in your local court system, you might talk to a judge or a criminal lawyer.

When you need information, consider interviews as a source. Then decide who would be the best available expert for you to interview. You might refer to the yellow pages of your telephone directory or the city directory in your library; you might ask if one of your teachers could recommend someone, or go to the chair of the department that teaches the subject you are investigating. Local firms and nonprofit organizations with interests in your subject are other sources. Once you have decided on someone who could help you, telephone or write that person requesting an interview. Introduce yourself and your interest in the subject, tell why you are contacting this person, and request the interview, suggesting a time you think will be agreeable to both of you.

Once the interview is arranged, prepare your questions carefully. For the most part, ask specific questions. A question like "What are the city's plans for improving street lighting?" may not give you the information you are seeking. If you want to know about the possibilities of improved lighting in a specific area, ask the specific question: "The sidewalks along Fifth Street are a major pedestrian traffic area, yet the street has several poorly lighted spots. Does the city have any plans to improve lighting in those places?" Whenever you ask a question calling for a yes or no answer, plan to follow up with another question if the information is not forthcoming: "What are those plans?" or "What can be done to change those plans?"

Arrive at the interview on time. Follow your plan, but be open to new, unexpected directions. If your interviewee wanders off the subject, however, get the interview back on track with one of your prepared questions. Let your interviewee do the talking. Listen carefully, taking only as many notes as necessary to help your memory later. If your interviewee doesn't object to a tape recorder and you can use one without distractions, consider taking one along. End the interview with a concluding question such as "Is there anything else you would like to tell me?" Depending on your purpose for the information you have collected, you may need to find out if your interviewee wants a copy of your report of the interview.

Immediately following the interview, make a complete record of it based on your notes. This is not your finished report or summary; it's your record made while the interview is fresh in your mind. You will probably write the report later, after you have thought more about the information or done more information gathering.

Two records of interviews follow. The first is a revised transcription, and the second is written in essay form using quotations and paraphrases of the interviewee's statements.

Reading

Here's a transcript of an interview between a reporter from *New Perspectives Quarterly* and the Reverend Jesse Jackson—a political, social, as well as religious spokesperson on drug use. As you read, observe how the interviewer directs the interview, seeks out specific answers, and leads into new directions.

Drug Use Is a Sin

New Perspectives Quarterly Interview with the Reverend Jesse Jackson

NPQ: By waging the first drug war battle in Washington, DC, Federal Narcotics Director William Bennett targeted the black population of the inner city. Is the focus in the right place?   1

Jesse Jackson: One hundred fifty billion dollars in illegal drugs flow into this country every year. Americans, which represent six percent of the world's population, consume half the world's drugs. The African-American population of the inner city does not have enough cash resources to buy up all those drugs.   2

Drug use and criminality are not solely the domain of the urban "underclass." To give the drug runner and the drug user a dark face merely offers false comfort, since the problem is truly elsewhere.   3

Furthermore, this drug epidemic is not just a problem of despairing youth from families broken over time by slavery and poverty. There is a crisis of values in the family structure of all Americans, not just the "underclass." And this crisis is reinforced by the culture: The betrayals, casual infidelities, and materialism promoted by TV programs like "Dallas" often have more access to the minds and impressions of our children than church, schools, or parents.   4

Drug lords are the masters and drug users are slaves. And the slaves   5
come in all colors, sizes, races, and sexes. It is simply misguided to ignore
the universal character of drug use—among pilots and train engineers,
public officials, ministers, doctors, stockbrokers, lawyers, college profes-
sors—and only focus on the black or the brown dimension of it.

New York Senator Alfonse D'Amato once went to the Bronx wear-   6
ing casual clothes to prove he could buy crack openly on any street
corner. Yet, he could just as easily have walked down to the bathroom
in the federal building in his usual suit. He could have gone to Battery
Park, overlooking the Statue of Liberty, and gotten any quantity or
quality of drug he wanted. Or, he could have gone to any suburban
school.

This said, in one respect William Bennett is right to focus on Wash-   7
ington, DC. When gangs bring their drug supply and weapons right into
the heart of our democracy they are displaying open contempt for the
government and the American people. To set up shop right in the face
of the president, in the very city where the justices of the Supreme Court
live and work, and where Congress presides, is a bold sign of contempt
for the whole American system.

This drug trade must be crushed and the drug lords must be busted.   8
If Communists were infiltrating us this way, causing the death of Americans in our capital, we would have a very different attitude. We still have
too much tolerance for drug-related death.

NPQ: While drug use is very widespread in America, it is also quite   9
dispersed. However, the focus seems to have fallen on the inner city and
the underclass because of the concentration and escalation of drug-
related crime and violence.

Jackson: There is no question that the combination of drug sickness,   10
greed, the availability of Uzi machine guns, and AK-47's is a formula for
disaster.

NPQ: After all, the violence isn't with the airline pilot or the. . . .   11

Jackson: The hell it isn't. When there is a train wreck, that's violence.   12
When a plane crashes, that's violence. When workers are mauled on the
assembly line, that's violence, or when their relatives are in jail or dead
because of drugs, that's violence.

It is a cop-out to focus only on gang violence and not on the extent   13
of drug-related violence around the country.

NPQ: To continue your analogy between the drug invasion and   14
Communist aggression, are you saying that the Bush Administration is
soft on drugs?

Jackson: No, I wouldn't say that they are soft. They are hard on what   15
they know, but their knowledge is soft and their resources are limited.

Bennett needs to have cabinet status and a real budget. He has 16
neither the authority nor the budget to fight a drug war. And, so far,
neither does he have the vision.

NPQ: What about Jack Kemp's proposals to evict drug users and 17
their families from public housing and to require ID cards for public
housing residents?

Jackson: Does that include those who have government subsidized 18
FHA and VA loans who get caught with drugs? Does that include those
who pay their rent with government salaries who get caught using drugs?
Does that include the middle class who, as beneficiaries of a government
subsidy, deduct their home mortgage payment from their taxes?

There is obviously a racial premise in this narrow and inadequate 19
solution.

NPQ: What is your program for stopping drug use? 20

Jackson: Cut the supply at the source, strengthen interdiction, edu- 21
cate the innocent, rehabilitate the sick, and enforce swift and tough
punishment for the purveyors of death—the drug lords who are nothing
more than terrorists.

Since the flow of drugs into the United States is an act of terrorism, 22
anti-terrorist policies must be applied. If someone is caught bringing
drugs into this country and selling them here, if someone is caught
transmitting the death-agent to Americans, that person should face wartime consequences. The line must be drawn.

NPQ: How do you propose to cut the supply and strengthen inter- 23
diction?

Jackson: Drug interdiction should be elevated to a central position 24
in our foreign policy. The Secretary of State should convene all the heads
of state from those nations where the drugs are grown, especially from
south of our border: Mexico, Colombia, Peru, and Bolivia. A multilateral
plan must be worked out that includes debt forgiveness and economic
development assistance, including programs for the development of alternative crops.

And the United States must supply military support, where needed, 25
because in countries like Colombia the drug lords have private armies
stronger than the standing armies.

We must also be more effective in stopping the flow of drugs. I have 26
been in Florida with Coast Guard officials. They know how 90 percent of
the drugs come into this country: In recent times, five of the six Coast
Guard cutters assigned to stop the flow of drugs have been deployed to
turn back Haitian boat people, not drugs. Five-sixths of the anti-drug
fleet that should have been devoted to chasing drug peddlers was, instead, chasing Haitians.

Finally, the $150 billion drug trade is being laundered in somebody's   27
banks. There is not an adequate challenge to the people who launder
money. Political authorities in the border areas, by and large, turn their
heads to these accomplices to murder.

NPQ: What about punishment?   28

Jackson: Swift punishment for pushers because they are terrorists.   29

NPQ: Meaning heavy sentences without the possibility of parole?   30

Jackson: Yes. Stiffer prison sentences and better nets.   31

NPQ: But isn't there a limit? Dr. Alim Muhammed, who runs the   32
Nation of Islam's "dopebuster" program in Washington's northeast section, told us that of the 200,000 black males who live in Washington,
10,000 of them are incarcerated.

Jackson: If prison is warranted, we have to use it.   33

NPQ: If pushers should be treated as terrorist purveyors of death,   34
does that mean they deserve the death penalty?

Jackson: I am not inclined to say pushers deserve the death penalty.   35
I am not sure that the state has the moral authority to kill.

NPQ: More than anything you have seen in your long career work-   36
ing for social change, does this drug scourge make you come the closest
to favorably considering the death penalty?

Jackson: Yes. This drug scourge makes me think that real punish-   37
ment is necessary. When people are openly unemployed but can flash
their expensive wares in the face of circumstantial evidence that they are
drug lords, it makes me think that there must be a drastic way to stop
them from manipulating our system.

The drug lords laugh at the system, which is not designed for people   38
who believe crime is something that pays.

NPQ: Beyond stiffer sentences and better nets, how can demand for   39
drugs be dampened?

Jackson: The whole environment that leads to drug use must be   40
changed. There is a need for prenatal care, day care, Headstart, job
training, affordable housing, jobs with some purpose, and the minimum
wage must be raised.

And there must be education against drugs to bolster moral   41
resistance.

NPQ: Where will that education come from? In our system, doesn't   42
moral resistance spring from the community and civil society—the
churches, family and parental authority, and so on? Government, after
all, is not a religious institution; the Constitution is not a moral code for
individual behavior, but a framework for protecting the chosen behavior
of individuals.

Jackson: The main responsibility for cutting supply falls on the 43 government. Cutting demand, I agree, must come more from the community.

NPQ: Okay. But who? How? For years you have been stumping the 44 country, preaching "down with dope, up with hope." Nancy Reagan has been pushing *Just Say No.* Nevertheless, drug use has risen in many areas.

Jackson: Well, there wasn't enough real work going on at enough 45 levels. I was crying out in the wilderness.

For too long, drugs were not seen as a national threat. Now, many 46 officials have gone from the extreme of ignoring the drug scourge to putting a racial label on it. So, the ready answer has been to kick suspected drug dealers and users out of their homes and lock them up.

NPQ: Some groups, including the Nation of Islam, seem to have an 47 effective approach to moral education and rehabilitation. Their objective is to restore cultural integrity to the community and the family, and to provide structure and discipline without government interference. They don't look to a white, Republican administration to solve the problems of their community.

Do you agree with their approach? 48

Jackson: Some people need cultural affirmation; discipline is also 49 important. This is one dimension.

I know that the Muslims have been effective in routing drug push- 50 ers by patrolling the housing projects. As long as this type of solution is within the law, it should be encouraged. Parents, in their off-time, should patrol the school areas so that drug pushers will determine that the area is too hot to sell drugs. Neighborhood patrols are also important.

NPQ: Where do you depart and where do you share common 51 ground with Drug Czar William Bennett's approach?

Jackson: This administration thinks it can get people off drugs by 52 threatening to evict them from their homes. People who crave drugs do not stop to consider where they live. They are already walking on air. The first thing the drug czar should know is the nature of drug addiction: Drug addicts are sick and sick people need medical care. Yet, where is the budget for care and rehabilitation?

Is the Bush Administration going to put them all in jail? Jail is also 53 public housing. What is the point of shifting people from one form of public housing to another form of public housing? In fact, jail is more expensive to the taxpayer.

Administration officials have jumped up with instant solutions before 54 they have an analysis. Why don't they convene a summit with leaders not only of drug-producing countries, but with mayors, police chiefs, health officials, and former users who have been wrestling with the drug problem long before it was on Bennett's mind? That would at least enable Bennett to get a grip on the nature and depth of the crisis. The approach should not be confrontational or racial. It should not focus on Washington, DC, and it should be bipartisan.

NPQ: Drug use seems such an intractable vice to some that they are   55
proposing decriminalization to remove the violence and the high illicit profits.

Might that be part of a solution, especially since so much drug use is   56
casual, not destructively addictive?

Jackson: I don't believe that. You may take away the profits but you   57
won't take away the poison. Drugs are poison. Taking drugs is a sin. Drug use is morally debased and sick . . .

NPQ: . . . Which means those Americans who use drugs—25 percent   58
of the population—are morally debased . . . ?

Jackson: It is true that Americans are willing allies to the drug   59
flow. Many of them are both enjoying and profiting from drugs. These same Americans wouldn't enjoy communism or fascism in the same way; they wouldn't enjoy an invasion and occupation by the Russians. But they seem to enjoy the occupation of drugs. Popping pills is pleasure. Taking drugs creates euphoria, happiness, good feelings, gratification.

With all the war-room strategies this nation has had for fighting   60
foreign enemies, we have never had an enemy this syrupy and slick. We have never had a time in which our own army wanted to engage the enemy for purposes of gratification. This enemy is more devastating than the enemy in the other uniform with the other ideology. This time the enemy is us. People are not being force-fed drugs. They are volunteering for this slow suicide.

NPQ: You are a religious man. Where does the moral resistance to   61
the short-term gratification of drugs come from?

Jackson: Values. They are taught by family, synagogue, temple,   62
church. There must be something ingrained that makes one resist the consumption of drugs; the same thing that makes one want to resist hating people and exploiting people. Drug abuse is a form of self-hatred and self-exploitation.

A commitment to life means a commitment to avoid the short-term   63
pleasure and long-term pain of drugs.

NPQ: But isn't the very ethos of this culture, in 1989, short-term   64
gratification . . . ?

Jackson: . . . Short-term pleasure, long-term pain, which means the   65
drug crisis, in the last analysis, is a cultural crisis.

Questions: The Community of Writers

1. Discuss whether the interviewer gets the expected answer from the first question.

2. Some of the questions seem to have been planned in advance and others developed in the process of the interview. Find examples of each kind of question.

3. What kind of information do the planned questions imply that *New Perspectives Quarterly* was seeking from Jackson?

4. Find an instance where the interviewer expresses an opinion, and consider what the purpose was. Does the interviewer achieve the purpose?

5. Jackson responds to the *NPQ* interviewer as a politician, a social activist, and a clergyman. Find examples of responses in each of these roles.

Analysis

The *New Perspectives Quarterly (NPQ)* interviewer clearly had planned some questions to ask. You can see them at places where the questioning takes a new direction rather than derives from Jackson's previous statement. One such question is paragraph 20: "What is your program for stopping drug use?" This question seems only loosely related to Jackson's statement in paragraphs 18 and 19 regarding the racial nature of Jack Kemp's proposals. Jackson's answer, however, seems to lead directly to the next question: "How do you propose to cut the supply and strengthen interdiction?" So, the interviewer's questions can be seen as originating in two ways: from advance preparation and from Jackson's statements.

The questions also seem to open up the possibility for Jackson to respond from his three public roles: politician, social activist, and clergyman. When the interviewer asks "Are you saying that the Bush Administration is soft on drugs?" (paragraph 14), a political response is solicited. Asking "How can demand for drugs be dampened?" (paragraph 39), the interviewer invites a social response. "Where does the moral resistance to the short-term gratification of drugs come from?" (paragraph 61) elicits a religious response. Such questions aid the interviewer in controlling the focus of the interview and even the role of the interviewee.

Paragraphs

Readers have certain expectations of *paragraphs:* that they won't be excessively long, that the first sentence or two will somehow orient them to the paragraph's content, that the sentences in the paragraph will be connected, and that the paragraph won't shift to a new subject without warning. Paragraph indentions are a graphic feature of written expression, usually with no correspondence in speech, and they are often a feature of revision, added where the text makes a slight shift in subject. Interviews are oral, because the transcriber, in addition to adding punctuation and spelling, must make decisions about paragraphing.

Jackson's reply to the first question is long—roughly 400 words, much too long for a single paragraph. Paragraphing, then, had to be added in the written transcription. What prompted the transcriber to indent? Each of the seven paragraphs can give us some inkling. The first paragraph concentrates on dollars spent on drugs, whereas the second amplifies the racial issue. The third paragraph shifts to a broader moral issue, and the fourth shows the spectrum of drug use. The fifth is devoted to Senator D'Amato. In the sixth Jackson returns to the question by addressing the drug war in Washington, D.C., and in the final paragraph he eloquently calls for stepping up the drug war. Each paragraph is connected to the one before it, but each addresses a slightly different aspect of the answer.

Style

This record of an interview probably had some editing before it appeared in *New Perspectives Quarterly.* At the same time, it's probably also an accurate record of the dialogue between the *NPQ* interviewer and Jesse Jackson. As a record, the transcript uses present tense verbs:

> *Is* the focus in the right place?
> Drug lords *are* the masters and drug users *are* slaves.
> *Do* you *agree* with their approach?
> The drug lords *laugh* at the system.

If this record were used in a report, many of the statements would be changed to past tense:

> *NPQ asked* if Jackson thought the focus *was* in the right place.
> Jackson *asserted,* "Drug lords are the masters and drug users are slaves."
> *NPQ questioned* whether Jackson *agreed* with the Muslims' approach.

Exceptions to this kind of change are direct quotations and statements of general truths or recurring actions:

> Jackson replied that the drug lords only *laugh* at the government's actions.
> Jackson answered, "This administration *thinks* it *can get* people off drugs by threatening to evict them from their homes."

Exercise: The Exploring Writer

Select a portion of the New Perspectives Quarterly *interview with Jackson (three or four questions and answers) and rewrite it as a report, making changes as necessary to move the interview from recording to reporting.*

Reading

In contrast to the preceding interview, which is a transcription of a dialogue, the following record is written in essay form. In it, John E. Cooney, having interviewed Robert Donnell for a feature in the *Wall Street Journal* (1974), describes Donnell's idiosyncratic work. As you read, observe how Cooney uses direct quotations and paraphrases to record the interview.

By Whom the Bells Toll

John E. Cooney

At 1:00 P.M. each weekday, Robert Donnell rushes to a small room high in Parliament Hill's Peace Tower in Ottawa where he erupts in a frenzy of activity:

Arms and legs flailing, he slides jerkily back and forth across a long oak bench. Like a masseur gone mad, he mercilessly punches, pounds, and slaps rows of short, broomhandle-like sticks jutting from a wooden panel in front of him. He furiously kicks and stomps wooden slats on the floor.

"I try . . . to put as much . . . of myself . . . into this . . . as I can," says a huffing Mr. Donnell, his face perspiring and nearly crimson after an uninterrupted fifteen minutes of such feverish activity.

That grueling routine is Mr. Donnell's way of giving a recital. He's Canada's official Dominion Carillonneur, the man who plays the Peace Tower bells that delight residents as well as foreign dignitaries and tourists who visit the nation's capital. He's the only full-time carillonneur in the country. But while most musicians enjoy audience acclaim, the carillonneur is hidden in the belfry so few folks know of his mighty exertion. In fact, most people who hear his performances don't even know he's playing.

"A lot of people think the bells are playing electrically," complains Mr. Donnell, a trim, dapper bachelor in his late fifties. "Whenever I overhear someone saying that I tell them 'No . . . It's me up in there doing that.'"

Indeed, it has been Mr. Donnell up in the Peace Tower doing that   6
since 1939, when he became only the second carillonneur ever appointed
to the civil service post that now pays $21,000 a year. (He's listed in the
federal phone book's yellow pages under "Branches & Services" of the
House of Commons.) And in the past thirty-four years, he has never
missed one of the fifteen-minute or hour-long recitals he schedules
nearly each week that he's in town.

"Fortunately, I'm very healthy," he says. "Anyway, there's nobody to   7
fill in for me if I get sick."

His good health may have something to do with the rigorous exercise   8
he gets on the job. A carillon—an outgrowth of small bells that struck
time in fifteenth-century clock towers in Belgium and the Netherlands—
must have at least twenty-three bells. The Peace Tower's has fifty-three,
weighing from 10 to 22,400 pounds. The carillonneur's strength goes
into banging away at the foot pedals and wooden keyboard—the instrument is modeled after a three hundred-year-old Flemish design—that
move bell clappers. The heaviest clapper is 504 pounds, and only the
strongest blows get it to gong.

"Playing can really prove exhausting," acknowledges Mr. Donnell,   9
exhibiting calluses like a karate expert's along the edges of his fast hands.

Besides the calluses, Mr. Donnell puts up with another drawback   10
most musicians don't have. He can't practice, at least not on the bells,
because he'd disturb Parliament—and much of the rest of the city as well.
To compensate, he has a keyboard not connected to the bells in a
practice room where he knocks out muted tunes. "It isn't exactly like
practicing on the real thing," he admits.

Playing, writing, and arranging music absorb most of his time. Even   11
his vacations are sort of a busman's holiday since he frequently spends
them in Europe searching for rare music that was composed just for
carillons. In addition, he keeps in touch with fellow carillonneurs
through the North American Guild of Carillonneurs, an organization
that—with the exception of Mr. Donnell and a handful of full-time
bellmen in the United States—consists of about two hundred part-time
carillonneurs. And since Mr. Donnell is recognized within his limited
circle as one of the best, he occasionally goes on concert tours that have
taken him as far away as Australia.

Although carillonneurs are relatively obscure today, from the six-   12
teenth through the eighteenth centuries carillons and the men who
played them were famous in many a Flemish town. There are accounts of
rival carillonneurs competing for honors. And one of the treasures of war
was to seize a city's carillon to be later ransomed back as the town's most
precious possession. When France's King Louis XIV captured the city of

Mons in 1691, for example, the formal treaty between the conqueror and the city calls for the ransom of the bells.

Today, "One thing that may deter people from studying the carillon 13 is that many bell towers have only stairs leading to the keyboard. By the time you get there, you're already tired," says Mr. Donnell, recalling the five hundred-step hike he had to the Michelin, Belgium, belfry where he studied. Now, he rides an elevator to work.

Since taking over the carillonneur post at Parliament, Mr. Donnell 14 has arranged and played literally hundreds of different works, including Bach's "Toccata in D Minor," Gershwin's "Porgy and Bess," and his own work, "Canadian Folksong Medley"—and, for Franklin Roosevelt, "Home on the Range."

He regularly performs when statesmen visit Parliament, but "I never 15 get to see the statesmen I play for," he says. "Their schedules are too tight to allow them time to come up for a visit."

Questions: The Community of Writers

1. What makes the work of a carillonneur "grueling"?
2. From this record, reconstruct the questions that Cooney might have taken with him to the interview.
3. If carillons can be played electrically, as most are today, what would be the advantage of having a carillonneur?
4. What kind of activity did each of you think Cooney was describing as you read the first three paragraphs?
5. Discuss what might have been the determining factors in Cooney's choice to sometimes use direct quotations and other times use paraphrases of Donnell's statements.

Analysis

"Interesting people with intriguing stories"—this is why *Wall Street Journal* interviews people like Robert Donnell with unfamiliar names but with stories that are evidence of the variety of life. This reading could just as easily fit in Chapter 14, To Praise or Censure.

Unlike the Jesse Jackson interview, this record of an interview is written as an essay. In such a record, much of the dialogue is probably lost in the writer's selection process; however, the reader also gains information that is not available in a transcription. Here Cooney uses not only direct quotation, as in a transcription, but description as well: he describes the exertion required for playing the bells, and he tells you a little about Donnell's appearance. Also, he paraphrases and summarizes a large part of the discussion, making a piece of writing briefer than a complete transcription of the interview would be.

Style

Cooney writes as if the interview is taking place in the present. He is in the bell tower with Donnell, watching him play and then talking with him. Notice, however, that Cooney's presence is only implied. (By contrast, in the Jackson interview the *NPQ* interviewer is identified with each question.) Nowhere does Cooney refer to himself.

Most of Cooney's verbs are in the present tense:

He *slides* jerkily back and forth.
Mr. Donnell *puts* up with another drawback most musicians *don't have.*

Cooney uses the past tense only to relate past experiences: "He *became* only the second carillonneur ever appointed to the civil service post." Quotations are set off in paragraphs, separating Donnell's words from Cooney's writing about the interview.

Exercise: The Exploring Writer

Cooney doesn't end his essay with a real conclusion; he just closes it with his last quotation from Donnell. Write an additional paragraph that makes an overall concluding statement about Robert Donnell as you perceive him from reading this essay.

Writing

Use interviewing as a method of getting information about a subject that interests you or one you need to report on for another class. Select your interviewee on the basis of qualifications to provide accurate information. After arranging the interview, write out the questions that will give you the information you need. During the interview, take enough notes to aid your memory; use a tape recorder if you have one and if your interviewee doesn't object. Immediately after the interview, fill out your notes.

If you were able to use a tape recorder, write a transcription like that of the Jackson interview. If you are writing your record from notes, you will need to paraphrase and summarize much of the interview, as Cooney does, quoting only when you were able to write down the exact words. Let your interviewee read your rough draft for accuracy and perhaps the addition of something you've omitted.

RECORDING GROUP ACTIONS

In school, most of your notetaking is probably for the purpose of recording lectures, assignments, and reading, as discussed in the introduction to this chapter. Sometimes, however, you may find yourself in the role of recording secretary, taking notes on the actions and discussions of a committee, an organization, or a collaborative group for one of your classes. Taking notes of this kind is like taking minutes of a meeting and then putting them in a form that others can read and that will be suitable for an official record.

If you are the recorder at a meeting, you will probably do more listening than speaking. You may want to use a tape recorder as a backup for your notes. Minutes must be accurate, complete, and objective. When recording discussions, you can summarize or paraphrase what members of your group say. At other times, such as for motions or specific decisions, you need a word-for-word record, including the names of the people who make and second the motions or suggest the decisions. When actions are to be taken, tell specifically what those actions are, who is to act, and when and where the action is to take place; for example, "Mary Carlin will report at the October meeting on the results of her telephone survey regarding new members."

Be objective in your recording, avoiding wording such as "Mary Carlin *generously* volunteered to conduct the telephone survey." And be consistent in your references to people. You can refer to them in one of several ways: by last name only (Carlin), by first name and last name (Mary Carlin), by first initial and last name (M. Carlin), by first name (Mary), or by a name preceded by title (Ms. Carlin). If you begin using first and last names, follow this form throughout the record.

As for the content of minutes, *Robert's Rules of Order* recommends the following:

1. The name of the group
2. The date, time, and place of the meeting
3. The names of the presider and the secretary
4. The fact that the previous minutes were approved or corrected
5. A separate paragraph for each subject
6. The exact wording of all motions and whether they were passed defeated, or tabled
7. The hour of adjournment
8. The signature of the recording secretary (and possibly of the chairperson)

Minutes may also show the names or the number of people present, a list of summary of reports read and approved, and the date and place of the next meeting.

A record of an informal meeting or of a collaborative group discussion in class would be less formal than the minutes just described, but it would contain some of the same elements: names, date, summary of the discussion, specific actions and decisions taken, work to be completed with the names of people assigned to carry out specific assignments, and whatever else is appropriate for the session.

Reading

Graduating seniors report that some of the most useful learning they acquired in college occurred as a result of volunteer activities—serving as officers of campus organizations, for example. Employers, likewise, consider voluntary service as valuable preparation for the responsibilities of the people they employ. The secretary of an organization has the opportunity to practice accuracy and clarity of reporting but often begins taking minutes with no previous experience or instruction.

What follows is the record of an informal organizational meeting for a new English club. In the form of minutes, the record shows who was present, what discussions and actions took place, and what was decided.

Minutes of the Organizational Meeting for a New English Club

Present: C. Burns, H. Dahlquist, M. Hagemeister, L. Juarez, M. Ledoux (Chair), E. Lee, J. Stang, H. Theis, R. White

M. Ledoux as convenor called the meeting to order at 1:05 P.M.

1. *Election.* By voice ballot, M. Ledoux was elected chair and H. Theis secretary.
2. *Purpose of club.* After an extended discussion concerning the purpose of the club and the fact that no English club on campus currently encourages writing and publication by its members, the following motion was made and passed:

    The purpose of this new English club will be to promote writing by its members, to encourage publication in campus newspapers and magazines, to attend plays as a group, and to report on new and interesting books. (H. Dahlquist, J. Stang)
3. *Name of the club.* Several possible names were suggested. Approved by voice ballot, The Writers' Circle will be the name of the new club.

4. *Meetings.* Following a discussion of the desirability and disadvantages of various times, the group agreed by consensus on the third Thursday of each month at 7:00 P.M. The chair will see if the English Department's conference room will be available as a meeting place.

5. *Sponsor.* For the purposes of advising and visibility in the English Department, the club agreed by consensus to have a faculty sponsor. The chair will ask Professor Janet Johnson if she will consent to be the sponsor.

6. *Promotion of the club.* Several means of promoting the club were proposed, among them speaking briefly at the next English Department meeting to ask faculty to promote the club, putting up posters in the English building to advertise the next meeting, sending postcards to English majors and minors, announcing the meetings on classroom blackboards, and asking faculty to read announcements of meetings. The following motion passed:

> That the chair speak briefly at the next English Department meeting to encourage faculty promotion of the club, that two volunteers make posters for the English building announcing the next meeting, and that two volunteers write announcements of the next meeting on classroom blackboards. (E. Lee, R. White)

E. Lee and H. Theis volunteered to make and put up the posters, and R. White and H. Dahlquist will write notices on the blackboards.

The meeting adjourned at 1:55 P.M. The next meeting will be held November 19 at 7:00 P.M. in the English Department conference room. Agenda: how to get published on campus.

—Harold Theis, secretary

Questions: The Community of Writers

1. Some aspects of these minutes conform to the recommendations in *Robert's Rules of Order,* such as the time of the meeting. Name others.

2. Some aspects of these minutes are a result of the secretary's (or organization's) choice, such as listing the names of everyone present. What are some choices not covered in the *Rules?*

3. Even though *Robert's Rules of Order* doesn't require the names of the people attending a meeting, Theis included them. What do you see as the advantages of doing so in the minutes of this meeting?

Analysis

The minutes of a meeting and notes of collaborative group discussions record actions. Both are evidence that speaking does things. Language is more than sounds formed by air passing over vocal cords and through the mouth. It's more than black marks on a page. When people use language, they are creating a relationship in which their words cause an effect.

To create the desired effect, speakers and writers must first use the appropriate words. If they say "Pugga woc" when they mean "Please pass me the popcorn," the effect will be bewildered glances. But if they say "Please pass me the popcorn," they will probably get the popcorn. Of course, they can also say something like "Would you mind closing the door?" in which case they would expect not the answer "Yes, I would mind closing the door" but the result of the door getting closed. "Would you mind closing the door?" is an accepted way of asking politely for someone to close the door.

Minutes and notes of group meetings record words as actions. In the English club minutes, the words spoken and recorded had the action of creating a new organization of people with mutual interests. The notes of a classroom group discussion may record contributions toward a paper you are writing together—the effect being a document. Even if there is no discernible product from the discussion, the effect on group members still exists. If, for example, your group has been asked to discuss ways of combating racial discrimination on campus, the words of each of you will affect the others in the group, and there will be a joint effect of greater awareness of discrimination, which the record will show.

Exercise: The Exploring Writer

The minutes for the new English club are written rather formally to serve as an official record. Suppose that you and a group of classmates are working together on an assignment to propose a new English club. You discuss the same matters recorded in these minutes, but the report is informal. As recorder, write that informal record, being as specific as necessary so that the chair of your group can report your decisions to the class as a whole.

Writing

Assume the role of recording secretary for an organization whose meetings you attend, and write minutes for one of the meetings. Include the information that *Robert's Rules of Order* recommends, summarizing discussions and recording motions word for word. Use a consistent format, either the one shown in the reading or another appropriate one.

ADDITIONAL READING FOR DISCUSSION

Reading

This student essay is the record of an interview. Like John E. Cooney's essay on the carillonneur Robert Donnell, this essay quotes some of the interviewee's words directly and records others indirectly; it also includes description and background. As you read, try to reconstruct Dulgar's interview questions.

Playin' Bones

Peter E. Dulgar

When fall comes to central Minnesota, so does fall festival; and when fall festival comes to St. Patrick's Church, so does Richard Bettendorf. Richard is a very special man, but it's hard to tell just by looking at him. A natural, sunny smile lights his face, the kind they used to grow a lot of on the plains. He wears dark baggy pants, one of those cardigan-things that all old men seem to wear sooner or later, and a speckled tweed hat. A hearing aid perches rather noticeably on his left ear, but anyone studying him that close will also notice his eyes and the way they gleam. His face is warm and brown, like old deerskin. On the surface nothing about him is extraordinary; he's just a wrinkled old country man, a lot like all old men. What Richard does with four small pieces of wood, however, is truly unique. [1]

He plays them. The pieces of wood are called "bones," and Richard plays music with them—like music heard nowhere else. He does it by holding them between his second and third fingers, two in each hand, and rolling his wrists until the bones vibrate together. The sound produced is somewhere between a clack and a chirp, and Richard plays like the fields are full of crickets wearing wooden shoes. "Playin' bones is easy," he says, "but ya gotta have it in ya ta get it out!" [2]

His bones are old and worn and slightly curved, like the bones of his body. They were made from a block of ebony wood, imported from Africa over fifty years ago. It cost him fifty dollars at the time, and that was enough to break his young bank account, but it was worth it for real ebony bones. "Ebony is the hardest wood in the world, ya know," he [3] explains, and no one cares if he's right or not. Years of sweat and good times have flowed from his fingers into these pieces of wood, and today they reflect a soft, warm happiness from the hard, black wood.

Richard taught himself to play when he was a young man in his 4 twenties, and he's been playing ever since, wherever people will listen. He's even been on the radio in Chicago. "I'd like to play 'Sweet Georgia Brown' over the loudspeaker at a Harlem Globetrotters game," he says, "but I just haven't been able to make it to Minneapolis yet."

This year he's accompanying Virg and the Eldoradoes, a Johnny Cash 5 style band hired to entertain at the festival. It doesn't matter what kind of band he plays with, though; the sound of bones goes good with anything.

Richard lives in Foley. He used to own the movie theatre with his 6 brother, but now he's retired and he gives his full attention to the bones. When the festival band takes a break, he strolls over to a group of old-timers under an oak tree. They all know him, for these are friends he's made over the last seventy years or so, and the conversation is rich with memories and old stories. One of his friends brought a banjo and he's playing with the band too. Richard teases him, switching his own tweed hat for his friend's baseball cap, as they improvise a little tune while waiting for the band to return.

Richard is seventy-seven years old, but you can't tell it when he plays, 7 kicking his heels up forwards and backwards and gyrating his shoulders in an effort to lift himself off the ground. He smiles when he plays, so widely the corners of his mouth endanger his ears, and it seems as if the combination of happiness and motion is enough to lift him above the ground, just a little bit. People stop to watch him play, some dance, others just smile and clap their hands, but nobody passes by.

Questions: The Community of Writers

1. Reconstruct the questions Dulgar might have asked Bettendorf when he interviewed him.

2. Discuss where the interview might have taken place.

3. This essay might appropriately be placed in Chapter 14, To Praise or Censure. What words and phrases show that Dulgar admires his interviewee?

4. Does this record of an interview work well as an essay, or would it be more effective in question and answer form like the Jesse Jackson interview? Discuss your opinions.

CHAPTER 10

Writing to Report

If in speaking to my friend I treat the events . . . as what happened, *the subject will necessarily partake a little more of my mind and a little less of the original matter. Although the order of events will still be chronological, it is now my memory and not my perceptual apparatus that is doing the selecting.*

—*James Moffett*

Reporting is a kind of writing you've no doubt had experience with. In school, you've probably written book reports, telling what books you've read and what they are about. You may have attended a lecture, address, or debate and written a report. In science classes you may have written lab reports after completing certain experimental procedures. For other classes, perhaps you have written research papers—reports of reading you did on specific topics with your analyses of that reading and your conclusions. **Reports** are accounts of something done, read, observed, discussed, thought, or experienced.

Unlike recording, in which an observer describes events while they are still happening, reporting usually tells *what happened:* where you went and what you saw on a trip to Mexico, for example; what book or story you read and how you responded to it; what chemicals you combined and what reactions you observed; how the play-off game was played and who was voted most valuable player; what happened when you auditioned for your first part in a play; what happened and how you felt at your first concert; and so on. All these events have already happened when you report them. What you write therefore depends not only on the accuracy of your observation but on your ability to remember the events as well.

Reports of past events, logically, are usually written in the past tense:

At first I *did* not *understand* J. M. Coetzee's *Foe,* but as I *continued* to read I *found* the events to be making more sense.

We *stayed* in a little village near the Pacific Ocean.

As I *stepped* onto the stage, I *didn't know* where to look: at the casting director, at the empty seats, or at the other people on stage.

Some reports, though, tell what something is like, and they are handled differently. When you return from your trip to Mexico, for example, you may report to your friends not only what you did but what Mexico is like as you observed it: "The villages *are* dusty but *have* a lot more character than you *see* in the packaged tours of the cities." Such descriptions are signaled by present tense verbs because, even though your observations took place in the past, you assume that what you observed is still true. If other travelers visit the parts of Mexico you visited, they may be able to view the same things you observed. Book reports similarly use present tense to tell what the book is about, because what you describe is still true: "The narrator of *Foe* is a woman castaway who *shares* Robinson Crusoe's island with Crusoe and Friday." If another reader picks up *Foe* and reads it, the narrator will still be a woman castaway.

Accuracy of Reports

As a reader and a writer of reports, you should be aware that a report filters information through the writer's mind and is only as accurate as the writer makes it. The account is influenced by three factors:

1. The writer's perceptions of the event,
2. The writer's memory of the event,
3. The writer's selection of details to include.

You may have observed how two people can report the same event in widely divergent ways, despite the fact that they both have attempted to report the facts accurately as they perceived, remembered, and selected them.

The writer's perceptions. As people observe events, their perceptions are influenced by their past experiences. A carpenter, for example, notices how a wooden structure disintegrates in an earthquake, whereas the owner of the crumbling building sees a distressingly expensive pile of rubble. An auto mechanic driving his car down the highway hears a hole in an exhaust pipe that would be just noise to someone with an untrained ear. Perceptions are also influenced by the observer's emotional state;

what a person sees is in part determined by whether that person is happy, depressed, angry, and so on. The owner of the damaged building, for example, has a great deal more emotional involvement than does the carpenter, who is only a bystander. And observations are influenced by a host of other factors, including seeing only what we want to see or expect to see, as well as being distracted by interruptions.

The writer's memory. What you remember for reporting is determined by various factors too: your physical and psychological state while remembering (as well as when the event occurred), your reasons for remembering, your ability to recall details, the degree of your interest in the event, and so on. Because memory is sometimes incomplete and inaccurate, written records are important aids for preparing reports. If you take notes of your impressions while reading a book, for example, you have more than your memory to work with when you write your report. For further discussion of notetaking, see Chapters 9 and 16.

The writer's selection. You may not want to use all the details you remember. Some are irrelevant to your purpose for reporting. Some would not interest your audience. And some are unnecessary for an audience's understanding of the subject. In most cases, however, college writers tend to include too few details rather than too many, and, as a result, readers are unable to see the situation as the writer intends. A prominent influence on what you remember and select for reporting is possible secondary purposes for reporting. Do you want to *persuade* someone to travel to Mexico (or not to travel to Mexico), to read a book (or not to read it)? Or do you want to *inform* readers about a good place to go in Mexico or a good book to read? Do you want to *entertain* readers about the humorous aspects of your trip? The details you remember and select are determined in part by your reasons for reporting.

Development

Events are often reported in *chronological* order. In narrating your report of a trip or an audition or an accident, you usually start at the beginning and proceed in time sequence to the end. In reporting what something is like, however, you may use some other means of development—*spatial*, for instance, in reporting what a certain Mexican village is like, or most important to least important for telling what a book is about. At times your report may be developed *causally*, showing how certain events brought about other events, or by *comparison*, showing how two events are similar. Reports are often developed in more than one way; a research report, for instance, is likely to use *definition, cause and effect, narration,* and other methods of development.

Reports frequently include direct quotations and other references attributable to other people. If you are reporting dialogue, for instance, you try to reconstruct the actual words of the people you are quoting; quote accurately, in other words, and enclose the statements in quotation marks. In other cases, you may want to report people's reactions to the events you are recounting. Any time you report the words or opinions of others, be careful to name those people so your reader understands that these are not your thoughts.

The readings and writing assignments in this chapter highlight several kinds of reports that you may have occasion to write: a narration of a personal experience, a description and narration of an observed incident, a description of a natural phenomenon, and a book report. The additional reading is a report on racism in the 1940s.

NARRATING A PERSONAL EXPERIENCE

One of the most common kinds of reports is the **narration** of a personal experience. Most people do a little of this nearly every day. Families, roommates, or friends get together and report on the interesting events of the day. We enjoy telling our stories and hearing someone else's. These stories are generally assumed to be true, so if we want to repeat someone else's story we can do so trusting its accuracy. But most of us know people who tend to exaggerate, and we're less likely either to believe their stories, no matter how interesting, or to repeat them.

Written reports of personal experiences are assumed to be true too. While readers acknowledge that the writer's account may omit some irrelevant details and may depend on how well the writer remembers the event, readers don't expect exaggeration and fabrication. If the experience is interesting enough to report, it doesn't require elaboration beyond what actually happened.

At the same time, reporters of personal experiences are free to express their own reactions to their experiences: "I was afraid I wouldn't get out of the bus alive." "There was once a time when I wondered what it would be like to float above the earth in a hot-air balloon." "Being a participant in the rally was one of the most significant things I have done." Readers welcome such expressions, because through them they are able to understand the significance of the narrated events.

Reports of personal experiences are usually developed in **chronological** order, from the beginning of the experience to its conclusion. When the narration makes up the entire essay, as it does in "Ever Green" in this chapter, the *thesis* may not be expressed but is implicit in the selection of details and the writer's expressed reactions to events. In this type of essay, the thesis may also be stated at the conclusion. Some essays use multiple reports of personal experiences to develop a theme or controlling idea, as in "Yes and No" in this chapter. In essays of this type, the thesis may be expressed in the introduction before being explained by short narratives.

Reading

The following essay is an example of a personal experience narration by a college student. Janice Anderson wanted to report an incident that still causes her some chagrin when she looks back on it yet gives her some pleasure for having participated in it. As you read, note how she develops her report and how she reacts to the incidents.

Ever Green

Janice Anderson

I had been wanting to do it for a long time. The first time I thought 1 to do it was at Valley Fair three years ago. I don't know why I didn't do it then. Maybe I thought it was silly or vain. Maybe I was just too cheap. But there I was at the State Fair, standing outside the "Superstar" booth handing over my ten dollars so I could record myself singing on professional sound equipment. Maybe someone important would hear my recording and offer me a fabulous contract! Surely at least the concession owners would want to use it to advertise.

My heart was racing just like when I had been a green soloist in my 2 junior high school choir. I couldn't believe my reaction. I'd had years of vocal training, had sung solos often, and had sung eight seasons with the finest civic choir in the city. I was a real musician! Why was I experiencing major stress over a simple two-minute recording? But maybe a little tension would get my adrenaline flowing, and that would help me. So, did I want to be Barbra Streisand or "The Jets"?

"What song d'ya wanna sing?" the matter-of-fact, gum-chewing 3 blonde behind the counter asked.

"Evergreen." I had decided to be Barbra. "Will I have sheet music?" 4

"No, ya'll have a word sheet. We've found sheet music just confuses 5 most people. They don't know how to read it. What's yer name?"

"Janice Anderson. I'd prefer sheet music, if you have it." 6

She typed my name on a label. How could anyone with such long 7 purple fingernails (obviously fake) type so quickly, flick the label off its paper backing so easily, and stick it on the cassette so accurately?

"Will I be able to hear the tape before I take it? My daughter had a bad experience at a recording booth once. There was something wrong with the tape. The sound was distorted somehow, or not mixed well." 8

"Sure. If ya' wanna, Janice. We'll play it over the loudspeakers after. Okay, Janice, just wait a minute and someone will call ya' when it's yer turn." 9

My heart picked up its pace. It seemed an eternity before I was called. 10

"Janice? Come with me." I can't remember what the young woman who took me into the booth looked like. I think her name was Sheena. She was very efficient. She had the instructions memorized and recited them as she led me down the miniature hallway, opened the door, and shooshed me into a carpeted upright coffin. 11

The shag wall was looped with electric cords that came together at the base of the microphone stand. They snaked up to a black bulbous microphone which took up most of the available space. The mesh covering made it look like the eye of a giant fly. A naked hook stared down at me from amongst carpet fibers, and a narrow vertical window exposed my bluejeaned rear to the world. 12

"You'll hear a singer through the headphones along with the music, but you'll hear only your own voice on your tape. Bill will play it once through for you to practice. Then you'll be recorded. Stand close to the mike. Sing loud and don't touch the microphone. Okay, Janice? Any questions?" She didn't wait for a response. "Good. Have fun. Remember, Janice, sing loud and don't touch the microphone!" She spoke to me as if I were a child or a nursing home resident with senile dementia. 13

"Okay," I guessed. It was strange how many questions I had before I entered, and how blank my mind had become in those few short steps from the outside world. 14

Sheena hung the plastic-coated word sheet on the wall hook. When I started to look at the words, she adjusted the microphone height and clapped the headphones over my ears. The almost soundless static coming through the headphones opened all eight of my sinuses and expanded my mind as well. My body was entombed, but my head was larger and lighter than a hot-air balloon. 15

"Sing loud and don't touch the microphone" kept repeating in my mind. 16

"Hi there, Janice," came a smoothly modulated, calm masculine voice. Must be Bill, I thought. I remember seeing a faceless back on a swivel chair with what seemed like at least four arms reaching about on a wide, tall control panel. He reminded me of the "Phantom of the Opera." I never saw his face, but I knew that, had he ever swiveled around, girls on the street would have screamed in horror. But he was very kind sounding, in spite of his obvious hurry. Bill repeated, word for word, what Sheena had said and asked if I was ready for the practice run. 17

"Okay, Janice. Remember, sing loud and don't touch the micro-   18
phone!"

An introduction began. In order to get my mouth near the micro-   19
phone and still see the word sheet, I had to crane my neck back, making
my Adam's apple stick out like an elbowjoint. I felt like a pelican trying
to swallow a fish. The music filled the airy space inside my head. So, with
fists clenched at my sides and muscles clenched in my throat, I sang loud
and *didn't touch the microphone!*

I could tell that the sounds coming from my mouth were horrible. I   20
did indeed sound like I had a fish stuck in my throat. As my heart beat
even faster in panic, I forgot every bit of vocal technique I had ever
learned. I sometimes hung under the pitch. Then other times I would
overcorrect and add too much vibrato. Sometimes my voice would patch
out, giving momentary interruptions of silence into a sustained note.
"You and I will make each night a first, every day a beginning" was the
only line that sounded okay. But one gorgeous line does not make a good
recording! I hadn't sounded so green since my first solos in junior high.

"Well, Janice. How did it go? Are you ready to record?" Bill asked with   21
his best disc jockey voice.

"Could you turn the volume down on the singer, please? It's kind of   22
distracting." I was sure that would help.

"Okay. Here we go. Remember, sing loud and don't touch the micro-   23
phone!"

Nausea accompanied my ever-quickening heart rate. I was afraid that   24
if it beat any faster, I'd pass out and throw up at the same time. I took a
deep breath, closed my eyes briefly in meditation, and told myself I could
handle it. I couldn't afford to make mistakes *this* time.

The recording was a little better than the practice in that I was closer   25
to the pitch more often. When I missed one of the entrances, I made up
for it by slipping in smoothly, as if I had wanted to come in late for a
dramatic effect. As before, "You and I will make each night a first, every
day a beginning" was great. However, the patching out continued and got
even worse, and my breath control left me. I was breathing in unnatural
places, like "Love, soft as (breath) an easy (breath) chair," and running
out of air at the end of phrases. In order to sustain the last note, I took a
big gulp in the middle of the final "evergreen."

I don't remember walking out. I only remember standing and waiting   26
on the sidewalk outside the booth. Everyone else's tapes sounded so good
as they were played over the loudspeakers. Maybe I'd been too critical of
myself, what with my trained ear and all. Maybe I'd sound just as good—
or even better!

I watched the gum-chewing blonde with the purple fingernails hand   27
a young woman her recording of "The Rose."

"Ya' sounded real great!" She flashed a smile as she thanked her for   28
her business.

I suppose she says that to everyone, just as she is trained to call all   29
customers by their first names, I thought. It was a pleasant rendition of
"The Rose," but far from "great."

The introduction to "Evergreen" started up. And so did my heart.   30
Then my heart sank when I heard what must have been my voice. It
sounded like a nervous junior high school soloist.

As I sheepishly stepped to the counter to claim my tape, I avoided   31
making eye contact with Ms. Purple-Nails. I just wanted to take the tape
and disappear. But she seemed to feel that saying a final word was part of
her job.

"Ya were, ah . . . pretty good, Janice," she said as she finally handed   32
me my tape.

The label read, "Janice Anderson. Evergreen." It should have said,   33
"Janice Anderson. Ever green."

When I go back next year, I'll try a different song. I plan to hold the   34
word sheet in my hand. And I might even touch the microphone.

Questions: The Community of Writers

1. Anderson does not state her thesis explicitly. In your own words, state the controlling idea of her essay, write it in a sentence, and then compare your sentence with those of your groupmates. How do you account for differences?

2. Anderson recalls experiencing several emotions during the incident she reports. What are those emotions, and to what is she reacting with each new emotion?

3. Describe each of the three people, other than the writer, who participated in this incident. Which one does Anderson characterize most vividly?

4. Does Anderson digress at all from her chronological development of her story?

5. Discuss the meaning of the title, "Ever Green."

Analysis

Anderson takes a simple event and makes a story of it that would interest a wide audience. To the basic report "I made a tape recording of myself singing 'Evergreen' at the state fair, and it was horrible" you would probably respond "So what?" But Anderson goes beyond the basic report by adding details and personal reactions. The story is still true and accurate—but more so. The expanded report gives readers a description of the recording studio and the people employed there, it recounts the conversations as Anderson remembers them, and it tells how Anderson felt from beginning to end. She had to remember and recount the details of the incident.

Whenever you narrate a personal experience, you have more details in your head than you put on paper. They may not readily come to the surface, but they're there. Most times writers don't prod their memories enough to take full advantage of what they know. Perhaps they're accustomed to telling their stories orally, with an audience beside them to coax out the details: "Then what did you say?" or "But what did she look like" or "How did you feel about that?" When you write, you need to put yourself in the role of audience as well as that of writer so you can see what details you should include—details that help your readers see the event as you do, or as you want them to. To assist your memory, try using some of the prewriting suggestions in Chapter 3: the journalist's questions, for example, or freewriting or brainstorming.

Thesis

Even after including as many descriptive and personal details as she did in this essay, Anderson still knows more about the incident than you do. She didn't say everything she could have. You don't know, for example, what all the choices of songs were, but Anderson does, or did. How did she decide what to include and what to omit? In revising narratives, writers often have to perform two actions. The first one (adding details) we've already discussed; the second one (deleting details) is just as important. Rough drafts of narratives often go on and on, off on tangents, touching on irrelevant information. In deciding what to add and what to omit, Anderson needed to think in terms of *thesis*—the overall controlling idea that holds the essay together and makes the impression on her audience that she is striving for.

In this essay, as often in narratives, the thesis sentence is unexpressed. Of course, not expressing a thesis is not the same as not having one. A writer must have a controlling idea to complete an essay—perhaps not when beginning to write but certainly during revision, when deciding what to add and what to delete. Often when a thesis is implied, the title expresses it. Anderson plays on words in using her title "Ever Green" to imply her thesis. Is she saying that she knows she showed herself to be an amateur yet that she enjoyed the experience anyway and knows she can do better? Such a thesis requires her to give a background of her singing experience, to make herself look a little foolish in her self-pride, to show how routine the recording is for employees of the makeshift studio, and to report her reactions throughout the experience.

Paragraphs

Another matter that frequently requires attention in revising narratives is paragraphing. When drafting a report of an event, you, like many writers, may compose one long *paragraph*. But long paragraphs are a problem for readers who like to encounter white space now and then as a rest. Paragraphs have a more important function, though, something like that of punctuation: they are a signal to the reader that here is a shift, that one part of the topic is completed and the writer is about to embark on another. This is why paragraphing in personal narratives is so difficult—the shifts are often minuscule.

In revising long narrative paragraphs, you need to look for these subtle changes. They may be shifts in time or location, as when Anderson shifts for paragraph 19, "An introduction began," and for paragraph 26, "I don't remember walking out." Another reason for beginning paragraphs accounts for most of Anderson's shifts. "Ever Green" consists of a great deal of quoted conversation, and writers conventionally begin a new paragraph for each new speech. So Anderson has separate paragraphs, for example, for the speeches of the receptionist and for her own responses.

Reading

In the essay that follows, a Korean student reports a problem he has in using English. Because of different conventions in Korean, a usage pattern that is common to Americans seems illogical to him. He uses two short narratives to illustrate his point.

Yes and No

Yong Il Song

After coming to America, I have suffered from the improper usage   1
of "yes" and "no." I sometimes confuse an affirmative response with a negative one because the usage of "yes" and "no" in Korean is different from English usage. For example, if I am asked, "Haven't you had dinner yet?" and I have not had dinner yet, then in Korean I usually say, "Yes, I haven't." But in English, I have to say, "No, I haven't." This different usage of "yes" and "no" in Korean and in English sometimes causes misunderstandings or even estrangements between my American friends and me.

Because of my misuse of "yes" and "no," I often find that my friends   2
misunderstand me: They perceive the exact opposite meaning from what I intend to give them. The following example will show how the misuse has embarrassed me. One day only a month after I came to the United States, I happened to have dinner with an American student, Bob, in a dining hall. He was living in the next room in the school dormitory. He asked me several questions about my background, including my family,

religion, and my nationality; I answered all the questions as sincerely as I could. Several days later, I found that some dorm residents thought that I came from North Korea. I was a little embarrassed. Even though North Koreans and South Koreans share common ancestors, the two nations have maintained serious competition for 30 years and are different in every respect: North Korea is the most chauvinistic country in the communist block, while South Korea is a leading developing country in the capitalist block. Thus, South Koreans do not like being regarded as North Koreans. I stopped by Bob's room and asked why he was spreading the wrong information on my nationality. Then he said, "Oh, you told me that you came from North Korea."

"No, I didn't," I replied. 3

"Don't you remember?" he continued. "When I asked you 'You are 4 not from North Korea, are you?' you clearly answered, 'Yes, of course.' Didn't it mean that you are from North Korea?" I was so confused that I did not even know whether I should say "yes" or "no" to his last question. He said that I pronounced "of course" so strongly that he could not ask me further; he thought that I was very proud of being a North Korean. I actually affirmed what I wanted to negate strongly.

The different usage of "yes" and "no" also causes estrangement be- 5 tween my friends and me. During the summer of 1989, my close friend Mark was a dorm-mate. He was in his late twenties and had gotten married about five years before. One sultry weekend night, he brought his son and daughter into the dorm. Playing with each other, his son and daughter made some noise while they were running up and down. I did not mind the noise since I was just watching TV. The next morning I came across Mark and his offspring in the doorway of the dorm. After we both said, "Hello," he introduced his children to me.

"Nice to meet you. How old are you?" I asked his son. 6

"He is three years old," Mark replied on behalf of his son and asked 7 me smiling, "Didn't they make noise last night? Didn't it bother you?"

Because I did not mind the noise at all, I clearly said "Yes!" How 8 stupid I appeared to be!

The mild smile suddenly disappeared from his face, and he said, "I 9 am sorry about that. They are going right now, so they will not bother you anymore. See you later."

He passed me by with his children. I could not understand what he 10 was sorry about, and again I stupidly said, "OK. Bye. Have a nice weekend!" After a moment of thinking, I recognized that I had misused "yes" and severely hurt his feelings. That evening, I had a hard time explaining my difficulty in using "yes" and "no" and apologizing for my impoliteness to Mark. After a short conversation, I found that if I had not realized my mistake and not apologized to him, he would have thought that I was a very rude person.

Grammatically, in Korea, people use a "yes" when they agree with the 11 literal meaning of a question regardless of whether the questioner uses a positive sentence or a negative one. In America, however, a "yes" is always followed by a positive sentence. This seemingly slight difference has made me confused and embarrassed more than any monstrous calculus problem has. To cope with this problem, I have set simple rules: First, take a five-second break if I am not sure of the proper word—"yes" or "no." Second, use the phrase "pardon me," so the person asking the question rephrases the sentences.

Questions: The Community of Writers

1. State Yong Il Song's thesis.
2. Which part of his thesis does his first narrative illustrate? His second narrative?
3. Think of another circumstance in which Yong Il Song's understanding of when to respond "yes" or "no" would present problems.
4. What is the effect of direct quotations in the essay's narratives?
5. Who would you guess is the intended audience? Use evidence from the essay to support your answer.

Analysis

Like Anderson, Yong Il Song uses simple events for his essay. He has been troubled by a specific problem in using English and illustrates that problem with two incidents. This use of **exemplification** is a common method of supporting points. Rather than limiting himself to a single incident, however, he has chosen to bring in a second occurrence. The effect is to amplify and strengthen his point about the difficulty of using the idioms of a second language. To first-language users, idioms are as fundamental, and often as unconscious, as word order in sentences. They are often illogical grammatically, meaning something different from the literal meaning of the words and can therefore pose difficulties for second-language usage. An example is "give someone a hand," meaning "help someone." When Yong Il Song responds to questions according to his Korean understanding of their meaning, his usage differs from the American English idiom.

Thesis

Yong Il Song states his *thesis* explicitly in his first paragraph. His statement illustrates all three components of thesis sentences explained on pages 58–60 of Chapter 3: subject, assertion, and method of essay organization:

> *Subject:* usage of "yes" and "no" in Korean and English
> *Assertion:* causes misunderstandings or even estrangements
> *Organization:* first misunderstandings, then estrangements

Yong Il Song's first narrative illustrates "misunderstandings" and the second potential "estrangements." As stated in Chapter 3, not all thesis sentences specify the writer's method of organizing the essay, but they do all express the subject of the essay and make an assertion about the subject.

Like Anderson's essay, "Yes and No" illustrates paragraphing with direct quotations. Yong Il Song has begun new paragraphs each time he quotes another speaker.

Exercise: The Exploring Writer

Report a conversation you have had recently, using direct quotations and making an effort to put down the exact words of both the other speaker and yourself. Begin a new paragraph each time the speaker changes. Note that commas and periods are usually written inside the closing quotation marks.

Writing

Report a personal experience. It may be something quite simple, like Janice Anderson's report of making a tape recording or Yong Il Song's difficulty with English idiom. Other personal narrative reports that might inspire an idea for you are at the end of the chapter: "The Patagonian Wind," " 'Little' Jimmy," and "The Principle." In recounting the details of the incident or incidents you choose to report and your reactions, keep your readers in mind. Prod your memory for details, perhaps asking the journalist's questions, brainstorming, or freewriting (See Chapter 3).

Begin as Yong Il Song does, with an introduction that includes your thesis, or as Janice Anderson does, plunging directly into the experience. As you compose, report the experience chronologically, from the beginning to end. Describe the setting for your readers, telling where the incident took place and what the circumstances were. Describe the other participants. Report conversations as direct quotations. Tell how you felt throughout the occurrence.

Select an expressive title, one that reflects your controlling idea whether or not you express that idea in a thesis sentence. Revise for paragraphing, so that you begin new paragraphs at shifts of time and place, as well as at shifts of speakers in conversation. Delete irrelevant details and add details where your readers might have questions.

REPORTING AN OBSERVED INCIDENT

If you were to think of all the reporting you do, next in frequency to personal experiences might be incidents you have observed. You witness an accident, or a fight, or a wedding, or a building being razed, and all these are worth reporting to another person. If you're like most people, you like to tell stories. And factual stories are usually easier to tell, because you don't have to invent details; you just remember them.

Sometimes your reports may be based on notes you've taken—on records, that is. In biology class, you record your experiments or observations and then write up your notes as a report. On your vacation trip, you may keep a journal, a daily account of your observations, and later report your experiences to a friend or relative. You may take notes on a painting or a play you've seen and then write a report about it.

How good are you at observing? Do you pay attention to details around you? If you witness a hit-and-run collision, for example, do you notice the model, make, and color of the car that fled? Or take another example, something less startling: the person who sits in front of you in English class has just had her hair cut and styled. Do you notice? Can you remember what her hair looked like before?

Reports of observations usually attend closely to details. They tend to be *descriptive* rather than narrative. Since they report what a person has seen, they may be developed **spatially** rather than chronologically.

Reading

The following essay reports close observations by a student of nature. Franklin Russell was a free-lance writer, born in New Zealand but commissioned by a Toronto magazine to observe life at a pond in Ontario, Canada. Before staking out his pond, he was no more experienced at pond watching than you probably are, but he learned to apply the objectivity of the scientist and the imagination of the artist. This essay, taken from his book *Watchers at the Pond,* reports his observations. As you read, watch for signs of the author's attitude toward his subject and of his presence in the report.

The Hunt

Franklin Russell

The pond swarmed with creatures whose lives depended on guile, 1
dissimulation, stealth, on strength and speed. The hunters ranged the
pond from the high upper air, where the red-tailed hawk hovered, to the
mud bottom, where dragonfly larvae lurked in endless ambush.

The death of the towhees in the southern forest was an insignificant 2
incident in one hunting day. Before dusk the sharp-shinned hawk had
killed again several times. But the towhees' death exemplified the perfection attained by some hunters in securing their prey.

Among these creatures were hawks, owls, wasps, robber flies, minks, 3
weasels, mantises, and crows. Perhaps the most imposing was the red-
tailed hawk. His scream in the hot sky gripped the senses, and the vertical
fall of his body terrified the forest. Another was the great horned owl
whose booming night call jerked sleeping crows out of their sleep. If
crows dreamed, they would have visions of great horned owls.

But size was no criterion of the hunter's skill and power. Few crea- 4
tures better personified the hunt than the robber fly. One had appeared
now, and his arrival had been so fleet that he was still unseen at the pond.
He was black, slender-bodied, hunch-shouldered, with enormous multi-
faceted eyes and long hooked legs. He stayed unmoving on a cattail stem,
his eyes glistening and watching. The pond sparkled. The trees mur-
mured in the wind of a new season. The frogs were silent at midday.

The fly was motionless one moment and gone the next. Only the 5
acutest eye could follow him low across the water on a course of intercep-
tion that ended at a droning bumblebee. The impact flung the bee into
the grass. He squirmed to sting the fly, but the powerful grip of hooked
legs held him tightly till a sting jabbed into his back. He was still struggling feebly when the fly inserted a sucking beak and began withdrawing
his body fluids.

Meanwhile, another robber fly arrived, flashed over the feeding fly 6
at pondside, and disappeared toward the northern trees. She saw a
large beetle scuttling over some bare ground and dropped and strad-
dled him before he even saw her. The beetle ran while the fly pushed
her sting at his heavy armor, seeking to find the chink that made him
fatally vulnerable. She found it, and as the beetle slowed his scuttling
run she unsheathed a cutter from her mouth and sawed a hole in his
back. Through this she inserted her beak and sucked. The beetle quiv-
ered and died.

It was a time of hunters lurking behind the peaceful façade of the 7
pond. A yellowthroat jerked out his song in a thicket. A volley of crow
calls rose from the marsh. A big green darner dragonfly hovered over the

feeding robber fly for a moment, then flicked over some blossoming chokeberries to the pond. He lowered a scoop formed by his hair-fringed front legs and drove through a swarm of gnats flying close to the surface of the water. A dozen of them were imprisoned in the scoop, and while still flying, the dragonfly chewed them dry and dropped their bodies in the water.

As long as a dragonfly patrolled the pond, no insect was safe. Some   8 of the hundreds of dragonflies there were as big as small birds, and all had double wings outstretched flatly from their bodies. All had great compound eyes that were almost omnipercipient, so widely and minutely did they see. The big green darner saw a wolf spider running through grass on the pond bank. At the same time and in the opposite direction, he was watching a monarch butterfly resting on a twig. The dragonfly's head was flexibly joined to his body so he could drop his head and look underneath and behind, and fly, as a result, with exceptional precision. He might be halfway across the pond and flick himself one hundred wingspans into the path of a butterfly. He would be eating before landing with his struggling victim.

The dragonflies were catholic hunters and cannibals. The green   9 darner paused over a leaf, then struck at a smaller, bright red dragonfly nearby. But his prey eluded him. He flew backwards, then whisked off sharply and hit a low-flying wasp. The two creatures tumbled into a mass of aquatic plants, the stingless dragonfly trying to kill the wasp before she could drive in her sting. The insects disappeared into the greenery, and the bright sun glittered on the tranquil pond.

The wasps greatly outnumbered the dragonflies at the pond and   10 were their antithesis. They were members of a great family of earth insects who had evolved lives of refinement and ingenuity, in contrast to the dragonflies' simple attributes of speed, power, and rapacity, which were virtually unchanged since primeval times. Some wasps, not seen at the pond, used small pieces of wood as tools to dig their burrows. Others, at the pond, were knowing enough to wrestle armor-sheathed victims till their bodies bent and a small crack appeared. The wasps would then sting through it. All the wasps were shelter builders, and they were both solitary and communal.

The silent struggle between wasp and dragonfly continued in the   11 greenery; nearby, six different wasps lingered on a cluster of lily pads. All had come to drink. A solitary wasp, black and skinny, his body longer than his wings and his head joined to his body by a short, exceptionally thin neck, rested on one leaf. He looked light and fragile, and a puff of wind moved him fractionally. Near him was a cicada killer three or four times his size, with massive abdomen, thorax, head, eyes, and wings. As a hunter of creatures equaling or exceeding her size and weight, she needed vigorous strength. Her shiny black body was half-circled by yellow bands, and she seemed remote, in the evolutionary process, from the fragile solitary wasp.

Elsewhere, communal wasps were working. The sun flickered over 12 the iridescent coat colors of the purple mud daubers, making them blue one instant, then green or purple. Potter wasps—shiny black and yellow, delicate and industrious—gathered clay to make small spherical nests. Paper wasps, with yellow stripes over green abdomens and red spots decorating their sides, were masticating wood fiber to make a nest. The puzzle of the wasps was why some collected into communities and fed their youngsters on nectar while others were solitary and fed their larvae on red meat.

The robber fly was still feeding on the beetle when a hunting wasp 13 hummed through the whispering green of oak and hickory. She had seen the shiny brown face mask of a large caterpillar bobbing up and down as he chewed on a leaf, his body invisible against it. The wasp alighted on the leaf, and the caterpillar tautened into a ball and dropped. Down he fell, glancing from leaf to leaf and then hitting a branch and ricochetting into the apparent safety of thick grass.

The wasp sank slowly after him. She found his rolled-up body wedged 14 between two grass stems, and with deliberation, she stung him twice. The stings might kill him or they might merely paralyze; it did not matter. His meat would still be edible when the wasp's egg hatched inside his body later. She gripped him now and pulled him free from the grass. In a moment she was in the air with him, headed for her subterranean burrow and the laying of one egg.

A yellow-banded wasp rose slowly and awkwardly from the pond 15 greenery. She had been severely bitten and partially blinded by the dragonfly, but she had killed him at last, driving her sting through a chink in the cluster of his six legs. The poison paralyzed the dragonfly's simple organs and stopped his long tubular heart. The wasp resumed her interrupted journey.

Questions: The Community of Writers

1. What kind of hunt does Russell describe? Who are the participants? Who are the hunters and who are the hunted?

2. At what point in this description does the actual report of events begin?

3. What do you learn about the author and his attitudes toward his subject? What is the tone of this essay? Discuss what the tone tells you about Russell's purpose.

4. The hunt Russell describes often ends in death. What does his attitude toward these deaths seem to be? How do you account for statements like "As long as a dragonfly patrolled the pond, no insect was safe" (paragraph 8) and "The death of the towhees in the southern forest was an insignificant incident in one hunting day" (paragraph 2)?

5. What does Russell's report tell you about the "peaceful façade" of the pond?

6. In writing this report, Russell probably did not rely totally on his memory. If you and your groupmates were assigned the task of reporting a pond observation, what kind of record might each of you keep?

Analysis

Try to imagine how Russell's notes might have looked. Like many reports, "The Hunt" probably began as notes recording the author's observations. He would have had jottings on the activities of the robber fly, the dragonflies, and the wasps. Probably watching with binoculars, he would even have observed in close detail the insects' appearances. Though he relies mostly on his vision, he paid attention to sounds too, such as the song of the yellowthroat and the calls of the crows. Notes are often not recorded in the same order as the report that utilizes them, and Russell's notes may not have been in the order of events reported here; he probably saw the dragonflies overhead while watching the robber flies and heard the yellowthroat and the crows throughout his observation.

You probably find, too, that the order in which you take your notes is the same order in which you use them. After you do some reading for a report, you probably shuffle your notes into an order that seems appropriate for your report. Because of this need to rearrange notes, notetakers often use note cards or small notepads for recording specific observations, descriptions, insights, summaries, and so on. (See Chapter 16 for a discussion of taking notes for reports.)

Thesis and Development

In writing his report, Russell may have rearranged some of the details in his notes, selected some details and omitted others, and added information that would connect this description with the previous chapter of his book plus giving significance to his observations. Was the robber fly the first hunter he observed? It seems so, although he may have been observing all three hunter groups at once—robber flies, dragonflies, and wasps. Since he can't report all his observations at once, he needs to begin somewhere. Connecting the dragonflies and the wasps is easy, because they hunt and attack each other. Beginning with the robber fly, Russell gives the impression of simultaneity by noting the dragonfly hovering over the feeding robber fly, then (paragraph 13) reporting that the robber fly is "still feeding on the beetle."

The first three paragraphs of "The Hunt" have a purpose other than to report and are probably not drawn from Russell's record, at least not in the form that is here. Paragraph 1 provides an overview of the essay, something that can't easily be accomplished while notetaking is in progress. In this paragraph Russell also states his *thesis:* that life on the pond depends on cunning and vigor. This is his insight into the events he observed; it may have occurred to him only after he had completed his observations or perhaps at some time while he was observing. But it would not have been at the beginning of his notes. The second sentence of this paragraph amplifies the first by defining the scope of the hunt, from the upper air to the bottom of the pond.

Paragraph 3 also defines the scope and setting, before the writer narrows down to the insect hunters. Paragraph 2 serves a double purpose: to link this chapter to the previous one, in which Russell reports that the towhees had been killed, and to emphasize again that success in the hunt depends on a highly developed skill.

Paragraph 4 begins the *chronological* report of what actually happens at the pond. Robber flies catch a bumblebee and a beetle, dragonflies "as big as small birds" catch any insect that strikes their fancy, including other dragonflies, and a wasp stings a caterpillar while another finally overcomes an attacking dragonfly. The report ends when the victorious wasp resumes "her interrupted journey." The entire report covers only minutes of an observation.

Exercise: The Exploring Writer

Be a close observer. Place yourself where you can record observations of people, animals, insects, or something else that has actions you can record, such as airplanes, taxis, and bicycles. Watch and listen, noting what happens. Record only your observation; don't interpret actions or impute motives.

Writing

Using your notes from the preceding exercise, revise them as a report. Read over your record and decide on an overall controlling idea that can serve as your thesis sentence. Like Russell, you may need to define the scope of your report. You may find it necessary to rearrange the details of your record, to delete some that seem irrelevant to your thesis, and to add some from your memory so that the connections between the details you report are clear to readers. You will probably find that a chronological or spatial arrangement works best.

Use coherence devices to help your reader fit events together. Note how Russell in paragraph 6 leads into his description of the actions of the second robber fly: "Meanwhile, another robber fly arrived." To introduce his report of the dragonflies, he shifts from the pondside to the sounds of the birds, then notes the hovering dragonfly. Later he links his report on the wasps back to his beginning by observing the wasp humming over the feeding robber fly.

Be descriptive. Use sight imagery so that your readers can see what you have seen. And use your other senses as appropriate: hearing, touch, smell, and taste. Use adjectives that evoke images and actions; Russell, for example, uses "*feeding* fly," "*stingless* dragonfly," "*shiny black* body," "*armor-sheathed* victims," "*spherical* nests." Like Russell, use verbs that denote specific actions: "the impact *flung* the bee," "a sting *jabbed* into his back," "a yellowthroat *jerked out* his song," "the two creatures *tumbled*," "the sun *flickered*." Use concrete nouns, too: "unsheathed a *cutter* from her *mouth*," "blossoming *chokeberries*," "whispering *green* of *oak* and *hickory*," "pond *greenery*."

DESCRIBING A NATURAL PHENOMENON

People often describe phenomena of nature. Whether you live in Minnesota or Florida, you like to hear how deep the snow was in International Falls—or how cold it was in January. Hurricanes in Florida or elsewhere are reported throughout the country. Earthquakes and mudslides in California make national news, along with fires in Wyoming, unremitting heat and humidity in the nation's midsection, floods on the Mississippi and other rivers, predicted melting of the polar ice caps and flooding of coastal cities, threats to the ultraviolet-screening capacity of ozone, and so on. Wherever we live, nature is part of us, part of our world; we want to read about it, and we often write about it.

An example of this kind of writing follows, in which Rachel L. Carson describes the legendary Sargasso Sea, a nearly stagnant part of the Atlantic Ocean. Reports like this one tell *what something is like,* as opposed to *what happened.* In reporting what something is like you generally use a spatial arrangement. This arrangement may be ordered, such as vertical or horizontal movement, or it may seem random—each part described as the writer encounters it. *Ordered* spatial arrangement might be exemplified by describing a person from head to toe or a garden from where you enter it to where you leave it. You might use a *random* spatial arrangement for describing a woods or a beach as each part registers in your consciousness.

Reports of what something is like are usually written with present tense verbs, as in the following sentences:

The beach only *seems* barren in the winter.
The river *rises* each year in proportion to the rains in the basin it drains.
Even though a hurricane *gives* plenty of warning of its arrival, it always *seems* to strike with an unexpected force.

These examples also demonstrate that when you describe what something is like, you do not report a specific incident; rather, you report the way something usually happens or acts or is.

Reading

In "The Sargasso Sea," noted nature writer Rachel L. Carson reports what the Sargasso is like: why it is such a weedy jungle in the middle of the Atlantic Ocean, what kinds of sea creatures live there, what it is, and what it is not. As you read, note how she arranges her description and how she writes in the present: what was true in 1951, when she wrote, is true today; the Sargasso Sea is still there, along with its weeds and their inhabitants.

The Sargasso Sea

Rachel L. Carson

The central oceanic regions, bounded by the currents that sweep around the ocean basins, are in general the deserts of the sea. There are few birds and few surface-feeding fishes, and indeed there is little surface plankton to attract them. The life of these regions is largely confined to deep water. The Sargasso Sea is an exception, not matched in the anticyclonic centers of other ocean basins. It is so different from any other place on earth that it may well be considered a definite geographic region. A line drawn from the mouth of Chesapeake Bay to Gibraltar would skirt its northern border; another from Haiti to Dakar would mark its southern boundary. It lies all about Bermuda and extends more than halfway across the Atlantic, its entire area being roughly as large as the United States. The Sargasso, with all its legendary terrors for sailing ships, is a creation of the great currents of the North Atlantic that encircle it and bring into it the millions of tons of floating sargassum weed from which the place derives its name, and all the weird assemblage of animals that live in the weed.

The Sargasso is a place forgotten by the winds, deserted by the strong flow of waters that girdle it as with a river. Under the seldom-clouded skies, its waters grow warm and heavy with salt. Separated widely from coastal rivers and from polar ice, there is no inflow of fresh water to dilute its saltiness; the only influx is of saline water from the adjacent currents, especially from the Gulf Stream or North Atlantic Current as it crosses from America to Europe. And with the little, inflowing streams of surface water come the plants and animals that for months or years have drifted in the Gulf Stream.

The sargassum weed is a brown alga that lives attached to rocks along the coasts of the West Indies and Florida. Many of the plants are torn away by storms, especially during the hurricane season. They are picked up by the Gulf Stream and are drifted northward. With the weeds go, as involuntary passengers, many small fishes, crabs, shrimps, and innumerable larvae of assorted species of marine creatures, whose home had been the coastal banks of sargassum weed.   3

Curious things happen to the animals that have ridden on the sargassum weed into a new home. Once they lived on a rocky shore, a few feet or a few fathoms below the surface, but never far above a rocky bottom. They knew the rhythmic movements of waves and tides. They could leave the shelter of the weeds at will and creep or swim about over the bottom in search of food. Now, in the middle of the ocean, they are in a new world. The bottom lies two or three miles below them. Those who are poor swimmers must cling to the weed, which now represents a life raft, supporting them above the abyss. Over the ages since their ancestors came here, some species have developed special organs of attachment, either for themselves or for their eggs, so that they may not sink into the cold, dark water far below. The flying fish make nests of the weed to contain their eggs, which bear an amazing resemblance to the sargassum floats or "berries."   4

Indeed, many of the little marine beasts of the weedy jungle seem to be playing an elaborate game of disguise in which each is camouflaged to hide it from the others. The Sargasso sea slug—a snail without a shell—has a soft, shapeless brown body spotted with dark-edged circles and fringed with flaps and folds of skin, so that as it creeps over the weed in search of prey it can scarcely be distinguished from the vegetation. One of the fiercest carnivores of the place, the sargassum fish Pterophryne, has copied with utmost fidelity the branching fronds of the weed, its golden berries, its rich brown color, and even the white dots of encrusting worm tubes. All these elaborate bits of mimicry are indications of the fierce internecine wars of the Sargasso jungles, which go on without quarter and without mercy for the weak or the unwary.   5

In the science of the sea there has been a long-standing controversy about the origin of the drifting weeds of the Sargasso Sea. Some have held that the supply is maintained by weeds recently torn away from coastal beds; others say that rather limited sargassum fields of the West Indies and Florida cannot possibly supply the immense area of the Sargasso. They believe that we find here a self-perpetuating community of plants that have become adapted to life in the open sea, needing no roots or hold-fasts for attachment, and able to propagate vegetatively. Probably there is truth in both ideas. New plants do come in each year in small numbers, and now cover an immense area because of their very long life once they have reached this quiet central region of the Atlantic.   6

It takes about half a year for the plants torn from West Indian 7 shores to reach the northern border of the Sargasso, perhaps several years for them to be carried into the inner parts of this area. Meanwhile, some have been swept onto the shores of North America by storms, others have been killed by cold during the passage from offshore New England across the Atlantic, where the Gulf Stream comes into contact with waters from the Arctic. For the plants that reach the calm of the Sargasso, there is virtual immortality. A. E. Parr of the American Museum [of Natural History] has recently suggested that the individual plants may live, some for decades, others for centuries, according to their species. It might well be that some of the very weeds you would see if you visited the place today were seen by Columbus and his men. Here, in the heart of the Atlantic, the weed drifts endlessly, growing, reproducing vegetatively by a process of fragmentation. Apparently almost the only plants that die are the ones that drift into unfavorable conditions around the edges of the Sargasso or are picked up by outwardmoving currents.

Such losses are balanced, or possibly a little more than balanced, by 8 the annual addition of weeds from distant coasts. It must have taken eons of time to accumulate the present enormous quantities of weed, which Parr estimates as about 10 million tons. But this, of course, is distributed over so large an area that most of the Sargasso is open water. The dense fields of weeds waiting to entrap a vessel never existed except in the imaginations of sailors, and the gloomy hulks of vessels doomed to endless drifting in the clinging weed are only the ghosts of things that never were.

Questions: The Community of Writers

1. What does Carson say the legendary Sargasso Sea is like? How does she compare the real sea to the legendary one?

2. What are the causes of this weedy sea?

3. Name some of the "curious things" that happen to the sea creatures inhabiting the sargassum weeds.

4. Carson attributes the natural adaptations of the Sargasso's inhabitants to the "fierce internecine wars" that take place in the weedy jungle. Compare these adaptations of hunters and hunted with those of the creatures Franklin Russell describes in "The Hunt."

5. In describing the Sargasso, Carson uses several methods of development. Find instances, perhaps more than one of each, of these methods: classification, contrast, cause and effect, definition, and process analysis. If necessary, refer to "Methods of Developing and Arranging Paragraphs and Essays" in Chapter 4.

6. Does Carson state her thesis? With your groupmates, phrase her controlling idea.

7. Discuss how the effects of Carson's essay would be changed if she had used past tense verbs to describe the Sargasso: *were* instead of *are, lay* instead of *lie,* and so on.

Analysis

Carson arranges her descriptive report spatially. In paragraph 1 she places the Sargasso Sea in the broader expanse of the Atlantic Ocean, moving inward to the Sargasso itself. Still progressing from larger to smaller, in paragraph 3 she describes the sargassum weed and then in paragraphs 4 and 5 the inhabitants of the weed. In the final paragraphs she moves back to the weeds, broadening out to account for them as part of the whole Atlantic. If you were not conscious of this orderly progression, you can credit Carson's skill in essay development and coherence.

Coherence

Carson clarifies the scope of her essay in the final sentence of paragraph 1: the Sargasso Sea, the sargassum weed, and "the weird assemblage of animals that live in the weed." Is this the sentence you identified as her *thesis?* It may well be so, since the purpose of this essay is to report what this natural phenomenon is like. Because Carson has clearly announced the scope of her essay, it is no surprise when in the next paragraph she launches into a description of the sea and its origins, nor when she progresses to discussing the weeds and then the animals. But her *coherence* doesn't rely only on her announcement of scope; she also links each new development to that announcement by *repetition of key words,* together with their synonyms, related words, and pronouns referring to them.

Notice the opening sentences of paragraphs 2, 3, and 4. Each one names the subject of its paragraph—"The Sargasso," "The sargassum weed," and "the animals" that inhabit the weed. Each mention of these key words links new paragraphs to the scope, or thesis sentence, and therefore to the essay as a whole. The opening sentences of other paragraphs also relate to the essay as a whole by means of this kind of repetition. Paragraph 5 refers to "the little marine beasts," paragraph 6 to "the drifting weeds," paragraph 7 to "the plants," and the final paragraph to "weeds."

Repetition achieves coherence within paragraphs as well. To see how the repetition of key words and related words connects sentences within a paragraph, take a closer look at paragraph 3. The key term here is *sargassum weed.* After mention of this term in the first sentence, thus linking the paragraph to the thesis, a synonym, *alga,* is introduced (*alga* is a Latin word meaning "seaweed," its plural being the more familiar *algae).* Sentence 2 uses a second synonym, *plants;* sentence 3 a pronoun, *they;* and sentence 4 a part of the original term, *weeds.* Study other paragraphs for similar uses of key word repetition to achieve coherence.

Exercise: The Community of Writers

Write a paragraph that patterns the style of paragraph 2 in "The Sargasso Sea." Begin "The _____ is a place _____ ," writing about a place you know in sentences similar to those Carson uses. When you have finished, compare your paragraph with those of your classmates and discuss the thinking you did while composing—how much you concentrated on your subject and how much on Carson's sentence patterns.

Writing

Write an essay that describes a place, perhaps the same one you described in the preceding exercise, for the purpose of reporting to readers what this place is like. In prewriting, try using the classical probes (see Chapter 3). Because they are related to methods of development, the probes may help you think of ways of classifying components of your subject, analyzing causes and effects, defining or identifying your subject, contrasting different aspects of it, or showing how the subject has developed into what it is now. Decide on the most appropriate manner of arranging your description—probably some spatial way. After drafting, check your methods of arrangement and development and the tense of your verbs. See whether your paragraphs are coherent: Are they all connected to a sentence that states the scope of your essay? Are the sentences within paragraphs related to one another?

WRITING A BOOK REPORT

You have probably written book reports before, and you will probably write them again. They're a common kind of school report because they achieve several purposes; you read the book (or enough of it to report on), you think about the subject of the book, and you write an essay. Under the best of circumstances, book reports also inform readers about the content of the book and interest them in reading the book.

Book reports, or reviews as they are sometimes called, do mainly two things: (1) *report* on the content and/or style of the book, and (2) *respond* to the content and/or style. Doing either requires that you read the book.

The main purpose of a book report is to report on content and/or style. You don't need to give a plot summary or try to cover every chapter. However, you do need to show an understanding of the entire book. You might give background on the occasion for its publication, such as new discoveries in the subject, or tell something about the author's credentials. You do need to give an overall view of the book, including the author's main point and emphasis, and you ought to tell readers what interested you most in the book.

Responding to the reading may be more difficult. To aid you in thinking about what you have read, use the Questions for Active Reading (page 6) and the Questions about Audience for Reading (page 26). When you ask questions such as "What is the writer's purpose in writing?" and "What does the writer do to stimulate my interest?" you will generate thoughts about the book. Continued use of questions like these is likely to produce the beginnings of a response, which can continue to develop as you write. (Summary and response are discussed in greater detail in Chapter 15.)

Reading

The book report that follows was written by a student in response to a book he read for his own enjoyment. The report consists mainly of information that interested him and that he thought might be of interest to other readers. Does Witzman give reasons for his favorable response?

Science Fact More Exciting Than Science Fiction

Paul Witzman

In 1985, Bob Ballard of Woods Hole Oceanographic Institute amazed the world with his announcement that he'd found the *RMS Titanic,* lost for more than seventy-three years. He substantiated his claim by showing pictures taken by an underwater robot. The wrecked ship was seen resting on the side of a mountain two and a half miles below the surface of the Atlantic Ocean. The next year Ballard, working with a group of French and American scientists, visited the *Titanic's* grave in a special deep sea diving submarine. *Her Name, Titanic* (New York: McGraw, 1988) is an exciting book written by Charles Pellegrino, one of the scientists who worked on the *Titanic* project. This book skillfully helps the reader understand why the *Titanic's* sinking in 1912 was so tragic, why the event is still significant today, and the incredible technology and effort it took to find and visit her.

Pellegrino provides his readers with a wealth of background information including a short biography of Bob Ballard, the expedition's leader, and how Pellegrino himself became involved in and affected by this project. Pellegrino is a scientist with many interests, the most compelling of which is space exploration and the search for alien life forms. It is his theory that there are oceans inside certain icy moons, especially Jupiter's moon Europa, and that life exists there. To develop a vehicle that could explore such an ocean he enlisted the help of Ballard, who had successfully designed machines that are able to probe the farthest depths of the Earth's oceans. That is when Ballard infected Pellegrino with his desire to find the *Titanic.*

The book transports the reader to April 15, 1912, and gives a feeling   3
of what it must have been like to be aboard the sinking ship—that feeling of total helplessness and regret that those who were aware of the ship's plight experienced. The *Titanic* had been warned by other ships at least six times that an ice field lurked in her path, yet she still proceeded at full speed. Her lookouts on the top deck were not provided with binoculars, making it impossible for them to spot hazards with enough warning to alter the huge liner's course. Once the iceberg, a glowing mountain of ice, was discovered to be directly in the *Titanic's* path, the captain steered the ship as far to the left as possible. The captain's reaction seemed wise at the time, but the 950-foot-long liner could only turn enough to prevent a direct impact, allowing the starboard side of the ship to scrape the iceberg.

The impact was hardly felt by most of the passengers. It wasn't known   4
that the ship had even suffered any damage until Thomas Andrews, the ship's designer, and the captain toured the lower decks a half hour later. There they found a 300-foot-long series of leaks in the *Titanic's* inch-thick steel-plated hull through which hundreds of gallons of water leaked each minute. As soon as Andrews surveyed the damage he knew that his unsinkable liner was going to sink and that, because the ship hadn't been fitted with enough lifeboats to save even half of her passengers and crew, there was going to be a great loss of life. What Andrews never knew is that a ship capable of rescuing everyone aboard the *Titanic* was only a few miles from her side and for some reason, believed by many to be fear of striking the same iceberg that doomed the *Titanic,* the *California* never responded to the distress flares and wireless SOS's that lasted almost two hours.

Most of the people aboard the sinking ship did not realize or believe   5
that the *Titanic* was sinking. They had so much faith in the claims that the ship was unsinkable that they refused to board the few available lifeboats. One survivor recalled that as the bow of the ship sank deeper and deeper in the dark water many of the cabins dipped below the water level long before they became flooded. She remembers looking over the side of her lifeboat and seeing a man peering out of a porthole that was five feet below the water level and that the light from his cabin cast an eerie greenish glow in the water.

Probably one of the least known and most troubling facts about this disaster is that the third-class passengers, most of whom were Irish immigrants bound for a new life in America, and the entire Italian kitchen staff were locked in their cabins on the lower decks and were never allowed to go up to the boat decks where there was some hope of survival. Consequently, most of these people had drowned in their cabins up to an hour before the first-class passengers were aware that the *Titanic* was sinking. Within two hours of striking the iceberg, she sank to the ocean floor, where she would rest in total darkness undisturbed until 1985.   6

Pellegrino tells about the space-age equipment employed in the search for the ship, which lasted from the beginning of June until September 1, when at one o'clock in the morning the *Titanic* was found. The underwater robot Argo, equipped with several 200,000 ASA cameras, virtually able to "see" in total darkness, sent the first pictures of the ship resting on the ocean floor. The first reaction of the ecstatic scientists was uncontrollable excitement and amazement at the photographs. This feeling, however, was soon replaced with a sense of mourning that affected the entire French and American crew aboard the *Knorr.* It was an emotion that no one had expected while on this adventure of a lifetime. Seeing the empty lifeboat davits that had last been seen the night fifteen hundred people perished in the cold and lonely Atlantic made time come unstuck for the explorers. For several days after their discovery many of the scientists couldn't eat or sleep as they pondered the terrible tragedy that had occurred in that place seventy-three years earlier. Ballard likened the mourning, which for him lasted nearly a year, to a nervous breakdown.   7

As a reader, one is able to experience somewhat the same mourning the scientists did in 1985. Pellegrino tells of the *Titanic's* sinking, using dramatic accounts given by survivors who are still alive today; of the exploration in 1985 and 1986; and of the wealth of technical information recently compiled that explains how the *Titanic* actually sank. These three different stories are perfectly fused into one, allowing the reader to know what the scientists knew and to experience what they experienced.   8

Questions: The Community of Writers

1. Book reports are sometimes written to persuade people to read the book. Does Witzman tell you enough about *Her Name, Titanic* to interest you in reading it? Discuss your answer, telling what interests each of you or why you are not interested.

2. This book report is more *report* than *response.* What is Witzman's response to the book?

Analysis

Witzman reports here on a book he enjoyed reading. This is the type of report you might make orally, in conversation with a friend: "I just read a good book; it's all about the sinking and rediscovery of the *Titanic*." Then if you're lucky your friend will say, "Oh? Tell me about it." And you can relate what really interested you about the book.

Your written report, of course, is more formal. First, it attracts an interested reader with an attention-getting title. Then an introduction gives enough details to keep the reader going. It names the book and its author and includes, in parentheses, other publishing information that may be necessary for the reader to locate the book in a bookstore. The introduction also gives a brief overview of the book, perhaps a little background on the author, and an assessment of the book. Then the body of the report recounts the aspects of the book that interested you the most and supports your assessment of the book.

In concluding, your written book report makes sure the reader knows how you feel about the book. In conversation you might say, "It was a really great book. You ought to read it." In writing, however, you would be more formal, as Witzman is: "These three different stories are perfectly fused into one, allowing the reader to know what the scientists knew and to experience what they experienced."

Exercise: The Exploring Writer

Select a book that you might be able to report on and explore your reactions to it by asking the Questions for Active Reading on page 6 and the Questions about Audience for Reading on page 26.

Writing

1. Write a report on a book you have read recently—one you've read either for school or for pleasure, possibly the one you explored in the preceding exercise. Report on what interests you about the book, assuming that a reader will be interested too. Include enough details so that a reader will get the flavor of the book and a sense of its treatment of the subject matter.

   Somewhere in your first paragraph, name the author and the title of the book and, in parentheses, its city of publication, the name of the publisher, and the date of publication.

2. Attend a lecture, address, debate, or some other special event, and write a report. Take notes on the event: what is said, the tone of the speaker(s), the issues addressed. Observe the audience too: their attention and responses, how many attended the event.

In your first paragraph, name the speaker(s), the occasion, the date, and the place. Name the title if there was one. Give an overall statement before moving on to the body of your report. Then give specific details—enough so your reader will understand the main issues and attitudes. Conclude with an overall summary and/or your own impressions of the event.

ADDITIONAL READING FOR DISCUSSION

Reading

This excerpt from Maya Angelou's *Gather Together in My Name* (1974) reports an experience of racism in the American South in the 1940s, shortly after World War II. Even though what she reports is a specific incident that she experienced, in recounting it Angelou reports much more. What does this story tell you about racism today?

The Principle

Maya Angelou

The days eased themselves around our lives like visitors in a sick-room. I hardly noticed their coming and going. Momma* was as en-grossed as she'd allow herself in the wonder of my son. Patting, stroking, she talked to him and never introduced in her deep voice the false humor adults tend to offer babies. He, in turn, surrendered to her. Following her from kitchen to porch to store to the backyard.

Their togetherness came to be expected. The tall and large dark-brown woman (whose movement never seemed to start or stop) was trailed one step by the pudgy little butter-yellow baby lurching, falling, now getting himself up, at moments rocking on bowed legs, then off again in the wave of Momma. I never saw her turn to stop to right him, but she would slow her march and resume when he was steady again.

My pattern had arrived from old exotic Texarkana. And I dressed for the trek downtown, and checked my hair, which was straightened to within an inch of its life and greased to desperation. From within the

1

2

3

_____

*Angelou's grandmother.

Store, I felt the threat of the sun but walked out into the road impelled by the missionary zeal.

By the time I reached the pond and Mr. Willie Williams' Dew Drop In, the plastic seemed to have melted to the exact shape of my feet, and sweat had popped through the quarter inch of Arrid in my armpits.   4

Mr. Williams served me a cold drink. "What you trying to do? Fry your brains?"   5

"I'm on my way to the General Merchandise Store. To pick up an order."   6

His smile was a two-line checkerboard of white and gold. "Be careful they don't pick you up. This sun ain't playing."   7

Arrogance and stupidity nudged me out of the little café and back on the white hot clay. I drifted under the shade trees, my face a mask of indifference. The skin of my thighs scudded like wet rubber as I walked deliberately by the alien white houses and on to my destination.   8

In the store the air lay heavily on the blades of two sluggish overhead fans, and a sweet, thick odor enveloped me at the cosmetic counter. Still, I was prepared to wander the aisles until the sun forgave our sins and withdrew its vengeance.   9

A tall saleswoman wearing a clerk's smock confronted me. I tried to make room for her in the narrow corridor. I moved to my left, she moved to her right. I right, she left, we jockeyed a moment's embarrassment and I smiled. Her long face answered with a smile. "You stand still and I'll pass you." It was not a request for cooperation. The hard mountain voice gave me an order.   10

To whom did she think she was speaking? Couldn't she see from my still-white though dusty gloves, my starched clothes, that I wasn't a servant to be ordered around? I had walked nearly three miles under a sun on fire and was neither gasping nor panting, but standing with the cool decorum of a great lady in the tacky, putrid store. She should have considered that.   11

"No, you stand still and I'll pass around you," I commanded.   12

The amazement which leaped upon her face was quickly pushed aside by anger. "What's your name? Where you from?"   13

A repetition of "You stand still and I'll pass around you" was ready on my tongue, when the pale woman who had taken my order slack-butted down the aisle toward us. The familiar face brought back the sympathy I had felt for her and I explained the tall woman into limbo with "Excuse me, here comes my salesgirl."   14

The dark-haired woman turned quickly and saw her colleague approach. She put herself between us, and her voice rasped out in the quiet store: "Who is this?"   15

Her head jerked back to indicate me. "Is this that sassy Ruby Lee you was telling me about?"   16

The clerk lifted her chin and glanced at me, then swirled to the older woman, "Naw, this ain't her." She flipped the pages of a pad in her hand and continued, "This one's Margaret or Marjorie or something like that."   17

Her head eased up again and she looked across centuries at me.   18
"How do you pronounce your name, gal? Speak up."

In that moment I became rootless, nameless, pastless. The two white   19
blurs buoyed before me.

"Speak up," she said. "What's your name ?"   20

I clenched my reason and forced their faces into focus. "My name"—   21
here I drew myself up through the unrevenged slavery—"is Miss Johnson.
If you have occasion to use my name, which I seriously doubt, I advise you
to address me as Miss Johnson. For if I need to allude to your pitiful
selves, I shall call you Miss Idiot, Miss Stupid, Miss Fool, or whatever name
a luckless fate has dumped upon you."

The women became remote even as I watched them. They seemed   22
actually to float away from me down the aisle; and from watching their
distant faces, I knew they were having trouble believing in the fact of me.

"And where I'm from is no concern of yours, but rather where you're   23
going. I'll slap you into the middle of next week if you even dare to open
your mouths again. Now, take that filthy pattern and stick it you-know-
where."

As I strode between the two women I was sheathed in satisfaction.   24
There had been so few critical times when my actions met my approval
that now I congratulated myself. I had got them told and told correctly.
I pictured the two women's mouths still open in amazement. The road
was less rocky and the sun's strength was weakened by my pleasure.
Congratulations were in order.

There was no need to stop at Mr. Williams' for a refreshing drink. I   25
was as cool as a fountain inside as I headed home.

Momma stood on the porch facing the road. Her arms hung at   26
her sides and she made no motions with her head. Yet something was
wrong. Tension had distorted the statue straightness and caused her
to lean leftward. I stopped patting myself on the back and ran to the
Store.

When I reached the one-step porch, I looked up in her face.   27
"Momma, what's the matter?"

Worry had forced a deep line down either side of her nostrils past   28
her stiffly held lips.

"What's wrong?"   29

"Mr. Coleman's granddaughter, Miss June, just called from the Gen-   30
eral Merchandise Store." Her voice quaked a little. "She said you was
downtown showing out."

So that's how they described my triumph to her. I decided to explain   31
and let her share in the glory. I began, "It was the principle of the thing,
Momma—"

I didn't even see the hand rising, and suddenly it had swung down   32
hard against my cheek.

"Here's your principle, young miss."   33

I felt the sting on my skin and the deep ache in my head. The greatest 34
hurt was that she didn't ask to hear my side.

"Momma, it was a principle." My left ear was clogged, but I heard my 35
own voice fuzzily.

The hand didn't surprise me the second time, but the same logic 36
which told me I was right at the white store told me I was no less right in
front of Momma. I couldn't allow myself to duck the blow. The backhand
swing came down on my right cheek.

"Here's your principle." Her voice had a far-away-tunnel sound. 37

"It was a principle, Momma." Tears poured down my burning face, 38
and ache backed up in my throat.

The hand came again and again each time I mumbled "principle," 39
and I found myself in the soft dust in front of the porch. I didn't want to
move. I never wanted to get up again.

She stepped off the porch and caught my arms. "Get up. Stand up, I 40
say."

Her voice never allowed disobedience. I stood, and looked at her 41
face. It glistened as if she had just dashed a pan of water over her head.

"You think 'cause you been to California these crazy people won't kill 42
you? You think them lunatic cracker boys won't try to catch you in the
road and violate you? You think because of your all-fired principle some
of the men won't feel like putting their white sheets on and riding over
here to stir up trouble? You do, you're wrong. Ain't nothing to protect
you and us except the good Lord and some miles. I packed you and the
baby's things, and Brother Wilson is coming to drive you to Louisville."

That afternoon I climbed into a horse-drawn wagon, and took my 43
baby from Momma's arms. The baby cried as we pulled away, and
Momma and Uncle Willie stood waving and crying good-bye.

Questions: The Community of Writers

1. What "principle" was Angelou standing up for? Discuss some corresponding modern-day principles. What principle motivated Angelou's grandmother to send her to Louisville?

2. What were your reactions as you read this narrative? What did you think when the narrator defied the woman at the General Merchandise Store? How did you feel when her grandmother struck and scolded her?

3. In his "I Have a Dream" speech (page 232), Martin Luther King, Jr., refers to a "bad check" to describe the rights of the people once enslaved in the American South. Discuss what Angelou's story tells about residual effects of slavery.

4. What do you learn about the narrator? What does she tell about herself at the time of the incident? Does she tell how she feels about the incident at the time of writing about it, about thirty years later?

5. The underlying theme of this narrative is Angelou's thesis. State it in your own words and compare with your groupmates' sentences.

CHAPTER 11

Writing to Inform

One of the best habits you can develop is that of studying the essays you find both enjoyable and informative.
—*Richard Marius*

Information surrounds us. From the bite-sized chunks of television news to the billboards we pass along the road, from public addresses to textbooks, we are bombarded every day with information. Can you think of any writing or speaking situation in which information of some kind is not passed on? You write your parents your grades this term, you read in your history textbook about the causes of the Civil War, you hear on television what the issues are in the senatorial elections, you read in the daily newspaper what's happening in Israel or South Africa or Atlanta, Georgia. Even when you just say "Hi, how are you?" you imply information: that you recognize the other person, that you acknowledge a social convention, and that you are inclined to be friendly. Much of what we read is written with informing as at least one of its purposes—on what's happening in politics, on what the newest trends in fashions or automobiles are, on how to judge the relative merits of blenders or television sets, and so on.

As shown in Chapter 10, much informational writing takes the form of *reporting*, relating what *has happened* or what has been done in specific circumstances. And as shown in Chapter 9, it also takes the form of *recording*, telling what *is happening*. The present chapter concentrates on communicating information in a more generalized sense—necessarily including what is happening or has happened but concentrating on *what happens* in given circumstances, implying that an audience needs to know or would want to know.

You inform when you take on a situation that needs to be changed—for example, inadequate day care for children of working mothers. You inform when you share something that you think others might profit from knowing, such as the effects of anorexia or bulimia on a person's social life, or the academic consequences of sports involvement, or the advantages of air bags in automobiles. You inform also when you define terms that may be unfamiliar to other people, such as *perestroika, endometriosis,* and *Judaism.* In short, you **inform** when your purpose is to communicate knowledge about situations that other people ought (in your opinion) to know about or might want to know about.

Information tells you something *new* and even surprising. Or it gives you a different perspective on something familiar. Most of what you read in this and other textbooks is meant to broaden your knowledge. Newspapers inform by keeping you current with world events, and magazine articles inform you about topics as wide-ranging as the magazines themselves.

If what you read is not new to you, either in the information it conveys or in its perspective, you are likely to lose interest. If, as sometimes happens with student readers, you are required to read or review writing that is not fresh and lively, you need to find ways of overcoming your lack of interest, forcing yourself to read actively, as Chapter 1 advises. It also often happens that writers build new information on old information, and if you give up too soon on the old information you will miss the new.

Whenever your purpose for writing is to inform, you probably have other purposes as well—to persuade, to instruct, to entertain, to praise, or to do something else. If you write, for example, to inform teenage girls about the dangers of anorexia nervosa, you undoubtedly also want to persuade them to get help if they find themselves with the symptoms. If you write to inform fellow college students about the stress that can result from working and attending college at the same time, you may also want to instruct them on ways to relieve that stress. If you write a mainly informative essay on shopping for a good used car, you may adopt a tone that makes the essay entertaining as well.

Sometimes writing that *seems* to be mainly informative is really something else. When you read about election issues, for example, the writer may be trying to persuade you to vote for a particular candidate, and awareness of that purpose will prompt you to search for bias in the selection of details and choice of words. Critical readers learn to look for underlying purposes in pieces of writing that seem to be informative, asking questions such as these:

- Why does the writer want to inform me about this subject?
- Does informing outweigh other purposes in amount of coverage?
- Do I find any exaggeration or discrepancies in the facts?

Having underlying purposes is not a bad thing; it's a common, often necessary, aspect of writing. When you write to your parents about your grades, your purpose may be in part to inform, but primarily you want to persuade them that you're doing as well in school as they should expect. These are dual purposes that both you and your parents are aware of. From the writer's perspective, you select details and choose words that may not give all the facts but will support your persuasive purpose. From the reader's perspective, your parents recognize that you have another, justifiable reason for wanting to impart the information you choose to include.

Informing is certainly a dominant purpose in writing. You will encounter it in almost all the essays in this book, as well as in most of the reading you do elsewhere. In this chapter you will see essays that inform about serious situations and common experiences, that seek to persuade as well as to inform, and that inform by definition.

INFORMING ABOUT A SERIOUS SITUATION

One of the most compelling reasons for writing is to inform other people about something the writer regards as a serious situation, with the understanding that informed people act responsibly. Much has been written about AIDS, or acquired immunodeficiency syndrome, for example, and about alcohol and drug abuse. You read something about the dangers to the earth's environment almost every day. You hear about increasing numbers of homeless people living on the cities' streets, about crime out of control, about growing numbers of teenage pregnancies. There is no lack of serious situations that some people know about and want to inform others about. In your own neighborhood or on your own campus, all you need to do is look around you to see serious situations: conflict over restrictions for drinking alcoholic beverages, inefficient registration procedures, deterioration of city neighborhoods or small-town shopping districts, depression among college students, and so on.

When you write about situations that you regard as serious enough to tell others about, you hope that by informing you can bring about change. Whether you specifically state that position or not, it is very likely an underlying purpose.

Reading

Try to imagine yourself not being able to read. You can't read the words on this page. You can't read the menu in a restaurant. You can't read the newspaper. You can't read the instructions on how to install your new stereo. In fact, when you go to buy your stereo, you can't read the list of comparative features of various stereo systems. Because you can't read, you also can't write. You can't get a college degree, and your job possibilities are limited. Illiteracy is a very serious situation; this is what Jonathan Kozol wants you to understand from reading this opening chapter from his book *Illiterate America*. In this chapter, he shares his concern about the problem and the need to do something to alleviate it. First read the essay to see what he says. Then be prepared to discuss the devices he uses for getting you involved.

A Third of the Nation Cannot Read These Words

Jonathan Kozol

He is meticulous and well-defended. 1

He gets up in the morning, showers, shaves, and dresses in a dark 2
gray business suit, then goes downstairs and buys a New York *Times* from the small newsstand on the corner of his street. Folding it neatly, he goes into the subway and arrives at work at 9:00 A.M.

He places the folded New York *Times* next to the briefcase on his desk 3
and sets to work on graphic illustrations for the advertising copy that is handed to him by the editor who is his boss.

"Run over this with me. Just make sure I get the gist of what you really 4
want."

The editor, unsuspecting, takes this as a reasonable request. In the 5
process of expanding on his copy, he recites the language of the text: a language that is instantly imprinted on the illustrator's mind.

At lunch he grabs the folded copy of the New York *Times*, carries it 6
with him to a coffee shop, places it beside his plate, eats a sandwich, drinks a beer, and soon heads back to work.

At 5:00 P.M., he takes his briefcase and his New York *Times*, waits for 7
the elevator, walks two blocks to catch an uptown bus, stops at a corner store to buy some groceries, then goes upstairs. He carefully unfolds his New York *Times*. He places it with mechanical precision on a pile of several other recent copies of the New York *Times*. There they will remain until, when two or three more copies have been added, he will take all but the one most recent and consign them to the trash that goes into a plastic bag that will be left for pickup by the truck that comes around during the night and, with a groaning roar, collects and crushes and compresses all the garbage of the occupants of this and other residential buildings of New York.

Then he returns upstairs. He opens the refrigerator, snaps the top 8
from a cold can of Miller's beer, and turns on the TV.

Next day, trimly dressed and cleanly shaven, he will buy another New 9
York *Times*, fold it neatly, and proceed to work. He is a rather solitary man. People in his office view him with respect as someone who is self-contained and does not choose to join in casual conversation. If somebody should mention something that is in the news, he will give a

dry, sardonic answer based upon the information he has garnered from TV.

He is protected against the outside world. Someday he will probably be trapped. It has happened before; so he can guess that it will happen again. Defended for now against humiliation, he is not defended against fear. He tells me that he has recurrent dreams.   10

"Somebody says: WHAT DOES THIS MEAN? I stare at the page. A thousand copies of the New York *Times* run past me on a giant screen. Even before I am awake, I start to scream."   11

If it is of any comfort to this man, he should know that he is not alone. Twenty-five million American adults cannot read the poison warnings on a can of pesticide, a letter from their child's teacher, or the front page of a daily paper. An additional 35 million read only at a level which is less than equal to the full survival needs of our society.   12

Together, these 60 million people represent more than one third of the entire adult population.   13

The largest numbers of illiterate adults are white, native-born Americans. In proportion to population, however, the figures are higher for blacks and Hispanics than for whites. Sixteen percent of white adults, 44 percent of blacks, and 56 percent of Hispanic citizens are functional or marginal illiterates. Figures for the younger generation of black adults are increasing. Forty-seven percent of all black seventeen-year-olds are functionally illiterate. That figure is expected to climb to 50 percent by 1990.   14

Fifteen percent of recent graduates of urban high schools read at less than sixth grade level. One million teenage children between twelve and seventeen cannot read above the third grade level. Eighty-five percent of juveniles who come before the courts are functionally illiterate. Half the heads of households classified below the poverty line by federal standards cannot read an eighth grade book. Over one third of mothers who receive support from welfare are functionally illiterate. Of 8 million unemployed adults, 4 to 6 million lack the skills to be retrained for hi-tech jobs.   15

The United States ranks forty-ninth among 158 member nations of the U.N. in its literacy levels.   16

In Prince George's County, Maryland, 30,000 adults cannot read above a fourth grade level. The largest literacy program in this county reaches one hundred people yearly.   17

In Boston, Massachusetts, 40 percent of the adult population is illiterate. The largest organization that provides funds to the literacy programs of the city reaches 700 to 1,000 people.   18

In San Antonio, Texas, 152,000 adults have been documented as illiterate. In a single municipal district of San Antonio, over half the adult population is illiterate in English. Sixty percent of the same population   19 sample is illiterate in Spanish. Three percent of adults in this district are at present being served.

In the State of Utah, which ranks number one in the United States 20 in the percent of total budget allocated to the education sector, 200,000 adults lack the basic skills for employment. Less than 5 percent of Utah's population is black or Hispanic.

Together, all federal, state, municipal, and private literacy programs 21 in the nation reach a maximum of 4 percent of the illiterate population. The federal government spends $ 100 million yearly to address the needs of 60 million people. The President has asked that this sum be reduced to $50 million. Even at the present level, direct federal allocations represent about $1.65 per year for each illiterate.

In 1982 the Executive Director of the National Advisory Council 22 on Adult Education estimated that the government would need to spend about $5 billion to eradicate or seriously reduce the problem. The commission he served was subsequently dismissed by presidential order.

Fourteen years ago, in his inaugural address as governor of Georgia, 23 a future President of the United States proclaimed his dedication to the crisis of Illiterate America. "Our people are our most precious possession. . . . Every adult illiterate . . . is an indictment of us all. . . . If Switzerland and Israel and other people can end illiteracy, then so can we. The responsibility is our own and our government's. I will not shirk this responsibility."

Today the number of identified nonreaders is three times greater 24 than the number Jimmy Carter had in mind when he described this challenge and defined it as an obligation that he would not shirk.

On April 26, 1983, pointing to the literacy crisis and to a collapse in 25 standards at the secondary and the college levels, the National Commission on Excellence in Education warned: "Our Nation is at risk."

Questions: The Community of Writers

1. Discuss what Kozol does to interest you in illiteracy. Does he make you want to do something about illiteracy? Does he convince you that illiteracy is a serious situation?

2. What reason might Kozol have for writing a book about illiteracy and for writing a chapter packed with as many details as this one?

3. What are the implications of the statement that "one million teenage children between twelve and seventeen cannot read above the third grade level" (paragraph 15)?

4. What does it mean to taxpayers that the cost of eradicating illiteracy in this nation could be billions of dollars? Considering the cost and the unlikelihood of those billions being allocated, how might the situation be relieved by other means?

5. Kozol's book was published in 1985. Do you think the problem has improved since then or worsened?

6. Discuss the methods of development that Kozol uses in this essay.

7. In your own words, write Kozol's thesis and compare your sentence with those of your groupmates.

Analysis

Illiteracy is a serious situation. The facts that Kozol presents are disturbing: One-third of adult Americans do not have survival literacy skills, one million teenagers read below the fourth-grade level, the number of illiterate people in the United States tripled from 1971 to 1985. Perhaps because readers' interests vary, Kozol has filled this first chapter of his book with facts to make certain he touches every one of its readers. Even before he gets to recounting the facts, he attracts reader interest with his short narrative of a day in the life of an unnamed illiterate graphic artist, a man who looks like any other New York office worker and commuter but lives in daily fear that someone will ask him about the words in the newspaper he carries.

Do you know someone who can't read? Try to imagine what it's like to be illiterate. How disabling would this inability be? What would you have to give up if you couldn't read? What would you not know? How would your life be changed? Inability to read can be a serious handicap. Still, if you are like many people, you will admit that you don't do much reading other than what you have to do.

How much *do* you read—beyond your class assignments, that is? Do you read a daily newspaper, subscribe to and read magazines? How often do you read a novel or other book? Perhaps you have never thought that this type of nonreading might be a disability too. Would your life be changed in any way if you did more reading? The answers to these questions are outside the scope of Kozol's essay, yet their implications are nearly as great as those of the issues he addresses. Nonreading is a serious situation.

Implied Thesis

Kozol does not state his *thesis*. He begins with a *narrative,* then devotes the remainder of the essay to relating *facts*. Yet the narrative and all his facts point to the unstated ideas that the rate of illiteracy in the United States is excessive and that something must be done to reduce it. The closest he comes to stating a thesis is in his last paragraph, where as a final warning he quotes from the National Commission on Excellence in Education: "Our Nation is at risk." This statement might be read as *informative,* meaning "The rate of illiteracy in the United States is excessive," or as *persuasive,* meaning "As a nation, we must act to correct the alarming rate of illiteracy." An informative thesis stresses information, whereas a persuasive thesis tries to move an audience to new thoughts or actions.

Even though Kozol's essay is openly informative, implying that readers want to know these facts, he clearly has another purpose. Even though he doesn't ever say that readers ought to attack the alarming problem of illiteracy, he clearly implies throughout the essay that this is what he intends.

Exercise: The Exploring Writer

Freewrite (see Chapter 3) for ten minutes on one of these topics:

- *How your life would be different if you couldn't read and how you would feel about the disability*
- *A serious situation that demands public attention*

Writing

Write about a problem that you regard as serious. Bear in mind that your primary purpose is to inform your readers, even though, like Kozol, you may well have persuasion as a second purpose. Use facts and narrative to make your point; do not tell your audience what to think or what action to take. Your informative thesis sentence, like Kozol's, may be implied, or you may state it explicitly. If you have a persuasive thesis as well, imply it.

The volume of information you have to communicate on your topic may not be as great as Kozol's; however, if you choose a topic that interests you, the chances are good that you can tell your readers something that is new to them. Here are some ideas for topics, but what you choose to write about may not be included:

- An AIDS epidemic
- Television news "shows"
- Drunk driving
- Drug addiction
- Effects of daytime "soaps" on children

These are all broad topics, as is Kozol's, but like Kozol you can select facts that are likely to achieve your purpose of informing your audience.

INFORMING BASED ON COMMON EXPERIENCE

People have many experiences in common. Worldwide, people know the feel and taste of water. Throughout the ages, sunlight has felt the same as it does today, the moon has looked the same, people have known the same kind of anger, love, and hate that we today know. Because we're human, we have common experiences. Yet how much do we actually know about those experiences—about water and the sun and the moon, even about our own emotions? We could probably learn something about all of them.

While much informative writing is intended to tell readers something outside their experience—something they don't know—a great deal of information tells readers something new about a subject they are already familiar with. You know the stars, for example; they're a familiar part of your world. Yet an essay on their components, relative ages, and so on would likely tell you something new. Pizza may be one of your favorite foods, but do you know its origins? Again, familiar subject, new information.

Sometimes, to write about new information on familiar subjects some special reading is necessary. For instance, if you were interested in writing about the history of pizza, you would probably have to do a little research. But there are many subjects that each of us knows a little better than most other people do. Those are subjects of informing based on common experience. You might know the characteristics of a good surfboard or good skis. You might know what baseball cards are most prized by collectors. You might know the components of good clean water for drinking, swimming, and other purposes. You might know the various kinds of hair that grow on people's heads. You might even know the history of pizza.

This section has two readings that explore things most people have in common. The first is on the physical senses and the second on the burning of firewood.

Reading

Unless one or another of your physical senses is impaired, you probably give little thought to the fact that you can see, hear, touch, taste, and smell. You're accustomed to seeing trees and grass turn green in the spring, water sparkle in the sunshine, traffic signals change from red to green. Neither is it remarkable that you hear the airplane flying over your head, the rush-hour traffic passing while you stand at the corner, the grackles settling into the trees for the night. You take your senses for granted.

In the essay that follows, George R. Harrison, a distinguished physicist specializing in optics, looks at our physical senses. Harrison concentrates mainly on vision to make his point about all the senses and to instill in his readers a fresh admiration for the capabilities of our ordinary physical senses. As you read the essay and encounter what may be new information about a familiar subject, notice the words and phrases that might be intended to persuade you to admire what your senses can do.

Senses

George R. Harrison

Now, what is a man? His body, "in form and moving" so "express and admirable," is made of protons, neutrons, and electrons; and he thinks with a brain composed of these and operating with the three fundamental forces of the physical world. To say this is not materialism, for if "God works in most mysterious ways His wonders to perform," not the least of His works, as we can see, involve protons, neutrons, and electrons. The study of their combinations helps us to understand our five senses, five paths of awareness to the brain, five "windows of the soul," by which we have our only contact with the external world.

Calling our senses five is an oversimplification, for we have more than five senses; we have at least three types of touch sensation: heat, pressure, and pain; and four types of taste, so that every flavor is a combination of sweet, salty, sour, and bitter. (The child who doesn't mind cod-liver oil and hates spinach is not being ornery; his taste buds merely respond differently from those of his mother.) We also have four types of vision, which all happen to involve the same pairs of eyes. The first type, night-vision, records no color, but paints its images in black and white on the retina; it operates best in faint light and is nearly 500 times as sensitive as the other three types of vision. These combine to give us more than 100,000 different sensations of color.

So sensitive are our retinas to green light—that is, to light whose waves are about one 50 thousandth of an inch long—that they can pick up as little as one 500 thousandth of a millionth of a millionth of a watt of power, and we can see a candle many miles away.

How was this sensitive detecting device developed, which is more elegant than any television camera? It contains a sharply focusing lens, surrounded by light-sensitive molecules which adjust it automatically to give the clearest image; self-regulating diaphragm, the pupil, and a shutter, the eyelid; and uses two projectors with which it introduced 3-D into vision some millions of years before the movies got around to this in 1953.

The marvelous twin cameras which send sensations to our brain from every object illuminated by even a millionth of the brightness of full sunlight sort out light rays so carefully that we get the fullest impact of reality through seeing. If necessary we can in addition verify the existence of an object by touching it, hearing it, smelling it, or tasting it. Beyond this, nature does not take us in contacting physical reality. And she has developed many forms of energy, such as cosmic rays and magnetic fields, which we cannot sense at all, yet which are no less real than those we sense directly.

So our senses are by no means perfect, and after exclaiming about the wonders of the eye, we must now examine its limitations. First, it is blind to more wave lengths of light than it can see. While insects can see somewhat with short-wave ultra-violet rays, humans cannot. (These insects, incidentally, have eyes consisting of multiple cones especially fixed for judging the direction of the sun for navigational purposes, and sometimes have polarizing filters to help steer by scattered light when the sky is overcast.) Also the sharpness of our vision is limited, and our lenses tend to deform and become cloudy. But now that nature has developed in man the brain needed to think scientifically, he can use this to extend his senses much beyond what nature has done.   6

Scientists have learned to supplement the sense of sight in numerous ways. In the front of the tiny pupil of the eye they put, on Mount Palomar, a great monocle 200 inches in diameter, and with it see 2000 times farther into the depths of space. Or they look through a small pair of lenses arranged as a microscope into a drop of water or blood, and magnify by as much as 2000 diameters the living creatures there, many of which are among man's most dangerous enemies. Or, if we want to see distant happenings on earth, they use some of the previously wasted electromagnetic waves to carry television images which they re-create as light by whipping tiny crystals on a screen with electrons in a vacuum. Or they can bring happenings of long ago and far away as colored motion pictures, by arranging silver atoms and color-absorbing molecules to force light waves into the patterns of the original reality. Or if we want to see into the center of a steel casting or the chest of an injured child, they send the information on a beam of penetrating short-wave X rays, and then convert it back into images we can see on a screen or photograph. Thus almost every type of electromagnetic radiation yet discovered has been used to extend our sense of sight in some way.   7

The evolution of the other senses is as interesting as that of vision, which nature has developed to nearly the maximum sensitivity permitted by the structure of light itself. Our ability to hear the commonest sound waves has reached its maximum possible sensitivity also. Some persons even are bothered by noises which arise from the random motions of molecules in the nerve endings of their ears. The threshold of sound awareness is said to be about the same in a human being, a catfish, or a bird, and the long-vaunted greater sensitivity of hearings of dogs and other animals probably arises from their ability to hear higher tones than we, and because they have less to distract them.   8

In many directions of evolution nature is stopped by limitations in   9
her own materials. There are some things that just take too long to work
out with protons and electrons by repeated trial and error, as, for example, to develop a wheel on a living creature. But often man can get
around such blocks by taking thought. We fasten wheels to ourselves with
automobiles, and our sense of hearing has been extended on radio waves
so that we can hear the sound of a dropped pin around the world.

Thus, though we sense directly only a few of the energy manifesta-   10
tions in the external world, science has taught us how to transform many
others so as not only to bring them into our ken, but to bend them to our
service. And science reveals man's physical body as a fascinating assemblage of the same protons, electrons, and neutrons that constitute a
stone, functioning in an even more remarkable cooperative effort. But
not yet is this the whole of Man.

Questions: The Community of Writers

1. Discuss new information about vision that you encountered in Harrison's
   essay.
2. Among the many facts that Harrison presents, what would you most like to
   remember?
3. What words and phrases express Harrison's admiration for the physical
   senses?
4. Of Harrison's several methods of development, which made his subject most
   interesting to each of you?
5. Locate several key words in "Senses" and discuss how their repetition links
   parts of the essay.

Analysis

Harrison clearly can speak with authority on optics. Writing on a
subject with which he has had much experience, he informs readers
about aspects of it they had not previously considered. He has this subject
in common with his readers; however, he is more informed about it than
we are.

Thesis

Harrison states a preliminary *thesis* in his first paragraph: that science
can help people understand their five senses. Then, after eight paragraphs using science to explain the senses, in particular vision, he concludes by stating his thesis more fully: Science not only helps us to
understand the senses but allows us to transform our perceptions for our
benefit.

Consider Harrison's attitude toward vision and the other physical senses. Beginning in his introduction, he uses words and phrases that express his admiration. Amid references to the Bible, he states that science can uncover some of the mysterious ways of God. He sees the five senses as "windows of the soul," through which an individual perceives the external world. Knowledge depends on them. Elsewhere in the essay, Harrison uses words like *marvelous* (paragraph 5) to refer to the eyes.

Development (analogy, comparison, exemplification)

Harrison develops his essay by several methods. In paragraphs 4 and 5 he uses the **analogy** of a camera, employing photographic terms to describe the parts of the eye. Writers often use analogy for describing something unfamiliar or difficult by means of something more familiar. Perceptions of the senses are particularly hard to describe. Analogy says, "Subject A (the function of parts of the eye) is like Subject B (the function of parts of a camera)," when Subject A is unknown and Subject B is known. If you want to tell someone what something smells like, you might say, "The flower smells like root beer." Analogous things are alike in enough ways to be useful in explaining, but they are never alike in all ways. Eyes and cameras, for example, have obvious differences, as do flowers and root beer.

In developing his essay, Harrison also uses a type of **comparison.** After extolling what he calls the "wonders of the eye," in paragraphs 6 and 7 he examines the eye's shortcomings: its blindness to certain wavelengths and its limited sharpness. Comparisons of this type look at pros and cons, pluses and minuses, advantages and disadvantages. Harrison devotes little space to the limitations of natural vision, using them instead as a transition to his next point, which examines what scientists have done to overcome these limits.

He develops the next paragraph, the seventh, by **exemplification,** suggesting several ways by which scientists extend the sense of sight. The paragraph begins with a topic sentence—"Scientists have learned to supplement the sense of sight in numerous ways"—indicating its direction, and it concludes with a reiteration of the topic—"Thus almost every type of electromagnetic radiation yet discovered has been used to extend our sense of sight in some way."

In paragraph 8 Harrison broadens his subject from vision to all the senses; then in paragraph 9 he again brings up limitations, this time regarding nature. He cites the example that nature has not been able to put wheels on living creatures but adds that nature has enabled the human brain to get around that limitation. In the final paragraph of this passage, Harrison summarizes his position on the physical senses before getting on to his next subject, the mind.

Coherence

New information builds on old information. This principle accounts for how you learn and remember. When you hear or read something new, you relate it to what you already know—comparing it, classifying it, chunking it in your memory with something similar. When Harrison tells you about the eye's sensitivity to green light, you probably try to remember any experiences you might have had seeing green light at a distance. Then you may consider the implications of this characteristic of vision. You put it away in your mind with something that is already there.

You can take advantage of this feature of learning by using it to make your sentences *coherent*. When you write a sentence, put the *old information,* a reference to what you've already said, at the beginning; then set down the *new information*. As an example of how this principle works, examine the sentences of the preceding paragraph. The first words of the first sentence, "New information," refer to an earlier discussion, and the remainder of the sentence, "builds on old information," makes a new assertion. The beginning of the second sentence, "This principle," encapsulates the first sentence, and the remainder makes a new assertion. Then the first part of the third sentence more or less rephrases what has already been stated and expands on it with new information. The final two sentences carry on with the new information begun in the third sentence. This paragraph illustrates one way to relate sentences to one another— through the "old information" connection. As you have seen, though, not all sentences work this way; they would be tiresome if they did.

Another method of gaining coherence is the use of *key words*. Notice how Harrison indicates relationships. Paragraph 2 begins, "Calling our senses five is an oversimplification," relating directly to his thesis reference to "our five senses," stated in paragraph 1. Paragraph 3 relates to paragraph 2 by repeated reference to retinas, a word introduced in paragraph 2. Harrison achieves overall coherence with every mention of the senses, because by so doing he connects new information to the key thesis word *senses*. Finally, his conclusion amplifies the simpler thesis stated in the introduction, completing the discussion of the senses and leading into the next section of the longer essay from which this portion was excerpted.

When you study how other writers achieve coherence, remember that you are examining *finished* essays, final drafts that, as a result of revision, are logically organized, adequately developed, clearly stated, and smoothly coherent. Harrison's essay, like those you write, was once a rough draft. Rough drafts usually are *not* logically organized, adequately developed, clearly stated, and smoothly coherent. When writers begin writing, they don't always know precisely where they are going, so all the parts of their essays or other writings don't relate to one another. In fact, writers often have to add parts and discard others before they're finished.

The coherence of a final draft is achieved with repeated revision and editing. In your composing and revising, you likely find the same to be true: Your rough drafts are *rough*. But one task to accomplish in revision is to make your connections clear, to show how sentences and paragraphs relate to one another, in other words, to make your writing coherent.

Exercise: The Community of Writers

1. *Begin with the key word* senses *and examine Harrison's essay for all repetitions of it in this and related forms (for example,* sensations*), including pronouns referring to it. How does repetition of this single word connect parts of the essay?*
2. *Practice using* analogy *for description. Choose one of the topics listed at the end of this exercise and, with your groupmates, write a short analogy using Harrison's fourth paragraph as a guide. To write an analogy, you need to use the terminology of the second, the known, subject to describe the first, the subject you want to clarify. The second subject is something familiar to most people; the first is something that is difficult to describe. Harrison, for example, describes the eye (first subject) as having parts like a camera (second subject): an automatically adjusting lens, a self-regulating diaphragm, a shutter, and two 3-D projectors.*

   If you want, think of your own group topic, something difficult to explain that you can describe in terms of something most people know. Or choose one of these:

   * *Hope is like . . .*
   * *A computer disk is like a . . .*
   * *Reading is like . . .*
   * *Sunlight is like . . .*
   * *Sight (hearing, taste, smell, touch) is like . . .*

Reading

We've all seen fires. We admire the flames even while we are fearful of their consequences. But do we really know what a fire is? Have you ever thought about what makes the flames? Or where the flames come from? What happens when something burns? In the paragraph that follows, an excerpt from a longer piece by the same name, John McPhee describes firewood burning in a fireplace: not how to make a fire but what happens to a log when it burns. Read it as an example of a familiar kind of writing, one that informs readers for greater understanding of common experiences.

Firewood

John McPhee

Science was once certain that firewood was full of something called 1
phlogiston, a mysterious inhabitant that emerged after kindling and
danced around in the form of light and heat and crackling sound—phlogiston, the substance of fire. Science, toward the end of the eighteenth
century, erased that beautiful theory, replacing it with certain still current
beliefs, which are related to the evident fact that green wood is half water.
Seasoning, it dries down until, typically, the water content is twenty per
cent. Most hardwoods—oak, maple, cherry, hickory—will season in six
months. Ash, the firewood of kings, will season in half the time. When
firewood burns, it makes vapor of the water. The rest of the log is (almost
wholly) carbon, hydrogen, and oxygen—the three components of cellulose, also of starch and sugar. When a log is thrown on the fire, the
molecules on the surface become agitated and begin to move vigorously.
Some vibrate. Some rotate. Some travel swiftly from one place to another.
The cellulose molecule is long, complicated, convoluted—thousands of
atoms like many balls on a few long strings. The strings have a breaking
point. The molecule, tumbling, whipping, vibrating, breaks apart. Hydrogen atoms, stripping away, snap onto oxygen atoms that are passing by in
the uprushing stream of air, forming even more water, which goes up the
chimney as vapor. Incandescent carbon particles, by the tens of millions,
leap free of the log and wave like banners, as flame. Several hundred
significantly different chemical reactions are now going on. For example,
a carbon atom and four hydrogen atoms, coming out of the breaking
cellulose, may lock together and form methane, natural gas. The methane, burning (combining with oxygen), turns into carbon dioxide and
water, which also go up the flue. If two carbon atoms happen to come out
of the wood with six hydrogen atoms, they are, agglomerately, ethane,
which burns to become, also, carbon dioxide and water. Three carbons
and eight hydrogens form propane, and propane is there, too, in the fire.
Four carbons and ten hydrogens—butane. Five carbons . . . pentane. Six
. . . hexane. Seven . . . heptane. Eight carbons and eighteen hydrogens—
octane. All these compounds come away in the breaking of the cellulose
molecule, and burn, and go up the chimney as carbon dioxide and water.
Pentane, hexane, heptane, and octane have a collective name. Logs
burning in a fireplace are making and burning gasoline.

Questions: The Community of Writers

1. In what ways has "Firewood" added to your understanding of fire?
2. What old information does McPhee build on?

3. What does McPhee say happens when a log burns? What makes the flames? What goes up the chimney?

4. In what ways is the modern understanding of what happens when a fire burns different from the old one? In what ways are the two understandings similar?

5. Discuss how McPhee's emphasis would change if his last sentence, "Logs burning in a fireplace are making and burning gasoline," were instead at the start of his paragraph, following his opening statement that science has erased the phlogiston theory with a new one.

6. Discuss whether McPhee, in addition to his purpose of informing, has a secondary purpose similar to Harrison's—to evoke admiration and a new understanding of his subject matter. Cite details from the paragraph.

Analysis

Like Harrison's "Senses," "Firewood" relates scientific discoveries about a familiar subject. Science can tell us what the substance of fire is. Take a closer look at "Firewood." McPhee first brings up an old term, *phlogiston,* then concludes with a new one, *gasoline,* for collectively describing the compounds that emerge in flames. Some people might say that the two terms are actually referring to the same thing and that science hasn't progressed much over the centuries. Others would argue that the term *gasoline* encompasses a much greater understanding of the substance of fire.

Development (chronological)

McPhee's method of developing his paragraph is **chronological,** to describe what happens when fire burns. After introductory facts about the characteristics of firewood, he begins the process: "When a log is thrown on the fire." Note the steps: agitation of molecules, breakup of molecules, formation of new molecules. At this point, McPhee says, "Several hundred significantly different chemical reactions are now going on"; the remainder of the paragraph describes some of these reactions.

The paragraph now moves from the **less emphatic** to the **more emphatic.** Note how McPhee begins with the production of methane out of one carbon atom and four hydrogen atoms, then gradually increases the numbers of carbon and hydrogen atoms as he names the compounds they produce. At the end it seems that he tries to surprise his readers a little with his identification of the burning compounds—pentane, hexane, heptane, and octane—as gasoline.

Secondary Purpose

The next time you watch a log burning in a fireplace, or some other kind of fire, give a little thought to the chemistry of burning, to the water vapor escaping up the chimney, and to the fact that that log is making and burning complex chemicals. Then ask yourself if McPhee might have a secondary purpose similar to Harrison's: to inspire admiration for the wonders of nature.

Exercise: The Exploring Writer

Writers influence audience response not only by their choice of words but by their sentence style as well. In the following series, McPhee uses two sentences only two words long to convey part of the intensity and the variety of molecular actions:

When a log is thrown on a fire, the molecules on the surface become agitated and begin to move vigorously. Some vibrate. Some rotate. Some travel swiftly from one place to another.

The two sentences "Some vibrate" and "Some rotate" may look like sentence fragments since they are so short, but because each has a subject, "Some," and a verb, they are truly sentences. Read the whole series of four sentences again, think about them, and then write four sentences of your own that follow this pattern. Write about something that also has a variety of actions, for example, a fish tugging on a line, people waiting in lines, or drivers stopped for a traffic signal. After these four sentences, write a few more to extend your description.

Writing

Write an essay about something that most people have in common but that you may be able to explain better than most. There are probably many familiar aspects of everyday life about which you can say something that not everyone knows. Your purpose, in addition to informing, could be to instill in your audience an appreciation for your subject. Here are some ideas for you to use as starters:

- Fast-food hamburgers—what's behind the wrapper
- Fingernails—what they are, how they grow, and so on
- Water—its components, its sources, and so on
- Ears—their parts, how they hear

After selecting a topic, explore it with one of the prewriting strategies discussed in Chapter 3—perhaps clustering. As your ideas begin to take direction, strike out those that no longer fit. Eventually you should be able to step back and ask yourself what idea holds all your thoughts on the subject together. At this point you may want to rearrange some of your connecting lines. State your central idea as a sentence, and you have a working thesis. Then you can arrange your ideas into what seems to be a workable order.

If you have trouble getting started, look again at how Harrison and McPhee begin. Both authors generate audience interest by first referring to something related to their subject, Harrison somewhat philosophically with his biblical references, McPhee bringing up the old word for fire. Harrison clearly states his subject and thesis in his introductory paragraph and again at the end, while McPhee ties his paragraph together at the end by naming the modern word for the substance of fire.

As you write, assume that your audience is familiar with your subject (just as they know what the senses and fire are) but will be interested in the new information you are sharing. In revision, give special attention to coherence, connecting related sentences and paragraphs with repetition of key words and application of the old information/new information principle.

INFORMING WITH A PERSUASIVE PURPOSE

How often do you read articles that have an ostensible purpose of informing but in fact, by means of absorbing you in the information, are meant to persuade you? This is a common type of discourse. Most advertisements and commercials, for example, *look* as if they are informing you—about the best sunscreen or the tastiest yogurt or the latest in blue jeans fashions—but in fact their purpose is to persuade you to buy the product. Commentaries and editorials in newspapers appear to reveal the latest facts about the most current issues—and indeed they do—but the commentators are also trying to convince you to agree with their opinions. For example, when you read an informative column about religious and satanic cults, the writer may be trying to persuade you to avoid organizations of this type. Editorials that inform you about dangers to the environment have a persuasive purpose also—to convince you to get involved in conservation.

Sometimes informing with an underlying persuasive purpose is deceptive, as in this paragraph from a sales letter:

Whether you're contemplating the purchase of additional life insurance now or at some future date, I have some interesting ideas to share with you that will be useful in your planning. In exchange for the opportunity to share these ideas, I will make and keep the following promises as a condition of our visit: (1) I will make no attempt to sell you anything in this visit, and (2) unless you specifically request it, no return call will be made. That's fair, isn't it, Mr. Brown?

The writer of this letter is surely not offering, only out of the goodness of his heart, to help Mr. Brown in his insurance planning. Such deception undercuts the writer's credibility and puts the reader on the defensive. If you were its recipient, you would likely file this letter in the wastebasket.

Usually, however, there is no deception in having dual purposes. Both writer and reader understand that the intention is to persuade with facts. Deception occurs when the writer pretends to be only conveying information, as in the example paragraph, and when the reader does not read actively enough to realize the writer's intention. (Persuasion as a primary purpose for writing is discussed in Chapter 7.)

Facts (Forms of Evidence)

Informative essays consist largely of facts, or evidence that can support statements of opinion. (See also the discussion in Chapter 7.) Facts are information that can be verified, such as examples, testimony, statistics, and historical evidence.

An *example* is a specific, concrete instance of the general principle or issue. It does not restate the issue; it illustrates it. In the following paragraph from an essay advising an informed use of euphemisms, the student writer's first sentence makes an assertion, and the remaining sentences illustrate it by examples:

> Workers view their jobs as being more respectable when certain euphemisms are used. "Sanitation men" collect the garbage, "animal welfare officers" catch stray dogs, and those who seek "counsel" need a lawyer. An "administrative aide" would probably type the boss's letters, while a "domestic engineer" would plan and prepare the family's evening meal.

A reader could corroborate these examples by listening to language use and by questioning other people about what the terms mean to them.

Testimony is a statement about the issue by an expert, either paraphrased or quoted. Television commercials have rugged-looking men selling auto mufflers, well-groomed women using laundry products, groovy kids eating lunchbox-sized packages of pudding and applesauce. And though we may disagree with such stereotyping, the advertisers' research shows that such testimony sells products. Writers often use testimony to bolster their credibility by reporting what people more knowledgeable than they have said on the subject. Testimony may come from interviews, letters, conversations, reading, and a variety of other sources. The authority of the expert is often cited; for example, the phrase "George R. Harrison, a distinguished physicist specializing in optics" tells you in what way the writer is qualified to write on the subject. The source of the information is usually named also, for example:

In *A Brief History of Time* (Toronto: Bantam, 1988), noted British physicist Stephen W. Hawking maintains that scientists have not yet answered the essential question, "How or why were the laws and the initial state of the universe chosen?" (173).

In addition to identifying the author and title of the source, the writer gives publishing information and the page number from which this information was drawn. (For more examples of source citation see Chapter 16.)

Statistics are numbers compiled competently and applied appropriately to the issue. Readers often expect statistics to be a part of the information conveyed in a piece of writing. Here is an example of how a student writer uses statistics in an essay urging people to wear seat belts:

Over 22,576 people die in car accidents each year. According to the National Highway Traffic Administration, 9,900 of those lives could have been saved if the occupants of the vehicles had been wearing seat belts.

Jonathan Kozol's essay on illiteracy in America shows how a writer uses statistics to inform and persuade (page 309).

Historical evidence is verifiable information concerning actual occurrences. It may come from our experience, observations, or reading. Like statistics, testimony, and examples, historical evidence must be true. Unlike fiction, where writers can invent, elaborate, and exaggerate details, informative writing is based on an implied contract between writer and reader ensuring the truth of the facts it reports. Violations of this contract destroy a writer's credibility. Writers therefore try to be sure of the truth of their information, while readers question any facts that appear to be inaccurate.

Facts—whether in the form of examples, testimony, statistics, or historical evidence—are persuasive in addition to their primary purpose of informing. Essays with a main purpose of persuading often use facts to support opinions; essays with an informative purpose use them less to back up opinions than to lead readers to form their own opinions.

Reading

The following short article from *Audubon* magazine informs readers about the effects of people releasing balloons to celebrate special events. It presents facts throughout and does not express the opinions of the writer or a position of the magazine. However, as you read, look for an underlying persuasive purpose.

Halftime Balloons a Pretty Problem

from *Audubon* magazine

Thousands of balloons released at sporting events may be a deceptive   1
threat to wildlife. The problem is hard to measure, says Peter Hibbard of the
Balloon Alert Project, an organization he runs with his wife, Susan, out of
their Toms River, New Jersey, home. A schoolteacher and part-time naturalist at Island Beach State Park, Hibbard says a sperm whale that washed
ashore three years ago died because a balloon it ate clogged its digestive
tract. Balloons also have been implicated in the deaths of both leather-
back and hawksbill sea turtles, which apparently mistake them for food.

Some measure of the amount of plastic waste added to the environ-   2
ment by balloon releases can be inferred from the numbers of balloons
launched: 20,000 at halftime festivities at Hawaii's Hula Bowl, a quarter-
million by the U.S. Bicentennial Committee on the nation's 200th birthday, 1.1 million by Disneyland, and 1.5 million by the city of Cleveland.

Released balloons travel fast and far, says Hibbard. He found a bal-   3
loon on the New Jersey shore that had traveled 150 miles in only three
and a half hours after escaping a realty company in Fairfax, Virginia.
What Hibbard finds particularly disturbing is that the releases are a form
of deliberate pollution that suggests to children that "it is okay to pol-
lute." The Balloon Action Project, he says, is supporting a bill in the New
Jersey Legislature that would ban promotional releases.

Questions: The Community of Writers

1. Point to facts in "Halftime Balloons" that are *example, testimony, statistic,* and
   historical evidence.
2. Discuss whether the facts are adequate. How could you verify them?
3. What does the writer of the article tell you about Peter Hibbard's authority to
   testify on the subject?
4. Compare the facts in paragraph 1 with those in paragraph 2. Which paragraph provides stronger evidence?
5. What do these facts tell you about balloon releases?
6. Given these facts, discuss what *Audubon* wants to persuade its readers to do.

Analysis

"Halftime Balloons" is not openly persuasive. The first sentence expresses an *informative* thesis: "Thousands of balloons released at sporting
events may be a deceptive threat to wildlife." Below the surface, however,
you may have detected another, a *persuasive,* thesis, something like "Balloons should not be released to promote special events." Or, stated more
forcefully, "Try to get promotional releases of balloons banned in

your state." The informative thesis is expressed; the persuasive thesis is implied.

Examine how the facts of the article support the contention about the dangers of balloon releases. There seems little doubt that the wildlife died as a result of balloon ingestion, as paragraph 1 states; autopsy could establish this as fact. There is also little disputing the numbers of balloons lofted, detailed in paragraph 2; verification could be achieved in a number of ways. The argument weakens, however, in establishing that the facts in paragraph 1 are caused by the facts in paragraph 2. That is, to the question of why the wildlife died after swallowing balloons, the answer is that large numbers of balloons were released at sporting and other events. Releases like these may well be the actual cause of the deaths, but skeptical readers would question the strength of the inferential link between both sets of facts.

The facts in "Halftime Balloons" are probably all true—verifiable, that is. But the causal link between them is weak. To show that balloon releases at sporting events are responsible for the deaths of wildlife, the article could connect the two incidents—perhaps with an additional fact, such as that the balloons removed from the digestive tracts of the dead animals were imprinted "Hula Bowl" or "U.S. Bicentennial" or something else that identified the lethal balloons with a particular large balloon release.

Development (cause and effect)

This article deals with **causes and effects.** It names a single cause—the releasing of large numbers of balloons—and several effects. Cause and effect is a common method of developing ideas, because it seems that people like to ask *Why:* Why did the Chernobyl nuclear reactor melt down? Why did my holiday photographs turn out so dark? Why is my car making that odd noise? Why did the sperm whale die, and why was it able to ingest a balloon? Or people want to know what the effects of an action will be: How will this tuition increase affect me? How will the new recycling law change my life-style? How would the proposed New Jersey bill on balloon releases affect unnecessary deaths of wildlife?

This article asks why the sperm whale and other wildlife died with balloons in their digestive tracts. The first sentence states the answer: "Thousands of balloons released at sporting events may be a deceptive threat to wildlife." This sentence implies cause and serves as the thesis for the article. The remainder of the first paragraph alleges effects of that cause, giving examples of wildlife deaths because of balloon ingestion, and the second paragraph again alleges causes by citing large balloon launchings. The final paragraph deals with causes and suggests a legal solution to the problem.

Exercise: The Exploring Writer

Rewrite "Halftime Balloons" for an audience other than Audubon *readers—perhaps readers of* Sports Illustrated, Money, *or your campus newspaper. Your facts may remain the same, but with a different audience you will probably use them differently to support a different underlying persuasive thesis.*

Exercise: The Community of Writers

You have examined the facts in "Halftime Balloons" for their type and verifiability. Now, with your groupmates, examine the facts in Jonathan Kozol's "A Third of the Nation Cannot Read These Words" on page 309, looking for examples, testimonies, statistics, and historical evidence and asking whether the facts seem verifiable to you.

Writing

Write a short essay that has the purpose of informing with a secondary purpose of persuading. Select a problem and ask Why? What is its cause? Then provide facts about both causes and effects. Make sure your connections are tight. If you like, begin with your informative thesis as "Halftime Balloons" does, and imply your persuasive thesis (whatever you want your audience to do). Here are a few problems to consider:

- Throwing away aluminum cans rather than recycling them
- Walking across grass rather than using sidewalks
- Arriving late for class (meetings, appointments, and so on)

INFORMING BY DEFINITION

Information sometimes comes in the form of definitions (see Chapter 5). You have seen this type of information in textbooks, magazines, newspapers—in any publication where informing is a purpose. You read about "good cholesterol" and "bad cholesterol," about illiteracy, about freedom versus responsibility, and so on.

Definitions identify. They tell what something is and how a writer is using a particular term. When you read about DNA, it's not enough to be told that the letters stand for deoxyribonucleic acid. You want to know what deoxyribonucleic acid is. Neither is it satisfactory to have only a dictionary definition telling you that deoxyribonucleic acid is some kind of "polymeric chromosomal constituent of living cell nuclei." In fact, by this time you might be more confused than ever. What you need is a description of DNA, an explanation of what it does, an example of how it works, a discussion of its variations and its effects, and so on. That might be an entire essay.

You frequently find definitions in textbooks. In a textbook on energy and society, for example, you would be likely to find definitions of kinetic energy, potential energy, nuclear energy, chemical energy, and so on. In a guide to the study of poetry, you would find definitions of imagery, figurative language, rhyme, meter, and other terms necessary to your understanding of the components of poems. As a reader of textbooks, you expect definitions of terms you don't know.

Writers often use definitions as only a portion of their books and essays, defining new terms or their specialized use of familiar terms. The textbook on energy does more than define terms, and the book on poetry is mainly a collection of poems. An essay on religious cults would define how the writer is using the term *cult* before discussing recruiting and indoctrination. An essay explaining how a friend died of hypothermia would first define *hypothermia*.

Reading

William Zinsser in his book *On Writing Well* defines *taste*—not the physical sense that detects sweet, salty, sour, and bitter, but an intuitive sense that enables people to do something right. Zinsser, after declaring that taste can't be defined, attempts to define it and to relate it specifically to writing. As you read, ask yourself: What is taste, as Zinsser defines it? At what point in his essay do you understand what he means by taste?

Taste

William Zinsser

What finally separates the good writer from the breezy writer is a   1
quality so intangible that nobody even knows what it is: taste. It can't be defined, but we know it when we see it. A woman with taste in clothes delights us with her ability to turn herself out every day in a combination that's not only stylish and surprising; it's also exactly right. Taste is the instinct to know what works and to avoid what doesn't.

In the arts, knowing what not to do is a major component of taste.   2
Two jazz pianists may be equally proficient at the keyboard. The one with

taste will put every note to useful work in telling his story; the one without taste will drench us in ripples and other unnecessary ornaments. A painter with taste will trust his eye to tell him what needs to be on his canvas and what doesn't; the one without taste will give us a landscape that's too pretty, or too cluttered, or too gaudy in its colors—anyway, too something.

I realize that I'm trying to pin down a matter that's highly subjective   3 and that has no firm rules. One man's beautiful painting is another man's kitsch. It's also true that taste changes with the decades— yesterday's charm is rejected today as junk, but tomorrow it will be back in vogue, certified once again as charming. So why do I even bring the problem up? Mainly to remind you that it exists. Taste is an invisible current that runs through all writing, and you should be aware of it.

Sometimes, in fact, it's not invisible. Every art form has a hard core   4 of verities that survive the fickleness of time. There must be something innately pleasing, for instance, in the proportions of the Parthenon; Western man continues to let the Greeks of two thousand years ago design his major public buildings. In music, the fugues of Bach have a timeless elegance that's rooted in the timeless laws of mathematics.

Does writing have any such guideposts for us? Not many—writing is   5 the expression of every person's individuality, and in general we can only say that we know what we like when it comes along. Still, as in the other arts, taste is partly a question of knowing what to omit. Clichés, for example. If a writer litters his prose with platitudes—if every idea is first and foremost and in the last analysis one that hits the nail on the head—we can safely infer that the writer lacks an instinct for what gives language its freshness. Faced with a choice between the novel and the banal, he goes unerringly for the banal.

Extend the point beyond clichés to include a writer's larger use of   6 words. Again, freshness is a critical factor. Taste chooses words that have originality, strength, and precision; non-taste veers into the breezy vernacular of the alumni magazine's class notes—a world where people in authority are the top brass or the powers-that-be. What exactly is wrong with "the top brass"? Nothing—and everything. Taste is knowing that it's better to call people in authority what they are: officials, or executives, or the president of the company. Non-taste reaches for the cute synonym.

But finally taste is a mixture of qualities that are beyond defining: an   7 ear, for instance, that can hear the difference between a sentence that limps and a sentence that lilts, or an intuition that knows when a casual phrase dropped into a formal sentence will not only feel right but will seem to be the inevitable choice. Does this mean that taste can't be learned? Yes and no. Perfect taste, like perfect pitch, is a gift from God. But a certain amount can be acquired. The trick is to study those who have it.

Questions: The Community of Writers

1. In your own words, define *taste* as Zinsser uses it and then compare your definition with your groupmates'.

2. If you wanted to produce writing that fits Zinsser's definition, how would you proceed?

3. With few guideposts (paragraph 5), how would you know if you had succeeded in producing tasteful writing?

4. How can you tell when something is strikingly new instead of overused and worn-out?

5. Discuss which of Zinsser's definitions of taste is clearest.

Analysis

Zinsser applies his definition of taste specifically to writing. Unfortunately, he asserts, there are very few guideposts to tasteful writing. And those guideposts depend on the writer's ability to tell the difference between the "novel" and the "banal," between a "sentence that lilts" and a "sentence that limps." It would seem that experienced writers have the advantage. Zinsser says further that perfect taste is "a gift from God."

However, all is not lost, for Zinsser adds, "a certain amount [of taste] can be acquired." You can acquire taste in writing from those who already have it, by studying how they write and learning from their style and usage. Like acquiring taste in clothes by observing how other people dress, in particular those you admire, you can acquire taste in writing by observing how writers you admire select and combine words and phrases. By "reading as a writer," as discussed in Chapter 1, you learn from those who already have acquired a certain taste in writing.

Development

Notice how Zinsser uses **exemplification** to develop his definition. In paragraph 1 he has an example of people with taste in clothing. In paragraph 2 he uses examples of taste in the arts—music and painting—and, in paragraph 4, examples of timeless taste. In each paragraph he makes a general statement and then illustrates it with examples. You'll find this pattern also in paragraphs 5 and 6. Paragraph 3 is a departure in which he focuses his discussion, and his concluding paragraph sums up his nebulous subject.

Exercise: The Exploring Writer

Practice Zinsser's style. Rewrite his second paragraph by substituting something else for "the arts." You might begin with this first sentence: "In baseball, knowing what not to do is a major component of taste." Or you might begin with "In dressing . . . " or with "In telling jokes . . . " or with some other topic. Follow Zinsser's sentence patterns throughout the paragraph, making changes where needed so the paragraph will fit your topic.

Writing

Define something not easily defined. Write a definition that comes out of your experience, one that you work out as you write. One effect of defining is that in telling someone else your understanding of a particular term, you clarify for yourself what that understanding is. By making tentative definitions in areas not yet fully explored, you may be constructing new knowledge. So, in carrying out this assignment, don't select a subject that is too easy for you. If you write on *perfection,* for example, you will probably develop your own understanding of what you think perfection is. Like Zinsser, you might want to admit to your reader that you are only experimenting with a definition.

Here are a few topics inspired by Zinsser's essay:

Taste	Armament
Perfection	Junk
Hope	Guidepost
Shoddy	Current
Typical	Gift
Novel (as an adjective meaning "new")	Kitsch

To assist in narrowing your topic and deciding what you can say, you may want to begin by brainstorming (see Chapter 3). Select an aspect of the topic that interests you the most, and continue brainstorming on the narrower topic, trying to think of examples that will illustrate it. Group the items on your list and formulate a tentative thesis. As you compose, you may find that exemplification is a particularly useful method of development, as it is in "Taste." Try developing your definition with examples rather than relying on your dictionary.

If in your writing you name a word as a word, instead of the thing it represents, underline (or italicize) the word. Here's an example: "The word *taste* is used in many ways other than to represent quality." But compare "Taste is the instinct to know what works and to avoid what doesn't." The first sentence refers to the word, the second to the thing the word represents, taste itself.

ADDITIONAL READING FOR DISCUSSION

Reading

This informative essay, published in January 1989, has a secondary purpose of persuasion. Notice how, like "Halftime Balloons a Pretty Problem," it has an underlying persuasive thesis and is developed by analyzing causes and effects.

~~Deadly Danger in a Spray Can~~

Michael D. Lemonick

When they were first synthesized in the late 1920s, chlorofluoro-   1
carbons (CFCs for short) seemed too good to be true. These remarkable chemicals, consisting of chlorine, fluorine, and carbon atoms, are non-toxic and inert, meaning they do not combine easily with other substances. Because they vaporize at low temperatures, CFCs are perfect as coolants in refrigerators and propellant gases for spray cans. Since CFCs are good insulators, they are standard ingredients in plastic-foam materials like Styrofoam. Best of all, the most commonly used CFCs are simple, and therefore cheap, to manufacture.

There is only one problem. When they escape into the atmosphere,   2
most CFCs are murder on the environment. Each CFC molecule is 20,000 times as efficient at trapping heat as is a molecule of CO_2. So CFCs increase the greenhouse effect far out of proportion to their concentration in the air.

A more immediate concern is that the chlorine released when CFC   3
molecules break up destroys ozone molecules. The ozone layer, located in the stratosphere, between 10 and 30 miles up, is vital to the well-being of plants and animals. Ozone molecules, which consist of three oxygen atoms, absorb most of the ultraviolet radiation that comes from the sun. And ultraviolet is extremely dangerous to life on earth.

The small amount that does get through to the earth's surface inflicts   4
plenty of damage: besides causing sunburn, the rays have been linked to cataracts and weakened immune systems in humans and other animals. Ultraviolet light carries enough energy to damage DNA and thus disrupt the workings of cells, which is why excessive exposure to sunlight is thought to be the primary cause of some skin cancers.

When scientists first warned in the 1970s that CFCs could attack   5
ozone, the United States responded by banning their use in spray cans. (Manufacturers switched to such environmentally benign substitutes as butane, the chemical burned in cigarette lighters.) But the rest of the

world continued to use CFC-based aerosol cans, and overall CFC production kept growing. The threat became far clearer in 1985, when researchers reported a "hole" in the ozone layer over Antarctica. Although the size of the hole varies with the seasons and weather patterns, at times Antarctic ozone has been depleted by as much as 50 percent in some spots. As a result of this disturbing development, twenty-four nations, including the United States and the Soviet Union, met in Montreal two summers ago and agreed to cut back on CFCs. The so-called Montreal Protocol is designed to achieve a 35 percent net reduction in worldwide CFC production by 1999.

That is not good enough, however. The same stability that makes 6 CFCs so safe in industrial use makes them extremely long-lived: some of the CFCs released today will still be in the atmosphere a century from now. Moreover, each atom of chlorine liberated from a CFC can break up as many as 100,000 molecules of ozone.

For that reason, governments should ensure the careful handling 7 and recycling of the CFCs now in use. Said Senator Albert Gore of Tennessee: "Much of what reaches the atmosphere is not coming from industrial sources. It's things like sloppy handling of hamburger containers." When plastic-foam burger holders are broken, the CFCs trapped inside escape. Discarded refrigerators release CFCs as well, and, noted Gore, a significant part of the U.S. contribution to CFC emissions comes from "draining automobile air conditioners and leaving the stuff in pans where it boils off." Such release of CFCs could be prevented if consumers and businesses were offered cash incentives to return broken-down air conditioners and refrigerators to auto and appliance dealers. Then the units could be sent back to the manufacturers so that the CFCs could be reused.

While recycling will help, the only sure way to save the ozone is a 8 complete ban on CFC manufacture, which should be phased out over the next five years. Fortunately, as the Montreal Protocol demonstrates, banning CFCs will be far simpler than reducing other dangerous gases. "The CFC producers are a small club of countries," said Brice Lalonde, France's Environment Secretary. But a ban could admittedly be economically disruptive to the entire world: the annual market for CFCs is some $2.2 billion. The Soviet Union, which is a heavy user of CFCs, will have a particularly tough time phasing out the chemicals. "I agree with the ban in principle," said Vladimir Sakharov, a member of the Soviet State Committee for Environmental Protection, "but in practice it will be extremely difficult. Our economy is not as flexible as others."

To make the transition easier, chemical companies are working hard 9 to find practical substitutes for CFCs. The most promising approach so far is to use CFC family members that are chemically altered to make them less dangerous to the environment. The chlorine-free substance HFC-134a, for example, is most likely to be used in refrigeration devices.

The major drawback to CFC substitutes is the high cost of making   10
them. It may be that until better manufacturing techniques are developed, consumers will have to pay more for affected products. The prospect is not a pleasant one, but it is a small price to pay for curbing the greenhouse effect and saving the life-preserving ozone layer.

Questions: The Community of Writers

1. What is the problem with chlorofluorocarbons (CFCs)?
2. What are the most common sources of CFCs?
3. What is the essay's informative thesis?
4. State the implied persuasive thesis of this essay.
5. What does Lemonick's selection of details tell you about his intended audience?
6. Name some of the implications, both direct and indirect, of people acting worldwide to significantly reduce CFCs.
7. Discuss the cause and effect development of this essay. Does the essay begin with cause or effect? What is the primary cause? The primary effect? What facts does Lemonick use to establish the link between cause and effect? Are these connections weak at any point?
8. What solutions to the problem does the author propose?

CHAPTER 12

Writing to Explain

Much of the writing we are asked to do in school or work involves explaining someone else's thinking. To do this well we must get inside that other person's idea.

—*Peter Elbow*

Explaining as a purpose for writing has aspects of both informing and instructing. **Explaining** tells *why* something is the way it is or *why* something works the way it does. Sometimes it analyzes *how* something works. If someone asks you how an accident happened, that person wants not just information about the accident but an explanation as well. *Information* gives answers to questions about *what,* instruction to questions about *how; explanation* gives answers to questions about *why* as well as *what* or *how.* Even when an explanation answers *what* or *how,* it implies *why.*

Television weather forecasts are an example of explanation. They tell you not only *what,* "it will rain tomorrow," but *why,* "a warm front is approaching and drawing moisture from the gulf." Elaborate maps and computer-enhanced satellite pictures assist the explanation. As another example, consider a magazine article that not only tells you about over-the-counter pain pills being a potential cause for damage in liver and kidneys but also explains why and how these effects occur. Or, a newsmagazine explains why employees' company loyalty is dying, and another tells why community activists take the drug war into their own hands. Explaining gives reasons, or causes.

Sometimes explanation takes the form of definition. Someone asks you, "What do you mean by *computer literate?*" and you explain what you mean when you use the term. Or an exam question asks you to define *metonymy,* so you explain its meaning as you understand it, giving some examples.

Like information, explanations are often an aspect of persuasive writing. A writer explaining the dangers of a combined dosage of aspirin and acetaminophen probably wants to persuade readers to be more aware of how they use over-the-counter pain pills. A writer explaining the latest oil spill urges greater government control, and one explaining the effects of cigarette smoking on health wants readers to quit smoking or not to start.

Explanations are a common part of schoolwork. First you learn, and then you explain. In quizzes and exams, explanation is often required as an accompaniment to *yes* or *no* answers: "Do you agree with the author? Explain your answer"; "Has the author convinced you of her position? Explain why or why not." Sometimes the exam question simply asks you to explain: "Explain the scientific method"; "Explain how the American ideal of self-help influenced the literature of the late nineteenth century." Sometimes in school the *student* asks for explanations. If an instructor's lecture or your textbook reading is unclear, you may ask for an explanation. Or you may ask the university administration for an explanation of a new policy, say on the repeating of courses.

An explanation presents the writer's understanding of the facts. Explanations therefore require information, or facts, *plus* a discussion of how or why the facts occurred. Explanations include a step of filtering the facts through the writer's mind that purely informative writing does not. Information states the facts as the writer perceives them, so it is influenced by the writer's mind. But explanation, in requiring the writer to account for the facts, requires not only the writer's perceptions and screening of the facts but even more the ability to analyze them and draw inferences from them.

For example, if you were writing an explanation of fatalities in automobile collisions, you would first collect information—possibly by finding statistics in almanacs, reading articles on causes of fatalities, and consulting with a traffic engineer on ways to prevent fatalities. While collecting your information, you would screen out some as irrelevant and, for various reasons, you might simply fail to notice other information that could have been useful to you. You would perceive on the basis of what interested you and what you expected to need in writing your explanation. After you had collected information on traffic fatalities, you would analyze it for causes and types of collisions, immediate causes of death in collisions, the process of impact, and so on, again according to your interests and needs. What inferences you would then draw from your information would be individual, as a result of your thinking processes.

Think of every member of your class starting out with the same statistics, articles, and so on, then each of you writing an explanation of the causes of traffic fatalities. You would each draw different inferences, and all your explanations would be unique. Explanations, then, demand careful, critical reading, with the reader asking pointed questions—such as these:

- Is the writer truly informed?
- Do the conclusions follow logically from the facts?
- Is the writer overlooking important information?
- What are some other possible conclusions?

Writers must be careful about the accuracy and relevance of the information they gather and the way they analyze that information and draw inferences from it.

Explanations utilize a variety of methods of development. Cause and effect analysis is common, as in explaining how pain pills affect the health of kidneys and liver or in discussing the reasons for the decline of employees' loyalty to their companies. Other methods are useful too. If you were explaining geothermal energy, you might use a combination of methods: *cause and effect analysis* to discuss the source of the heat energy; *exemplification* to show what geothermal energy is (geysers, volcanic eruptions, and hot springs); *classification* to explain the kinds of geothermal energy (hot water reservoirs, natural steam reservoirs, geopressured reservoirs, the normal geothermal gradient, hot dry rock, and molten magma); *comparison* with other types of energy; *process analysis* to show how geothermal energy has developed and how it is mined; and *analogy* to explain how geothermal energy is like energy from other sources.

If you were explaining hyperactivity in children, you might begin by *defining* what hyperactivity is as you perceive it, conjecturing *causes,* delineating *effects,* and providing *examples.* You might consider the effects and side effects of drug therapy, you might quote the opinions of medical experts, and you might refer to teachers' experiences with hyperactive children. Thus, in explaining hyperactivity, you tell *what* it is, *how* it affects children, and *why* it is an elusive problem.

The essays in this chapter illustrate the broad range of explanation. Almost anything can be the subject of explanation—how a writer intends to use a word, reasons for relinquishing custody of one's children, how one views one's friends. These essays also illustrate how broad-ranging the means of developing explanations can be—for example, cause and effect analysis, classification, narration of personal experience, exemplification, and definition (as explained also in Chapter 4).

EXPLAINING BY ANALOGY AND EXEMPLIFICATION

Probably from time immemorial people have been explaining what it is like to be human. Early Christians tried to explain what true love, or *agape,* was like. Hebrews explained original sin. Plato, in his "Allegory of the Cave," explained the difficulty of perceiving truth. Every now and then, someone comes up with a new explanation of intuition or cognition or pain—or desire, fear, anger, or any of the other emotions that human beings share. These characteristics have one thing in common: They are difficult to describe. If they were easy to explain, the explanations would now be common knowledge. Each time someone attempts to explain one of these human characteristics, he or she must analyze available data and then make an inferential leap, acquire an insight to say something new about a familiar yet enigmatic subject. Then, to make that insight clear to readers, the writer might use *analogy,* showing how the characteristic is like something already understood, or *exemplification,* giving specific instances of the characteristic as the writer views it. (See Chapter 4 for further discussions of methods for developing ideas.)

Reading

In the essay that follows, philosopher-physician-scientist Lewis Thomas attempts to explain the human ability to discern by intuition—sidelong glances that put two and two together without resort to calculation, that provide insights based on unconscious knowledge, that deal with ambiguity as no computer can. As you read, note how Thomas uses this idea to explain what human beings know and how they could use their knowledge to meet new challenges to understanding the earth.

The Corner of the Eye

Lewis Thomas

There are some things that human beings can see only out of the corner of the eye. The niftiest examples of this gift, familiar to all children, are small, faint stars. When you look straight at one such star, it vanishes; when you move your eyes to stare into the space nearby, it reappears. If you pick two faint stars, side by side, and focus on one of the pair, it disappears and now you can see the other in the corner of your eye, and you can move your eyes back and forth, turning off the star in the center of your retina and switching the other one on. There is a physiological explanation for the phenomenon: we have more rods, the cells we use for light perception, at the periphery of our retinas, more cones, for perceiving color, at the center. 1

Something like this happens in music. You cannot really hear certain sequences of notes in a Bach fugue unless at the same time there are other notes being sounded, dominating the field. The real meaning in music comes from tones only audible in the corner of the mind. 2

I used to worry that computers would become so powerful and sophisticated as to take the place of human minds. The notion of Artificial Intelligence used to scare me half to death. Already, a large enough machine can do all sorts of intelligent things beyond our capacities: calculate in a split second the answers to mathematical problems requiring years for a human brain, draw accurate pictures from memory, even manufacture successions of sounds with a disarming resemblance to real music. Computers can translate textbooks, write dissertations of their own for doctorates, even speak in machine-tooled, inhuman phonemes any words read off from a printed page. They can communicate with one another, holding consultations and committee meetings of their own in networks around the earth. 3

Computers can make errors, of course, and do so all the time in small, irritating ways, but the mistakes can be fixed and nearly always are. In this respect they are fundamentally inhuman, and here is the relaxing thought: computers will not take over the world, they cannot replace us, because they are not designed, as we are, for ambiguity. 4

Imagine the predicament faced by a computer programmed to make language, not the interesting communication in sounds made by vervets or in symbols by brilliant chimpanzee prodigies, but real human talk. The grammar would not be too difficult, and there would be no problem in constructing a vocabulary of etymons, the original, pure, unambiguous words used to name real things. The impossibility would come in making the necessary mistakes we humans make with words instinctively, intuitively, as we build our kinds of language, changing the meanings to imply quite different things, constructing and elaborating the varieties of ambiguity without which speech can never become human speech. 5

Look at the record of language if you want to glimpse the special qualities of the human mind that lie beyond the reach of any machine. Take, for example, the metaphors we use in everyday speech to tell ourselves who we are, where we live, and where we come from. 6

The earth is a good place to begin. The word *earth* is used to name the ground we walk on, the soil in which we grow plants or dig clams, and the planet itself; we also use it to describe all of humanity ("the whole earth responds to the beauty of a child," we say to each other). 7

The earliest word for earth in our language was the Indo-European root *dhghem,* and look what we did with it. We turned it, by adding suffixes, into *humus* in Latin; today we call the complex polymers that hold fertile soil together *humic* acids, and somehow or other the same root became *humility.* With another suffix the word became *human.* Did the earth become human, or did the human emerge from the earth? One answer may lie in that nice cognate word *humble. Humane* was built on, extending the meaning of both the earth and ourselves. In ancient Hebrew, *adamha* was the word for earth, *adam* for man. What computer could run itself through such manipulations as those? 8

We came at the same system of defining ourselves from the other direction. The word *wiros* was the first root for man; it took us in our vanity on to *virile* and *virtue,* but also turned itself into the Germanic word *weraldh,* meaning the life of man, and thence in English to our word *world.*   9

There is a deep hunch in this kind of etymology. The world of man derives from this planet, shares origin with the life of the soil, lives in humility with all the rest of life. I cannot imagine programming a computer to think up an idea like that, not a twentieth-century computer, anyway.   10

The world began with what it is now the fashion to call the "Big Bang." Characteristically, we have assigned the wrong words for the very beginning of the earth and ourselves, in order to evade another term that would cause this century embarrassment. It could not, of course, have been a bang of any sort, with no atmosphere to conduct the waves of sound, and no ears. It was something else, occurring in the most absolute silence we can imagine. It was the Great Light.   11

We say it had been chaos before, but it was not the kind of place we use the word *chaos* for today, things tumbling over each other and bumping around. Chaos did not have that meaning in Greek; it simply meant empty.   12

We took it, in our words, from chaos to cosmos, a word that simply meant order, cosmetic. We perceived the order in surprise, and our cosmologists and physicists continue to find new and astonishing aspects of the order. We made up the word *universe* from the whole affair, meaning literally turning everything into one thing. We used to say it was a miracle, and we still permit ourselves to refer to the whole universe as a marvel, holding in our unconscious minds the original root meaning of these two words, miracle and marvel—from the ancient root word *smei,* signifying a smile. It immensely pleases a human being to see something never seen before, even more to learn something never known before, most of all to think something never thought before. The rings of Saturn are the latest surprise. All my physicist friends are enchanted by this phenomenon, marveling at the small violations of the laws of planetary mechanics, shocked by the unaccountable braids and spokes stuck there among the rings like graffiti. It is nice for physicists to see something new and inexplicable; it means that the laws of nature are once again about to be amended by a new footnote.   13

The greatest surprise of all lies within our own local, suburban solar system. It is not Mars; Mars was surprising in its way but not flabbergasting; it was a disappointment not to find evidences of life, and there was some sadness in the pictures sent back to earth from the Mars Lander, that lonely long-legged apparatus poking about with its jointed arm, picking up sample after sample of the barren Mars soil, looking for any   14 flicker of life and finding none; the only sign of life on Mars was the Lander itself, an extension of the human mind all the way from earth to Mars, totally alone.

Nor is Saturn the great surprise, nor Jupiter, nor Venus, nor Mercury, nor any of the glimpses of the others. 15

The overwhelming astonishment, the queerest structure we know about so far in the whole universe, the greatest of all cosmological scientific puzzles, confounding all our efforts to comprehend it, is the earth. We are only now beginning to appreciate how strange and splendid it is, how it catches the breath, the loveliest object afloat around the sun, enclosed in its own blue bubble of atmosphere, manufacturing and breathing its own oxygen, fixing its own nitrogen from the air into its own soil, generating its own weather at the surface of its rain forests, constructing its own carapace from living parts: chalk cliffs, coral reefs, old fossils from earlier forms of life now covered by layers of new life meshed together around the globe, Troy upon Troy. 16

Seen from the right distance, from the corner of the eye of an extraterrestrial visitor, it must surely seem a single creature, clinging to the round warm stone, turning in the sun. 17

Questions: The Community of Writers

1. How does Thomas explain looking "out of the corner of the eye"? What examples does he give? Have you ever noticed this phenomenon before? Can you think of other examples?

2. Why is Thomas not worried about computers taking the place of human minds?

3. Discuss how Thomas uses language for relating earth and humanity. Which of these explanations of our language is most helpful in understanding his point about the human mind?

4. What is the "deep hunch" that separates computers and human minds?

5. Thomas says that the greatest puzzle yet to be comprehended is the earth itself. How can we perceive this familiar world out of the corner of our eyes in order to discover new and surprising things?

6. What do you learn about Thomas from reading this essay? How does he use the first-person pronouns *I* and *we*?

7. Discuss intuition from your own experience.

Analysis

There is a Persian fairy tale about three princes from an island once called Serendip (now Sri Lanka). Every time these princes went on a journey, they discovered something valuable quite by accident. While looking for one thing, they unexpectedly found another. From the experiences of these mythical princes derives the word *serendipity* to describe unexpected and fortunate discoveries. Thomas seems to be describing such discoveries when he says that by focusing on one object we can see another more clearly. He uses examples of looking at stars and listening to music. What other examples can you think of?

Computers, Thomas says, can't see out of the corners of their eyes—not because they don't have eyes but because they don't have intuition, or hunches, those mysterious flashes of knowledge synthesized from expertise and experience. With this kind of knowledge, people understand metaphors (for example, "rained cats and dogs") and ambiguities, such as the many meanings for the word *earth*. They can also be surprised at new discoveries concerning the rings of Saturn, amazed at the birth of a child, awed at the splendor of another sunset. For this reason, Thomas is no longer frightened at the possibilities of computer brains. They can never equal the capabilities of the human brain.

Development (analogy, exemplification)

In developing his explanation of the capability of the human brain to discover new things and to be surprised at its discoveries, Thomas employs several approaches. He uses the **analogy** of seeing "out of the corner of the eye"—that peculiar ability to see stars and listen to music by concentrating on different stars and other components of the music. Insights often come this way: while we're studying one thing, we understand something else. This is a distinctly human capability, he says, in contrast to that of a computer brain, which cannot handle perceptions gained by this means. For several paragraphs Thomas then illustrates by **exemplification** the human capability for comprehending the ambiguities of language and understanding what our words say about our lives. Earth and humanity, he says, are conceptually intertwined by the similar roots of the words we use to describe them. All these illustrations show how we see out of the corners of our eyes: while using the word *humane* we think of a peculiarly *human* feature; when using the word *earth* for any one of its many meanings we are cognizant also of all the related meanings.

In paragraph 13 Thomas moves to considering the capacity of the human brain to discover the universe and to marvel at discoveries, using as an example the discoveries concerning the rings of Saturn. To identify "the greatest surprise" not yet fully explored (paragraph 14), Thomas first contrasts what it is *not*—the great surprise is not Mars, Jupiter, or Venus. In paragraphs 16 and 17 he states the point of his essay, that the earth is more amazing than any other discovery in the entire universe could be and that if we just look at it out of the corners of our eyes we will be able to see how splendid it is.

Exercise: The Exploring Writer

Experiment with looking "Out of the corner of the eye." Try looking at stars, tree branches, windows or other features of buildings, or a distant geographic feature. Then write a page, in your journal or elsewhere, describing the physical and psychological aspects of the experience.

Writing

Explain a characteristic that human beings share. Like Thomas, you probably have no definitive knowledge on the subject, but you can explain the characteristic as you understand it. Choose something that interests you and that is still largely open to consideration. Here are a few topics that might spark ideas for you:

- Intuition
- Pain
- Fear
- Attitudes toward pets
- Attitudes toward gardening
- Smiles

After selecting a topic, observe the attribute in yourself and others and speculate about how and why it happens. Begin asking questions about it, perhaps using the classical probes (see Chapter 3), because they lead to various methods of developing ideas as well as discovering them. Ask some questions like these:

1. What is x?
2. How many varieties of x do I know of?
3. What are the components of x?
4. How does x compare with similar things?
5. How does x differ from similar things?
6. How does x work?
7. What are some examples of x?
8. What are the causes of x?
9. What are the effects of x?

As ideas emerge, think about a point for your explanation. Thomas's point is that by looking out of the corners of our eyes, we can discover new things about our world. That's an important point, and, once you get going on your topic, you can probably make one that is equally important. You may be able to think of an analogy for explaining your subject, for example "fear is looking over your shoulder all the time." Whether you use analogy or not, try to include enough examples that your readers will understand your point. Consider using more than one method of development to cover your subject as thoroughly as necessary. In your essay, express your point wherever it seems appropriate—near the beginning or, as Thomas does, near the end. (Analogy is discussed also on pages 76–77, 177, and 318; exemplification on pages 80–81, 85, and variously throughout the book; see index.)

EXPLAINING CAUSES OR REASONS

Do you sometimes feel compelled to explain why you made a particular choice about a personal matter? Not that it's anybody's business, but you still feel the pressure of questions and criticisms from friends, relatives, acquaintances, perhaps even society: Why did you decide to go to this school? Why did you choose to have an abortion? Why did you start smoking cigarettes? Why do you want to live at home? Why? Why? Why?

So you write to explain your choice. You may write your explanation in the form of a letter, an essay, or a journal entry. Sometimes your explanations will influence other people to make similar choices, sometimes absolve you from criticism, and sometimes make you feel better for having written them.

Explanations of personal choices usually give the background for the decision—what your life was like before the choice, what the choices were, how you weighed them, how you made your decision. Explanations of this kind may be developed by narrative, giving the chronological history leading to the choice. They may be developed by cause and effect, showing the causes of your choice. And they may use classification in describing the various choices available.

However you choose to develop an explanation and whatever form it takes, what you write comes from your personal experience. You likely don't need to do any background reading, and you probably don't need to consult with anyone on the details. What you do need to do is search your own mind and emotions to try to discover why you made the choice and what your attitudes toward it are. It is very likely that you will need to write several drafts to get an explanation that accurately reflects your reasons for making the choice.

Reading

In the essay that follows, a nontraditional student writer explains why she made a particular choice. Pressured by family, friends, acquaintances, and even strangers to account for what they considered an "unnatural" choice for a mother to make, Coral Watercott thought long and hard about her reasons. In explaining her choice, she wrote several drafts and sought feedback from a variety of readers, among them her classmates and her ex-husband. Here is her final draft. As you read it, consider the difficulty of writing such an essay and observe how she develops her explanation.

Responsible Choices

Coral Watercott

In a society of tradition and accepted ways of doing things, I have chosen in my life to do some things in a very nontraditional way. I am a divorced woman and the noncustodial parent of two daughters and a son. Crystal is ten, Marisa is nine, and Ricky is five. I pay child support and pick up my children every other weekend and alternating holidays. I call them on the phone once a week to connect with them and find out how they are doing at home and in school. 1

When I relinquished custody of the children to my ex-husband, Richard, I was met with open hostility and indignation from many women. Even those I anticipated getting some support from turned away from me, not able to understand how I, as a mother, could do such a thing. I was verbally abused by some women and scorned by many. Each woman who learned of my status as a noncustodial parent, those with children and those without, put up an invisible wall and would not hear when I attempted to explain my reasons for the choices I had to make. 2

Women I respected and thought were my friends openly expressed their anger. I was told by my mother that children belong with their mother, no matter what the situation is. A neighbor came to my place of employment and yelled at me for being so selfish. She couldn't understand how I could do such a thing to my children and still be able to sleep at night knowing the pain I had inflicted on my own flesh and blood. I was pointed at in restaurants and whispered about in the grocery store where I worked. 3

I spent the first two years of the separation justifying my actions, trying to live with my decision, and struggling to understand why this was such a horrible decision on my part. I was guilt-ridden, ashamed; I began to question my own identity as a woman. I tried to learn why I was different, how I could do this when so many of my own gender were telling me how wrong it was. 4

I had many reasons for not obtaining custody of my children. Before my separation and divorce, I had to take a long, hard look at my life and what I had to offer the children as their mother and a responsible adult. The only choice I could make was to have the children live with their father. 5

I grew up in a dysfunctional home. My mother and father were   6
divorced when I was twelve years old, and my mother remarried. My
father, mother, and stepfather all have serious drinking problems. My
parents were all abusive in one form or another, and their abuse had a
huge effect on my life, both as a child and as an adult.

When I married Richard, I felt that by moving out of my parents'   7
home and into my own all my problems would disappear. I was going to
leave the abuse and the alcohol behind and begin my own life with my
own family. I decided then that my life would be very different from that
of my parents. My children would never have to suffer the abuse that I
had to and I would be the "perfect" parent. I would never abuse my own
children the way that I had been abused, and I vowed to myself that I
would be just the opposite of my parents.

Six years and three children later, I realized that I was miserable. My   8
life was falling apart and I felt as though I were going crazy. I was drinking
heavily and my marriage had disintegrated. One morning, I looked in the
mirror and found that I was the one person I never wanted to be—my
mother. It was at that moment I realized that I needed help and began
to try to put my life back together.

After seeing the damage done to my marriage, I knew there was no   9
way that I could ever save it. I made the decision to separate from my
husband. Then the only decision left to make was who the children were
going to live with.

I knew in my heart that I had to deal with the issues of abuse in my   10
childhood and that those issues made me an unhealthy parent. Although
at that point I had not physically abused my children, I knew that there
had to be some emotional abuse inflicted upon them. I also knew that I
was not capable of raising three children alone. I was afraid that there
would come a time when I would lose control and hit my children. I had
no idea what a good parent was because I had had no role models to
learn from. I didn't want my children to grow up as I did. I wanted a
better life for them.

Society dictates that mothers obtain custody of their children. Moth-   11
ers that do not have custody of their children are obviously rotten parents
and don't care about their children. Knowing that "good" mothers keep
their children, I was in a dilemma. I wanted to be a good mother and give
my children a happy life. Yet I knew that I couldn't be a good mother
until I worked on the issues of my past. I would be a better mother if I
left the children with their father.

I did the only thing I could do and still sleep at night. I left the   12
children with their father. He was loving, caring, and sensitive to their
needs. I felt secure knowing that the kids would be in his care, that they
would be well taken care of and loved.

Since that time five years ago, I have dealt with many issues from my   13
childhood and I am now a confident, healthy mother. I have learned how

to be a good mother, how to take care of my children and not to make the same mistakes my parents did when they raised me. I have also learned what normal children are like and how they behave. I no longer expect myself to be a perfect parent or expect my children to be perfect kids.

I know now that I made the right decision. I still deal with attitudes   14
from women who do not understand my choices and turn away from me. I no longer believe that just because I was born female I make a better parent. I know that men make excellent parents. They have just as much love for their children as women do. I don't feel guilty or ashamed of my decision. In fact, I am proud that I had courage to be honest with myself and loved my children enough to let them go. I am closer now to my children than I ever was. We have a healthy relationship, and they know the reasons they live with their father.

If a woman asks me how I could let my children go, I tell her that I   15
did it because I loved them. When I'm asked if I'll obtain custody some day, I reply that it depends on what my children want and how their father feels about it. As long as the kids are happy and healthy, that is all I need to know.

I hope that women in today's society faced with issues I have been   16
faced with will look at their situations honestly. Women do have choices and we have the responsibility to make the choices that are best for us, not ones that fit best into the norms of society. Women are not born with innate parenting qualities; these qualities are taught to us by our parents. Women have to learn as much as men about how to be healthy parents. Many of us were raised in dysfunctional homes, and many have yet to deal with the issues of our own childhoods. To raise healthy children for tomorrow's world, we have to work at being healthy parents today.

Questions: The Community of Writers

1. Why does Watercott feel the need to explain her decision to give custody of her children to their father?
2. Discuss your reactions to Watercott's explanation. Does she adequately explain her reasons for the decision?
3. What are some of the cause and effect relationships in this essay?
4. Whom does Watercott assume as an audience?
5. Discuss Watercott's purpose for explaining her choice: to persuade, to justify herself, or something else.
6. If you had been in Watercott's position, what choice would you have made?

Analysis

The people we associate with have certain ideas of what individuals should do in particular circumstances. Married couples should have children. Couples with children should be married. Mothers should have primary responsibility for child care. When someone goes against the accepted ideas, others in the society exert pressure in the form of disapproval and ostracism. Sometimes the disapproval can be cleared up with an explanation of the reasons for the frowned-upon action. Sometimes the explanation accomplishes no more than to make the explainer feel better.

Watercott seems to have a purpose other than to silence criticism or to make herself feel better. Her repeated references to society and what roles women expect of other women point to a persuasive purpose—perhaps to change attitudes, perhaps to encourage women in similar circumstances to do what they know is right.

Writing an explanation like Watercott's is difficult. In her first draft Watercott didn't face her real reasons for giving up her children. She brought up things like her husband's nice house in the country and his propensity toward fatherhood. She mentioned that she felt the need to return to school. She totally omitted any reference to her childhood, her alcoholism, and her own doubts about her nurturing abilities. The essay was flabby, mainly an attack on society's criticisms. In the revision, however, she was more willing to deal with the issues squarely and was more honest about her shortcomings. The second draft required some editing and a little shuffling of paragraphs, but it was essentially the draft you have read here.

Thesis and Development (chronological)

Watercott's essay explains reasons for an action. She organizes her explanation from the **specific to the general,** with an overall narrative, **chronological** structure. Throughout most of the essay she writes about her experience; this sentence from paragraph 5 might be considered her thesis: "I had many reasons for not obtaining custody of my children." After explaining her own case, however, she concludes with a much broader, more general statement: "I hope that women in today's society faced with issues I have been faced with will look at their situations honestly." At this point she addresses other women who might be in similar circumstances: "Women are not born with innate parenting qualities; these qualities are taught to us by our parents." At this point the essay seems to have a purpose other than to justify Watercott's own actions.

Within its narrative structure, Watercott's explanation develops *causally.* She begins with an effect, the relinquishment of custody of her children, and proceeds to discuss causes: her childhood in a dysfunctional and abusive family, her fears that she would become an abusive parent, her alcoholism, her lack of appropriate role models for either parents or children. At paragraph 13 she begins discussing the effects of her decision to give up her children and search for her own identity: she is now a confident, knowledgeable, loving parent, and her children are happy and well cared for. (In an essay later in this chapter, a young African-American woman explains a choice she made.)

Exercise: The Exploring Writer

Write a journal entry on social pressures, freewriting (see Chapter 3) until you discover a specific instance in which a decision of yours was subject to social pressure. If you do the following writing assignment, this freewriting can open up ideas for you.

Writing

There have probably been times when you were misunderstood, when a choice you made was disapproved of by family, friends, or acquaintances. You may have taken a stand on an unpopular issue, befriended a person outside your social group, refused to go along with your friends' activities. At such times, you probably felt that you wanted to explain your position—to tell others why you were convinced that the choice you made was right, and perhaps to encourage others to follow their own conscience and reasoning, not the pressures of the social group.

Write your explanation, either as an essay or as a letter to someone who would be an appropriate audience, someone you want to convince of the merits of your decision. You will probably use cause and effect analysis at least in part. You may also use some narrative as you give background.

Because explaining actions is difficult, you may be dissatisfied with your first draft, so allow plenty of time for heavy revision. If you can, get feedback from two kinds of readers: someone who knows you and the circumstances and someone, like a classmate, who is only an acquaintance. If their advice makes sense, follow it, but rely mostly on your own sense of what needs to be said.

EXPLAINING BY DEFINITION

It is often necessary for people to explain their terms when they write. A report on the morphinelike effect of endorphins would explain what these brain chemicals are and how they affect the body's reaction to pain.

A discussion of attention-deficit hyperactivity disorder (ADHD) would define this medical term for a particular condition in children. Explanations often accompany a piece of writing that has another purpose: to report, to persuade, and so on. Like other forms of explanation, explanatory definitions tell *why* and *how* something is the way it is. By telling how endorphins work, a writer defines the word. By telling how hyperactivity affects children and why they may be affected, a writer explains what hyperactivity is.

(Definition as a method of development is explained on pages 81–82 and 168–69. You'll find another example of definition on pages 330–31.)

Reading

Elliott Aronson, a noted behavioral psychologist, wrote a chapter on human aggression in his book *The Social Animal* (1984). He began his chapter by introducing the idea that "we humans have shown ourselves to be an aggressive species. With the exception of certain rodents, no other vertebrates so consistently and wantonly kill members of their own kind." At this point, before going further in his discussion of the psychology of human aggression, he paused to devote three paragraphs to defining aggression. What is his explanation of what aggression is?

Aggression Defined

Elliott Aronson

It is difficult to present a clear definition of *aggression* because the term is used in so many different ways in common speech. Clearly, the Boston Strangler, who made a hobby of strangling women in their apartments, was performing acts of aggression. But a football player making a tackle is also considered aggressive. A tennis player who charges the net is called aggressive. So, too, is a successful insurance salesperson who is "a real go-getter." The young girl who staunchly defends her own possessions against the encroachment of other children and the young girl who goes out of her way to clobber her brother are both considered aggressive. On a more subtle level, if a neglected husband sulks in the corner during a party, this may be an act of "passive aggression." Also, a child who wets the bed, a jilted boy friend who threatens suicide, or a student who doggedly attempts to master a difficult mathematical problem could conceivably be labeled as illustrations of an aggressive tendency in human beings. And what of the violence exerted by the state in its attempt to maintain law and order—and the less direct forms of aggression through which people of one race or religion humiliate and degrade people of different races or religions? If all these behaviors are to come under the blanket term *aggression,* the situation is indeed confused. As a way of increasing our understanding of aggression, we must cut through this morass and separate the "assertive" aspects of the popular definition from the destructive aspects. That is, a distinction can be made between behavior that harms others and behavior that does not harm others. Accordingly, the go-getting salesperson or the student doggedly sticking to the mathematical problem would not be considered aggressive, but the Boston Strangler, the clobbering child, the suicidal boy friend, and even the sulking, neglected husband would all be defined as aggressive.

But this distinction is not altogether satisfactory because, by concentrating on an outcome alone, it ignores the intention of the person perpetrating the act, and this is the crucial aspect of *aggression.* I would define an act of aggression as a behavior aimed at causing harm or pain. Thus, by definition, the football player is *not* considered to be performing an act of aggression if his aim is simply to bring down his opponent as efficiently as possible—but he *is* behaving aggressively if his aim is to cause pain or injury, whether or not he succeeds in doing so. To illustrate, suppose a three-year-old boy slaps at his father in anger. The slap may be totally ineffectual—it may even cause his father to laugh. But it is, nonetheless, an aggressive act. Similarly, the same child may, in total innocence, thrust a sharp elbow into his father's eye, causing severe pain and colorful contusions. Because its painful consequences were unintentional, this would not be defined as an act of aggression.

It might be useful to make one additional distinction regarding intentional aggression, namely, a distinction between aggression that is an end in itself and aggression that is instrumental in achieving some goal. The first we will call *hostile aggression;* the second we will call *instrumental aggression.* Thus, a football player might intentionally inflict an injury on the opposing quarterback in order to put him out of the game and thus increase his own team's probability of winning. This would be instrumental aggression. On the other hand, he might perform this action on the last play of the last game of the season to "pay back" the quarterback for some real or imagined insult or humiliation; this is hostile aggression since the aggressive act is an end in itself. Similarly, dropping a bomb on a ball-bearing factory in Munich in World War II can be considered an act of instrumental aggression, while shooting down defenseless women and children in a Vietnamese village can be considered an act of hostile aggression. The "hit man" working for the Mafia who guns down a designated victim is probably behaving instrumentally; thrill killers, such as members of the Manson family, probably are not.

Questions: The Community of Writers

1. According to Aronson, what are the problems in trying to define *aggression?*

2. Which of his definitions do you favor—those in the first paragraph, the one in the second, or those in the third?

3. Applying Aronson's definition of *aggression* as behavior aimed at causing harm or pain, decide whether the following acts are aggressive:
   a. A man beating his wife in an alcoholic rage
   b. A twelve-year-old hanging himself
   c. A couple pushing to the front of a line at a movie theater
   d. A teenager stealing an automobile
   e. A two-year-old striking his sister with a stick

4. What effect do the aggressive behaviors described in the first paragraph have on their recipients?

5. What is the tone of Aronson's definition? What does his tone tell you about his purpose?

6. In what ways does Aronson explain the *how* and *why* of aggression?

Analysis

In this essay Aronson begins by showing why he needs to define *aggression:* the term is used so broadly that it could mean almost any assertive act. Given different contexts it could mean a tennis player's manner on the court, a child's wetting the bed, and a student's determination to solve a math problem. With such wide-ranging meanings, definition is necessary, so Aronson defines the word as he uses it. You may not totally agree with Aronson's definition of *aggression,* but in the context of his chapter on the psychological aspects of the behavior, the definition is correct.

Development (exemplification, comparison)

Aronson develops his definition from **general to specific,** beginning with a broad definition and gradually narrowing it to one he can work with. From his opening definition of *aggression* as many kinds of assertive acts, he redefines and narrows the term as behavior that harms others, then narrows it still more as behavior *intended* to harm others; finally he divides his definition into two specific kinds of aggressive behavior, hostile and instrumental. From the general, he has developed a very specific definition, one he can use for his extended discussion.

To clarify his definition at each point, Aronson uses another method of development—**exemplification,** explaining each definition with numerous examples. In the final paragraph he uses **comparison**—contrasting hostile aggression with instrumental aggression.

Thesis

Aronson's definition of *aggression* is found in his second paragraph: "I would define an act of aggression as a behavior aimed at causing harm or pain." This is not his thesis, however. Remember that a thesis is (1) a statement of the subject and (2) an assertion about the subject. The subject of the essay is defining aggression, and this sentence is part of the subject—it defines aggression. It is not an assertion about defining aggression.

A sentence that *does* state the subject and make an assertion about it is the first sentence of the essay: "It is difficult to present a clear definition of *aggression* because the term is used in so many different ways in common speech." Here the subject is defining aggression and the assertion about it is that such definition is difficult. The remainder of the sentence tells how the definition will be developed, by showing the "many different ways" the word is used.

Exercise: The Community of Writers

With classmates, brainstorm (see Chapter 3) a list of aggressive acts and then classify them first as intending to harm others or not, and then as hostile or instrumental. For ease in visualizing your classification, lay out a chart something like this:

Brainstormed list	Intentional harm	Not intentional harm	Hostile aggression	Instrumental aggression

Finally, discuss whether Aronson's definition is adequate for explaining aggressive acts as you and your classmates know them.

Writing

Definition is usually part of a larger piece of writing. A writer defines a word because it needs to be clarified in its context. Aronson couldn't discuss the psychological aspects of aggression without first explaining how he was using the term. You're not writing a chapter of a book as Aronson did, but you do have contexts that sometimes require definition. In one of the subjects you are studying (other than English), select a word that must be precisely defined in order to understand the subject. It may be a word that has multiple meanings, as *aggression* does, or it may be one that is difficult to comprehend without clarification and examples. Here are some idea starters:

- History
- Energy
- Pollution
- Radiation
- Noise

If doing so is appropriate for your context, develop your definition from general to specific, beginning with the broadest use and narrowing to something more particular. However you decide to arrange the development of your essay, you will probably want to use a number of examples to assist you. As you write, remember that this is *your* definition. Other people in other contexts may use the word differently, but in your context you use it the way you define it.

Conventional usage in definitions is that words named as words are underlined or italicized, as you have seen with *aggression*. Words referring to the thing itself, for example the act of aggression, are not underlined or italicized. (See an example on page 352.)

EXPLAINING BY CLASSIFICATION

One way we make sense of our world and manage all the information we encounter is to divide and classify. We classify trees as deciduous and coniferous, and we further classify deciduous trees as oaks, maples, elms, and so on, with coniferous trees having other classifications. We could take each item in a class and divide it still further: burr oaks, pin oaks, and so on if we're working with oak trees. We classify much of our world: automobiles, dogs, music, athletics, magazines—most of what we encounter daily. By classifying, we organize information and thus know more about it and make it easier for us to remember. If we classify automobiles as foreign made and American made, each new car that comes along will go into one category or the other. If we classify American-made cars by maker, the distinctions will be even finer, and, as a result of our experience, we may know certain things about items in each class: the durability of parts, for example, the dependability of service, or the likelihood of recalls.

Classification occurs on the basis of shared characteristics, and these characteristics enable us to understand the items of the class. We understand certain things about country music that are not true of jazz. We know things about team athletics that are not true of individual sports. If you were to classify computers, you would look at types of operating systems, kilobyte capacities, the computers' main purposes compared with your purpose, and so on. Knowing that a Zenith is more like an IBM than like an Apple, you would classify the Zenith with the IBM.

Shared characteristics are determined by *principles of classification,* and these principles are dependent on needs. If you were considering buying a computer for word processing, you would classify differently than if you wanted primarily data-processing and spreadsheet capabilities. You would concentrate more on the computers that have features particularly attractive to word processing, making finer distinctions in classifying those features. Your principles for classification might be how functional the keyboard is for word processing, how easy the monitor is on the eyes for long periods, what types of word-processing software can be used with the computer, and whether the software is included in the purchase price. If you were to classify friends, as Judith Viorst does in the essay that follows, your principles of classification might be the locale of the friendships, their intensity, and their function. And because you would be classifying from your own perspective, you would do it according to the kinds of friends you have and how you view friendships. (Classification as a method of developing ideas is also discussed in Chapter 4, pages 73–74.)

Reading

In this essay, Judith Viorst explains women's friends by classifying her own. As you read, try to discover the principles of classification that determine Viorst's categories and her perspective on friendships.

Friends, Good Friends—and Such Good Friends

Judith Viorst

Women are friends, I once would have said, when they totally love 1 and support and trust each other, and bare to each other the secrets of their souls, and run—no questions asked—to help each other, and tell harsh truths to each other (no, you can't wear that dress unless you lose ten pounds first) when harsh truths must be told.

Women are friends, I once would have said, when they share the 2 same affection for Ingmar Bergman, plus train rides, cats, warm rain, charades, Camus, and hate with equal ardor Newark and Brussels sprouts and Lawrence Welk and camping.

In other words, I once would have said that a friend is a friend all the 3 way, but now I believe that's a narrow point of view. For the friendships I have and the friendships I see are conducted at many levels of intensity, serve many different functions, meet different needs and range from those as all-the-way as the friendship of the soul sisters mentioned above to that of the most nonchalant and casual playmates.

Consider these varieties of friendship: 4

Convenience friends. These are the women with whom, if our paths   5
weren't crossing all the time, we'd have no particular reason to be friends: a next-door neighbor, a woman in our car pool, the mother of one of our children's closest friends, or maybe some mommy with whom we serve juice and cookies each week at the Glenwood Co-op Nursery.

Convenience friends are convenient indeed. They'll lend us their   6
cups and silverware for a party. They'll drive our kids to soccer when we're sick. They'll take us to pick up our car when we need a lift to the garage. They'll even take our cats when we go on vacation. As we will for them.

But we don't, with convenience friends, ever come too close or tell   7
too much; we maintain our public face and emotional distance. "Which means," says Elaine, "that I'll talk about being overweight but not about being depressed. Which means I'll admit being mad but not blind with rage. Which means I might say that we're pinched this month but never that I'm worried sick over money."

But which doesn't mean that there isn't sufficient value to be found   8
in these friendships of mutual aid, in convenience friends.

Special-interest friends. These friendships aren't intimate, and they   9
needn't involve kids or silverware or cats. Their value lies in some interest jointly shared. And so we may have an office friend or a yoga friend or a tennis friend or a friend from the Women's Democratic Club.

"I've got one woman friend," says Joyce, "who likes, as I do, to take   10
psychology courses. Which makes it nice for me—and nice for her. It's fun to go with someone you know and it's fun to discuss what you've learned, driving back from the classes." And for the most part, she says, that's all they discuss.

"I'd say that what we're doing is doing together, not being together,"   11
Suzanne says of her Tuesday-doubles friends. "It's mainly a tennis relationship, but we play together well. And I guess we all need to have a couple of playmates."

I agree.   12

My playmate is a shopping friend, a woman of marvelous taste, a   13
woman who knows exactly *where* to buy *what*, and furthermore is a woman who always knows beyond a doubt what one ought to be buying. I don't have the time to keep up with what's new in eyeshadow, hemlines, and shoes and whether the smock look is in or finished already. But since (oh, shame!) I care a lot about eyeshadow, hemlines, and shoes, and since I don't *want* to wear smocks if the smock look is finished, I'm very glad to have a shopping friend.

Historical friends. We all have a friend who knew us when . . . maybe   14
way back in Miss Meltzer's second grade, when our family lived in that

three-room flat in Brooklyn, when our dad was out of work for seven months, when our brother Allie got in that fight where they had to call the police, when our sister married the endodontist from Yonkers, and when, the morning after we lost our virginity, she was the first, the only, friend we told.

The years have gone by and we've gone separate ways and we've little in common now, but we're still an intimate part of each other's past. And so whenever we go to Detroit we always go to visit this friend of our girlhood. Who knows how we looked before our teeth were straightened. Who knows how we talked before our voice got unBrooklyned. Who knows what we ate before we learned about artichokes. And who, by her presence, puts us in touch with an earlier part of ourself, a part of ourself it's important never to lose.

"What this friend means to me and what I mean to her," says Grace, "is having a sister without sibling rivalry. We know the texture of each other's lives. She remembers my grandmother's cabbage soup. I remember the way her uncle played the piano. There's simply no other friend who remembers those things."

Crossroads friends. Like historical friends, our crossroads friends are important for *what was*—for the friendship we shared at a crucial, now past, time of life. A time, perhaps, when we roomed in college together; or worked as eager young singles in the Big City together; or went together, as my friend Elizabeth and I did through pregnancy, birth, and that scary first year of new motherhood.

Crossroads friends forge powerful links, links strong enough to endure with not much more contact than once-a-year letters at Christmas. And out of respect for those crossroads years, for those dramas and dreams we once shared, we will always be friends.

Cross-generational friends. Historical friends and crossroads seem to maintain a special kind of intimacy—dormant but always ready to be revived—and though we may rarely meet, whenever we do connect, it's personal and intense. Another kind of intimacy exists in the friendships that form across generations in what one woman calls her daughter-mother and her mother-daughter relationships.

Evelyn's friend is her mother's age—"but I share much more than I ever could with my mother"—a woman she talks to of music, of books, and of life. "What I get from her is the benefit of her experience. What she gets—and enjoys—from me is a youthful perspective. It's a pleasure for both of us."

I have in my own life a precious friend, a woman of sixty-five who has lived very hard, who is wise, who listens well; who has been where I am and can help me understand it; and who represents not only an ultimate ideal mother to me but also the person I'd like to be when I grow up.

In our daughter role we tend to do more than our share of self-revelation; in our mother role we tend to receive what's revealed. It's

15

16

17

18

19

20

21

22

another kind of pleasure—playing wise mother to a questing younger person. It's another very lovely kind of friendship.

Part-of-a-couple friends. Some of the women we call our friends we never see alone—we see them as part of a couple at couples' parties. And though we share interests in many things and respect each other's views, we aren't moved to deepen the relationship. Whatever the reason, a lack of time or—and this is more likely—a lack of chemistry, our friendship remains in the context of a group. But the fact that our feeling on seeing each other is always, "I'm so glad she's here" and the fact that we spend half the evening talking together says that this too, in its own way, counts as a friendship.   23

(Other part-of-a-couple friends are the friends that came with the marriage, and some of these are friends we could live without. But sometimes, alas, she married our husband's best friend; and sometimes, alas, she is our husband's best friend. And so we find ourself dealing with her, somewhat against our will, in a spirit of what I'll call *reluctant* friendship.)   24

Men who are friends. I wanted to write just of women friends, but the women I've talked to won't let me—they say I must mention man-woman friendships too. For these friendships can be just as close and as dear as those that we form with women. Listen to Lucy's description of one such friendship: 25

"We've found we have things to talk about that are different from what he talks about with my husband and different from what I talk about with his wife. So sometimes we call on the phone or meet for lunch. There are similar intellectual interests—we always pass on to each other the books that we love—but there's also something tender and caring too."   26

In a couple of crises, Lucy says, "He offered himself, for talking and for helping. And when someone died in his family he wanted me there. The sexual, flirty part of our friendship is very small, but *some*—just enough to make it fun and different." She thinks—and I agree—that the sexual part, though small, is always *some*, is always there when a man and a woman are friends.   27

It's only in the past few years that I've made friends with men, in the sense of a friendship that's *mine*, not just part of two couples. And achieving with them the ease and the trust I've found with women friends has value indeed. Under the dryer at home last week, putting on mascara and rouge, I comfortably sat and talked with a fellow named Peter. Peter, I finally decided, could handle the shock of me minus mascara under the dryer. Because we are for each other. Because we're friends.   28

There are medium friends, and pretty good friends, and very good friends indeed, and these friendships are defined by their level of intimacy. And what we'll reveal at each of these levels of intimacy is calibrated   29 with care. We might tell a medium friend, for example, that yesterday we had a fight with our husband. And we might tell a pretty good friend that this fight with our husband made us so mad that we slept on the couch. And we might tell a very good friend that the reason we got so mad in that fight that we slept on the couch had something to do with that girl who works in his office. But it's only to our very best friends that we're willing to tell all, to tell what's going on with that girl in his office.

The best of friends, I still believe, totally love and support and trust each other, and bare to each other the secrets of their souls, and run—no questions asked—to help each other, and tell harsh truths to each other when they must be told.   30

But we needn't agree about everything (only twelve-year-old girl friends agree about *everything*) to tolerate each other's point of view. To accept without judgment. To give and take without ever keeping score. And to *be* there, as I am for them and as they are for me, to comfort our sorrows, to celebrate our joys.   31

Questions: The Community of Writers

1. Viorst classifies friends according to variety and level of intensity. What eight varieties of friends does she discuss? How many levels of intensity does she describe? Would her system of classification work for classifying men's friends?

2. Is Viorst's perspective on friendships the same as yours? Which varieties would you omit if you were classifying friends? What categories would you add?

3. What do you learn about Viorst from what she says about friends?

4. What kind of male friendship does Viorst describe? Discuss whether friendships of this kind are possible.

5. Can you see any advantage to classifying friends according to variety and intensity? What might have prompted Viorst to write an essay about friends?

6. In what ways does Viorst explain the *how* and *why* of women's friendships?

Analysis

Have you ever told a friend some intimate detail of your life and then discovered that soon everyone you know was talking about it? Have you ever got into trouble by going along with the actions of your friends when your wiser self was telling you not to? These might be some reasons to sit down and examine your friendships. If you talk intimately with a "medium" friend or a "pretty good friend," one who has no close relationship with you, that person may, for a variety of reasons, discuss the details of your life with other people. If your friends are doing things you disapprove of, these friends may not be as close as you thought. To distinguish between friends of this kind and "best of friends" has some advantages. And to classify your friends according to what you do with them might help you to say no when they want you to do things you're not comfortable with.

We don't know what Viorst's reason was for examining her friendships, but with her emphasis on topics of discussion, it might have been betrayal of a confidence. Her introductory paragraphs may support such a view. More to the point for you as a reader, however, is what reason she had for explaining her **classification** of friends in a published essay. She undoubtedly assumed that readers could profit from, or at least be interested in, her explanation. Her purpose for explaining may therefore be to prompt readers to examine their own friendships to see what types they may be.

Thesis and Development (classification)

After two background paragraphs on what Viorst "once would have said," the third paragraph and the single-sentence fourth paragraph express the thesis and organization of this essay. Here we have a statement that says there are many varieties of friendship and these varieties are based on such characteristics as levels of intensity, functions, and needs.

For each category, Viorst explains its functions and needs. Convenience friends, for example, are people who do little things for us because it is handy to have such mutual aid available from neighbors, but they're people we don't discuss private matters with. With cross-generational friends, by contrast, we may discuss private matters, though it seems from Viorst's description that mainly the younger member of the pair does the discussing, while the older member seems to have the role of adviser.

In keeping with her introductory background about not all women's friends being "soul sisters," Viorst explains the kinds of conversations that might be had with each type of friend. With historical friends, she talks about old times, with special-interest friends she discusses that special interest and rarely anything else, and with part-of-a-couple friends she discusses a variety of subjects but only when they get together as couples. With her men friends she can discuss intellectual interests and enjoy the small flirty part of the relationship.

Viorst's final variety of friendship is the "best of friends." She develops this category within her second principle of classification: intensity of friendships, or "levels of intimacy." Only to the best of friends do we "tell all." Only the best of friends can be trusted not to compromise our secrets, can be relied on to comfort us when we need comforting, and can be expected to honestly tell us when we're wrong. These are the friends Viorst once would have said were the only kind of friends. Her essay thus brings the discussion back to the beginning, where she refutes her older idea about friends.

Exercise: The Community of Writers

Combine Viorst's major principles of classification: variety and level of intensity. Make a chart of "medium friends," "pretty good friends," and "very good friends," and then, weighing functions, place each of the eight varieties in one of these levels. Discuss your decisions and the reasons for your classifications.

Writing

Respond to Viorst's classification of friends with your own perspective on how friends should be classified. Begin with a brainstormed list, jotting down as many kinds of friends as you can think of (see Chapter 3). Push yourself until you have a long list—twelve to fifteen items. Then group your items and eliminate those that don't apply. Compare your list with Viorst's and note differences. Discuss your categories with friends or classmates to get their perspectives. Then begin thinking what you can say about the varieties, functions, or intensities of friendships that may be different from what Viorst has said.

Your introductory paragraphs, like Viorst's, may provide the background for the discussion; in your case, it may be that you disagree with Viorst's categories, that her classification doesn't apply to unmarried college students, that the female perspective isn't relevant to men, that there is no such thing as a "best friend" as Viorst describes her, and so on. Then state your position—how you classify friends.

Determine a specific purpose for writing, such as to show the categories of friendship for college students and to explain why these categories differ from those of mature women. Your purpose might be to explain why no friends can be trusted to keep silent about intimate details of their friends' lives, or why women can't be close friends with men without the relationship becoming sexual. As you consider what to write, decide on a specific audience—such as fellow college students, any men, or any women.

Be specific in your development of each category, explaining how each is different from the others, perhaps quoting friends, giving examples, discussing what you talk about or do with friends in each category. When you have a rough draft, have a classmate read it and tell you if you've omitted something important, if you haven't been clear enough, if you have been unnecessarily wordy, and whatever else you might want to know before completing your revision for a final draft.

ADDITIONAL READINGS FOR DISCUSSION

Reading

In the following essay, an African-American woman explains her decision to leave her Chicago neighborhood to attend school in Minnesota and the effects of making that choice. Her decision, like Coral Watercott's in "Responsible Choices" (page 347), receives an explanation because some people might question her reasons.

Never Leave Your Past Behind

BernaDette Wilson (student writer)

I grew up in a low-income, single-parent family on the far south side   1
of Chicago. My sister and her family also lived with us. They needed a place to stay while they looked for a more affordable house. One thing my family doesn't do is turn our backs on each other. Sociologists who claim to be experts on non-white families have their own word for this type of situation. They derogatorily label this as a poverty-stricken, black matriarchal extended family who lives in the ghetto. Yet all in all, we were happy because we helped each other. We were not the type of family who wondered what the next meal would be. We always knew we would have food on the table, but the type of food was a different story.

Plain and simple, our goal was to survive. Survival to us was to get a   2
job and hopefully wake up the next morning. I didn't think about college. Why should I? I didn't even like high school. But, somehow, somewhere an idea was instilled in me. "To be 'somebody,' I must go to college; if I didn't go, I would be a nobody." Because I believed this, I became more distant from my family and friends. I felt ashamed of my family because no one went to college right out of high school except for me. I felt my friends were not worthy of my time because I was in college and they were not. My biggest mistake in life was when I tried to leave my past behind me. It took me nineteen long, painful years to believe and learn never to be ashamed of who I am or where I came from.

Since I lived in an area where there were only Blacks, I wanted to   3
get away from them. I didn't want to witness another murder in front of my house. I couldn't tolerate another ten-to-twenty-year-old drug seller stopping me and asking, "Hey baby, wanna buy this 'caine?" I could no longer look at pregnant teenagers with their kids, walking around and looking for the mailman and their welfare checks. I got tired of staying up past 2:00 A.M. waiting for house parties to end. The

polluted, chemical-like air was getting to me. I even got tired of my next door neighbor wanting to borrow sugar. She actually told me, "I borrow it because it cost too much to buy." This is why I came to St. Cloud, Minnesota, to get away from that environment and to be around people who were achievers like myself.

Ahh! I was in a white, religious, middle-class area with people who understand the true meaning of education and who were going to get "true" success. These were my role models, people who lived in a nice clean place. However, I soon found out they didn't feel as highly about me as I felt about them. 4

The second day I was in St. Cloud, a white man stared at me in disgust and very abruptly dug his finger in his nose. At first I looked him straight in his eyes; then feeling intimidated, I lowered my head and kept walking. I did the complete opposite of what my grandmother told me. She said, "Always walk up straight, and hold your head up high because you are a beautiful black woman." That same week, I couldn't believe what I heard. Two older white men walked past me and one of them said, "Those fucking niggers shouldn't be here." As much as that hurt me, I smiled at both of them and kept walking. 5

My friends at St. Cloud State criticized the way I talked. They said, "You talk like a Southerner." However, my friends in Chicago said, "You sound white." I also couldn't understand why most of my instructors used me as an example. One instructor said, "BernaDette doesn't feel happy her ancestors were enslaved." And, another instructor would stare at me during lecture as if I were stupid. By that time, I felt out of place. I felt like a failure because no matter what I did, I didn't have what it took to be accepted. I didn't have white skin. But what kept me in the race was my mind. I was smart and intelligent, and as my mother used to say, "Nobody can take away what you already know." 6

At St. Cloud, I used my mind to my advantage. I kept my grades up. I talked to people as if I was sure of myself. I tried to be extra nice so people would like me. But during all that "role-playing," I still wasn't happy because I couldn't be myself. The two most important things I realized were to love myself and to love my family. After I knew my family supported me whatever I did or said, my life began. Mentally, I grew stronger. I no longer felt ashamed of my family or friends. Most of all, I no longer was ashamed of being black. In fact, I love myself because I am black. 7

I feel empowered because of what I have seen and experienced. I am proud because I am the first one in my family to attend college. I am happy because the people I love have helped me the best way they knew how. The only thing I needed to do was love myself for who I am and where I came from. In order to do that, as my favorite high school teacher said, "You have to know where you came from before you know where 8 you're going. And, you can't do that by acting like someone else." After all these years, I am proud to announce that I am a black woman who knows where she's going.

Questions: The Community of Writers

1. What reason does Wilson give for her decision to go to college? How does her decision compare with yours?

2. Wilson explains *causes* for her decision to go to college. She also describes *effects*. What are some of those effects? How do they compare with your first weeks at college?

3. St. Cloud State University is a mid-sized university in central Minnesota. Why do you suppose Wilson went to school there? What might her experiences have been if she had elected to attend your school?

4. Wilson's primary purpose seems to be to explain an aspect of her life. What other purpose might she have for writing this essay?

Reading

Student writer Terry Splett explains why her family celebrated both Chanukah and Christmas when she was growing up. As an adult remembering what it was like growing up in a Judeo-Christian home, she writes mainly from the child's point of view, trying to understand the differences between being a Christian and being a Jew. As you read, notice how she develops her explanation by comparison.

We Celebrated Chanukah and Christmas

Terry Splett

"Because he's Jewish" was Mom's reply when I asked her why Daddy   1
never went to church with us on Sundays. She explained that he went to a different church with Grandma Nancy and Grandpa Aaron and that when I got older I would understand. So, from the time we were old enough for Sunday School until the time we got confirmed, Mom would pack up the four of us kids and cart us off to church on Sunday mornings. Wishing that he was coming with us and hoping that he wouldn't be lonely while we were gone, we'd all kiss Daddy goodbye as he sat in the easy chair reading the paper. We were used to doing everything together, and somehow leaving him alone on Sunday mornings seemed wrong. But we knew that when we came home Daddy would be in the kitchen putting the final touches on the breakfast that he had made especially for us, and we would all be together again.

The other kids at church would always ask where my Dad was, and 2
I'd answer proudly that he was Jewish and didn't have to come. Then I'd
tell them that he was at home cooking eggs and hash browns for us,
knowing how jealous they'd be because they didn't have a Jewish Daddy
who had breakfast waiting for them when they got home from Sunday
School.

I didn't know what Lutheran was, much less Jewish, but I suspected 3
that being Jewish had something to do with the times when we got all
dressed up and went to Grandma and Grandpa's house for what Daddy
called the High Holidays. We'd all sit down to dinner, but we wouldn't
eat right away because Grandpa and Daddy had to say prayers, and we
had to be very quiet. Grandpa would sit at the head of the table. He wore
a scarf around his neck, which was funny because it wasn't cold in the
house, and he always sat on a pillow. Both Grandpa and Daddy wore
round, black hats. The hats were so small that I always thought they'd fall
off their heads, and I kept warning my dad. My brothers got to wear hats
too, but my sister and I couldn't because they were only for boys.

Grandma gave each of us a little book, and Grandpa and Dad would 4
take turns reading from the book and taking small sips of wine. Even we
kids got to drink wine. We didn't like it but drank it anyway because it
made us feel grown up. We couldn't understand what Grandpa and Dad
said because they spoke in a different language, but we could follow
along in the book that had English underneath the strange letters that I
knew they were reading. I remember Daddy had to correct me once when
I turned a page because I didn't know that the books were backwards and
I was going the wrong way. It always seemed like the prayers took a long
time, but finally everyone would say Amen, just like in church, and
Grandma would start serving the food.

Most of the food was the same kind that we had at home, like 5
chicken, potatoes, and beans. But there were other items that we had
only at Grandma's, like gefilte fish and matzo ball soup. We especially
liked the round, hollow crackers called mandalah that were meant to be
put in the soup but that we ate as snacks.

We enjoyed those holidays. It made us feel like we were helping 6
Daddy be Jewish, and I think that made him happy too. There were other
holidays that we celebrated as well, Passover and Chanukah. Over the
years, Dad would explain the importance of each occasion in a way that
we could understand, and that made us enjoy them all the more. Chanukah came around Christmas time each year, and we celebrated both. At
home, we had a Christmas tree and Santa always came as we expected,
and at Grandma's we had a Chanukah bush, and the Chanukah Man
came with presents as well. As children, we loved that time of year. When
I grew up, Dad told me that there was no Chanukah Man or Chanukah
bush. He said that Grandma had invented them especially for us kids
because she knew how much children love Santa Claus and Christmas

trees, and she didn't want us to feel left out when we went to her house for the holidays. No one could love us more.

Eventually, I began learning the religious importance of Christmas in Sunday School. I began to learn what Lutheran was, and what Jewish was from the Christian point of view. Somehow, what I was learning seemed to contradict everything that I had learned at home, and I was scared. Mom and Dad had taught us about good and bad, and right and wrong. We knew that it was bad to steal and to swear and to lie. They told us that when good people died they went to heaven, which was a good place. It was where God was. They also told us that when bad people died, they went to a different place, a bad place; Mom called it hell. We didn't want to go to hell. We wanted to go where God was, so we tried very hard to be good.   7

At church, they talked about good and bad, and heaven and hell as well. They talked about being saved, and that being saved meant going to heaven. They said only Christians would be saved, only good Christians, and all I could think about was my daddy. At home we learned about good people and bad people. At church we learned about good Christians and bad Christians, and I wondered about everyone else, especially my daddy. I didn't understand and wanted to go to my dad's church for answers.   8

He took me to his church, the synagogue. It reminded me of the Lutheran church in some ways, but in others it was very different. The rabbi wore a long black robe, just like the pastor in church, but he had a long beard and wore one of those hats, a "yarmulke," Dad said. I noticed that all the men wore yarmulkes, and many wore scarfs like Grandpa did. There weren't many children there, and the men sat in a different part of the synagogue from the women. What I remember most was the scrolls. They were beautiful, and the men that held them during different parts of the service handled them with such care that I knew they were very special. I couldn't understand. They never talked about Christians in the synagogue. They talked about the Jewish people. They were the chosen people and were waiting to be saved. The Jewish people would go to heaven. I was relieved because that meant Daddy, but I wondered about Mom and me and the rest of the kids. I was still confused.   9

After the service, Daddy introduced me to more people than I could remember. He was so excited that I was with him. Everyone was kind and friendly, and I couldn't see any differences between the people here and the people at church. They seemed happy and loving and honest. We were all people, and I was glad that I learned about people the way I did at home. I never learned to separate kinds of people. I wished that churches and synagogues didn't. If they didn't, maybe they'd understand each other better. I knew that I would never completely understand the church or the synagogue. In my own mind I decided that in the end we would all be taken care of because we all believed in God and in Good and in Love.   10

I told Mom and Dad what I had learned and they were so proud. 11
They both agreed with what I had come to believe, but they warned me
that many people would never understand. That wasn't important to me.
What was important was that my family would always be together, and
now I knew that we would.

In the following years we continued to celebrate both the Christian 12
holidays and the Jewish holidays, and they were all very special times for
my family. One year for Christmas I received a gold cross on a chain to
wear around my neck. The following year, for Chanukah, I received a
small Star of David. I put it on the gold chain I had received earlier, and
for years I never took the chain off. I loved the way the cross and the Star
of David hung together from that chain, touching one another. They
represented everything that I had learned over the years.

Questions: The Community of Writers

1. In what ways does Splett compare Chanukah and Christmas? What do the two
   holidays have in common? In what ways are they different? What was special
   about the way her family celebrated them? What other holidays does she
   compare?

2. In what ways does Splett compare Jewish people and Christian people? Why
   does she have such a hard time seeing the differences?

3. What does the symbolism of the cross and the Star of David on a single chain
   represent for Splett?

4. What does Splett's experience say about prejudice toward groups of people?

5. What is the tone of this essay?

6. Splett does not explicitly state a thesis. Discuss what her unstated thesis, or
   controlling idea, is.

CHAPTER 13

Writing to Instruct

To teach is to learn twice.
—Joseph Joubert

As a purpose for writing, **instruction** generally tells a reader *how to do something* or how something is done. This kind of writing might tell you how to make a paper airplane, as the first reading in this chapter does, or how to put your test answers on a computer data sheet, how to assemble a bicycle, or how to use a new stereo system. We are surrounded by instructions—many of them clear and concise, others poorly written and difficult to follow. Have you ever tried to set a digital watch with instructions that were more of a hindrance than a help? Have you ever tried to play a new game on the basis of instructions from your opponent and found new rules cropping up every time you seemed about to win?

Writing to instruct requires careful work. The writer must know the task well, be able to present the steps of the task in sequential order, write them clearly enough so someone who knows nothing about the task can follow them, and omit nothing important. In so doing, the writer will probably learn something new about the task too. Instructions have an obvious pattern of development: They start with the first step and proceed to the last, simple chronological order. They do not include irrelevant details, because such information might be confusing. If materials are required, they are listed.

Writers of instructions must not only know the subject well but must also understand the reader's level of knowledge. If your reader knows nothing about the subject of your instructions, you will need to define your terms and explain each step in detail, whereas if your reader is more knowledgeable, you can feel free to use specialized terminology. At the same time, instructional language must always be exact and correct. This sentence would be difficult to follow because of its inexactness: "Drill a small hole in the support frame." What size is "small"? Where in the support frame should the hole be drilled? Also, for the sake of clarity, avoid using vague words like *this, it,* and *they* to refer to specific actions. The following instructions are unclear because of vague pronouns:

> The names of files are kept in directories on a disk. *They* also contain information on the size of the files.

> MS-DOS will display a status report and any errors that it has found. An example of *this* can be found in Chapter 5.

To prevent your reader from being confused, sometimes you will want to give your instructions in the form of a list, as the writer of these instructions for beginning a card trick does:

1. Have someone remove any two cards from a shuffled deck.
2. Return the cards to the top of the deck.
3. Shuffle the cards, keeping the two cards on top of the deck.

When you don't list your instructions, use coherence devices to keep your reader with you: *first, next, now that you have completed the first step.* Also give your reader clues for especially critical points: *This is the most important part. Be sure that the thermometer records exactly 238 degrees.* If two operations need to be done at the same time, tell your reader so: *meanwhile, while the sauce is simmering, at the same time.*

Instructions generally speak directly to the reader with the pronoun *you* and imperative voice.

> *Drill* a small hole.
> *Shuffle* the cards.
> *Hold* the control key down while *you* press the F1 key.

Try to avoid using *should,* as in "You should hold the control key down." To consider the needs of your readers and the approach to take in writing your instructions, apply the Questions about Audience for Writing (page 26).

The readings and writing assignments in this chapter all have the purpose of instruction; in a way they are all "how-to" assignments, yet they differ in a number of ways, from having multiple purposes to being only ostensibly instructive.

FOLLOWING AND WRITING INSTRUCTIONS

How good are you at following instructions? Have you ever done the exercise that begins by advising you to read all the instructions first, tells you to write your name at the top of the page, then has you do a lot of stupid things like clapping your hands, staring at the ceiling, or yelling out loud, only to tell you at the end to disregard all the instructions except the first two? It may seem as if the only reason for the exercise is to make you look silly, but actually the exercise conveys an important point: It's generally easier to follow instructions if you read them through first so you have some idea of where they're going and what you need to do.

Reading

Here are some instructions by Campbell Morris on making a paper airplane. Take the time to make the "Smooth Flyer" and to fly it. But don't just *make* the plane; also observe *what you do* while you make it: where your problems are, how much you refer to the diagrams, where you have trouble with terminology, where the instructions are easy and where difficult to follow.

Smooth Flyer

Campbell Morris

Your average, everyday kind of dart is unstable and unsuitable to prolonged smooth flying. Here is another glider that is so simple to make but flies incredibly well — even the teacher will be impressed!

1.
Use a sheet of 8½" x 11" paper folded in half lengthwise. Fold the corners in as shown.

2.
Fold the leading edges in as shown.

3.
Fold in half.

4.
Fold wings down, slightly angled as shown. Give the fuselage around 2 cm height. Both height and angle can be experimented with if you wish.

5.
Fold the leading edge of the wing into a long fin. The fin is shown folded upwards. You can fold the fin downwards for an even smoother flight. See which way you think is best. Bring the wings up for the next step.

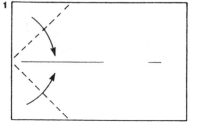

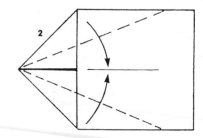

6.
*Invert the fold. The dots show
the hidden flaps inside the
fuselage. Where they meet at
the bottom edge of the fuselage
is point C. Fold your inverted fin
from point C to point A. A is the
tail end of the wing crease AB.
Of course you must crease CA
well to invert the fold.*

7.
*Bring the wings level. The
finished Smooth Flyer should
look like this. (The fin can be
folded downwards as
mentioned in step 5.)*

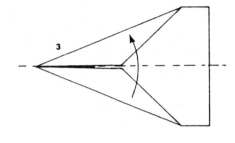

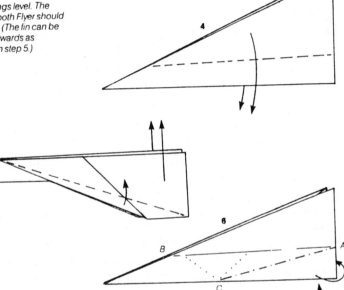

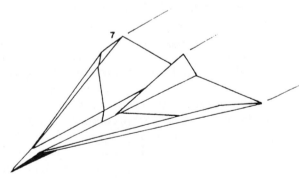

Throwing Instructions
*Throw with slight force in a
straight direction. Make sure
the wings are level or slightly
raised.*

Questions: The Community of Writers

1. How did your paper airplane turn out? Does it look like Morris's diagram of the finished Smooth Flyer? Does it fly?

2. Where did you have problems following Morris's instructions?

3. How often did you refer to the diagrams? Where would you make changes in the instructions? Was any terminology a problem for you?

4. Did you read all the instructions before beginning?

5. What have you learned about the way people follow instructions?

Analysis

Instructions are not always easy to follow. Some people have trouble making the Smooth Flyer, while some don't. Reasons for the difficulty vary. Some people seem to be more visually oriented, paying more attention to diagrams than to verbal instructions, while others prefer written guidance. This is why instructions often include both a written guide and diagrams. Diagrams are *not* meant to supplement poorly written instructions.

Unfamiliar terminology is sometimes a problem in following instructions. When you write instructions, make certain that your terms are clear—by explaining them, using synonyms or diagrams, or employing other means. Terms such as "leading edges" and even "the fold" are not transparently clear to all readers. Perhaps some of the terminology in "Smooth Flyer" made carrying out the instructions difficult for you. As a writer of instructions, be patient with your readers. If this is their first time performing the task, everything may be unfamiliar. Give them encouraging words: "You're now halfway finished" or "You've now finished the most difficult part."

Sometimes people have trouble following instructions because they don't read carefully. Readers may skip over words and sentences because they think they already know what the instructions say. They ignore the part, for example, that tells them to attach Wire A to Receptacle C because they've installed enough electronic equipment to know where Wire A should be attached—and proceed to attach it to the wrong receptacle. Writers can forestall this kind of misreading with such directives as "Most important," "Performing this step correctly is critical," or "Make sure you have the section marked 'top' in upper position."

People have many reasons for misreading instructions—some of them the fault of the writer, some the fault of the reader. As a reader, you probably occasionally misread—to your detriment, because you might have to repeat the task. As a writer, you need to take the responsibility of considering how your readers might misread and of trying to prevent any misreading.

Exercise: The Community of Writers

Working with a partner, rewrite the "Smooth Flyer" instructions, revising any parts that either of you found difficult to follow.

Writing

Write instructions on how to make something. Choose something that can be done in seven to ten steps, something that will have a finished product, something that you know well enough to be absolutely clear about. You might choose another paper-folding activity, like making a box or a different kind of airplane; you might consider how to cut paper dolls or paper snowflakes, how to build a house of cards, or some other activity that involves *making* something. Use diagrams if you wish, but remember if you do that *both* the diagrams and the verbal instructions must be clear. Be careful of technology, defining any terms your readers may not understand. Keep in mind that not everyone uses even familiar terms in the same way.

Number your steps and use chronological development, presenting the steps in the exact order in which they must be done. Remember that people don't always follow instructions the way we expect them to; try to anticipate what your readers might do—and not do—and what kinds of difficulties they might have. The task you are describing may be easy for you to do, but writing instructions that someone else can follow easily is another matter. Assume an intelligent audience but one that doesn't know what you know about making this thing.

Before making a final copy, read your instructions through, carrying them out in your mind. Try to be an uninformed reader relying on your instructions for performing the task.

WRITING INSTRUCTIONS FROM EXPERIENCE

Most instructions are written from the writer's own experience. We are able to tell someone else how to make a pizza because of having successfully made pizzas ourselves. If we tell a reader how to change the oil in an automobile, we do so out of our experience in changing oil. It's very difficult to tell someone "do as I say" if you can't also say, or imply, "do as I do."

But it seems that we can always learn something new. Even while writing about something we know well, we learn about it. You may have changed the oil in cars many times and be able to perform the task without thinking much about it, but when you try to tell someone else how to do it, someone who doesn't know what the parts under the car look like, much less what they're called, you will test your own knowledge of this task. It has often been said that if you want to know something really well, you must teach it to someone else.

Reading

In the essay that follows, a professional writer and teacher of writing, Roger Garrison, instructs apprentice writers on how to use punctuation. Because these instructions grew out of his own experience as a writer, and because writers, when writing, punctuate according to practice not rules, Garrison presents guidelines for ways other writers can think of punctuation. He gives only one rule.

Punctuation

Roger Garrison

There are not many precise rules, despite grammar manuals, for commas, semicolons, and other typographical marks we use to indicate pauses in written speech. We have only a few stops (places for a reader to pause or take note): period, semicolon, colon, dash, question mark, and parentheses. (An editor once said, "Forget the exclamation point. It should be used only for swearing or direct commands. Otherwise, it reminds me of a kid jumping around the page on a pogo stick. Makes me nervous.")   1

These few punctuation marks are remarkably easy to understand, if you strip away the finicky rules that have grown up around them.   2

Punctuation marks are signals to readers. They tell them when to pause, when to stop, when a question has been asked. Except for direct quotations, or quotes within quotes, there are two simple ways to think about these marks.   3

1. Think of punctuation as breathing or pausing: 4

Comma	,	Half a breath.
Semicolon	;	Three-quarters of a breath.
Period	.	A full breath.
Colon	:	"Stop, a list is coming."
Dash	—	"Emphasis, side comment, definition coming."
Parentheses	( )	"I want to tuck a quick fact or comment here."

2. Or think of punctuation as traffic signals: 5

Comma	,	Flashing yellow light: Slow down; look right and left.
Semicolon	;	Flashing red light: Come almost to a stop; then go.
Period	.	Stop sign: Stop full, then go.
Colon	:	Arrow or road sign: "Food, Fuel, Lodging, Next Right."
Dash	—	Detour—be alert.
Parentheses	( )	"Caution, alternate route."

If you wonder how to punctuate a sentence, read it aloud. Where are   6
the natural pauses? How long do you want your reader to breathe, to
pause? Learn to read your own writing aloud to yourself, slowly, sentence
by sentence.

One simple rule: You may put a full sentence (independent clause)   7
on either side of a semicolon, a colon, a period, or a dash, or within
parentheses—but *not* on either side of a comma, unless you have a
compound sentence with a conjunction such as *and* or *but*. The comma
splice, or comma fault, places a comma where we need a period (usually)
or a semicolon. It "splices" (fastens together) two complete sentences.
Example: The car swerved off the road, it went into a ditch.

Most Common and Annoying Error

The most persistent mechanical error is a punctuation mistake as in   8
"The elephant lifted *it's* trunk." *STOP!* One of the easiest rules to remember is: *The total number of possessive pronouns that have an apostrophe is one:
one's.* So it's always *ours, yours, hers, theirs, its, whose, oneself.*

Personal Favorite

I like the semicolon as the most flexible of punctuation marks. (It's   9
a journalist's favorite, too.) It can separate independent clauses (full
sentences); it can serve as a longer stop than a comma in a series of
phrases where you want separate emphasis; or it can either link or
contrast logically connected elements within a sentence—as in this one.
But be careful not to overuse it. On an early draft of this book, my editor
said, "You scatter semicolons with wild abandon." He was right.

Questions: The Community of Writers

1. What is Garrison's "one simple rule"?
2. Discuss whether Garrison's guidelines can be more useful than rules.

3. Of Garrison's two ways of thinking about punctuation, which do you prefer: pause marks or traffic signals?

4. What would be the effect of writing the listed information in paragraphs 4 and 5 in normal paragraph form?

5. In paragraph 8 Garrison identifies the error he considers the "most common and annoying." What kind of error disturbs each of you the most?

Analysis

Garrison makes an important point about punctuation marks: They are *signals* for readers. As such, they are no more interchangeable than road signs and traffic signals are. If a state department of transportation were to put up a red octagonal sign to signal a road curving to the right, drivers would be confused about how to proceed. The same happens with writing. If a writer inserts a period (a stop sign) to signal the end of a phrase (for example, "Picking up the mail."), readers are confused: Did they misread? They wonder what the writer means by the period.

Development

After the topic sentence in paragraph 3, "Punctuation marks are signals to readers," Garrison gives two ways of thinking about punctuation marks: as breath marks corresponding to speech (paragraph 4) and as traffic signals (paragraph 5). The appropriate mark gives the necessary signal. In presenting these two ways of thinking about punctuation, Garrison uses a numbered list form, with three columns in each list: one naming the punctuation marks, one illustrating them graphically, and a third interpreting the marks. As seen in Morris's "Smooth Flyer" instructions, writers often rely on lists to draw attention to points in their instructions.

Garrison gives only one rule. When writers follow this rule, they indicate to their readers that they know where their sentences end, and readers then can know where to end them too. Other people writing about punctuation, if they were to reduce their instructions to one rule, would likely name something else: "Use two commas, not one, to set off interrupting modifiers," perhaps, or "Don't use a period until you come to the end of your sentence."

There may be disagreement on the "most common and annoying error" too. For Garrison that error is the faulty *it's*. *It's* and *its* are two entirely different words, the first meaning "it is" or "it has" and the second indicating possession. Using the one with the apostrophe when you need the other gives a faulty signal, something like writing *course* when you mean *coarse*. For further discussions of punctuation, see Lewis Thomas's "Notes on Punctuation" in Chapter 8 and Punctuation in the handbook of usage at the end of this book.

Exercise: The Exploring Writer

Identify your "most common and annoying error" and write a brief explanation of how writers can remember to avoid it. Compare errors and explanations with your classmates.

Writing

Write instructions out of your experience. Everyone can do certain things better than other people can. Garrison wrote as an experienced writer to less experienced writers. You might be quite an expert at repotting a plant or repairing an electrical cord. There is something that you know how to do that other people would like to be able to do too. Write a paper about it, assuming an interested audience.

Begin your paper with a paragraph that, like Garrison's first paragraph, makes an attempt to interest your audience, presenting your subject in a fresh way. In explaining your instructions, consider using numbered lists, but don't attempt to use columns unless they're right for your subject. If headings are appropriate, use them. Like Garrison, use the second-person pronoun *you* when addressing your reader, and use the first-person pronoun *I* when referring to your own preferences and practices.

WRITING INSTRUCTIONS ON NEW USES FOR FAMILIAR THINGS

Instructions sometimes tell readers about new uses for familiar things. People write articles and books about how to use common household materials for unsuspected purposes. There is an entire book on how to use vinegar, from cleaning water stains to rinsing hair and so on. People occasionally read about how to decorate their homes and rooms with "found" objects, such as rocks, weeds, and driftwood.

Written instructions of this kind often first convince readers that the familiar items are useful for new purposes: Forget about the fact that vinegar smells sour; if it rinses your hair clean of soap residue, why not use it? And weeds are not just *weeds;* if you find the right ones they will look quite attractive stuck in a fruit jar. Writers sometimes expose commonly held beliefs so they can instruct their readers on new ways to do things.

Reading

In the essay that follows, Suzette Haden Elgin, retired professor of applied psycholinguistics, tells readers how to detect a lie, and in doing so she promotes a new use for a familiar item—the telephone. First she must refute the commonly held belief that it's easier to lie over the telephone than in face-to-face conversation. In refuting the myth about lies, she instructs readers on how to use the telephone for detecting lies. The author of several books on "verbal self-defense," Elgin calls her writings "first-aid" manuals on what to do when under verbal attack, or how to avoid letting other people get the better of you. As you read this essay from her book entitled *The Last Word on the Gentle Art of Verbal Self-Defense,* notice how she establishes her authority: She summarizes "research studies," then goes beyond them to suggest her own explanation.

Telephone Listening

Suzette Haden Elgin

Life is filled with things that are assumed to be true because they are   1
"obvious" or "self-evident." It's always a shock to learn that one of those things is not true at all. It gives you a chance to imagine what it was like to hear from the town crier that the world was round rather than, as was obvious and self-evident, flat.

Among the set of self-evident myths is the idea that if you want to lie   2
you're better off doing it on the phone, where people can't see you and you are therefore more likely to get away with it. That happens to be false; it is in fact easier for people to spot a lie when they hear it on the phone than when they hear it from a person present at the time.

The research studies suggest a number of reasons for this. For example: 3

1. There is less distraction in telephone speech, so the listener can concentrate more easily.
2. There is less emotional involvement in telephone conversation, which eliminates yet another sort of distraction.
3. Pitch changes, which are important to the detection of deceit, are easier to hear when attention is focused entirely on the voice.

I agree with all three of these proposed explanations; they are surely   4
accurate. But I think that the generalization we can draw from them is this: *Without body language feedback, a person who lies cannot obtain the necessary data for the constant fine-tuning required to make lies work.* The

auditory (ear) channel of communication alone does not provide enough information for this purpose. The speaker who would like to deceive can't even watch for body syncing or other obvious clues to attention. Which means that on the phone you *can* fake listening!

In person, it's easier for speakers to deceive and very difficult for listeners to do so. On the telephone, this is reversed—it is the listener who can deceive more easily, and the speaker who has difficulty. The ear is a much better judge of lying than the eye is, contrary to what is often assumed—and the very best channel of all for lying is the *face*, which is of course invisible in telephone communication. (It's interesting to consider what this may mean for people who do teleconferencing with video and can see one another as they talk, but we don't yet have enough data on that to come to any firm conclusions about it.)

Knowing this gives you crucial strategic information about the method you choose for carrying on language interactions when you suspect that you might be dealing with a Phony Leveler.* You are better off having your conversation by telephone. The telephone will keep you from being influenced by the perfect match between the Phony Leveler's speech and body language, which is so convincing when you can see it. And it will keep the Phony Leveler from being able to observe your reactions and make constant linguistic adjustments based on them. That gives you a much better chance in such an interaction than you would have if it were carried on face-to-face.

Used properly, this is a major advantage for the listener. But unless you listen with your full attention, the advantage will be canceled. Half-listening on the phone, while you read a magazine or watch television or daydream, will be no more effective than half-listening in person. Listen carefully for changes in the pitch of the voice; research indicates that when people are trying to deliberately deceive others the pitch of their voices will rise.

This does not mean that high pitch is a clue to the detection of deception, however. A rise in pitch in the speech of someone who has a naturally low-pitched voice is just as significant. It is the deviation from the pitch level established by the speaker as the norm—the *mismatch* between what has been established as typical and the higher pitch—that warns the listener to be wary.

Your best strategy as a listener, when you're not certain that you can trust a speaker with whom you plan some sort of interaction, is to have at least one discussion of the issues by telephone before you have the face-to-face meeting. That will give you an opportunity to listen for deception in a situation where the speaker can't use body language and associated feedback skills as tools to influence your perceptions.

---

*Phony Leveler means "liar."

Questions: The Community of Writers

1. What reasons does Elgin say the "research studies" give for its being easier to detect lies over the telephone than face to face? Do these reasons make sense to you? Do they make sense to Elgin?
2. How does Elgin suggest using telephone conversations for detecting lies? Do you agree that liars need body language feedback to make their lies work?
3. Have you ever been told a lie over the telephone? Could you tell that it was a lie? If so, what gave the lie away?
4. Discuss other unusual uses for the telephone.
5. What is the tone of this essay? What is Elgin's attitude toward her subject? How does she use the first-person pronoun *I*?

Analysis

To present her method of detecting lies, Elgin must first refute the commonly held belief that it's easier to lie over the telephone. Based on your own experience as a liar or as someone being lied to, can you say that Elgin convinced you that the telephone is better for detecting lies than telling them?

Purpose and Development

What is Elgin's purpose for writing? As the author of a book entitled *The Last Word on the Gentle Art of Verbal Self-Defense,* Elgin is probably not primarily interested in telling you about research on lying or even telling you that it's harder to lie over the telephone than face to face. Her purpose is more likely evidenced in the last four paragraphs: to *instruct* you and other readers on how to avoid being deceived. Her *thesis* is probably something like this: "To tell whether or not someone is lying to you, concentrate on the quality of that person's voice over the telephone." She develops her essay with three main parts:

1. Refuting the commonly held myth "If you want to lie you're better off doing it on the phone" (paragraphs 1 and 2),
2. Presenting new evidence (paragraphs 3 and 4),
3. Instructing the reader on how to use this evidence to handle a difficult problem (paragraphs 5 through 9).

Exercise: The Community of Writers

Make a body language observation. Go to a public place where you can observe two people in conversation but not overhear them. Concentrate on one person, taking notes on how that person uses his or her hands, face, and other body parts in the act of communication—both as speaker and as listener. Without knowing what has been said, write your perceptions about the attitude and purpose of that person in carrying on the conversation. Then meet with your group to discuss what things our body language tells others.

Writing

Elgin recommends telephoning in some cases rather than conversing face to face. In this writing, think about the advantages of face-to-face conversation, and then write an essay that presents this kind of dialogue in preference to another kind. Like Elgin on using the telephone for exposing liars, select particular circumstances for the conversation you're recommending. First state the advantages as you see them; then write two or three paragraphs that advise readers how to carry on this kind of conversation to achieve their purposes. Use Elgin's essay as a guide. In writing, you will have two aims: to persuade your readers of a special use for face-to-face conversation and to instruct them on the best way to have this conversation.

USING HUMOR IN INSTRUCTION

Instructions are usually serious and straightforward; they tell readers how to do something that needs to be done. But, like many other kinds of writing, instructions are often used simply for the sake of humor. Such essays are more common in popular magazines than in academic writing, but sometimes in English classes students have an opportunity to try writing just for fun.

Writing of this kind *looks like* instructions but usually has an unexpected subject, such as "how to roast a hot dog over an electric range," or takes an exaggerated viewpoint. Readers know from the beginning that this is not serious fare, and they accept it for what it is. (Writing for entertainment is covered in more detail in Chapter 8.)

Reading

Tom Bodett is a humorist who lives in Homer, Alaska. You may have heard his commentaries on public radio's "All Things Considered" or his ads on commercial radio. Whether you live in Alaska or not, you will probably appreciate the humor of "Ditch Diving," because it's more about drivers than about a particular locality. Bodett tells you how to be good at a "sport" not often described. The essay has three parts, plus introduction and conclusion—in other words, it is a variation of the standard five-paragraph essay. Try reading it as a caricature of both winter sports and the essay form.

Ditch Diving

Tom Bodett

The graceful winter sports of skiing, skating, and dog-sledding get a lot of attention around Alaska, but there's another winter activity that nobody seems to appreciate for the art that it actually is—ditch diving. We all become practitioners of this art at one time or another, but none of us seems to hold proper appreciation of what we're doing, perhaps because its aesthetics have never been fully defined for us. Allow me.

To dive you need a road, a ditch, some snow on the ground, and any licensed highway vehicle or its equivalent. Nothing else is required, but a good freezing rain will speed up the process.

The art of the dive is in the elegance with which you perform three distinct actions. The first one, of course, is that you and your car *leave the roadway*. Not so fast there, hotshot—remember, this is an art. The manner and theme of your dive are weighed heavily in this maneuver.

For instance, the "I wasn't looking and drove into the ditch" dive will gain you nothing with the critics. The "He wasn't looking and drove me into the ditch" dive is slightly better, but lacks character. The "It sucked me into the ditch" dive shows real imagination, and the "We spun around three times, hit the ditch going backwards, and thought we were all going to die" dive will earn you credits for sheer drama. The "I drove in the ditch rather than slide past the school bus" dive might win the humanitarian award, but only if you can explain to the police why you were going that fast in the first place.

Okay, so now you've left the road. Your second challenge is to *place the vehicle*. Any dumbbell can put a car in a ditch, but it takes an artist to put one there with panache. The overall appeal of your installation is gauged by how much the traffic slows down to gawk at it.

Nosed-in within ten degrees of level won't even turn a head. Burrowed into a snowbank with one door buried shut is better, and if you're actually caught in the act of climbing out a window, you're really getting somewhere. Letting your car sit overnight so the snowplows can bury it is a good way of gaining points with the morning commuter traffic. Any wheel left visibly off the ground is good for fifty points each, with a hundred-point bonus for all four. Caution: Only master-class ditch divers should endeavor to achieve this bonus positioning.

All right, there you are, nicely featured alongside your favorite roadway. The third part of your mission is to *ask for assistance*. Simply walking to a phone and calling a tow truck will prove you a piker and not an artist at all. Hit the showers, friend. The grace and creativity you display getting back on the road must at least equal those you employed while leaving it.

Let's say you were forced into the ditch and are neatly enshrined with   8
one rear wheel off the ground and the hood buried in the berm. Wait until any truck bigger than your bathroom happens along and start walking in that direction with a pronounced limp. Look angry but not defeated, as if you'd walk all night to find the guy who ran you off the road. Look the driver in the eye like it would have been him if he'd been there sooner. This is a risky move, but it's been proven effective. If the truck has personalized license plates and lights mounted all over it, you're in good shape. Those guys love to show how hard their trucks can pull on things.

I prefer, however, to rely on the softer side of human nature. Addle-   9
brained people hold a special place in our hearts, and I like to play on these protective instincts. If my car is buried beyond hope, I'll display my tongue in the corner of my mouth and begin frantically digging at the snow drift with my hands until someone stops to talk me out of it. If my hands get cold and still nobody's stopped, I'll crawl head-first into the hole I've dug and flail my legs around like I was thrown clear of the wreck. This works every time and has won me many a ditch-diving exhibition over the years.

I certainly hope I've enlarged your appreciation of this undervalued   10
creative medium. I warn against exercising this art to excess, but when the opportunity arises, remember: Hit 'er hard, sink 'er deep, get 'er out, and please, dive carefully.

Questions: The Community of Writers

1. Outlining a completed essay is sometimes useful for analyzing the essay's structure (see Chapter 5). Working with other members of your group, analyze Bodett's essay by making an outline that accounts for the subject of each paragraph and shows how each paragraph relates to others.

2. Would you agree that Bodett's primary purpose is *not* to instruct? Explain your answer.

3. Discuss at what point the essay began to be funny for each of you.

4. What are Bodett's techniques for achieving humor? Note vocabulary, word combinations (like "buried in the berm," paragraph 8), and selection of details.

5. In what ways does Bodett make fun of sports?

Analysis

Bodett uses instruction as a means of entertainment. He sets the tone in his first paragraph, where he compares ditch diving to other "graceful winter sports" and requests permission to define its "aesthetics" for you.

Later he calls you, the reader, "hotshot" and implies that you're about to plunge headlong into the nearest ditch before you read the remainder of the instructions. Bodett achieves humor with vocabulary, selection of details, and a familiar essay form.

Development

"Ditch Diving" is easily recognizable as a variation of the standard five-paragraph essay. In fact, the exaggeration of the form may be considered part of the humor by establishing expectations of what is to follow. Bodett's introduction sets the tone, subject, and circumstance; then a short paragraph, as in any good how-to essay, lists the necessary "equipment." A clear-cut *thesis* is expressed at the beginning of paragraph 3: "The art of the dive is in the elegance with which you perform three distinct actions." This thesis sentence establishes reader expectations by stating the subject ("the art of the dive"), making an assertion about the subject ("is in the elegance with which you perform"), and declaring the method of development ("three distinct actions").

Bodett then discusses the "three distinct actions" that are part of ditch diving:

1. The dive, paragraphs 3 and 4;
2. The style of placement, paragraphs 5 and 6;
3. The call for help, paragraphs 7, 8, and 9.

He concludes in the traditional five-paragraph-essay way—with a summary paragraph.

Coherence

Not only is Bodett's essay tightly structured but it is closely *coherent* as well. Each time Bodett shifts from one aspect of ditch diving to another, he clearly signals the reader:

> Okay, so now you've left the road. Your second challenge is to *place the vehicle.* (paragraph 5)

> All right, there you are, nicely featured alongside your favorite roadway. The third part of your mission is to *ask for assistance.* (paragraph 7)

What he does in these *transitional sentences* is summarize what he just said and then proceed with the next step. This is an obvious way of achieving coherence, but it does ensure that the reader will keep up.

Exercise: The Exploring Writer

Brainstorm (see Chapter 3) a list of things people do not *want to do, things like burning toast or getting a sunburn (see topics under the following writing assignment). Then select one topic that interests you and explore some ways of achieving the undesired end. Try clustering (see Chapter 3) to discover some "steps" or "actions" in achieving the end.*

Writing

Write a humorous how-to essay on something that people do *not* want to do, using the topic you explored in the preceding exercise. Adopt a basic essay form with five divisions represented by five or more paragraphs. Introduce your essay in such a way that your reader does *not* take it seriously, list any equipment that is necessary, state your thesis explicitly, and use an obvious means of coherence. Explore your own experience for possible topics, but here are a few ideas to get you started:

- How to burn toast
- How to get a sunburn
- How to spill ketchup on the front of your favorite shirt
- How to lock yourself out of your room, house, or car

As already noted, Bodett's thesis sentence is transparent, being absolutely explicit on how he will develop his essay. While not all thesis sentences have all three parts, for this assignment try including in your thesis all of them—subject, assertion, and method of development.

CHAPTER 14

Writing to Praise or Censure

What we admire we praise, and when we praise, advance it into notice.

—William Cowper

"Out on the ski slopes they look like hand grenades." This statement describing people wearing down-filled coats is not complimentary. Rather, it seems to express disapproval, to censure those people who don't dress and act as Tom Wolfe would have them do, as you will see if you read the remainder of his short piece "The Down-Filled People" later in this chapter. Wolfe's censuring paragraph is paired with one of praise by Gretel Ehrlich. She stands up for cowboys.

Praising and **censuring** are common purposes for writing. Letters of recommendation are a familiar example of praise; in them the writer recounts the positive features of the candidate, downplaying or ignoring the negative. Other examples are obituaries, eulogies, commencement addresses, award ceremonies, "roastings," and book or movie reviews. Censuring comes often in the form of newspaper or television exposés: the governor is charged with spending millions on the official residence, a television evangelist with immoral acts, a senator with accepting illegal gifts. Whatever form this purpose for writing takes, praise or censure, the writer says something about an individual or a group of people—sometimes good things, sometimes bad.

Audience and Writer

When people write to praise or censure, they often have a specific audience in mind, as with commencement addresses, award ceremonies, and "roastings," but at other times the audience is more general, as with obituaries and reviews—which usually appear in newspapers for a wide audience. In some cases, the audience is the subject of the praise or censure. For example, the primary audience of a commencement address is usually the graduating class, and the class is also the subject of that address; at award ceremonies and "roastings," the subject is present and part of the audience but not necessarily the primary audience. With reviews, who the audience is depends on the reviewer's purpose. Reviews usually praise or censure someone's *work*, not the person; reviews of plays, movies, or books concern the work of playwrights, directors, authors, and so on. When you review a classmate's writing, you praise or criticize the work, not the person. (Reviews, or "critiques," are covered in Chapter 15.)

For an audience to willingly accept what a writer says about an individual or an individual's work, the writer must usually establish his or her credentials. If, for example, you as a writer are censuring the makers of a movie, you need to establish at least that you've seen the movie, better yet, that you've seen similar movies—and, even better, that you've written other movie reviews. You may at times have heard speakers or have read writers praising or censuring someone without taking the trouble to learn some basic information—a commencement speaker, for example, who knows nothing about the graduating class, or the reviewer of a concert who doesn't understand the type of music being performed. To be credible in your praise or censure, you must know the subject.

Secondary Purposes

Writing to praise or censure usually has more than one purpose. In a "roasting," the purpose would be not only to praise or censure but to entertain as well; in a eulogy, to inform readers about a death; in a review, possibly to inform, possibly to persuade. In one of the essays in this chapter, British writer W. J. Weatherby's eulogy in praise of Marilyn Monroe, a secondary purpose is to inform readers about the troubled life of this film star. In Wolfe's "Down-Filled People," a purpose in addition to censure might be to persuade people not to try to dress and act and talk like all the people they associate with.

Descriptive Details

In essays that praise or censure, you'll find a great deal of description, an abundance of specific details. You can't very well praise a classmate's rough draft without some details illustrating how the essay is effectively written. You can't censure a movie or book unless you give some specific details showing how bad it was. Here are some examples of concrete descriptive phrases taken from essays in this chapter:

> No matter what she said, those teeth never parted. I suspected they were dentures because they were too straight and too white.

> If a cow is stuck in a boghole, he [a cowboy] throws a loop around her neck, takes his dally (a half hitch around the saddle horn), and pulls her out with horsepower.

> The woman sat on a straw bale next to the short, thin man and listened to his story.

Since the subject matter of each of these essays is a person or group of people and the purpose to acquaint the reader with those people, the specific details are essential to the essays. There must be enough of them, and they must be clear and vivid.

Praise and censure also make abundant use of the connotations that words acquire—not just their dictionary meanings but the emotional reactions they conjure up as well. Compare "great sensitivity" with "exaggerated frenzy." Don't you react much more favorably to the first phrase? And compare "too straight and too white" with "straight and white." Can teeth be "too straight" and "too white"? Even though straightness and whiteness are to be prized in teeth, perfection in this context is a negative quality.

In addition to the writings by Wolfe, Ehrlich, and Weatherby, this chapter has a student essay that is clearly censure, "The Poetry of Sister Margarete." The additional readings at the end of the chapter are further examples of praise.

REGISTERING DISAPPROVAL

Expressions of disapproval are common, especially around election time. Sometimes, in fact, political mudslinging is so dominant that issues are never addressed. On most days, you can pick up the newspaper and find articles that censure someone. Closer to your own experience, you may be able to remember from childhood or your teen years times when you either criticized someone not in your group or received such criticism. When people register disapproval, it is sometimes done in a kindly manner and sometimes not.

Reading

"The Poetry of Sister Margarete" is a student essay in which the writer registers her disapproval of a teacher she once had in school. You have probably wanted to do the same thing at times—and maybe even did, at least orally with your friends and classmates. Susan Wollack criticizes her teacher and tells why she disliked her, filling in with enough details that you can imagine yourself in the classroom.

The Poetry of Sister Margarete

Susan Wollack

I didn't like her. She was pretty enough and petite, but she seemed 1 to lack confidence and overcompensated by trying to make everyone around her feel inadequate. Sometimes I would just stare at her, and my attention would be drawn to her mouth as she talked with her teeth clenched together. No matter what she said, those teeth never parted. I suspected they were dentures because they were too straight and too white. I mused that perhaps she had used Super Poli-Grip in confusion one morning and they were permanently fused together. It was easy to tune her out when she spoke, particularly when her face became a blur except for those teeth.

Her cool green eyes were like ice. They were not unattractive eyes: 2 rather they seemed to hold no intensity, no emotion. I don't recall if she ever really looked at anyone directly; surely there was nothing of recognition in those eyes.

Her face was, I must admit, flawless and perfectly proportioned with 3 her high colorless cheekbones. There was something restrictive about her monotoned voice, which went on and on. Those generous lips would move in exaggerated frenzy to ensure that each word, each syllable and vowel, was pronounced correctly and with emphasis, as if all words held equal importance.

I sat in the front of Sister Margarete's class, so there was no mistaking 4 her presence, no hiding behind anyone so that she could not catch me dozing off in the stuffy classroom of the Old Building, which had been constructed in the 1800s. Did she know that opening a window might tend to refresh us at the last hour of the day's classes? Was she so insecure that she feared that the appearance of an inquisitive fly might distract one of us from her lecture?

I played games with her sometimes. I acquired a manner of napping 5 with my eyes open in a state of semi-comatose whereby I could hear what she was saying as if she were in my dream. I delighted in the knowledge that she would lose control if she caught anyone napping in her class and hoped that she would try to embarrass me by calling on me to repeat what she had said. It happened only once, and the look of surprise at my unabridged recollection of her words was pleasure enough for me to last a lifetime.

"Tell me the three ingredients necessary in writing a short story, Miss Thompson," Sister Margarete hissed, the emphasis on "Miss." 6

"Beginning, plot, and ending," I recited. "In each short story there should contain a dramatic episode which leads to a crucial moment between two characters or a character and a situation. If the characters have been developed properly and the meaning of the story is clear, the story should be remembered by the reader." 7

"And how do you make certain that the reader will remember the story, Miss Thompson?" she shot back with the velocity of a returned Ping-Pong ball. 8

"It is important that the story is complete so that the reader doesn't feel cheated at any point and the dramatic portion of the story holds the reader's interest. It is mandatory that the characters are described so that they are understood and the reader may identify with the characters to a certain extent." 9

Sister Margarete's lips tightened in an almost invisible line beneath her nose. I knew she hated me for that instant; I'm sure she had to say many Our Fathers and Hail Marys that night during prayertime in order to reinstate herself in God's grace. 10

Following my glorious triumph, her patterned pace among the desks quickened; I could see her black shrouded figure out of the corner of my eye as she glided to the back of the room to continue her discussion of English. 11

It was difficult for us seniors to concentrate on our studies as thoughts of graduation and illusions about life after graduation consumed our attention. Although it was already May, the heat was still pouring in from the four-foot-high heating vents which stretched along the entire length of the windowed wall. We knew that beyond the confines of the high ornamental ceiling and the surgery-blue walls, a real world was at work. We belonged out there, not in this prison. Sister Margarete's words fell on deaf ears, but still she persisted in her torturous ordeal of teaching. 12

We were studying poetry the day she lost the restricted discipline that she usually controlled our minds with during last period. She stopped in mid-sentence, which had the effect of abruptly shaking me awake for the first time that semester. The unnerving persistence of silence caused shivers to travel up and down my freckled arms, and the last ten minutes of class dragged on. Even the hands of the IBM clock appeared to be stuck. I nearly felt sorry for her as she tried unsuccessfully to recapture her unattentive audience. 13

The next day we reported to a classroom empty of our instructor. On 14
the chalkboard was a hastily scrawled message written in blue chalk. Blue,
mind you! We were to report to the hill overlooking the river.

"I wonder what is going on?" we discussed in hushed tones as we 15
gathered in front of the chalkboard. With much confusion and some
amount of disbelief, we picked up our books and filed out in orderly
fashion.

There she was, sprawled out on the grass, her black veil billowing in 16
the early May breeze. Her white face betrayed a hint of pinkness as she
beckoned us to come closer. Dutifully, we surrounded her and cautiously
sat in ladylike fashion on our notebooks.

"Tell me what you see and hear and smell and taste," she began. 17
"Look around you and become one with your environment. Now this
(and she spread her hands like the Lady of Fatima) is poetry! This is
poetry." And she smiled.

The days which followed were full of the usual anticipation of the 18
ending of the school year. Yearbooks were signed, party plans were
discussed, and caps and gowns were issued. Even though Sister Margarete
never again deterred from her lesson plan for the remainder of the year,
we all knew that there was more to her than she probably wanted us to
be aware of. I still did not like her, but I was pleased that now I felt I knew
her.

Questions: The Community of Writers

1. How does Wollack (Miss Thompson) show her disapproval of Sister
   Margarete's classroom manner?

2. In the "napping" incident, Wollack reveals as much about her own character
   as about Sister Margarete's. Characterize Sister Margarete; then characterize
   Miss Thompson. What character features do they share?

3. Discuss reasons for the writer's dislike of Sister Margarete. Did it have anything to do with her own character?

4. What does Wollack do to make it possible for you to visualize Sister Margarete?
   Name some of the specific words and sentences that help you to see her as
   the writer does.

5. In addition to describing teeth that were "too straight and too white," in what
   ways does Wollack use connotations of words to influence the reader to see
   Sister Margarete as she does?

Analysis

Wollack's *thesis* evolves from a simple opening statement, "I didn't like
her," to a fuller understanding at the end: "I still did not like her, but I
was pleased that now I felt I knew her." The simple statement is enough
at the beginning for the reader to know how to approach this essay, but

it would not be enough at the end after the reader has experienced two incidents that reveal the complexities of the relationship between the characters. The fuller, evolved thesis at the end complements the simple one at the beginning.

Development

Wollack develops her essay through **exemplification**—specific examples of her relationship with Sister Margarete. In the first example, the napping incident, she describes a demanding, vindictive, authoritarian interrogator, and in the second she seems not quite sure how to present the puzzling contrast of the poetic nun. In both cases, we are seeing Sister Margarete exclusively through the eyes of a student who admittedly didn't like her. We can therefore learn as much about the writer as we can about the subject of the writing. Why would a student "play games" by pretending to be napping and hoping the teacher would pounce on her so she could delight in the thought of the teacher losing control?

Style and Tone

Wollack uses concrete words and phrases to describe Sister Margarete: "cool green eyes were like ice," "high colorless cheekbones," "lips tightened in an almost invisible line beneath her nose," "black veil billowing in the early May breeze." Words like these make it possible for readers to see the subject as the writer does. Words with negative connotations influence the reader too. For example, Wollack describes Sister Margarete's eyes as cool like "ice" rather than comparing them to something admirable like a "refreshing brook" or an "aspen woods in summer." Wollack says that Sister Margarete "Controlled our minds"; a less negative statement might have been "kept order in the classroom."

Wollack's *tone* in the essay is objective and impertinent at the same time. She accomplishes this dichotomy by writing from a mature stance while capturing the attitude of the teen. She "recites" in a singsong manner the teacher's definition of a short story. She recalls that the teacher "hissed" her question. She describes the school as a "prison" and a "torturous ordeal." The "triumph" over Sister Margarete was "glorious." From the adult perspective, Wollack looks back on the experience and tries to understand why it was important to her, why she wants to write about it now. She sees the teen "playing games," and she acknowledges that after the poetry incident, even though she still disliked the teacher, she knew the complexities of the nun's personality better. This increased understanding makes it possible for Wollack to conclude by expanding her thesis.

Exercise: The Exploring Writer

Think about someone you disliked while growing up. Brainstorm (see Chapter 3) and list as many words as you can think of to describe that person. Force yourself to make a list of at least thirty items.

Writing

Write an essay that describes someone you disliked while growing up. Use your brainstormed list from the preceding exercise to help you get started. Then freewrite (see Chapter 3) one encounter between you and that person that can reveal the antipathy between you. Use direct quotations if they're appropriate. Try to recall a second encounter that reveals another aspect of your relationship, and jot down some notes about what you remember. When you begin to draft, you can organize and pull together the various aspects of your prewriting. Your thesis, like Wollack's, may be a simple statement at the beginning, but as you reveal the complexities of your feelings, your thesis will need to evolve into a statement that reflects those complexities. Coming to this understanding of your own feelings toward the individual you describe may be the most difficult part of this writing. You will need to know why you dislike the person and why that dislike is still important to you.

In your descriptions, use concrete words and phrases—words that name things we can identify with our senses, like "blue chalk" "black veil," and "eyes like ice." As you revise (and this may mean going back over your writing at any time), ask yourself questions like these:

1. Am I using concrete words and phrases?
2. Is my tone too harshly critical?
3. What am I revealing about myself in this essay?
4. Is my thesis stated clearly?
5. Do my descriptions and my incidents develop my thesis as I have expressed it?
6. Does my evolved thesis reflect those descriptions and incidents?

PRAISING OR CENSURING A GROUP OF PEOPLE

You have no doubt encountered the censure or praise of groups of people. Perhaps a newspaper article praised rescuers after a natural disaster or contributors to a charitable fund. Letters to the editor of your campus newspaper might censure students who participated in a protest demonstration—or praise them. In a history class, you might read the "Letter from Birmingham Jail," in which Martin Luther King, Jr., censures eight clergymen who had censured him for his actions on civil rights. Other people have written letters or articles of censure directed at groups who take a position on civil rights, women's rights, abortion, capital punishment, and so on. You find letters or articles of praise on the opposite side.

People sometimes praise or censure groups of people not for their positions but for what they are. In argument, censure of this type is called *ad hominem,* an attack on the person or persons instead of on the issue. When either praise or censure is directed at a *group* of people, it usually addresses a single issue—for example, their taste in music, the way they dress, the way they talk, and so on. When praise or censure extends beyond the single issue, it is usually a result of *stereotyping,* or treating all members of the group as if they have all the same characteristics. An extreme example would be censuring someone's politics because of his or her taste in music.

Readings

The two next readings are short pieces, one censuring a group of people, the other praising a group of people. As you read the two, think about the purposes of their writers. What does Tom Wolfe want you to think as you read "The Down-Filled People"? What effect does his brief essay have on you? How does Gretel Ehrlich want you to think about cowboys? Does reading her paragraph change your attitudes? What does "The Down-Filled People" tell you about Wolfe? What does "Cowboys" tell you about Ehrlich?

The Down-Filled People

Tom Wolfe

They wear down-filled coats in public. Out on the ski slopes they look like hand grenades. They have "audio systems" in their homes and know the names of hit albums. They drive two-door cars with instrument panels like an F-16's. They like High-Tech furniture, track lighting, glass, and brass. They actually go to plays in New York and follow professional sports. The down-filled men wear turtleneck sweaters and Gucci belts and loafers and cover their ears with their hair. The down-filled women still wear cowl-necked sweaters and carry Louis Vuitton handbags. The down-filled people strip wood and have interior walls removed. They put on old clothes before the workmen come over. In the summer they like cabins on fresh water and they go hiking. They regard *Saturday Night Live* and Steve Martin as funny. They say "I hear you," meaning "I understand what you're saying." They say "Really," meaning "That's right." When down-filled strangers are at a loss for words, they talk about real-estate prices.

Cowboys

Gretel Ehrlich

A cowboy is someone who loves his work. Since the hours are long—ten to fifteen hours a day—and the pay is $30 he has to. What's required of him is an odd mixture of physical vigor and maternalism. His part of the beef-raising industry is to birth and nurture calves and take care of their mothers. For the most part his work is done on horseback and in a lifetime he sees and comes to know more animals than people. The iconic myth surrounding him is built on American notions of heroism: the index of a man's value as measured in physical courage. Such ideas have perverted manliness into a self-absorbed race for cheap thrills. In a rancher's world, courage has less to do with facing danger than with acting spontaneously—usually on behalf of an animal or another rider. If a cow is stuck in a boghole he throws a loop around her neck, takes his dally (a half hitch around the saddle horn), and pulls her out with horsepower. If a calf is born sick, he may take her home, warm her in front of the kitchen fire, and massage her legs until dawn. One friend, whose favorite horse was trying to swim a lake with hobbles on, dove under water and cut her legs loose with a knife, then swam her to shore, his arm around her neck lifeguard-style, and saved her from drowning. Because these incidents are usually linked to someone or something outside himself, the westerner's courage is selfless, a form of compassion.

Questions: The Community of Writers

1. Which paragraph do you prefer, Wolfe's or Ehrlich's? Analyze why you prefer one over the other.
2. What purposes other than to praise or to censure might these writers have had?
3. Compare the tone of Wolfe's paragraph with that of Ehrlich's.

Analysis

Wolfe and Ehrlich each describe a group of people, Wolfe to censure and Ehrlich to praise. Wolfe's piece is complete as it is, Ehrlich's excerpted from a book called *The Solace of Open Spaces*.

Tone

In writing, *tone* is something like the sound of your voice. When you speak, sometimes you sound angry, sometimes gentle, sometimes whining, sometimes sarcastic, and so on. All these tones are truly *your* voice. Even though your voice has its own characteristics, you adjust it to the speaking situation—your subject matter, your audience, your relationship to that subject matter and that audience, and your purpose in speaking. Your tone reflects your attitude. How do you read Wolfe's tone? Is it cynical? sarcastic? demeaning? He probably makes you want to find ways of convincing yourself you're not one of *them,* the down-filled people. Ehrlich's tone is different. In using words like *selfless* and *compassion,* she shows an attitude toward her subject that is caring and respectful.

Multiple Purposes

We've already established that Wolfe's primary purpose is to *censure,* Ehrlich's to *praise.* Ehrlich might also want to *inform*—to set the reader straight on what cowboys and their work are really like, to denounce the "iconic myth," or popular image, of rugged, trigger-happy men who, if they're lucky, ride off into the sunset at the end of the movie. Ehrlich shows that, though they are rugged, cowboys are also tender and compassionate. Wolfe probably has other purposes too—entertainment, or *persuasion.* Do you suppose he wants to make you feel guilty if you wear a down-filled coat or enjoy Steve Martin's humor? Or might he have another point?

Exercises: The Exploring Writer

Writers achieve particular tones by conscious use of words and details. In these exercises, you can gain insight into how tone is achieved.

1. Keeping the subject matter of down-filled people, rewrite Wolfe's paragraph to make its tone more like that of Ehrlich's paragraphs. You might begin with a sentence like this:

   They wear down-filled coats to protect themselves from the bitter cold winds that blow in the harsh winters of the North Country.

   Continue rewriting until you have a paragraph that praises instead of censures.

2. Keeping the subject matter of cowboys, rewrite Ehrlich's paragraph to make its tone more like that of Wolfe's paragraphs. You might begin with a sentence like this:

A cowboy is someone who is obsessively infatuated with his work.

Continue rewriting until you have a paragraph that censures instead of praises.

Writing

Select a group of people that you're familiar with, and describe them twice—once to censure and once to praise, writing one short essay for each purpose. For each writing, adjust your tone and your treatment of details.

Here are some possible topics:

- Customers
- Drivers
- Joggers
- Dog owners
- Cat owners

PRAISING THE DEAD

Some people think that any mention of death is morbid. Other people are preoccupied with death. Between these two poles is a healthy acceptance of the fact that life comes to an end. Pets die, grandparents die, parents die, friends die. Somehow the survivors need to accept the fact and go on living.

It is common to praise people who have died. *Obituaries,* a staple of daily newspapers, mainly give the facts about a person's life. *Eulogies* are often spoken at funerals, extolling the virtues of the deceased and overlooking shortcomings.

Reading

Since the death of Marilyn Monroe in 1962, much has been written about her life as sex symbol and movie star of the fifties. The essay that follows was written shortly after her suicide and appeared in the London *Manchester Guardian.* Its writer, W. J. Weatherby, praises the film star and mourns her passing. As you read it you will encounter some unaccustomed features of style, in part because the article was written in the United Kingdom, in part because it was written nearly thirty years ago.

Marilyn Monroe

W. J. Weatherby

Marilyn Monroe's death at thirty-six is a real Hollywood tragedy,   1
unlike most of those the film studios try to fabricate. It seems now to have
the same inevitability as Hemingway's a year earlier, and just as death by
shotgun gave his life a classical finish, so an overdose of sleeping tablets
seems now the only ending we might have expected to this tragedy. The
heartrending fact is that many of the friends of this doomed film actress
have been afraid for over a year that something like this might happen
and nobody seemed able to help. At least the gossip columnists who had
begun to ask "What will Marilyn do when she's middle-aged?" have their
answer now.

It is questions like that which help to explain the tragedy of Marilyn   2
Monroe, for it is much more than an unhappy young actress who has
died. News of her death will probably reach more people than that of
anyone for years because she was an international symbol and, as such,
had to bear an appalling burden. This was worth while in the early days
of her career, for it was only as a sexual figure, everyone's dream blonde,
the world's cover girl, that she could reach stardom in Hollywood. But
when she had got there and then had a chance to act rather than pose,
she found herself still trapped as a symbol. To understand what this
meant you had to go out in public with her. Even a casual drink meant
being under the spotlight; to go to a theatre could cause a riot. It was as
though she had to help to pay for every sexual frustration in our kind of
society, every neurotic that clutches at such symbols and has helped to
create the Hollywood dream factory. In that sense many people had a
hand in her death.

Many a Hollywood actress would have revelled in this role, but it was   3
the elusiveness of Monroe—a quality that reflected the shy, sensitive side
of her—that helped to make her into this sex symbol, probably the most
famous ever created by Hollywood with the possible exception of
Valentino (and in the last year or two of his short life he felt the pressures
on him to be unbearable). But she was a Hollywood symbol in a much
deeper sense than that, for she was born in Los Angeles in the Hollywood
shadow, her mother worked—as a negative cutter—in one of the film
studios, and she grew up brainwashed, as it were, into the belief that the
dream of every girl should be to become another Mary Pickford. And she
had plenty of outside incentives to escape into such a dream world. Her
parents were not married and she never knew her father; when she was
a child her mother had to go into a mental hospital, and she had to go
the round of foster parents. It is hardly surprising that she got married
as soon as she could—at sixteen—though she was divorced by the time
she was twenty. By that time she had seen more of the grey side of life

than most people ever do. What an escape to a Technicolor view Hollywood must have seemed. She had committed herself to it long before she ever learnt the price she would have to pay.

Model, bit player, larger rôles, fledgling star—it was a fairly conventional route to Hollywood fame. But she had a quality that made her stand out in the crowds of equally pretty girls competing for attention and this gave her the advantage she needed—though it was years before anyone ever suggested that quality might be talent. Those years—when she was a star but not credited with anything but symbolism—were the critical ones. By the time she had a chance to make use of the acting lessons she took so earnestly, it was as if her experiences had split her personality too much for her ever to feel secure. She had a distressing habit of discarding people after a few years as if she could never count on loyalty or trust. It seems true to say that she was by then a schizophrenic—part of her still the innocent girl next door in her Hollywood dreamland and part of her the career woman, the woman who had decided to accept life as a jungle and live in it on those terms. This was revealed in her attitude towards her position as sex symbol. There were times when she seemed to enjoy it, to make the most use of it she could, and then suddenly you would see the other side of her which had to pay for it—the very attractive mixed-up girl clinging to her pills and her psychoanalysis.

There was, of course, a history of mental disorder on her mother's side—both maternal grandparents were committed to mental institutions and an uncle killed himself, Some will try to explain away her problems in terms of heredity. But the influence of this on Marilyn Monroe was rather a fear that she might have inherited something than any sign that she had. But an unbalanced personality like that should never have had to endure the pressures firstly of her rootless early years, an introduction to sex as a child that amounted to rape, and then the Hollywood symbolism. She must in fact have been an extraordinarily strong person to have pulled herself up from such beginnings and to have endured so long and to have continued to grow as an actress.

It was Sybil Thorndike who made the shrewdest remark about her talent when they worked together (with Sir Laurence Olivier as fellow star) in *The Prince and the Showgirl.* "You watch her do it in the studio and it doesn't seem much—too vague and underplayed," said Dame Sybil. "But when you see it on the screen, her performance seems perfect. She really opens out. It is as if she were made for the cinema." The same elusive quality that made her such an extraordinary sex symbol also gave her a unique comic style. By *The Seven Year Itch* and *Some Like It Hot,* she had developed a style of her own, a style of wit and charm that was laced together with a very effective off-beat timing that could sometimes madden directors in rehearsals. In her last film, *The Misfits,* written by her third husband, Arthur Miller, she tried to adapt this technique to serious drama and, though not wholly successful, gave a performance in much greater depth than ever before. She had hoped it would justify all her claims to being a serious actress, not a symbol, and so she took the poorish reviews very much to heart.

"Heart" is the word that comes to mind in trying to describe her as a   7 person—she perhaps responded and felt too much for her own good. When she was truly herself she could have an afternoon spoilt by seeing a passing cruelty—such as a fish caught and dangling—that the rest of us would hardly notice. Her marriages reflected her. Not for her those inbred Hollywood marriages. She married Joe Di Maggio, the baseball star and American hero, and then, going to the opposite extreme of American heroes—from sport to the intellectuals—she married Arthur Miller. This seemed to be the perfect complementary marriage—the marriage of beauty and brains. It bewildered those who thought of her as a sex symbol. It delighted those who knew the real Marilyn Monroe—as it saddened them when the marriage broke up over a year ago. Norma Jean Baker (her mother's name was Baker and her father's Mortenson and so she took her mother's) then seemed alone in the crowd—the crowd of Hollywood symbols (and symbols of our society?) bearing down on her.

Questions: The Community of Writers

1. What does the essay say about Weatherby's attitude toward Monroe?

2. Are there any clues in the essay to the writer's being a man or a woman? Does it matter whether you know?

3. What does Weatherby tell you about Monroe? Discuss some facts that interest each of you.

Analysis

In this brief biography, Weatherby eulogizes Marilyn Monroe by praising her virtues and excusing her weaknesses. After an introductory paragraph, Weatherby seems to answer a series of questions:

1. Who was Marilyn Monroe?
2. Why did she become a film star?
3. How did she become a sex symbol?
4. How did being a symbol affect her?
5. Was she a good actress?
6. Why did she die?

The thesis that ties all the questions together is stated in the second paragraph: "for it is much more than an unhappy young actress who has died." Questions are often helpful in deciding what to write, and when we have a controlling idea—a thesis—to hold the answers together, questions can assist us in organizing our writing.

Purpose

Weatherby praises Monroe so that readers may know this film star better and appreciate her talents. Eulogies are usually written at or near the time of someone's death, but when they are written and published they reach not only the present audience but future audiences as well. Even though this essay was written in 1962, it still praises Monroe. Eulogies, perhaps more than most other types of praise, are meant for future audiences as well as present ones.

Weatherby seems to have known Monroe well. It is not clear, however, whether this knowledge was personal or drawn from public documents. The details are treated sensitively and sympathetically. Reread the essay and mark any words that indicate the writer's attitude toward the subject—words like *tragedy* and *heartrending*.

Exercise: The Exploring Writer

Writing style is a little different in the United Kingdom than it is in the United States. Spelling is one readily apparent difference. Read Weatherby's essay again and note all the words that are spelled differently than they would be in an American newspaper, like theatre, *for instance.*

Writing

Write a eulogy, an essay in praise of someone who has died, someone you knew either publicly or privately. Concentrate on the good that person did while alive, the positive effects of that person's life, perhaps why that person was the kind of person he or she was. To help you discover ideas and arrange them, you might think of questions like those answered in the Monroe essay. Don't focus on the person's death; write about his or her life—in a positive way. For another example of a eulogy, refer to the one about James Baldwin at the end of this chapter.

PRAISING THE LIVING

Perhaps we don't praise the living often enough. How often do we miss opportunities to say something really complimentary—sincerely—to someone we know? We probably *think* thoughts like "Didn't he do a great job of washing that car?" or "That was a really great idea" but let the opportunity for saying those words of praise pass by. Sometimes parents forget to praise their children, and sometimes children overlook opportunities to compliment their parents. Teachers may forget to praise their students, and students may forget to praise their teachers. We all know people who are doing ordinary things extraordinarily well or extraordinary things that we never expected to see done. These are things to praise.

Praise, unlike flattery, is genuine. Praise takes note of a person's accomplishments or admirable characteristics, and it is not given on a quid pro quo basis; praise doesn't expect something in return.

ADDITIONAL READINGS FOR DISCUSSION

Reading

The recommendations that follow are copies of real summary remarks on a standard placement service recommendation form; only the names have been changed. As you read, determine which letter is the most likely to get a job for the applicant.

Two Letters of Recommendation

I. Toni Prescott is one of the best students I've known. She is studious, bright, well-read. She meets challenges with enthusiasm; she deliberately takes on the more difficult project. She seems to know her abilities and capabilities and appears unwilling to engage in either the easy task or the one that demands more time or ability than she can bring to it. She doesn't hesitate to speak out when something needs to be said, yet she is a highly personable young woman, pleasant and cheerful with a positive nature.

I know Toni from two of my classes: Freshman Composition and The Rhetoric of Writing. In both classes her work was superior in every way. She participated intelligently and readily in class discussions, attended class regularly, and completed her work on time. Her writing was always well done, revealing the work of a thoughtful mind engaged in a particular problem.

I am confident that Toni Prescott will succeed in whatever endeavor she takes on.

II. Ted Grange was an asset to my business writing class: always sitting in the front row, always prepared, always a willing participant in class discussions, always alert. I was glad to have him there. He worked well in various modes: individually, in groups, or in pairs.

Questions: The Community of Writers

1. Which of the two recommendations would you rather have in your file?

2. Writers of letters of recommendation try to be as positive as they can about the person recommended. Prospective employers, by contrast, try to read between the lines to determine what has not been said. Reread Ted Grange's letter and try to discover what the writer is *not* saying.

3. Toni Prescott's letter is highly positive. Can you detect any omissions that a prospective employer or graduate school might wonder about?

Reading

The following short piece is an obituary from *The New York Times*. Notice that it states facts, not opinions, about Margie Inman; it neither praises nor censures.

Margie Inman Is Dead at Seventy-six; Walked on Wings of Planes

Davie, Fla., October 7 [1987] (AP)—Margie Lynn Inman, who performed on the wings of airplanes in her youth and later battled local officials for the right to live in a lean-to with a menagerie of pets, has died at the age of seventy-six. 1

Mrs. Inman died September 30, the day she was to have entered a nursing home after weeks of failing health, friends said. 2

She performed as a wing-walker in the 1920s and '30s in the Inman Brothers Flying Circus with her husband, Rolley Roger Inman, a pilot. He died in a crash in 1944. 3

Mrs. Inman began living in a lean-to on her property near Fort Lauderdale after her house collapsed in 1976. She spent much of her Social Security checks on food for her pet cats, dogs, and rats, which she called "my kids." Her disputes with neighbors and local officials over the animals ended when local people pitched in to help her clean up the property. 4

Questions: The Community of Writers

1. In chronological order, list the facts this obituary gives about Margie Inman.

2. What do these facts tell you about Inman's character?

3. Compare this obituary with the eulogy for James Baldwin that follows.

4. How could you use the facts in this obituary to write a eulogy praising Margie Inman?

Reading

As opposed to the factual, objective obituary, a eulogy includes praise of the virtues and accomplishments of the deceased person. An obituary is a brief biography, a eulogy an article of praise. A eulogy includes biographical information, but from the writer's point of view. The following eulogy for James Baldwin appeared in *The New York Times* on December 1, 1987. As you read it, try to distinguish between facts and the writer's opinions.

James Baldwin, the Writer, Dies in France at Sixty-three

Lee Daniels

James Baldwin, whose passionate, intensely personal essays in the 1950's and 60's on racial discrimination in America helped break down the nation's color barrier, died of cancer last night at his home in southern France. He was sixty-three years old.   1

Mr. Baldwin's brother, David, was with him at his home in St. Paul de Vence when he died, according to Cynthia Packard, a friend and former assistant to the author, who said she talked with David by telephone last night. Mr. Baldwin died at 6:15 P.M. New York time, according to Ms. Packard.   2

At least in the early years of his career, Mr. Baldwin saw himself primarily as a novelist. But it is his essays that arguably constitute his most substantial contribution to literature.   3

Mr. Baldwin published his three most important collections of essays—*Notes of a Native Son* (1955), *Nobody Knows My Name* (1961), and *The Fire Next Time* (1963)—during the years when the civil-rights movement was exploding across the American South.   4

Some critics said his language was sometimes too elliptical, his indictments sometimes too sweeping. But then Mr. Baldwin's prose, with its apocalyptic tone—a legacy of his early exposure to religious fundamentalism—and its passionate yet distanced sense of advocacy, seemed perfect for a period in which blacks in the South lived under continual threat of racial violence and in which civil-rights workers often faced brutal beatings and even death.   5

Mr. Baldwin had moved to France in the late 1940's to escape what he felt was the stifling racial bigotry of America.   6

Nonetheless, although France remained his permanent residence, Mr. Baldwin in later years described himself as a "commuter" rather than an expatriate.   7

"Only white Americans can consider themselves to be expatriates," he said. "Once I found myself on the other side of the ocean, I could see   8 where I came from very clearly, and I could see that I carried myself, which is my home, with me. You can never escape that. I am the grandson of a slave, and I am a writer. I must deal with both."

Despite the prominent role he played in the civil-rights movement in the early 1960's—not only in writing about race relations but in organizing various sorts of protest actions—Mr. Baldwin always rejected the labels of "leader" or "spokesman." 9

Instead, he described himself as one whose mission was to "bear witness to the truth." 10

"A spokesman assumes that he is speaking for others," he told Julius Lester, a faculty colleague at the University of Massachusetts at Amherst, in an interview in *The New York Times Book Review* in 1984. "I never assumed that I could. What I tried to do, or to interpret and make clear, was that no society can smash the social contract and be exempt from the consequences, and the consequences are chaos for everybody in the society." 11

This serene sense of independence was not simply a political stance, but an intrinsic part of Mr. Baldwin's personality. 12

"I was a maverick, a maverick in the sense that I depended on neither the white world nor the black world," he told Mr. Lester. "That was the only way I could've played it. I would've been broken otherwise. I had to say, 'A curse on both your houses.' The fact that I went to Europe so early is probably what saved me. It gave me another touchstone—myself." 13

Mr. Baldwin did not limit his "bearing witness" to racial matters. He opposed American military involvement in Vietnam as early as 1963, and in the early 1960's he began to criticize discrimination against homosexuals. 14

Mr. Baldwin's literary achievements and his activism made him a world figure and to the end of his life brought him many honors in this country and abroad. The French Government made him a Commander of the Legion of Honor in 1986. 15

Yet, Mr. Baldwin was also clearly disappointed that, despite his undeniable powers as an essayist, his novels and plays drew decidedly mixed reviews. 16

Go Tell It on the Mountain, his first book and first novel, published in 1953, was widely praised. Partly autobiographical, it tells of a poor boy growing up in Harlem in the 1930's under the tyranny of his father, an autocratic preacher who hated his son. 17

Mr. Baldwin said in 1985 that in many ways the book remained the keystone of his career. 18

"*Mountain* is the book I had to write if I was ever going to write anything else," he remarked. "I had to deal with what hurt me most. I had to deal, above all, with my father. He was my model. I learned a lot from him. Nobody's ever frightened me since." 19

Questions: The Community of Writers

1. This eulogy is considerably longer than the obituary for Margie Inman. What kinds of facts does the eulogy contain that the obituary does not?

2. What words tell you Daniels admires Baldwin?

3. Name some of Baldwin's accomplishments that Daniels seems to admire.

4. Daniels quotes Baldwin on writing and on his civil rights activities. Which of these quotations most significantly tells you what kind of man Baldwin was?

5. Compare the Baldwin eulogy with the Marilyn Monroe eulogy by W. J. Weatherby. What kinds of information do you learn about the subjects? What attitudes do the writers have toward their subjects?

CHAPTER 15

Writing to Summarize and Respond

> *Writing is thinking made tangible, thinking that can be examined because it is "on the page" and not all "in the head," invisibly floating around.*
>
> —*John T. Gage*

Much academic writing is done in response to other writing: You summarize an assigned chapter, analyze and respond to an article or book you have read, answer an essay question on an exam, or summarize and paraphrase sources for a research paper. In each case, you show what you know about a subject. To get along in school, you must be able to summarize and respond and to ask and answer questions. There are good reasons why such seemingly routine writing is so common in instruction. First, writing of this type assists learning: By summarizing and responding and by asking and answering questions, you read more actively and understand more thoroughly. Moreover, such writing is common in the professional world—summarizing reports, answering inquiries, responding to a colleague's proposal, and so on—so this kind of school writing not only assists learning but also prepares you for writing on the job.

This nuts-and-bolts academic writing has much in common with other kinds of writing. Even though emphasis is usually on the subject, you still must consider the entire rhetorical situation: the purpose, the audience, and your own role—as well as the subject. The purpose of academic writing is usually to show that you understand the material or to assist you in learning and examining the material. By covering the material thoroughly and thoughtfully, you establish your role as a knowledgeable student.

The audience is almost always the teacher and must be considered when you write. Be sure you know what your teacher is looking for, and don't expect one teacher to have the same expectations as another. (This, again, is good preparation for the job, because supervisors don't all have the same expectations either.) Teachers have individual preferences, and emphasis varies too by course and discipline. Some teachers will not accept writing that contains first-person pronouns (*I, we*); others want you to use *I* and *we,* but they reject passive verbs. Documentation of references varies by discipline, so it's not wise to question a teacher who requests MLA (Modern Language Association) even though another teacher has specified APA (American Psychological Association) or something else. If your teacher asks for a particular format, follow that format, even if you think you know a better one. If the assignment specifies a length, observe that length (within reason); longer is not necessarily better, and shorter may be a result of your having overlooked something important. In school as in the world of work, there are many appropriate forms for writing, and their appropriateness is determined by the situation.

The opening pages of this chapter will discuss and illustrate three kinds of school writing: summaries and abstracts, essay examinations, and critiques and responses. This discussion will be followed by several examples of student and professional writing, concluding with a variety of writing assignments. Exercises will be interspersed throughout.

SUMMARIES AND ABSTRACTS

Summarizing is an essential skill for academic writing. You summarize lab or lecture notes, reading assignments, articles you've read in your library research, and individual or group activities. Summaries often accompany other kinds of writing: essay exams, critiques, and reports, to name a few. This discussion concentrates on summaries that may stand alone or be a part of a larger piece of writing.

A **summary** presents in condensed form the substance of another piece of writing. It usually begins with a *nutshell* statement, or overall summary, then presents the essential points of the writing, not necessarily in the same order as in the original. Related to the summary is the **abstract,** or précis, which gives a concentrated essence of the larger piece of writing. An abstract generally covers the main points in the same order as the original and usually does not begin with a nutshell statement. An abstract is usually written from the same perspective as the original, whereas a summary is often written from the perspective of the summarizer.

Compare these brief examples of a summary and an abstract of Judith Viorst's essay "Friends, Good Friends—and Such Good Friends" in Chapter 12:

Summary

In "Friends, Good Friends—and Such Good Friends," Judith Viorst classifies women's friends according to varieties and levels of intensity. She identifies eight varieties of friends: convenience friends, special-interest friends, historical friends, crossroads friends, cross-generational friends; part-of-a-couple friends, men who are friends, and best of friends. Only best of friends share total trust and love and are completely honest with one another. All other varieties of friendships are at a lower level of intensity.

Abstract

The varieties of women's friendships are convenience friends, special interest friends, historical friends, crossroads friends, cross-generational friends, part-of-a-couple friends, men who are friends, and best of friends. Only best of friends, at the highest level of intimacy, share total trust and love and are completely honest with one another.
—Judith Viorst, "Friends, Good Friends—and Such Good Friends"

The *summary* is written from the perspective of the summarizer: "Judith Viorst classifies," "she identifies." It tells what Viorst *does,* as well as what she *says.* The *abstract,* by contrast, does not refer to Viorst; rather it reports the content of the essay as if Viorst were writing. It reports only what she *says.* Also, the summary begins with a nutshell statement, whereas the abstract begins with Viorst's first classification, the varieties of friendships. Notice too that the nutshell statement of the summary names the source of the summary but that such information is outside the abstract. (An alternative in the abstract would be to include the source in parentheses at the end of the first sentence, as in the example on page 415.) Neither summary nor abstract expresses opinions of the summarizer or abstractor.

Whether you write a summary or an abstract depends on your purpose. As a part of a larger piece of writing, such as a report, summary is more effective. One reason is that stylistically a summary is written from the same point of view as the rest of the report, and as the writer you can select as much information from the original as you need for your purpose. Abstracts usually stand alone—at the beginning of a report, for example—to give readers a quick view of the entire entity. If you were writing a report, then, you would *summarize* other pieces of writing that support your points and provide the necessary background, and you would *abstract* your own report. Both summaries and abstracts should accurately reflect the meaning and sense of the original. Summaries, however, can be more selective, concentrating on particular aspects of the original rather than giving a complete overview.

Conciseness

One feature that summaries and abstracts share is *conciseness*. They omit details, descriptions, illustrations, and sometimes explanations. Although some of these features may have attracted your attention while you read the original, you should omit them from your summary unless they are essential support for the main point. In striving for conciseness, be especially careful, when revising, to cut all unnecessary words. Notice how the second sentence below says the same as the first but in fewer words:

> *Wordy.* Almost all of the reading that people do is a single form of information processing that takes place when the person's mind selects information from the page and then stores it away in the mind; in the process, the mind relates the new information to what the reader already knows.

> *Concise.* Most reading is a form of information processing in which the mind selects and stores new information, relating it to what the reader already knows.

Among the ways in which summaries and abstracts gain conciseness, coordination and subordination are the most useful. *Coordination* relates two or more ideas at an equivalent level, often using the coordinating conjunctions *(and, but, or, nor, so, for, yet);* commas separate items in a series, and semicolons sometimes separate equivalent clauses. Here is an example of coordination in the Viorst summary: "Only best of friends *share total trust and love and are completely honest with one another."* This sentence has two coordinate pairs. "Trust" and "love" combine the ideas of what best of friends share, and "share total trust and love" and "are completely honest with one another" make assertions about the same subject, "best of friends," joined by the connecting *and.* The summary paragraph has other instances of coordination; notice especially the parallel list of varieties of friends.

Subordination relates ideas that are not equivalent, making one idea dependent on another. The following sentence from the Viorst abstract illustrates how an idea comprising several sentences in the original is compressed into a subordinate portion of a sentence: "Only best of friends, *at the highest level of intimacy,* share total trust and love and are completely honest with one another." In this sentence, "at the highest level of intimacy" has become a modifying phrase set off by commas.

Other common elements of subordination are participial phrases and subordinate clauses. **Participial phrases** are useful for making writing more concise. "Relating it to what the reader already knows" is a participial phrase in the sample sentence above, condensing the longer "The mind relates it to what the reader already knows." **Subordinate clauses** are of two types: those that begin with conjunctions such as *because, when, after, if,* and *although,* and those that begin with relative pronouns such as *that, who,* and *which.* Here are two examples that show how these clauses contribute toward conciseness:

> *Wordy.* Computer information is stored on small disks. As a result of this compact storage, the information may be kept longer than paper records.
>
> *Concise.* Because computer information is stored on small disks, it may be kept longer than paper records.

> *Wordy.* Much of the data gained from telephone monitoring is hearsay. This hearsay information could be potentially damaging.
>
> *Concise.* Much of the data gained from telephone monitoring is hearsay, which could be potentially damaging.

For additional discussions, see Style in the handbook at the end of this book.

Writing a Summary

To write a summary, you must understand the original and your purpose for summarizing it. Sometimes we summarize a complete article and sometimes only a portion of it. The instructions here are for summarizing an entire article, though you can apply them also to summarizing a portion of an article or a book.

1. *Read.* First read the article through to get its gist; make no notes or marks at this time. After you've finished reading, write in a single sentence what you think is the main point. Then look for a thesis sentence in the article and underline it; does it agree with your nutshell statement? Make sure your view of the article isn't slanted toward a minor point.

2. *Underline.* Once you have a clear understanding of the writer's main point, read the article again, this time underlining major points in support of the thesis and transitional phrases that show how parts are connected. Omit specific details, examples, description, and unnecessary explanations. Go through the article another time if necessary.

3. *Write.* Now begin writing your summary. Open with your nutshell statement, including a reference to the writer and the title of the article (as in the preceding Viorst summary). Then write your summary, using your underlines as a guide, writing with your own words and phrases, not those of the original. This is one place where many people go wrong in

summarizing: they lift a series of sentences or phrases from the original instead of writing in their own words. In a summary you can use phrases like "Viorst classifies" and "Burgess describes," but be careful not to include your own opinions or thoughts. For now, don't worry about length; you can cut later. To conclude, make a final statement that reflects the significance of the article from the original writer's view.

4. *Revise.* Read your summary for accuracy; if it doesn't make the same point as the article or if you have omitted something important, revise. Read your summary for coherence; if it doesn't read smoothly, with all parts clearly related, refer to the transitional phrases you marked in the original and use them or others to relate your sentences. Read for length; if your summary is more than one-fourth the length of the original, start cutting, using subordination and coordination to compress ideas, deleting all repetitious and unnecessary words. Write another draft and ask someone else to read it for sense and comprehensibility. Ask for criticism and accept it graciously.

5. *Edit.* Correct spelling and punctuation errors, and look for other errors, especially those that you know commonly occur in your writing. Write a clean draft and proofread for copying errors.

Writing an Abstract

Writing an abstract is similar to writing a summary. First read the article for comprehension, then begin marking key points. In writing your abstract, you may find it helpful to draft a summary sentence for *each paragraph,* combining all your single sentences with appropriate connecting words or phrases. Try to end up with a shortened version of the larger whole, omitting nothing important. To keep your abstract in the original writer's perspective, avoid words such as "Viorst classifies" and "Burgess describes"; refer to the preceding Viorst abstract and the abstract that follows.

Sample Summary and Abstract

(original essay appears in Chapter 11)

Summary

In "Senses," physicist George R. Harrison discusses a physical feature common to all people, their senses, focusing primarily on one of the senses, vision, to show the complexity of all of them. The eye, he says, is so sensitive that it can detect light from a candle at a distance of many miles. Yet the eye is limited as to the wavelengths of light it can see, and the lens frequently becomes deformed and clouded, further limiting vision. Science, however, has invented ways for extending the capabilities of the eye by means of magnification and other methods. As with vision, science has extended and transformed the capabilities of the other senses, expanding the understanding and use of the external world.

Abstract

The five senses enable people to connect with the world (George R. Harrison, "Senses"). Each sense, however, has more than one type, so that the number is actually more than five. The eye has four types of vision. Extremely sensitive retinas receive light through a focusing lens that is adjusted by a diaphragm called a pupil and is shielded by a shutter called an eyelid. Vision is supported by the other senses, allowing a person to sense an object by touching it, hearing it, smelling it, or tasting it. The eye is limited by the wavelengths it can detect and its own deformities. Scientists, however, have invented means for overcoming these limitations, utilizing magnification and other methods. Scientists have also extended and transformed the capabilities of the other senses, enabling people to better know their world.

Exercise: The Community of Writers

Contrast the summary and abstract of Harrison's "Senses." Find examples of how they differ in perspective and content and how they both use coordination and subordination. Refer to the original essay in Chapter 11.

ESSAY EXAMINATIONS

Essay examinations are a specialized type of writing for which answering questions is the major purpose. You write an essay exam to show what you know about a given subject, not to inform someone about that subject. It goes without saying, then, that all the advice in the world about writing the exam is of no use unless you know the material.

Preparing for an Essay Exam

Cramming for an essay exam will help only if you have kept up with your reading and notetaking throughout the term. Students who are experienced at preparing for college essay exams advise that you do your assigned readings when you receive them and review your notes frequently. For particularly difficult material, they recommend summarizing both your reading and your notes. (For tips on efficient notetaking, refer to Chapter 9, where experienced student notetakers share some advice.)

Close to exam time, review your notes and summaries. Study your assigned readings, picking up points that your teacher covered in class. To aid your review, use one of the methods of invention described in Chapter 3. The classical probes might be especially helpful, or the more visually oriented cubing. Apply them to your subject: identify it, classify it, compare and contrast it, analyze it, use it, give some examples of it. Aim for a broad understanding of the subject, but also try to file away a number of important details; it is mainly for drilling yourself on details that cramming can be useful. To aid your broad understanding, write some questions that you could expect to find on the exam and then work out answers to them.

And get sleep, and food. A rested and alert mind is better able to meet the challenge of utilizing your knowledge of the subject in response to a difficult question. Then go to class confident that, even though you may not know all the material, you know enough of it to answer most questions.

Writing an Essay Exam

Don't panic. Take time to read the exam carefully and to determine what is required. If you have several questions to answer, budget your time according to the percentage points of the questions—half of your time for a 50 percent question, for example. Allow some time for planning, most of it for writing, and some for revising and editing. Here are some tips for managing the condensed writing process.

1. *Prewrite.* Read each question carefully, letting key words tell you what the examiner expects. If the question asks for causes and effects, for example, a listing of examples will not do the job. If it asks for a list, several paragraphs on one item will not do. Study the following key words and see how they differ in their instructions.

Key Words in Essay Exams

Analyze	Separate the subject into its parts and examine each part, relating each to the whole and to each of the others.
Compare	Show similarities.
Contrast	Show differences.
Define	Give the meaning, keeping in mind the class of the thing and how it differs from others in its class.
Describe	Give physical and factual characteristics.
Discuss	Give a complete and detailed answer by examining, analyzing, defining, and doing anything else appropriate.

Enumerate	List concisely the points required.
Evaluate	Make a judgment, either pro or con, and explain your decision.
Explain	State the how and why, clarifying and interpreting the material.
Illustrate	Explain or clarify by means of examples or diagrams.
Outline	In a concise and systematic form, give main ideas and important supporting material.
Summarize	Give the material in a condensed form.

If you draw a blank while reading the question, try stimulating your mind with the same invention questions you used for studying (classical probes or cubing, for example). Jot down ideas as they come to you. Even though you think you will remember your good ideas, they probably will slip away. Make a list of topics you want to cover. But work quickly. Spend about 10 percent of your time prewriting, or planning.

2. *Write.* When you're ready to start writing, use your prewriting list as a guide. Make your first sentence a rephrasing of the question: "Explain several ways in which science and transportation are related" becomes "Science and transportation are related in several ways." This sentence then serves as your thesis. Write an organized essay, the method of organization determined by the key words of the question, and include specific details wherever appropriate. Make sure that you don't get off your topic and that all your paragraphs follow your thesis. Save about 10 percent of your time for revising and editing.

3. *Revise.* An essay exam is necessarily a quick process. But it's amazing how much better you can make your essay in only a few minutes. There are mainly two things you must do in revision:

    a. Make sure that all your paragraphs relate to your thesis and that the end of your essay makes the same point you began with. If one of your paragraphs is widely off the topic, you may have to scrap it; *X* it out and write "omit" in the margin. But the paragraph may be salvageable—by adding a topic sentence that relates the paragraph to your thesis and/or by rewriting your thesis to encompass the paragraph. If your ending makes a point different from your thesis, adjust either the end or the thesis. It's extremely important that all parts of your essay be related. Don't skip this step in your revision.

    b. Check for errors and make corrections. Look for the kinds of errors you commonly make, because you probably have some in this essay. Cross out the error, and make the correction neatly above it or in the margin. Don't write over the error, because your correction will probably be illegible. Editing for errors is extremely important. It can make the difference of a full letter grade or more.

One final point: for writing essay exams, use a pen, not a pencil. Penciled writing may seem easier to erase and revise, but it usually ends up smudged. Even under the best of conditions, penciled writing is harder on the reader's eyes; ink is brighter and clearer.

Exercise: The Community of Writers

With your classmates, discuss the following essay question to determine (1) what it is asking, (2) what the first sentence of an answer might be, and (3) how the answer should be developed. Use blank spaces for items of subject matter you don't know.

Analyze three forms of fossil fuel, comparing their methods of formation, the extent of existing resources, their roles in meeting energy needs, and their roles in future energy needs.

CRITIQUES AND RESPONSES

A **critique** is an analysis of and a commentary on another piece of writing; it generally focuses on technique as well as on content. A **response** is a commentary on another piece of writing that may address technique but generally focuses on content. Book reviews are a type of critique, analyzing both technique and content; book reports tend to be in the response category, focusing more on content. In school writing, both critiques and responses are common. Their subject matter is another piece of writing; they usually show that the writer has read and understood the work. Both critique and response may include summary, analysis, interpretation, and evaluation. Expressions of personal disagreement are uncommon in critiques but may be found in responses, especially if the writer can back them with evidence.

Whether you write a critique or a response depends on your purpose. It's important that you find out precisely what the assignment calls for. A literature assignment may ask you to write a critique of a short story, and a freshman composition assignment may request a response to a newspaper commentary. The critique assignment calls for analysis of the story's theme, form, characters, and plot, plus interpretation and evaluation. The response may look for analysis of the purpose in the newspaper commentary and evaluation of the validity of the writer's position plus a statement of supporting or opposing position. But critiques are not restricted to literature, nor responses to newspaper commentaries. If you were to write a critique of a newspaper commentary, you would address such rhetorical concerns as the writer's sense of audience, attainment of purpose, authority on the subject, and accuracy and sufficiency of evidence. And if you were to write a response to a short story, you would react particularly to the content, perhaps relating it to your own experience, perhaps noting the validity of the theme and realism of the characters, perhaps commenting on the value of the piece. As you can see from the sample essays in this chapter, the distinction between critique and response is frequently blurred.

Writing a Critique or a Response

To write either a critique or a response, you must be informed, having carefully read the piece in question and having enough experience in the subject matter to determine your criteria for analysis. The process is in some ways similar to summarizing, since both deal with another piece of writing, but the critique and response require the additional measures of analyzing and evaluating.

1. *Read.* First read the piece through just for enjoyment and information, making no notes. Read actively and thoughtfully, seeking answers for such active reading questions as "What is the writer's main point?" and "What is the writer's attitude toward the subject?" (Refer to the Questions for Active Reading on page 6.) Upon completing your first reading, write a brief reaction.

2. *Analyze.* Read a second time, trying to be more thorough, more analytical of both detail and technique, making notes now and underlining details you may want to remember. Try to answer the Questions for Active Reading on page 6, plus the Questions about Audience for Reading on page 27. To heighten your understanding of the piece, apply one of the invention methods in Chapter 3—the classical probes, the journalist's questions, or cubing, perhaps. Determine your specific criteria for analysis, such as

    a. Does the writer appear to be informed about the subject?

    b. Is the writer's purpose clear?

    c. Does the writer appear to understand the audience?

    d. Does the writer's technique support the purpose?

        (1) How is the essay organized?

        (2) How are the major points supported—with examples, observations, quotations, statistics, or something else?

(3) What are the major features of sentence structure in terms of length, pattern, and variety?

(4) How does word choice relate to subject, purpose, and audience?

(5) What is the tone of the piece? Is the tone consistent?

If necessary for an informed reaction, read related materials.

3. *Evaluate.* Step back from your work now to allow yourself time and space to ruminate on what your analysis means, how the piece you've read relates to your knowledge and experience, how you feel about what the writer has said. Determine your specific criteria for evaluation based on your purpose. You might consider these questions:

a. How informed is the writer about the subject?

b. Is the writing appropriate for the time and environment when the piece was written?

c. How competent is the writer's technique?

d. How well does this piece compare with similar writings?

e. How thoroughly does the writer support major points?

Write another reaction, and discuss your thoughts with other people. Make a working outline of how you plan to proceed. Here's a basic structure that you might be able to adapt:

a. Introduction: title, author, preliminary information, summary, your main point

b. Background: facts, issues, biographical data, essential definitions

c. Strengths of the writing

d. Weaknesses of the writing

e. Conclusion: final statement reinforcing your main point

4. *Write.* Using your notes, reactions, and working outline, begin writing a draft. As in summary, begin with an introduction that states your thesis and names the author and title of the work you are writing about. Here's an example:

> During my twenty-five years of experiencing life, I don't believe a woman has ever called me for a date. Granted, the first fifteen years or so didn't really hold much potential, but the last ten have failed to produce also. Therefore, I've decided that women just don't call men for dates. In his July 31, 1989, *Newsweek* "My Turn" article, "Women, Pick Up the Phone!" Gerald Nachman has come to the same conclusion.
>
> —Peter E. Dulgar

In this introduction to an essay that appears later in this chapter, Dulgar names the author, the title, the magazine, and the point of his response—that he and Nachman agree.

As with most of your writing, in your critique or response you have a thesis and major supporting points. These points may be derived from your *analysis* of the work and the writer's credentials for writing it, your *interpretation* of the work and its implications, and your *evaluation* of its worth.

Paraphrase

Critiquing and responding require abundant support from the work itself. This support may be in the form of summary, paraphrase, and direct quotation. The amount of *summary* you use depends on whether your reader has read the work or not; the more familiar the reader, the less summary needed. **Paraphrase** is similar to summary in that you put the writer's ideas in your words. It is different from summary in that it is not condensed; sometimes it is even longer than the original. Observe in the following paraphrase how the original idea is stated in different words:

Original

Certainly more people fail because they do not know the requirements of being an employee than because they do not adequately possess the skills of their trade; the higher you climb the ladder, the more you get into administrative or executive work, the greater the emphasis on ability to work within the organization rather than on technical competence or professional knowledge.

—Peter F. Drucker, "How College Helps You to Be an Employee"

Paraphrase

According to Peter F. Drucker, an essential job requirement is knowing how to be an employee. More people fail on the job, he says, because they don't know how to work within a firm's organization than because they don't have the skills or knowledge of their trade. The ability to work in the employ of a company becomes especially necessary as one is promoted to higher levels of responsibility.

Paraphrase and summary sometimes utilize **direct quotation.** Quotation ought to be used sparingly, but it is appropriate when the writer's words are especially apt, highly technical, or strongly opinionated. In the preceding paraphrased sentence, for example, Drucker uses the term "being an employee" in a specialized way, and the paraphrase might quote it directly, as this revision of the first sentence illustrates:

According to Peter F. Drucker, knowing "the requirements of being an employee" is essential to job success.

When you are critiquing or responding, the bulk of your support will come from the piece you are working with. Naming it once at the beginning may be the only documentation necessary, with the possibility of a work cited notation at the end. If you refer to other sources, however, you will need to name them. A works cited entry includes the name of the author, the title of the work, and publishing information. Here are two examples:

Drucker, Peter F. "How College Helps You to Be an Employee." *Fortune* May 1952: 74–76.

Brill, Steven. *The Teamsters.* New York: Simon, 1978.

(See also how Tracy Wallack, on page 435, documents the article she responds to and the additional article she has read. Other examples can be found in Chapter 16.)

Throughout your writing, strike a tone that is courteous, serious, and respectful. Avoid sarcasm, anger, and pathos. Think of yourself as a scholar writing for other scholars.

5. *Revise.* Read your draft through to remind yourself of what you have said. Then reread the work you are responding to; you may discover new ideas or find out you were off base somewhere along the line. Ask yourself if you need new evidence. Check your tone for an appropriate level of courtesy and seriousness. See if you use present tense verbs whenever you refer to what the other writer says, for example:

Gore *writes* with urgency and conviction as he *explains* the consequences of our misuse of the earth.

But use past tense verbs when referring to your own reading:

Its content *was* so riveting that it *brought* me to deep introspection as I *read.*

Have a friend read your essay and give you critical comments: Is it clear? Is it fair? Is it accurate?

6. *Edit.* As with all your writing, look for the kinds of errors that you normally make and correct them. Write a clean draft and proofread for copying errors.

Exercise: The Exploring Writer

Write a paraphrase of the following paragraph. Keep the meaning the same, but use your own words and writing style. Begin by referring to the author. Since this is not a summary, your paraphrase may be as long as, or longer than, the original.

Generally speaking, people can be grouped into two categories of intellectual preference. The first group prefers explorations which require a precision of logical processes. These are the people who become interested in the natural sciences and mathematics. They do not become scientists because of their education, they choose a scientific education because it gratifies their scientific mental set. The second group prefers explorations which involve the intellect in a less logically rigorous manner. These are the people who become interested in the liberal arts. They do not have a liberal arts mentality because of their education; they choose a liberal arts education because it gratifies their liberal arts mental set.

—Gary Zukav, *The Dancing Wu Li Masters*

READINGS

Reading

Critiques analyze and comment on another piece of writing, generally focusing on technique as well as on content. Responses comment on another piece of writing, generally focusing on content and how it agrees with the responder's own experience and knowledge. Given these definitions, read student writer Peter E. Dulgar's essay to determine whether it is a critique or a response to the *Newsweek* article that follows it. (The title of Nachman's article is the original; the one in parentheses is the title *Newsweek* used.)

Please . . . Pick Up the Phone!

Peter E. Dulgar

During my twenty-five years of experiencing life, I don't believe a   1
woman has ever called me for a date. Granted, the first fifteen years or so didn't really hold much potential, but the last ten have failed to produce also. Therefore, I've decided that women just don't call men for dates. In

his July 31, 1989, *Newsweek* "My Turn" article, "Women, Pick Up the Phone!," Gerald Nachman has come to the same conclusion.

It seems as if I've made an infinite number of calls to women I've been interested in—although I'm sure that in reality the total was somewhere under a million. I'm not an especially brave person when it comes to that type of thing, but I think I've been making a pretty good effort. It usually takes me about a day to work up the nerve to actually make the call. In the meantime I experience a full range of nervous side effects, from pseudo-ulcers to a peculiar arm spasm which causes me to repeatedly pick up the phone and then slowly place it back in its cradle.

Society's recipe for men must have something to do with these feelings. It's written somewhere in the rulebook for Western Civilization that men will be confident and commanding. Someone must have edited out the sections on fear and rejection.

I can't imagine true equality for women until they have experienced the thrill of making the call. This is the "final secret barrier to true equality," as Nachman describes it. Women can have all the equality they want, but they also have to assume their share of the telephone burden.

I'm sure women are afraid of rejection too, but the only way to achieve equality is to take risks. I can honestly say that calling a woman on the telephone—actually picking up the phone, dialing, and talking to a woman I don't really know—is about the riskiest thing I've done as a man.

This transition could benefit the equality of men too. We'd learn what it's like to have three grandmothers die in the same week, and our hair would have to suffer an unnatural amount of washing.

So pick up the phone, women! We'll pick it up too, and the combination should keep us all happy.

Warm Hearts, Cold Feet
(*Newsweek* title: "Women, Pick Up the Phone!")

Gerald Nachman

The last sexual taboo—yes, it appears there's still *one* left—is the brazen hussy who calls a man for a date.

High up on the roster of things that single women hate most about men they've just met is the lout who promises he'll call and doesn't. This is a horrid and thoroughly ungentlemanly practice, to be sure, but I have a radical solution that seems not to have occurred to any females I know, otherwise fearless and resourceful creatures: Why don't women call the men who don't call them?

Well, I know why and I'll tell you. It's because they can't. They're simply incapable, as in psychologically paralyzed. The very thought terrifies most women and turns their dialing fingers to stone. The females I've talked to—modern in every politically correct way—don't quite know why, either, but each concedes, almost shamefully, that she can't bring herself to do it. Few women seem not even to have seriously entertained such an outrageous concept. I would wager that Gloria Steinem has never called a man she met at a party and might like to see again.

What gives here, female persons? 4

A good deal of grief could be avoided—misunderstandings, miscal- 5 culations, and just plain misery—if women awaiting that all-important ring could pick up the phone and call the man who seems, for his own vague and snarled reasons, unable to call her. I don't mean women in relationships, or those who have been out once with someone. No, I mean telephone virgins who have never, you know, done *it:* called a guy cold.

One reason for the reluctance to use the phone, undoubtedly, is that 6 women assume that the lack of a call equals rejection. But permit me to reassure them that when a man does not call, usually it isn't that at all.

Part of the time it's sloth or indecision. Part of the time it's good old 7 cowardice. Part of the time he loses the number (never write anything crucial on a cocktail napkin). Part of the time he can't quite remember what the woman looked like and why he wanted her phone number in the first place. Part of the time he just forgets. Part of the time he lets so much time pass that he's afraid the woman will forget *him.* And yes, OK, part of the time he changes his mind.

But in this one silly little convention, it remains forever 1959. De- 8 spite a generation of feminist thought and deed, there is still this ar- chaic unwritten hush-hush ladies-and-gentlemen's agreement, this final secret barrier to true equality, this quaint vestige of dainty telephone etiquette.

Women will still ask men to dance and buy them drinks and take 9 them to dinner; they will even start conversations with them on street corners and in grocery stores; they will wink and carry on in a semi- scandalous manner at cocktail parties—but they will not telephone them first.

For whatever reasons of propriety, rather than make a direct call, a 10 woman can much more readily write a man a note, suggesting ever so nonchalantly (the deftly placed "P.S.," the coy parenthetical aside) that they "get together sometime." I have done a little research in this field (and for the purposes of today's study, specifically polled a dozen certifi- ably advanced females), and the results reveal that a woman would sooner ask a guy to marry her than telephone a man she met at dinner the night before.

Hey, I'm a sensitive guy and I'm aware of their worries, but the basic 11 reason for all the fear and trembling seems to be based on antiquated teenage training, the old mom's tale that maintains: *It's the gentleman's place to call, dear.*

Perhaps one way to get the ball rolling here is for women to ask for   12
a man's business card. Not, mind you, merely as a sly ploy, a coquettish
flutter of interest—the dropped hanky of networking—but for the
avowed purpose of actually putting it to use.

The proffered card even provides a built-in safety catch: a man who   13
hands out a card to a woman he's unsure about (or hasn't the foggiest
interest in) at least has been warned and can begin rehearsing his excuse should she indeed phone: "Of course I remember you, Gloria, and
you're *real* sweet to call, but, well, I'm sort of involved with someone right
now. . . ."

Quite apart from the very real fear of being considered a bimbo or   14
wacko, a woman understandably is hesitant to call a man due to possible
rejection, one she's brought on herself—that hollow hello at the other
end of the line, the halfheartedly cheery "*Oh . . . hi*" that men have had
to endure since the invention of the telephone. Having been the recipients of such calls, women are all too aware of the little deceptions that
can occur at the receiving end.

Female fears are not altogether groundless. Women are afraid that if   15
they do muster the courage to dial first, the man will be so mortified he
won't know what to say. Many men—indeed, even the most technically
liberated and right-thinking ones—are likely to be struck mute when
women begin calling for dates, but we'll get over it, I feel certain, and, in
no time, learn to perfect a flirtatious titter and say, "Why, hello there.
What a surprise!"

If the caller turns out to be someone the man had an inkling he just   16
might call himself but was worried that she wouldn't be interested or had
forgotten him, he is going to be one happy boy. If the hoped-for female
call fails to materialize, it's probably a good thing for men to learn what
it's like to watch a silent telephone.

I concede it's going to be rough sledding for these bold pioneer   17
women who make those first intrepid calls. And until we get used to the
idea, men are bound to sound baffled and weird for a while. Once the
concept catches on, though, as I'm sure it will with a little courage on
each side, it could revolutionize the women's movement (at least the
single women's movement) and free both sexes from the manacles of
rampant phoneism.

Questions: The Community of Writers

1. Is Dulgar's essay a critique or a response? Support your answer with evidence
   from his essay.

2. Reconstruct Dulgar's criteria for analyzing Nachman's essay.

3. What purpose does Dulgar achieve with "Please . . . Pick Up the Phone!"?
   Who do you think is his intended audience?

4. Characterize the tone of Dulgar's essay and, with a classmate, analyze the essay for details and words that contribute to that tone.

5. Notice how Dulgar cites the Nachman article. Does he give you enough information for locating the article if you needed to?

Reading

"Latin America from the Bleachers" reviews a book about baseball in Latin America. The reviewer, Tom Miller, has written books about Latin America himself. The review appeared in the *New York Times Book Review* in 1989. Read the review to determine what Miller's criteria for analysis might have been and what his evaluation of *El Béisbol* is.

Latin America from the Bleachers

Tom Miller

El Béisbol: Travels through the Pan-American Pastime.
By John Krich.
272 pp. New York: The Atlantic Monthly Press. $18.95.

One day last fall I was talking with the groundskeeper at the baseball   1
stadium in Agua Prieta, a Mexican border town joined at the navel with
Douglas, Arizona. Just beyond the ball park's outfield wall stand two
parallel fences separating the United States from Mexico. A gully runs
between the two. In the early 1970's, according to the custodian, a player
for the hometown Vaqueros named Montoya slugged a homer out of the
park all the way to the United States. "There've been five home runs into
the ditch," the fellow said, waving a hand, "but this was the only one over
the second fence. We call it 'the international home run.' "

The notion of baseball as an international sport is a comforting one;   2
it is our most benevolent, least expensive, and most accessible export. It
is neutral but not neutered, peaceful but not passive. John Krich has
taken this idea and headed south with it into Mexico, the Caribbean,
Central America, and all the way to South America to determine the
influence our benign pastime holds on Latin America.

Mr. Krich, a Sunday morning softball player, seems well suited for the   3
task. One previous book, *Music in Every Room,* gained acclaim for its
offbeat, sly travel writing. Another, *A Totally Free Man,* is an energetic
fictionalized autobiography of Fidel Castro.

In *El Beisbol,* Mr. Krich juggles no fewer than five hardballs at once—   4
the sport, the lands he visits, international relations, the players he
encounters, and himself. While it seems obvious early on that he has

difficulty keeping them all in the air simultaneously, I wanted to cheer him on anyway, all the way to Venezuela, secure in the knowledge that something new would be revealed and hopeful that his strong writing would rise to the task.

Mr. Krich becomes a wandering sports fan, free of genuine curiosity   5
and patronizing good will as he zigzags from ball park to ball park, country to country: "To carry an American passport in the Americas is to follow a trail cleared by the Marines. What a set of groundskeepers!"

Baseball, not New York schooling, taught him about countries to our   6
south. "My first inklings of our continental neighbors," Mr. Krich writes, "came from the glorified seasonal workers who traveled North following the summer game, the migrant *braceros* who helped pick crops in green outfields."

In his first stop searching for the source of these seasonal workers,   7
hoping to blend the symbolic with the historical, he finds the spot where Columbus landed in the Dominican Republic. He stays only long enough to get bored by a local freelance historian and note that the Indians Columbus encountered were probably the first to yell, "We wuz robbed!" He also begins the unfortunate habit of quoting innumerable cabdrivers.

In Puerto Rico almost everybody claims Roberto Clemente as having   8
been his closest friend, and *El Béisbol* overflows with stories about the Pittsburgh Pirate who went down with a planeload of goods destined for earthquake relief in Nicaragua on New Year's Eve, 1972. A visit to the Roberto Clemente Sports City near San Juan ends up with its director suggesting the island prepare for independence. On a ride across Puerto Rico Mr. Krich argues about the Cuban revolution with his driver. In Ponce on New Year's Eve his "search for authenticity" caves in, and he joins some youngsters on a family back porch as they watch videos of Sting. Interviews with Vic Power and Ruben Gomez, who starred with the Cleveland Indians and the New York Giants, respectively, make the author's visit to Puerto Rico worthwhile, as they describe major league racism from teammates, cops, and circumstances in the 1950's and 60's.

Back in the Dominican Republic, a "country disguised as a tryout   9
camp," he makes it to San Pedro de Marcorís, the port city whose welcoming billboard claims it has "given the most major leaguers to the world." Mr. Krich observes: "All roads in this republic lead to baseball—no matter how rutted or circuitous, no matter how many times you get stopped. . . . This is one Latin country where the suspects dragged from their homes in the dead of night are usually coveted shortstops."

The heart of *El Béisbol* thumps in Nicaragua, where the author is part   10
of a good-will group of Americans touring that beat-up country to play sloppy baseball and give away bats, balls, and gloves. The "Baseball for Peace" team plays clubs organized by a Nicaraguan farmers' union, and loses its opener, 14-0. The fields are pretty terrible; at one, oxen graze in left field, and "the right field line is your basic malarial swamp. . . .

The infield is rutted, the bases wherever we imagine." The author, who warms the bench for most of the tour, finally pinch-hits. He gets hit by a pitch just above the elbow and ends up on the disabled list. But the most profound injury to these merry peaceniks schlepping through enemy territory comes not from the pitcher's mound but from the mouth of a *campesino:* "Why do you bring us baseballs when we need spare parts for our Italian tractors? Do you know we haven't been able to lay irrigation ditches in a year? What good are bats and balls to people who are starving?" The questions go unanswered.

It is in Venezuela that Mr. Krich, by now apparently tiring of his own mission, rebounds as he searches for "the end of baseball." "Who's to say that going from ballpark to ballpark is an any less edifying form of tourism than traipsing from battlefield to battlefield, cathedral to cathedral?" he asks. Indeed, if his quest wears thin at times, it never wears out, and at Ciudad Piar, 325 miles southeast of Caracas as the ball flies, he finds what he takes to be the southernmost baseball diamond in the Americas: "I spring from the cab and do a lap around the bases. . . . I find safety tagging first, second, third, home." *El Béisbol* closes with a terrific fantasy of the baseballization of the Americas.

But something is troubling here. Throughout his journey the author never seems uncomfortable with his bare-bones Spanish, yet he mocks Spanish speakers' limited English. "Gringo," he writes, "have no fear that you can't speak the language." A disturbing pattern of superficial observation occasionally surfaces and comes across as condescension. Mr. Krich writes: "Latin culture looks remarkably, distressingly homogeneous"; and, "I still don't know what to make of this culture that is not very efficient at anything except song, color, commotion." Shallow perceptions like these tarnish what is otherwise a book of integrity and pleasure. Did the author learn nothing more from his exceptional odyssey than coups may come and coups may go, but baseball lives forever?

Questions: The Community of Writers

1. Miller opens his review with a personal experience. Do you regard this as an effective beginning? In which paragraph of his several-paragraph introduction does he state his thesis—his reaction to Krich's book? In addition to a personal experience and a statement of thesis, what does Miller include in his introduction?

2. Notice the newspaper format for a book review. Set off at the head of the review is the book title, the author's name, the number of pages, the place of publication, the publisher, and the price. How does this information differ from the last entry shown in the works cited example on page 434?

3. Discuss Miller's credentials to write an informed review of Krich's book. Locate evidence of his authority.

4. How does Miller use quotations and summaries in his review?

5. On what criteria does Miller criticize Krich's book? What does he like about the book? What does he regard as its weaknesses?

6. What is Miller's overall evaluation of the book?

Reading

In the following essay, student writer Traci Teas responds to a newspaper article by Al Sicherman, "Be Scared for Your Kids" (see Chapter 8). Teas relates Sicherman's column to her own experience.

Fatal Trip

Traci Teas

Minneapolis *Star Tribune* columnist Al Sicherman usually brightens Sunday mornings with his off-the-wall humor and witty, albeit zany, interpretations of everyday occurrences. On Sunday November 15, 1989, however, his column had a serious tone. The subject, his son's fatal LSD-induced fall, had so much emotional appeal that it made the front page as a human-interest story. Its content was so riveting that it brought me to deep introspection as I read. Though Sicherman's focus is to warn parents to "be scared for [their] kids," the column does hold a vital message for us as college students as well. This message, of the devastating effect upon unsuspecting parents when they find that their otherwise bright college student's death was due to recreational drug use, is one that should teach all of us to look at what our drug or alcohol use is doing to others.

College students before us were destroying themselves and their fruitful futures by allowing their drug use to take over, or at least hinder, their judgment. Still the message has not sunk in. Not until we are smacked in the face with an incident such as Joe Sicherman's death do we realize the impact that it would have on our parents and others who love us if we were to die because of a mind-altering substance.

Sometimes we forget why we are in college. We hurry through classes, homework, and studying to go out, socialize, and experience life independent from our parents. Though making new friends, experiencing new things, and enjoying the newfound privileges of adulthood are all a part of college life, so are advancing ourselves, excelling, and broadening our horizons. How can we do these things when we are drunk at the bar most nights of the week, stoned in class, or flying out a window on an acid trip?

Perhaps Joe Sicherman lost his focus and found himself imbibing too much in the recreational side of college life. Evidently, he was enjoying himself as a freshman at a Wisconsin college. He was an extremely funny, bright kid who, like his father, had the potential to be an excellent journalist. Humorous anecdotes displaying his sense of humor decorate his father's article. These asides make the piece all the more tragic as we realize that this humor no longer will be created to brighten the lives of those around him. Moreover, Joe's death has put a damper on his father's light, funny writing style: "I probably won't be writing a humor piece for a while," he says (10). For that reason, all of us who are fans of Sicherman are losing out because of Joe's fatal experimentation with LSD. This should make us both angry with Joe for causing so much pain in his father's life and aware of the large number of people affected by the careless death of a young adult.

Should college students never take drugs or drink alcohol? Should they always act in a mature, responsible way and constantly avoid inappropriate behavior? No. No one can put those restrictions on young adults, and we do have to learn from our mistakes. Should college students be aware of the ramifications of their behavior on others? Very definitely. That is the essence of Sicherman's message to college students. He wants us to realize that "it is parents' worst fear that something terrible will happen to their kids; it is kids' constant struggle to be free of the protection of their parents" (10).

Something terrible happened to Sicherman's child. Sicherman had dreams for his son that will never be realized. Now he has only memories of an eighteen-year-old son who thought it would be all right to try LSD, a son who plunged through a seventh-story dorm window to his death. Meanwhile, the father is left feeling guilty, as if he had somehow caused, or could have prevented, his son's death. Is that fair? Is the father to blame, or is it we, the younger, college-aged generation, who perpetuate the idea once again that it is cool to take drugs until we pass out or vomit—or die? Let's take a good, hard look at our behavior, and let's not take from our parents what they have given us, our lives.

Work Cited

Sicherman, Al. "Be Scared for Your Kids." *Star Tribune* [Minneapolis, MN] 5 Nov. 1989: A1, 10.

Questions: The Community of Writers

1. Although Teas responds mostly to the content of Sicherman's article, she does refer also to his technique, commenting, for example, on the serious tone, so unusual for Sicherman's columns. Name one or two other comments on technique.

2. What is Teas's thesis?

3. A key word in Teas's thesis is *should*. What influence does this thesis have on the tone of the essay? Characterize the tone.

4. Is Teas convincing? What else might she have done to lend additional support to her thesis?

5. Locate two instances of direct quotations followed by a parenthetical page number.

Reading

Student writer Renee Walsh writes about a short story, "I Stand Here Ironing" by Tillie Olsen. As you read, try to determine Walsh's criteria for analysis and evaluation. What is her evaluation of the story?

Ordinary Heroes

Renee Walsh

A friend of mine approached me the other day, discouraged by life's trials. She was looking for something to admire, something or someone to look up to. She said there weren't any heroes anymore. Looking around at the modern world, I had to agree with her.

Shortly thereafter, I read something that made me change my mind. That something was the story "I Stand Here Ironing" by Tillie Olsen. When I first read it, it struck so many familiar chords in my own life that I had to read it a second time. Olsen writes with an imagery and sensitivity that is rare, with an honesty that is almost never seen. Through her story she showed me that there are plenty of heroes today.

The character of the mother in the story is not the stereotypical hero that most people would think of. She has made mistakes, she has done the wrong thing, even when she knew it was wrong, and she has not always been there for herself or her children. A stereotypical hero would always do the right thing and would always, unlike real people, know what that was. In this story, however, there is considerable evidence that both mother and daughter are real heroes.

It has always been my opinion that if something feels right at the time, or if it is all you can do, then it is right. If something is true in your heart, then it will be true to your life. Critic Joanne Frye says in her essay about this story that Olsen writes of "the problems of selfhood in the modern world" (287). The character of the mother has difficulty finding and holding on to her "self" largely because of external events such as the war, the depression, and her abandonment by her husband. These are events beyond her control, yet she perseveres, and survives with her "self" intact. If this were not so, she would not be able to come to the conclusions that she does at the end of the story. She comes away from all of it a little wiser and a lot stronger. Despite the mistakes she may or may not have made, she is a hero.

In the story, the mother speaks of when she had to send her daughter Emily away to nursery school. She realized at the time that this was probably not the best thing for Emily, but at the same time she knew that it was the only thing available to her. As the mother states: "It was the only way we could be together, the only way I could hold a job" (Olsen 812). It truly was the only way, and, as one source says, "gauging the hurts and needs of one human being against the hurts and needs of another: this is the pattern of parenthood" (Frye 288). The mother balanced their need to stay together with the pain of being separated by the nursery school for part of the time, and decided to go with the latter for as long as they could. Both mother and daughter survived this pain: survival of pain is what makes heroes.

Another way the mother acts heroically is using her insight toward the end of the story to see into Emily's life and make a beneficial decision. Ann Charters says that by saying to the counselor "Let her be," when the counselor says that Emily needs help, the mother is recognizing that Emily will be better off finding her own way than receiving the type of "help" they have thus far received (141). I agree with Charters; the help they have received has seldom benefited them. The mother sets a good example of caring and understanding by letting Emily help herself without interference.

Emily has more of a parallel to the typical hero than her mother does. Emily has largely overcome the events of her past and used them to find herself and her talents. According to one source, Olsen "presents a convincing case for the influence of external circumstances on human achievement" (Yalom 59). In her character of Emily, Olsen also shows us how one particular person overcame and went beyond those circumstances.

There is a point in the story where the mother says she doesn't recognize her daughter. Emily is on stage performing, and what the mother sees is someone confident, commanding, and strong. Emily is there behind the act, and the mother should recognize her, because Emily has many of the same qualities that she herself has. Both have overcome great difficulty, both have seen and survived great pain, and both have gone beyond their external circumstances to become more than what the world would have them be.

By yesterday's standards, they are anti-heroes. They are not Superman or Superwoman, but super women. I applaud Tillie Olsen for showing us what largely goes unnoticed. Olsen shows us that we are all heroes, that we all have worth, despite hardship, despite flaws, despite mistakes. "I Stand Here Ironing" is a story which, while forcing the reader to see, also comforts and soothes. My reaction to this story cannot be totaled, because that reaction is still happening. The story has made me look inside myself and answer questions I never knew I had; it has also made me question answers I thought I was sure of. It is a story I will always think of as the one that made me look around and see people for what they really are . . . and can be.

Works Cited

Charters, Ann, William E. Sheidly, and Martha Ramsey. Instructor's Manual to Accompany *The Story and Its Writer: An Introduction to Short Fiction.* New York: St. Martin's, 1987.

Frye, Joanne S. " 'I Stand Here Ironing': Motherhood as Experience and Metaphor." *Studies in Short Fiction* 18 (Summer 1981): 287–92.

Olsen, Tillie. "I Stand Here Ironing." *The Story and Its Writer: An Introduction to Short Fiction.* Ed. Ann Charters. 2nd ed. New York: St. Martin's, 1987. 811–17.

Yalom, Marilyn, ed. *Women Writers of the West Coast: Speaking of Their Lives and Careers.* Santa Barbara: Capra, 1983.

Questions: The Community of Writers

1. What criteria does Walsh use for evaluating Olsen's story "I Stand Here Ironing"?

2. Walsh uses present tense verbs to describe actions in the story except for actions that occurred before the time of the story. How does she use verbs to describe her own reactions to the story? Locate verbs at several points in the essay. What effects do these variations in tense have on reading the essay?

3. What is Walsh's thesis? How does she develop her essay in support of her thesis?

4. Show how Walsh's conclusion reiterates and reinforces her thesis.

5. Walsh cites her sources for both paraphrase and direct quotation. Find at least one instance of each. In the parenthetical citations, she names the author when she does not name her in the sentence; locate examples that include the author's name with the page number.

Reading

This student essay responds to a *Time* magazine article by Senator Albert Gore entitled "What Is Wrong with Us?" (see Chapter 7). The writer also refers to a second article in the issue, and both articles are named in her works cited list at the end.

An Urgent Need

Tracy Wallack

The *Time* magazine article "What Is Wrong with Us?" (66) by Senator   1
Albert Gore expresses the global need for environmental action to save our earth from humanity's own destruction of it. Gore writes with ur-

gency and conviction as he explains the consequences of our misuse of the earth. Gore's active participation in making the public aware of the approaching environmental crisis is a good example of quality leadership and should be credited as such.

Gore discusses five political barriers that must be overcome before political action is warranted. He says the first barrier is psychological; people are unwilling to accept the fact that the earth, because of people, has been and continues to be severely damaged. In a desperate plea for help, Gore bluntly states, "We are at an environmental boiling point" (66). Gore feels that a change in political thinking is required to save the earth.

Skeptics like Kenneth E. F. Watt, professor of environmental studies at the University of California at Davis, call the greenhouse effect "the laugh of the century" (Sancton 28). Thomas A. Sancton, on the other hand, agrees with Senator Gore: "The skeptics could be right, but it is far too risky to do nothing while awaiting absolute proof of disaster" (28).

Other experts, such as Harvard biologist E. O. Wilson, have compared humanity's destruction of the earth to the great mass extinction of the dinosaurs (Sancton 28). Sancton, like Gore, states that humanity is in a war for survival and that this war can be won only if all nations become one and attack the problems globally (30).

Senator Gore is rightfully concerned about the earth. After all, the future generations of all living things depend for their survival on the continued health of the earth. The threat our environment is facing is real and will not go away. As Sancton says, "Now, more than ever, the world needs leaders who can inspire their fellow citizens with a fiery sense of mission, not a nationalistic or military campaign but a universal crusade to save the planet (30). Sancton's statement is true, but I also agree with Gore that resolving our environmental problems will be "unimaginably difficult" (66).

Works Cited

Gore, Albert. "What Is Wrong with Us?" *Time* 2 Jan. 1989: 66.
Sancton, Thomas A. "What on Earth Are We Doing?" *Time* 2 Jan. 1989: 24–30.

Questions: The Community of Writers

1. Direct quotations are effective in critiques and responses when the words of the original are particularly apt, highly technical, or personal opinions. Wallack has several quotations in her essay. Analyze the effectiveness of each one on the basis of these criteria. Would the essay be improved if any of the statements were paraphrased instead of quoted?

2. In what ways does Wallack use the Sancton article to support her response to Gore's article? Do you think this is an appropriate use of a second article?

3. What do you learn about Wallack in her essay?

4. What assumptions does Wallack make about her audience?

Reading

In the following essay, a student writer analyzes two essays about hunting, both of which can be found in Chapter 7. In carrying out her analysis, she makes a subject-by-subject comparison, first analyzing one essay, then the other. Notice how she uses parenthetical page citations to document references to the articles—for direct quotations, paraphrases, and summaries. At the end, she includes a "Works Cited" list, naming the two articles as she found them in the first edition of *The Purposeful Writer.*

The Hunting Controversy

Karolyn Skudlarek

Hunting has been controversial ever since civilized people no longer needed to hunt for food in order to eat. In his essay "Heroes, Bears, and True Baloney" (179), John Skow asserts that hunting as a wildlife management measure is "true baloney" and that people who hunt innocent animals are "pests" (180). James Kilpatrick, on the other hand, proposes in his essay "Some Hunting Protesters Are Overzealous Hypocrites" (181) that wildlife is a natural resource that many people depend on to sustain their families, and that people who protest hunting are not the "animal lovers" they claim to be (182). Both writers are effective in making their points, but they are slanted in their views. I have recently been taking a gun safety course in which hunter ethics are discussed, and I feel that both writers bring up ideas that are worth exploring.

Skow was prompted to write his essay when the bears migrating into his county in New Hampshire became the target for hunters during a five-week hunting season initiated to control the bear population (179). He describes hunters as irresponsible and proposes that they are likely to do more damage than the bears (180). He would like the opportunity to see the bears and had been told that a female and two cubs were close to his home. He describes the bears as "smart, cute, hungry corn thieves and garbage raiders, happy to be in the suburbs and virtually harmless" (179). What he fails to point out is that bears migrate into other areas because of overpopulation and shortage of food supplies. They don't dig through garbage cans as a playful act; it's a matter of survival. A female is very protective of her cubs, and should she feel they are being threatened by small children who may encounter these animals in their own back yard, a tragedy could occur. Hunting is a wildlife management measure which helps to control the bear population so that food supplies are adequate. Hunting season is

limited to ensure that the population remains stable and is not depleted to a point which would endanger the species.

Skow does make a good point about the dangers of encountering the   3
irresponsible hunters (180) that gun safety instructors refer to as "slob
hunters." These are people who ignore hunter ethics and the important
rules of gun safety. They are the small percentage of hunters who ruin it
for the others by their thoughtless attitudes and disrespect for nature.
But Skow fails to point out that these people are in the minority. Gun
safety instructors introduce hunter ethics to children at an early age in
order to stress the importance of being polite and considerate when
hunting and having respect for nature.

Taking a different view, Kilpatrick was angered by the fanatic animal   4
rights demonstrators protesting deer hunting in front of TV cameras
while hunters were out in the fields. The protesters stated they had just
as much right to be there (making loud noises to scare off the deer) as
the hunters did (181). But Kilpatrick aptly points out that "no one has a
constitutional right to interfere physically with the lawful conduct of
another" (181). Kilpatrick generalizes that self-proclaimed "animal lovers" are hypocrites because they eat meat and wear leather belts or shoes
(181). But most people who call themselves animal rights activists are
protesting the inhumane treatment and senseless killing of animals
which Kilpatrick himself objects to. Like Skow, he generalizes and in
doing so gives a slanted view of these protesters. Their demonstrations
have raised public awareness of the senseless killing of endangered species for their furs, the thoughtless killing of dolphins in the tuna industry,
and the inhumane treatment of laboratory animals. Although I agree
that a small percentage of protesters are fanatics and that they have no
right to interfere with legal hunting practices, I'm grateful for their
publicized demonstrations, and I don't question their motives as Kilpatrick does.

The controversy over hunting will probably always be with us. When   5
writers as effective as Skow and Kilpatrick withhold information and give
slanted views, they contribute to the dispute. We need to consider the
important points of both sides in order to make an informed decision.
Education about hunter ethics and gun safety at an early age may help to
alleviate the tension between these different points of view.

Works Cited

Kilpatrick, James. "Some Hunting Protesters Are Overzealous Hypocrites."
   The Purposeful Writer: A Rhetoric with Readings. By Donna Gorrell. Boston:
   Allyn and Bacon, 1991. 181–82.
Skow, John. "Heroes, Bears, and True Baloney." *The Purposeful Writer: A
   Rhetoric With Readings.* By Donna Gorrell. Boston: Allyn and Bacon, 1991.
   179–81.

Questions: The Community of Writers

1. What is Skudlarek's thesis, and where does she state it? How does she expand it in her conclusion?

2. Skudlarek devotes paragraphs 2 and 3 to Skow's article and paragraph 4 to Kilpatrick's—a subject-by-subject comparison. On what points does she compare the two articles?

3. What is Skudlarek's authority for analyzing essays about hunting? Discuss how she draws on that authority and whether you think her authority is adequate.

4. Direct quotations must be exact, word for word, and paraphrases must be true to the original. Compare Skudlarek's direct quotations and paraphrases in paragraph 4 with the words of the original on page 201. Discuss her possible reasons for using the quotations and paraphrases as she did.

WRITINGS

Writing a Summary

Following the steps outlined under "Writing a Summary," write a summary of the following essay from *Time* magazine (5 February 1991). Read the essay before beginning to make notes. Open your summary with a nutshell statement, and support that statement with the major ideas of the essay. Write from your perspective, not Chavira's, but do not express your opinions. Conclude with a reinforcing statement. Make your summary approximately one-fourth the length of the original. Use coordination and subordination to compress ideas and reduce wordiness.

The Rise of Teenage Gambling

Ricardo Chavira

Amid the throngs of gamblers in Atlantic City, Debra Kim Cohen   1
stood out. A former beauty queen, she dropped thousands of dollars at blackjack tables. Casino managers acknowledged her lavish patronage by plying her with the perks commonly accorded VIP customers: free limo rides, meals, even rooms. Cohen, after all, was a high roller. It apparently did not disturb casino officials that she was also a teenager and—at 17—four years shy of New Jersey's legal gambling age.

Finally, Kim's father, Atlantic City detective Leonard Cohen, com-   2
plained to authorities. Kim was subsequently barred from casinos. But by then the damage had been done. "She was an addicted gambler," Cohen says of his daughter. Moreover, Kim had squandered all her money, including funds set aside for college. Officials at the five casinos where she gambled claimed that her case was an anomaly.

On the contrary, Kim's sad case is only too common. Gambling researchers say that of the estimated 8 million compulsive gamblers in America, fully 1 million are teenagers. Unlike Kim, most live far from casinos, so they favor sports betting, card playing and lotteries. Once bitten by the gambling bug, many later move on to casinos and racetrack betting. "We have always seen compulsive gambling as a problem of older people," says Jean Falzon, executive director of the National Council on Problem Gambling, based in New York City. "Now we are finding that adolescent compulsive gambling is far more pervasive than we had thought." 3

Just 10 years ago, teenage gambling did not register even a blip on the roster of social ills. Today gambling counselors say an average of 7% of their case loads involve teenagers. New studies indicate that teenage vulnerability to compulsive gambling hits every economic stratum and ethnic group. After surveying 2,700 high school students in four states, California psychologist Durand Jacobs concluded that students are 2½ times as likely as adults to become problem gamblers. In another study, Henry Lesieur, a sociologist at St. John's University in New York, found eight times as many gambling addicts among college students as among adults. 4

Experts agree that casual gambling, in which participants wager small sums, is not necessarily bad. Compulsive betting, however, almost always involves destructive behavior. Last fall police in Pennsauken, N.J., arrested a teenage boy on suspicion of burglary. The youth said he stole items worth $10,000 to support his gambling habit. Bryan, a 17-year-old from Cumberland, N.J., recently sought help after he was unable to pay back $4,000 he owed a sports bookmaker. Greg from Philadelphia says he began placing weekly $200 bets with bookies during his sophomore year in college. "Pretty soon it got to the point that I owed $5,000," he says. "The bookies threatened me. One said he would cut off my mother's legs if I didn't pay." Still Greg continued to gamble. Now 23, he was recently fired from his job after his employer caught him embezzling. 5

Why does gambling fever run so high among teens? Researchers point to the legitimization of gambling in America, noting that it is possible to place a legal bet in every state except Utah and Hawaii. Moreover, ticket vendors rarely ask to see proof of age, despite lottery laws in 33 states and the District of Columbia requiring that customers be at least 18 years old. "You have state governments promoting lotteries," says Valerie Lorenz, director of the National Center for Pathological Gambling, based in Baltimore. "The message they're conveying is that gambling is not a vice but a normal form of entertainment." Researchers also point to unstable families, low self-esteem and a societal obsession with money. "At the casinos you feel very important," says Rich of Bethesda, Md., a young recovering addict. "When you're spending money at the tables, they give you free drinks and call you Mister." 6

Efforts to combat teen problem gambling are still fairly modest. Few 7
states offer educational programs that warn young people about the
addictive nature of gambling; treatment programs designed for youths
are virtually nonexistent. In Minnesota, where a study found that more
than 6% of all youths between 15 and 18 are problem gamblers, $200,000
of the expected income from the state's new lottery will go toward a
youth-education campaign. That may prove to be small solace. Betty
George, who heads the Minnesota Council on Compulsive Gambling,
warns that the lottery and other anticipated legalized gambling activities
are likely to spur youth gambling.

Security guards at casinos in Atlantic City and Nevada have been 8
instructed to be on the alert for minors. But it is a daunting task. Each
month some 29,000 underage patrons are stopped at the door or ejected
from the floors of Atlantic City casinos. "We can rationally assume that if
we stop 29,000, then a few hundred manage to get through," says Steven
Perskie, chairman of New Jersey's Casino Control Commission. Commission officials say they may raise the fines imposed on casinos that allow
customers under 21 to gamble.

Counselors fear that little will change until society begins to view 9
teenage gambling with the same alarm directed at drug and alcohol
abuse. "Public understanding of gambling is where our understanding of
alcoholism was some 40 or 50 years ago." says psychologist Jacobs. "Unless
we wake up soon to gambling's dark side, we're going to have a whole
new generation lost to this addiction."

Writing a Critique

Following the guidelines under "Writing a Critique or a Response,"
write a critique of "Literature's Black Heroes All Needn't Be Racial Mar-
tyrs" by George Will (*Time* 13 Dec. 1990). After reading the essay for the
first time, establish your criteria for analysis and evaluation, considering
such aspects as purpose, intended audience, writing style and technique,
and use of terminology. As you write your critique, support your thesis
with evidence from Will's essay, using summary, paraphrase, and quotation as appropriate. Use parenthetical citations as in "Ordinary Heroes,"
pages 432–34, with this book as your source. Here's an example of your
"Work Cited":

> Will, George. "Literature's Black Heroes All Needn't Be Racial Martyrs." *The
> Purposeful Writer: A Rhetoric with Readings.* 2nd ed. By Donna Gorrell.
> Boston: Allyn and Bacon, 1992. 441–42.

You may want to relate the content of the essay to your own experience
or other material you have read on the subject.

Literature's Black Heroes All Needn't Be Racial Martyrs

George Will

Rutherford Calhoun is one of those rapscallions who have enlivened   1
American literature since Huck Finn decided civilization made him itch,
and lit out for the territories. Calhoun is a ne'er-do-well who instead of
going down a river on a raft stowed away on a ship to escape the twin
horrors of debts and marriage. The ship turned out to be bound for
Africa to collect cargo; slaves. And Calhoun is black.

So is his creator, Charles Johnson, who teaches at the University of   2
Washington and has written, without setting out to do so, an emancipation proclamation for black writers. It is his novel "Middle Passage,"
winner of the National Book Award. It is an example of triumphant
individualism, on the part of both Calhoun and Johnson.

Calhoun is a freed slave from southern Illinois whose former master   3
assuaged his guilt by tamping great gobs of learning into Calhoun.
Calhoun arrived in New Orleans around 1830 speaking like Spinoza but
determined not to be "a credit to his race," a phrase that made him gag.
He lived for pleasures, particularly the thrill of theft, until forced to
choose either domesticity or punishment by a frightening creditor. Instead, he went to sea, a free black on the crew of a ship bringing slaves to
American investors, one of whom was black. Johnson wants you to know
that black experiences have been various.

"Middle Passage" reflects Johnson's years of research in the literature   4
of the sea and the hair-raising facts of slavery. The verisimilitude about
the smells, sanitation and diseases aboard ship includes details about the
captain, who is a "tight packer" (of slaves; Johnson explains how it was
done). When a slave died in transit, the Captain would cut off the ears to
verify to the investor that the victim had been aboard.

In opaque remarks opaquely reported, a National Book Award juror   5
suggested that the politics of ideology and ethnic entitlements, a poison
in the teaching of literature nowadays, had seeped into the NBA process.
But in felicitous remarks made when accepting the award, Johnson made
clear what his novel itself makes clear: The "message" of the book is the
absence of the sort of "message" that stultifies art.

Johnson noted that he is the first black male to win the award since   6
Ralph Ellison won in 1953 for "Invisible Man." Ellison's aim, says Johnson, was creation of "a black American personality as complex, as multi-
sided and synthetic as the American society that produced it."

A black literature of protest, stressing victimization, appeared about   7
three decades ago. It was, says Johnson, inevitable and important—and
limiting. Literature, he says, should by a form of discovery. A writer
should not know in advance what, or at least all of what, he is going to

say. Literature that is an extension of an ideology, that is didactic to the point of preachiness, lacks the power to change the reader's perceptions as the writer's perceptions change. A serious writer ought to be not only surprising, but himself surprised.

In "Invisible Man" (perhaps the finest American novel since "The 8 Great Gatsby"), Ellison made vivid how blacks are made "invisible" where racial perceptions obliterate perceptions of individuality. That is what white America did to black Americans.

But there is a form of suffocation that blacks can inflict upon them- 9 selves. It is to insist on a literature of orthodoxy, a literature of protest which insists on group consciousness. Against this, Ellison was adamant: "Our task is that of making ourselves individuals."

Calhoun learns from his voyage, and especially from his encounter 10 with the dignified but inaccessible (to him) culture of the slaves. He learns that he is a Yankee sailor.

A white crew member tells Calhoun: The slaves, too, are black, but 11 they are not like you. The crew members call him Illinois, and by the end of the novel Calhoun knows that somewhere in America, perhaps Illinois, is home. The novel is about—quietly about—patriotism.

"If," Calhoun muses, "this weird, upside-down caricature of a country 12 called America, if this land of refugees and former indentured servants, religious heretics and half-breeds, whoresons and fugitives—this caul-dron of mongrels from all points of the compass—was all I could rightly call home, then aye: I was of it. There, as I lay weakened from bleeding, was where I wanted to be."

Johnson anticipates in the 1990s a black fiction "of increasing intel- 13 lectual and artistic generosity, one that enables us as a people—as a culture—to move from narrow complaint to broad celebration." I think he means celebration of the possibilities of American individualism. I know that his novel, and the award, are reasons for celebration.

Writing an Essay Examination

Select one of your courses, particularly one for which you are likely to be required to write an essay exam, and prepare for an exam according to the guidelines under Essay Examinations. Write several questions that could be asked on the exam, then write an essay on one of them, again following the guidelines.

CHAPTER 16

Writing a Research Paper

Many students have written a research paper of some type by the time they get to college. It may have been a short paper using three or four sources of information, a report on published critiques of a novel, poem, or short story, or even a fairly long paper that was a culmination of several weeks or months of work. But some students have never written any kind of research (or "term") paper. If you are one of them, you are not at a disadvantage. In this new situation—writing the college research paper—expectations are different from those in high school or junior high school. Whatever your past experience, your instructor and this chapter will guide you through the process of research and writing so that you can end up with a significant piece of writing and the satisfaction of knowing that from your own hard work you have acquired and reported a body of knowledge that others may find interesting and informative.

The Community of Scholars

You are about to enter a community of scholars—people who ask questions and seek answers. In a way, research is something everyone is familiar with. If you want to buy a computer, you ask a variety of questions: Which type will best suit my needs? How much can I afford? What do the experts say about particular brands? Then you try to answer those questions—by studying computer magazines, checking your bank account, browsing the computer stores and talking with the salespersons, consulting a teacher of computer courses, and so on. On the basis of your research, you come to a decision—one that can be stated somewhat like a **thesis sentence**: Considering my needs, my available funds, and the best advice I could get, I will buy XXX computer.

Scholars ask questions too: What do the critics say about the published writing of Barbara Kingsolver? How do the Democratic and Republican parties compare on racism issues over the past five years? What are the psychotherapeutic benefits of meditation? What caused the onset of Graves' disease in both George and Barbara Bush? Then the scholars seek answers to their questions—sometimes in the library, sometimes by surveying groups of people, sometimes with scientific experiments. They do whatever is necessary to answer their questions. Sometimes the questions go unanswered, whereupon they may ask new questions or drop the subject for a time—or forever. But for the most part, questions can be answered with the right kind and the right amount of research.

Then scholars generally report their research. In other words, they write a research paper. In their paper they describe the problem, why it was important to find an answer, how they sought their answers, and what they learned. They can usually summarize the results of their research and tell their readers what they learned from their experts, statistics, or hands-on experiments. They can state an answer to their question or admit that as yet they have discovered no answer. Some research ends in a persuasive document. Researchers who want to persuade someone else to see an issue the way they do will collect evidence that supports their position and then use that evidence in a documented paper that is essentially persuasive in purpose.

For people at colleges and universities, scholarship is our job. Whether we're students or teachers, neophytes or sophisticates, we engage in scholarship. We ask questions. We study what other scholars have written. We do our own observations or experiments. And by doing these things, we seek answers to our questions. If all this sounds too heavy for you, remember that the questions scholars ask are generally of their own making. Scholars are *interested* in their questions, and, like the consumer wanting to buy a computer, they are even excited about the process of finding answers. Their questions are related to their career field or other interests, and they have some tangible knowledge when they have completed their research.

In school, your research topic is often assigned, depending upon the course of study, while at other times you have an open choice of topic. Most commonly, however, you are given a choice of topics limited to the subject under study: In a World War II history class your topic is limited to the second world war; in an anthropology class, it is limited to the origin, development, and behavior of humankind. By searching a particular field, you develop a familiarity with the scholarship in that field: You learn who the scholars are, how to find your way around in the journals that publish their work, what the experts have said about the topic you are researching, and so on. If this field happens to be your major, you may be laying the groundwork for further work toward your career.

Primary and Secondary Research

The preceding paragraphs intimate that answers to research questions can be sought in a number of ways. These ways are often classified as being of two types: primary and secondary.

Primary research is hands-on work, with no go-between to interpret information. Primary researchers locate and interpret their own information. Some of their methods are interviews, surveys, controlled experiments, observations, and study of original documents. They deal with *primary evidence*: interview transcripts, survey statistics, observation records, and published documents. Chapter 9 has two interview reports. The first, a transcribed record of a conversation between the interviewer and the interviewee, Jesse Jackson, is primary evidence that could become part of a report. Chapters 10 and 15 also explain and illustrate some of these methods of primary research.

Secondary research uses the primary research of other people. All the evidence produced by secondary research is termed *secondary evidence*, which may contain interpretations and be a limited selection of the information available to the researcher. When you engage in secondary research, you read the published reports of others' research—found generally in scholarly journals and books. For example, a review of Carolyn Chute's *The Beans of Egypt, Maine* is secondary evidence; Chute's book itself is primary evidence. A chart showing the distribution of seat belt wearers by age and sex is secondary evidence in the health care pamphlet it appears in; the source of the statistics in the chart—the researcher's report of a survey—is primary evidence.

Sometimes secondary research takes a third step away from primary evidence in the form of published condensations or reactions to published secondary research. Encyclopedias are almost always secondary evidence, often to the extended step of being summaries of other secondary research. They are generally most useful at the beginning of research, when the researcher wants to acquire an overview of a subject.

Library research, then, is often secondary research. Unless you are using original documents, you are engaging in research that depends on the credibility, accuracy, and fairness of the authors of the work you are studying. Limiting yourself to one or two sources and failing to evaluate everything you read can therefore cause a decided slant, and perhaps even unintended untruth, in your paper. But secondary research, done well, has value. To justify the need for additional information, primary researchers often begin their firsthand studies with secondary research (sometimes called, in their reports, "reviews of related literature"). It makes available the responses of experts to primary and other secondary research; it collects, summarizes, compares, and otherwise digests the reported research on a given subject; it provides information that might not otherwise be accessible to nonprofessionals. Whether your research is primary or secondary, it can report useful information.

Overview of the Research Process

At first glance, the process of writing a research paper seems quite linear: First you select a topic, then you do your research, and finally you write the paper. In practice, however, much of the activity overlaps and even falls back on itself. Some people call the process recursive, to describe the falling back, recurring action. A better term might be *concursive*, meaning that several of the research activities may occur at the same time. For example, while you're reading and taking notes, you may also be formulating and revising a tentative thesis, jotting down a working outline, and even doing some preliminary drafting. One step is not necessarily completed before you begin another.

Figure 16-1 is a schedule chart that illustrates how one person's research process might look. The process is roughly linear, progressing in a downward diagonal toward submission of the final copy at the end of the term. But the process is also concursive, with several activities happening at once. While in the process of selecting a topic, this student spends a little time at the library, takes a few notes, and writes a tentative thesis. In the midst of reading and notetaking, the student continues to search the library, plus revising the tentative thesis twice, performing a preliminary organization of notes, and even making a stab at a portion of the first draft. However, some parts of the process obviously must follow other parts: Getting the assignment comes before researching and writing, and proofreading comes after the final copy has been typed or printed.

Your process may be similar to the one shown here; it may also be different. It is probably best if you avoid a strictly linear process. Begin reading and notetaking before you have completed your library search; begin writing a tentative thesis early and revise it as often as necessary; return to the library any time you discover you need more, or different, information. But do avoid changing your topic midway or near the end of the process (some teachers don't allow it anyway). To avoid getting deeply entrenched in research you cannot conclude, do a preliminary library search to find out whether information is available. If your topic is not working out after you are already deep into your research, alter it somewhat so that you can utilize the work you have already completed.

The remainder of this chapter will guide you through the research process, ending with a completed paper. To avoid working "like a hen following a chalk line," as one professional writer put it, give the entire chapter a quick reading to see where the process is leading you.

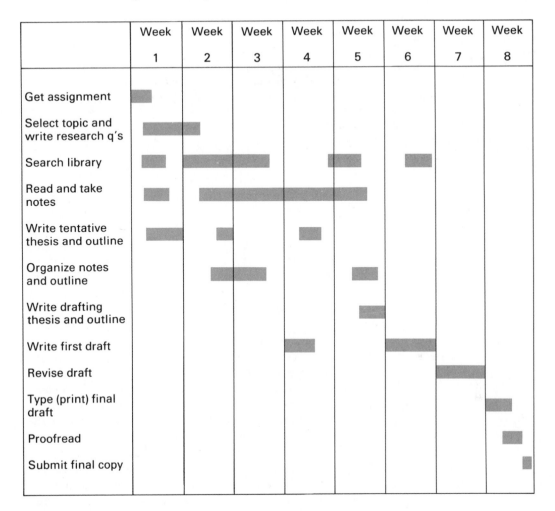

Figure 16-1. Schedule Chart of One Person's Research.

Exercise: The Exploring Writer

Draw a schedule chart. On an 8½ by 11 sheet of paper, divide the time available to you into evenly spaced periods, allowing space at the left for listing the research activities. After your quick reading of this chapter, draw up a list of your anticipated research activities in a column at the left of your chart. Draw vertical lines to separate the weeks and the left column. Use horizontal bars to indicate the period of time you anticipate working on each activity. In drawing your bars, you may want to work from both the top and bottom of the chart, beginning with your two firm dates: getting the assignment and submitting the final draft.

Exercise: The Community of Writers

Compare your schedule chart with those of a group of classmates. Try to account for differences and similarities. What do your charts tell you about your process of writing? Do the activities represented as concurrent seem that they can (or should) be done at the same time? Do the lengths of the horizontal bars seem like reasonable guesses as to the time that will be required for the activity? In what ways have the schedule charts of you and your classmates differed from the one in Figure 16-1?

The Rhetoric of Research Reports

In Chapter 2 you read about the rhetorical components of writing situations: the writer, the audience, the subject, and, overall, the purpose for writing. Depending on its purpose, some writing emphasizes the writer, some the audience, and some the subject. Autobiographical writing and personal expressive writing emphasize the writer, writing that seeks to persuade or entertain concentrates on the interests of the audience, and writing to inform or explain emphasizes the subject in an objective, impersonal style. All writing has aspects of all these components, but most writing emphasizes one or the other.

Research writing, where the purpose is often to inform or explain, usually emphasizes the subject, though sometimes, when the purpose is to persuade, it has strong elements of emphasis on the interests of the audience. When you get your assignment, hold off considering your subject and the narrowed topic you will write on and first consider the entire rhetorical situation: what your role as writer and researcher is expected to be, who your primary audience will be, how much choice you have in topic selection and on what basis you are expected to make your topic choice, and, finally, the purpose for the research.

Your Role as Writer

In a subject matter course such as anthropology or business ethics, you are usually expected to assume the role of a student of that subject matter—a beginning anthropologist or a future corporation employee, for example. You are expected to find books and journal articles by recognized professionals in the field and to use them with confidence and comprehension, citing their work as required by conventions of scholarship and, where appropriate, acknowledging their contributions to their field. Using the vocabulary characteristic of the field further boosts your credibility. In an English class devoted to writing, you are equally expected to be a serious student of whatever subject you or your teacher selects for your research. You must search out the applicable sources of information and use them knowledgeably.

Such a role may be an unfamiliar one for you, but it is not an impossible one. The research process itself assists you in assuming it. By reading numerous sources of information on a given subject, you become somewhat of an expert. Plan to read more than you can possibly include in your paper, knowing that the additional reading will improve the authority of your written voice. After a while, you will also find yourself able to use the vocabulary of your subject with ease, and you will learn which names keep coming up in references and which ones are most respected. You will develop a sense of what experts in that field consider common knowledge, and you will learn to evaluate what you read. When you write your research paper, you will be able to convey this newly established credibility. You will confidently state your own research question, use the vocabulary that is appropriate, and use only those sources you need for answering your question.

Since the emphasis of a research paper is generally on the subject, and because the genre itself is usually more formal than the short essay, most teachers advise that writers avoid the first person *I* so that the focus remains on the subject. Another form often avoided in research papers, and again because of their level of formality, is contractions. While words like *can't* and *won't* are acceptable in most informal writing, they lower the level of formality expected for research papers and are best spelled out in their full form.

Your Audience

Your assignment will tell you something about the expectations of your audience, who in most cases of college research writing is the teacher. It is important for you to understand (and accept) that teachers differ in their expectations. Because Professor James, your history teacher, wants you to leave two-inch margins on left and right and to number your pages on the bottom, you are not to assume that this format is right for all situations. As another example, some teachers want you to lead into every piece of borrowed information by naming its source; others don't notice whether you do or not. In some disciplines, mainly the humanities, the format of the Modern Language Association (MLA) is followed; in others, mainly the social sciences, that of the American Psychological Association (APA); and in others, still other formats. In a matter as conventional as the research paper, it is extremely important for students to learn what the expectations are and to follow them. Expectations differ according to disciplines, schools, and individuals. Outside of school, they differ from corporation to corporation and from institution to institution. Learning to adapt in school will lead the way for getting along as an employee.

You also need to know how much your audience knows about your subject and how detailed you should be in your writing. Sometimes teachers want you to assume a public audience, one that has no previous knowledge of the subject. In that case, you would be thorough in your descriptions and background information and carefully define any specialized terms you use. At other times, the teacher is a knowledgeable audience who wants you to display what you have learned about the subject. In this case, you also must be thorough, giving details, background, and defined terms to show your understanding of them. Sometimes, however, the teacher wants you to assume an audience of like-minded scholars who know the terms and background and want to know what you have discovered that is new. You may not encounter this assumption until later in your college career, after you have studied for a while in your major.

Your Subject

A research paper is something you have to live with for a sizable chunk of your life. So if you have any choice at all, choose something that interests you, something you won't tire of next week. Don't pick a subject just because it seems easy to research or because a friend is choosing it or because someone in your family has some books on it. Choose something that you want to learn about—something that interests you personally or something that will get you started toward your career interests. The next major section will give you some guidance in topic selection.

Your Purpose

Central to the rhetoric of the research paper is the purpose for researching and writing. Sometimes people want to **report** what has been written on a given subject; their reports are often called "reviews of literature" or, as part of a larger piece of research, "reviews of related literature." They briefly summarize each item, noting contributions to the subject and often comparing and relating items. Sometimes such reports take the form of annotated bibliographies—a list of sources briefly summarized and described. Another kind of report is an account of the writer's primary research—an experimental study, an observation, a survey, an interview, and so on. Such reports include reviews of related literature.

Many research papers are written to **inform** readers about a subject. The researcher draws together what is known and available on the subject and puts it in a readable, coherent form. Examples of research written for this purpose might be "Effects of Grades on Motivation in Tenth Graders," "Thomas Jefferson's Views on Slavery," and "The Uses of Doppler Radar for Tracking the Weather." Since the primary emphasis is on the subject, these papers are written with an objective, impersonal tone.

The major purpose of some research papers is to **persuade** the audience to a particular action or opinion. By means of the information gleaned from the research, the writer hopes to make some changes in the audience—to stop smoking, for example, or to become a vegetarian. The tone of such papers is often apparently objective because of the wealth of facts reported, but close inspection may reveal loaded words and slanted information. Whether you are a reader or a writer of such persuasive research papers, look for supportive evidence based on reasoning, facts, and statements from authorities in the field. See Chapter 7 for further coverage of writing to persuade.

Selecting and Narrowing the Topic

You can't do research, of course, unless you have something to research: your topic. Two major sources of topics are yourself and your library.

Exploring Your Own Interests

If your assignment does not specify a topic for your research, you need to begin exploring your own interests. To bring them to the surface, begin with one of the prewriting activities described in Chapter 3: brainstorming, perhaps, or asking *who, what, when, where, why,* and *how.* (Refer to Chapter 3 for details on how to practice these techniques for discovering ideas.) And don't overlook the assistance you can gain from talking about research possibilities. Classmates, friends, and family can be sounding boards for your ruminations.

In making your selection, avoid subjects that are overworked or that may involve you emotionally. Abortion, gun control, capital punishment, and legal drinking age are a few topics that may be on your teacher's "avoid" list. These topics are difficult to narrow without getting involved in larger, emotional issues.

Exploring in Your Library

You can also use your school library for finding a topic. Several of the library tools for locating material on given topics are useful also for suggesting subjects you might like to pursue. For subjects at the most general level, use your library's classification system for its central catalog. There are two major cataloging systems: Dewey decimal, based on numbers, and Library of Congress, based on a combination of letters and numbers. If your library uses the Dewey decimal system, you will find ten major headings:

000	General works
100	Philosophy
200	Religion
300	Social sciences
400	Language
500	Natural sciences
600	Technology and applied sciences
700	Fine arts
800	Literature
900	History and geography

Each major heading in the Dewey system is subdivided into related categories: 530 for physics, for example, and 340 for law. Further divisions are indicated by more specific numbers, such as 538.112 and 342.2384.

Many college and university libraries use the Library of Congress classification system, divided into twenty major groups:

A	General works
B	Philosophy and religion
C	General history
D	Foreign history
E–F	American history
G	Geography and anthropology
H	Social sciences
J	Political science
K	Law
L	Education
M	Music
N	Fine arts
P	Language and literature
Q	Science
R	Medicine
S	Agriculture
T	Technology
U	Military science
V	Naval science
Z	Bibliography and library science

Categories are further classified by combinations of letters and numbers—for example, PS3823. Once you have identified a major subject that interests you, you can begin browsing the subclassifications—on a classification list in your library, in your library's card or online catalog (see descriptions on pages 460–62), on the books on the shelves, or on your library's shelf list, which names all the books in your library by classification.

Another useful tool for discovering research topics is the *Library of Congress: Subject Headings,* a large reference book listing subjects for classifying books according to the Library of Congress scheme. Still other useful sources are the *Reader's Guide to Periodical Literature* and other indexes to periodicals. Again, just scan subject listings until something sounds interesting to you.

Once you have a general subject, you can use some of the same tools for narrowing your subject to manageable size as those you used for discovering it in the first place: one of the prewriting techniques described in Chapter 3, your library's classification system, or your library's catalog and indexes. If you are considering the broad subject of space stations, for example, by looking in the *Reader's Guide* you find such subheadings as "equipment" and "industrial use," plus a cross reference to "space colonies." At this point, you may decide that space colonization is what you're really interested in learning more about, so you shift your focus to the narrower subject. With a preliminary search of this kind, you also get a sense of the amount of published material on your subject. If there is a great deal, your subject is probably too broad; if you're finding very little, you may have to broaden your subject or shift it to a related topic.

Exercise: The Exploring Writer

If you don't have an assigned topic, browse in your library, using Library of Congress: Subject Headings *and* Reader's Guide to Periodical Literature. *Make a list of five or six topics that interest you and seem to have a promising number of entries in the* Reader's Guide.

Phrasing Your Research Question(s) and Tentative Thesis

As you narrow your topic, begin asking questions that you want to answer and that can lead to a focus for your research. If you ask questions about subjects that genuinely interest you, the search for answers will not be tedious; they'll be an important part of your life. Your preliminary search will present questions, but it will also answer questions. Those that are answered readily are not subjects for research. Continue asking questions suggested by your early reading and for which you can supply only a tentative answer. Such questions might be:

Is pornography "natural"?
What is the danger of toxic wastes?
How do children acquire values?
Will Social Security be there when I need it?

Such questions have no ready answers but promise suggested answers that might come with further reading and searching.

At this point, try adding encyclopedias to your research tools. While these sources of information are not always acceptable as references in a research paper, they can be extremely useful for providing background information at the beginning of the project. They can tell you what is generally known about a subject, what is not known, what its history is, who its leading figures are, and so on. Encyclopedia articles also usually include bibliographies of standard sources for further reading. Among the most respected general encyclopedias are

Collier's Encyclopedia
Columbia Encyclopedia
Encyclopedia Americana
Encyclopaedia Britannica
World Book

From your research questions, formulate a tentative thesis that will lend further focus to your research. A thesis sentence, as explained in Chapter 3, expresses both the subject and an assertion about the subject, and it implies purpose. The following thesis sentences promise an informative paper:

Psychotherapeutic meditation reduces anxiety and neuroses.
The nuclear accident at Chernobyl resulted from incompetence.

These more likely presage a persuasive paper:

A national health insurance program that covers everyone would provide better medical care for all citizens.
Hopelessly ill people should have the right to decide whether to live or die.

Both kinds of thesis sentences state the subject and make a point. The way they are phrased indicates whether the writer's purpose is to use reasoning, facts, and authority to **inform** the reader or to **persuade** the reader to new actions or opinions. However, some writers disguise a persuasive purpose under an informative thesis and use information to attempt persuasion. (See pages 136 and 324–28 for additional discussions of informative versus persuasive statements of thesis.)

Exercise: The Community of Writers

With several of your classmates, discuss the following thesis sentences. Decide on the subject and assertion of each, the purpose of each as informative or persuasive, and the research question(s) that each might answer. As a group, rewrite persuasive thesis sentences to indicate an informative purpose, and rewrite informative sentences to announce a persuasive purpose. Discuss the advantages and disadvantages (to both readers and writers) of a thesis phrased to suggest a purpose other than the intended one. Is such a practice ethical?

1. The nuclear accident at Chernobyl could happen at other nuclear plants.
2. A controlled diet can reduce the risk of heart attack.
3. Left-handed people are an oppressed minority.
4. Single-sex schools should be permitted because they are beneficial to the students they serve.
5. "Killer" bees are not as dangerous as sometimes thought.
6. Flexible leave policies benefit both employer and employee.
7. Gambling among teenagers is an epidemic of staggering proportions.
8. Feminism aims at making the world better for all people.

Developing Your Bibliography

One of the keys to competent research is a well-developed working bibliography. A working bibliography, made at the beginning of your research and built throughout the process, is a compilation of places where you are likely to find information on your narrowed topic. The items for your bibliography come from a number of sources: periodicals indexes, your library's general catalog, computer searches, and so on. Additional valuable sources are all the articles and books you read, because very often their authors list bibliographies for further reading. Usually these sources are valued by the experts in the field and are gold mines for new researchers.

Many experienced researchers recommend keeping the working bibliography on three-by-five-inch index cards, one item to each card. Cards have the advantage of sorting flexibility. For example, after you have compiled them in random order as you discover sources, you can sort them by call number for ease in locating the items in the library, sort them again to set aside those references you haven't yet located, again according to your order for using them as you write, and yet again alphabetically for writing your list of works cited, setting aside those you didn't actually use in your paper. Throughout your research, you can easily add items. In addition to sorting flexibility, the size of your cards makes them easy to carry in your pocket and set down in the library while you're looking for an item.

Figure 16-2 shows sample working bibliography cards for a book and for a journal article. They include all information that will be needed for the list of works cited: author, title, and publishing facts. In addition, they have the call numbers for ease in locating the items, and the book card has a note reminding the researcher that the book includes a bibliography. It is important to make these cards accurate and complete; otherwise you may need to locate the item again during the late stages of preparing your paper. (For more details on what information to include on your cards, see "Documenting Your Sources" beginning on page 473.)

Searching the Library

Your school library will probably be your primary source of information for answering your research questions and supporting your thesis. To complete your research successfully, you should be familiar with the reference room, the system for using periodicals, and the catalog of books. If you need help in using any of the library's tools, ask a librarian. The reference librarian has special training to assist library users in researching a wide range of subjects.

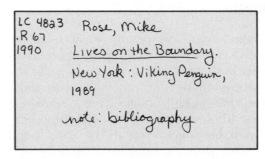

Call number

LC 4823
.R 67
1990

Rose, Mike

Lives on the Boundary.
New York : Viking Penguin,
1989

note: bibliography

Author

Title of book

City of publication
Publisher
Date of publication

Researcher's note

Edsall, Thomas Byrne, and
Mary T Edsall. "Race"
Atlantic Monthly
May 1991 : 53-86

Authors of article

Title of article

Title of magazine

Date and page
numbers

Figure 16-2. Sample Annotated Bibliography Cards.

The Reference Collection

A good place to begin your research is the reference room. In the area of your library set aside for reference works, you will find dictionaries, encyclopedias, biographies, yearbooks, atlases, and gazetteers. It would be worth your while to browse the collection to discover the wealth of sources available to you. The works, you will find, are arranged according to your library's classification system, whether Dewey or Library of Congress (see pages 451–53). The reference room offers advantages to the beginning college researcher. First, you become acquainted with an important part of your library, including the reference librarian and the information collected and stored here. Second, reference works, encyclopedias in particular, can give you a helpful overview of your subject. These books are written by experts in their subjects and often, in accompanying bibliographies, list further sources of information, suggesting areas for study and giving your research a real boost.

Some of the major general encyclopedias have already been named. Listed here is a sample of other general reference tools widely used on a variety of subjects:

Current Biography
Dictionary of American Biography
Information Please Almanac
Oxford English Dictionary
National Atlas of the United States of America
Statistical Abstract of the United States
Webster's Third New International Dictionary of the English Language
Who's Who in America
World Almanac and Book of Facts

In addition, most encyclopedias publish annuals that review the events of the preceding year.

Beyond general works, each reference collection also has specialized works for major fields of study. For example, there are encyclopedias for art, astronomy, biological sciences, chemistry, computer science, dance, earth sciences, economics, education, film, history, law, literature, mathematics, medicine, music, philosophy, physics, psychology, religion, and social sciences. Most of these fields also have specialized dictionaries. By using specialized reference works you can begin to acquire knowledge of the field, its major issues, and the vocabulary common to its practitioners.

Periodicals

The core of your research will probably be articles in periodicals. If you use scholarly articles published in journals respected in the field you have chosen to research, you will be consulting the experts in that field. Scholars doing primary research publish their findings first in journals, later in books. Because of the longer publishing process, books usually lag at least two years behind journal articles. It is therefore imperative that you become acquainted with your library's periodicals system.

Articles in periodicals (publications issued at intervals: magazines, scholarly journals, newspapers) are listed in indexes. The most common general index is the *Reader's Guide to Periodical Literature*, which lists over 170 periodicals mostly of the popular type, such as *Reader's Digest* and *Sports Illustrated*. Such magazines have limited use in scholarly research, because, among other reasons, they rarely cite their sources, though some of the magazines listed in this guide can be used with confidence, such as *Scientific American*, the *Atlantic*, and the *New York Review of Books*. If you have a question about the respectability of any source, consult your teacher.

The *Reader's Guide* is a good place to begin your periodicals search. First, it leads you to information written for the general public—information that will be easy for you to read and understand while you're still getting acquainted with your subject. Remember that everything you read does not need to be cited in your paper. A second advantage of the *Reader's Guide* is that most specialized indexes follow the same format, so familiarity with one index will aid you in using another. The following description of the *Business Periodicals Index*, arranged much like the *Reader's Guide*, can help you use an index appropriate to the subject you are researching.

As Figure 16-3 illustrates, indexes are arranged by subject—shown in bold type at the left margins. Broad subdivisions often have subdivisions, indicated in centered bold type, and further divisions marked by centered italic type. Each entry gives the title of the article, the author, the title of the periodical, its volume number, the page numbers of the article, and the date. Other features such as illustrations and bibliographies are noted. You also find cross references to other locations of the information you are looking for, introduced by *See*, and to related entries, in the form of *See also*. At the front of the index are lists of abbreviations, so if you don't know what *J Mark Res* means, you can find it listed as *Journal of Marketing Research*. Seeking further information, you find in the list of periodicals indexed that the journal is a publication of the American Marketing Association, located in Chicago.

Most subject areas have specialized periodicals indexes. Examples are *Art Index*, *Education Index*, *Humanities Index*, and *General Science Index*. In many fields, there are also abstracts: serially published summaries of journal articles. Many libraries have reference sheets listing indexes for various subjects. When using a periodicals index, first locate appropriate

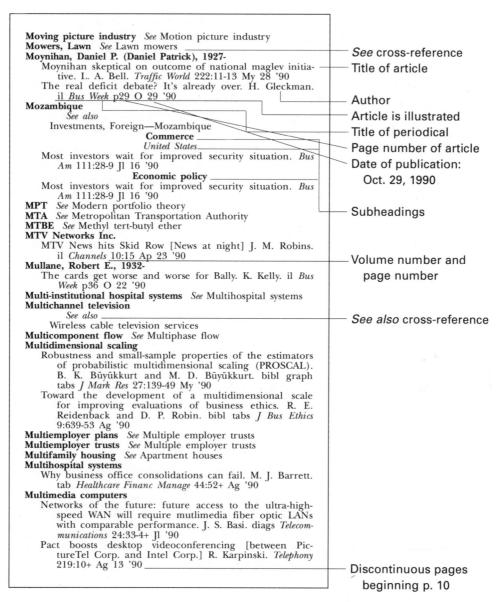

Figure 16-3. Annotated Excerpt from *Business Periodicals Index*.

subject headings by using a bound volume, because it has more numerous headings than the current paperbound issues. Use the *See also* cross references to locate headings that suit your search. Look also at subheadings for narrower, perhaps more suitable, listings. Then begin your search for articles, beginning with the most recent issues and working backward as far as appropriate for your topic, copying all the information in each entry you want to locate (see "Documenting Your Sources" on page 473).

Another source of information, particularly for historical or current events, is newspaper indexes. Your library probably carries several that are respected for their news coverage and editorial commentaries: probably *New York Times, Wall Street Journal, Christian Science Monitor,* and *Los Angeles Times.* Your library's copies of the newspapers are undoubtedly on microform—usually microfilm (long rolls of film negatives) and microfiche (cards with many pages represented in reduced form on each card). Both forms require the use of reading machines, which your librarian will assist you with if you are using them for the first time.

To locate the articles you've found listings for, copy down all the information for each listing; then use your library's serial holdings list to find out which periodicals you'll be able to find, where they are located, and in what form. Many periodicals are bound and shelved like books, several issues or a volume under a hard cover. Current issues would be shelved in a current periodicals section. Other periodicals are available only in microform.

The Central Catalog

All the books shelved in your school library are listed in the central catalog; also included are non-print items such as videotapes and sound recordings. At one time, all library catalogs listed books on three-by-five-inch cards shelved in drawer after drawer—called the "card catalog." Card catalogs list items three ways: by author, by title, and by subject. Some libraries divide the three lists into two catalogs: author-title and subject.

Figure 16-4 shows a card from the subject catalog. The top line of the card names the subject—one of those listed near the bottom of the card. The title card would have the title on the top line, and the author card would begin with the author line. This card is from a library that uses the Library of Congress classification system (see page 452). The HV call number indicates that the book is shelved in the area of the library designated for social sciences. In addition to the full title and the name of the publisher, the card gives the date of publication (allowing you to question whether the information is too old for your purpose), and other descriptive data.

Many libraries have replaced their card catalogs with online catalogs. Instead of drawers and cabinets, these libraries have computer terminals throughout the library accessing listings of all their holdings. Users follow the instructions beside the terminal to locate items by author, title, and

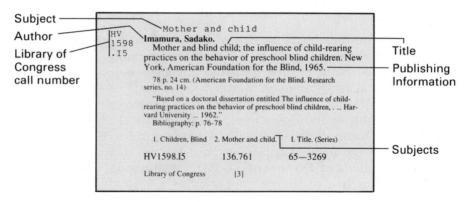

Figure 16-4. Annotated Sample of a Catalog Card.

subject. Entering the "subject" command and a short subject heading, you would receive a listing of all the library's holdings on that subject (or as many as can be held on a screen; another command would bring up the next screen). When you select a particular title, the screen displays the same information given on a catalog card, including the call number. Entering another command, you would learn the status of the book—whether it is on the shelves, checked out, on reserve, and so on. If your library has an online system, you need to learn how to use it. It is not difficult, and using it can be much quicker than a card catalog search. Figure 16-5 shows an example of an online printout describing a book and its availability status.

```
Screen 001 of 001  Record 0021 of 0024 SCS                    Catalog SCS
LOCATION:   BF21 .W56
AUTHOR:     Wolman, Benjamin B       ed.
TITLE:      Scientific psychology; principles and approaches. Ernest Nagel:
            consulting ed.
PUBLISHER: New York, Basic Books [c.1965]
DESCRIPTN: xv, 620 p. 25 cm.
BIBLIOG:   Includes bibliographical references.
SUBJECT:   Psychology--Addresses, essays, lectures.
----Type  DS  to Display availability Status /  RE  to Recall index
SCS=)PRINT ON
PRINTER ON?
SCS=)DS
BAR-CODE-ID        AREA/FLOOR     COPY   DUE--DATE-TIME   HOLDS   RESERVE-ID
30102000073153     CIRC-4th        01   *ON SHELVES       000
30102000073161     CIRC-4th        02   *ON SHELVES       000
SCS=)PRINT OFF
```

Figure 16-5. Online Catalog Entry.

Government Publications

Another useful source of information is government publications, though in using them you should remember that they represent an official point of view. Probably the biggest problem in using them is their massive number. You can avoid some of the frustration by using the *Monthly Catalog of United States Government Publications* (published monthly by the Government Printing Office) and *Public Affairs Information Service Bulletin* (published semimonthly). If your library does not carry the items that interest you, you can order them from the Superintendent of Documents, G.P.O., Washington, DC 20402, at nominal cost or free of charge.

Computer Searches

Your library probably has two kinds of computer searches: CD-ROM and online. With *CD-ROM*, your library has the database on compact disk (CD) and probably will not charge you for using it. Common CD-ROM databases are *Periodicals Abstracts*, indexing 450 popular and scholarly journals from the United States, Canada, and England in all subject areas; *Government Publications Index*, indexing the *Monthly Catalog* named in the preceding paragraph; *General Periodicals Index*, indexing 1100 magazines and journals; and ERIC (Education Resources Information Center), the largest education database. There are many more; find out what is available at your library.

Online searches access huge databases from a central location. They are done usually with a librarian, who works with you in determining appropriate search terms. There is usually a charge, depending on the length of the search, but in exchange you get access to millions of items, which your combination of terms limits to a printout of titles suitable to your search.

Exercise: The Exploring Writer

Develop a working bibliography for the subject you will research. Although you will find that some types of sources will be more fruitful for you than others, begin by searching each of the types discussed above: the reference collection, periodicals (using the Reader's Guide *and at least one specialized index), and the central catalog. Your teacher may also request that you investigate government publications and carry out a computer search.*

Taking Notes on Your Reading

The notes you take will be your source of information as you write your research paper, so make them accurate and thorough. Actively read for answers to your research questions, making notes on relevant material—perhaps providing definitions of key terms, examples of important concepts or events, analogies to things your reader may be familiar with, apt quotations from respected authorities on the subject, an account of how a plan would work, and so on. What you need for developing your research paper are the same types of information you have used for writing formal essays. The difference is that some of information for the research paper comes from other people. (See also "Notes" in Chapter 9, pages 238–42.)

Index Cards

Index cards are useful for notetaking for the same reason they are handy for the working bibliography: flexibility. Cards bearing single-item notes can be collected as you do your research, held together in a packet or with a rubber band and thus easily transported. When you begin organizing your paper, you can arrange your cards according to your outline. Drafting, then, becomes an orderly process of turning note cards over as you use them instead of tearing through a notebook trying to find the appropriate note.

Some students, rather than using three-by-five cards, find the four-by-six size preferable, giving them more space for each note. Some like to use several colors of cards: organizing their notes with a different color for each type of note (quotation, summary, etc.) or for each heading. Some researchers like the flexibility and convenience of a four-by-six notepad, the advantage being that the pages hold together during notetaking and can be separated later for sorting and organizing.

To simplify sorting later, put only one item of information on each card, and in a top corner label the card with a key-word heading signifying its content, as illustrated in Figure 16-6. In the other upper corner write the author's name, to correspond to the bibliography card, and the page number. If you have more than one item by an author, number the items—Rose 1, Rose 2, and so forth—and mark the bibliography cards in the same way. To avoid late trips back to the library, be sure you include the page numbers for all notes except your own; you will need them when you use the information in your paper.

Key-word
heading

Quotation

Researcher's
note

Key-word
heading

Quotation

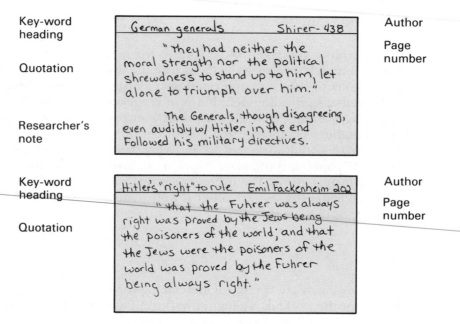

Author

Page
number

Author

Page
number

Figure 16-6.   Sample Annotated Note Cards.

Other Notetaking Systems

Some of your articles will be so important for your topic that you want
more than your notes on their content. In that case, make a *photocopy* so
you will have the entire article for your use. Then you can make notes in
the margins and highlight particularly relevant sections. As useful as
photocopies are, do not consider them alternatives for note cards. Cross
reference them to cards on which you note a heading, the author's name,
and observations on how you will use the material. Be sure to reference
the photocopied article to a bibliography card.

For books that you plan to use heavily, you can use *self-sticking note
sheets* to mark relevant pages. As with photocopied articles, reference your
note sheets to corresponding note cards and bibliography cards. Since
the pages you have marked are likely to cover more than one aspect of
your topic, you may well have several note cards for one book, each with
separate headings.

More and more researchers are using *computers* for recording their
notes. To avoid a disarray of notes like those taken randomly on notebook
paper, pattern your computer notes after note cards, one note to a page,
referenced by subject, author, and page number. You can print your notes
and arrange them manually as you would note cards, then block-move
them as you write your draft.

Quotation, Paraphrase, and Summary

The notes you take will no doubt be of four kinds: exact quotation, paraphrase of the original, summary, and your own thoughts. To assist yourself later in knowing which kind of note you are using, adopt a system that makes sense to you. Enclosing quotations in quotation marks is obvious, and for your own notes you might use parentheses; then everything else would be the author's ideas in your words.

Quotations, summaries, and paraphrases must be accurate, and meaning must not be altered when taken out of context. Be sure to enclose in **quotation marks** all word-for-word notes, and double-check to be sure you have every word and punctuation mark right. If an author is quoting someone else, include the second person's name in your note. When the quotation continues onto a second page, mark on your note where the page break occurs in case you don't use the entire quotation in your paper. While you may wish to take many of your notes as direct quotations, the ideas of other people will fit into your paper better if you write them in your own words.

A **paraphrase** is a restatement in approximately the same number of words as the original, whereas a **summary** is a shortened version of the original, written in the summarizer's words. After writing a paraphrase and a summary, review what you have written to be sure it accurately reflects the original—that it does not alter meaning by your word choice or selection of details. (For more on summaries, see Chapter 15.)

When you write paraphrases, be careful to use your own words and phrases, not just a rearrangement of the original. Illustrated below is a faulty paraphrase, followed by a better one.

Original

> Scientific revolutions are forced upon us by the discovery of phenomena that are not comprehensible in terms of the old theories.—Gary Zukav, *The Dancing Wu Li Masters;* New York: Bantam, 1979, p. 192

Faulty paraphrase

```
Scientific revolutions, says Gary Zukav, are forced upon us
when we discover phenomena that we cannot comprehend in
terms of the old theories.
```

Better paraphrase

```
In The Dancing Wu Li Masters, a book about physics for the
unscientific person, Gary Zukav observes that revolu-
tions in science occur when old theories can no longer
explain new knowledge (192).
```

The first paraphrase is just a reworking of the original, using much of the same language, and it does not adequately cite the source (see "Documenting Your Sources" on page 473). In contrast, the second gives evidence of another mind working on the sentence and then restating it. It also correctly cites the source, which would be named in a list of works cited. Sometimes, when paraphrasing, it is necessary to use particularly apt or technical words exactly as they are used in the original. In that case, enclose the quoted words:

> In The Dancing Wu Li Masters, a book about physics for the unscientific person, Gary Zukav observes that revolutions in science occur when old theories can no longer explain new knowledge. "Old Ideas die hard," he says (192).

Plagiarism

Plagiarism is the use of someone else's words or ideas as if they were one's own. It constitutes dishonesty. An obvious type of plagiarism is the presentation of another student's work under one's own name. Most students recognize this practice as dishonesty and refrain from engaging in it—although, when pressed for time, they may be tempted to take what they see as an easy way of getting their work done. Don't be tempted; your writing assignments are learning experiences, and when you don't do them, you don't learn. As a consequence, most schools have serious penalties for plagiarism. Look at it from a long-term perspective: No one wants to build a career on a degree that involves cheating.

In research papers, plagiarism occurs when students don't take the trouble to learn and practice the conventions of documentation. The rules are simple—though, admittedly, their practice is more complicated. Conventions of scholarship require that everything borrowed from another source be cited. That means not only direct quotations but summaries and paraphrases as well. The sources of words and ideas that are not your own must be named. In addition, quotations must be exact and all borrowings must not alter the meaning of the original. Study the section on documentation carefully and refer to it frequently as you draft and revise your paper.

The primary reason usually given for citing sources is to give credit where it is due. This is a valid reason. Whatever you write belongs to you, whether or not you register a piece of your writing with the U.S. Copyright Office. If somebody else uses your idea in a piece of his or her writing without citing you as its source, the idea appears to belong to that person. In writing, everything you do not cite is assumed to be your own knowledge. This is the first reason for citing sources. The second is related. Citing the source answers a reader's question: "How do you know this?" And the third reason is related to the second: You back up your knowledge and experience with that of experts, greatly increasing your credibility on the subject. If these reasons are not enough to convince you that documentation is worth the trouble, there is one more: Documentation is expected of scholars and researchers. Students who are serious about their college work are careful about documentation.

Some kinds of information do not need to be documented. One, of course, is your own knowledge, acquired from your own experience, observations, and education. Even so, it is often useful to give the context for the acquisition of your knowledge; for example, "In the two years I've worked as a volunteer in Friendly Acres Nursing Home, I have never observed abuse of patients." Another type of information that does not require documentation is common knowledge: historical facts that can be found in reference books (such as, "Maya Angelou was born in St. Louis as Marguerite Johnson"), familiar truisms (such as "Writing improves with revision"), and common maxims (such as "Birds of a feather flock together"). *Opinions* of other people are always cited, as well as facts resulting from another's research. Any time you are in doubt about whether or not to cite a source, cite.

In recent years, a new question of scholarly ethics has arisen from frequent use of collaborative projects. If you and a group of classmates work out a solution to a problem and one of you writes the report, who gets the credit? If you bring drafts of your papers to class for peer review and as a result of your classmates' contributions you turn in a greatly improved paper, should you give them any credit? In both cases, honesty would require naming all contributors—for the same reasons you cite print sources. The others have made a real contribution, and naming them tells your readers how you happened to have such a wonderful paper. If you think your credibility is at stake for saying you had help, how much more is it at stake if your reader suspects that help but you don't admit it? You may have noticed in the prefaces of books a section called "acknowledgments," where the authors acknowledge the assistance they have received from others. Early drafts may have been reviewed by experts in the field, ideas may have developed from discussions with colleagues, somebody may have typed the manuscript— all of these contributors are usually acknowledged. Such a practice for student writing may be a new idea for you. If so, discuss it with your teacher.

Exercise: The Community of Writers

In a collaborative group, analyze the following paraphrases and discuss (1) whether they are true to the original and (2) whether they are too close to the original phrasing. Revise any problem sentences. (Assume that each paraphrase is referenced to a Works Cited list.)

1. *Original:* "Although one would not know it from consulting various recent proposals on how to mend the educational system, this point—that reading books and watching television differ entirely in what they imply about learning—is the primary educational issue in America today."—Neil Postman, *Amusing Ourselves to Death* (New York: Viking Penguin, 1985, pp. 144–45).

   Paraphrase: According to Neil Postman, the most serious educational issue in America today is that reading books and watching television tell American students very different things about what learning is (144–45).

2. *Original:* "The first potential distortion when you are feeling guilty is your assumption you have done something wrong. This may or may not actually be the case."—David D. Burns, *Feeling Good: The New Mood Therapy* (New York: NAL, 1980, p. 179).

   Paraphrase: Guilt, says psychiatrist David D. Burns, involves assumptions that may or not be true. One of these potential distortions is the feeling of having "done something wrong" (179).

3. *Original:* "Upward progress within any corporate hierarchy of management depends, of course, in large part on talent. But a number of informal considerations—some of them social—often weigh heavily in promotions and hiring."—Vance Packard, *The Status Seekers* (New York: Pocket, 1959, p. 107).

   Paraphrase: Reporting corporate practices prevalent in the 1950s, Vance Packard declares that social factors were often as important to promotion and hiring as competence to do the job (107).

Organizing Your Notes: Thesis and Outline

As noted earlier in the chapter, many of the steps in doing research occur at the same time. You may begin organizing your notes while you are still reading and taking notes. You formulate a tentative thesis after your preliminary reading and are likely to revise it during your in-depth reading. You probably see your paper taking shape as you note headings for each of your note cards. The time does come, however, when you need to sit down with your notes and begin to shape an outline.

After you've completed what you perceive to be the greatest part of your reading, try to write a thesis sentence suitable for drafting your paper. By this time, your head is full of information about your subject and you should be ready to make your statement about it. Write a sentence that states your subject and the assertion, or point, you want to make about it (see pages 58–60). Make your statement narrow enough and specific enough that you can develop it adequately in the assigned length of your paper. Here are thesis sentences that state both the subject and the assertion, narrowly and specifically.

> Although some changes have been made in recent years, the amount of medical research with female subjects is still inadequate.
>
> Regarding the use of time and resources, American and Japanese school systems can learn from one another.

Your thesis sentence should help you decide how to organize your paper. The paper following the first of these thesis sentences would describe recent changes in medical research, then show how little is still being done, concluding that present research with women as subjects is inadequate. The second sample sentence implies a comparison between American and Japanese school systems on the matter of how they use time and resources. The methods for developing research papers are similar to those for developing informal essays, as described in Chapter 4: exemplification (first sentence), comparison (second sentence), chronology, definition, emphasis, and so on.

Exercise: The Exploring Writer

Write a rough outline of how you think your thesis should be developed. (See outline patterns on pages 55–58). Sort your note cards according to your subject headings, spreading them out on the floor or on a table so you can see each heading. Then look for subcategories, placing these cards next to those they are related to. As you work, you will probably see the shape of your paper begin to emerge. Revise your rough outline to fit your groups of cards, make adjustments as necessary in the headings of your cards, and look for areas where you will need to do additional reading.

Evaluating Your Sources

With your research questions in mind, evaluate the quality of your notes. Do they address your questions in some way? Do they give you some means of developing your thesis? Set aside notes that may have seemed relevant when you made them but which, it is now clear, will not be needed for the paper. Don't regard the time taking them as wasted—the information you gained will increase your authority on the subject, providing your written voice with a more knowledgeable tone.

Evaluate the authority of your authors. Have they been cited by other authors? Do the things they say jibe with what others in the field say? In cases of disagreement, do the differences exist in the facts or in the way the facts are interpreted? As you form your own opinions on your subject, you are likely to find that authorities differ with one another and you must make your choices. For example, astronomers interpret the evidence for the origins of the universe in various ways, each opinion contributing to knowledge in the field but none being confirmed as the decisive truth until more evidence is available. Be aware of the issues and disagreements regarding your subject.

Question how your sources use facts. What do they omit? Do you detect any bias in their selection of details or their use of loaded words? They may give you facts on AIDS education in the schools, for example, but if they use phrases like "usurping the authority of the family" you know they have a one-sided perspective on the facts.

After carefully evaluating your notes as they relate to your research questions and, overall, to what you have learned about your subject, take whatever additional notes you need and set aside those your judgment has rejected. Revise your outline and thesis sentence to the form you want to use for writing your draft. Block out a period of time without interruptions—a few hours if you can manage them. Gather all your information—bibliography cards, note cards, thesis sentence, and outline—and prepare to write.

Drafting Your Paper

During the process of reading, notetaking, and organizing, your head becomes full of ideas. You know a great deal more about your subject than when you started. Using your thesis sentence and your outline as guides, begin drafting your paper. Begin wherever you feel confident about what you want to say. That may be with your introduction, if you know how you want to begin. Otherwise, begin by writing your thesis and proceeding with your first main point.

Since drafting a research paper is a bigger project than most people can complete in one sitting, plan to do your writing in chunks, a section of your outline at a time. Whenever you must interrupt your writing, try to leave it with a beginning of what you intend to say next. When you return to writing, read over at least the last paragraph or so, enabling you to maintain your tone and coherence. Don't allow your outline to confine you; use it for what it is—a guide—but if at any time you see a need to diverge from your preliminary plan, do so, making sure, of course, that you don't get into irrelevancies.

Using Your Sources

In writing a paper that uses information outside your own knowledge and experience, it is crucial for you to keep in mind that *this is your paper.* Because it goes out under your name, whatever you write is yours. One implication of this principle is that whatever you do not attribute to another source is taken to be from your own knowledge and experience. Source citation is therefore one of the most important things for you to do (see the section on "Documenting Your Sources" that follows). Another implication is that a series of quotations loosely strung together is not going to cut it. You have your own thesis, your own outline, your own purpose for writing, your own opinions; your quoted, paraphrased, and summarized material just supports what you have to say. A third implication is that paraphrases and summaries are preferable to direct quotations—for the reason that paraphrases and summaries are written in your own words and therefore make it easier to maintain your own style and purpose. So use quotations sparingly. If it is necessary to quote several lines, block indent them. Set in the entire quotation ten spaces, double-spaced, and omit quotation marks.

Cite your sources as you use them, making the parenthetical notation as discussed under "Documenting Your Sources." On separate paper—or at the end of your document if you're using a word processor—add the entry to your reference list. People who put off these notations often overlook references that require citations.

Introduction, Conclusion, and Title

There are no special rules for writing **introductions** to research papers. As in shorter essays, introductions use narratives, anecdotes, questions, definitions, statistics, and so on—whatever is appropriate for setting the tone for the paper, establishing the writer's authority, and announcing the subject. As stated earlier in the chapter, a research paper usually strikes an objective tone, very often not using the pronouns *I* and *you* and avoiding contractions, colloquialisms, and other features of everyday speech. These features vary somewhat according to situations, so be sure you know what is expected of your research paper. An appropriate tone plus a familiarity with the facts and vocabulary associated with the subject establishes your authority to write your paper. If your introduction is well done, by its end there should be no doubt in your reader's mind about what your subject is and what your perspective on that subject is.

As with your shorter essays, you need to conclude your research paper with something that sounds like an end—a summary of your main points, a restatement of your thesis, a recommendation for action or further study, implications of your report, and so on. A **conclusion** should not just rehash what you've just said; anything said now should draw together— conclude—what you've presented in the paper. If in your introduction you asked a question, answer it here. If you narrated a relevant incident or presented a problem, resolve it here.

Both introductions and conclusions should be short as compared to the rest of the paper—in most cases no more than a paragraph. If your introduction runs more than two-thirds of a page, it is probably too long; a conclusion longer than half a page could probably be shortened.

Sooner or later, your paper must have a **title**. Your title, like all titles, should both describe and stimulate interest in your topic. If you still don't have one when you start drafting, don't worry about it; something will probably come to you sooner later. If nothing has come by the time you are ready to type or print your final draft, talk it over with a friend; between you, you are likely to discover something. (For more on introductions, conclusions, and titles, see pages 86–90.)

Coherence and Clarity

Because of its relatively greater size, the research paper can present some problems in coherence and clarity that are not troublesome in shorter papers. Unless you use an outline as a guide for drafting, you may set off on tangents unrelated to your thesis, forget how you were using terms and begin using them differently, thoughtlessly repeat statements and details, and even lose your sense of direction. In addition to letting an outline be your guide, work in sections—solid chunks of your paper— and for blocks of time. After a break, rereading your last-written paragraphs helps you make connections.

Coherence means that your paragraphs are internally unified, developing a single aspect of your subject, and that all your paragraphs connect to one another and relate to your thesis. You can achieve these connections, as noted elsewhere in this book, with repetition of key words (expressed in your thesis sentence and topic sentences) and related synonyms and pronouns, with transitional words and phrases, and by stating old, or familiar, information before making new assertions. (See pp. 106–08, 296–97, 319–20, 386, and "The Making of English Sentences" at the end of this book.

Clarity means that you adequately explain everything that needs explaining, define whatever words your reader may not understand or read the way you intend them, write sentences that are not unnecessarily complicated, and use words that are not unnecessarily technical or obscure. It means having everything right—your thesis, your organization, the development of your ideas, your grammar and mechanics, *everything*—so that nothing stands in the way of your reader grasping your meaning.

Documenting Your Sources

In scholarly research, sources of information are always documented. Methods of documentation, however, differ according to discipline. In the humanities, MLA (Modern Language Association) is common; in the social sciences, APA (American Psychological Association); in history, the *Chicago Manual of Style.* Each of the physical sciences has its own method. The methods described in this chapter are MLA and APA, but when you write research papers in other disciplines you will need to learn what documentary style to follow.

Both MLA and APA have easy-to-use parenthetical styles of citing sources. In most cases, for MLA all you need do is conclude borrowed information with a parenthetical page number or, if you haven't named the author, include the name in your parentheses. With APA, you give the publication date in parentheses, along with the author's name if you didn't include it in your sentence; page numbers follow direct quotations. These parenthetical references correspond to items fully cited at the end of your paper.

Before examining formats in greater detail, remember that *everything you borrow must be documented*—whether you paraphrase it, summarize it, or directly quote it. The only exception is common knowledge (see page 467). The discussion that follows, then, applies to all instances of borrowed information.

Both MLA and APA are parenthetical systems of documentation. Instead of footnotes, they name the source in a parenthetical note that follows the borrowed information:

MLA

Michael Ruse observes that humans are the "most interesting" of all organisms biologists might study (63).

Humans are interesting subjects of biological study (Ruse 63).

APA

> Michael Ruse (1988) observes that humans are the "most
> interesting" of all organisms biologists might study
> (p. 63).
>
> Humans are interesting subjects of biological study (Ruse,
> 1988).

MLA calls for the author's last name and the page number of the reference; if the author has been named in the text, only the page number is
placed in parentheses. APA calls for the author's name and the date of
publication; like MLA, if the author is named in the text, the name is not
repeated. In both MLA and APA, the sentence period follows the parentheses. MLA uses no comma between the name and the page number, but
APA style takes a comma before the date.

At the end of the document, the list of sources is called "Works Cited"
in MLA, "References" in APA. Both styles include only the sources actually
cited in the paper. What follows are examples of some of the most
common types of source citation in papers using MLA or APA styles.
Observe the examples in close detail: spacing, punctuation, abbreviations, capitalizations, indentations, underlines, as well as content.

Sample MLA and APA Forms

Books

Book by a Single Author

MLA

> Ruse, Michael. Philosophy of Biology Today. Albany: State
> U of New York P, 1988.

APA

> Ruse, M. (1988). Philosophy of biology today. Albany:
> State University of New York Press.

Two or More Works by the Same Author

MLA

> ---. The Philosophy of Biology. London: Hutchinson U
> Library, 1973.

APA

Ruse, M. (1973). <u>The philosophy of biology</u>. London: Hutchinson University Library.

[Note: References are arranged by year of publication; this reference would precede that of 1988; both entries would give complete citations.]

Book by Two or More Persons

MLA

Mitsch, William J., and James G. Gosselink. <u>Wetlands</u>. New York: Van Nostrand, 1986.

APA

Mitsch, W. J., & Gosselink, J. G. (1986). <u>Wetlands</u>. New York: Van Nostrand.

Edited Book

MLA

Fishman, Joshua A., Charles A. Ferguson, and Jyotirindra Das Gupta, eds. <u>Language Problems of Developing Nations</u>. New York: Wiley, 1968.

APA

Fishman, J. A., Ferguson, C. A., & Das Gupta, J. (Eds.). (1968). <u>Language problems of developing nations</u>. New York: Wiley.

Work in an Anthology

MLA

Passin, Herbert. "Writer and Journalist in the Transitional Society." <u>Language Problems of Developing Nations</u>. Ed. Joshua A. Fishman, Charles A. Ferguson, and Jyotirindra Das Gupta. New York: Wiley, 1968. 442-57.

APA

Passin, H. (1968). Writer and journalist in the transitional society. In J. A. Fishman, C. A. Ferguson, & J. Das Gupta (Eds.), <u>Language problems of developing nations</u> (pp. 442-457). New York: Wiley.

Translation

MLA

> Nemirovitch-Dantchenko, Vladimir. My Life in the Russian
>   Theatre. Trans. John Cournos. 1936. New York: Theatre
>   Arts, 1968.

[Note: The book was originally published in 1936 by another publisher.]

APA

> Nemirovitch-Dantchenko, V. (1968). My life in the Russian
>   theatre (J. Cournos, Trans.). New York: Theatre Arts.
>   (Original work published 1936.)

Article in a Reference Book

MLA

> Hartl, Daniel L. "Heredity." World Book Encyclopedia.
>   1989 ed.

[Note: If the article is unsigned, alphabetize the item under the title.]

APA

> Hartl, D. L. (1989). Heredity. In World book encyclopedia.

Pamphlet

MLA

> Cohen, Pauline. How to Help the Alcoholic. Public
>   Affairs Pamphlet No. 452. New York: Public Affairs,
>   1970.

APA

> Cohen, P. (1970). How to help the alcoholic (Public
>   Affairs Pamphlet No. 452). New York: Public Affairs.

Government Publications

MLA

> United States. Bureau of Land Management. State of
>   Arizona. Wilderness Status Map. Washington: GPO, 1991.

APA

> United States Bureau of Land Management, State of
> Arizona. (1991). <u>Wilderness status map</u>. Washington,
> DC: U.S. Government Printing Office.

Articles

Article from a Magazine

MLA

> Wiley, J. P., Jr. "Time Is Running Out for Forest
> Birds." <u>Smithsonian</u> Feb. 1990: 28+.

[Note: The + means that the article was paged discontinuously throughout the issue.]

APA

> Wiley, J. P., Jr. (1990, February). Time is running out
> for forest birds. <u>Smithsonian</u>, pp. 28+.

Article from a Scholarly Journal with Continuous Pagination

MLA

> Kennedy, Liam. "Farm Succession in Modern Ireland:
> Elements of a Theory of Inheritance." <u>Economic
> History Review</u> 54 (1991): 477-99.

APA

> Kennedy, L. (1991). Farm succession in modern Ireland:
> Elements of a theory of inheritance. <u>Economic History
> Review</u>, <u>54</u>, 477-99.

Article from a Scholarly Journal, Each Issue Paged Separately

MLA

> Jensen, Rick K. "Service Screens Delinquent Youths for
> Placement in Treatment Programs." <u>Corrections Today</u>
> 53.5 (1991): 172-78.

APA

> Jensen, R. K. (1991). Service screens delinquent youths
>   for placement in treatment programs. Corrections
>   Today, 53(5), 172-178.

Article from a Newspaper

MLA

> "Tokyo Single Life: A Dormitory." New York Times 17 Jan.
>   1991: C7.

APA

> Tokyo single life: a dormitory. (1991, January 17). New
>   York Times, p. C7.

Letter to an Editor

MLA

> Pearson, Hugh. Letter. Wall Street Journal 12 July 1991:
>   A11.

APA

> Pearson, H. (1991, July 12). Letter. Wall Street
>   Journal, p. A11.

Information Service

MLA

> Coombe, Christine A. "A Global Perspective in the
>   Foreign Language Classroom." ERIC, 1990. ED 326 066.

APA

> Coombe, C. A. (1990). A global perspective in the
>   foreign language classroom. (ERIC Document
>   Reproduction Service No. ED 326 066)

Interview

MLA

```
Williams, Catherine. Personal interview. 5 Nov. 1992.
```

APA

Personal interviews are not cited as references. Include pertinent information in the text:

```
(Catherine Williams, personal communication, Nov. 5,
    1992).
```

Revising Your Paper

By the time you get to the point of revision, you may have spent weeks working on your research paper. You may be getting tired of the whole project and just want to see it ended. Considering that you have other things going on in your life too, such an attitude is understandable. At the same time, the very fact that this paper represents such a large chunk of your life is the best reason for taking the additional time to revise it carefully. All too often, student work is downgraded simply because of too many mistakes (of one kind or another) in the final draft. Allow time for revision, and then revise your paper carefully.

This section consists of two revision checklists: the first a review of topics covered in the drafting section, the second some reminders on style and accuracy. A third checklist is included in the next section, "Format of Your Final Paper."

Revision Checklist on Content

1. *Thesis.* Now that you have written your paper, does your thesis still accurately signal your subject and the position you are taking on it? If not, reword it. Reread pages 58–60 and 468–70 if necessary.
2. *Support.* With your outline in hand, examine your main supporting points. Have you dealt with all the major issues or facets of your subject? Are there any paragraphs or sections that drift off the subject and would be better eliminated? Does the organization of your points still seem logical to you, or would they be clearer if you did some reorganization?

Revision Checklist (continued)

3. *Paragraph development.* Is each paragraph or section developed as fully as necessary? Have you defined terms that may be unfamiliar to your audience? Have you included details to explain and exemplify your topics? Do your paragraphs each center on a single aspect of your subject?

4. *Integration of sources.* Have you fully integrated all your borrowed information into your text? If your assignment requires you to announce your sources as a way of leading into your quotations, summaries, or paraphrases, be sure you have used such phrases as "According to Michael Ruse in *Philosophy of Biology Today...*" and "Michael Ruse observes that...." Whether or not such lead-ins are required of you, all your borrowed information must be integrated. Consider them as *support* for your points, not as substitutions for your own ideas. If your paper appears to be a series of strung-together quotations and summaries, you still need to do some serious thinking about what you mean to say and then say it, using quotations and summaries only to back you up.

   Make sure too that you have marked the end of each piece of borrowed information with an appropriate citation, as described in the "Documenting Your Sources" section. This is critical; well-researched and otherwise carefully written papers have failed because all sources have not been cited.

5. *Introduction and conclusion.* Take a look at your introduction and conclusion together. Because they are separated by several pages (and probably several days in the writing process), they may appear to be going in different directions. Make sure they read as if they are both parts of the same paper. While your conclusion may state your point more completely and more finally than your introduction, they should both make the same point. Reread the section on introductions and conclusions if you need to.

   In addition, question whether your introduction and conclusion accurately reflect your finished paper. Pay particular attention to your introduction. Because you may have written it while you were still "cold," it may be a little stiff and slightly off topic. You may be able to delete parts or to add something—an apt illustration or statistic, for example.

After revising the content of your paper according to this checklist, you will probably have a much stronger paper. However, despite the hours you've already devoted to revision, you still have work ahead of you. While you revise according to the following checklist, you are likely to continue revising on content as well.

Revision Checklist on Style

1. *Tone.* Read your paper for tone. Have you been objective throughout, avoiding inappropriate references to first person (*I*) and your beliefs and preferences, plus inappropriate references to the reader (*you*)? Have you avoided casual, everyday language (contractions, colloquialisms, slang, and so on), relying, instead, on usage that is appropriate for publication? Have you used with confidence the terms integral to a discussion of your subject? Have you written with assurance throughout, as one who knows the subject well?

2. *Coherence.* Have you related all parts of your paper to their surrounding parts and to your thesis? If one part is related to another by cause and effect, show that causal relationship (perhaps by phrases such as "A result of this action was . . ." or "This simple act had a number of unfortunate repercussions"). One section may exemplify another, compare one thing to another, present an analogy to explain another, and so on. Make sure these relationships are clear.

   Since you have already revised, if necessary, your thesis and organization (the primary coherence devices), you can go back now to see if you have used them as fully as you might for achieving coherence. Do you repeat the key words of your thesis and topic sentences (plus synonyms, related words, and pronouns with clear reference)? Does the first sentence of each paragraph tie into the preceding paragraph in some way (such as "Another example of this circumstance is . . ." and "This decision may be compared to . . .")? In connecting paragraphs with one another, as well as sentences with one another, have you taken advantage of the "old information/new information" principle, recapping what is known before asserting something new (see page 319)?

> ### Revision Checklist (continued)
>
> 3. *"Works Cited" or "References" format.* First make certain you have included all the sources you have cited in your text and that all the sources listed have been cited. Do not include other sources unless your assignment calls for a "works consulted" list too.
>
>   Then check the format of every entry. See that each one conforms in all particulars to the style you are using: information, order of items, punctuation, capitalization, spacing, underlining, and abbreviations. Documentary format is similar to spelling or punctuation in that readers expect words to be spelled in certain ways, punctuation marks to mean certain things, and parts of a citation to stand for certain publishing elements. Be consistent with the style you are using.

Format of Your Final Draft

Unless your instructor tells you otherwise, observe these guidelines for the form of your final draft.

Type or print your paper on good quality 8½ by 11 white paper; do not use lightweight or erasable paper. Have a fresh black ribbon in your typewriter or printer. Use only one side of the paper. Margins should be one inch on all sides for MLA style and 1½ inch on all sides for APA. Do not justify the right margin; leave it uneven. Double-space throughout the entire text, including long quotations and your list of references. Number every page in the upper right corner by simply typing the number, plus, for MLA style, your last name, and, for APA, a short title.

MLA	*APA*
Johnson 1	Telekinesis
	3

Type the number half an inch down from the top of the page for MLA and one inch down for APA.

Title pages are usually not necessary for term papers. Instead, at the top left corner of your first page, on separate double spaced lines, type your name, the name of your instructor, the course number, and the date. If your assignment calls for a title page, your instructor will tell you what elements to include. Your instructor will also tell you if you need to include any other items, such as outline, abstract (see pages 410–18), or table of contents. Begin your "Works Cited" or "References" on the page following the last page of text and continue numbering consecutively.

If, when you proofread, you need to make corrections in your typed copy, draw a clean line through the error and insert the correction in the line above it (never in the margins), either typed or written in ink. Strike-overs are never acceptable, but you may use correcting liquid or tape to cover and type over an error. If you find extensive errors, retype the page.

Before typing your final draft, apply the first item of the following checklist. While typing, refer often to the sample student paper at the end of the chapter, using it as a guide for style and format.

Revision Checklist on Format and Usage

1. *Grammar.* You may need to go over your draft several times, concentrating each time on different potential problems. On one trip through, check for unclear *pronouns*, making certain that each pronoun stands for an identifiable noun. Avoid masculine pronouns (*he, him*) referring to antecedents of either or unidentified sex; recast the sentence to plural, use *he or she*, or avoid the pronoun altogether. (See Style in the handbook.)

   Check your **verbs**. References to the work of other writers are usually introduced with present-tense verbs: "As Ruse *points out,* classification is necessary if we are to make sense of our world." Past-tense verbs refer to completed activities: "Ruse *delivered* a shortened version of his book as a memorial address at York University."

   Unless your teacher permits them, avoid **contractions** (such as *won't* for *will not* and *shouldn't* for *should not*) and the pronouns *I* and *you*. Check for all grammar and punctuation problems that sometimes occur in your writing. (Refer to handbook as necessary.)

2. *Format.* There is little room for creativity in the format of research papers. Apply the guidelines described in the section on format and all your instructor's specifications. Double-check your list of works cited (or references) to be certain you have been consistent in following the MLA (or APA) documentary style.

3. *Appearance.* Look at your finished paper with a critical eye. Does it look good? Do your margins look right? Is your type clear and black? Are the pages free of smudges and creases? If not, redo those pages. Does any page have more than two or three corrections? Retype or reprint that page. If you were on the job, you would want to submit a product that represented you as a careful worker; your teacher expects that kind of care.

The End

Read your paper over one more time—yes, *one more time*—to make sure you have no typing errors. If you do find any, make the corrections as noted already; your paper won't look as neat with a penned-in correction, but it will read better. Then follow your teacher's instructions for fastening the pages of your paper. Some people want only a paperclip in the upper left corner, some prefer a staple, and some advise a binder of some type. If your teacher has not specified a fastener, use a paperclip. Putting that on is truly the end. Your research paper is completed.

Sample Student Research Paper

The following paper is printed here as a guide on format and style for a paper using MLA documentation. Do not think of it as a model paper, because instructors' guidelines differ and this paper was written under an assignment different from yours. Marginal annotations point out pertinent features of the paper. Following the full MLA-style paper are a few pages of the same paper reformatted according to APA style. Again, use this sample only as a guide, not as a model.

Sample Student Research Paper
MLA Format

Woods 1

Brian J. Woods

Professor Lynn Bryce

English 163

14 November 1991

The Central Importance of Anti-Semitism

in Nazi Ideology

Anti-Semitism is a thread which runs through the entire Holocaust. But to say this is not to describe the effect that anti-Semitism had on the Holocaust. Was the Holocaust the culmination of centuries of anti-Semitism? Was rabid anti-Semitism spurred on by other beliefs? Many questions can be asked, and answers seem hard to come by. Yet anti-Semitism, the Holocaust, and Nazism have been inseparable since World War II. It is necessary in discussing them to find some connection between them. In this paper I will argue that anti-Semitism was the basis from which the Nazis logically worked out their ideology.

Since anti-Semitism preceded Nazism, the first area to examine is general anti-Semitism. One important aspect of anti-Semitism is religious hatred and intolerance. The European Christian culture seemed to explain the Jews' unacceptance of Christianity in the darkest ways. Norman Cohn, in his book Warrant for Genocide, contends that since the first crusade the Jews were depicted as children of Satan. Furthermore, the Jews were "accused of murdering Christian children, of torturing the consecrated wafer, and of poisoning the wells" (22). These unfounded accusations are bad enough, but the Jews were also accused of the most hideous crime--the murder of God through the crucifixion of Jesus, i.e., deicide. Leon Poliakov, a Holocaust scholar, notes that the charge of deicide implies a criminal people, beyond salvation, who are therefore destined to servitude ("Weapon" 834).

Author's last name and page number

Double-spacing throughout

Centered title

Introduction announces subject of paper, asks pointed questions

Thesis

Topic sentence to orient reader

Source citation, summary, then direct quotation

Identifies authority of source

Woods 2

Cultural intolerance also plays a large part in anti-Semitic belief. The Jews had different norms under which they lived. Eugen Weber, in an article on anti-Semitism, points out that these differences caused strong resentments from non-Jews (165). Moreover, Poliakov argues that an anti-Semitic atmosphere forced Jews closer together, exacerbating the separateness of the Jews ("Weapon" 834). However, while the Jews were bound culturally in groups they were separated physically throughout many countries. Anti-Semitic belief postulated a secret Jewish conspiracy working internationally which controlled "political parties and governments, the press and public opinion, banks and economic development" (Cohn 22-23). The imagined Jewish threat seemed to be one of "internationalism and individualism" (Poliakov, Harvest 6). The Jews were hated for both their closeness and their dispersion.

A third aspect of anti-Semitism is the association of Jews with political movements. Cohn observes that in pre-World War II Europe individual Jews leaned toward liberal democratic beliefs because these provided the best hope for their liberty. The Jews needed some kind of protection from anti-Semitic practices. But there were groups, for example the aristocracy and the clergy, who viewed this Jewish liberalism as a grave threat to their interests and values (24). Hitler believed the Jews were trying to become spokesmen for progress, a threat to the old, presumably better, ways (314). Anti-Semites did not just disagree with certain political views, however; they hated the Jews as a group because of some nebulous threat they represented. Sarah Gordon, in her study of the Nazi Holocaust, suggests this when she describes Hitler's idea of the "Jewish spirit" as comprising "democracy, parliamentarianism, liberalism, rationalism, individualism, legalism, bolshevism, humanism, and intellectualism" (91).

The last of the elements of the "Jewish spirit" presents a

Topic sentence followed by support from four sources—summaries incorporating direct quotation

Topic sentence, connecting to preceding paragraph and announcing new paragraph

Paraphrase

Page number

Direct quotation, page number

Woods 3

problem. If Hitler distrusted intellectualism, can an underlying Nazi ideology be found? This is a real problem because of the central position Hitler occupied in the Nazi party. William Shirer, a noted scholar on the Third Reich, illustrates this with his description of an early attempt to limit Hitler's power within the party. When Hitler discovered an attempt to merge the Nazis with other, similar parties, he offered to resign. When his resignation was refused, he abolished the party committee and assumed dictatorial powers, which lasted until the end of the Third Reich (72-74). Hitler himself in Mein Kampf writes that for political questions "the decision will be made by one man" (449). This situation is further complicated by the emotional nature of the appeals of Hitler and Nazism. Gordon insists that the Nazis gained support through appeal to the hatreds and tensions which Germans felt toward the Jews (152). And J. J. Schokking, in an essay on Nazi methods, confirms that Nazism's appeal seemed to be in its offer to "replace material and spiritual despondency by a new hope" (481).

Although there is no concrete written ideology which can be pointed to, this does not mean there was no ideology underlying Nazi aims and actions. Perhaps Hitler, as supreme dictator, could set whatever program he liked. But Alan Bullock, in his discussion of Hitler's political ideas, warns that it is a mistake to ignore the content of Hitler's appeal to the more than one third of the German people who voted for him ("Political" 350). Throughout the reign of the Third Reich there were several aims which remained consistent, the most notable being the problem of the "Jewish question." Mein Kampf, which an official paper of educators called "our infallible pedagogical guiding star" (Shirer 344), sets out these aims or ideas. Three of the major ideas guiding Nazi action were race theory, nihilism, and the unifying theme of Weltanschauung. These three ideas made up part of a decidedly evil theory. Together they relied

Authority of source leads into summary

Topic of next several paragraphs

upon each other for impact and justification, but separately they
could stand on their own.

    Nazi race theory held to an inherent difference between the
races. The racial character could not be altered but could be
weakened through interbreeding (Gordon 25). Naturally, the Nazis
put forth that the Germans were the representatives of the Aryans,
the master race. Furthermore, as Leni Yahil points out in her book
The Holocaust, according to Nazism "race was the factor that
governed men's lives" (37). Thus race theory provided the central
conflict in life which Nazism proposed to overcome. Certainly,
Nazism was not the originator of the idea of racial inferiority; one
need only look to slavery in the United States to see this. Yet
coexistent with Nazi race theory was a perhaps unprecedented
moral stance, that of nihilism. Wilhelm Grenzmann, in his study of
the link between the philosopher Friedrich Wilhelm Nietzsche and
National-Socialism, keeps to the traditional meaning of nihilism: a
rejection of previous and current moral theories, and a rejection of
distinction in moral values. Grenzmann asserts that "National-
Socialism is nihilism in politics in its extreme form" (217). Nazi
nihilism encompassed a belief that living entailed the domination of
the stronger being, and the right of the stronger to set morality
(Grenzmann 204). Nazism characterized traditional Judeo-
Christian morality as weak and cowardly, and, as will be seen,
blamed the Jews most especially for the development of traditional
morality (Yahil 654).

    Race theory and nihilism lay in the background of Nazi
ideology, whereas Weltanschauung was the up-front, social aspect
of Nazi thought. According to Martin Needler, in his political study
of Hitler's anti-Semitism, the Weltanschauung was a basic core of
positions on specific issues which the voters could be confident the
parties would adhere to. All parties in pre-World War II Germany

Topic sentence for
paragraph

Paraphrase followed by
author's name and
page number

Woods 5

had a Weltanschauung (332). Hitler's Weltanschauung was "the
granite foundation of all [his] acts" (Hitler 22). The Nazi
Weltanschauung encompassed many ideas directly and
peripherally, but three may be separated out as important and
implying the rest. Emil L. Fackenheim, in his article questioning
why the Nazis carried out the Holocaust, identifies these three as
the need for lebensraum, the Fuhrerprinzip, and anti-Semitism
(201-02). Lebensraum is the need for living space, something the
Nazis would obtain through armed conquest. Hitler himself said:
"Germany's future [is] . . . wholly conditional upon the solving of the
need for space" (qtd. in Shirer 419). The Fuhrerprinzip was
founded upon the belief that one great man would be needed to
lead Germany to its destined greatness. This idea became
intimately tied to anti-Semitism as Nazism developed. Fackenheim
points out that only two things remained solid as the Reich
collapsed and all lebensraum had been lost: "the Fuhrerprinzip,
and the murder of more, and ever more, Jews" (203).

Within the Weltanschauung, anti-Semitism steps forward as a
distinct ideological belief. This, however, need not have been the
case in Nazi race theory. Indeed, in an influential work explaining
the theory of racial differences, H. S. Chamberlain explains that the
Jews are different yet not inferior to the Teutons, the other "pure"
race he identifies.[1] However, in analyzing the Jews, "Chamberlain
slips into the very vulgar anti-Semitism which he condemns in
others" (Shirer 155). And the Jew as inferior subhuman, the "vulgar
anti-Semitism" of which Shirer speaks, is a central obsession in
Nazism. Gordon explains that in Hitler's eyes history involves
nationalistic needs for living space or world domination. The Jews
were a scattered nation, seeking "racial supremacy through
dominance, subjection, and extermination" (95). It is easy to see,
then, that the Nazis felt a need to do something about this inferior

Quotation from a
secondary source

Square brackets for
interpolated words

Ellipsis dots to indicate
omission

Paraphrase, including
direct quotation

Footnote number for
content note (following
text)

Woods 6

anti-Aryan, who would destroy the Aryans given a chance. This belief marks a turn from the supernaturalism of the deicide charge to, as Poliakov points out, the "science" of race theory ("Weapon" 834).

The Jews were more than just the anti-Aryans, they were also the polluters of the pure race. Hitler writes that interbreeding had weakened the Aryan strain in Germany (328). The Germans were at a disadvantage as long as they were not pure Aryans, and "it was partially this fear that prompted his obsession with destroying European Jews himself before further degeneration weakened [the] 'Aryans'" (Gordon 92). The Nazis called for a repurification of the Aryan race, and this process necessarily entailed the removal of the race-weakening Jews. Although the pseudo-scientific race theory does not make clear exactly why the Aryans are superior, it is more clear what the Nazis wanted: a Europe dominated by Germany, whose resources would be used only for the benefit of Germany (Shirer 1223). Thus, within the Nazi system it was a logical conclusion to destroy the Jews in order to pave the way for the future German empire.

Nazi race theory provided for the hatred of all Jews by lumping them all in one category of race. This analysis, helpful from a Nazi viewpoint, also extended into the area of politics and economics. As noted earlier, Jews generally tended toward liberalism, and this did not sit well with conservatives, who saw the Jews as bearers of unwanted change (Gordon 26). But the Jews were also seen as allies of Marxism, the antithesis of liberal capitalism (Poliakov, "Weapon" 833). In fact, there were few social threats, real or perceived, for which the Jews were not blamed. From starting World War I to causing the great depression, "the Nazis harped on the theme of Jewish culpability ad nauseam" (Gordon 151). Just as the threat of racial weakening required a response, so did the threat

Short title for identifying one of two sources by same author

Author plus page number, since author is not named in text

Woods 7

of unwanted political and economic systems brought about by the Jewish "race." This response was the political aspect of race theory.

Just as there are superior and inferior races, whose basic differences are of the utmost importance, so within a race the differences between individuals are important. To Hitler, "the inequality of individuals and of races" was a law of nature (15). Furthermore, it is the duty of the state to raise the superior individuals and, equally importantly, to subordinate the inferior (446). Thus rulers have an inherent right and duty to rule; they are not chosen by the majority. In Hitler's words, "There would be no 'democratic nonsense'" (qtd. in Shirer 125). Authoritarian rule was the natural outcome of this belief, for there were no objective means of determining who the superior individuals were. Fackenheim notes that within this system there would be one individual who would wield overall authority, being the most clear-minded and superior. From the inception of Nazism it was Hitler who played this role (202). Hitler formed a movement of "fantastic differentness" (Needler 2) against the "new" ideas as represented by the Nazi caricature of Judaism. Joining the Nazi party, for any reason, meant being drawn into a dictatorial framework which demanded an overall outlook of anti-Semitism.

Beyond their anti-Semitic race theory and its authoritarian implications, the Nazis needed a moral grounding wholly different from Judeo-Christian beliefs. "Do unto others as they do (or you would have them do) unto you" would not fit into their scheme. Nazi nihilism went against, and was a reaction to, Judeo-Christian morality. Friedrich Nietzsche labeled traditional morality as "slave morality" long before the rise of the Third Reich (qtd. in Grenzmann 205).[2] The so-called slave morality involved concepts antithetical to eventual Nazi tenets: the equality of all individuals before God, the

Source of common maxim is not cited

Footnote number for content note (following text)

Woods 8

concept of an objective measure of good and evil, and the primary responsibility of the individual to act and be held responsible for his or her actions. The Nazis viewed the old morality as an attempt by the weak to dominate. Hitler asserts that activity must not be aimed at "philanthropic flim-flam," but instead toward strengthening the race-oriented state, which leads "to the degeneration of the individual" (29-30).

In rejecting Judeo-Christian morality, the Nazis placed a special emphasis on its Jewishness. Poliakov notes that "in the eyes of the neo-pagans [i.e., the Nazis], the chosen people symbolized the dishonored morality of the Gospels and the Judeo-Christian tradition" (Harvest 6). Moreover, there is also an implicit notion of a conspiracy theory. For if the Jews are after world domination through racial interbreeding, and the Jewish morality was a weakening, slave morality, then traditional morality could be seen as further Jewish treachery. But if traditional morality was part of Christianity as well, why single out the Jews? Needler confirms that Hitler was a sincere anti-Christian, but this conviction was not part of Hitler's visible election campaign (335). Since Christians made up most of the German population, surely Hitler could not gain power based on a program which espoused hatred of the electorate. The Jews, on the other hand, had a history of oppression, and their population was but 1 percent of the entire German population (Gordon 8). History, numbers, and beliefs combined to make the Jew the perfect anti-Nazi. As Herman Rauschning, an early party leader, said, "If the Jew did not exist, we should have to invent him" (qtd. in Poliakov, Harvest 2-3).

The Nazis did not merely rebel against the Jewish morality; on the contrary, they had an underlying view in keeping with their attitude toward race and authoritarianism. Chamberlain's race theory had room only for biological facts of existence. Alfred

Square brackets for interpolated words

Citation of indirect source; short title for identifying one of two sources by same author

Woods 9

Rosenberg, a follower of Chamberlain, made this claim clear by
postulating that the ultimate phenomenon accessible to mankind is
that of the struggle "between blood and its environment, between
blood and blood" (Grenzmann 210). Thus, morality does not come
from outside mankind but from within, imposed by the race theory in
which man "recognize[s] the obligation imposed upon him by
Nature" (Hitler 401). Duty and honor become the central tenets of
Nazi morality, with no room for the Judeo-Christian ideas of guilt
and sin (Grenzmann 213). Race and the racial organization, i.e. the
state, become all important, and the individual loses all value except
as part of the state.

    Grenzmann points out that in this naturalistic scheme "endless
struggle is its only law. Might is always right" (208). How, then, did
this Nazi morality work to bring about the German-Aryan nation?
Fackenheim argues that all moral decisions were reduced to the
question of what the Fuhrer would do in the doer's place (201).
Thus, murdering Jews in cold blood became morally acceptable
because it was what the Fuhrer willed; and the Fuhrer willed it to
protect Aryan racial purity. Gordon quotes George Kren and Leon
Rappoport as insisting that the Holocaust was not "irrational" but an
example of logic losing touch with human feeling (91). Within
Nazism, a hideous act of murder could be construed as moral by
appeal to the logical framework of Nazi moral theory. The Nazis
needed but one thing more to prove the justice of their moral
theory. This, of course, was the anti-Reich, the Jew (Poliakov,
Harvest 2).

    Race theory and nihilism provide the background against which
the Nazis worked, but the Weltanschauung remained to set the path
along which the Nazis would tread. Shirer emphasizes that "the
blueprint of what the Almighty had called upon [Hitler] to do in this
cataclysmic world . . . , the Weltanschauung. . . . [was] set down in

Square brackets for
interpolated letter to
make quotation
conform to textual
sentence

Textual reference to
indirect source

Ellipsis dots to show
omission from original;
square brackets for
clarifying words

cold print for all to ponder" (163). The cold print was Mein Kampf.
As noted above, three major points in the Weltanschauung are
lebensraum, the Fuhrerprinzip, and anti-Semitism.

The Nazis needed lebensraum, or living space, for their grand
Germany, and armed conquest was in accordance with nature's
laws for achieving this goal (Fackenheim 201). Bullock quotes
Hitler saying that "there is no historical injustice where soil is
concerned," which fits very well with the nihilistic theory of morals
("Political" 354). Armed conquest was to be the means by which
Germany grew, but what of the conquered peoples? Gordon points
out that the hierarchy of race decided this dispensation. The
English and French were to be treated relatively well, while the
Poles and Slavs were to be enslaved and partially exterminated.
The Jews, as history would show, were to be completely
exterminated whenever possible (99-100). The Jews needed to be
completely cleared out of the lebensraum in order for the Nazis to
fulfill their Aryan destiny. Hitler notes that "all who are not of good
race in this world are chaff" (Shirer 129).

The fact that the Germans did begin a massive campaign to
gain ever more lebensraum is due in large part to the Fuhrerprinzip.
Hitler was supreme leader, with everyone in Germany ultimately
answering to him through lesser authorities. Though the German
generals voiced dissent at the military aims of Hitler again and
again, they inevitably carried them out. Shirer writes that the
generals "had neither the moral strength nor the political
shrewdness to stand up to [Hitler]" (438). In this capitulation to the
Fuhrer, "Hitler's own ideas, and above all, Hitler's anti-Semitism
became orthodox belief in Nazi Germany. Michael Marrus, in his
study of anti-Semitism, asserts that race theory and anti-Semitism
need not necessarily have led to murder, much less the Holocaust
(175). Something needed to be added to the base of anti-Semitism

Woods 11

which would stir the people of Germany to, if not abject hatred, at least a willingness to allow the heinous crimes of the Holocaust. The Fuhrerprinzip as catalyst seems to go a long way as explanation.

In the final analysis, Nazism always comes back to the "Jewish problem" for justification of their aims. Needler contends that Hitler needed a sort of glue to hold together the "half-baked ideas" which the Nazis shared with other parties on the "lunatic fringe." This glue was anti-Semitism (333). Gordon points out that the Jews could be blamed for all the "evils" the Nazis chose to identify (151). Indeed, the Jews could even be blamed for contradictory actions, such as defending both capitalism and Marxism, as noted earlier. "Like all obsessions, the Jew is not a partial, but a total explanation" (Hitler 15). To the Nazis, the Jews were scapegoat, justifier, and eternal enemy. The Nazis relied upon the "truth" of anti-Semitism, as well as the "truth" of the system built on anti-Semitism. Fackenheim puts it very succinctly when he writes: "That the Fuhrer was always right was proved by the Jews being the poisoners of the world; and that the Jews were the poisoners of the world was proved by the Fuhrer being always right" (202).

Concluding summary, ending with apt quotation

Woods 12

Notes

[1]Shirer writes that Chamberlain is "quite wooly in his definitions" (155). But it seems that the Teutonic qualities Chamberlain identifies are seen to reside most strongly in the German Aryans. The ideas Shirer discusses are found in Chamberlain's 1200-page book <u>Foundations of the Nineteenth Century</u>. An ideological predecessor of Chamberlain, Count Joseph Arthur de Gobineau, wrote another mammoth work, the four-volume <u>Essay on the Inequality of the Human Races</u>. These two works are important for understanding the development, depth, and intricacies of race theory as it relates to Nazism. However, the outcome remains obvious: the German people's greatness lies in their connection to Aryanism, and the Aryans, being the greatest race, must recover their purity (Shirer 150–58).

Grenzmann is very careful in pointing out a strong ideological link between Nietzsche and Nazism. However, he does argue that Nietzsche is a figure who "contributed more than most to the disaster" (204). Further, many ideas within Nazism fall into Nietzschean terminology, e.g. "slave morality," the "band of blond beasts." Indeed, a whole line from Nietzsche was lifted by Goebbels: "Anything that does not weaken me strengthens me" (205).

Content notes, providing reader with useful information not directly related to the writer's thesis

Woods 13

Works Cited

Bullock, Alan. <u>Hitler: A study in Tyranny</u>. New York: Perennial-
    Harper, 1971.

---. "The Political Ideas of Adolf Hitler." International Council
    350-80.

Cohn, Norman. <u>Warrant for Genocide</u>. New York: Harper, 1966.

Fackenheim, Emil L. "Holocaust and Weltanschauung:
    Philosophical Reflections on Why They Did It." <u>Holocaust and
    Genocide Studies</u> 3.2 (1986): 197-208.

Gordon, Sarah. <u>Hitler, Germans and the "Jewish Question."</u>
    Princeton: Princeton UP, 1984.

Grenzmann, Wilhelm. "Nietzsche and National-Socialism."
    International Council 203-42.

Hitler, Adolf. <u>Mein Kampf</u>. 1924. Boston: Houghton, 1971.

International Council for Philosophy and Humanistic Studies. <u>The
    Third Reich</u>. Facsimile printing. London: Weidenfeld, 1967.

Marrus, Michael R. "The Theory and Practice of Anti-Semitism."
    <u>The Nazi Holocaust</u>. Ed. Michael Marrus. Vol. 2. London:
    Meckler, 1968. 172-84. 15 vols.

Needler, Martin. "Hitler's Anti-Semitism: A Political Appraisal."
    Marrus Vol. 2, 331-35.

Poliakov, Leon. <u>Harvest of Hate</u>. Westport: Greenwood, 1975.

---. "The Weapon of Anti-Semitism." International Council 832-
    51.

Schokking, J. J. "Nazism's Way to Success." International Council
    479-503.

Shirer, William L. <u>The Rise and Fall of the Third Reich</u>. New York:
    Fawcett, 1983.

Weber, Eugen. "Jews, Antisemitism, and the Origins of the
    Holocaust." Marrus Vol. 1 , 162-78.

Yahil, Leni. <u>The Holocaust: The Fate of European Jewry</u>. Trans.
    Ina Friedman and Haya Galai. New York: Oxford UP, 1990.

Book by one author

Second title by same author; cross-reference to book in which it was found

Article in a scholarly journal

Article in a collection; cross-reference to book in which it was found

Reprint of an older book

Collection of articles, corporate author

Multivolume work

Translation

Sample Pages from a Student Research Paper
APA Format

Central Importance

1

Running title plus page number

The Central Importance of
Anti-Semitism in Nazi Ideology
Brian J. Woods
St. Cloud State University

Title

Central Importance

2

The Central Importance of Anti-Semitism

in Nazi Ideology

Anti-Semitism is a thread which runs through the entire Holocaust. But to say this is not to describe the effect that anti-Semitism had on the Holocaust. Was the Holocaust the culmination of centuries of anti-Semitism? Was rabid anti-Semitism spurred on by other beliefs? Many questions can be asked, and answers seem hard to come by. Yet anti-Semitism, the Holocaust, and Nazism have been inseparable since World War II. It is necessary in discussing them to find some connection between them. In this paper I will argue that anti-Semitism was the basis from which the Nazis logically worked out their ideology.

Since anti-Semitism preceded Nazism, the first area to examine is general anti-Semitism. One important aspect of anti-Semitism is religious hatred and intolerance. The European Christian culture seemed to explain the Jews' unacceptance of Christianity in the darkest ways. Norman Cohn (1966) contends that since the first crusade the Jews were depicted as children of Satan. Furthermore, the Jews were "accused of murdering Christian children, of torturing the consecrated wafer, and of poisoning the wells" (22). These unfounded accusations are bad enough, but the Jews were also accused of the most hideous crime--the murder of God through the crucifixion of Jesus, i.e., deicide. Leon Poliakov (1967), a Holocaust scholar, notes that the charge of deicide implies a criminal people, beyond salvation, who are therefore destined to servitude.

Cultural intolerance also plays a large part in anti-Semitic belief. The Jews had different norms under which they lived. Eugen Weber (1988), in an article on anti-Semitism, points

Running title plus page number

Centered title

Date of publication immediately following author's name

Page number for direct quotation

Central Importance

3

out that these differences caused strong resentments from non-Jews. Moreover, Poliakov (1967) argues that an anti-Semitic atmosphere forced Jews closer together, exacerbating the separateness of the Jews. However, while the Jews were bound culturally in groups they were separated physically throughout many countries. Anti-Semitic belief postulated a secret Jewish conspiracy working internationally which controlled "political parties and governments, the press and public opinion, banks and economic development" (Cohn, 1966, 22-23). The imagined Jewish threat seemed to be one of "internationalism and individualism" (Poliakov, 1975, 6). The Jews were hated for both their closeness and their dispersion.

A third aspect of anti-Semitism is the association of Jews with political movements. Cohn observes that in

Author's name, date, and page numbers for direct quotation not textually attributed to the author

Central Importance

4

References

Bullock, A. (1971). <u>Hitler: A study in Tyranny</u>. New York: Perennial-Harper.

Bullock, A. (1967). The political ideas of Adolf Hitler. In International Council for Philosophy and Humanistic Studies (Ed.), <u>The Third Reich</u>. Facsimile printing. London: Weidenfeld.

Cohn, N. (1966). <u>Warrant for genocide</u>. New York: Harper.

Fackenheim, E. L. (1986). Holocaust and Weltanschauung: Philosophical reflections on why they did it. <u>Holocaust and Genocide Studies</u>, 3(2), 197-208.

Gordon, S. (1984). <u>Hitler, Germans and the "Jewish Question."</u> Princeton: Princeton University Press.

Grenzmann, W. (1967). Nietzsche and National-Socialism. In International Council for Philosophy and Humanistic Studies (Ed.), <u>The Third Reich</u>. Facsimile printing. London: Weidenfeld.

Hitler, A. (1971). <u>Mein Kampf</u>. Boston: Houghton Mifflin. (Original work published in 1924)

Marrus, M. R. (1968). The theory and practice of anti-semitism. In M. Marrus (Ed.), <u>The Nazi Holocaust</u> (vol. 2, pp. 172-184). London: Meckler. 15 vols.

Needler, M. (1968). Hitler's anti-semitism: A political appraisal. In M. Marrus (Ed.), <u>The Nazi Holocaust</u> (vol. 2, pp. 331-335). London: Meckler. 15 vols.

Poliakov, L. (1975). <u>Harvest of hate</u>. Westport, Conn.: Greenwood Press.

Poliakov, L. (1967). The weapon of anti-semitism. In International Council for Philosophy and Humanistic Studies (Ed.). <u>The Third Reich</u>. Facsimile printing.

Book by one author

Second title by same author; article in an anthology

Article in a scholarly journal

Reprint of an older book

Multivolume work

Central Importance

5

London: Weidenfeld.

Schokking, J. J. (1967). Nazism's Way to Success. In International Council for Philosophy and Humanistic Studies (Ed.). The Third Reich. Facsimile printing. London: Weidenfeld.

Shirer, W. L. (1983). The rise and fall of the Third Reich. New York: Fawcett.

Weber, E. (1968). Jews, Antisemitism, and the origins of the Holocaust. In M. Marrus (Ed.). The Nazi Holocaust (vol. 1, pp. 162–178). London: Meckler. 15 vols.

Yahil, L. (1990). The Holocaust: The fate of European Jewry (I. Friedman and H. Galai, Trans.). New York: Oxford University Press.

Translation

APPENDIX A

HANDBOOK: A GUIDE TO CLEAR SENTENCES

This handbook is a reference tool on questions of English usage. It focuses on the sentence as the basic material of written and spoken discourse. Because the clear expression of ideas depends on the clarity of sentences, writers concentrate a great deal of attention on their sentences—revising until they feel they have expressed those ideas precisely and unambiguously. In making their revisions, writers sometimes depend on their own sense of correctness and appropriateness, and sometimes they refer to the tools of their profession: usage guides, handbooks, dictionaries, and so on.

This usage guide builds on the assumptions that you as a writer already know what English sentences look like and how they are made (see a discussion of these matters in Appendix B, which begins on page 548) and that you have already learned the parts of speech and parts of the sentence. But this guide assumes, too, that you, like other writers, sometimes have problems getting your sentences to come out right. These are problems in *usage*: how to use verbs, modifiers, and pronouns, for example. This discussion focuses on those problems, explaining the *how* more than the *what,* treating those problems as matters of writing, not of grammar. It avoids grammatical jargon as much as possible but defines terms where necessary for understanding the problem. This guide also gives you a quick review of punctuation, mechanics, spelling, and style. Refer to this guide while writing and when your instructor suggests sections for you to study.

Here's how the sections are arranged:

1 SENTENCE BOUNDARIES

Section Guide

1A Fragments

   1Aa Subordinate clause fragment

   1Ab Phrase fragment

   1Ac Incomplete thoughts

   1Ad Acceptable fragments

1B Comma splices and fused sentences

Sentence boundaries are marked by **end punctuation (7A):** periods, question marks, or occasionally exclamation points. Because they mark the ends of sentences, each mark of end punctuation must be preceded by at least one independent clause (a complete statement containing a subject and a verb and not beginning with a subordinating word). Errors in sentence boundaries involve inappropriate punctuation: periods where commas or no punctuation should go, and commas or no punctuation where periods or semicolons should go. To develop your own sense of which marks to use, think of periods, semicolons, and commas as *strongest* to *weakest*. The weakest mark, the comma, is not interchangeable with the strongest mark, the period, and usually not with the semicolon. But periods and semicolons, depending on the writer's choice, *are* often interchangeable. The following discussions regarding sentence boundary errors are based on this reasoning.

1A Fragments

Sentence **fragments** are errors in which partial sentences are treated as sentences—begun with a capital letter and ended with a period. The fragment may be a subordinate clause, a phrase, or a combination of subordinate elements. What makes each a fragment is that it lacks a subject or a verb, or that it begins with a subordinating word. Only independent clauses can make independent statements.

1Aa Subordinate Clause Fragment

Recognition. A subordinate clause has a subject and a verb but cannot make an independent statement because of the connector that implies it is only part of a sentence. Here are two lists of the most common subordinating connectors.

Subordinating conjunctions, arranged by function

Time	*Place*
after	where
before	wherever
once	*Cause*
since	as
until	because
when	since
whenever	*Condition*
while	even if
Contrast	if
although	unless
even though	whereas
though	*Result*
while	in order that
Alternative	so
than	so that
whether	that

Relative pronouns	
who (whom, whose)	whoever (whomever, whosever)
which	whichever
that	
what	whatever

where	wherever
when	whenever
why	

Any clause beginning with one of these words is *subordinate* and should not be written as a sentence. Here are examples of clause fragments (italicized):

> The Vikings revolutionized shipbuilding with the keel. *Which allowed their ships to go faster and farther without stopping for supplies.*
>
> Norway's Lapps are believed to be a nomadic people of Asian heritage. *Who follow reindeer herds through Norway's cold, rugged land.*
>
> *Because the northern part of Norway is so far north.* It has long periods during the summer when the sun shines 24 hours a day.

Before you can correct sentence fragments, you must be able to recognize them—a difficult thing to do when you know what you meant to say and, as a result, think the missing words as you read. The trick to recognition is to read differently. Some people suggest reading the text backward, sentence by sentence, because fragments tend to stand out when the context is different. Another way is to line up all the sentences in a list, like this:

> The Vikings revolutionized shipbuilding with the keel.
>
> Which allowed their ships to go faster and farther without stopping for supplies.
>
> Norway's Lapps are believed to be a nomadic people of Asian heritage.
>
> Who follow reindeer herds through Norway's cold, rugged land.
>
> Because the northern part of Norway is so far north.
>
> It has long periods during the summer when the sun shines 24 hours a day.

Lined up in this way, fragments stand out more than they do in the context of a paragraph. This technique works especially well with a word processor because of the ease of reformatting.

Correction.   There are mainly two ways of correcting clause fragments: (1) attaching them to the preceding or following sentence and (2) removing or changing the subordinating connector. These sentences illustrate both types of correction:

> The Vikings revolutionized shipbuilding with the keel. *This innovation* allowed their ships to go faster and farther without stopping for supplies. [The subordinating word of the fragment is changed.]
>
> Norway's Lapps are believed to be of Asian heritage—nomadic people who follow reindeer herds through Norway's cold, rugged land. [The fragment is connected to the preceding sentence with a dash.]
>
> Because the northern part of Norway is so far north, it has long periods during the summer when the sun shines 24 hours a day. [The fragment is connected to the following sentence with a comma.]

1Ab   Phrase Fragment

Phrase fragments lack a subject, a verb, or both. The most common phrases written as fragments are *verbal phrases* and *prepositional phrases.*

Recognition.   A *verbal phrase* is a word group made up of a verb form and related modifiers and other words. As opposed to *verb phrases,* which are made up of verb parts (such as *has been gone*), a verbal phrase is constituted with a *verbal,* a word formed from a verb but not functioning as a verb. *Going,* for example, is a verbal, as is *gone.* You probably wouldn't write "Charles going to St. Louis" or "Charles gone to St. Louis." Instead, you would add helping verbs: "Charles *is going* to St. Louis" and "Charles *has gone* to St. Louis."

There are three kinds of verbals: gerunds, participles, and infinitives. Gerunds end in *-ing,* participles end in either *-ing* (present) or *-ed* (regular past); infinitives have no ending but are usually introduced by *to.* Here are a few examples of how verbals are formed from verbs:

Verb	*Present participle and gerund*	*Past participle*	*Infinitive*
snap	snapping	snapped	to snap
look	looking	looked	to look
want	wanting	wanted	to want
go	going	gone	to go
has	having	had	to have

Verbals function primarily as adjectives and nouns, most often in verbal phrases.

In the following examples, the italicized verbal phrases are fragments because they are written as sentences:

Eero Saarinen designed the 630-foot Gateway Arch for the St. Louis riverfront. *Imagining a giant stainless steel arch.* [*Participial phrase* modifying *Eero Saarinen*]

Critics said that cranes could not reach high enough. *To lift the steel sections into place.* [*Infinitive phrase* modifying *high*]

Under Saarinen's plan, a derrick would creep up the side of each leg of the arch. *Lifting each plate into position.* [*Participial phrase* modifying *derrick*]

Saarinen knew that precision was of utmost importance. In *building the arch.* [*Gerund phrase* as object of preposition *In*]

A *prepositional phrase* is a word group made up of a preposition and its object. Together they contribute meaning to a sentence, usually modifying a noun or a verb. Like subordinating conjunctions, prepositions show relationships, such as time, place, condition, cause, and so on. Here are some of the most common prepositions:

about	along	because of
above	along with	before
according to	among	behind
across	around	below
after	as	beneath
against	at	beside

between	in place of	regarding
beyond	in spite of	since
but	inside	through
by	instead of	throughout
by means of	into	till
concerning	like	to
despite	near	toward
down	next	under
during	of	underneath
except	off	unlike
except for	on	until
excepting	onto	up
for	out	upon
from	out of	up to
in	outside	with
in addition to	over	within
in back of	past	without

In the following examples, prepositional phrases have been written as sentences and are therefore fragments:

The Vikings were descendents of Teutonic settlers. *Like most of today's Norwegians.*

Norway is a land of natural beauty. *From its fjord-lined coast to frigid Lapland.*

Correction. Phrase fragments can be corrected in one of two ways: (1) by connecting them to a related sentence or (2) by expanding them to a sentence. Both ways are illustrated below.

Verbal fragments corrected:

Eero Saarinen designed the 630-foot Gateway Arch for the St. Louis riverfront. *He imagined a giant stainless steel arch.* [The verbal fragment is expanded to a sentence.]

Critics said that cranes could not reach high enough *to lift the steel sections into place.* [The verbal fragment is connected to a related sentence.]

Under Saarinen's plan, a derrick would creep up the side of each leg of the arch, *lifting each plate into position.* [The verbal fragment is connected to a related sentence.]

Saarinen knew that precision was of utmost importance in *building the arch.* [The gerund phrase, object of the preposition *In,* is connected to a related sentence.]

Prepositional phrase fragments corrected:

The Vikings were descendents of Teutonic settlers, *like most of today's Norwegians.* **or** *Like most of today's Norwegians,* the Vikings were descendents of Teutonic settlers. [The prepositional phrase is connected to a related sentence.]

Norway is a land of natural beauty. *Its charm extends from its fjord-lined coast to frigid Lapland.* [The prepositional phrase is expanded to a sentence.]

1Ac Incomplete Thoughts

Sometimes fragments are simply errors in punctuation: The writer uses a period when a comma or no punctuation would be correct. In the examples in **1Aa** and **1Ab,** each fragment could be attached to the accompanying independent clause. A more difficult type of fragment to correct is the incomplete thought, such as this one:

> *A large concrete dock 50 feet short of a wooden platform anchored in the middle of the bay.*

In this fragment, something is missing, and, as a result, a reader doesn't know what to make of the words "large concrete dock." With fragments of this sort, the writer needs to insert the missing information. The fragment might be revised like this:

> A large concrete dock juts out, stopping 50 feet short of a wooden platform anchored in the middle of the bay.

1Ad Acceptable Fragments

You probably encounter fragments every day. Titles are often fragments, as are answers to questions and expressions of strong emotion.

> Titles: *The Purposeful Writer,* "A Fire in the Woods"
>
> Answer to question: "How many more chairs do we need?" "Fifteen."
>
> Expression of strong emotion: "What a great concert!"

And much advertising utilizes fragments:

> Intricate, delicate, exquisite. Extravagant in every way.
>
> Another successful client meeting. Par for the course.

Common as they are in everyday life, fragments are usually unacceptable in academic or business writing. Even though professional writers and advertising writers sometimes use them for emphasis, there are rarely cases when you will need intentional fragments for effective expression of your thoughts in school or business.

1B *Comma Splices and Fused Sentences*

Comma splices and fused sentences are incorrectly punctuated compound sentences. Two independent clauses (clauses that can stand alone as sentences) side by side in the same sentence can be punctuated in one of only two ways:

1. With a comma and a coordinating conjunction
          or
2. With a semicolon (with or without a transitional adverb).

Here are two examples of comma splices:

> *The economy of Algeria is in trouble, many citizens blame the government.*
>
> *The death of any soldier is tragic, however, death by friendly fire is particularly disturbing.*

Both sentences could be corrected by substituting a semicolon after the first independent clause; the first could also be corrected by adding the coordinating conjunction *and* and keeping the comma.

> The economy of Algeria is in trouble; many citizens blame the government.

> The economy of Algeria is in trouble, and many citizens blame the government.

> The death of any soldier is tragic; however, death by friendly fire is particularly disturbing.

Fused sentences, sometimes called *run-on sentences,* are like comma splices without the comma between the two independent clauses. Here are examples:

> The United States has 281 lawyers per 100,000 people Japan has only 11 attorneys per 100,000.

> *The economy of Algeria is in trouble many citizens blame the government.*

Like comma splices, fused sentences can be corrected by inserting a semicolon between the two independent clauses or by adding a coordinating conjunction plus a comma:

> The United States has 281 lawyers per 100,000 people; Japan has only 11 attorneys per 100,000.

> The economy of Algeria is in trouble, and many citizens blame the government.

The list of *coordinating conjunctions* is short:

and	or	for	yet
but	nor	so	

You can begin a second independent clause with one of these conjunctions preceded by a comma.

Unlike coordinating conjunctions, *transitional adverbs* are not conjunctions and therefore do not join sentence elements. They do, however, connect ideas by showing how they relate to one another. Like conjunctions, they can show addition, contrast, result, and other relationships. Here are some of the common transitional adverbs, arranged by function:

Addition	*Contrast*
in addition	however
also	nevertheless
moreover	on the contrary
next	on the other hand
then	otherwise
finally	*Result*
Comparison	therefore
likewise	consequently
similarly	then
in comparison	as a result

Examples	*Time*
for example	meanwhile
for instance	subsequently
in fact	finally
specifically	then

Transitional adverbs are used most commonly to connect the ideas expressed in independent clauses, as in the following sentences:

> Air bags are effective in head-on collisions; *however,* they offer little or no protection in a side-impact crash or a roll-over.

> Air bags deflate within one second after inflation; *therefore* they do not interfere with control of the car.

Notice that when a transitional adverb begins a second independent clause, it is preceded by a *semicolon.* Failure to practice this rule of punctuation results in a comma splice or a fused sentence. The transitional adverb is usually *followed by a comma,* although sometimes, as in the second sentence above, the comma is omitted.

Some comma splices and fused sentences result when writers use transitional adverbs as if they were coordinating conjunctions. If you have trouble distinguishing transitional adverbs from coordinating conjunctions, here are two tests you can make:

1. None of the coordinating conjunctions is longer than three letters, and all the transitional adverbs are four letters or longer.
2. Transitional adverbs are *movable* within the sentence, and coordinating conjunctions are not. In the first example above, *however* could be moved to the end of the sentence or after *protection.*

Recognition. The first step in avoiding comma splices is to identify them. Because they happen only in sentences with at least two independent clauses, you can test your sentences by substituting periods for your commas. If you end up with complete sentences, you probably have a comma splice or a fused sentence. Here is an illustration testing one of the preceding example sentences:

> The economy of Algeria is in trouble.

> Many citizens blame the government.

Both statements are obviously complete standing alone. They therefore cannot be connected with a comma or no punctuation. *Remember this simple rule of punctuation: Periods and commas are not interchangeable, but periods and semicolons often are.* If a period is correct, a comma is not. Here is another example of a comma splice, followed by a test of the clauses and two corrections:

Comma splice

The United States has 281 lawyers per 100,000 people, Japan has only 11 attorneys per 100,000.

Test showing two complete sentences

The United States has 281 lawyers per 100,000 people.

Japan has only 11 attorneys per 100,000.

Corrections

The United States has 281 lawyers per 100,000 people; Japan has only 11 attorneys per 100,000.

The United States has 281 lawyers per 100,000 people, but Japan has only 11 attorneys per 100,000.

For a further discussion of how coordination and subordination work to make up English sentences, see Appendix B, "The Making of English Sentences," page 548.

2   SENTENCE INCONSISTENCIES

Section Guide

2A Faulty parallelism

2B Mixed sentences, faulty predication

2C Shifts

Sentences pose difficulties for readers when the grammar is confused or inconsistent. Such problems happen when writers pay attention to what they are saying and not to how they are saying it. Such attention is a natural condition of writing, and careful revision usually takes care of any problems.

2A Faulty Parallelism

Parallelism results when two or more grammatically equivalent sentence elements are joined. (See the section on Coordination in Appendix B.) Here is a sentence with parallel elements:

> In a country where college education becomes increasingly everybody's chance, where executives and refrigerator salesmen and farmers play golf together, where a college professor may drive a cab in the summertime to keep his family alive, it becomes harder and harder to guess a person's education, income, and social status by the way he talks. —Paul Roberts

Here is the same sentence with the parallel elements arranged to be more visually accessible:

> In a country
>   {where college education becomes increasingly everybody's chance,
>   {where {executives
>   and {refrigerator salesmen
>   and {farmers play golf together,
>   {where a college professor may drive a cab in the summertime to keep
>   his family alive,
>   it becomes {harder

and {harder to guess a person's {education
{income,
and {social status
by the way he talks.

This sentence has parallel clauses (each beginning *where*), parallel subjects (*executives, refrigerator salesmen,* and *farmers*), parallel adverbs (*harder* and *harder*), and parallel direct objects (*education, income,* and *social status*). As this sentence illustrates, the principle of parallelism does not require that elements be alike in every way. Some of these nouns have modifiers, for example, and the clauses have different structural patterns.

Parallelism becomes a problem when dissimilar elements are joined, as in these examples:

> *Bolivia has three distinct geographical areas: the Andean Highlands, the Yungas, and the third is the Oriente.* [The last element is not parallel.]
>
> *Bolivia is a country of contrasts in people, plant life, and in tropical products.* [The second element is not parallel.]
>
> *The Bolivian high plateau—about 500 miles long and being 80 miles wide—is about 12,000 feet above sea level.* [The two interrupting elements are not parallel.]

Faulty parallelism can be corrected in various ways:

> Bolivia has three distinct geographical areas: the Andean Highlands, the Yungas, and the Oriente. [Unparallel words are omitted.]
>
> Bolivia is a country of contrasts in people, in plant life, and in tropical products. [A word is added.]
>
> The Bolivian high plateau—being about 500 miles long and 80 miles wide—is about 12,000 feet above sea level. [A word is moved.]

Revision of faulty parallelism is usually fairly easy to achieve. What is difficult is recognizing it, and unfortunately there are no tricks to easy recognition. Even experienced writers find that in their own writing they need to make an editing trip through their drafts looking just at their parallel structures. The absence of faulty parallels is a sign of careful writing.

2B Mixed Sentences, Faulty Predication

In mixed sentences, sometimes called faulty predication, two or more parts do not make sense together. Like other inconsistencies, this kind of problem usually occurs when writers concentrate harder on meaning than on grammar. Study the inconsistencies in these sentences:

> *By driving to the movie was how we saw the accident happen.*
>
> *Just because Johnson smoked marijuana doesn't mean he won't be a good mayor.*
>
> *A CAT scan is when a medical technician takes a cross-sectional x-ray of the body.*

These constructions are common in everyday speech and may not seem inconsistent to you. And in casual speech they are usually acceptable. In writing, however, they require a closer analysis. In the first sentence, the subject of the verb *was* is the prepositional phrase *By going to the movie*; grammatically, prepositional phrases cannot function as subjects. In the second sentence, the subject of the verb *does mean* is the adverb clause *Because Johnson smoked marijuana*; adverbs, being modifiers, cannot logically function as subjects. In the third sentence, an adverb clause, *when medical technicians take cross-sectional x-rays of the body*, is a complement of the subject—another function that adverbs cannot serve. Here are the sentences revised:

> While driving to the movie, we saw the accident happen.
>
> We can't conclude that Johnson won't be a good mayor just because he smoked marijuana.
>
> A CAT scan is a cross-sectional x-ray of the body.

In each of the revised sentences, the subjects and predicates are now logically consistent.

2C Shifts

Shifts occur when writers lose track of their sentence elements. Shifts occur in a variety of ways:

In person

> In music, where left-handed people seem to be talented, the right-handed world puts *you* at a disadvantage. [Shift from *people,* third person, to *you,* second person]

In tense

> Even though many musicians *are* left handed, instruments *had been designed* for right handers. [Shift from present tense to past perfect]

In number

> A left-handed *violinist* has to pay extra to buy *their* left-handed violin. [Shift from singular to plural]

Once recognized, shifts are often easy to revise:

> In music, where left-handed people seem to be talented, the right-handed world puts *them* at a disadvantage.
>
> Even though many musicians are left handed, instruments *have been designed* for right handers.
>
> Left-handed *violinists* have to pay extra to buy their left-handed violins.

3 PROBLEMS WITH MODIFICATION

Section Guide

3A Dangling and misplaced modifiers

3B Restrictive and nonrestrictive modifiers

3C Adjectives and adverbs

One part of a sentence can be *modified* by another part. A part that is modified is changed in some way: limited or broadened, perhaps, or described, defined, identified, or explained. Adjectives and adverbs always serve modifying functions, but clauses and phrases also can be modifiers. This section deals with problems in modification. For a fuller discussion of how modifiers work, see Appendix B, on page 548.

3A Dangling and Misplaced Modifiers

Dangling and misplaced modifiers are words and word groups that, because of their position or the way they are phrased, make the meaning of a sentence unclear and sometimes even ludicrous. These troublesome modifiers are most commonly verbal phrases, prepositional phrases, and adverbs. Here are examples:

> *Reaching to pick up the saddle,* the obnoxious horse may shake off the blanket. [The dangling verbal phrase appears to relate to *horse.*]
>
> *To extend lead out of the eversharp pencil,* the eraser cap is depressed. [The dangling verbal phrase implies that *the eraser cap* does something.]
>
> The eversharp pencil is designed to be used permanently, *only periodically replacing the lead.* [The dangling verbal phrase implies that the pencil replaces the lead.]
>
> Dick *only* had to pay ten dollars for his parking ticket. [The misplaced adverb should immediately precede *ten.*]
>
> Theodore caught a giant fish in the very same spot where he had lost the ring *two years later.* [The misplaced adverb phrase confusingly appears to modify the last part of the sentence instead of, correctly, the first part.]

Errors of this type are difficult for writers to recognize because to the writers they are not ambiguous.

Recognition. Verbal phrases always have implied subjects; in other words, somebody is performing the action. For clarity, that implied subject should be the same as the subject of the sentence or clause. To recognize your own dangling verbal modifiers, make sure that the implied subject of the verbal phrase is the same as the subject of the sentence. In the first example above, the implied subject of *Reaching* is not *the horse.* In the second example, the implied subject of *To extend* is not the *eraser cap.* And in the third example, the implied subject of *replacing* is not the *pencil.* Also check passive voice, because in a passive sentence the subject is not the doer of the action. In the second example, the dangler can be corrected when the verb, changed from passive to active voice, tells who should depress the eraser (see correction below).

Correction. Correcting dangling and misplaced modifiers depends on the type of error. Misplaced modifiers can often be moved to a more appropriate position:

Dick had to pay *only* ten dollars for his parking ticket.

Two years later, Theodore caught a giant fish in the very same spot where he had lost the ring.

Dangling modifiers usually require some rewording:

As you reach to pick up the saddle, the obnoxious horse may shake off the blanket. [The dangling verbal phrase is converted to a clause.]

To extend lead out of the eversharp pencil, *depress the eraser cap.* [The main clause is revised so that *you* is the implied subject of *depress* (as it is for *To extend*).]

The eversharp pencil is designed to be used permanently, *only periodically needing the lead replaced.* [The dangling verbal phrase is revised so that implied subject of *needing* is *pencil.*]

3B *Restrictive and Nonrestrictive Modifiers*

Some modifiers are essential to a sentence because they *restrict,* or limit, the meaning of the words they modify; others, while adding important information, are not essential to the meaning of a sentence. The first type is called *restrictive* and the second *nonrestrictive.* The terms usually refer to subordinate clauses and phrases. Here are examples of restrictive and nonrestrictive modifiers:

Restrictive

People *who plan to visit Europe* should take time to see Belgium. [Relative clause modifying and identifying *People*]

The industrialized country *between the Netherlands and France on the North Sea* is constitutionally a kingdom. [Prepositional phrases modifying and identifying *country*]

The Kempenland was thinly populated *before coal was discovered there.* [Subordinate clause modifying *was populated* and giving meaning to the sentence]

Language and cultural differences have created friction *that has existed for centuries.* [Relative clause modifying and identifying *friction*]

Nonrestrictive

Belgium has two major populations: the Flemings, *who live in the north and speak Flemish,* and the Walloons, *who live in the south and speak French.* [Two relative clauses, the first modifying *Flemings* and the second modifying *Walloons*]

With Brussels in the middle of the country, both groups inhabit the city. [Prepositional phrases, together modifying *inhabit*]

NATO's headquarters is in Brussels, *where it has been since its beginning in 1950.* [Subordinate clause modifying *Brussels*]

Covering southeastern Belgium, the sandstone Ardennes mountains follow the Sambre and Meuse rivers. [Participial (verbal) phrase modifying *mountains*]

These examples illustrate several aspects of restrictive and nonrestrictive modifiers:

1. They *modify* a word in the clause or sentence; they therefore function as adjectives or adverbs.

2. They can appear at the beginning, somewhere in the middle, or at the end of a sentence or clause.
3. Most types of subordinate elements can be restrictive and nonrestrictive.
4. Whether a clause or phrase is restrictive or nonrestrictive depends on its function in the sentence.
5. Restrictive elements are not set off with punctuation; nonrestrictive elements are set off with commas (and sometimes dashes).

If you think the distinction between restriction and nonrestriction is not worth making, consider the following sentences, the first restrictive and the second nonrestrictive:

People who wear braces on their teeth should not eat caramel apples.

People, who wear braces on their teeth, should not eat caramel apples.

Set off with commas, the *who* clauses implies that all people wear braces on their teeth and should not eat caramel apples. It does not *restrict,* or limit, the meaning of *people.* In the first sentence, however, the *who* clause does restrict, or limit, the meaning of *people* to only those who wear braces on their teeth. Often only the writer knows the intended meaning and therefore needs to make the distinction by setting off, or not setting off, the modifier.

Here are a few guidelines that might help you in making this fine distinction:

1. A modifier that modifies a proper noun (one that names a person or thing) is usually nonrestrictive, because the name is sufficient identification. Notice *Flemings* and *Walloons* in one of the preceding examples.
2. A *that* clause is almost always restrictive. See the fourth example.
3. Adverbial subordinate clauses (those beginning with subordinating conjunctions such as *because* and *when;* see list on page 505) are almost always restrictive and usually not set off with commas when they appear at the end of their sentences. If they appear at the beginning of sentences, they are almost always set off with commas.
4. A nonrestrictive modifier at the beginning of a sentence is followed by a comma, one at the end is preceded by a comma, and one in the middle is enclosed with two commas. See example sentences with *before, where,* and *who.*

3C Adjectives and Adverbs

Adjectives and adverbs, often called *modifiers,* describe nouns and verbs. *Adjectives* modify nouns; that is, they describe, limit, explain, or alter them in some way. By modifying, they *limit* the meaning of the nouns: *red car* is narrower in meaning than *car,* and *fast red car* is narrower than *red car. Adverbs* modify verbs, adjectives, and other adverbs, telling more than the words by themselves would tell: drive *carefully* (adverb modifying a verb), *unexpectedly* early (adverb modifying an adjective), drive *very* carefully (adverb modifying an adverb). Adverbs usually tell how, where, when, and how much.

Adjectives and adverbs occasionally present some problems for writers. Be careful not to use adjectives when adverbs are needed, as in this sentence:

> *The governor suspected that the legislators were not taking him* <u>serious</u>. [*Seriously* is the form required for modifying the verb *were not taking*. (If you're not sure whether a word is an adjective or an adverb, check your dictionary, which probably labels parts of speech.)]

Another problem in form concerns the *comparative* and *superlative* degrees. The comparative form of adjectives and adverbs shows a greater degree between two things:

> Your luggage is *stronger* than mine. [Adjective comparing *your luggage* and *mine*]
> Your luggage survives airport baggage handling *better* than mine does. [Adverb comparing how the two *survive* handling]

The comparative degree is formed by adding *-er* to shorter adjectives and adverbs (*strong, stronger, hard, harder*); longer words are preceded by *more* (*beautiful, more beautiful; seriously, more seriously*). Do not use *-er* with *more* (not *more harder*).

The superlative form shows a greater degree among three or more things:

> This is the *strongest* luggage I have ever seen. [Adjective comparing the present luggage to all other luggage the writer has seen]
> Your luggage survives airport baggage handling *best* of all luggage I've seen. [Adverb comparing how all luggage the writer has seen survives handling]

The superlative degree is formed by adding *-est* to shorter adjectives and adverbs (*strong, strongest; hard, hardest*); longer words are preceded by *most* (*beautiful, most beautiful; seriously, most seriously*). Do not use *-est* with *most* (not *most strongest*).

Do not use adjectives and adverbs gratuitously, just to fill space or because you think you ought to. They are effective only when they add meaning.

4   VERBS

Section Guide

4A   Tense
4B   Subject-verb agreement
   4Ba   Intervening subordinate element
   4Bb   Subject complement
   4Bc   Compound subject
   4Bd   Indefinite pronoun as subject
   4Be   Inverted sentence order
   4Bf   Intervening relative clause

Verbs are the central core of a sentence; together with subjects, they make statements. Verbs often tell what the subject is doing:

> The company *agreed* to plead guilty to criminal charges.
> Nearly every miner *can name* a casualty of black lung disease.

Another common function of verbs is to link subjects to complements:

> Logan *is* an isolated county in the corner of the state.

Sometimes the verb tells something about the subject, as the following passive verb does:

> Casualties of mining *cannot be measured* only by injuries.

By changes in form, verbs can tell the time of the action (past, present, future), the number of the subject (singular or plural), and the person of the subject (first person, *I, we*; second person, *you*; third person, *he, she, it, they*).

4A   Tense

The problems that writers sometimes encounter when using verbs in writing result from the fact that verbs, unlike most other words in English, have many forms, and a slight shift in form can alter meaning. Notice how the meanings of the following pairs of sentences change as the verbs change:

> The fish *has jumped* into the boat.
> The fish *have jumped* into the boat.
> The concert *starts* at 8:15 p.m.
> The concert *started* at 8:15 p.m.

In the first pair, the meaning changes from one fish to more than one fish jumping into the boat. In the second pair, the first verb implies that the concert has not yet begun; the second, that it has already begun. It is important, therefore, to use the verb form that conveys the intended meaning. Observe how the verb *vanish* changes in the following sentences to indicate differences in time, or *tense*:

Present:	Many agricultural jobs *vanish.*
Past:	Many agricultural jobs *vanished.*
Future:	Many agricultural jobs *will vanish.*
Perfect:	Many agricultural jobs *have vanished.*
Past Perfect:	Many agricultural jobs *had vanished.*
Future Perfect:	Many agricultural jobs *will have vanished.*

To omit an *-ed* ending or use the wrong helping verb gives readers a false message.

Helping (auxiliary) verbs.   It is also important to use a form that is a *finite*, or an actual, verb. In the following example, the word that appears to be a verb (italicized) is not a finite verb:

> The fish *jumping* into the boat.

The word *jumping* does not have one of the primary functions of verbs—telling time of the action, called *tense*. The time of the occurrence could have been the past (*the fish were jumping*), present (*the fish are jumping*), or the future (*the fish will* *be jumping).*We also don't know whether the writer meant one fish or many. The *-ing* form is a *verbal* and requires a helping, or auxiliary, verb to make it finite, or able to tell time: words such as *am, is, are, was, were* (forms of *be*). Other helping verbs are *do* (*Do* you *want* the paper? She *doesn't want* the paper) and *have* (I *haven't seen* the paper; *has* she *seen* it?).

Irregular verbs.   Most verbs change forms in a regular way: *want* in the present becomes *wanted* in the past, *wanting* with the auxiliary *be* (i.e., *is wanting*), and *wanted* with the auxiliary *have* (i.e., *have wanted*). Many verbs change irregularly, however—internally rather than at the ending. Here are a few of the most common irregular verbs:

Base form	Past tense	Present participle	Past participle
be (is, am, are)	was, were	being	been
come	came	coming	come
do	did	doing	done
drink	drank	drinking	drunk
give	gave	giving	given
go	went	going	gone
grow	grew	growing	grown
lie	laid	lying	lain
see	saw	seeing	seen
take	took	taking	taken
teach	taught	teaching	taught
throw	threw	throwing	thrown
wear	wore	wearing	worn
write	wrote	writing	written

Check your dictionary for the forms of other verbs you suspect may be irregular.

The verb form that is perhaps the most troublesome is the *-s* form in the present tense. This form is used for all singular nouns and the pronouns *he, she,* and *it.* It is discussed in section **4B.**

4B   Subject-Verb Agreement

Clauses are made of subjects and verbs plus their modifiers and other related words. A fundamental principle of usage is that verbs agree with their subjects. In most cases, this principle presents no problem: You say "Birds *have* feathers," not "Birds *has* feathers." But all sentences are not this simple. Before getting into the problem areas, consider first that errors in subject-verb agreement occur only with present-tense verbs and those verb tenses that use present-tense forms of helping verbs (such as *have* and *be*). And, except for the irregular verb *be* (with its forms *am, is, are, was, were*), the problem centers on third-person singular verbs with their *-s* ending. Here is the problem illustrated. Notice that only the verbs in the third-person singular are different. The unfortunate thing is that all nouns are third person and, when singular, require this form in the present tense.

	Present		*Present Perfect*	
	singular	*plural*	*singular*	*plural*
first person	I work	we work	I have worked	we have worked
second person	you work	you work	you have worked	you have worked
third person	**he works**	they work	**he has worked**	they have worked
	(she, it)		**(she, it)**	

It is the *-s* form, then, that you need to watch for to avoid errors in subject-verb agreement. Here are some situations that may cause problems.

4Ba   Intervening Subordinate Element

When a subject and a verb are side by side, they usually do not present a problem. Often, however, writers separate them with subordinate elements, such as clauses, prepositional or verbal phrases, and other elements. The result may be a verb error. The following sentence illustrates this problem:

> *The realization that life is a series of compromises never <u>occur</u> to some people.* [The subject is *realization*, a singular noun, and should be followed by the singular verb *occurs*. The corrected sentence would read "The realization that life is a series of compromises never occurs to some people."]

4Bb   Subject Complement

Subject complements follow some verbs and rename the subject, though they are not always in the same number as the subject. Because a singular subject may have a plural complement, and vice versa, confused writers might make the verb agree with the complement instead of the subject. Here's an example:

> *The result of this mistake <u>are</u> guilt, low self-esteem, and depression.* [The subject is *result*, not *guilt, low self-esteeem, and depression*; the singular subject should be followed by the singular verb *is*. The corrected sentence would read "The result of this mistake is guilt, low self-esteem, and depression."]

4Bc   Compound Subject

Two or more words may be compounded to make a subject. Whether they are singular or plural depends on their connector. Subjects connected by *and* and *but* are plural, but those connected by *or* and *nor* are singular or plural depending on whether the item closer to the verb is singular or plural. Here are examples:

> The young mother and the superior student *are* both candidates for compulsive perfectionism. [Two subjects, *mother* and *student,* are joined by *and* and take a plural verb.]

> Promotions or an employee award *tells* the perfectionist he or she is achieving personal goals. [When two subjects, *promotions* and *award,* are joined by *or,* the verb agrees with the nearer one; in this sentence a singular verb is required.]

An employee award or promotions *tell* the perfectionist he or she is achieving personal goals. [Here the plural verb, *tell,* agrees with *promotions,* the closer of the two subjects.]

4Bd   Indefinite Pronoun As Subject

Indefinite pronouns are defined and listed under **5Cb.** Though these words often seem plural in meaning, most of them are singular grammatically. When indefinite pronouns are the subjects of sentences or clauses, their verbs are usually singular. Here are examples:

Everyone *has* at some time worried about achieving goals. [The singular indefinite pronoun *everyone* takes a singular verb, *has.*]

Each car and truck on the highway *was* creeping along on the icy pavement. [The singular indefinite, *each,* requires a singular verb, *was.*]

Neither of us *is* going to worry about being late. [The singular indefinite, *neither,* takes a singular verb, *is.*]

Nevertheless, some of us *are* going to be very late. [The indefinite *some* (like *all, any,* and *none*) is singular or plural depending on context; compare "Some of the book *is* boring."]

4Be   Inverted Sentence Order

Inverted sentence order can confuse your natural inclination to subject-verb agreement. Examples of inverted order are questions, plus sentences beginning with *there.* Sentences like these demand closer attention to agreement.

Have the results of the test come back yet? [The plural subject, *results,* takes a plural verb, *have.*]

There *are* many special services provided just for kids at hotels, ski lodges, and restaurants. [The plural subject, *services,* takes a plural verb, *are. There* is never a subject; it only holds the place for the subject in an inverted sentence.]

4Bf   Intervening Relative Clause

Subordinate clauses that begin with the relative pronouns *who, which,* or *that* present special problems in subject-verb agreement. Their verbs must agree with their own subjects, not with a word in another clause. These subordinate clauses demand special attention because whether the pronouns are singular or plural depends on their antecedents. These sentences illustrate agreement within relative clauses:

Every person who *attends* the baseball game will receive a free cap. [*Who,* the subject of *attends,* means "person," a singular noun.]

John is one of the few people I know who *care* about frogs. [*Who,* the subject of *care,* means "people," a plural noun.]

John is the only one of all the people I know who *cares* about frogs. [*Who* in this sentence means "one."]

5 PRONOUNS

Section guide

5A Pronoun case

5B Pronoun reference

5C Pronoun agreement

    5Ca Compound antecedents

    5Cb Indefinite pronouns as antecedents

    5Cc Shifts in person

Pronouns can have all the same sentence functions as nouns; the difference is that pronouns do not have the meaning that nouns have. Nouns name things; a noun stands for the thing itself. Pronouns, however, refer only to nouns. Whenever that reference is ambiguous or inconsistent, there is a problem in clarity.

5A Pronoun Case

Case is a grammatical term for the way nouns and pronouns show their relationships to other parts of a sentence. In English, nouns have only two case forms: the regular form (the one listed in a dictionary, such as *year*) and the possessive form (used to show ownership or connection, such as *year's*; possessive nouns are discussed at **8Ca**).

Pronouns, however, have retained their case forms. Here are the forms for personal and relative pronouns:

	Nominative	*Objective*	*Possessive*
Personal	I	me	my, mine
	you	you	your, yours
	he	him	his
	she	her	her, hers
	it	it	its
	we	us	our, ours
	they	them	their, theirs
Relative	who	whom	whose
	whoever	whomever	whoever

Notice, first, that possessive pronouns, unlike possessive nouns, do not take apostrophes—none of them. Sometimes writers confuse possessive pronouns with contractions, which do have apostrophes (such as *it's,* meaning *it is* or *it has*; and *who's,* meaning *who is*; for a further discussion, see **8Cb**).

Another problem writers sometimes have with pronoun case is using a nominative form when they need the objective or using an objective form when they need the nominative.

Nominative Case. Use the *nominative* forms for subjects and for words referring to subjects, as in these examples:

Among the patients a nutritionist sees are the grossly overweight people *who* have tried all kinds of diets. [*Who* is subject of the verb *have tried* in its own clause.]

They have a life history of obesity and diets. [*They* is the subject of *have.*]

He and the patient work out a plan for permanent weight control. [*He* and *patient* are the compound subjects of *work.*]

The patient understands that the ones who work out the diet plan are *he* and the nutritionist. [*He* and *nutritionist* refer to *ones*, the subject of the clause.]

Notice that pronoun case is determined by the function of the pronoun in its own clause and that compounding (*he and the patient*) has no effect on case.

Objective Case.   Use the *objective* forms for objects of all kinds:

"Between *you* and *me*," said the patient to his nutritionist, "I'm ready for something that works." [*You* and *me* are objects of the preposition *between.*]

An exercise program is usually assigned the patient for *whom* diet is prescribed. [*Whom* is the object of the preposition *for.*]

The nutritionist gives *her* a suitable alternative to couch sitting. [*Her* is the indirect object of *gives.*]

Modest exercise combined with modest dieting can affect *him or her* dramatically. [*Him or her* is the direct object of *can affect.*]

Having advised *them* about diet and exercise, the nutritionist instructs dieters about behavioral change. [*Them* is object of the participle *having advised.*]

Notice again that the case of a pronoun is determined by its function in its own clause and is not affected by compounding (*you and me*).

5B Pronoun Reference

Personal and relative pronouns (see list under **5A**) must refer to nouns. By themselves they have no meaning. As a result, they can cause problems in clarity for writers. If you were to read "She teaches technical writing at her local technical college," you would know only that *someone*, a woman, teaches technical writing at the college. But if the sentence were preceded by one like this, "After getting her master's degree, my mother has achieved one of her life goals," the pronoun *she* would have meaning. In this case, *mother* is the antecedent of *she*. The antecedent gives meaning to the pronoun. For this reason, it is essential that pronouns refer unambiguously to their antecedents and that pronouns and antecedents agree.

Ambiguous pronoun reference may occur in various ways: more than one possible antecedent, adjective as intended antecedent, implied antecedent, and too great a separation between antecedent and pronoun. Here are sentences in which the pronouns do not clearly refer to their antecedents:

The immunologist refused to admit fraudulence of the data reported by a former colleague in a paper he *had cosigned.* [*He* could refer to *immunologist* or to *colleague.*]

In Carolyn Chute's book The Beans of Egypt, Maine, *she* treats poverty with concern and understanding. [Possessive nouns function as adjectives; in this case

> *Carolyn Chute's* modifies *book* and cannot serve as antecedent of the pronoun *she.*]

> It *says in the newspaper that the economy will not improve soon.* [There is no antecedent for *it.*]

> At Ajax they *have tires on sale till the end of the month.* [There is no antecedent for *they.*]

> This *only reinforces public skepticism about the credibility of scientists.* [There is no antecedent for *this.*]

> *One of the primary rules for using humor in advertising is often broken,* which *is that the ad doesn't make fun of the product.* [The antecedent of *which, rules,* is too distant for the reference to be clear.]

Faulty pronoun reference is corrected by clarifying the relationship between the pronoun and its intended antecedent. Observe how the example sentences have been revised:

> The immunologist refused to admit fraudulence of the data reported by a former colleague in a paper *the immunologist* had cosigned. [*The immunologist* replaces the unclear pronoun *he.*]

> In *her* book *The Beans of Egypt, Maine, Carolyn Chute* treats poverty with concern and understanding. [The possessive pronoun replaces the possessive noun and refers to the noun subject, *Carolyn Chute.*]

> *The newspaper* reports that the economy will not improve soon. [The unclear pronoun *it* is replaced by its implied antecedent, *newspaper.*]

> *Ajax* has tires on sale till the end of the month. [The unclear pronoun *they* is replaced by *Ajax.*]

> This *kind of waffling* only reinforces public skepticism about the credibility of scientists. [The unclear pronoun *this* is replaced by the adjective *this* modifying the intended antecedent *kind of waffling.*]

> That the ad doesn't make fun of the product is an often-broken primary rule for using humor in advertising. [Parts of the sentence are moved around until they are clear.]

Revising unclear pronouns is sometimes like working a jigsaw puzzle: finding and adding a missing piece or moving parts around to achieve the best fit. Often only the writer can make the right connections.

5C Pronoun Agreement

Some pronoun errors result because the pronoun and its antecedent do not agree. In this sentence, "When a student is late for this class, they find the door locked," the plural pronoun *they* refers to a singular antecedent, *a student.* There no agreement in *number.* In this sentence, "When a student is late for this class, you find the door locked," again the pronoun, this time *you,* does not agree with the antecedent. This time the problem is *person.* Pronouns must agree with their antecedents in both number and person. (See the list of pronouns in **5A.**)

5Ca   Compound Antecedents

Problems sometimes occur with compound antecedents. If the antecedents are joined by *and,* the pronoun is plural; if joined by *or,* the pronoun agrees with the nearer antecedent. Here are examples of correct usage:

> In the pediatric trauma center, the head doctor and head nurse direct *their* medical team. [The pronoun *their* refers to both *doctor* and *nurse.*]

> The head doctor or the head nurse directs *his or her* team. [The pronouns *his or her* refer to the closer antecedent, *nurse* (since the gender of the nurse is not known, the neutral alternatives are used).]

> The head doctor or the other doctors give *their* help when it is needed. [The pronoun *their* agrees with the closer antecedent, *doctors.*]

5Cb   Indefinite Pronouns as Antecedents

A particularly troublesome kind of agreement is that between personal or relative pronouns and *indefinite pronouns.* As their name implies, indefinites do not refer to particular persons or things; grammatically they are usually singular but are often intended as plural. Here are the common indefinite pronouns:

all	every	none
any	everybody	nothing
anybody	everyone	one
anyone	everything	some
anything	neither	somebody
each	no one	someone
either	nobody	something

Like nouns, these pronouns can serve as antecedents of personal and relative pronouns. But because most of them are grammatically singular, they can be troublesome in sentences. Here are examples of correct usage:

> Everyone in the trauma center has *his or her* specific job to do. **or** All the personnel in the trauma center have *their* specific jobs to do. [The neutral, though wordy, alternative *his or her* agrees with the singular indefinite *everyone.* The second sentence illustrates the use of plural when gender is unknown.]

> *Each* of them does *his or her* job efficiently and competently. **or** *All* of them do *their* jobs efficiently and competently. [*Each* is singular, but *all* is either singular or plural, depending on context (compare "*All* literature has *its* place").]

5Cc   Shifts in Person

Agreement errors in *person* are shifts between *I* or *we* (first person), *you* (second person), and *he, she, it,* and *they* (third person). These errors are probably more often a result of carelessness than of imperfect knowledge. Being more familiar with casual speech than formal writing, writers sometimes shift from *I* to *you,* for example, when only one of them is meant, as in these sentences:

> Last summer *I* went on a canoeing trip to northern Manitoba. It was *my* first trip that far north, and it was so peaceful *you* could forget all the problems back home. [The person represented by *you* was not present. The writer means *I.*]

See also **2C,** which discusses shifts.

6 STYLE

Section Guide

Style in writing, like style in clothes, art, or anything else, is individual and develops with use and awareness. But even individual writers vary their style, depending on the situation. At school and work, the preferred style tends to be more formal and objective. The readings in this book provide abundant examples of this style. It is neither stuffy nor patronizing nor coldly analytical. It is simply clean, direct, and clear. This handbook section treats a few of the obstacles to a good writing style.

6A Conciseness

Nobody wants to read more words than necessary. When you write concisely, therefore, you are considerate of your readers. To achieve **conciseness,** you do not need to eliminate details and other content; rather, you cut empty words, repetition, and unnecessary details.

6Aa Empty Words and Repetition

In the following passage, all the italicized words could be omitted without altering the meaning.

> *In the final analysis, I feel that* the United States should have converted to the *use of the* metric system *of measurement* a long time ago. *In the present day and age,* the United States, except for Borneo and Liberia, is the *one and* only country in the *entire* world that has not yet adopted this measurement system.

Repetition of key words is an effective technique for achieving emphasis and coherence, but mindless repetition serves only to bore the reader.

6Ab   Introductory Expletives

Unnecessary and repetitive use of *there is, there are, there was* and related constructions contributes to wordiness. Here is an example, with a revision.

There are many people who think the metric system is un-American.

Revise to Many people think the metric system is un-American.

The most effective use of this construction is to announce something:

There are three reasons for switching to metric now.

6Ac   Active/Passive Voice

English sentences are usually written in the **active voice,** in which the subject of the sentence is the doer of the action of the verb:

Scott misplaced the file folder. [*Scott,* the subject of the sentence, performed the action, *misplaced.*]

With the **passive voice,** the doer of the action is the object of a preposition or is omitted entirely:

The file folder was misplaced by Scott. [*File folder* is now the subject of the sentence.]

The file folder was misplaced. [The person doing the action is not named.]

At best, the passive voice is wordier than the active voice; at worst, it fails to acknowledge who performs the action of the verb. Use the passive voice when you do not know or want to name the doer or when you want to keep the subjects consistent within a paragraph.

To avoid the passive voice, look for *by* phrases near the ends of your sentences; if you find any, see if the subject of your sentence performs the action of your verb. If not, revise the sentence so that it does. Another way to find occurrences of the passive voice is to look for forms of *be*: *am, is, are, was, were, been, being.* Not all these verbs will be passive, but if they function as part of an action verb, see if the subject performs the action. If it does not, and if your sentence would be clearer with the subject performing the action, revise to the active voice.

6B   Sexist Language

As the number of women in the workplace continues to increase, terms such as *policeman* and *chairman* are no longer acceptable to many readers. Writers who are sensitive to their audience, therefore, will avoid such terms, replacing them with expressions such as *police officer* and *chairperson* or *chair.*

6Ba   Masculine Nouns

Do not use *man* and its compounds generically. For many people, these words no longer mean both male and female persons. Here are some examples of substitutions:

mailman	mail carrier
businessman	business person, executive, manager, or other specific term
fireman	fire fighter
man hours	work hours
mankind	humanity, people
manmade	manufactured, synthetic
salesman	salesperson, sales representative, sales agent, or other specific term
Congressman	Member of Congress, Representative

Often the effect of such substitutions is to use a more specific word, which thus makes writing more specific.

6Bb   Masculine Pronouns

The masculine pronouns *he, him,* and *his* are no longer acceptable to many readers in a generic sense, meaning both male and female. Avoiding them poses some difficulties, however, because English does not have a generic singular pronoun to use instead. So writers select the most suitable of several options.

1. Eliminate the pronoun.

   Every writer has an individual style. **instead of** Every writer has his own style.

   A writer uses a dictionary when necessary. **instead of** A writer uses his dictionary when necessary.

2. Change to plural forms.

   Writers have their individual styles. **instead of** A writer has his individual style.

3. Sparingly use *he or she, one,* or *you.*

   Each writer has his or her own style. **instead of** Each writer has his own style.

   When writing, one adopts an individual style. **instead of** When writing, a writer adopts his individual style.

   When you write, adopt your own style. **instead of** When a writer writes, he adopts his own style.

6Bc   Stereotyping and Patronizing Terms

Avoid terms that cast men or women in particular roles or that imply that women are subordinate to men. Here are some examples and sample substitutions.

lady lawyer	lawyer
male nurse	nurse
career girl	professional woman, attorney, manager, or other specific term
coed	student
maiden name	birth name, family name
housewife	homemaker, consumer, parent, or other specific term

gal Friday	assistant, secretary, or other specific term
Dickens and Miss Austen	Dickens and Austen

7 PUNCTUATION

Section Guide

Punctuation is a system of signals telling readers how the parts of written discourse relate to one another. They are similar to road signs that tell the driver what to expect: A sign with an arrow curving left means that the road makes a left curve, a "stop ahead" sign that a stop sign is imminent, a speed limit sign what the legal speed is. Drivers trust that the signs mean what they say: They don't expect a curve to the right, or they prepare to stop, or they adjust their speed close to the announced limit. Readers, too, expect punctuation marks to mean what they say: A period means the end of a sentence, a colon that an explanation will follow, a comma that the sentence is not finished. Punctuation is a way for writers to help readers understand their words in the intended way.

Punctuation corresponds roughly to intonations and other physical signals in speech. When you speak, you utilize pitch levels, pauses, hand signals, head movements, and facial expressions to make sure your audience understands you. At the end of a sentence, you unconsciously let your voice drop—not just pause but decidedly drop in pitch. With some questions, your voice rises at the end, as in "Do you want to go?" With other questions, the pitch drops, as in "Do you want to go or not?" You can have brief pauses, or you can lengthen them to increase the drama of what you are saying. You can increase or decrease the sound volume of your words. None of these signals are available to writers. To make their situation even more difficult, writers do not have their audience right in front of them to look puzzled or to question them when meaning is unclear. So writers use punctuation.

Ends of sentences are punctuated with periods, question marks, or exclamation points. Semicolons function as "soft" periods, usually marking the end of independent clauses (as periods do) but not of complete thoughts. Commas show relationships within sentences, as do colons, dashes, quotation marks, parentheses, brackets, and ellipsis dots. These marks are explained in the sections that follow. Other marks, those used within words (apostrophes, hyphens, underlining [italics], and slashes) are explained in Section 8 on mechanics and spelling.

Figure A-1 (see page 532) serves as a quick guide to sentence punctuation. For explanations, refer to the relevant entry.

7A End Punctuation: *period, question mark, exclamation point*

A **period** is the normal mark for ending sentences. A **question mark** ends a sentence that asks a direct question, and an **exclamation point** ends forceful assertions.

7Aa Period

Sentences normally end with a period.

Studies suggest that eating fish two or three times a week may reduce risk of heart attack. [Statement]

Eat two or three servings of fish a week. [Mild command]

The patient asked whether eating fish would reduce risk of heart attack. [Indirect question]

Avoid inserting a period before the end of a sentence; the result will be a fragment (**1A**). Sentences can be long or short; their length does not determine their completion. Both of the examples below are complete sentences.

Eat fish. [Mild command; the subject, *you*, is understood.]

In a two-year study of 1,000 survivors of heart attack, researchers found a 29-percent reduction in mortality among those who regularly ate fish or took a fish oil supplement. [Statement; one sentence]

7Ab Question Mark

A sentence that asks a direct question ends in a question mark.

How does decaffeinated coffee differ from regular coffee?

Do not use a question mark to end an indirect question:

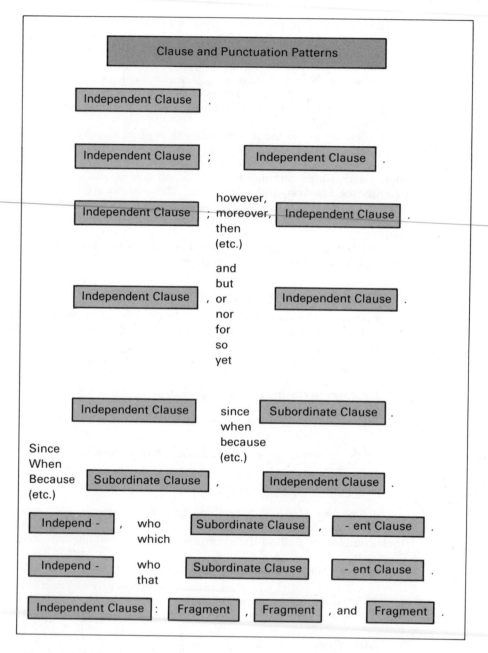

Figure A-1.

The customer asked how decaffeinated coffee differs from regular coffee.

With quoted questions, place the question mark inside the final quotation marks:

The customer asked, "How does decaffeinated coffee differ from regular coffee?"

7Ac   Exclamation Point

The exclamation point ends forceful assertions.

Fire!
Shut that door immediately!

Because they give the impression of shouting, exclamation points are rarely needed in formal business and academic writing.

7B   *Semicolon*

The main use for a semicolon is to connect two closely related independent clauses.

Dengue hemorrhagic fever is a viral infection common to Southeat Asia; it kills about 5,000 children a year.

Sometimes the second clause contains a **transitional adverb (1B):**

Dengue has existed in Asia for centuries; *however,* it grew more virulent in the 1950s.

Do not use a comma where a semicolon or period is required; the result is a comma splice **(1B)**. In contrast, a semicolon used in place of a comma may result in a type of fragment **(1A):**

In populations where people have been stricken by an infectious virus, survivors have antibodies in their bloodstreams; *which prevent or reduce the severity of subsequent infections.* [The semicolon makes a fragment of the *which* clause.]

Do not confuse the semicolon with the colon **(7D).** While the semicolon connects independent clauses, a colon ordinarily does not.

On occasion, the semicolon is used to clarify sentences that have parts set off with commas:

Scientists are researching the effects of staphylococcus bacteria, which cause infections in deep wounds; influenza A virus, which causes respiratory flu; and conjunctivitis bacteria, which have at times caused fatal purpuric fever.

7C   Comma

The **comma** is probably the most troublesome mark of punctuation because it has so many uses. It is a real workhorse for punctuation within a sentence. Its main uses are explained below.

7Ca   Compound Sentences

A comma joins two independent clauses connected with a **coordinating conjunction (1B):**

Martinique is a tropical island in the West Indies, and it attracts flocks of tourists annually.

Do not use the comma between independent clauses without the conjunction, even if the second clause begins with a **transitional adverb (1B):**

Faulty: Martinique is a tropical island in the West Indies, it attracts flocks of tourists annually. [Two independent clauses with no conjunction; it is a comma splice **(1B)**]

Faulty: Martinique is a tropical island in the West Indies, consequently it attracts flocks of tourists annually. [Two independent clauses with transitional adverb; it is a comma splice **(1B)**]

7Cb   Introductory Sentence Elements

Commas set off a variety of introductory sentence elements, as illustrated below:

When the French colonized Martinique in 1635, they eliminated the native Caribs. [Introductory subordinate clause **(1Aa)**]

Choosing death over subservience, the Caribs leaped into the sea. [Introductory participial (verbal) phrase **(1Ab)**]

Before their death, they warned of a "mountain of fire" on the island. [Introductory prepositional phrase **(1Ab)**]

Subsequently, the island's volcano erupted. [Introductory transitional adverb **(1B)**]

Short prepositional phrases are sometimes not set off:

In 1658 the Caribs leaped to their death.

Sometimes, however, there is the risk of misreading when a writer omits the comma:

Before, they had predicted retribution. [Comma is required to prevent misreading.]

7Cc   Nonrestrictive and Parenthetical Elements

Words that interrupt the flow of a sentence are set off with commas before and after. If they come at the end of a sentence, they are set off with one comma.

In this class are nonrestrictive modifiers **(3B)**, transitional adverbs **(1B)**, and a few other types of interrupters. Here are examples:

This rugged island, *which Columbus discovered in 1502,* exports sugar and rum. [Nonrestrictive *which* clause; commas before and after]

A major part of the economy, *however,* is tourism. [Interrupting transitional adverb; commas before and after]

Tourists, *attracted to the island by its climate,* enjoy discovering its culture. [Interrupting participial (verbal) phrase **(1Ab)**; commas before and after]

A popular tradition in Martinique is the Carnival, *which occurs just before Lent each year.* [Nonrestrictive *which* clause; one comma]

Martinique is an overseas department of France, *a status conferred in 1946.* [An absolute, ending the sentence (participial phrase plus the noun it modifies)]

7Cd Series

Commas separate items in a series:

Martiniquans dance to *steel drums, clarinets, empty bottles, and banjos.* [Four nouns]

Dressing in colorful costumes, dancing through the streets, and thoroughly enjoying the celebration, Martiniquans celebrate Carnival with enthusiasm. [Three participial (verbal) phrases **(1Ac)**]

Martinique has a population of over 300,000, its main religion is Roman Catholic, and its languages are French and Creole dialect. [Three independent clauses **(1B)**]

Various sentence elements can make up a series, but the elements joined should be equivalent grammatically (see **2A,** which discusses faulty parallelism). Common practice calls for a comma before the conjunction joining the last item in the series.

7Ce Quotations

Commas set off quoted sentences from the words that introduce them:

"A wise man," says David Hume, "proportions his belief to the evidence."

According to Plato, "Writing will produce forgetfulness" in writers because "they will not need to exercise their memories." [The second clause is not set off with a comma.]

"*X* on beer casks indicates beer which paid ten shillings duty, and hence it came to mean beer of a given quality," reports *The Dictionary of Phrase and Fable.*

Quotations introduced with *that* and other connectors (such as *because* in the second sentence above) are not set off with commas. Commas at the end of quotations go inside the quotation marks.

7Cf Coordinate Adjectives

Commas separate adjectives that equally modify a noun:

The "food pyramid" was designed as a *meaningful, memorable* way to represent the ideal daily diet. [Two adjectives modify *way* equally.]

When you're not sure about using a comma, try inserting the coordinating conjunction *and* between the two adjectives to see if they are truly coordinate (*meaningful and memorable*). Another test is to reverse the order of the adjectives (*memorable, meaningful*). Do not use a comma between adjectives that are not coordinate or between the last adjective and the noun being modified. (See also **3C,** which discusses adjectives and adverbs.)

7Cg   Addresses and Dates

Use a comma to separate city and state in an address, but do not set off the ZIP Code:

Glen Ridge, New Jersey 07028   **or**   Glen Ridge, NJ 07028

In a sentence, state name is enclosed in commas:

The letter from Glen Ridge, New Jersey, arrived by express mail.

Dates are treated similarly:

January 5, 1886   **but**   5 January 1886

The events of January 5, 1886, are no longer remembered. [When other punctuation is not required, the year is followed by a comma.]

7Ch   Commas to Avoid

Some people mistakenly believe that commas should be used wherever they might pause in speech. A comma does mean pause, but not all pauses are marked by commas. Use a comma only when you know you need one. **Avoid** the following comma uses:

1. To set off restrictive sentence elements:

   People*, who want a balanced diet,* can use the food pyramid as a guide. [The *who* clause is necessary to identify *people* and should not be set off with commas; see **3B.**]

2. To separate a subject from its verb and a preposition from its object:

   People who want a balanced diet*,* can use the food pyramid as a guide. [The comma following the *who* clause separates the subject, *people,* from its verb, *can use.*]

   The bottom level of the food pyramid contains food from grains, *such as, bread, cereals, rice, and pasta.* [The preposition *such as* should not be followed by a comma.]

3. To follow a coordinating conjunction (**1B**):

   The food pyramid describes a new approach to a balanced diet. But*,* the meat and dairy industries opposed it. [The coordinating conjunction *but* should not be set off with a comma.]

4. To separate two independent clauses (**1B**) not joined with a coordinating conjunction:

> The pyramid shows fewer servings of dairy and meat products, therefore consumers would buy less of these higher-priced foods. [The sentence requires a semicolon (**7B**); see also **1B** on Comma splices.]

5. To set off coordinate elements joined with a coordinating conjunction: Vegetables and fruits are near the bottom of the pyramid, *and should be eaten several times a day.* [The coordinating conjunction *and* joins a second verb, *should be eaten,* not a second independent clause; see **7Ca** on compound sentences.]

7D Colon

The **colon** is used most often to introduce an explanatory element, often in the form of a list:

> The space shuttle *Challenger* lifted off on January 28, 1986, with a seven-member crew: Francis R. Scobee, Michael J. Smith, Ronald E. McNair, Ellison S. Onizuka, Judith A. Resnik, Gregory B. Jarvis, and Christa McAuliffe. [The list explains *crew.*]

> A twelve-member investigating team discovered the cause of the disaster: a leak in one of the shuttle's two solid-fuel booster rockets. [The phrase explains the *cause of the disaster.*]

Do not use colons interchangeably with semicolons (**7B**). Semicolons separate two independent clauses (**1B**); colons ordinarily are followed by a phrase or phrases. Also avoid using colons after verbs and prepositions (**1Ab**):

> The two causes of the O-ring failure were cold temperatures and design deficiencies. [No colon after *were*]

> The commission investigating the disaster noted a number of failures in communication, such as one within the National Aeronautics and Space Administration. [No colon after *such as*]

Colons have a few other set uses:

Time	10:15 a.m.
Salutation in a business letter.	Dear Patricia Morton:
Biblical reference	Genesis 2:3

7E Dash

The **dash** separates sentence elements with greater emphasis than a comma:

> In *The War of the Worlds* (1898), science-fiction writer H. G. Wells described an intense beam of light that destroyed objects on contact—the laser.

It is also used to set off a nonrestrictive sentence element (**3B**) that might be confusing if set off with commas:

A number of medical uses—performing eye surgery, removing tumors, and unclogging coronary arteries—make the laser more than a destructive weapon. [The three explanatory items separated by commas are set off from the rest of the sentence with dashes.]

Like commas that set off nonrestrictive elements within a sentence, dashes are used in pairs—at the beginning of the interruption and at the end.

A dash is sometimes used in place of a colon when a colon might seem too formal:

Besides its medical uses, the laser serves many other functions—reading price codes, playing compact audio disks, and sending telephone messages.

Use the dash with caution; overuse gives the impression that you aren't familiar with alternative means of punctuation.

7F   Quotation Marks

The main use for **quotation marks** is to set off direct quotations:

Professor Charlotte Johnson announced, "Interdisciplinary science is combining fields of scientific knowledge to make up new disciplines."

"Biochemistry," she went on to say, "combines biology and chemistry."

Quotations within quotations are marked with single quotation marks:

"The term 'interdisciplinary science' thus describes a change in how processes are investigated," she concluded.

Use quotation marks correctly with other punctuation marks. Periods and commas (see **7Ce**) always go inside the end quotation marks; colons and semicolons almost always go outside the quotation. Dashes, question marks, and exclamation points go inside or outside depending on meaning—inside if the mark applies to the quotation and outside if it applies to the surrounding sentence:

"Do you know the various branches of the physical sciences?" asked Professor Johnson.

Did the professor say, "Histology deals with tissues and cytology with the fine structures of individual cells"?

Do not use quotation marks to set off indirect quotations:

The professor said that histology and cytology are different branches of study.

Another use for quotation marks is to enclose titles of works that are not published separately, including short stories, poems, and essays:

"You Are a Man" by Richard Rodriguez

"The Incident" by Countee Cullen

Do not enclose titles of your own essays when they are in title position. (See **8D** for treatment of titles of works that are published separately.)

Quotation marks are sometimes used to enclose words used in a special sense, but be careful not to abuse this function:

The "right" way to do a thing is not always the best way.

(For a further discussion of using quoted material within your papers, see Chapter 16.)

7G Other Marks

7Ga Parentheses

Parentheses enclose interrupting elements, setting them off from the rest of the sentence or discourse with a greater separation than other enclosing marks such as commas and dashes. They usually add explanatory information that might seem digressive to the topic.

> The Particle Beam Fusion Accelerator *(PBFA II)* is a device designed to produce energy by fusion. [Parentheses set off an abbreviation that will henceforth be used in place of the full term.]
>
> The PBFA II stores up to 3.5 million joules of energy. *(One joule is the amount of energy expended by a one-watt device in one second.)* [Parentheses set off an explanation framed as a complete sentence.]

Parentheses are always used in pairs. They might have internal punctuation (as in the second example above), but marks related to the sentence as a whole go outside the parentheses. Parentheses are almost never preceded by a comma. Note the following example:

> During fusion *(joining of two atomic nuclei to form a larger nucleus),* mass is converted to energy. [Parenthetical element is followed by a comma, showing that it relates to *fusion*. If it had been preceded by a comma, it would appear, illogically, to relate to *mass*.]

7Gb Brackets

Square **brackets** have limited uses and are not interchangeable with parentheses. Their most common use is to mark insertions in quoted material:

> Describing the Great Depression, Frederick Lewis Allen says, "The total amount of money paid out in wages *[in 1932]* was 60 percent less than in 1929." [The words *in 1932* were not part of the original text.]

Some writers use brackets to enclose brief parenthetical material within parentheses:

> Jules Verne (*Journey to the Center of the Earth* [1864]) described giant apes and a vast subterranean sea at the core of the earth. [The date of publication is parenthetical to the title of the book.]

7Gc   Ellipsis Dots

Ellipsis dots (spaced periods) are used in quotations to indicate where words have been omitted. Three spaced dots mark omissions within a sentence. If the omission comes at the end of your sentence but not at the end of the original sentence, use four spaced periods.

> One of the legacies of the Great Depression, says Frederick Lewis Allen, is that "if individual Americans are in deep trouble, . . . their government [should] come to their aid." [Words following a comma in the original sentence are omitted within the sentence. The brackets **(7Gb)** enclose an inserted word.]
>
> This idea, adds Allen, "was fiercely contested for years. . . ." [Allen's sentence did not end at *years,* where the quoted sentence ends.]

When using ellipsis, be careful not to distort the meaning of the original by your selection of what to include and what to omit (see also Chapter 16).

8   MECHANICS AND SPELLING

Section Guide

8A Capitalization

8B Abbreviation

8C Apostrophe

    8Ca Possessive nouns

    8Cb Contractions

    8Cc Special uses

8D Italics (Underlining)

8E Hyphens

8F Spelling

    8Fa Doubling a final consonant

    8Fb Words Containing -*ie* or -*ei*

    8Fc Final *e*

    8Fd Final *y*

    8Fe Plurals

    8Ff Homonyms

Some "rules" of writing are flexible, allowing choices, but this is not the case with spelling. With the invention of the printing press in the fifteenth century and the publication of dictionaries in the eighteenth century, flexibility in spelling all but vanished. Dictionaries spell almost all their words in exactly the same way as other dictionaries, and readers expect writers to do likewise. We have expectations about the way hyphens compound words, the way apostrophes show possession or contraction, the way suffixes are added to root words, and so on. This section treats the formation of words—capitalizing, abbreviating, punctuating (apostrophes, italics, and hyphens), and spelling.

8A Capitalization

The rules for **capitalization** are relatively fixed. Shown below are examples of situations calling for capitalization.

Beginning of a sentence
In 1929, the whole credit structure of the American economy was shaken.

Proper names
With the onset of the Great Depression, President Hoover at first tried to organize national optimism. [Historical period or event; person]

Bankers on Wall Street, manufacturers in Detroit, and legislators in Washington all had an effect on the economy. [Place]

The Great Depression was part of a worldwide collapse, ending only with World War II. [Historical period or event]

President Hoover set up the Reconstruction Finance Corporation to aid banks and businesses. [Person; institution]

In 1900, most of the African-Americans in this country lived in the South. [Races and nationalities; geographical region]

Jell-O, Pepsi, Rice Krispies [Trade names]

Aunt Beatrice; Grandmother Dietz; Dad [Relationships when they are part of the name; **but** *my dad* and *my aunt and uncle*]

Titles
Death at an Early Age by Jonathan Kozol; *The Dancing Wu Li Masters: An Overview of the New Physics* by Gary Zukav [Capitalize first and last words, words following colons, and all other words except articles (*a, an,* and *the*) and conjunctions and prepositions of fewer than five letters.]

Avoid capitalizing in circumstances like the following:

For many people, the winter of 1902 was bleak. [Seasons]

Many people moved south to a warmer climate. [Compass directions]

My great grandparents were among those who moved. [Relationships]

Simon Waterson was a professor of history at the time. [Titles that are not part of proper names]

8B Abbreviation

While **abbreviations** are part of the language, they are are not all acceptable in all circumstances. A general guideline is that they are less common in formal prose than in less formal circumstances. The examples shown below are arranged from most acceptable to least acceptable in written prose.

Titles with proper names
Dr. Paul Gordon   Paul Gordon, Ph.D.
George Grossman, Jr.

Times and dates

11:15 A.M. or 11:15 a.m.   53 B.C.   A.D. 371

Names of organizations and countries

NATO   CIA   NBC

U.S. as an adjective (*in a U.S. city*) but *United States* as a noun (*a city in the United States*)

Latin abbreviations (write out except in source citations and parenthetical comments)

etc.	and so forth (*et cetera*—applies to things)
i.e.	that is (*id est*)
e.g.	for example (*exempli gratia*)
cf.	compare (*confer*)
et al.	and others (*et alii*—applies to persons)
N.B.	note well (*nota bene*)

Abbreviations to be avoided in most prose

The school board [not *bd.*] met on Tuesday [not *Tues.*] February 3 [not *Feb.*].

William [not *Wm.*] Townsend was a guest lecturer in the economics [not *econ.*] class.

Townsend arrived from Pittsburgh, Pennsylvania [not *PA* or *Penn.*], late last night. [For letters and envelopes, use the U.S. Postal ZIP Codes, such as PA for *Pennsylvania* and IL for *Illinois*. Note that both letters are capitalized and are not followed by periods.]

Consult your dictionary when you have questions about specific abbreviations. For the use of abbreviations in source citations, see Chapter 16.

8C Apostrophe

The **apostrophe** has two main uses in English—to mark possessive nouns and to show contractions—plus a few specialized uses. Avoid all other uses.

8Ca Possessive Nouns

Ownership or connection is marked on nouns with apostrophes:

Norton's resume is short and concise. [The resume belongs to Norton.]

This week's newsletter will be a little late. [The newsletter of this week]

The article's title is confusing. [The title of the article]

To make nouns possessive, follow one of these steps:

1. For singular nouns, add *'s: nature* + *'s* = *nature's*; *Tess* + *'s* = *Tess's*.
2. For plural nouns ending in *s*, add *': strangers* + *'* = *strangers'*.
3. For plural nouns not ending in *s*, add *'s: men* + *'s* = *men's*.

Do not use apostrophes to make nouns plural: not *The Harris's are in Florida.* (See **8Fe**.) And do not use apostrophes with possessive and relative pronouns: not *The family lost it's home in the fire.* (See **5A** on pronoun case and **8Cb** on contractions.)

8Cb Contractions

Apostrophes stand in place of omitted letters in contractions:

doesn't	does not
isn't	is not
I'd	I would
you've	you have
it's	it is **or** it has
who's	who is **or** who has
let's	let us
we'll	we will

Because contractions reflect a casual style, they are usually not acceptable in formal writing. Do not confuse the contracted *it is* (*it's*) and *who is* (*who's*) with the possessive pronouns *its* and *whose*. (See **5A** on pronoun case.)

8Cc Special Uses

Plurals of letters, numbers, and words used as terms

I am hoping to get all A's this year.

The memo had four misspelled *there*'s. [See **8D**, which discusses underlining words used as terms.]

All the 7's are upside down in the 1990s catalog. [The plural for years is usually formed without apostrophes.]

Omitted letters or numbers

We'll never forget the summer of '78. [Restrict to informal writing.]

"Be seein' ya," Charlie said. [Dialect in quoted speech]

8D Italics (Underlining)

Italic type slants to the right and is used in printed material in the same way that underlining is used in handwritten or typed copy. It has specialized uses.

Titles of works published independently

The Atlantic Monthly (magazine)

A Farewell to Arms (book)

The Wall Street Journal (newspaper)

Northern Exposure (television program)

Cats (play)

Ships, aircraft, spacecraft, and trains

Challenger (spacecraft)

Leasat 3 (communications satellite)

San Francisco *Zephyr* (train)

Words used as terms

The process of heat transfer is called *conduction.*

The Latin words *et cetera* mean "and other things."

Emphasis [Use sparingly]

"I said '*Did* you buy the tickets?' not '*Would* you buy the tickets?'"

Many people writing with word processers use italics instead of underlining. If you are writing a documented paper for class, find out if your teacher approves of italics for titles.

8E Hyphens

Hyphens have three main uses: to divide words at the ends of lines, to form compound words, and to connect spelled-out numbers.

Dividing words [Always divide between syllables.]

dis-	physi-	condi-	symp-
tance	cian	tion	toms

stopped	ruled	(Don't divide one-syllable words.)

particu-   **not**   particular-
larly   ly   (Don't carry over
                                           only two letters.)

Forming compound words

ex-husband   twentieth-century fiction
self-confident   a well-written essay
all-inclusive   brother-in-law
pro-Communist   high-risk investment
anti-Christian   secretary-treasurer

but

postmortem   the twentieth century
minicomputer   an essay that is well written
antimissile   highly risky investment
prorate   executive secretary

Connecting spelled-out numbers

twenty-fifth time

fifteen-page paper

one hundred thirty-two

132-page report [when the spelled-out number is more than two words]

Whenever you have a question about dividing words and hyphenating compound words, use your dictionary. Dots usually mark syllables, and hyphens mark hyphenated compounds.

8F Spelling

One of the unfair facts of life is that the ability to spell is not equally distributed: Some people spell easily and some don't. If you're one of the latter, you'll need to put more time into getting your words right. A spell-checker is helpful, because it flags most misspelled words and suggests alternatives. If you are using one of these aids, however, be especially careful to look for misspelled homonyms **(8Ff).** Rules of spelling sometimes help, though too many of them are probably a hindrance. Therefore only the most useful and dependable ones are included here.

8Fa   Doubling a Final Consonant

When adding a suffix such as *-ing* or *-ed* to a word that ends in a consonant, double the final consonant to keep the internal vowel short; for example, *permit, permitted; stop, stopped.* Double the final consonant when all three of the following are true:

1. The word ends in a consonant preceded by a vowel.
2. The word is one syllable or the accent is on the final syllable.
3. The suffix begins with a vowel.

Here are some other examples:

hop	hopped	begin	beginning
sit	sitting	prefer	preferred
put	putting	occur	occurrence
win	winner	recap	recapped

8Fb   Words Containing *-ie* or *-ei*

The familiar rhyme about using *-ie or -ei* is true most of the time—enough times that it is worth remembering: *i* before *e* except after *c* when the sound is long *e.* Thus words such as these follow the rule:

receive	believe	weight
ceiling	chief	beige
conceited	siege	eight

There are a few common exceptions: *caffeine, either, neither, seize,* and *weird.* Another common word that the rule does not address is *friend* (spelled *-i* before *-e,* but the sound is not long *e).*

8Fc   Final *e*

To add an ending to a word that ends in a silent *e,* drop the *e* when the ending begins with a vowel:

believe + able = believable   believe + ed = believed

move + able = movable   move + ment = movement
hope + ing = hoping   hope + ful = hopeful

When the consonant preceding the final *e* is a soft *c* or *g,* the *e* is dropped only when the ending begins with *e* or *i:*

change + ing = changing   change + able = changeable
notice + ing = noticing   notice + able = noticeable
manage + er = manager   manage + ment = management
nice + er = nicer   nice + ly = nicely

8Fd   Final *y*

To add an ending to a word with a final *y* preceded by a consonant, change the y to *i* except when your ending is *-ing:*

happy + ly = happily   study + ing = studying
apply + s = applies   apply + ing = applying
vary + ous = various   vary + ing = varying
try + ed = tried   try + ing = trying

When the final *y* is preceded by a vowel, keep the *y:*

play + ed = played   play + ful = playful
employ + ed = employed   employ + ment = employment

but

say + s = says   say + d = said
pay + ment = payment   pay + d = paid

Never change the *y* when adding an ending to a proper noun: *the Barrys.*

8Fe   Plurals

Plural nouns ordinarily have an *s* ending:

boy + s = boys   car + s = cars

Words that end in *ch, s, sh, x,* or *z* require *-es:*

box + es = boxes   church + es = churches

Words ending in *o* are a little more troublesome. If the *o* is preceded by a vowel, add *s:*

radio + s = radios   video + s = videos

If the *o* is preceded by a consonant, ordinarily add *-es:*

hero + es = heroes   potato + es = potatoes

A few common words take either *s* or *-es*:

tornados, tornadoes   zeros, zeroes   volcanos, volcanoes

Some words form their plurals internally or do not have a plural form. Do not add an *s* to these words:

child, children   deer, deer
man, men   fish, fish
mouse, mice   moose, moose

Compound words ordinarily have an *s* at the end of the compound:

textbook, textbooks   snowshoe, snowshoes
text edition, text editions   snow goose, snow geese

But when the first word of the compound is the main word, add the *s* to it:

sisters-in-law   attorneys-general

Whenever you are in doubt about the correct plural ending, check your dictionary.

8Ff   Homonyms

Some of the most troublesome words to spell are **homonyms,** words that sound alike but are spelled differently. Here is a partial list of the most common ones:

accept, except   maybe, may be
affect, effect   of, 've (have)
already, all ready   passed, past
cite, sight, site   than, then
forth, fourth   their, there, they're
it's, its   to, too, two
know, no   whose, who's
lead, led   your, you're

A few other words, not exactly homonyms, are sometimes confused:

breath, breathe   lightning, lightening
choose, chose   loose, lose
clothes, cloths   precede, proceed
dominant, dominate   quiet, quite

Use your dictionary to check the meanings of any sound-alike words you are unsure of.

THE MAKING OF ENGLISH SENTENCES

For writers, most sentence relationships are of two types: **coordination** and **subordination**. In other words, the parts of a sentence are *grammatically equal* to other parts (coordination) or *grammatically dependent* on other parts (subordination). For example, two independent clauses in a sentence are *coordinate*; but when a sentence has an independent clause and a dependent clause, the dependent clause is *subordinate*. The following discussion centers on how coordination and subordination make up English sentences. Specific aspects of usage are covered in Appendix A.

COORDINATION

When two or more equivalent grammatical elements are connected, they are coordinate. These elements can be clauses, phrases, or single words. Only parallel elements can be coordinated—verbs joined to verbs, nouns to nouns, similar phrases to similar phrases, similar clauses to similar clauses.

Coordination has a number of features:

1. A variety of sentence elements can be coordinated, from independent clauses (clauses that can stand alone as sentences) to phrases and single words.
2. Any number of equivalent elements can be coordinated—from two on up.
3. Coordinated elements are parallel—verbs joined to verbs, nouns to nouns, phrases to phrases, clauses to clauses.
4. Coordinated elements are connected, in most cases, with a coordinating conjunction.

Careful writers avoid overusing coordination because writing lacks emphasis, variety, and shades of meaning when all assertions are equivalent.

Clauses

Clauses are word groups that have a subject and a verb and other related words. Clauses are *independent*, or main, and *dependent*, or subordinate. Independent clauses can function as sentences; dependent clauses must be accompanied by an independent clause. Both types of clauses can be coordinated within sentences—independent clauses with independent clauses, and dependent clauses with dependent clauses—as the following sentences illustrate:

> Most newspapers are still published for a local audience; they print news and happenings of community interest. [Two independent clauses joined by a semicolon]

> The term "Big Bang" is common usage now with scientists, but it originated as a sarcastic rejection of the theory. [Two independent clauses joined by a comma and coordinating conjunction *but*]

> The Food and Drug Administration has concluded that aspartame does not cause tumors but that further study is needed. [Two subordinate clauses beginning with *that* and joined by *but*]

These examples show that coordinate clauses of both kinds can be joined by coordinating conjunctions (*and, but, or, nor, for, so, yet*) and that independent clauses can also be connected by semicolons.

Phrases

Phrases of like types can be coordinated: prepositional phrases, verbal phrases, verb phrases, and so on. Here are examples:

> Connors *went* wide for a ball, *slugged* a winner, *was carried* into the next court by his momentum, *saw* a ball from the other match coming at him, and *hit* that for a winner too. —*Time* [Series of six *verb* phrases joined by commas and a final coordinating conjunction]

> American medical devices are equally remarkable, *giving life to those with terminally diseased organs, giving mobility to those crippled with arthritic joints and deadened nerves,* and even, miraculously, *restoring the sense of hearing to those deprived of it.* —*Atlantic* [Series of three participial (verbal) phrases joined by commas and a final coordinating conjunction; also, embedded in the second participial phrase are two coordinate noun phrases, *arthritic joints and deadened nerves,* joined by a coordinating conjunction]

Phrases are joined by coordinating conjunctions. In a series of three or more, they are separated by commas.

Words

Words of like types can be coordinated: nouns with nouns, verbs with verbs, adjectives with adjectives, and so on. Here are examples:

> *Broccoli and related vegetables* contain beta-carotene, a substance that may reduce the risk of heart attack. [Two nouns joined by a coordinating conjunction]

The Japanese have a reputation for manufacturing *cars, camcorders,* and *computers.* [Series of three nouns, joined by commas and a final coordinating conjunction]

Coordinating Connectors

Coordinate sentence elements, such as paired or serial clauses, phrases, and words, are ordinarily joined by coordinating conjunctions. Omission of the conjunction between two independent clauses may result in a comma splice or a fused sentence. Transitional adverbs relate ideas but do not serve as conjunctions.

Coordinating Conjunctions.   Coordinate sentence elements are usually connected with coordinating conjunctions: *and, but, or, nor, for, so,* and *yet.* The connector tells readers how the connected elements are related: *and* means addition, *but* and *yet* contrast, *or* and *nor* alternatives, *for* cause, and *so* result. Note how the conjunctions in the following sentences affect the meaning:

The elevator goes to the top, *but* you can get off at any floor.

The elevator goes to the top, *so* you can get off at any floor.

Coordinating conjunctions can join two sentence elements or a series of three or more. Usually only one conjunction is used with a series, although writers occasionally use a conjunction between all the elements in the series. Compare the following sentences:

Caffeine withdrawal symptoms can include headache, fatigue, *and* occasional muscle pain.

Headache *or* fatigue *or* occasional muscle pain can be symptomatic of caffeine withdrawal.

On occasion, writers may entirely omit conjunctions when they write a series:

Caffeine withdrawal symptoms can include headache, fatigue, occasional muscle pain, even flu-like symptoms.

A common fiction about coordinating conjunctions is that they cannot begin sentences. There is no rule against this usage; as a matter of fact, these connectors are often quite effective as transitions between sentences, as in this example:

Small North Dakota potholes are home to many species of birds, crustaceans, and insects. Yet, because of their potential for making money, these ponds are also valued by farmers and developers.

Transitional Adverbs.   Transitional adverbs (listed at **1B** in Appendix A) are not true connectors; they are adverbs rather than conjunctions. Although they do not connect parts of sentences, they join ideas by showing relationships. *However,* for example, relates a contrasting idea, and *therefore* relates a result. They are thus useful in compound sentences as an alternative to connecting clauses with coordinating conjunctions. When using one of them, punctuate the end of the first clause with a semicolon.

Compound Sentence

A compound sentence contains two or more independent clauses. The clauses may be joined by a comma plus a coordinating conjunction or by a semicolon with or without a transitional adverb. Here are some examples of compound sentences:

> Seventy-five percent of the nicotine in a cigarette ends up in the atmosphere; only 25 percent goes into the smoker's lungs and brain. [Two independent clauses joined by a semicolon]

> The prosecuting attorney charges, the public defender defends, but together they almost always negotiate. [Three independent clauses linked by commas and a final coordinating conjunction]

> Ask any group of tough whip-and-spur-clad horse trainers to define "gentling," and they will probably not understand you. [Two independent clauses connected by a coordinating conjunction]

> The United States has been called a melting pot; however, in many ways we are very far from having melted into one. [Two independent clauses joined by a semicolon with a transitional adverb]

The following sentence, though it contains coordination, is *not* a compound sentence:

> To learn social behaviors, children watch other people and imitate their behavior.

This sentence coordinates the two verb phrases beginning with *watch* and *imitate*. It does not contain two independent clauses.

SUBORDINATION

Subordination is an essential aspect of sentence relations. If all parts of a sentence were grammatically equivalent, the sameness would be tedious. Subordinate elements add spice and variety to a sentence and lend emphasis to the main elements. A subordinate part of a sentence depends on other parts for its meaning. At the same time, it often provides a fuller meaning than could be achieved by the independent elements alone.

Clauses

Clauses are word groups that have a subject and a verb and other related words. Clauses are *independent* (or *main*, discussed in the sections on Coordination and Compound sentence) and *dependent* (or subordinate). Only subordinate clauses are discussed in this section. Here are examples of subordinate clauses:

People *who exercise on a regular basis* change certain enzyme systems *so that they are more likely to burn fat than sugar.* [Two subordinate clauses, one beginning with *who* and modifying *People,* and one beginning with *so that* and modifying the verb *change*]

Because sedentary people are more likely to burn sugar than fat, they tend to become hungry sooner and to overeat. [Subordinate clause beginning *Because,* modifying the verb *tend*]

Walking, jogging, swimming, and cycling each has different energy rates, *which depend on a number of variables.* [Subordinate clause beginning *which,* modifying *rates*]

These examples illustrate several aspects of subordinate clauses:

1. They modify (describe, limit, explain, alter) a word in the main, or independent, clause. Each clause contributes an important meaning to the sentence.
2. They are unable to stand alone, having incomplete meanings on their own. Here are the examples without their main clauses:

    who exercise on a regular basis

    so that they are more likely to burn fat than sugar

    Because sedentary people are more likely to burn sugar than fat

    which depend on a number of variables

3. Something in the clause makes them subordinate: *who, so that, Because,* and *which.* These words connect the dependent clauses to the main clauses and show relationships. Without these subordinating words, some dependent clauses could be independent:

    They are more likely to burn fat than sugar.

    Sedentary people are more likely to burn sugar than fat.

    Clauses beginning with *who, which,* and sometimes *that* cannot have the subordinating word removed without a drastic effect on meaning:

    exercise on a regular basis

    depend on a number of variables

4. Subordinate clauses can appear in various places in the sentence: beginning, middle, or end. But those beginning *who, which,* or *that* usually must immediately follow the words they modify.

Phrases

Phrases are word groups without subjects and verbs. They may be verbal phrases, prepositional phrases, adverbial phrases, and so on. They usually add important meaning to a sentence. Here are examples of phrases:

For walking and jogging, the calorie expenditure is greater for people of greater body weight. [Prepositional phrase modifying *is greater*]

Increasing both speed and effort in aerobic activities, the exerciser burns more calories. [Verbal phrase, modifying *exerciser*]

A tired exerciser may expend more calories *because of less efficient performance.* [Prepositional phrase modifying *may expend*]

To lose weight, you should try aerobic exercise. [Verbal phrase modifying *you*]

These examples of verbal and prepositional phrases illustrate similarities with clauses in how they relate to other parts of a sentence:

1. They modify (describe, limit, explain, alter) a word in the independent clause (or in another clause). Each phrase contributes an important meaning to the sentence.
2. They are unable to stand alone, having incomplete meanings on their own. Here are the examples without the clauses:

   For walking and jogging

   Increasing both speed and effort in aerobic activities

   because of less efficient performance

   To lose weight

3. Something in the phrase makes them subordinate: *for, -ing, because of,* and *To.* These words connect the phrases to the main clauses and show relationships.
4. Phrases can appear almost anywhere in a sentence.

Words

Single words are often subordinate to other words, especially when they serve a modifying function:

Exercise time is a *complex* variable. [Two adjectives modifying the nouns they precede]

Exercise is *more* effective when done *regularly.* [Two adverbs, the first modifying the adjective *effective*, the second modifying the verb *done*]

Uncoordinated swimmers may expend *more* energy because of *wasted* effort. [Two verbals modifying the nouns they precede, plus an adjective modifying the noun *energy*]

Adjectives and adverbs are integral parts of sentences, filling out the meaning of the words they modify. Try reading the example sentences without the italicized words, and you'll see that the sentences are very empty indeed—of not just variety but meaning itself. The familiar advice to add adjectives and adverbs to our sentences is appropriate, therefore, only when we take it to mean "add meaning," not fluff or filler. The following sentence, for example, would read just as well without the italicized words—better, in fact, because the reading would be more efficient:

From a *very* practical point of view, most *seriously* determined exercisers would be *far* better off choosing an aerobic exercise that they *positively* enjoy.

Subordinating Connectors

Subordinating connectors are of three types: (1) subordinating conjunctions and (2) relative pronouns, which connect clauses, and (3) prepositions, which connect phrases. All three types of connectors show how clauses or phrases relate to the rest of the sentence.

Subordinating Conjunctions.   Some subordinate clauses begin with subordinating conjunctions. Like coordinating conjunctions, they connect clauses to the rest of a sentence by showing relationships: time, place, cause, contrast, and so on. Unlike coordinating conjunctions, of which there are only seven, subordinating conjunctions are numerous. Some of the most common are listed in Appendix A, section **1A.**

Subordinating conjunctions begin their clauses and are not set off from their clauses by any mark of punctuation. As conjunctions, they have no other function than that of connector. Consequently, if they are removed, their clauses are still complete. Notice how the first sentence below can be made into two sentences:

> *Although the benefits of walking have been recognized for centuries*, walking is being rediscovered by joggers and runners with injuries.

> *The benefits of walking have been recognized for centuries.* Walking is being rediscovered by joggers and runners with injuries.

Even though the revision is correct grammatically, it illustrates the advantage of using subordination in writing. The conjunction *although* shows a contrasting relation between the two clauses, whereas in its absence the two statements are related only by the fact that one follows the other.

Relative Pronouns, Adjectives, and Adverbs.   Relative pronouns, adjectives, and adverbs connect relative (subordinate) clauses to their sentences. They are listed in Appendix A, section **1A.** Since these connectors are not conjunctions, they have grammatical functions within their own clauses:

1. As a pronoun standing for a word in the main clause and having a noun function in its own clause.

    > Walking is being rediscovered by joggers and runners *who have sustained injuries.* [The pronoun *who* means *joggers and runners* and is the subject of *have sustained.*]

    > Brisk walking can prevent many work-related aches *that are both annoying and disabling.* [The pronoun *that* means *aches* and is the subject of *are.*]

2. As an adjective standing for a word in the main clause and having an adjective function in its own clause.

    > The person *whose job requires sitting or standing all day* can profit from this kind of exercise. [The adjective *whose* means *person's* and modifies *job.*]

3. As an adverb referring to a word in the main clause and having an adverb function in its own clause.

    > Find a time *when you can get away for half an hour and walk.* [The adverb *when* refers to *time* and modifies *can get.*]

Because of these essential functions within their own clauses, relatives, unlike conjunctions, cannot be removed without radically altering the clause.

Prepositions. Prepositions (listed in **1A** in Appendix A) relate their objects to other sentence elements. Together with their objects, they make up *prepositional phrases,* the function of which is usually to modify a noun or a verb. In the following sentences, observe how each preposition represents a differing relationship between its object and the word the phrase modifies.

The explanations given *by bioenergetics practitioners* are unacceptable.

The explanations given *to bioenergetics practitioners* are unacceptable.

The explanations given *about bioenergetics practitioners* are unacceptable.

The explanations given *among bioenergetics practitioners* are unacceptable.

Using the appropriate preposition is something learned mainly through reading other writers and listening to other speakers, although dictionary entries can be helpful too.

Complex and Compound-Complex Sentences

You already use a variety of sentences. Instead of speaking and writing entirely in simple sentences made up of only one independent clause, you probably freely use subordinate clauses, such as those beginning with *because, who, that,* and *when*. And whenever you do, you are using complex or compound-complex sentences. A complex sentence is made up of an independent clause and at least one subordinate clause. A sentence that is compound-complex contains more than one independent clause and at least one subordinate clause. Here are examples of both kinds of sentences:

Complex Sentences

Biologists have a difficult time defining *what life is* and *what it is not*. [Two subordinate clauses following an independent clause]

While a virus is basically a dead particle, it becomes active and reproductive once established in another creature. [A subordinate clause preceding an independent clause]

Anyone *who has had the flu or even the common cold* knows how active a virus can be. [A subordinate clause modifying the subject of the independent clause]

Compound-Complex Sentences

Several traits are common to living things; among them are the ability to grow, to move, to metabolize, to reproduce, and to adapt to *whatever conditions may enter their environment*. [Two independent clauses; the second has a subordinate clause embedded as object of the preposition *to*.]

Not all life forms have all these traits, and some objects *that are known to be inanimate* have several of the traits. [Two independent clauses; the second has an embedded subordinate clause modifying *objects*.]

For guidance on punctuating complex and compound-complex sentences, see **7B** and **7C** and Figure A-1 on page 532 in Appendix A.

Coordination and Subordination

Effective writing has both coordination and subordination—coordination that sets equivalent elements side by side, subordination that makes some elements dependent. Both are useful writing tools; the one you use depends on your purposes. When you subordinate one idea by phrasing it as a subordinate clause or a phrase, you emphasize the idea expressed in the main, or independent, clause. By the nature of the subordinating connectors, you also show how the subordinate idea relates to the main idea. When you coordinate two or more ideas, you emphasize each one equally. Make use of all your stylistic options.

Glossary

Listed below are brief definitions of terms used in *The Purposeful Writer.* Words in boldface type indicate other entries in the glossary. Parentheses enclose examples for some entries. To locate discussions that are more complete, use your index and, for questions of usage, the brief handbook in Appendix A.

Abstract A condensation of another piece of writing; similar to **summary,** usually written from the same perspective and in the same order of development as the original.

Active reading A way of reading that seeks answers to questions and interacts with the text.

Active voice See **Passive voice.**

Addition A form of **revision** in which a writer inserts in an earlier draft explanations, illustrations, transitions, and so on as words, punctuation, sentences, or paragraphs.

Agreement A principle of grammar that **verbs** correspond to their subjects, singular verbs for singular subjects ("A *record is* sometimes *revised* as a report") and plural for plural ("*Records are* sometimes *revised* as reports"), and that **pronouns** correspond to the words they stand for ("When *writers* proofread, *they* read for errors").

Analogy A means of developing and arranging ideas that explains one subject through references to a second subject ("Writing is like growing a plant").

Answering questions A common type of academic writing in which the audience usually knows more than the writer and the writer shows what he or she knows about the subject, as in **essay examinations.**

Appeal of character (*ethos*) An aspect of **persuasion** that presents the **writer** as informed, respectable, and trustworthy.

Appeal of logical reasoning (*logos*) An aspect of **persuasion** in which a writer presents a well-reasoned argument based on **facts (examples, testimony, statistics,** and **historical evidence)** and relevant **opinions.**

Appeal to the minds and emotions of the audience (*pathos*) An aspect of **persuasion** in which the writer identifies with the **audience** and calls on its needs and interests.

Arguable proposition A stance on an undecided issue, one that can be argued on the basis of **facts** and relevant **opinions.** An arguable proposition can serve as the **thesis** of a **persuasive essay.**

Audience A component of a **rhetorical situation.** Depending on the other components, the writer adjusts discourse to a particular audience. See also **purpose, subject,** and **writer.**

Brainstorming See **Listing or brainstorming.**

Cause and effect analysis A means of developing and arranging ideas that examines causes or effects of particular circumstances.

Censure See **Praise or censure.**

Chronology A means of developing and arranging ideas according to the sequence of events; simple time order.

Citation of sources See **Documentation.**

Classical probes A means of **inventions** related to the mental processes. Ideas are discovered and explored by identification, comparison, classification, cause and effect analysis, process analysis, and exemplification. As a method for **revision,** the classical probes can assist a writer in discovering undeveloped ideas in a draft.

Classification A means of developing and arranging ideas according to their categories.

Clustering See **Mapping or clustering.**

Coherence The aspect of a composition in which all parts relate and are connected to one another. Coherence is achieved by a clearly stated **thesis sentence,** topic sentences, repetition of **key words,** review of **old information** before statement of **new information,** insertion of **transitional expressions,** and other devices.

Comma splice An error in punctuation that joins two sentences with a comma ("Sometimes freewriting is used without a focusing topic, you begin writing whatever is on your mind"). A writer can correct a comma splice by replacing the comma with a period or a semicolon, or by adding a conjunction after the comma. Similar to a fused sentence, which is two sentences joined without any punctuation between.

Comparison A means of developing and arranging ideas by comparing them to one another and showing how they are similar and different; contrast is a type of comparison that focuses mainly differences.

Conclusion The end of a composition, often reiterating the main idea.

Connotations The associations conjured up by a word that, in addition to its explicit meaning, make up an audience's understanding of what a writer is saying.

Contrast See **Comparison.**

Critical reading **Active reading** directed either to the meaning of a text or to its **style** and structure.

Critique An analysis of a commentary on another piece of writing. The critique usually focuses on technique as well as on content.

Cubing A means of **invention** allowing a writer to visualize a subject enclosed in a cube whose six sides require the writer to examine the subject by classifying it, analyzing it, describing it, differentiating it, locating it, and using it.

Dangling modifier A modifying phrase, usually at the beginning of a sentence, that does not modify the word the writer intended ("*Studying humorous essays,* they often have breaks in the humor"). This syntactic error can usually be corrected by revising the sentence to make its subject the same as the implied subject of the phrase ("*Studying humorous essays,* you find that they often have breaks in the humor").

Definition A statement of meaning, or the characterization of a class of something—for instance, an essay explaining taste or aggression.

Deletion A form of **revision** in which a writer removes words, punctuation, sentences, or paragraphs to make the composition clearer and more concise.

Development Methods of expanding and arranging ideas, occurring often during **drafting** but also during **prewriting** and **revising.** See also **Analogy, Answering questions, Cause and effect, Chronology, Classification, Comparison, Definition, Exemplification, Problem and solution, Question and answer,** and **Space.**

Documentation References to sources of information, such as books and journal articles. Scholarly courtesy requires showing sources of **quotations, paraphrases,** and **summaries,** usually by renaming the author, title, page numbers, and publishing information—sometimes parenthetically following the reference and sometimes in footnotes or endnotes. A list of works cited or references usually follows a paper that borrows words and ideas from other writers.

Drafting The act of putting words on the page or word processor screen, often preceded by **prewriting** and followed by **revising.**

Editing The act of removing errors in a draft, usually in words and punctuation, ordinarily following **revision.**

Emphasis A method of arranging ideas that places the most important at the beginning or the end of a composition. Also, the focus of a piece of writing: the **writer,** the **audience,** or the **subject.**

Entertain A **purpose** for writing that appeals to the mind or emotions of the audience to create pleasure.

Essay A composition that expresses the views of a **writer** on a single **subject.** The essay usually consists of an **introduction** to the subject, a **thesis sentence** that expresses the writer's position on the subject, and several **paragraphs** of thesis development, often concluding with a reiteration of the main idea.

Essay examination A **subject**-emphasis form of writing in which the writer shows an **audience** who already knows the subject matter that the writer also is informed about it.

Ethos See **Appeal of character.**

Exaggeration A stylistic feature common in humor and writing that **appeals to the emotions of the audience,** found notably in parody, sermonic addresses, and satire.

Example A type of **fact,** or support for an **opinion,** that may be drawn from personal experience, experience of others, reading, or observations.

Exemplification A means of developing and arranging ideas in which **examples** illustrate and explain statements.

Explain A **purpose** for writing in which the **subject** is emphasized, telling the **why** and **how** of something.

Facts Verifiable statements that are true and therefore inarguable. Types of facts are **examples, testimony, statistics,** and **historical evidence.**

Fallacies Errors in logic, such as broad generalization, oversimplification, question begging, either-or reasoning, post hoc cause, and ad hominem.

Feedback Response from readers on how they perceive a composition; useful in **revision** for telling where the draft needs to be improved.

Fragment An incomplete sentence, lacking a subject, a verb, or both ("Applying Bradley's words to the present context"). A fragment can be corrected by adding the missing part or by attaching the fragment to a nearby sentence ("Senator Gore applies Bradley's words to the present context" or "Senator Gore quotes General Omar Bradley, applying Bradley's words to the present context").

Freewriting A means of **invention** in which a subject is explored by means of preliminary writing done rapidly and without concern for **style** or correctness.

Fused sentence See **Comma splice.**

General to specific and specific to general Related methods of arranging ideas. General to specific begins with a statement of thesis or topic followed by specific explanations and **examples,** and specific to general first accumulates illustrations and explanations and concludes with a generalized statement.

Historical evidence A type of **fact,** or support for an **opinion;** verifiable occurrences.

Imitation A means of **invention** that enables a writer to discover new ideas while following the **style** of other writers.

Inform A **purpose** for writing in which the **subject** is emphasized and the **audience** is assumed not to know the information conveyed.

Instruct A **purpose** for writing in which the **subject** is emphasized, telling *how* something is done.

Introduction The beginning of a composition, establishing the **subject,** the **writer**'s relationship to the **audience** and to the subject, the **thesis** and **purpose** of the composition, the **tone,** and usually some means of heightening audience interest.

Invention Methods of discovering and exploring ideas and how to express them. See also **Classical probes, Cubing, Freewriting, Imitation, Journalist's questions, Listing, Mapping, Outlining, Questions about audience,** and **Reading.**

Journal A record of personal experiences and impressions for purposes important only to the **writer;** an academic journal might serve as a record of school-related analyses, **summaries,** insights, and so on.

Journalist's questions A means of **invention** in which ideas are discovered and explored by questions beginning *who, what, where, when, why,* and *how.* As a method for **revision,** the questions can assist a writer in discovering undeveloped ideas in a draft.

Key words A **coherence** device that links ideas by repeating words that are significant in expressing those ideas.

Listing or brainstorming As a means of **invention,** a rapid itemized recording of thoughts related to a particular subject.

Logos See **Appeal of logical reasoning.**

Mapping or clustering As a means of **invention,** an itemized recording of thoughts on a particular subject which are then related by connecting lines. As a reading technique, mapping can assist a reader in understanding what has just been read. As a method of **revision,** mapping can reveal irrelevant information or undeveloped ideas.

Move A **purpose** for writing that appeals to the emotions of the audience to bring about action or to engender compassion, anger, or other feelings toward others.

Narration Storytelling by means of **chronological** development. Narration is used to introduce a composition, to illustrate a point, and to compose an entire essay.

Old information/new information A **coherence** device based on the principle that new ideas build on ideas already expressed. A writer recaps an idea already stated before making a new statement.

Opinion A position on an issue that if supportable by **facts** is arguable and thus can be stated as a **thesis.** Relevant, fact-based opinions can serve as support for arguments.

Outlining A means of organizing one's thoughts in a conventional format. An outline can serve as a guide for writing; as a means of **invention** or **revision** it can show gaps in the development of ideas.

Paragraphs Divisions of prose compositions that develop single aspects of the subject; units of writing of unspecified length.

Paraphrase A rewording of another piece of writing. Unlike **summary,** a paraphrase is usually not a condensation.

Participial phrase A word group consisting of a participial and it's modifiers or complements ("swimming quickly to shore," "known to be true").

Passive voice A sentence arrangement in which the subject does not perform the action of the verb ("Events were described by an observer"). Usual sentence arrangement would be active voice, with the subject performing the action of the verb ("An observer described events").

Pathos See **Appeal to the minds and emotions of the audience.**

Persuasion Writing for the **purpose** of moving an **audience** to action or changing the audience's views on an issue, accomplished with three appeals: **appeal of the writer's character (***ethos***), appeal to the minds and emotions of the audience (***pathos***),** and **appeal of logical reasoning (***logos***).**

Praise or censure A **purpose** for writing in which the **subject** is a person who receives approval or disapproval.

Prewriting A period of thinking that precedes **drafting,** usually to explore the subject, how to approach it and organize it, what **style** and **tone** the writer should assume, how to phrase sentences, and so on.

Problem and solution A means of developing and arranging ideas in which a writer describes a perplexing situation and then proposes a way or ways of remedying it.

Pronouns Words that stand for nouns. To have meaning, pronouns' relation to their antecedents must be clear (examples of pronouns that are not clear: "All *this* led Timex to look around for new worlds to conquer." "We entered the lower-price watch market to convince buyers that *they* don't have to be expensive"). If the reference of the pronoun is not clear, it may be necessary to substitute a noun. ("All *this success* led Timex to look around for new worlds to conquer." "*Timex* entered the lower-price watch market to convince buyers that *good watches* don't have to be expensive").

Proofreading The act of correcting typing or scribal errors in a composition; usually the final step in preparing a manuscript.

Purpose The determining factor in how the other three components of the **rhetorical situation (writer, audience,** and **subject)** relate to one another.

Question and answer A means of developing and arranging ideas in which a writer asks a question and then answers it.

Questions about audience A means of **invention** in which ideas are generated by the writer's knowledge of the **audience.** As a method for **revision,** the question can assist a writer in seeing whether a draft has adequately considered the needs and interests of the intended audience.

Quotation An exact copy from another piece of writing, enclosed in quotation marks to show that it is borrowed.

Reading As a means of **invention,** a major source of ideas for writing.

Reading as a reader A method of **revision** that puts the writer in the **audience's** place to see whether the writing is clear and understandable.

Reading as a writer **Active reading** directed to the **style** and structure of the text rather than its meaning.

Rearrangement A form of **revision** in which a writer rearranges the words, punctuation, sentences, or paragraphs of an earlier draft.

Record A **purpose** for writing in which the **subject** is emphasized and which coincides with the occurrence of an event.

Reflective writing A **purpose for** writing in which the writer is emphasized and which derives from the writer's own thoughts and perceptions.

Repetition A stylistic feature common in writing that **appeals to the emotions of the audience,** drawing on a sense of rhythm.

Report A **purpose** for writing in which the **subject** is emphasized; objective writing that is usually done after an event occurs.

Response Impressions and interpretations of another piece of writing. See also **Critique.**

Revision The act of reconsidering what one has written and making changes in the form of **addition, deletion, substitution,** or **rearrangement.**

Rhetoric The principles of communication, balancing the relations among **writer, audience, subject,** and **purpose.**

Rhetorical situation An occasion for communication, in which **writer** (or speaker), **audience, subject,** and **purpose** are the principal components.

Space A means of developing and arranging ideas according to placement—vertically, horizontally, or circularly.

Statistics A type of **fact,** or support for an **opinion;** relevant data.

Style The distinctive way a writer uses words and their combinations to convey a particular **purpose,** persona, and **audience** relationship. See also **Tone** and **Voice.**

Subject A component of a **rhetorical situation.** Other components influence the writer's attitude toward and coverage of the subject. See also **Audience, Purpose,** and **Writer.**

Substitution A form of **revision** in which a writer substitutes words, punctuation, sentences, or paragraphs for those in an earlier draft.

Summary The key points of a piece of writing, reduced for another writer's purposes.

Testimony A type of **fact,** or support for an **opinion;** a quotation from an expert on the issue.

Thesis sentence The main idea of an **essay,** stated in a single sentence that expresses the **subject** and makes an assertion about it. The thesis sentence may also state the essay's method of development.

Title The name of a composition, identifying and describing it, often written to attract **audience** interest.

Tone An aspect of writing that is roughly comparable to the sound of the writer's voice. It reflects a writer's attitude toward the **subject**—for instance, objective, cynical, or humorous. See also **Voice.**

Transitional expressions **Coherence** devices that connect thoughts by relational words, such as *however* and *but* showing contrast, *therefore* and *so* showing result, and *moreover* and *and* showing addition. Transitions are sometimes better achieved by an entire sentence or even a paragraph.

Unexpressed assumptions Underlying suppositions of a **thesis** that may or may not require support.

Voice That which makes a person's writing individual, comparable to the sound of a person's voice in speech. While each writer's voice is individual, it can be varied depending on the writer's attitude toward the **subject** and the **audience** (for instance, an angry voice or a friendly voice). See also **Tone.**

Writer A component of a **rhetorical situation.** A writer may project various roles depending on the other components. See also **Audience, Purpose,** and **Subject.**

Index

*Italicized page number indicates that the term introduced on that page is listed in the glossary.

Credits *(continued)*

Pages 129–31. Henry David Thoreau, "A Fire in the Woods," from *The Journal of Henry David Thoreau,* Volume II, 1850. From a collection edited by Bradford Torrey and Francis Allen, copyright 1962. Reprinted by permission of Dover Publications, Inc.

Pages 134–35. Aldo Leopold, excerpt from *A Sand County Almanac, With Other Essays on Conservation from Round River* by Aldo Leopold. Copyright © 1949, 1953, 1966, renewed 1977, 1981 by Oxford University Press, Inc. Reprinted by permission.

Pages 138–40. Mark Baker, "The Taste of Evil," from *Nam: The Vietnam War in the Words of the Men and Women Who Fought There.* Copyright © 1981 by Mark Baker. Reprinted by permission of William Morrow & Company, Inc.

Pages 146–48. Lewis Thomas, from *Late Night Thoughts on Listening to Mahler's Ninth Symphony* by Lewis Thomas. Copyright © 1980, 1981, 1982 by Lewis Thomas. Reprinted by permission of Viking Penguin, a division of Penguin Books USA Inc.

Pages 152–54. Teri Anderson Brown, "Walking Point." Reprinted by permission of the author.

Page 159. Steve Crow, "Painting Minnesota." Reprinted by permission of the author.

Page 160. Countee Cullen, "Incident." Reprinted by permission of GRM Associates, Inc., Agents for the Estate of Ida M. Cullen. From the book *Color* by Countee Cullen. Copyright © 1925 by Harper & Brothers; copyright renewed 1953 by Ida M. Cullen.

Page 169. Jack J. Kraushaar and Robert A. Ristinen, excerpt from *Energy and Problems of a Technical Society,* rev. ed. Copyright © 1988 by John Wiley and Sons, Inc.

Pages 174–76. Albert Gore, "What Is Wrong with Us?" *Time,* January 2, 1989, p. 66. Copyright 1988 The Time Inc. Magazine Company. Reprinted by permission.

Pages 181–82. Neil Postman, "What 'Sesame Street' Teaches," from *Amusing Ourselves to Death.* Copyright © 1985 by Neil Postman. Reprinted by permission of Viking Penguin, a division of Penguin Books USA Inc.

Pages 186–87. Ellen Goodman, "Protection from the Prying Camera," from *Close to Home.* Copyright © 1979 by The Washington Post Group. Reprinted by permission of Summit, a division of Simon & Schuster, Inc.

Page 195. Sydney J. Harris, "High Cost of Compromise," excerpt from *The Best of Sydney J. Harris* by Sydney J. Harris. Copyright © 1975 by Sydney J. Harris. Reprinted by permission of Houghton Mifflin Co.

Pages 196–98. Milton Friedman, "Prohibition and Drugs." Originally published in *Newsweek,* May 1, 1972. Reprinted by permission. Milton Friedman is Professor Emeritus of Economics, University of Chicago, and Senior Research Fellow, Hoover Institution.

Pages 198–200. John Skow, "Heroes, Bears, and True Baloney," *Time,* November 13, 1989, p. 122. Copyright 1989 The Time Inc. Magazine Company. Reprinted by permission.

Pages 200–02. James Kilpatrick, "Some Hunting Protestors Are Overzealous Hypocrites," excerpt from the Universal Press Syndicate, December 1, 1989. Reprinted by permission.

Pages 203–05. Barbara Ehrenreich, "Teach Diversity—with a Smile," *Time,* April 8, 1991. Copyright 1991 The Time Inc. Magazine Company. Reprinted by permission.

Page 209. Martin Luther King, Jr., excerpt from "I Have a Dream." Reprinted with permission of Joan Daves Agency. Copyright © 1963 Martin Luther King, Jr.

Pages 214–16. Lewis Thomas, "Notes on Punctuation," from *The Medusa and the Snail* by Lewis Thomas. Copyright © 1979 by Lewis Thomas. Reprinted by permission of Viking Penguin, a division of Penguin Books USA Inc.

Pages 220–21. Loren Eiseley, "The Winter of Man," *New York Times,* 1978. Copyright © 1978 by The New York Times Company. Reprinted by permission.

Pages 223–27. Al Sicherman, "Be Scared for Your Kids," from the *Minneapolis Star Tribune,* November 5, 1989, pp. 1A, 10A. Reprinted with permission of the *Star Tribune,* Minneapolis-St. Paul.

Pages 232–35. Martin Luther King, "I Have a Dream." Reprinted with permission of Joan Daves Agency. Copyright © 1963 Martin Luther King, Jr.

Pages 243–46. Lynda Van Devanter, excerpted from *Home Before Morning* (Beaufort Books, 1983). Copyright © 1983 by Lynda Van Devanter. Reprinted by permission of the author.

Pages 249–51. Joan Didion, excerpt from "Los Angeles Notebook," from *Slouching Towards Bethlehem* by Joan Didion. Copyright © 1967, 1968 by Joan Didion. Reprinted by permission of Farrar, Straus and Giroux, Inc.

Pages 255–60. (interview with) Jesse Jackson, "Drug Use Is a Sin," *New Perspectives Quarterly,* Summer 1989, pp. 8–14. Reprinted by permission.

Pages 263–65. John E. Cooney, from *The Best of the Wall Street Journal.* Reprinted by permission of the *Wall Street Journal,* © 1974 Dow Jones & Company, Inc. All Rights Reserved Worldwide.

Pages 287–89. Franklin Russell, "The Hunt," from *Watchers at the Pond.* Copyright © 1961 by Franklin Russell. Reprinted by permission of Alfred A. Knopf, Inc.

Pages 293–95. Rachel Carson, "The Sargasso Sea," excerpt from *The Sea Around Us,* Revised Edition, by Rachel L. Carson. Copyright © 1950, 1951, 1961 by Rachel L. Carson; renewed 1979 by Roger Christie. Reprinted by permission of Oxford University Press, Inc.

Pages 302–05. Maya Angelou, "The Principle," from *Gather Together in My Name* by Maya Angelou. Copyright © 1974 by Maya Angelou. Reprinted by permission of Random House, Inc.

Pages 309–11. Jonathan Kozol, "A Third of the Nation Cannot Read These Words," from *Illiterate America,* copyright © 1985 by Jonathan Kozol. Used by permission of Doubleday, a division of Bantam, Doubleday, Dell Publishing Group, Inc.

Pages 315–17. George R. Harrison, "Senses," excerpt from "Faith and the Scientist," published in *The Atlantic Essays,* copyright © 1958 by D. C. Heath. Used by permission of Elizabeth C. Harrison.

Page 321. John McPhee, "Firewood," from *Pieces of the Frame* by John McPhee. Copyright © 1963, 1969, 1970, 1971, 1972, 1973, 1974, 1975 by John McPhee. Reprinted by permission of Farrar, Straus and Giroux, Inc.

Page 327. Excerpt from "Halftime Balloons a Pretty Problem," *Audubon,* September 1988, p. 18. Reprinted from *Audubon,* the magazine of the National Audubon Society.

Pages 330–31. William Zinsser, "Taste," from *On Writing Well.* Copyright © 1976, 1980, 1985 by William K. Zinsser. Reprinted by permission of the author.

Pages 334–36. Michael D. Lemonick, "Deadly Danger in a Spray Can," *Time,* January 2, 1989, p. 42. Copyright © 1989 The Time Inc. Magazine Company. Reprinted by permission.

Pages 340–43. Lewis Thomas, "The Corner of the Eye," from *Late Night Thoughts on Listening to Mahler's Ninth Symphony* by Lewis Thomas. Copyright © 1980, 1981, 1982 by Lewis Thomas. Reprinted by permission of Viking Penguin, a division of Penguin Books USA Inc.

Pages 352–53. Elliott Aronson, "Aggression Defined," excerpt from *The Social Animal,* 4th ed. Copyright © 1984 by W. H. Freeman and Company. Reprinted by permission.

Pages 357–61. Judith Viorst, "Friends, Good Friends—and Such Good Friends." Copyright © 1977 by Judith Viorst. Originally appeared in *Redbook.* Reprinted by permission of Lescher & Lescher, Ltd.

Pages 372–73. Campbell Morris, "Smooth Flyer." Reprinted by permission of The Putnam Publishing Group from *More Best Paper Aircraft* by Campbell Morris. Copyright © 1987 by Campbell Morris.